American Capitalism

Politics and Culture in Modern America

Series Editors: Michael Kazin, Glenda Gilmore, Thomas J. Sugrue

Books in the series narrate and analyze political and social change in the broadest dimensions from 1865 to the present, including ideas about the ways people have sought and wielded power in the public sphere and the language and institutions of politics at all levels—national, regional, and local. The series is motivated by a desire to reverse the fragmentation of modern U.S. history and to encourage synthetic perspectives on social movements and the state, on gender, race, and labor, on consumption, and on intellectual history and popular culture.

American Capitalism

Social Thought and Political Economy in the Twentieth Century

EDITED BY NELSON LICHTENSTEIN

PENN

University of Pennsylvania Press

Philadelphia

10 9 8 7 6 5 4 3 2 1

Published by
University of Pennsylvania Press
Philadelphia, Pennsylvania 19104-4112

Library of Congress Cataloging-in-Publication Data

American capitalism : social thought and political economy in the twentieth
century / edited by Nelson Lichtenstein.
    p.   cm. — (Politics and culture in modern America)
    ISBN-13: 978-0-8122-3923-2
    ISBN-10: 0-8122-3923-7 (cloth : alk. paper)
    1. Capitalism—United States. 2. Right and left (Political science). 3. United
States—Economic policy. I. Lichtenstein, Nelson. II. Series
HB501 .A57   2005
330.12'20973—dc22   2005045654

Contents

Introduction:
Social Theory and Capitalist Reality in the American Century

Nelson Lichtenstein

At the opening of the twenty-first century, the power and pervasiveness of American capitalism and of the equation that links open markets to democratic institutions has become a large part of the common wisdom. Words like reform and liberalization now denote the process whereby a global market in labor, capital, and ideas replaces the regulatory regimes, either authoritarian or social democratic, that were erected during and after the Great Depression. In 1960, when Daniel Bell famously announced an "end of ideology in the West," he was noting that the debate about the viability of capitalism, which had consumed intellectuals and social theorists for two generations, had been transformed into a calculation that subordinated the market to a purposeful, yet well-constrained set of social and political compromises.[1]

But thirty years later, when Francis Fukuyama coined his now (in)famous catchphrase, "the end of history," he spoke for an ideologically self-confident set of policy intellectuals who saw the capitalist market itself as culturally and politically determinative. "Liberal democracy combined with open market economics has become the only model a state can follow," wrote Fukuyama in the months just before the fall of the Berlin Wall. This was another way of arguing for what Margaret Thatcher had also asserted, when her efforts to deregulate business and dismantle the welfare state ran into Labour Party resistance, "There is no alternative."[2]

The events of September 11, 2001, have done little to alter such self-confidence. "The sort of people who work in financial markets are not merely symbols but also practitioners of liberty," wrote Michael Lewis in the *New York Times Magazine* shortly after the attack. "They do not suffer constraints on their private ambitions, and they work hard, if unintentionally, to free others from constraint. . . . It tells you something about the world-view of the terrorists that they crashed half their arsenal into the World Trade Center. They believed that the bond traders are as critical as the U.S. generals and the politicians to extending liberty's influence in the world. They may be right. And that should make you feel proud."[3]

The essays in this collection, most of which were talks first delivered at a conference at the University of California, Santa Barbara in March 2003, have all been written when such sentiments are commonplace, if not triumphant. Most reject this overweening self-confidence, but all take as a starting point the cognizance that we live in a world in which a capitalist market in labor, land, goods, and ideas has become so normalized and naturalized that it almost vanishes from our consciousness, both lay and academic. The U.S. model of global capitalism has proven supremely attractive because its gravitational pull is now almost entirely unimpeded by the weight of any other competing entity. Not only did the Soviet Union collapse during the early 1990s, but so too did competition, both economic and ideological, from a Japan-centered Pacific Rim.

From a model-building perspective, the collapse of the Soviet Union had been discounted long before its dramatic political demise. For almost half a century few critics of American capitalism had looked east of the Elbe for inspiration or advice. Still the demise of this empire, and the increasing marketization of the Chinese economy that preceded it, seemed to demonstrate that any organization of society that substituted economic planning for a market mechanism was bound to lead to a disaster of the first order.[4] Indeed, the elimination of this world-historic rival devalued the ideological role played by those Keynesian, social-democratic programs and compacts that in the early Cold War years had been a vital component of the claim that in the world of actually existing capitalism the sharp elbows had been tucked and the market forces tamed. The collapse of the Soviet Union and its satellites thus made possible the celebration of a globalized capitalism with nary a backward glance, especially when all this was accompanied by the eclipse of organized labor in the Atlantic world, the corrosive impact of America's uniquely bitter racial divide on social and economic policy, and the cunning élan with which Ronald Reagan and Margaret Thatcher mobilized elements of the working class on behalf of laissez-faire principles.[5]

The demise of a Japanese-centered "Pacific Century" has been equally dramatic and perhaps even more significant in advancing the idea that there no longer exists any alternative to a distinctively American version of global markets and capitalist social mores. Japan has been the world's second largest economy for more than thirty years, and in the 1970s and 1980s the entire East Asian model for advanced capitalism, with its quasi-planning from the top, its innovative and seemingly cooperative labor relations, and its technological prowess, represented the real challenge, and alternative pathway, for an American capitalism that was growing frustrated with a Keynesianism that seemed increasingly ineffectual. But the collapse of Japan's real estate, banking, and technology bubble in 1990 inaugurated more than a decade of stagnation and crisis for America's great economic rival. Despite the manipulation of every fiscal and monetary lever at its command, the Tokyo planning ministries and the highly politicized Japanese banks, which had once been given such credit for shaping the entire economic miracle, have found their recovery efforts repeatedly frustrated.[6]

The United States has had its own share of corporate bankruptcies and stock market gyrations, but today few take such economic shocks as an indication that capitalism is in danger of a fundamental transformation. In the wake of the scandal bankruptcies of Enron and Comcast there was much finger pointing from the business press and from Democratic critics of "crony capitalism," but most thought that only a beefed up regulatory apparatus was necessary to resolve the problem. Bush administration officials congratulated themselves for doing little to avert the disaster, asserting that the disappearance of Enron et al. actually vindicated the free market. Bush's first treasury secretary, Paul O'Neill, not a loyalist when it came to the Iraq war or the administration's tax policies, nevertheless saw the bankruptcy of the nation's sixth largest corporation as more of a vindication than an indictment of contemporary capitalism. "Companies come and go," he said. "Part of the genius of capitalism is people get to make good decisions or bad decisions and they get to pay the consequences. . . . That's the way the system works."[7]

But seeing the way the system works has always been as much a product of the intellect as it has been of testable reality. This book is therefore as much a study of imaginative social thought as it is of political economy. By this we mean the ways key writers and intellectuals, from across the political and aesthetic landscape, have historicized, conceptualized, and projected the trajectory of the social system that we commonly denote as capitalism, certainly as it manifests itself in the West, and specifically within the United States. With few exceptions, the individuals who are the subjects of these essays—Talcott Parsons, Clark Kerr, C. Wright Mills, Peter Drucker, Friedrich von Hayek, C. L. R. James, to name just a sample—did not think of themselves as economists or even as traditional social scientists. They shared few ideological or political ideas in common, but they were all historically minded enough to see that the economic system in which they lived was an evolving, changeable construct with a future that promised to be very different from its past. This historicized sensibility, so alien to the triumphalism and stasis of our own time, is the subject that this essay collection seeks to recapture. Such a reassessment will demonstrate that the capitalist present has been surprisingly different from that projected for it in the past; indeed, it may well stand at considerable variance from the many possible futures that lie before us.

There have been three moments during which American intellectuals have most forcefully engaged themselves in a debate over the essential character and possible futures for American capitalism. In the long generation that extended from the railroad strikes of 1877 until the First World War, the United States became an industrial juggernaut, with all the class strife and economic inequality that was characteristic of big cities, huge mills, and transcontinental markets. This was the era in which the word "capitalism" was first deployed to describe a system in which market, profit, social structure, and ideology were inexorably linked. Marx had never actually used the word, preferring "capitalist mode of production" or "capitalist accumulation" in its stead, but a later generation of Germans, including Werner Sombart and Max Weber, put forward the idea that capitalism was not just an economic mechanism for the creation and distribution of land, labor, and capital but a social and cultural system that shaped every aspect of human existence.[8]

Such a broadly defined usage was welcomed in the United States, especially among reformers and radicals who sought to resolve "the social question," sometimes called the "the labor question," in those late nineteenth-century years when an understanding of the economy and its social consequences seemed so essential. To use the word capitalism in this context implied that the contemporary world was an impermanent state of affairs, historically delimited and possibly ready for a transmutation into something else. But until the turn of the twentieth century neither the critics nor the defenders of American capitalism could see much possibility for an evolutionary transformation of the status quo. The orthodox economists of that era were largely ahistorical proponents of a market whose future looked very like the recent past. In rejoinder, writers like Henry George, Edward Bellamy, or Henry Demarest Lloyd, as well as those who advocated a more scientific brand of socialism, searched for the economic or legislative lever that would precipitate a social crisis and resultant ethical redemption, thus ushering in a commonwealth whose operative principles were at Manichean odds with that of the present order. Although most of these reformers saw the centralizing, monopolizing tendencies apparent in fin de siècle capitalism as indicative of a future dystopia, their understanding of the early twentieth-century economy was that of a largely static system whose reform would require its absolute negation.[9] After the turn of the twentieth century, Progressive reformers put forth a far more incremental and successful reform agenda, but as a system of both power and production, they too held out little hope that capitalist social structures could evolve from within. The state might well play a forceful and effective role, but even in its best incarnation it functioned as a diligent policeman who curbed capital's baser instincts without fundamentally reconstituting the nature of capitalist enterprise itself.[10]

The long generation that stretched from the end of World War I until the height of the Cold War constitutes a second era in the modern history of the capitalist idea in America. This was truly an "Age of Reform," to use and extend the phrase coined by Richard Hofstadter more than half a century ago. This was an epoch in which a new cohort of reformist intellectuals and policy makers came to appreciate the power of social mores, organizational structures, and political initiatives over and above that of the market, the entrepreneur, and the corporation. During five decades of growth in the size and legitimacy of the American state, in which the specter of militarism, Stalinism, and fascism hovered just offstage, it is not surprising that Atlantic intellectuals, both left and right, thought of capitalism as an inadequate phrase for a political economy that was highly politicized and increasingly corporatist. It was in these years, Howard Brick reminds us, that capitalism, the word, fell out of favor, to be replaced by a set of circumlocutions, some quite defensive in character, such as "free enterprise," "industrial society," "machine age," and "private sector."

It is useful to divide this age of reform into two phases. The first is that of the Progressive-New Deal impulse, in which reformist officials and their brains trusts saw the transformation of American capitalism as a political, ideological project linked to popular enthusiasms and conscious planning initiatives. The locomotive of history seemed to be running particularly fast during the Great War, when even Theodore Roosevelt thought "socialized government action . . . absolutely necessary for individual protection and general well-being under the conditions of modern industrialism."[11]

In a second phase, running from the end of World War II until the early 1970s, intellectuals also thought the capitalist system might transmute itself into something quite beyond markets and property. But among the postwar liberals, and even many of the radicals, who forecast the shift to a postindustrial order beyond ideology and class conflict, this shift in history's tectonic plates was less a product of conscious political action, and certainly not social mobilization, than it was a function of capitalism's own malleability, its capacity for incremental calibration at the hands of an expertise that commanded administrative will. President John Kennedy captured this ethos even better than Daniel Bell when he told a 1962 Yale audience that the economic problems facing contemporary society were "technical issues, complicated problems" not subject to the great enthusiasms of yesteryear.[12]

In both phases, liberal intellectuals, from Walter Lippmann and Adolph Berle to John Kenneth Galbraith and Clark Kerr came to believe that the market really had been subordinated, either to a warfare/welfare state or to an organizational revolution that put growth-oriented managerial bureaucracies at the heart of economic decision-making. This wishful accommodation between a generation of intellectuals and the essential features of Western capitalism did not make people like Talcott Parsons, Daniel Bell, or even Peter Drucker pro-capitalist ideologues. Rather, they came to see the hard substance of postwar capitalism as simply of far less consequence or danger than in earlier decades. When it came to a structural understanding of the political economy, most theorists worried far more about a claustrophobic bureaucratism than an uncontrolled market capitalism. Thus in the 1950s, many on the left were consumed in a furious debate over, and condemnation of, the "mass culture" that seemed such a rotten fruit of the economic success generated by postwar corporate capitalism. For John

Kenneth Galbraith, Paul Goodman, Vance Packard, and Dwight Macdonald, organization, expertise, and status anxiety trumped markets, profits, and social conflict.[13]

Because many intellectuals and opinion makers saw the iron cage of Weber as a more informative guide to society's postwar pathologies than the class antagonisms of even a much reformed Marx, they helped prepare the ideological ground for the social and cultural insurgencies of the 1960s. Indeed, in the 1940s and 1950s a deradicalization of social theory, a shift away from an economic or class analysis, made possible and palatable the dramatic reinsertion of race and gender issues into the mainstream political and social agenda. Gunnar Myrdal's liberal idealist construction of the American racial dilemma effectively marginalized the Marxism of men like Oliver Cox, C. L. R. James, and W. E. B. DuBois, thus preparing the way for the patriotic, rights-conscious universalism so effectively championed by Martin Luther King and his civil rights generation. Likewise, Betty Friedan played a decisive role in legitimizing modern feminism, but only after this former left-wing labor journalist had thoroughly psychologized "the woman question" and isolated it from a larger, long-standing critique of work, sex, and family in market society.[14]

If this eclipse of the market in mid-twentieth-century social theory generated creative new ways to think about culture and identity, it made liberals and the left poorly prepared for the turbulence that characterized the world economy in the 1970s and after. Capitalism may have faded from sight after 1950 during what Eric Hobsbawm has identified as the "Golden Age of Capitalism."[15] But it was still capitalism, with all its surprises and instabilities. Thus in the last third of the twentieth century we encounter a third moment when our ideas about the trajectory that American capitalism might follow were significantly transformed. The idea that American society was fundamentally capitalist was rehabilitated on both the right and left. As Howard Brick points out in his essay, the year 1965 might serve as a starting point. That was the moment when *Forbes* magazine, perhaps feeling the first winds of the conservative revival that would soon give Hayek and Milton Friedman the Nobel Prize, launched an advertising campaign that asserted that *Forbes* was indeed a "capitalist tool." Likewise, those inspired by the New Left sought a more systematic analysis of the meaning and character of the system in which they struggled. Growing impatient with incremental reformism and pluralist social science, SDS leader Rennie Davis told a 1965 antiwar rally that in order to understand the ills that beset America, we must "name the system" that had produced Vietnam, racial inequality, and the nuclear arms race.

So when stagflation and stagnant living standards arrived in the 1970s, both the left and the right were ready to once again think of their society as a fundamentally capitalist order. For a time academic Marxism energized the study of labor and legal history, corporate governance, social stratification, and the economics of global capitalism. But the real ideological winners were found on the right. Not only did they have their free-market advocates within the academy, especially in economics, political science, and within the highly influential law schools, but the right generated a popular political constituency that celebrated entrepreneurship, devalued government regulation, and linked the idea of an unfettered capitalism to maintenance of democratic rights and the health of civil society. Triumphal proponents of twenty-first-century capitalism have argued that as the international flow of labor, capital, and information becomes more efficient, the capitalist marketplace has finally become a universal phenomenon, generating a single pathway to wealth and democracy. Exhibit A in this globalization of what had once been an Atlantic-centered world is China, which seems on track to overtake Japan as the world's second largest economy.

An important ideological trope accompanying this forecast is the argument that democratic institutions are bound to flourish in a market society composed of numerous nodes of autonomous economic and institutional power. This perspective is sometimes linked to a kind of technocratic utopianism in which the spread of information technology enhances the market power of individuals and niche producers in a fashion very much at odds with the oligarchic structures that dominated the managerial imagination forty or fifty years ago. Thus by the last years of the twentieth century, both the left and the right could "name the system." Today, when the World Trade Organization or a similar transnational institution meets in Seattle, Sydney, or at some other highly contested venue, both the ministers inside the hall and the demonstrators in the streets know that the subject of their ire, admiration, and debate is pretty much the same world capitalist order.

This book contains thirteen essays that discuss how a number of American intellectuals have thought about the trajectory that capitalism in this country might well follow. These essays do not constitute a history of twentieth-century capitalism in the United States, although the contributors to this collection are well aware of the ebb, flow, and reconfiguration of the American political economy. Rather their variegated perspectives will serve an illuminating purpose if they historicize how we have thought about twentieth-century capitalism, therefore also problematizing the contemporary ideas and sentiments that sustain the sense of inevitabiity that so often characterizes twenty-first-century discussions of global market capitalism.

The opening essays discuss a central theme that runs through many of the contributions: why and how the idea of capitalism became eclipsed by sociological or political constructs encompassing the idea of a "postindustrial" or even "postcapitalist" society. We usually think of such ideas as a product of Cold War tensions, and as David Engerman demonstrates, studies of Soviet industrialization did indeed owe much to federal funding of social science research in the years after 1947. However, Howard Brick uncovers a richer provenance for such views. He traces the roots of what he calls the "post-capitalist vision" back to the intellectual and political crisis that followed World War I, when men like Walter Lippmann were convinced that "a silent revolution is in progress." As Brick points out intellectuals in the post-World War I era questioned both the centrality of capitalism and the distinctiveness of that system. Unlike so many nineteenth-century theorists, from Marx to Sumner, they came to distinguish between the economic order and the social/cultural organization of society. This "shift away from economics," most notable and influential in the work of Talcott Parsons, gave intellectuals, including men like Franz Boas, David Riesman, and Daniel Bell the space to think about culture, psychology, and race. Although liberals and former socialists were most adept at making such prognostications, this sense that capitalism was in the midst of an evolutionary and perhaps conflict-free transformation was also common to conservative icons, including Joseph Schumpeter and Friedrich von Hayek, although they mourned rather than celebrated this effortless shift to a world of postbourgeois power and values.

The onset of the Cold War initially advanced the idea of a postcapitalist vision. At a time when the CIA supported the non-Communist left in Europe, when the Marshall Plan subsidized the growth of the welfare state and the nationalization of key industries, it was easy for many intellectuals, not only those on the left, to believe that capitalism was but a transitory structure of culture, power, and distribution. They saw industrialism and modernity as far more enduring and fundamental, characteristic of societies to the east as well as the west of the Elbe.

As David Engerman makes clear, the idea that the social structures in the Soviet Union and the United States were moving toward a sociological convergence was initially a Western conceit, but the idea eventually turned some social scientists against the Cold War's deepening polarities. If the Soviet Union and the United States were headed in the same direction, then why all the fuss? As a founder of Harvard's influential Russian Research Center, Talcott Parsons, the most important sociologist in the postwar United States, came to believe that the process of industrial modernity within the Soviet Union would eventually transform an authoritarian society into one of "democracy, pluralism, and rationalism." Just as Parsons came to think that Marxism had little leverage in the West as an ideology, so too did he believe that in the Soviet Union aspirations for a revolutionary transformation would be replaced by economic instrumentalism and scientific pragmatism, a posture not all that different from the ideas that guided the mixed economies of the United States and Western Europe.

Indeed, the idea of transnational convergence—along some axis involving mass consumption, industrial complexity, and social pluralism—became a hallmark of post-World War II liberalism. But as Engerman shows us, the same Parsonsian architecture that might forecast convergence along liberal democratic lines, could also take on a darker coloration if the bureaucratization, manipulation, and authoritarian corporatism associated with industrialism would transform the capitalist West into something not all that different from the Stalinist East. This was the "nightmare" vision of the convergence forecast by C. Wright Mills, Herbert Marcuse, and Alvin Gouldner.

The replacement of the idea of capitalism by an ideologically neutered "industrialism" had a profound impact on American liberalism and on the way in which social problems were defined and tackled during that era—between 1930 and 1980—when liberalism represented the dominant political and intellectual discourse in the United States. This is made abundantly clear in the essays covering three key figures: the prolific, high profile economist and public intellectual John Kenneth Galbraith, the labor economist and educator Clark Kerr, and the management theorist Peter Drucker, whose conservatism accommodated an understanding of capitalist industrialism that liberals might well endorse themselves. All shared in the postcapitalist vision identified by Howard Brick and they all believed in an optimistic, Whiggish variant of the convergence hypothesis that Parsons and his Harvard-MIT colleagues advanced.

Clark Kerr is best known as the University of California educator who confronted a successful student insurgency in the fall of 1964. Kerr's conception of the corporate multiversity seemed oppressive and claustrophobic to Berkeley students, who fought for freedom of speech, supported civil rights, and sought a larger, more authentic degree of personal autonomy within the highly organized social structures that seemed so characteristic of education, work, and even play. Kerr's obtuseness in that crisis, argues Paddy Riley, can only be understood if one takes into account his own theory of postwar industrialism. Kerr's World War II experience as a young arbitrator-mediator convinced him, and the cohort of labor economists who would prove so influential in the postwar years, that neither Marxist theory nor market-oriented economics could explain the practical fashion by which self-interested institutions—labor, management, the government—fought to manipulate and reshape the political economy.

Instead, Kerr shifted his gaze from the world of industrial conflict that he had sought to mediate in the 1940s to a world of knowledge-based institutions and interests that he saw in the 1950s as key to the system of "pluralistic industrialism" that was replacing the class polarities that had been characteristic of early twentieth-century capitalism. Not unexpectedly, Kerr believed that knowledge was the key to social progress, and like so many social theorists of the mid-twentieth century, he believed that societal convergence was taking place at home as well as abroad. For Kerr, the trajectory all industrial societies were bound to follow put nations in the third world and the Soviet bloc on the same path as the capitalist West. But in similar fashion, Kerr believed that the imperatives privileging knowledge and skillful management were also driving all the organizational components at the core of an advanced industrial society like the United States. Thus a kind of efficacious convergence was taking place between the modern business corporation and the research university. "The elites all wear grey flannel suits," quipped Kerr. Instead of conflict at the picket line or the ballot box, "The battles (in the new knowledge society) will be in the corridors instead of the streets, and memos will flow instead of blood."[16]

If Clark Kerr's sunny expectations were shaken by the rise of an impatient New Left, not all liberals in the 1950s and 1960s shared the Californian's Whiggish determinism. Like Kerr, John Kenneth Galbraith believed that history was moving in his direction, but as Kevin Mattson makes clear, he remained an engaged intellectual who disdained the complacency that had crept into the outlook of men like Kerr and the administrative liberals of his generation.

Galbraith's intellectual pedigree descended from Thorsen Veblen as well as Adolph Berle and Gardiner Means, whose landmark 1932 book, *The Modern Corporation and Private Property*, offered New Dealers so much analytical firepower. From the former Galbraith took his faith in what he would call the "educational and scientific estate," and from the latter his argument, on display most clearly in the *New Industrial State* (1967), that in the modern corporation ownership had been effectively divorced from control, making the shareholders marginal to the trajectory of modern American capitalism. Like Parsons and Kerr, Galbraith was a pluralist, but he never allowed the complacent determinism of his social scientific contemporaries to color his politics. Mattson is entirely right to emphasize that Galbraith remained a combative, activist liberal even during the 1950s when the Harvard economist was most confident that a New Dealish, ideologically consensual politics had become hegemonic across a fair slice of the policy spectrum. This was because Galbraith, true to the spirit of Veblen and his austere Scotch-Irish forbearers, remained skeptical of economic growth per se and the privatized consumerism that by the late 1950s had come to seem both aesthetically repellant and socially dysfunctional. In shifting a critique of American capitalism to those grounds, Galbraith shared much with the cultural and ecological New Left, but the very success of this brand of post-scarcity liberalism left American liberals unprepared for the renewed arguments over market fundamentalism that the right would advance when in the 1970s it became clear that American capitalism was not on automatic pilot.

Peter Drucker, the foremost management theorist of the last half of the twentieth century, shared an intellectual companionship with liberals like Kerr and Galbraith because, like them, Drucker believed that capitalism had transformed itself into a system that successfully subordinated both market and property to the technocracy and bureaucracy engendered by industrial society. As Nils Gilman argues with much insight, Drucker's great task was the legitimization of the corporation in an era when capitalist enterprise seemed responsible for the twin catastrophes of the 1930s, the onset of the Great Depression and the rise of Central European fascism. Drucker saw that the Nazis attracted mass support because they provided an alternative to the mechanistic, economic conception of man characteristic of classical liberalism.

Thinking along lines that paralleled those of Kerr, Galbraith, and Parsons, Drucker also threw out the market, marginalized the engine of profit, and defined industrialism as an organic system of mutual obligations. But unlike the self-conscious liberals, Drucker put his politicized reconceptualization of Western capitalism at the service of the modern corporation, which he thought of as a kind of constitutional regime that, in the best of hands and circumstances, might stand athwart the atomizing, existentially harsh modernity that was the hallmark of twentieth-century economic life. He was a man of the right, concludes Gilman, who understood "that conservatives had to develop a democratic theory of industrial organization if they wanted to save capitalism from existential implosion." In 1940s America, Drucker therefore endorsed collective bargaining, high wages, and the welfare state.

Left-wing intellectuals were not absent from the mid-twentieth-century debate about the character and trajectory of capitalism. They were more self-conscious in their critique, and gave to their analysis a moral, as well as a sociological, incisiveness, but in many respects they shared important points of commonality with the mainstream liberals. During the 1950s C. Wright Mills may well have been the nation's foremost social critic, and in the decades since his untimely death in 1962 Mills's reputation as a radical analyst of the American social structure has made a steady advance.

However, as Daniel Geary makes clear, Mills was influential because he replaced the phraseology of capitalist exploitation with a set of social structures and psychological categories that were rooted much more in a Weberian than an economic analysis of power in America. Indeed, Mills was just as much a student of Max Weber as Talcott Parsons, and like the Harvard sociologist, Mills helped move mid-twentieth-century social science away from economics and toward a study of "total social structures." Of course, whereas Parsons and other liberals highlighted those Weberian arguments stressing social cohesion, Mills and the radicals who followed him emphasized the Marxisant element within Weber's social thought, pointing to the compulsive character of large-scale economic, military, and political institutions. The Mills of *White Collar* and *The Power Elite* saw American society bound together not by common values à la Parsons but by "big chains of authority." They were rational, bureaucratic, and universalistic, but for all that modernism still oppressive and claustrophobic.

Although he did fieldwork in Puerto Rico, Mills, like so many left-wing social scientists of his generation, ignored issues of race and region. Yet two of the greatest theorists of capitalist transformation were products of the Caribbean diaspora whose ideological legacy remains potent half a century after their productive apogee. Both C. L. R. James and Oliver Cox imported into their understandings of world capitalism a racial dimension sorely lacking in that of most mid-twentieth-century theorists. They put at the center of their analysis the dichotomy between the trans-Atlantic core and the agricultural, colonized periphery where divisions of wealth and labor were determined by a racially embrocated structure of power that these intellectuals did so much to put at the center of late twentieth century consciousness and then deconstruct in such a forceful, telling manner.

C. L. R. James is known for his great history of race, class, and revolution in San Domingo, which appeared in 1938 as *The Black Jacobins*; and in more recent decades his understanding of a rich and autonomous world of working-class sport and culture has been rediscovered by scholars involved with postcolonial theory and subaltern studies. But as Christopher Phelps shows us, James was also a participant in the debate over the trajectory of world capitalism during those mid-twentieth-century decades just before its stability became a widely accepted hypothesis. James was not an academic and he did not write for the mainstream press, so his argument that a form of "state capitalism" characterized regimes East of the Rhine was largely confined to the debates that so ardently engaged Trotskyist intellectuals in the U.S. and Europe.

But if in the 1930s and 1940s few were aware of such polemical exchanges, Phelps nevertheless demonstrates that much was at stake. The character and fate of the Bolshevik Revolution—the "Russian Question"—was never about the Soviet Union alone. As was the case with Parsons, Kerr, and Mills, studies of the USSR became part of the debate over the future of Western capitalism as well, and over the leverage of those forces that might transform it. For James and his circle, therefore, the understanding that the Soviet regime was "state capitalist" meant that it was still subject to the internal conflicts and contradictions common to all capitalist regimes. It was not an immutable totalitarianism that only a militarized West could contain and defeat. James therefore looked to those oppositional impulses that remained outside the structures of power. As Phelps shows so well, he retained an abstract faith in the potency of the traditional working class, but his lasting fame would rest upon his exploration of those seemingly apolitical, culturally resonant impulses that he first observed in the Caribbean struggle against British imperialism.

Oliver Cox was also a product of the ideologically fertile Caribbean, and he too proved to be a scholar whose work gained far more influence after his death than before. Like James, Cox understood race and caste as categories that derived far more from the imperatives of the labor market than they did from any cultural or social traditionalism. They were hardly an example of the cultural lag that liberals believed the market or the industrial bureaucracy would necessarily dissolve. Although once eclipsed by James, Oliver Cox's multivolume exploration of the division of labor and profit in the Atlantic world has become increasingly relevant to those who study global capitalism. It is not surprising that Cox had little influence when theories of developmental modernization and industrial rationality were hegemonic on the liberal left, but in the early twenty-first century Cox's racially inflected world systems schema, his critique of what we would today call globalization, offers us an analytical weapon with which a deconstruction of the Washington consensus and the World Bank's privatization agenda might begin.

Just as Cox and James began to see racial constructions as endemic to world capitalism, so too does Daniel Horowitz demonstrate that the feminist founders of U.S. women's history were all engaged in a dialogue with classical Marxism, a conversation in which the structural claims of a Friedrich Engels, an August Bebel, or even a Charlotte Perkins Gilman gave way before an explosion of scholarship that emphasized historical contingency and literary meaning. In this realm of feminist politics and scholarship, autonomous cultural, social and ideological patterns of subordination and power superseded the more structuralist hierarchies that were characteristic of a Marxist mode of analysis. Horowitz, who has made a parallel argument in his celebrated biography of Betty Friedan, here examines four feminist writers whose ideas on gender, economics, and power were shaped by Popular Front culture and Communist Party practice. In their early work, Eleanor Flexner, Carl Degler, Gerda Lerner, and Aileen Kraditor all explored the question with which a generation of scholars and activists had once grappled, "Does capitalism liberate women?"

Whatever their answer, the centrality of the question itself demonstrated that this cohort of feminist historians all thought that issues involving the division of labor, the relationship of property to patriarchy, and the fate of the working class were keys to understanding the history of women and the meaning of gender in the modern world. Politically, these intellectuals tended toward political liberalism and a Whiggish historiography, with the possible exception of Kraditor, who opted for a cynical neoconservatism in her later years. As with Kerr and Galbraith, a bureaucratic industrialism became the vague societal category that replaced the polarities of power and ideology once found in their analysis of capitalist patriarchy. The cultural superstructure had emerged as autonomous while the structural imperatives of a capitalist organization of work and family faded from center stage. This ideological trajectory helped mainstream the history of women in U.S. scholarship, but in the process the feminist academy lost a certain analytical edge, or rather, issues of power, wealth, and class dropped from view in the post-1970s era, as they had for many other liberals.

But just as the left was beginning to emphasize the autonomy of a set of cultural, racial, and gender structures within modern society, the American right was beginning to rediscover the virtues of the market, and to celebrate, with little apology, the inequalities and conflicts that were the necessary fruit of a free and unfettered capitalism. Friedrich von Hayek is an essential figure in this battle of ideas: his 1944 book *The Road to Serfdom* has achieved canonical status as the work that gave rise to the modern conservative movement and the reemergence of laissez-faire economics. *The Road to Serfdom* was an energetic antisocialist, anti-welfare state polemic, but it achieved a huge resonance because it linked that critique of Anglo-American economic regulation to an attack on the fascist and Stalinist evils of that era.

As Juliet Williams demonstrates in her contribution to this volume, Hayek's reputation as a libertarian extremist is somewhat exaggerated, although this is largely a consequence of his own self-popularization among audiences attuned to such views. He actually held that the modern liberal state must exercise some regulatory power if capitalist markets and social stability were to be preserved. For example, Hayek supported Social Security during the same season, in the early 1960s, when Barry Goldwater first put its privatization on the Republican political agenda. But Hayek eclipsed the nuance and complexity of his political economy by indulging in rhetoric that misrepresented his own theorizing, such as his well-known warning that "so soon as one moves an inch in the planned direction you are necessarily launched on the slippery path which will lead you in due course over the precipice." In the end, concludes Williams, Hayek was not a closet authoritarian, but a reluctant democrat who was torn between his neoliberal philosophy and his elitist politics.

The conservative, antistate populism from which Hayek drew such acclaim was also fertile ground for a mid-twentieth-century assault upon a set of institutions that were emblematic both of the preservation of great wealth as well as the advancement of the postwar brand of economic regulation advocated by so many of the liberal intellectuals discussed in this volume. There was a double irony here, as Alice O'Connor makes clear in her discussion of the political controversy in which big philanthropies like Ford and Rockefeller found themselves embroiled in the 1950s and 1960s. On the one hand, the invention of the modern philanthropic foundation came in the era of the robber barons. Sustained by tax policy and a benign regulatory environment, these institutions allowed a class of extraordinarily rich Americans to perpetuate their influence from one generation to the next. But on the other hand, the ideological outlook adopted by the old-line foundations ran parallel to that of the Parsonian intellectuals: differences in economic power and wealth were marginal to the values and roles played by individuals in a mass society, even as a cosmopolitan elite assumed key posts in government, business, and academe.

An embittered critique of this brand of liberal philanthropy soon emerged on the right, for which the big foundations came to represent the subversion of free-market capitalism and the rise of planning, internationalism, and racial integration, all orchestrated by a cadre of intellectuals and professional bureaucrats, just the sort of people Kerr and Galbraith thought essential players in the construction of a modern, knowledge-based society. We have in this controversy the kernel of a "new class" analysis of liberalism and the welfare state, later advanced by neoconservative intellectuals in the 1970s and 1980s. Wedded to an ideology of social science empiricism and consensual politics, the big foundations had few tools with which to respond to this ideological assault. Indeed, as O'Connor points out, foundations like Ford and Carnegie became increasingly timid after 1969, especially as a phalanx of overtly ideological, self-consciously conservative think tanks and foundations began to make their weight felt in the Washington policy arena. Conservative foundations like Bradley, Olin, and Scaife funded the ideas that would legitimize the Reagan-Bush ascendancy. Their work achieved an ironic victory early in the twenty-first century when the administration of George W. Bush slashed the federal estate tax, which had been premised upon the Progressive-era idea that great wealth, in purely private hands, should not descend unfettered or untaxed from one generation to the next.

To explain the popular success for this kind of raw market ideology, the careers of two influential right-wing propagandists bear close examination. Lemuel Boulware was the personnel director of General Electric in the 1940s and 1950s. Like Peter Drucker, he sought to legitimize the corporation in an age of labor, war, and government planning. But unlike Drucker, whose starting point was the catastrophic failure of liberal capitalism in Europe, Boulware was a product of that self-confident, technically advanced business civilization that was but momentarily shaken by the Great Depression in the United States. And whereas Drucker welcomed the voice of labor as a kind of junior partner, whose calibrated accommodation would itself reinforce the legitimacy of corporate hegemony, Boulware thought of labor power the way Hayek, in *The Road to Serfdom*, thought of state planning: give an inch and you are well on the way to a collectivist dystopia.

In Kim Phillips-Fein's fascinating portrait of Lemuel Boulware, we see the way in which the ideas of conservatives like Hayek and Ludwig von Mises are invoked to propagate an increasingly conservative corporate agenda. Drucker was honest enough to recognize that America's giant corporations were planning regimes whose inner life was that of a paternal autocracy relentlessly seeking to subordinate the market to a larger corporate purpose. Boulware, like so many other American business conservatives, indulged himself in the useful fantasy that a corporation like General Electric was but a weak and pliant instrument of other forces: customer choice, labor market pressures, and technological innovation. Trade unionism, powerfully entrenched among the skilled workers in the key General Electric plants, seemed a particularly egregious assault upon market rationalism and management prerogative. Radicals like Mills and liberals like Galbraith were equally skillful in their evisceration of such managerial mythmaking, but Boulware was more successful in the long run, for it was his linkage of a steadfast anti-unionism with a radical ideological assault upon the New Deal that carried the day in late twentieth-century America.

That an audience of militant libertarians was ready to endorse a celebration of market capitalism became clear, as Jennifer Burns reminds us in her splendid story of Ayn Rand's rise and fall within the hothouse world of American conservatism. Rand was an amazingly influential novelist whose *The Fountainhead* (1943) and *Atlas Shrugged* (1957) sold in the millions. Her works of radical individualism and militant hostility to planning, unionism, and the New Deal defended capitalism as efficient, democratic, and ethically moral. A Jewish refugee from the Bolshevik Revolution, her libertarianism was nevertheless bound tightly to the atheism that was a hallmark for the rationalistic humanism of those early twentieth-century decades. She was therefore a fierce, high-profile proponent of "Godless capitalism."

Rand's posture and her popularity were a challenge to the generation of conservatives who took their lead from William F. Buckley's new *National Review* magazine. Seeking a fusion of capitalist markets and Christian traditions, these conservatives found themselves thwarted and embarrassed by Rand's disdain for the church, its theology, and the community of believers. Her novels had highlighted the contradictions between a dynamic, egotistical capitalism and Christian "virtue," but it was just this combination that the new conservatives thought both morally defensible and politically expedient. Most of the writers at Buckley's *National Review* were convinced that as an atheist, Rand missed the central truth offered by the new conservatism: that religion was the only viable foundation for victory over the collectivist madness of Stalin's terror, or even the creeping estatism that was advancing in the West. In a devastating, dismissive 1957 review of *Atlas Shrugged* Whittaker Chambers drove home this point, arguing that Rand's "materialism of the Right" differed little from "a materialism of the Left." Rand would command a large audience for yet another decade, but the Catholic conservatives who pioneered the modern linkage between Christian religiosity and capitalist markets had successfully marginalized Rand's secular libertarianism. The path was now clear to a revival of laissez-faire politics and growth of a religious constituency massive enough to advance those anti-welfare state policies.

Contemporary American politics seems to confirm both the triumph of the capitalist imagination and the simultaneous extent to which that ideological construct has become so completely embedded within the conventions of public discourse as to render it invisible. "The forces of the market are just that," pronounced the Chicago school economist Arnold Harberger on a Public Broadcasting Service interview show early in the current century, "they are like the wind and the tides . . . if you want to try to ignore them, you ignore them at your peril."[17]

One might not think that orthodox sentiments of this sort played much of a role in the rightward lurch of American politics, including that of the 2004 election, but as Thomas Frank, Harold Meyerson, and other pathologists of Democratic Party decline have observed, liberalism's incapacity to historicize this kind of market absolutism, to offer hard-pressed voters a larger analysis, both moral and ideological, of what ails them renders even the most cautious left-of-center politicians defenseless against the culture-war attacks continuously, and creatively, generated on the right. The liberal default is not just a question of program: of a failure to push for universal health care, a substantial rise in the minimum wage, or a reform in the labor law. These proposals gain little traction, even among supporters, because they are not offered as part of a structural explanation for the state of the economy and the dynamic that drives contemporary American capitalism. Thus when Frank conducted a 2004 tour of West Virginia, a state where the primitive polarities inherent in an extractive brand of capitalism once ensured a rough kind of class politics, he found working-class cabins and trailers plastered with George Bush posters.[18]

West Virginia residents still imagined a world in which they were confronted by a set of alien oppressors, but in the early years of the twenty-first century these were far more likely to be found among the bicoastal cosmopolitans than the mine-owning barons of old or the Wal-Mart manager down the street. Unlike the liberals, the culture warriors in the GOP have successfully imagined a social and economic universe, full of strife and tension, in which the future really is up for grabs. If libertarian-tending conservatives like Lemuel Boulware and Friedrich von Hayek could not quite pull this off, William Buckley and his heirs did figure out how the right could finally wed laissez-faire markets with Christian morals in modern America. All this is highly ironic, of course, because the ideological eclipse of market capitalism, and the class politics that inevitably accompanied it, was in some small but significant part a product of liberal and left-wing efforts to move beyond ownership and exchange and into a world in which knowledge, status and culture played a much larger role in structuring consciousness, politics, and the postcapitalist future.

No collection of scholarly essays can expect to serve as a particularly effective vehicle for authors intervening in contemporary political debate. But historical consciousness remains one of the intellect's most potent subversions, which is why it is our hope that an historicized understanding of twentieth-century capitalism can unsteady a few twenty-first-century verities and provide a glimpse of a possible future that is something more than a return to the political economy of a pre- New Deal era that we once thought long-buried.

Part I
Theorizing Twentieth-Century American Capitalism

1

The Postcapitalist Vision in Twentieth-Century American Social Thought

Howard Brick

Since the Cold War's end, paeans to the victory of capitalism have brought us to a peculiar pass in modern social thought. The term itself was not always widely embraced. Early modern Europe knew "capital" and "capitalist," but naming a whole socioeconomic order "capitalism" began only in the mid-nineteenth century, usually linked with left-wing dissenters and hence anathema to leaders of, and pleaders for, a modern, private property, free-market system.[1] Only in the early twentieth century, particularly as the work of Max Weber, Werner Sombart, and Henri Pirenne became widely known, did "capitalism" gain some legitimacy in the academy, suggesting even a slight leftward tilt there, for the term still implied two things that many of the system's defenders wished to deny: that the private market economy was historically specific (one could speak of the "rise of capitalism" and thus perhaps its "fall") and that it was socially constituted, based on a specific arrangement of institutions, motives, and actions other than allegedly natural "propensities" for trade and gain.[2]

Nonetheless, American businessmen and their publicists also began using the term "capitalism" unapologetically in the 1920s, though it frequently appeared next to, or interchangeably with, alternatives such as "the competitive system" or "the American system."[3] By the 1940s, business circles became somewhat more circumspect, and some spokespeople considered the euphemistic "free enterprise" a friendlier term, with "capitalism" serving as the special usage of the more "hard-boiled" conservatives who insisted on upholding a strict doctrine of laissez-faire—and who felt on the defensive for much of the postwar period.[4] Thus the late 1970s campaign to market *Forbes* magazine as a "capitalist tool" was self-consciously brash, embracing a term originally sensed to be (and used again in the 1960s as) a left-wing insult, while it also signaled the right turn of public discourse, back to the world of 1920s business publicists and the 1940s Taft Republicans.[5] Now in the early twenty-first century, even the memory of insult has fled. My students define their society as "capitalism" and are surprised to hear the word ever seemed off-color *or* that capitalism has a history. They doubt the idea

that capitalism may not reflect natural impulses brought to fruition in en-
lightened modernity. Even at this moment, despite embarrassment over the
late-1990s stock market bubble and creeping corporate scandals, "capitalism" seems unexceptionable, suggesting permanence, not transience.

Neither today's confidence in the permanence of capitalism nor the old-
fashioned nineteenth-century discomfort with implications of its transience,
however, defined the cast of mind that marked mid-twentieth-century liberal American social thought. During the postwar period (1945–1973), many
social theorists and observers claimed that "capitalism" no longer adequately
described the key traits of social life in the United States or other "advanced"
countries. Part of the problem lay in the term itself, which appeared to them
either too vaguely defined or too prejudicial in presuming what it had to
prove (i.e., that economic relations defined the nature of a society). But
they also believed that contemporary society, empirically, had changed in
ways that escaped the limits of capitalism. Something new and unheralded
was afoot, hard to name and variously defined: in Western Europe, a few
discussed "postcapitalist" society; Americans began talking of "postindustrial" society (displacing "capitalism" from the center of attention); others
settled simply on "modern society," intending to show that the ubiquity of
bureaucratic or professional organization carried more weight than property relations.[6] Euphemistic impulses were not paramount in these circles.
This midcentury mode of thought emerged *after* the concept of capitalism
had achieved some legitimacy in academic social thought in the 1920s, and
it arose not among those wishing to defend the private property system but
among thinkers and writers reared in various styles of criticizing that system.
They dispensed with "capitalism" not because they viewed socioeconomic
relations as given and fixed but because they saw those relations profoundly
in flux—and even the name "capitalism," they thought, rendered the indefinite character of present social relations too sharply, rigidly, and statically.

This broad, long-running current of writers speculating on the obsolescence of the concept of capitalism or the transmutation of capitalist reality
might be summed up as "the postcapitalist vision," though this phrase would
refer to a wider group than those in the 1950s who explicitly promoted the
name "postcapitalist society," such as Anthony Crosland, intellectual leader
of the British Labor Party's "new right," and the liberal German sociologist
Ralf Dahrendorf. Crosland in particular welcomed the new "statist" order
he said had displaced "capitalism."[7] Given partial nationalizations and a
substantial measure of social provision, Crosland saw an end to "the absolute autonomy of economic life." Furthermore, he wrote, "the dominant
emphasis ceases to be on the rights of property, private initiative, competition, and the profit motive; and is transferred to the duties of the state,
social and economic security, and the virtues of cooperative action."[8]

Yet, while claims like this provide something of a touchstone for the
current of thought at issue here, the "postcapitalist vision" would include

writers who simply argued that advanced Western societies were no longer adequately understood as "capitalist," or that these societies were witnessing the decline in the social salience of capitalist institutions, or indeed more boldly, that they had passed (or were about to pass) a boundary beyond the characteristic structures and processes of capitalism. Writers of the latter sort cited various markers of change: the appearance of new institutional forms for organizing enterprise that were not entirely "private"; the rise of the regulatory state that increasingly limited the sway of market mechanisms and ultimately deprived them of the power to determine social affairs; the role played in motivating social change by noneconomic forces (i.e., not by capital accumulation as such), forces such as scientific knowledge or egalitarian values of civic inclusion, participation, and social provision; the apparently collectivizing impact of advanced technology; the waning of economics as the privileged sphere of social action and analytical understanding; and so forth.

Such propositions were not unique to Crosland's milieu, a left-leaning Europe in an age of postwar reconstruction, but characterized American observers as well. Despite our tendency to view the 1940s through the 1960s as a "golden age" of capitalism, in which war-sparked growth resurrected the repute of private enterprise and crushed all pretenders to collectivist futures, a fairly robust reformist vision survived in the United States and read the future through other than procapitalist lenses.[9] Moreover, while this current of social thought undoubtedly became intertwined with the political conditions of the Cold War, it was neither spawned by, nor can it be reduced to, Cold War anticommunism. Midcentury social theorists in this vein had a pedigree, we will see, that linked them to an older intellectual current, emerging around the first world war and running through the 1920s and 1930s. Brought into the postwar world and lasting until the 1970s, the postcapitalist vision made up one of the most enduring, yet overlooked or misunderstood set of ideas of the twentieth century.

Discerning the Postcapitalist Vision

The first task is to recognize the salience of this set of ideas in midcentury intellectual life and to outline some of its dimensions. Some sense that capitalism—the concept and the reality of the thing—was growing obsolete filtered through academic and public discourse after World War II. Writing in an American magazine in 1953 on the alpine sanitorium, the Berghof, depicted in his novel, *The Magic Mountain*, Thomas Mann cast "capitalism"—in fullest health identified with an old bourgeois way of life—as a fading order:

Such institutions as the Berghof were a typical pre-war [World War I] phenomenon. They were only possible in a capitalistic economy that was still functioning well and normally. Only under such a system was it possible for patients to remain there year and year at the family's expense. *The Magic Mountain* became the swan song of that form of existence.[10]

American writers too thought that a "normal" capitalism no longer existed. The leading sociologist Talcott Parsons began his career in the 1920s fascinated by Sombart's and Weber's work on the nature of capitalism and declared that understanding "capitalism as a social system" was the key to building a modern social science.[11] Yet, by the early 1940s, Parsons had concluded that "the capitalism/socialism dichotomy" no longer applied, for American society was not *simply* capitalist, and in ways bound to grow in significance as time went on, had already surpassed the norms of capitalism.[12]

Reasons for doubting the relevance of "capitalism" to the contemporary social order varied. Long-standing debates about which traits most essentially defined capitalism—be it economic individualism, the expansion of market exchange, laissez-faire principles, the process of capital accumulation and the generalization of wage labor, or an ethic of work, saving, and private investment—struck some observers as fruitless and too weighted with political bias.[13] In any case, if it were agreed that capitalism defined an *economic* system, did it make sense to name a whole *society* "capitalist," disregarding the relative weight of different elements—besides the economic sphere, the political, cultural, familial, and psychological aspects—that make up a complex social order? Observers wondered, that is, whether the competitive, profit-driven, market mechanisms of capitalism any longer dominated social life as they once had, thus questioning the *centrality* of capitalism in contemporary society. Others questioned the *distinctiveness* of capitalism. The Cold War coexistence of market and command economies devoted to mass production suggested to some observers and social critics that a generic "industrial society," rather than capitalism in particular, became the most salient object of analysis in the modern era.[14]

At the same time, and in a somewhat different sense, influential writers thought that the capitalist form of contemporary Western society had itself grown indistinct, blurred by the advent of "mixed" systems in the West or by prospects for a "convergence" of capitalist and noncapitalist orders on some new, third term. Having emerged in the 1930s and 1940s among social democrats eager to combine elements of market and plan, the idea of a "mixed economy" initially meant more than a homeopathic dose of government regulation in a private property economy. It suggested an admixture of economic principles and institutions that created something new.[15] Thus even the hard-nosed realist of French sociology, Raymond Aron, wrote in 1954, with reference to the postwar order encompassing regulation, state enterprises, and limited planning, that "socialism has ceased in the West to be a myth because it has become a part of reality."[16] As a vision of convergence, on the other hand, a New York sinologist discussing U.S. relations with East Asia in 1964 foresaw an "integrated world" coming, marked by "new world forces—post-Marxian and post-capitalist—twenty-first century, not nineteenth."[17] George Lichtheim called postwar Western Europe "post-bourgeois," a society where "what underlies the whole movement is the persistent tension between social and market values, with the former gradually getting the upper hand."[18] These various ways of doubting the applicability of "capitalism" in contemporary social analysis were complemented by those who continued to use the term capitalism but nonetheless saw it as a *passing* order: Liberal economist Robert Heilbroner wrote *The Limits of American Capitalism* (1966), arguing that its growth capacity had diminished and new socioeconomic forces had appeared on the scene that pressed beyond its bounds. Earlier, Heilbroner's well-known survey of modern economic thought, *The Worldly Philosophers* (1953), had ended with a chapter hopefully entitled "Beyond the Economic Revolution," suggesting an upcoming time when market calculation of price-based efficiency, as the key to allocating scarce social resources, would lose its grip on modern life.

The postcapitalist vision was not a socialist one—especially because doubt about the significance of "capitalism" usually carried skepticism about the meaning of its customary opposite, "socialism," as well. There was a good deal of modesty, uncertainty, or hesitation in judging the outcome of present developments, hence the utility of the prefix, "post-," which typically signals a degree of reticence in prediction.[19] Nonetheless, for most advocates of the postcapitalist vision, their skepticism or modesty regarding the name of the emergent order was linked to a remarkable progressive confidence in some sort of evolution toward a "social economy" or a society that had gotten beyond the unalloyed supremacy of markets and private wealth. To be sure, the postcapitalist vision still owed something to styles of socialist thought known as "revisionist" in the early twentieth century, associated particularly with the "evolutionary" perspectives of Eduard Bernstein. Bernstein's gradualist notion of capitalism "growing over into" socialism lent the postcapitalist vision its characteristic understanding of change: that the present marked a transition where no clear divisions or boundaries were evident.[20] French social democrat Jean Jaurès had vividly captured this conception of change: moderns, he wrote, would experience the advent of socialism as navigators "crossed the line of a hemisphere—not that they have been able to see as they crossed it a cord stretched over the ocean warning them of their passage, but that little by little they have been led into a new hemisphere by the progress of their ship."[21] For postcapitalist theorists, similarly, gradual changes in degree could usher in world-shifting transformations barely sensed until they had come to pass. Contemporary society was perpetually reinventing itself, eluding old labels and practices.

The postcapitalist vision also possessed a good deal of political lability. So far in this description, it has appeared as a reformist current welcoming the transitional developments of the moment for the promise they held of a greater social democracy. Yet a more critical or pessimistic counterpoint had emerged as well, imagining a new order of politically regulated markets as an unheralded, but oppressive—even totalitarian—regime. Speculation since the early 1940s about a "managerial revolution" (James Burnham), "administered society" (Max Horkheimer and Theodor Adorno), and the like emerged alongside postwar social-democratic aspirations, and while the pessimistic current countered the hopes of liberal postcapitalist theorists, it shared the assumption of having passed a watershed that rendered old definitions of capitalism obsolete.[22] The "critical sociology" of C. Wright Mills, for instance, occupied one corner in the field of postcapitalist vision, rather than standing outside it, since Mills "sidestepped the issue of capitalism," as Daniel Bell has put it.[23] The "power elite" of government chiefs, top military men, and corporate executives that Mills assailed appeared in his rendering to be untroubled by either class conflicts or business cycles. Rather than focusing on issues of property, inequity, exploitation, and destructive economic development, Mills criticized above all the "bureaucratization and centralization of the means of political power," historian Kevin Mattson writes.[24] Furthermore, Mills's suggestion around 1960 that a "New Left" would "center, first of all, upon the cultural apparatus and the intellectuals within it," along with his advocacy of a "public Science machine, subject to public control," shows his proximity to those of his contemporaries who described a "postindustrial" society defined, as we will see below, by its peculiar dependence on knowledge production and the growth-fostering impact of "science" as a social good.[25]

Indeed, the American New Left of young radical intellectuals might be considered part of the postcapitalist vision too. No one evoked the sense of unsettled social analysis for a coming new age better than Paul Potter, president of SDS, addressing an antiwar demonstration in 1965:

What kind of system is it that justifies the United States or any country seizing the destinies of the Vietnamese people and using them callously for its own purpose? What kind of system is it that disenfranchises people in the South, leaves millions upon millions of people throughout the country impoverished and excluded from the mainstream and promise of American society, that creates faceless and terrible bureaucracies and makes those the place where people spend their lives and do their work, that consistently puts material values before human values—and still persists in calling itself free and . . . fit to police the world? . . . We must name that system. We must name it, describe it, analyze it, understand it and change it.[26]

Potter had no suggestions for a name and later remarked, "capitalism was for me and my generation an inadequate description of the evils of America."[27] In this respect, although New Leftists served as harsh critics of the postcapitalist liberals, the young radicals shared their conviction of inhabiting a profoundly new stage of social evolution, following a recent sea-change that brought them beyond old capitalist standards of market autonomy and class conflict to a highly organized order that called for a new kind of opposition.

The postcapitalist vision does not represent the *main* current or the sum total of American social thought in this period. It was largely limited to left-liberal intellectuals and some of their more radical critics. Most economists, unconventional social analysts such as Barrington Moore, Jr., as well as certain distinctive trends in economic anthropology and the beginnings of attention to world systems, lay outside it. Relatively small circles of Marxists sustained the critique of Western society as capitalist, and even smaller circles of radical writers like that around C. L. R. James answered liberal convergence theories with an alternative convergence view of the Soviet Union as "state capitalism," highlighting how fraught the very definition of capitalism was.[28] Despite these varieties of terminology and diagnosis, the postcapitalist vision constituted one of the prevalent moods among postwar Western intellectuals, and it seeped into a broader milieu of public discourse through those thinkers' ties to elite magazines and newspaper writers and their subtle influence on how reformers framed their aspirations.[29] Not only did this mode of thought deem conservative faith in "private enterprise" out of touch with the currents of change in modern society; it also trumped more traditional left-wing arguments that the lineaments of bourgeois society had survived the constant alterations of modernity and the stresses of twentieth-century wars and depressions intact.

The prominence of this discourse in postwar American intellectual life prompts a new look at the social history of ideas in the twentieth century. Intellectual life after World War II is often described in terms of a broad conservative drift and collapse of social criticism, pending an unexpected renewal of dissent, circa 1960, that cast aside the conformist spirit of the Cold War years.[30] But insofar as the renewed dissent of the 1960s shared a sense of inhabiting a new order which old categories of social analysis failed to grasp, it is reasonable to inquire into the hidden sympathy between postwar liberalism and radicalism—and even to imagine that the new radicalism arose not merely in opposition to new forms of social control in an overorganized age (though that impulse undoubtedly gave the New Left much of its distinctive spirit), but also with hopes aroused by the potential that postcapitalist reformers hailed, the immanent forces of change in an order of life pushing against and beyond the bounds of capitalism. As Mike Davis has written, "It is necessary to recall that the revolutionary rhetoric of the 1960s was sustained by the real promise of reformism."[31]

Moreover, the postcapitalist vision directs our attention to something like a "long wave" in intellectual life. The postcapitalist vision after World War II actually harked back to an earlier time when observers had hailed a breakthrough to a "new order," when American intervention in World War I capped the quickening reform spirit of the late Progressive years and the war's aftermath unleashed a worldwide labor insurgency that raised both the prospect of "industrial democracy" as well as questions about the perpetuity of private property in modern society.[32] This conjuncture gave rise

to influential strains of interwar social thought, such as institutional economics, anthropological culture critique, political pluralism, and a new
structural-functional sociology. These in turn laid the basis for future developments, since the intellectual leaders of the American academy after the
1940s were reared intellectually in the 1920s and 1930s and carried that
heritage into another "new era" after World War II.

Charting the linkages in this chain leading from the 1910s up to and
including the postwar era may best be done in terms of genealogical descent.
In this sense the postcapitalist vision appears as the sum of a limited set of
themes, motifs, terms, expectations, and arguments handed down in time
from one intellectual cohort to another—at each step replicated, deployed
in new ways, or reshuffled, recast, and supplemented by new additions.
This set of themes, motifs, and so forth included characteristic notions regarding the changing nature of economic organization and of property;
so-called "silent revolutions" transforming the old order; the cultural mal-
ady of competitive individualism and the expanding scope of social solidarity that might check or reverse it; the decay of old ruling classes; the
emergence of new forces of productivity and new impulses to economic
dynamism; the perpetual reinvention of modernity; a break with economistic standards of public policy and of conceiving social order; the declining imperatives of scarcity; and the coming centrality of social rights in the
definition of citizenship. Select arguments or phrases like these echo each
other uncannily all the way from 1914 through the 1950s and 1960s, until
the 1970s or 1980s, when capitalist triumphalism finally marked the exhaustion of postcapitalist confidence.

Figures of Descent in the Postcapitalist Vision

The lineage of the postcapitalist vision begins, then, roughly when the concept of capitalism itself achieved at least some degree of legitimacy in conventional intellectual discourse, in the 1910s and 1920s. That a burgeoning
discussion of the nature and history of "capitalism" coincided with new
speculation on the evanescence of capitalism should occasion little surprise.
The tumult of the Great War, the Bolshevik Revolution, and the ensuing
worldwide labor insurgency made the status quo appear markedly less stable than heretofore, and the notion of entering capitalism's twilight made
it more compelling to question what capitalism, after all, *was*. More generally, though, the theory of capitalism, at least as it developed through the
work of Marx, his disciples, and related fields of thought, had always been
concerned to note the forces moving to transform or negate capitalism.
Marx was one of the first to reflect on the course of change immanent in
capitalism, referring for instance to the development of the corporation
(or "joint-stock company") in cryptic Hegelian style as "the abolition of
the capitalist mode of production within capitalist production itself," and

commenting in his *Grundrisse* on the role played by science and technology in creating, ultimately, a *social* order of production where privatized wage-labor became obsolete.[33] For Marx, these trends were part of the subterranean forces of socialization that could only be fully realized by overthrowing the power of private capital.[34]

Subsequent Marxists persistently probed such trends of development, notably Rudolf Hilferding in his 1910 study, *Finance Capital*, and in his later speculations regarding the transitional implications of a developmental stage he called "organized capitalism."[35] Tellingly, socialists tended to divide into revolutionaries, whose orthodox insistence on the necessity of a political break with capitalism may have led them to overlook the ways its form mutated over time, and revisionists like Eduard Bernstein, influenced by British Fabians, whose inclination to gradualism set him on the lookout for new institutional forms but also led him to an oversimple optimism that the world was going his way. If reformers in the 1920s, then, asked about the nature of capitalism while discerning, at the same time, ongoing forces of change liable to alter it beyond recognition, they followed in the footsteps of a tradition of speculation and dispute within the ranks of socialists and among Marxists themselves.

Similarly, at this juncture of the 1910s and 1920s, attention to the primacy of economics in governing social affairs coincided with anticipations of a time to come when the force of market economics would wane and a new order would emerge marked by a more distinctly social consciousness. The concepts of economy and society had been wedded together from the eighteenth-century birth of modern social science to the early twentieth century. Even though late Victorian middle-class reformers typically evoked "society" to justify their aims of modifying, ameliorating, constraining, or overcoming the communally destructive effects of expanding market relations, major theorists such as Veblen and Weber still considered economy and society conjoined. By the mid-twentieth century, however, a subtle but weighty intellectual revolution took place aiming to distinguish society and economy, to define a social realm in terms distinct from economic exchange, and to posit an autonomous social sphere that gained ascendancy over mere economics. The rise of sociology in the American academy by the 1940s and 1950s, combined with social psychology and cultural anthropology to chart a broad field called "social relations" outside politics and economics, marked this shift in modern consciousness. In the mundane realm of organizing academic departments, casting aside the central role of economics in defining society mimicked a development that Marxists thought required revolutionary change: for Marx and his followers, struggle against a capitalist order that reduced social relations to the terms of the cash nexus was required to usher in a new society that would see the withering away of political economy.[36] Yet by the mid-twentieth century, the new academic field constituted by an autonomous "social realm" helped make it easier for theorists and reformers to imagine a postcapitalist future, and the idea of a society that gradually moved "beyond economics" became virtually a constant of the postcapitalist vision.

The confidence that economics had lost much of its determinant force was not yet a feature of reformist thought in the 1910s and 1920s. The centrality of rapid industrialization and labor strife from the 1870s to the 1920s (known then as "the *social* question") sustained the robust conceptual link between economy and society, making it imperative to understand the structure and processes of capitalism. Yet this imperative also directed attention to the possibility of capitalism's transformation, and reformers were aroused by the war crisis to expect a new departure in modern social development. When John Dewey supported American intervention in World War I, he wrote, "We are fighting for freedom to transact business, though this war may easily be the beginning of the end of business. In fifty years, it is altogether probable, the whole system which we know as 'business' today will have vanished from the earth."[37] His periodization at least neatly marked out the time in which such *beliefs* about the drift of things retained some sway. Disappointment at the end of the war with Woodrow Wilson's leadership did not quash the hopes of those, like Dewey, whom we call "left Progressives."[38] The young churchman Reinhold Niebuhr wrote in November 1920 that American politics and society were heading toward "some kind of democratization of industry and some degree of socialization of property."[39] Even in the quiescent 1920s, reformist intellectuals thought "the place which private property is to take in the world of the future" was up for grabs. In the 1930s, some expected its decay.[40] This milieu and mood sets a starting point for the genealogical descent of the postcapitalist vision, which I will outline in a series of narrative moments.

From Old Order to New

Associated with "revisionist" ideas of capitalism "growing over" into a social economy, a postcapitalist vision appeared amid the reformist fervor of Progressivism at high tide, to be glimpsed in the work of young Walter Lippmann and his *New Republic* mentor Herbert Croly; in some respects their manner of formulating evolutionary expectations helped set the stage for half a century of speculation. Educated in part by Fabians (notably his Harvard instructor Graham Wallas) and by Thorstein Veblen (though he lacked Veblen's radical pessimism), Lippmann argued that "a silent revolution is in progress" and only a lack of will, fortitude, and intelligence would prevent the forces of change from knocking over the decadent "old order." In his view, the coming of the great corporation had "played havoc with the older political economy" and made fools of the economists precisely because it rendered "private property" ineffectual. Since the "corporation has separated ownership from management" (many shareholders stood as "feeble representative[s] of the institution of private property" while "managers on salary" administered complex organizations), "most of the rights of property [have] already disappeared."[41]

Not exactly an advocate of what subsequent critics called "corporate liberalism," Lippmann foresaw the direct transformation of corporations into pillars of a social economy. Start with the railroads, he suggested, where it would be easy to exchange stock certificates for government obligations, and commence the transition to a time "sure to come when the government will be operating the basic industries." Combine such easy nationalizations with a full range of social security measures and it would be possible to liberate "mankind . . . from a fear economy." Croly went further, forecasting "the day . . . when citizens can forget the economic aspects of life"—a telling notion that posited a vision of society beyond economy. Furthermore, Lippmann and Croly suggested that theirs was a time when reality moved faster than thought, and in pragmatic fashion claimed that the "elusive and changing" quality of experience rendered all settled doctrines suspect: "there is a weakness which clings to stiff and solid frames of thought because the subtlety of life is distressing," Lippmann wrote.[42] And among those indicted for social analyses that froze rather than liberated the forces of change, Lippmann fingered Marx, and his old concept of capitalism, for offering such "solid frames of thought" to his slavish followers. In this germ of a "postcapitalist" vision, Lippmann denied the relevance of capitalism while forecasting its imminent demise.

INTERWAR SOCIOECONOMICS

However chastened by the outcome of war mobilization, the peace settlement, and the conservative turn of 1920, this prewar reformist milieu survived well into the 1920s. The critique of traditional economics glimpsed in Lippmann's scenario of a coming social economy remained central to the institutionalists, followers of Thorstein Veblen and other heterodox economists such as Simon Patten, whose work in the 1920s marks another moment in the descent of the postcapitalist vision. Rexford Tugwell, a student of Patten's and a young Columbia University economist in 1924, led a group of dissenters in preparing a volume entitled *The Trend of Economics*, asserting that abstract, deductive economic theory, preoccupied with ideal conditions of market equilibrium, would have to give way to a new "inductive" science in which "the central problem of economics [is] the cumulative change of economic institutions." Even in these "days of reaction," Tugwell's senior colleague Wesley Clair Mitchell remarked in his contribution, "we cannot regain implicit faith in the stability of our prewar institutions." Mitchell, Tugwell, and others in this optimistic volume advocated an "experimental economics" that would "attack the problem of controlling the business cycle" and provide new methods of "social cost accounting" so measures of common well-being would serve as the benchmark for judging and reforming "property rights, contract forms, social organization and so forth." They aimed also to challenge "that abstraction, the economic man" that narrowed the vision of social science and in practice, they believed, rendered much of work and social life a mortifying experience, the reduction of persons to economic factors, to "hands."[43]

For Tugwell, it was the very ambition of this reformist agenda that led him to question the meaning of the term "capitalism." He had, he wrote, an "acquired taste for raw life in the making" and knew that "reality conforms pretty badly to theory." No one could understand the American economy, he insisted, by identifying it with "Alfred Marshall's or J. B. Clark's system" and even classifying the going order as "capitalism" tempted one to mistake the real economy for the "finished and symmetrical" model the bookish economists offered. Analogously, he wrote, one could not understand Soviet Russia in the late 1920s by calling it "communist" and assuming its workings adhered to Marxist principles. On guard against tendencies to reify theory, Tugwell wrote, "Perhaps communism is, in itself, something; perhaps capitalism, is also, in itself, something. I cannot somehow understand these systems in that way."[44] Reifying theory in such a way as to classify discrete, rigidly defined economic systems was precisely the error committed by orthodox adherents of laissez-faire principles: *this*, Tugwell suggested, was the greatest roadblock obstructing the kind of radical reform needed in modern industrial economies.

The Trend of Economics exaggerated the institutionalists' chances in their bid to dominate the American economics profession, but institutionalism's greatest literary monument, *The Modern Corporation and Private Property* (1932), by Adolf A. Berle and Gardiner C. Means, had a more enduring impact. Best remembered for its remarks on "the dispersion of stock ownership," Berle and Means's book actually refined the logic in Lippmann's claim that the separation of ownership and management opened a path toward socializing the corporation. The flipside of dispersed stock ownership, they stated, was the concentration of "control" in the hands of a small elite, an "economic autocracy" or "corporate oligarchy" (these phrases derived directly from the war-era discussion of "industrial democracy" and its dreaded opposite, concentrated economic power), which acted unchecked in a legal no-man's land. And according to Berle and Means, that oligarchy could *not* claim, as traditional doctrine had it, that property ownership, risk of one's own resources, and responsibility for managing the works—taken together—entitled them to enjoy the winnings of enterprise. For all intents and purposes, Berle and Means wrote, when "active and passive property relationships attach" to different persons—anonymous shareholders on the one hand and the all-but-anonymous "control" on the other—"private property in the instruments of production disappears." In fact, corporate enterprise is not private enterprise at all, they argued, but "the organized activity of vast bodies of individuals, workers, consumers, and suppliers of capital." Corporations "have become more nearly social institutions."[45] When the clique supervising such an organism lacked a rationale for autonomy rooted in property ownership, "the problems of control have become problems in economic government." This evolving separation of ownership and control, Berle and Means wrote, has "cleared the way for the claims of a group far wider than either the owners or the control. They have placed the community in a position to demand that the modern corporation serve not alone the owners or the control but all society. . . . [W]hen a convincing system of community obligations is worked out and is generally accepted, in that moment the passive property right of today must yield before the larger interests of society."[46]

The notion that corporations could be compelled to bear "responsibility" to society clearly did not equal a socialist or communist program of state ownership, but Berle and Means remarked that "the difference in all of these lies only in degree," for "private property" had lost its grounding and "collective" means of organizing economic life were ascendant.[47] In this sense, they believed they had brought attention—here echoing Lippmann's phrase—to one of those "revolutions of the more silent sort that . . . are unrecognized until they are far advanced."[48]

PSYCHOCULTURAL CRITIQUE

Let us call Berle and Means's discourse a distinctive interwar style of "socio-economics," which served as one of two key props of the reformist imagination. The other lay in cultural theory. The "social planning" advocate George Soule showed the link between the two when he remarked in Tugwell's *Trend of Economics*:

The classical schools [of economics] were without the benefit of modern anthropology, which has revealed so many varieties of communal life and economic mores. . . . At present the structure of systematic knowledge which in the end will enable us to order human relationships is hardly begun. Much of the material has not arrived. There is not even a good ground plan. By the same token, *very little is yet surely known to be impossible.*[49]

In other words, relatively new notions of cultural pluralism could be mobilized on behalf of the idea that modern economic civilization was not a fixed form of nature but rather a set of conventions, norms, or institutions that might be profoundly altered. At this time, the portrait of the *kula* ring of exchange relations in Bronislaw Malinowski's *Argonauts of the Western Pacific* (1922) was typically read as a challenge to both the old Smithian idea of a human "propensity to truck, barter, and exchange" and the associated conception of *homo economicus*, the psychological model of human action based on instrumental rationality, economic calculation, and self-interest.[50]

For French sociologist Marcel Mauss, in his 1925 work *The Gift*, Malinowski's *kula* showed that exchange might be conducted not on the basis of trading economic equivalents or seeking private gain but rather for purposes of enriching social solidarity. Such lessons, illustrating the mingling of morality and economy, were eagerly embraced by social democrats aiming to undermine the metaphysics of laissez-faire doctrine and legitimize a thoroughgoing social regulation of economic affairs.[51]

While reformers generally construed the link between socioeconomics and culture in this fashion, interwar American anthropology produced a more specific cultural critique of competitive individualism that marked another step in the descent of the postcapitalist vision. The program of studying the relation between culture and personality that Franz Boas initiated (and his favored students pursued) after the war, had a mildly left-romantic tinge. Edward Sapir's essay "Culture, Genuine and Spurious," first published in the iconoclastic postwar journal *The Dial*, manifested it: contemporary industrial civilization was a "spurious culture," he wrote, for it failed to provide individuals with either a sense of community or the means to integrate their spiritual yearnings and material practices. Aimed at the deracinating effects of industrialism, this critique evoked William Morris's standards of what made a "true society" and, more broadly, sustained the tradition of "culture against capitalism" that Raymond Williams recognized in nineteenth-century English letters.[52] Further left-romantic echoes are discernible in work conducted by the most prominent figures in Boasian culture and personality studies, Ruth Benedict and Margaret Mead, as they collaborated with the émigré psychoanalysts Karen Horney and Erich Fromm as well as Sapir's student John Dollard.[53] In her 1937 book, *The Neurotic Personality of Our Time*, Horney argued that social norms of extreme individualism fostered free-floating aggression and consequently neurotic anxiety. The same analysis figured in Dollard's *Caste and Class in a Southern Town* (1937), for he claimed that the anxiety spawned by competitive individualism (i.e., the offspring of the repressive Protestant ethic, or as Fromm might have put it, the bourgeois ego) expressed itself in white aggression toward blacks.[54]

In another venue, Ralph Linton, Franz Boas's successor at the helm of Columbia University's Anthropology department, sought to synthesize the culture and personality school with the anthropological functionalism of A. R. Radcliffe-Brown, drawing on the common coin of cultural critique to argue that Western civilization was in fact dysfunctional (in Sapir's terms, "spurious"), hobbled by inadequate means of social and cultural integration. Published in 1936, his summa of contemporary anthropology, *The Study of Man*, featured the hopeful inscription on its dedication page, "To the Next Civilization."[55] Interwar anthropology, especially as the international political crisis deepened, imagined that it inhabited a turning point, a watershed in social change. Any successful issue from the current crisis would almost inevitably be taken to represent a way of life somehow fundamentally transformed.

Parsons's "Shift Away from Economics"

By the early 1940s, Talcott Parsons was able to bridge the two key elements of the interwar reformist imagination (socioeconomics and psychoanalytic anthropology), and hence furthered the course of the postcapitalist vision. Parsons had entered the social sciences as a college student in the early 1920s, trained by institutional economists at Amherst College. With their recommendations, he went abroad after college to study at the London School of Economics, a venture intended to introduce him to the British social democrats R. H. Tawney and Harold Laski (whose sojourn in the United States from 1915 to 1920 had made him a familiar of American reformers, particularly in the *New Republic* circle).[56] Parsons took Malinowski's courses there as well. A second year abroad at Heidelberg introduced him to the work of Max Weber, and his first professional publications were articles summarizing for an American audience Sombart's and Weber's theories of capitalism. Parsons's writing soon assumed an increasingly abstract, rarefied tone and rarely dealt explicitly with the analysis of capitalism. Yet his masterwork of 1937, *The Structure of Social Action*, remained rooted in interwar socioeconomics: it offered a forceful critique of economistic conceptions of social affairs (i.e., *homo economicus* and the centrality granted to instrumental rationality by the schema of utility maximization) and it made an attempt to justify the social regulation of economic affairs to a society too ideologically wedded to a narrow individualism.[57]

During the late 1930s and early 1940s, Parsons moved toward integrating concepts of anthropology and psychoanalyis into his notion of social inquiry. The result, curiously enough, was a *turn* to frankly jettison the concept of capitalism. By 1940 and 1941, Parsons had concluded, as he later put it, that "the capitalism/socialism dichotomy" no longer served the social analysis of modernity. His concerns were partly political, even in the blunt ideological sense: in that crucial period from summer 1939 to summer 1941, as Parsons and other liberal colleagues at Harvard sought to justify aid to Britain and finally intervention in the world war, he saw the political scene as one strained between right-wing "isolationists" and left-wing war opponents. Associating the isolationists with such quasi-fascist populists as Charles Coughlin, he was convinced that both extremes bore a misguided hostility toward capitalism, when contemporary society no longer merited that label. His early hopes for promoting the social regulation of economic affairs had, in fact, demonstrated to him that productive enterprises were increasingly organized along lines of bureaucratic administration rather than private ownership (clearly borrowing from Berle and Means) and that modern society offered sufficient resources for fostering collective solidarity and responsibility (making regulation feasible). These expectations of immanent evolutionary change showed his ties to the interwar reformist milieu, and he made it clear that his desire to quiet factional debate and assure social harmony in the face of war demands did not entail freezing the status quo. Borrowing the psychocultural critique of competitive individualism, he argued that American norms of equality of opportunity and differential outcomes (i.e., inequality of result justified as "finding one's own level") spawned disappointments, anxieties, and resentments that fueled social conflict—and that the proper means to assure harmony involved wide-spread social provision (something like a guaranteed annual income) in order to markedly reduce the kind of insecurity that rendered American society unstable.[58]

Thus even while casting out the relevance of "capitalism," Parsons imag-ined the creation of a social economy. In doing so, however, he also fur-thered the development of the postcapitalist vision by contributing to the conceptual separation of society from economy. In making his move to embrace the psychoanalytic anthropology of the late 1930s, he concluded that social analysis in the future had to focus on phenomena that political economy per se could not understand: namely, the phenomena of social-ization whereby cultural norms become "internalized" to shape the per-sonality for social roles. In the late 1940s, as he led the reorganization of Harvard's social sciences in the creation of a new interdisciplinary Depart-ment of Social Relations—combining sociology, cultural anthropology, and social psychology—he fostered what he called the coming "shift of empha-sis away from economics." The same shift occurred elswhere as scholars focused attention on the study of "self, culture, and society."[59] A new "be-havioral" bent in social science examined society in terms of subjective norms people observed in everyday life and the organization of those nor-mative standards in institutions and social interactions in the home, school, church, neighborhood and other venues.[60] In fact, the midcentury shift away from economics, while far from universal in social thought, was so widespread that it appeared even in Marxist circles, as Antonio Gramsci, although never doubting the centrality of capitalist development, generated the notion of "hegemony" (a kind of power working in the field of civil society, defined in noneconomic terms) and the Frankfurt Institute of Social Research analyzed culture and personality as a key to domination.[61]

The generality of this shift away from economics suggests that more was at stake in the rise of sociology and "social relations" than merely a reor-ganization of academic turf in American universities. The emerging breach between concepts of society and economy, wedded together since the origins of modern social thought in the Scottish Enlightenment, transformed the terms of diagnosing social structure and processes of change. Subsequently it might appear that "capitalism" defined only economic mechanisms and could not comprehend other, distinctly *social* dynamics (e.g., the rise of meritocracy and professionalism) that allegedly equaled or exceeded economic forces in their impact on human affairs. Or one might argue that "economic" relations of market exchange steadily paled before growing demands for communal belonging or the security offered by public services. Although the milieu of postcapitalist theory was a varied one, some impulse to surpass the dominance of economics in thought and practice figured prominently in almost all its exponents, from Croly and Lippmann on. In Harvard's Department of Social Relations and the academic reorganization that paralleled it elsewhere, Parsons in effect inscribed that postcapitalist impulse in the fundamental concepts of modern social science, pioneering a *noneconomic concept of civil society.*[62] This theoretical move mirrored and made feasible diagnoses of the declining significance of economic necessity and the possibility of postcapitalist arrangements.

Although it now seems counterintuitive to promote a noneconomic concept of society in a period so marked by economic boom (and widespread propaganda for the productive prowess of "private enterprise") in the 1950s, Parsons responded to the postwar age of plenty with an analysis that persisted in displacing economics from the center of attention. Writing with Neil Smelser in their 1956 book, *Economy and Society,* Parsons argued that the most significant lesson of Keynesianism was that the economy is not a self-sufficient mechanism (always righting itself) but rather is deeply embedded in social institutions. While most economists persisted in using an individualistic frame of reference for understanding the economic actor, Parsons and Smelser insisted that all economic concepts—purchasing power, productive power, utility, and cost—must be reinterpreted in terms of social resources, needs, and alternatives. In other words, they relied on a kind of social Keynesianism to suggest that the sphere of economy be viewed as a social function (or instrument) subjected to moral and political direction. The individualistic bias of economics, they wrote, was related to the fact that "the opinion of most economists remains within the framework of the capitalism-socialism alternative" that Parsons and Smelser rejected. For reformers of their stripe, economy increasingly appeared not to be a coercive force, a recalcitrant order of impersonal exchange, but an instrument taken in hand to achieve socially chosen goals—or at least potentially so if the political will could be mustered to that effect.[63]

As Parsons's example suggests, hopes for social reform and the evanescence of capitalism did not vanish after the Depression decade. Although the rise of totalitarianism and the stresses of war brought American intellectuals closer to embracing "American democracy," the democratic ideology of the war and postwar years still promoted the hope of "building a better world." In his 1944 book, *The Great Transformation* (published first in the United States), émigré Karl Polányi welcomed "the disintegration of a uniform market economy" and predicted, "Out of the ruins of the Old World, cornerstones of the New can be seen to emerge."[64] In the summer of 1947, the anticommunist liberals of Americans for Democratic Action were content that the world was "moving toward socialism." One of their leading members, Arthur Schlesinger, wrote in 1949, "Britain has already submitted itself to social democracy . . . and the United States will very likely advance in that direction through a series of New Deals,"[65] a view ADA liberals thought confirmed by the robust interventionist rhetoric of Harry Truman's Fair Deal and his 1949 inaugural address. The complaint of Taft Republicans about "creeping socialism" seemed to confirm the left-liberal vision of ascent to a social economy by virtually imperceptible gradations, crossing Jaurès's invisible hemispheric line. The sense of passing a boundary infected observers in other quarters as well. In *The Church and Contemporary Change* (1950), Methodist bishop G. Bromley Oxnam wrote that the present generation was witnessing "a new beginning . . . as significant as was the passage from slavery to feudalism, and from feudalism to capitalism."[66] To be sure, the enthusiasm of reconstruction right at war's end paled under the late 1940s pressures of the Cold War and the demands it placed on intellectuals and reformers to "choose the West"—a commitment facilitated for a generation of social-democratic liberals like Schlesinger (or other young intellectuals fleeing revolutionary ideology) by a conviction that the going order was itself yielding to a social economy.

Thus Cold War imperatives did not finally suppress, and indeed before long fostered a modus vivendi with, a modern American reform tradition already several decades old. Rather than arising under Cold War impulses to mount a euphemistic defense of American life against either Soviet broadsides or against radical critics at home, the postcapitalist vision rested on late-Progressive and interwar reformist currents that had always been (as Tugwell's remarks above suggested) nonrevolutionary and anticommunist. In time, this heritage helped assure an elective affinity between the postcapitalist vision and pro-Western Cold War polemics, since reformers considered as given the drift toward a social economy. Specters of a "silent revolution" still aroused comment.[67] The British economic journalist Andrew Shonfield wrote in 1965 that the United States, even in light of New Deal and Fair Deal reforms, was "the outstanding laggard in the general movement of the Western world towards the eager acceptance of a vastly enlarged role for the central government in economic affairs."[68] Although Shonfield still described this order as "modern capitalism," his identification of a "general movement" bound to take over the United States as well as Europe served to identify modernity with trends usually cast as social-democratic.

"THE INVENTIVENESS OF OUR TIMES"

The infiltration of what I've called a postcapitalist vision into social-scientific work defined by a noneconomic concept of civil society can be sighted quite clearly in one of the landmarks of American social science in the 1950s,

David Riesman's *The Lonely Crowd*. Riesman stood firmly in the emerging intellectual current I have already sketched, and his work signaled another moment in the descent of the postcapitalist vision. Though trained as a lawyer, he gravitated toward psychocultural theory by the early 1940s. He was analyzed by Fromm and commenced an avid and intimate correspondence with Margaret Mead, fascinated by "culture and personality" analysis. By 1946, he had found his way to the University of Chicago, where he organized the core college course later known as "Self, Culture, and Society." By 1956, Riesman moved to Harvard where he found a comfortable home in Parsons's Department of Social Relations.[69]

The Lonely Crowd was a study in "characterology" but also a diagnosis of social change, an argument that the contours of American life were altered as values based on the primacy of production gave way to those associated with consumption. Although consumption depended on a highly productive industrial economy, Riesman claimed that the lineaments of a typical capitalist society had been left behind. To begin with, contrary to left-wing or "populist" conventions, he insisted the United States lacked a ruling class based on "pelf and power." The managerial revolution had undermined the old sources of authority in privately held wealth; moreover, he even doubted that the profit motive really explained behavior in the economic sphere. As an indication that *homo economicus* no longer ruled, he offered evidence that corporate employees had to be *motivated* to greater performance by distinctly "social" concerns of security, status, teamwork, and so forth—rather than by, for instance, the promise of higher sales commissions.[70]

This critique of economism went further in the book's core analysis—the epochal shift from the "inner-directed" to the "other-directed" personality as the modal form of the American character. Inner-direction was another term for the Protestant ethic, the capitalist work ethic, the bourgeois ego, and there is little doubt in reading the text that Riesman never meant to sing its praises. Very much in line with the 1930s cultural critique developed by Horney and others, Riesman regarded the inner-directed personality to be rigid, repressive, and productive of violent impulses, whether hidden or open. His apparent scorn for the newer model, the other-directed personality and its "conformist" texture (a critique also rooted in the Boasians' interwar concern over cultural orthodoxy) tended to obscure, however, the hopeful prospects Riesman saw in the new order.[71] For he regarded the other-directed personality as a more *socialized* person, one "sensitive to others"; if that kind of sensitivity, which made possible a more flexible personality than the old steely and private bourgeois ego, could be fused with what he called "autonomy"—a kind of individuality based more on creativity and self-expression than acquisition—there would emerge a genuine "social individual," both free and integrated in vital communities. Never a radical, Riesman nonetheless championed Paul and Percival Goodman's utopian-anarchist book, *Communitas*. He valued individuality but rejected economic individualism, writing in subdued tones about a social life that might be imagined beyond the rule of the old bourgeoisie.[72]

The left-liberal intelligentsia of the postwar years in fact maintained its own variety of buoyant optimism. Among chastened ex-radicals, the new postwar theme of an "end of ideology" did not mean an "end of history" or an end to significant change, but rather a continued search for more modest ways—gradual, evolutionary ways by all means—of imagining the ongoing transformation of modern society beyond classical capitalism. Political scientist Robert A. Dahl, who had written a doctoral dissertation in 1940 promoting a vision of market socialism from a Deweyan, pragmatic point of view, sustained the mood of interwar socioeconomics in the ponderous volume he authored with economist Charles Lindblom, *Politics, Economics and Welfare: Planning and Politico-Economic Systems Resolved into Basic Social Processes* (1953).[73] There, they insisted that all the old "isms"—particularly "capitalism" and "socialism"—no longer applied. Yet, in this new period, their hopes for democracy were high—and contrary to some interpretations of Dahl's later theory of "polyarchy," they did not conceive democracy as something limited to a regulated competition among political elites. Democracy, they wrote, had to offer what they called "appropriate inclusion" to a broad and diverse populace, security measured in a full range of social services, and "subjective equality" for all citizens based in values such as "control [i.e., self-control], respect, status, and dignity." But more important, for our purposes, the contemporary scene in Western societies also offered a wide range of institutional forms for property, enterprise, and services, from the private corporation to the regulated utility, the public authority under tripartite governing boards, cooperatives, national health services, and so forth—all "attest[ing] the inventiveness of our times."[74] The demise of "isms" they supposed (another phrasing of an "end of ideology") was premised on a notion that social change had indeed passed beyond the absolute rule of private property and market relations and issued in a new era of experimentation and reform in social relations.

THE POSTINDUSTRIAL PROMISE

Persisting through the 1950s, such notions blossomed in the 1960s, which in many ways marked the culmination of the postcapitalist vision in time. At its inception in the late 1950s and early 1960s, the idea of "postindustrial society" conveyed a sense of social change far more substantive than the mere technological euphoria associated with the term today.[75] The core of postindustrialism lay in the notion that economic dynamics as traditionally understood—namely the primacy of market exchange and economic calculation in terms of efficient allocation—were giving way to new principles of organization as social development came to depend more on "social goods," notably science and higher education. Postindustrial advocates tended to assume that since productivity gains now relied on scientific knowledge and scientifically trained workers, public funding of research and education became the central motive force of economic development, calling forth a more socialized order. Daniel Bell, who still insists that post-industrial society did *not* mean "postcapitalist" society, nonetheless claimed that the university as a public resource would replace the corporation as the central institution of postindustrial society.[76] This order was to be government-centered, future-oriented, and dependent on planning the cultivation of knowledge and expertise in terms of social needs rather than old economic norms of efficiency. Such visions found many exponents. Even Berle, by now a dogged defender of the political establishment, still had high expectations of social reform. In the preface to the 1968 edition of *The Modern Corporation and Private Property*, he described the

emergence of the American state partly as an administrator of wealth distribution, partly as a direct distributor of certain products. In notable areas *production for use rather than production for profit* is emerging as a norm. Education, scientific research and development, the arts, and a variety of services ranging from roads and low-income housing to nonprofit recreation and [public] television constitute a few illustrative fields.

Strikingly, in light of our sorry condition nearly forty years later, he continued, "Health will probably be . . . such a field."[77]

Since Berle can be situated on the *right* of the reformist milieu I have sketched, we should note others who more boldly plied the themes of post-capitalist discourse, particularly ideas of society beyond economy. Columbia University sociologist Amitai Etzioni, in a 1968 book dedicated to his radical students in New York and Berkeley, described what he called an "active society," reforming itself in order to approximate more closely its most cherished ideals of equality, liberty, and belonging. Such ongoing processes grew from the prevalence of self-conscious individuals with flexible ego boundaries who were open to change and fellowship (another echo of the interwar social-psychological critique), and from the growing capacities of centralized government to control resource use and social development. According to Etzioni, particularistic economic interests were bound to play ever less of a role in governance, and the trend of the future moved toward declining inequalities of wealth and income as bounds of inclusion in social citizenship widened.[78]

American and trans-Atlantic thought in the 1960s typically focused on science and technology as a new, institutionalized basis of social and economic dynamism. Two principles were implied here: first, that science and technology were profoundly social—or socialized—resources, not reducible to the terms of commodity exchange and requiring some degree of collective decision-making or "planning" to guide their development and application; second, that contemporary society had entered a period marked by the primacy of change as such, a kind of perpetual reinvention of social structure and social norms. Ideas first bruited in the 1930s, '40s, and '50s regarding the growing significance of social solidarity and consequently the reshaping of modal personality away from bourgeois norms of self-reliance and the autonomous individual returned to the scene and flourished, cropping up in all sorts of literature. The British Indianologist Richard Lannoy, writing optimistically in 1971 of his hopes that economic development in India might bypass the socially destructive effects of early industrialization, described a kind of convergence between Eastern communal traditions and advanced industrial (or postindustrial) societies: "The irony is that in the West electronic technology and complexity of organization no longer permit the survival of individualism, but encourage unified-field awareness and interdependence."[79] Such McLuhanesque views of electronic media here fused with ideas about the consequences of modern organization that date back at least to Berle and Means and Lippmann, as well as conviction in the obsolescence of competitive individualism and the isolated self that followed the Horney/Fromm cultural critique.

The End of Transitional Hopes

It is perhaps ironic that the theory of postindustrial society—replete with its connotations on an increasingly social economy—reached its widest audience in the 1970s, just as the postcapitalist vision was entering a precipitous decline. Bell's major work, *The Coming of Post-Industrial Society*, appeared in 1973, followed three years later by *The Cultural Contradictions of Capitalism*. Critics at the time asked (sometimes jeeringly) why capitalism now came back into focus as an object of analysis. Bell protested that the second book represented no shift, no surrender of his postindustrial theory, since the two publications were really companion volumes, both drawn from a common manuscript drafted in 1969. Yet Bell's decision to dwell a bit on the concept of "capitalism" at this time said a great deal. In the spirit of the reformist age of the postwar years, Bell still regarded capitalism as a decadent system, though its lingering standards and consequences (viz., an acquisitive consumer ethos that eroded obligations to the commonweal) might prove to be the spoiler that obstructed or aborted the hoped-for postindustrial transition.[80] Bell's recognition of the limits or inhibitions on profound social-structural change spelled trouble in the field of postcapitalist vision. The deepening of economic crisis in 1970s helped accelerate the waning of that vision, not so much because the postcapitalist vision depended on growth but because the most severe recession since World War II made crystal clear how recalcitrant the economic realm remained and how mistaken Crosland and others had been in asserting its autonomy had ended.[81] The tendency of the "new social sciences" (Parsons's "social relations" field) after World War II to trumpet their ascendancy and promote a noneconomic concept of civil society was embattled by a revival of political economy, a reassertion that matters of property, wealth, and exchange, economic development, inequality, and the uses of power, stood close to the center of social structure. This revival appeared both on the Left, in the renewal of academic Marxism, and on the Right in the return of new varieties of Smithian market ideology.[82] Needless to say, the shift back, away from the postwar liberal noneconomic concept of society, was accompanied by a rapid decline in confidence that Western society had *already* entered a transitional phase of development leading *beyond* capitalism. In the wake of the 1970s crisis, commencing a policy shift toward deregulation, privatization, and open market practices, it became increasingly commonplace and unobjectionable to recognize Western society as capitalist indeed.

CODA

Throughout the 1970s, Talcott Parsons, then in retirement, worked on a manuscript, *The American Societal Community*, focused on that dimension of social life (aside from the economic, political, and cultural spheres) which constituted the main object of his science, sociology. He defined the "societal community" as that aspect of the total system which gave a large, diversified arrangement of people and organizations the norms that made sense of their roles and assured a sufficient degree of "harmony" and "coordination" among them. It was the sphere that defined the substance of collective identity, that legitimated rights, and that offered the sense of belonging or "membership" usually called citizenship. And he announced that, given the trend of recent reform in the 1960s toward inclusion, equality, and generalized "social rights," the societal community was "the core" of modern society *as* a system, the vanguard or source of the most significant innovations motivating social change.[83] In the manuscript, he sought to defend this posture against the revival of perspectives he regarded as economistic, either market ideology or—what actually took more of his fire—left-wing theories focusing on inequality of wealth and power as the key dimensions of analysis.[84]

On a visit to Germany in 1979, intended by his hosts to celebrate the fiftieth anniversary of his doctoral dissertation on the concept of capitalism in Sombart and Weber, Parsons died, leaving *The American Societal Community* unfinished. During the same year, another scholar of trans-Atlantic renown (born the same year as Parsons), Fernand Braudel—heir to Henri Pirenne— published his magisterial three-volume work, *Civilization and Capitalism, 15th–18th Century*. As Braudel put it, one of his most telling contributions was "to introduce the word *capitalism* . . . as an *essential* model" to the study of early modern history.[85] Braudel admitted that the word was "ambiguous, hardly scientific, and usually indiscriminately applied," and yet, "after a long struggle, I gave up trying to get rid of this troublesome intruder. I decided in the end that there was nothing to be gained by throwing out along with the word the controversies it arouses, which have pertinence to the present-day world."[86]

Braudel's culminating achievement symbolized the return of "capitalism" in the 1970s, but he was far from alone in making that concept essential to contemporary analysis. Defenders such as Milton Friedman, Michael Novak, and Irving Kristol cheered for capitalism, while the socialist economist Ernest Mandel offered his notion of "late capitalism" as a Marxist account of just that phase of development which postcapitalist and postindustrial theorists (mistakenly in his view) judged to be transitional. Capitalism figured in the work of "world-systems" theorists who followed Braudel, such as Immanuel Wallerstein and Giovanni Arrighi, as well as their critics, such as the influential historian of early modern Britain Robert Brenner. A new generation of economic sociologists also began a literature dealing with "varieties of capitalism," distinguishing the institutional forms capitalism took in the contexts of different social settings, developmental regimes, and historical paths.[87]

Aware that the economic crisis of the 1970s marked a historic turning point, perhaps threatening the survival of modern capitalism but more likely merely initiating a new stage in its development, Braudel returned at the end of his trilogy to the question of the word itself: "Was I right to welcome it in? To use it as an *essential* model, applicable to several centuries? A model is like a ship: built on land, launched on water. Will it float? Can it sail? If it is seaworthy, perhaps its analytical cargo will be valid too."[88] Indeed, the concept of capitalism had returned, as object of analysis, of critique, and—by the 1990s—of uncritical celebration too.

Historicizing the Postcapitalist Vision

How can we account for the endurance of the postcapitalist vision over so many discrete and to some extent disparate periods of the twentieth century? Important clues to the origins and significance of the postcapitalist vision can be found in Charles Maier's renowned analysis of efforts to reconstruct the order of political economy after World War I. War mobilization in all the major European countries, and especially the class upheavals before and after the armistice, rendered the status of prewar elites "precarious," Maier wrote, though those elites managed an adroit reclamation of power in a few years' time. Having pushed back working-class insurgency and quashed reform socialist plans for nationalizations or empowered factory councils, European liberals and conservatives won a "restabilization" of Europe but "no simple restoration." In place of the open and direct rule of society and politics by a proud and jealous bourgeoisie, new

administrative forms for regulating political economy fell into place that
entailed "dealing with unions . . . giving state agencies control over the
market, building interest-group spokesmen into the structure of the state,"
and in general allowing "the interpenetration of state and economy within
each national unit." Maier concluded, "Rescuing bourgeois Europe meant
recasting bourgeois Europe," or even, as he also put it, engineering a move
"from bourgeois to corporatist Europe."[89] Yet this outcome of hard-fought
battles from 1919 to 1922 was not evident at their start, when voices in varied keys—"men of left, right, and center," Maier said—found a place within
a widespread discourse of reconstruction. They all "noted the new tendencies . . . the growing web of interest groups and cartels, the obsolescence
of the market economy, the interpenetration of government and industry," and their visions ranged from the left's hopes for "a less coercive and
more egalitarian economy" to authoritarian state corporations and the
Hooverian vision of a technocratic "community of abundance." According
to Maier, "History was to play tricks on each group," as the resulting corporatist system fit none of their models.[90]

It is telling that in describing the order of institutionalized administration he called corporatism, Maier self-consciously cited a range of European literature from Rudolf Hilferding to Ralf Dahrendorf—authors from
the 1920s to the 1950s of a *postcapitalist* vision—as those who had most
clearly grasped the movement toward a new "organized" political economy.
Yet in 1975 when Maier wrote, he did not accept their diagnosis. Looking
back from the economic crisis of his own time, he saw the struggles in the
wake of World War I commencing a "transformation that carried *capitalist*
societies through a half-century transit."[91] In a sense, a left-liberal discourse
of "reconstruction" lasted as well throughout the same half-century. The
irony of Maier having recourse to postcapitalist theorists to describe a regime
he understood nonetheless as capitalist helps us recognize the cast of the
social-liberal consciousness that emerged in the era of the first war and
lasted through the mid-twentieth century: it insisted on interpreting the
institutional form of liberal corporate capitalism as a transitional stage
promising something beyond capitalism itself. Every temporary revival of
reformist political energy, in 1917–1920, the 1930s, 1945–47, and 1958–68,
reheated the air under this balloon of theoretical conjecture.[92] Indeed, the
postcapitalist tradition always had a left-liberal valence, a bent confirmed
by the fact that today virtually the only exponents of a postcapitalist vision
stand on the left among a few idiosyncratic Marxists or post-Marxists.[93] They
serve to remind us of a basic proposition in Marx's critique of capitalism:
that a deep contradiction in modern development lies between the socializing trends fostered by capitalism itself and the regime of privatized accumulation. By insisting on one side of the matter, highlighting the steady
course toward a social economy (or the diminution of economics per se),
the postcapitalist vision bent the stick so far as to obscure the persistence

of yawning inequities in power and wealth. Yet when we pull the stick back toward criticizing the unbalanced structures and processes of capital accumulation that wreak havoc on social life, let us not forget that the socializing dynamics of capitalist development, the emergence of the new within the old, provide the only real means we have to imagine a different future. The deeply flawed twentieth-century postcapitalist vision had its own virtues, sustaining a polemic against absolutist market theories of society and insisting that ongoing institutional changes justified at least the feasibility of collectivist measures. Rudimentary perhaps, but such arguments, freed of wishful thinking and tied to new struggles for change, play a part sustaining hope in a world, like ours, burdened by capitalist triumphalism.

2

To Moscow and Back: American Social Scientists and the Concept of Convergence

David C. Engerman

The field of Soviet Studies grew from practically nothing into a major intellectual enterprise in the decades after World War II. While the field clearly benefited from the desire to know the Cold War enemy, the American intellectual encounters with the USSR had effects far beyond foreign policy. Indeed, scholars in Soviet Studies fashioned or refashioned some of the central concepts of American social sciences in the postwar period. Even terms typically connected to Western society took new life and new forms as a result of intellectual encounters with the Soviet Union. "Industrial society" is one such term. As leading sociologists sought to define modern life, they turned increasingly to the Soviet Union, which they saw as an industrial society similar in many ways to western societies, especially the United States. Studying the Soviet Union, then, could teach us about ourselves as well as the Cold War adversary.

The broad intellectual implications of studying the Soviet Union were hardly lost on American scholars and foundation executives, even in the early years of the Cold War. When the Carnegie Corporation provided a grant to create Harvard University's Russian Research Center (RRC) in 1947, it had far grander aims than merely influencing foreign policy. The Carnegie Corporation wanted to advance research in the social sciences using Russia as a case study. The first director of the center, not surprisingly, echoed its benefactor's concerns; he saw Harvard's contributions "both from the point of view of scholarship and the national interest."[1] These dual ambitions, scholarly and political, go a long way in explaining how it came to be that America's best-funded institution for Soviet studies was initially led by a group containing no experts in Russian and Soviet affairs, and indeed no one who could speak or read Russian. The main attraction for the Carnegie Corporation was Harvard's new Department of Social Relations (DSR), which brought together social psychologists, sociologists, and cultural anthropologists in the ill-defined but well-funded field of the behavioral sciences. Both administrative and intellectual leadership in this field came from sociologist Talcott Parsons, whose works of social theory dominated postwar social scientific thought in the United States.

Carnegie officials secured Parsons's participation in the Russian Center's Executive Committee; he remained a member until retiring from Harvard in 1973.

In part to redress its own lack of expertise on Russia, the RRC devoted its first semester, spring 1948, to an ongoing seminar about future research possibilities. Inviting a variety of guest speakers, center members engaged in serious if unsystematic (and occasionally desultory) analyses of how different fields of scholarship could contribute to American knowledge of the USSR—and how that knowledge would contribute to the different social sciences.

Existing scholarship on the USSR offered few ideas in line with the RRC's plans. American understandings of the Soviet Union emphasized its great distance from and differences with the West. Could one apply any general rules (as social scientists did) to the society that Winston Churchill famously called a "riddle wrapped in a mystery inside an enigma"? One common view of the USSR saw Stalin's rule as but one chapter in a seemingly eternal history of despotism in Russia, stretching back to Ivan the Terrible or even earlier. Other views emphasized instead the Soviet commitment to Marxism, making the USSR not so much a society as an incarnation of a political idea.[2] Few scholars suggested that Russia had anything in common with the capitalist world.

In contrast to these approaches, Harvard's Russian Research Center sought to root its work in the latest techniques of social science. Behavioral scientists, especially in the Department of Social Relations, worked with the RRC in pursuit of a testing-ground for new approaches to the social sciences.[3] Clyde Kluckhohn—a founding member of the DSR and the first director of the RRC—noted that the Center's principal goal was "interdisciplinary research on a high academic level."[4] This agenda would pay off handsomely. Harvard trained many of the leading scholars in Soviet Studies, including at least a dozen future leaders of the American Association for the Advancement of Slavic Studies. But few scholars or participants have recognized the important role Harvard's RRC played well beyond its immediate field. That broader impact can be measured in the success of many RRC affiliates who rose to prominence in fields other than Soviet Studies, including philosopher Herbert Marcuse, sociologists Alex Inkeles and Barrington Moore, and labor economist Walter Galenson. These successes were the result of both individual creativity and an institutional orientation toward broad analysis.

The center's agenda-setting seminar, which exemplified this breadth, was a success in both financial and intellectual terms. At the end of the semester, the Carnegie Corporation agreed to support the RRC for five years. And in the course of their explorations, scholars outlined an agenda for studying the Soviet Union that would carry the field not just through its first five-year plan but through much of the Cold War. At the same time, they introduced concepts that would become central to the social sciences more generally, a trend especially visible in Parsons's work.

Parsons's background and career prepared him well to connect studies of the USSR to the social scientific mainstream. Sympathetic to left-wing causes in his youth, Parsons recalled joining the ranks of "enthusiasts for the Russian Revolution and the rise of the British Labour Party" while a student at Amherst College.[5] Educated in Germany, in the spiritual if not physical presence of Max Weber, he became the undisputed leader of postwar American sociology. His election to the presidency of American Sociological Association in 1949 marked only the beginning of his prominence. He trained many if not most of the key scholars in the behavioral sciences and its constituent disciplines. Most of the major scholarship in sociology, social theory, and the behavioral sciences built on or took inspiration from his penetrating but impenetrable prose.[6] Parsons's cosmopolitan vision shaped both his theoretical and empirical work. At home in European social theory, Parsons was also one of the very rare American sociologists who extended his studies outside the United States and Western Europe; in the words of two recent analysts, Parsons was "one of the few genuinely modern and global minds of the twentieth century."[7] This broad vision extended to his studies of the USSR. Parsons's extensive and intensive connections to the RRC—reinforced by his wife's long-term service as the center's administrator—facilitated the cross-fertilization of the behavioral sciences and research on the USSR. With Parsons at the forefront, a generation of American intellectuals reconsidered modern life as they observed the USSR.

Themes of Parsons's Early Work

The widening of Parsons's analytical horizons in the postwar years is best observed in contrast to his scholarship of the preceding decades. Before 1950, he had already begun to engage the key themes he would later bring to his analysis of the USSR: the importance of the professions, the structures and functions of industrial society, and the possibilities for human agency in modern society. Yet these early writings had both an abstractness and especially a provincialism that are strikingly absent in much of his later work.

Parsons's prewar writings on industrial society focused only on the capitalist societies of the West. References to industrialism in his first book, *The Structure of Social Action* (1937), seem to employ it as a synonym for capitalism. For instance, his discussion of Weber's theories of capitalism focused especially on what Weber called "rational bourgeois capitalism." This form of capitalism entailed not only a particularly economic structure—industrial enterprises—but also a bureaucratic form of organization. Similarly, his description of British economist Alfred Marshall relied on a simple equation of free enterprise and industrial organization. Most pointedly,

Parsons addressed the nature of industrial society—and betrayed his hopes for alternatives—in the book's introduction. He deemed nineteenth-century social theorists like Herbert Spencer irrelevant to modern social science because they envisioned progress and evolution independent of human agency. Spencer's laws of competition meant that social change would move inexorably "in the same direction," with no human activity able to steer its course. He hoped that the future promised more than "'bigger and better' industrialism"—that his generation might have the opportunity to direct the course of social change. This basic hope for reform infuses the subsequent 800 pages of the book, in which Parsons developed what he called a voluntaristic theory of action.[8]

Another one of Parsons's earlier concerns—the special place of professions in industrial societies—also set the stage for his later writings on the USSR. He sought to show how professions were an essential part of modern society and not mere atavisms destined to be overrun by acquisitiveness in the surrounding society. At the same time, he celebrated the distinctive motivations and actions found in professional spheres. Modern professions included "many of our most important social functions," he wrote, including the pursuit and application of both scientific and humanistic knowledge. While Parson's work on the professions used little if any empirical material, it implicitly dealt only with liberal societies of the West—a point noted critically by one sociologist, Russian émigré Nicholas Timasheff, who claimed that Parsons's formulation was "valid in the wider world" of all modern societies. There was no need, Timasheff continued, for sociologists to limit their discussions to "liberal society." Years later, Parsons himself would eventually reach a similar conclusion.[9]

World War II marked a new stage for Parsons's work. He served as the founding chairman of the Department of Social Relations, which brought together scholars interested in the relationship between humans and their societies. Parsons's work in new department (and discipline) represented a key moment in what historian Howard Brick identifies as Parsons's "shift away from economics."[10] Only by combining the insights of social psychology, cultural anthropology, and sociology, Parsons believed, could scholars conquer the major intellectual problems of the day. Foremost among these problems was the question of social stability: under what terms, and with what mechanisms, would individuals put aside their own narrower interests in the name of social cohesion? Economic questions, such as conflicts over resource allocation, had only a minor place in the DSR worldview. Drawing on European theorists (with heavy doses of Weber and Freud), behavioralists elaborated a theory of human nature that they applied with little regard for cultural differences. In spite of the catholicity of application, this scholarship drew its inspiration from analyses of the West; as historians Ron Robin and Ellen Herman have suggested, the project of the behavioral scientists was universal without being cosmopolitan.[11]

Whatever the limits of his work in the late 1940s and early 1950s, Parsons referred to that era as his "golden age." His scholarly output in 1951 alone suggests how fruitful the early years of the DSR had been for him. He published a long theoretical volume, *The Social System*, which built on his earlier works to suggest some polarities between pre-modern and modern societies. The book outlined the essential attributes of a modern way of thought: favoring impersonal rationality over personal connections, valuing achieved over inherited status, and willing to think in universal rather than particularistic terms. Though the book devoted one section to dynamic processes, *Social System* was about maintaining social equilibrium, not promoting social change.[12]

Parsons and his DSR colleagues (together with some visiting scholars) also co-edited a book on the theory of action that was intended to be a foundation text for the behavioral sciences.[13] Taking his work in a more psychological direction, he also edited a volume of readings on personality, in part the outcome of his encounters with Freudian thought. His publications of the early 1950s show the high point of his engagement with psychology and psychiatry, as he published in specialist journals in those fields and covered topics like the superego and the Oedipus problem.[14] And Parsons's "golden age" also saw the first glimmerings of effort to conceptualize industrial society in a comparative framework.

Discovering Industrial Society

At a meeting of the RRC's inaugural seminar in early March 1948, Parsons posed a question revealing his own interest in Soviet studies. Ever the grand theorist, he called for an examination of the Soviet Union on a "broad comparative front." Studying present-day Russia, he claimed, would enhance historical knowledge about industrialization and urbanization; processes long since completed in the West could be "caught in an earlier stage" in the Soviet Union. Parsons was well aware of the tumultuous changes in Soviet Union in preceding decades—a wholesale effort to remake an agricultural nation into a modern industrial state through rapid industrialization, forced collectivization, and transformation of culture. Although these changes had taken place under the banner of Communism, Parsons wondered whether the Soviet Union was building Communism or creating an industrial society. To what extent, in short, did ideology explain Soviet events?[15] This question got at the root of Western understandings of the USSR: was it sui generis or was it just another variant of that common species, the industrial society? Efforts to answer this question—his own as well as those of other writers—shaped work in social theory for decades to come.

The revamped category of industrial society emerged from an understanding of the USSR along the lines that Parsons had introduced in spring

1948. As his views of the Soviet Union evolved over the next decade, especially in response to Soviet events, his definition of "industrial society" grew more precise. Ideas about the Soviet Union shaped Parsons's thought in two ways. First, reckoning with the USSR led him to elaborate on issues already of importance to him. Well before 1948, he was interested in the place of professions in capitalist society. Only in the 1950s, however, did he follow Timasheff's lead and examine the professions outside the capitalist world. (Living up to his reputation for confusing nomenclature, Parsons at first called industrial societies "capitalist," explaining that he took the term to mean capital-intensive; he soon abandoned this unusual use of the word.) Second, and more importantly, analyzing the Soviet Union led Parsons's work in new directions. After a decade or more of implicitly confining modern society to Western Europe and the United States, by the 1950s Parsons recognized that industrial societies existed beyond the shores of the North Atlantic. Studying the rise of the first industrial societies might reasonably be restricted to Western Europe, but exploring the further evolution of modern societies required a broader scope.[16]

The Social System incorporated Parsons's perspective on the Soviet Union. Indeed, he fit the USSR into his taxonomy by noting its universalistic aspects but also its tendency toward nationalism. He offers the Soviet Union as one of a very few empirical cases of social change, citing two factors leading to major changes in Soviet society. Borrowing heavily from the young Harvard sociologist Barrington Moore, Jr., Parsons noted how the responsibilities of power would force changes to Soviet ideology; it would continue shed its "utopian" elements in order to rule. He also echoed the arguments of another junior colleague, Harvard's Alex Inkeles, to suggest a second motor for change: industrialization. Economic transformation, he wrote, would lead to new forms of individualism inconsistent with revolutionary ideology. Whether by the fact of Soviet rule (per Moore) or by the forms of Soviet economic organization (per Inkeles), Soviet ideology would undergo major change in the coming years, Parsons concluded. He even offered a bold (if poorly worded) forecast: "This particular sociologist's prediction is that 'communism' will not be realized and that the increasing realization that there is no prospect of its realization will force far-reaching modifications in the ideology." Even before Stalin's death, then, Parsons identified some important features of the Soviet past that would shape the Soviet future.[17]

By the time Parsons published more extensively on the Soviet Union, in the late 1950s, his views of that nation had changed. In 1948 he had seen the Soviet Union as a society in the "early stages of industrialization." A decade later he categorized it unambiguously as an industrial society. Important changes in the Soviet Union account for this reconsideration. Economically, the USSR boasted growth rates far above America's, according to widely discussed analyses by Western economists; the Soviet economy was in fact becoming more industrial.[18] Just as important for Parsons, though, was the death of Joseph Stalin five years to the day after his seminar discussion of 1948. While Stalin was still alive, few western observers envisioned a Soviet Union drastically different than the one he ruled. The term "totalitarian," ubiquitous in the early 1950s, seemed to imply that such states did not evolve significantly, especially in the direction of decreased control. Stalin's death in March 1953 prompted careful reexamination of these assumptions. Even scholars like Merle Fainsod, who dismissed talk of liberalization as a "tactical maneuver" designed to allow the regime to "consolidate its authority," admitted that modifications of Soviet totalitarianism might be possible in some distant future.[19] Other scholars suggested that the Soviet Union without Stalin needed a different frame of analysis.[20] The concept "industrial society," encompassing the USSR, and the notion that American and Soviet societies might converge, found both new adherents and new audiences in the context of de-Stalinization and the Thaw.[21]

When social scientists of the decade explained the demise of Stalin and the system named after him, they reconsidered intellectual categories well beyond Soviet life. Recognition of the USSR as a modern society forced Parsons to place his once-static notion of social structure in a historical framework. It eventually required that he distinguish between capitalism and industrialism as distinct if overlapping societal types. His emerging definition of industrial societies, in fact, seems closely tied to his analyses of the Soviet Union.

Parsons made the connections between his conceptions of the USSR on the one hand and industrial society on the other especially clear in his contribution to a classic work applying modernization theory to Soviet studies: *The Transformation of Russian Society*, edited by Cyril Black.[22] Parsons's background paper revealed his determination to define industrial society in accordance with his understanding of the Soviet Union. More than any of his prior writings, this paper, "Some Principal Characteristics of Industrial Societies," carried Parsons's work from an analysis of "action systems" to outlining "some of the principal features of the structure of that still small, but increasing, group of societies which can be called 'industrial.'" Even more importantly, this essay reveals a new attention to the historical development of industrial societies.[23]

Parsons's enumeration of the key elements of industrial societies built on his prior analyses of social systems. While his definition included strictly economic criteria, he devoted more space to sociological aspects like institutions and "value-commitments" that supported industrialization. He also offered considerations that corresponded closely to the pattern-variables that he had theorized in *The Social System*. Modern societies, he suggested, would value universalism over particularism, achievement over ascription, affective neutrality over affectivity, and specificity over diffuseness.[24]

In spite of all of the similarities Parsons identified among modern societies, he also observed some variations. Sharp contrasts among different societies might appear, especially as industrialization began. The United States and Britain maintained "economic primacy" in the opening stages of becoming industrial societies. Other societies, in contrast, relied heavily on "political agency" in the early stages of industrialism; here the USSR was a "paradigmatic example." Parsons believed that capitalism accounted for the emergence of very first industrial society; later societies, though, did not require capitalism and might fruitfully undertake government-led industrialization. Government intervention, he concluded, could be functional for lagging nations. As they caught up with the leaders, however, differences would diminish.[25] As a society became increasingly industrial, its distinctive attributives would fade. This argument added a new sort of historical specificity to his arguments about the emergence of modern societies. Even if industrialization itself might take different forms, Parsons suggested, societies that underwent the process shared important structural similarities and would grow to share even more. By expanding his compass to include industrial societies other than Western ones, Parsons also began to develop a historical approach to modern societies.

"Some Principal Characteristics of Industrial Societies" used a parallel argument to explain the importance of socialist ideology in Soviet life. Ideology, Parsons concluded, served the crucial function of legitimation, breaking down traditional loyalties to "reinforce [the] motivation to participate in higher-order" organizations. Ideology, then, was primarily a means of promoting the institutionalization of new values and norms appropriate to an industrial society.[26] Ideology was no longer set in opposition to industrial progress (as he had implied in 1948), but was a functional tool for mobilizing masses mired in tradition. As important as it was for promoting industrialization, though, ideology had little place in mature industrial societies. In exploring the functions of ideology, Parsons also reconsidered the roots of Soviet doctrine, Marxism. Prior to the mid-1950s, his writings on Marxism focused primarily on theories of action. From that perspective, Marx's ideas about social change left him in the same camp as the obsolete Spencer: an evolutionist with no place for human agency. As he grew more interested in industrial society, however, Parsons reconsidered Marx's role, viewing him instead as a primitive forebear of modern social scientists. This new view is especially visible in an unpublished paper from 1955, "The Social Sciences and Modern Industrial Society."[27] Building on his earlier interest in the professions, Parsons identified the emergence of the "scientific study of human behavior" as a crucial attribute of modern societies.[28] As a scientific tool, Marxism had a mixed record. It was, on the one hand, "an advance at the level of general theory." In its universal scope and comprehensive aims, Marxism was "definitely superior to anything else in its time." To his credit, Marx was among the first to identify "the general industrial complex emerging in Western society." Yet scientific theories—not least,

Parsons's own action theory—became more specialized as they progressed. Such was not the fate of Marxism, which never developed as a scientific theory even if it had "ideological appeal" among workers and intellectuals. Indeed, its broad following beyond the ranks of scientists eliminated the possibility that Marxism could provide a "base for further scientific development." Marx was "one of the symbolic 'grandfathers' of the theory of action," though had been relegated to a remote garret by the behavioralist branch of the family.[29]

Marxism's transit from social science to ideology had major implications in the postwar world. It posed no direct threat in the West, where "the development of social science is too deeply grounded" to permit ideological commitments.[30] Outside the industrial world, however, ideology presented a clear and present danger. "Immature" societies, such as those in the third world, offered a perilous breeding ground for ideological pestilence. Even if western societies were immune to ideological blandishments, other nations might be susceptible. This concern, of course, was not Parson's alone; sociologists Edward Shils celebrated (and Daniel Bell acknowledged) ideology's irrelevance in the industrial world even as they worried about its impact elsewhere.[31]

But what about the role of ideology in the Soviet Union, which some writers saw as ideology incarnate? Parsons believed that the Soviet Union, like the United States, had already been inoculated against this dangerous threat: "the Communist societies have gone too far in positively institutionalizing science" to be further seduced by ideological sirens. The power of scientific thinking, he suggested, would eventually lead Soviet society away from its pursuit of ideological fantasies and toward the incremental improvements appropriate to modern industrial societies. New modes of thinking in the USSR would soon enough subject Marxism to "the kind of critical reexamination which scientific development inevitably entails." Parsons added another historical dimension to his own views of the Soviet Union as a modern society. It had originally been a society shaped—or was it misshaped?—by its ideological predilections. By the mid-1950s, though, the Soviet Union was well on its way to becoming an industrial society that had abandoned ideological exuberance in the name of scientific knowledge. Thus, he predicted in the unpublished essay's closing lines, "it seems likely that East and West in the present ideological sense . . . are more likely to converge than to continue to diverge."[32]

Coming to Convergence

Parsons reiterated this theme in a variety of presentations in the late 1950s. He suggested that Cold War tensions—running especially high in those years—would fade as superpowers' similar structures and values mitigated their differences. A talk prepared for Radio Free Berlin offered his most direct statement about convergence. In that talk, he argued that both the United States and the Soviet Union promoted modernization as well as a general pattern of "'human freedom and welfare' which transcends their differences"; the two nations were "very closely related." Now that they had solved the problems of industrialization, both nations sought answers, albeit in different ways, to the problem of equality. Those factors that defined western societies but were absent from their adversary—property rights, democracy, and freedom of expression—would soon emerge as challenges to Soviet rule. Comparing Communism to other ideologies of "reform" (Calvinism and Jacobinism), Parsons argued that such radicalism must inevitably fade: "it seems as certain as such things can be that communism also will prove to be short lived." According to Parsons's emerging theory of industrial societies, a scientific mindset would replace ideological fervor. An industrial society would be both a paragon and a promoter of rationalism, evidenced in the spread of science, the rise of education, and the growth of rational bureaucracies. Because the Soviet Union had become increasingly rationalized in recent years, Parsons concluded that it would continue on the path toward a full-fledged industrial society: "From its own internal dynamics," he wrote, communism would yield to political democracy, pluralism, and rationalism. The Soviet Union, in short, would become more and more like the United States. The "major polarization of the world" would slowly give way to recognition of common ground. His own broadcast from Berlin, he concluded with typical modesty, might even help promote this recognition.[33]

Parsons's notion of convergence assumed that the adjustments would be only on the Soviet side. What he identified as a "core . . . pattern" of industrialism—which would represent the Soviet future—amounted to an encapsulation of his view of the United States. This pattern included political norms emphasizing participation, the spread of scientific thinking, and the rise of mass consumption as essential elements of modern societies. Though Soviet levels of consumption trailed Western levels by a large margin, the Soviet leadership had nevertheless committed, like all industrial societies, to improving the "standard of living of the masses."[34] At the height of the Cold War, then, Parsons argued that geopolitical antagonisms obscured important structural similarities.

Diverging on Convergence

Parsons was hardly the first writer to postulate a convergence between capitalist and socialist societies. Since the late 1930s, observers had described common traits and tendencies. Most of these theorists of convergence give primacy to social structure and institutions, though they disagreed radically about the value and benefit of such convergence.

"Nightmare" theorists like philosopher Herbert Marcuse and sociologist

C. Wright Mills saw the convergence of the United States and the Soviet Union as part of a global trend toward spirit-sapping bureaucracies. They drew indirect inspiration from the debates in Trotskyists circles on the eve of World War II. In a brilliant polemic of 1937, Leon Trotsky blamed the Soviet bureaucracy for betraying the revolution. His followers expanded this argument beyond a diagnosis of Soviet ills. Bruno Rizzi warned of the imminent "bureaucratization of the world" while James Burnham feared a "managerial revolution" that had already overtaken not just the USSR but much of the industrial world. Rizzi and Burnham differed in particulars of crucial importance to Trotsky's followers. Did the bureaucrats constitute a new class? Was bureaucratic rule a new form of property relations? Yet the parallels were close enough that the Italian later accused Burnham, by the 1950s a leading American conservative, of plagiarism.[35] Notions of convergence were hardly the exclusive province of the left; in 1944 Friedrich von Hayek called the rise of collectivism in capitalist nations the first step on the "road to serfdom" in 1944.[36]

Herbert Marcuse picked up this argument in his analyses of Soviet ideology that also drew attention to parallels with the United States. Even before publishing his influential book *Soviet Marxism* (1958), he emphasized the ways that "industrial civilization" shaped the Soviet Union as a social system as well as Communist ideology. In his book, he did not go so far as to equate the Soviet Union and the United States, though he did stress the "common requirements of industrialization" that shaped both societies. Like the Trotskyists of the 1930s, Marcuse emphasized the "common features of late industrial civilization," most notably bureaucratic rule, centralization, and regimentation. Ultimately, he feared, these industrial societies might diminish not just freedom but the desire for freedom. Most importantly for his later work, Marcuse outlined how industrial societies hampered the free expression of individuality.[37] These latter issues, which one academic reviewer praised as "brilliant and disturbing remarks about the features and trends of Western industrial society," soon became the central thrust of Marcuse's influential *One-Dimensional Man* (1964). Offering few distinctions between Western and Soviet versions of industrial society, that book railed on tendencies toward "totalitarian" organization in modern societies that seek to shape not merely individual behaviors but individual aspirations. This critique soon became very influential in New Left attacks on American society.[38]

Another New Left icon, C. Wright Mills, offered a view of Soviet-American convergence that echoed Marcuse's critique. Mills accused industrial societies of a "materialism" that organized the world in the interests of social efficiency rather than human individuality and growth. The Soviet Union and United States "apparently differ" in ideology, he wrote, but "in structural trend and in official action they became increasingly alike."[39] In a short book and in a series of articles for *The Listener*, Mills outlined a critique of industrial societies for turning technology into a "fetish" and for alienating work "in the name of efficiency." In a comment that revealed his disdain for Soviet ideology, he remarked that Communism was not about equality or revolution but about "forced industrialization."[40] Publication of his book, *The Causes of World War Three* (1958), brought Mills into direct conflict with his one time mentor Irving Howe. Howe accused Mills of ignoring the power of political ideas by minimizing the differences between the USSR and the West so much that the analysis verged on proposing "moral coexistence." Mills's reply revealed little interest in finding common ground. He famously accused Howe of being an "Old Futilitarian of the dead American left." Even worse, he accused Howe, who had founded *Dissent* in the darkest days of McCarthyism, of being no better thant a Cold Warrior: "But Irving, as regards foreign policy, from what, tell me, do you dissent?"[41]

Mills, more than Marcuse or most other writers, faced direct attacks for his suggestion that industrial societies had more common ground than differences. Both "nightmare" theorists combined a heretical view of the West with an increasingly conventional view of the Soviet Union as a modern society outgrowing ideology.

Meanwhile, more optimistic convergence theorists saw the emergence of modern industrial societies as a structural shift that augured a new era of peace and stability. The best-known of these "sunshine" theorists was economist (and later policy-maker) Walt Whitman Rostow, who famously described a five-step development program suitable for all countries. Each nation, he declared, would pass through a "take-off" on its way from traditionalism to the "age of high-mass consumption." Most importantly for the purposes here, Rostow proclaimed the five stages as universals: all nations would pass through the same stages in the same order; only timing would distinguish one nation's take-off from another's. As he quoted his namesake in the conclusion of one book, his vision was one in which "All peoples of the globe together sail, sail the same voyage, / Are bound to the same destination." Even the Soviet Union fit into the "common growth experience" he had outlined, and was headed to the same "destination" as the U.S., if slightly later than its nemesis.[42]

Princeton historian Cyril E. Black marked perhaps the extreme of optimism about what modernization could accomplish. In his 1966 primer, *The Dynamics of Modernization,* Black predicted that the "revolution of modernization" would proliferate around the world. National traditions that had once inhibited social and economic change would fall before the juggernaut of this revolution. The death of these traditions would, in turn, end sources of international tension. If the revolution of modernization proceeded far enough, Black wrote, national governments might go the way of national traditions, yielding a truly global culture and the rise of a world government.[43]

Other convergence theorists focused on sociological rather than economic mechanisms. Parsons's protégés Marion Levy and Alex Inkeles worked in very different fields but shared a tireless dedication to the claim that the social structures of all industrial societies would converge.[44] Inkeles was especially important to Parsons's understanding of the Soviet Union. Trained in both sociology and Russian language, he was one of the first faculty members working in both DSR and RRC; his prolific writings appeared frequently in Parsons's footnotes. Inkeles's abiding attachment to convergence grew out of his studies of the USSR as well as his broader comparative work.

Parsons's view of the USSR owed a special debt to Inkeles, whose influential analyses of Soviet society underscored that Russia exhibited "many of the general features of the modern industrial order." Using data from interviews with former Soviet citizens, Inkeles challenged the notion that the USSR was a completely foreign society where western social-scientific theories did not apply.[45] His description of the key elements of the modern industrial order balanced positive and negative. On the one hand, he dismissed concerns about "atomization" and alienation (à la Marcuse and Mills). Industrial societies would certainly create new forms of sociability, but there was no reason to view what he called the new "super-community" as inferior to smaller social formations. On the other hand, Inkeles noted that an industrial society might have totalitarian tendencies, thus rejecting the claims of sunshine convergence theorists (like Rostow and Black) who expected modernization to reduce social suffering and international tensions in the long run. Inkeles instead worried that "totalitarianism may be *too* compatible with the characteristic features of industrial society."[46] In any case, political organization should not exclude the USSR from the ranks of industrial societies.

Inkeles's early work on the Soviet Union focused on questions of popular attitudes toward government. Finding little evidence of "concern with 'civil liberties' per se," he noted that some features of the Soviet system "win strong, widespread support and approval." A combination of coercion and citizens' "adjustive habits" had yielded the general "stability of the Soviet system." This new stability would permit either the rise of a rational bureaucracy in the hands of "managerial technicians" or the gradual movement of the USSR toward accommodations and eventually convergence with the West.[47]

Inkeles continued to focus on the USSR as an industrial society in his 1960s publications. One of his most widely read articles argued that the reigning perspectives of Soviet society, especially the totalitarianism model, offered inadequate insight into recent Soviet life. Instead, he argued, observers needed to consider the model of "mature industrial society." The Soviet Union itself was shifting gears, from a totalitarian regime under Stalin to a stable industrial society; Western observers needed to follow suit.[48] Inkeles's professional successes in the 1960s coincided with the increasing acceptance of his model of modernization, especially as applied to the USSR.

At the same time he analyzed the Soviet Union as an industrial society, Inkeles also pursued empirical research on other societies. As early as 1956, for instance, he and a coauthor argued that hierarchies of occupational prestige varied only minimally among industrial societies.[49] His multinational research project culminated almost two decades later with the publication of *Becoming Modern*, which provided evidence that the process of economic modernization would reduce cultural differences. Even after the publication of that book, Inkeles continued to report on the global cultural convergence created by the spread of industrialism. As the century ended, he collected many of these reports into a volume appropriately entitled, *One World Emerging?* That volume gathered evidence from all over the world to support his hypothesis that "the industrial societies of the world are converging on a common social structure."[50] For Inkeles, as for Levy, Mills, Marcuse, Black, and (to a lesser degree) Rostow, this process of convergence would take place independently of human action or direction.

While Parsons is frequently associated with macrosociological argumentation along the lines that Inkeles suggested, his own views about the convergence of American and Soviet societies combined structural elements and individual agency. As he had done in his first monograph, *Structure of Social Action*, Parsons attempted to find a role for human action even in the burgeoning modern states he was describing. He located that agency in a group of great personal and professional significance to him: social scientists. With its attention to scholars, and its mood squarely between the sunshine and nightmare versions, Parsons's theory might earn the nickname of "sherry hour" convergence theory. At whatever hour, though, his analysis of the USSR, and with it his ideas about convergence, provided not just a spur but also a convenient summation of his ideas about modern industrial society.

Parsons's Soviet Journeys

Parsons's deepening interest in the USSR culminated in two visits there in the mid-1960s. These trips brought together his central scholarly concerns: the importance of the sociological profession (and his own role within it), the functions and limits of ideology, and the convergence of industrial societies.

In 1964, he received an invitation to participate in a Soviet-American scholarly exchange program. His eighteen days in the Soviet Union—following celebrations in Germany for the Weber centennial—included a stay in Moscow with short trips to Leningrad, Kiev, and Yalta. The main purpose of the trip was to inform Soviet scholars about the state of knowledge in American sociology. In a series of small seminars and one large public lecture, Parsons described recent American work along both empirical and theoretical lines. In spite of various logistical difficulties (which he attributed, curiously enough, to the "Russian Character"), his talks were well received.[51] While his discussions with Soviet sociologists revealed many areas of significant disagreement, Parsons chose to emphasize common ground in his reports. Both American and Soviet scholars, he wrote, employed similar methods in their empirical work; indeed, each side could learn from the other. Their research often focused on similar topics, especially those related to industrial sociology or to generational conflicts. Yet Soviet sociology had yet to catch up with, let alone overtake, the Americans. Citing assessments of the field by Robert Merton and George Fischer, Parsons concluded that Soviet sociology was in its very first years as a true scholarly discipline. Indeed, at the time of his visit, sociologists had no institutions of their own. They worked instead in institutes and faculties of philosophy and published in philosophical journals.[52] The differentiation of sociology from philosophy would provide further proof of the Soviet Union's status as a modern society.

Parsons drew obvious satisfaction from the rise of academic sociology in the USSR. Almost a decade earlier, he had identified the serious pursuit of social knowledge as a symptom of modern societies. Seeing Soviet sociology emerge ("crystallize," in Fischer's language) confirmed for him that the USSR was itself fully modern.[53] There is a certain degree of narcissism in this response. Browsing in the Academy of Sciences library, Parsons saw an impressive collection of the central texts of Western sociology, including his own. Similarly, he noted on multiple occasions how many Soviet scholars were familiar with the main trends of Western sociologists—meaning works by Parsons, his students, and his colleagues.[54] Beyond any self-congratulatory element, though, he hoped that the emergence of scientific sociology would further propel the USSR to modernity.

Among the lecture notes and letters of introduction that he brought back from Russia is a handwritten reflection on his Soviet experience entitled "General Idea: Close Parallel of Communism to Calvinism."[55] At one level, the notes amount to a simplistic comparison between the liberalization of Prussian Calvinism and the (projected) transformation of Soviet Marxism. In the context of his earlier writings about the sociological profession, though, the notes show what place the social sciences would have in the Soviet liberalization he foresaw. The emergence of sociology from faculties of philosophy demonstrated a new stage of differentiation, a process which Parsons had long associated with modern societies. But this particular distinction held special importance: it amounted to "admitting [the] canons of science . . . into what had previously been matters of faith." The field of philosophy, the guardian of Marxism-Leninism and official Soviet ideology, was giving birth to a scientific field that would be organized around an empirical research agenda rather than deducing scientific truths from Soviet doctrine.[56] The rise of sociology in the USSR, then, was tantamount to the separation of church and state in early modern Western Europe. Proper understanding of Soviet trends shed light on the evolution of modern societies—and vice versa.

Parsons's trip to the Soviet Union also contributed to his renewed efforts to diagram and document the emergence of modern societies in historical perspective. He worked out new aspects of a historical framework in an important 1964 article, "Evolutionary Universals in Society."[57] These universals were institutions that different social systems would "hit upon" independently, but were so important that they would immediately become core elements of modern social systems. The institutions he outlined in the article, as it happens, all accorded closely to his conception of American society and thus made for unlikely "universals." At the same time, though, Parsons devoted the final pages of the article to a discussion of the Soviet case. His four features of a modern society are familiar from his earlier theories: bureaucratic organization, money and the "market complex," a universalistic legal system, and a democratic political system. Independently or together, these developments would increase a society's adaptive capacity, its ability to continue to grow and modernize. Parsons recognized, however, that these criteria did not describe all modern societies in the present. For instance, in his discussion of markets, he noted that modern socialist societies were able to achieve high productivity with "relatively minimal reliance" on the market—by relying instead on other universals, namely bureaucracy. Further growth, he believed, would require a turn toward a market-based system of resource allocation. He made a parallel argument about the role of democracy in modern societies, suggesting that "communist totalitarian" states maintained a nondemocratic political system only at the price of limiting the possibility of continued development. Here he hazarded a prediction: nondemocratic societies would "prove to be unstable." To avoid economic stagnation or even collapse, they would have to make adjustments in the direction of democracy and pluralism.[58] Even when theorizing at a general level about industrial societies, Parsons drew out the implications for the Soviet Union, a subject of his increasing interest.

Parsons identified the expansion of education as another factor promoting Soviet liberalization. The Soviet Union had devoted significant energy and resources to educating its citizens, creating a sophisticated population that would eventually demand its own political role. Efforts to accommodate these demands, Parsons argued, meant "the single monolithic party must [eventually] relinquish its monopoly" of political control. Highlighting the expansion of Soviet education, in short, led him to an optimistic conclusion that democratic reform in the Soviet future. "Evolutionary Universals," published only months before a group of conservative party officials deposed Nikita Khrushchev, cited the changes of the Soviet system since Stalin to argue for continued (even accelerated) transformation.[59] Soviet politics, then, would ultimately yield to the imperatives of a modern society. The educated citizenry and the desire for continued economic growth would spur political change.

Parsons's increasing attention to the evolution of industrial societies like the USSR also shaped his historical views on the emergence of such societies in the first place. Unfortunately, he never wrote another magnum opus along the lines of *The Structure of Social Action* or *The Social System*; no broad theoretical work incorporated his evolving ideas. There are, however, two books written for undergraduates that deal with the emergence of industrial societies; these are the closest thing to a statement of Parson's evolutionary theory. Invited by Inkeles to contribute a volume on "societies" to a textbook series called "Foundations of Modern Sociology," Parsons's new historical consciousness actually created significant editorial problems. Unable to write a single short volume on the prehistory and evolution of modern societies, he eventually split the manuscript in two.[60] The distance that his social theory had traveled in the previous decade is evident from the tables of contents. Whereas *Social System* began with a discussion of action theory and its relevance to social theory, the outlines for his new work opened with a historical section. His view of the nature of social systems had not changed significantly over the decade, but he was now attempting to describe the emergence of modern social systems in an evolutionary framework. This framework was intertwined with Parsons's travels to and thinking about the USSR.

He carried draft outlines of his projected volume on "societies" to Moscow. The volume, unlike his previous works, devoted a significant section to the antecedents of modern society. First came primitive and archaic societies, then "intermediate empires," and finally "seed-beds" for modernity in ancient Israel and Greece. But it was his historical analysis of modern societies (and not merely their antecedents) that marked a shift in his thinking.

Parsons's description of the history of modern societies (in what became *The System of Modern Societies*) revealed how considerations of the USSR had informed his newest theories of social change. When dealing with the evolution of modern societies, he applied his familiar model of social functions in a dialectic mode. Each modern society, he argued, excelled in advancing some but not all of the functions. Thus the first modern system in Holland, England, and France introduced religious tolerance, national identity, and a parliamentary system. All of these contributed to the dual industrial and democratic revolutions of the eighteenth century. The counterpoint to this inaugural system emerged to the east—in Prussia—in the early nineteenth century. Prussia's innovations included new forms of collective organization, most notably its bureaucratic administration. Inculcating a "stringent" sense of duty to the state, the Prussian monarchy was able to mobilize its highly stratified population for a single goal. As the Prussian model spread across Europe, it increased the adaptive capacity of modern societies.[61]

The next step for modern societies came with rise of a new lead society for the West, the United States, in the late nineteenth century. The United States represented, like France and England, a model for a democratically organized modern society. But soon the East—this time the Soviet Union—presented a variation. It is here that Parsons's analogy between Prussian Calvinism and Soviet sociology becomes most significant. Both Calvinism and Communism represented "counterpoints" to the main (Western) line of historical development. For Parsons, the Soviet Union further improved modern societies' capacities to organize and mobilize their populations around collective goals. His optimism about the future liberalization of Soviet political control, then, suggested that it too would soon incorporate the innovations of the democratic revolution. This roughly sketched analogy shaped the direction of *System of Modern Societies*, as he compared the post-Stalin thaw to religious toleration, and predicted an "ecumenical" future for the Soviet Union. The Soviet Union might then represent a synthesis of two modern traditions, Eastern and Western. It could thus become the lead society in a new stage of modern life.[62] Parsons's dialectic of modernity looked to the USSR to advance beyond the accomplishments of American society.

This advancement in the Soviet Union could take place only through the spread of scientific thinking, which was in turn the responsibility of social scientists. The differentiation of sociology and philosophy was a harbinger of the "secularization" of Soviet ideology. In the social sphere, industrialization and education had eradicated much of the localism and built up a sense of collective Soviet identity. Changes in the Soviet economy also suggested that the Soviet Union was heading toward more Western forms of social organization. Citing recent studies by Western experts on the Soviet economy, Parsons noted the rising standard of living for Soviet citizens; in his estimation, this meant that the USSR had entered Rostow's vaunted age of high mass consumption. The major lag for the Soviet Union, Parsons admitted, was in the political sphere—but even there he noted tremendous political progress and placed great hopes that the Soviet Union might "run broadly in the direction of western types of democratic government." The keys to Soviet developments in this direction were twofold: widespread education and the emergence of effective social sciences.[63] These issues would emerge even more strongly after his next trip to Russia, in 1967.

After returning from the USSR in 1964, Parsons sporadically pursued research on the state of sociology in Soviet bloc countries—a project hampered not only by innumerable other demands on his time but also by his lack of facility in the Russian language. Reading through the growing number of English-language monographs on Soviet sociology and working with a Russian-speaking research assistant, Parsons envisioned a project that would substantiate his high hopes for the future of Soviet sociology. He was especially excited to see how his Soviet colleagues had adopted many of the elements that he saw in his own work: a determination to shed ideology in the name of science, a focus on theoretical as well as empirical questions, and a desire to consider the sources of social stability.[64]

Parsons had similarly high ambitions for continued exchanges with the USSR. He believed that scholarly exchanges sped advances in Soviet sociology—by which again he meant the Soviets' continued trend toward American sociology. At the same time, the exchanges would provide opportunities for productive contacts across the Iron Curtain, helping to reduce Cold War tensions. True to his interest in elevating the role of social scientists in both countries, he was particularly anxious to see American and Soviet sociologists compare notes on methods of social forecasting. Looking at future convergence rather than present-day differences would provide, in his words, "a means of bypassing traditional conflict between East and West." Envisioning the bright future would ease the tensions of the more problematic present. As he told a Ford Foundation official when requesting funding for his travels to the USSR, the process of bringing scholars together would offer "one way to minimize East-West ideological conflict and polemics."[65] Scholarship itself could solve the Cold War.

Parsons's second trip to the USSR, in 1967, was far briefer and less involved than his one three years earlier. Traveling with a group of scientists promoting disarmament (an offshoot of the international Pugwash movement), he reestablished contact with the hosts of his 1964 trip as well as with a handful of Soviet sociologists whom he had met at International Sociological Association conferences. His conversations focused on methods of social forecasting, as well as on possible exchange initiatives that would bring small groups of Soviet and American scholars together to discuss history, sociology, and economics.[66]

These meetings clearly exceeded even Parsons's high expectations. Reporting afterwards to the American ambassador in Moscow, he repeated his enthusiastic appraisal of Soviet scholarship, and especially its newfound social-scientific bent. Most importantly, he saw in Soviet academic life the symptoms of a society that was becoming more modern, shedding puerile ideological posturing for mature scholarship. He identified this trend in Soviet intellectual life as a sign that convergence with the United States might be coming sooner rather than later. Soviet scholars' determination to master the techniques and approaches of western social science, Parsons predicted, "may prove to be of very substantial significance in easing some of the tensions inherited from the Cold War period."[67] Universalistic science would at last conquer ideological divisions.

The extent of his hopes for Soviet-American academic exchanges is best illustrated in a remarkable letter Parsons wrote to fellow academic Walt W. Rostow, then in his final year as national security advisor in President Johnson's White House. Parsons began by updating Rostow, whom he knew personally and professionally, on his most recent trip to the USSR. Celebrating the spirit of joint scientific enterprise he had recently experienced,

Parsons attributed this newly productive relationship with Soviet scholars to changes in Soviet life. Soviet interest in developing the field of sociology, he wrote, marked the "'secularization' of the political religion of Marxism-Leninism." Ideology had yielded to science, and there was no going back. Yet the shift in Soviet scholarship toward Western social-scientific techniques faced a grave threat. This threat came not from the Soviet side but from Parsons's own: the escalation of the Vietnam War might isolate Soviet scholars and thereby prevent their new belief in science from reaching full flower. Already, war-related tensions had scotched one prominent Soviet Academician's visit to the United States; any further delays in the academic exchange programs would be "truly tragic." The answer, he told Rostow, was simple: stop the Vietnam War, which was impeding the efforts of serious scholars to bring about significant changes in Soviet life.[68] Parsons's letter insisted that the ivory tower, and not the Pentagon, was best suited to winning the Cold War.

Parsons's second trip to Moscow was the high-water mark of his own efforts to build connections between modern sociology and modern society. From his earliest moments of focus on modern societies in the 1930s, through his more systematic efforts to theorize modern social structures in the 1950s, he saw sociology—by which he meant his own attention to social structures and their functions—as both an effect and a cause of modernity. The emergence of sociology as a scientific enterprise indicated that a society had reached a certain level of modernity. And the work of sociologists to replace ideology with rationality furthered a society's progress toward modernity.

Convergence Critiqued

While Parsons responded to Soviet sociology's turn to structural-functionalism with a combination of satisfaction and hope, other Western critics reacted very differently. Most prominent and prolific was sociologist Alvin Gouldner, who devoted almost half of his book *The Coming Crisis of Western Sociology* (1970) to an attack on Parsons and his brand of "academic sociology." In spite of the bulk and bluster of his criticisms, his views shared important assumptions and limitations with Parsons. Gouldner traces two broad traditions of sociological thinking from the mid-nineteenth century through the 1960s. What he called academic sociology began with Auguste Comte and culminated in Parsons. Counterposed to this was "Marxist sociology," which had been cast out of academic discourse in the West but was still represented by the social-scientific work taking place in the Soviet Union and Eastern Europe. The former represented the forces of stability; the latter, Gouldner's preference, the forces of change. By the 1960s, Gouldner warned, the two traditions had come close to merging into one—and on terms distinctly favoring western, or academic, sociology.

Gouldner continued in the tradition of nightmare convergence theory. Restricting his focus to the social sciences, Gouldner reached the same conclusion as Mills and Marcuse had: the Soviet Union was becoming an alienating mass society organized around economic production. In acknowledging the newfound popularity of academic sociology (structural-functionalism) in Soviet intellectual circles, he traced the origins of the trend to the society itself; "social science is a *part* of the social world as well as a *conception* of it," Gouldner wrote in the book's early pages. Like, Parsons, Gouldner saw the articulation of sociology in the USSR as an indicator of a new sort of social structure: "The emergence of a 'Western-type' Academic Sociology in the Soviet Union . . . is premised on the development of the Soviet economy and its industrial basis." Gouldner's claims about this new social structure also paralleled Parsons's: the stability of the Soviet system, claimed the former, required a sociology of the status quo: "Soviet industrialization is the central premise of Soviet sociology." Gouldner criticized this new emphasis in Soviet scholarship: "the Soviet Union's internal need for the stabilization of its own society" was "conducive to an academicization of Marxism that dulls its critical and revolutionary edge."[69] Like Mills and Marcuse, Gouldner foresaw convergence and recoiled in horror. Even if a shared interest in functionalist sociology "contribute[d] to peaceful cooperation" between the Cold War adversaries, wrote Gouldner, it marked a nightmarish convergence, the rise of an unchallenged "culture dominated by spiritless technicians."[70] Gouldner admitted that he had done more in criticizing other sociologists than he had in laying out a new approach to the field. His final chapter, though, did outline a sociology that abandoned the pretense of objectivity in favor of "reflexivity," of consideration of the role of theorist in the shaping of the theory. This reflexive sociology, of course, differed greatly from Parsons's tendency to abstraction and self-proclaimed detachment from his time and place.

Though Parsons hardly shared Gouldner's views of proper sociological work, let alone his apocalyptic vision, the two sociologists had much in common. Both scholars saw the rise of structural-functionalism as not just an intellectual issue but as a crucial indicator about social life and social structure. Like Parsons, Gouldner also defined industrial society — and not the capitalist order — as the reference point for discussions of social and political change. And finally, both Parsons and his critic found crucial support for their theories of industrial society in their analyses of the Soviet Union.[71]

It is fitting that Parsons, the theorist of convergence, was himself part of an intellectual convergence by the early 1970s. As his student Clifford Geertz pointed out, Parsons had built much of his impressive scholarly career on one or another variant of that concept.[72] He and Gouldner both found in the USSR important harbingers for the future. For Parsons, the Soviet Union had entered the ranks of industrial societies, and thus faced the same sets of problems that the industrial nations of the Atlantic faced: urbanism, labor control, education and socialization, management, and the like. For Gould-ner, the Soviet Union represented—as it had for Burnham three decades earlier—the final resting place for dreams of social change. Marxist soci-ology, in which Gouldner had placed such high hopes, had given way to the sociology of stasis; the Soviet Union was no longer a force impelling change but instead a force of inertia.

But the most striking convergence between Gouldner and Parsons is that they both saw their own field as the solution to the problems of modernity. Of course, they defined those problems differently; Parsons worried about vestigial irrationalities and even ideological distractions, while Gouldner concerned himself with the end of ideology. Yet they found the same solu-tion: sociology. Gouldner devoted the programmatic aspects of his book to the promotion of a "reflexive sociology"; self-awareness in scholarship was his way out of the dead-end of modern problems. Parsons saw sociologists as the solution to American-Soviet antagonisms; by serving as a model for Soviet sociology, they would help make the Soviet Union more like the United States. Gone was any broader vision of political or social change, whether brought about by mass action or revolutions from above. Gould-ner's critique of Parsons, for all of the punches it lands on its target, has a similarly narrow range of possible solutions. Gouldner and Parsons mark the arrival of the "end of ideology," at least in the west. Both theorized about social change that began in their own departments.

How Gouldner and Parsons came to converge, and how the category of industrial society expanded beyond the capitalist states of the north Atlan-tic, cannot be told without reference to the Soviet Union. Building on schol-arship on Soviet life by Inkeles and other social scientists, Parsons came to treat the USSR as an industrial society, similar in all important respects to the United States. What differences the two superpowers had was the result of survivals that would soon pass out of existence because they retarded social functions.[73] The future would be not only bright but monochromatic.

Parsons, as the leading sociologist of his generation, helped set the re-search agenda for the American social sciences in the postwar era. That his reflections on the USSR shaped the evolution of his thought suggests that key social scientific concepts emerged in the context of Soviet changes. The impact of the Soviet Union on American thought, therefore, deserves a wider consideration, one that looks beyond foreign policy and the politiciza-tion of academic life. Observing the Soviet Union, American social scien-tists reacted to the growing stability of the Soviet Union with an optimism (however unwarranted) that industrial societies were the sole possibility for the future. At the same time, academics, whether promoting or attack-ing the status quo, saw themselves as the solution to the problems of the day. American social science had met the Cold War enemy, and yet focused primarily on itself.

Part II
Liberalism and Its Social Agenda

Clark Kerr: From the Industrial to the Knowledge Economy

Paddy Riley

Ever since its publication in 1963, Clark Kerr's *The Uses of the University* has been an exemplary document of its era. Written when college enrollments were skyrocketing, federal funding for scientific research was abundant, and predictions about a burgeoning "knowledge economy" were novel, Kerr's book is a prototypical account of the golden age of the American research university. Of course, since it was followed so closely by the Free Speech Movement at the university over which Kerr presided, most scholars tend to read *The Uses of the University* with a fair amount of irony. After all, Kerr's impassive confidence in the future of the "multiversity" led him to describe an incipient student movement as but a "mild counter-revolt."[1]

Interpretations of Kerr's career as an educator follow those of his most famous book. On the one hand, Kerr is the liberal administrator who brought universal access and international distinction to higher education in California; on the other, he is the bumbling bureaucrat who mismanaged campus unrest and ignored the legitimate political dissent of university students. While each of these views has its merits, the debate surrounding Clark Kerr lacks historical sophistication. Since criticisms and praise both tend to gravitate toward the climacteric years of the 1960s, little attention has so far been paid to Kerr's early career as a labor economist and arbitrator and its relationship to his later role in the university.[2] This disregard is surprising, since the portrait of the "multiversity" Kerr would become famous for in the 1960s grows directly out of his earlier work in the field of industrial relations. From a historical perspective, in other words, *The Uses of the University* is not only a product of its time, but the outcome of a long intellectual and vocational development. It marks the culmination of Clark Kerr's analytic shift from the industrial to the knowledge economy.

This intellectual development began in the middle of a Central Valley cotton-picker's strike in 1933, when Kerr, a young graduate student at Berkeley, first became interested in the peaceful resolution of labor disputes.[3] His faith in mediation was ramified by his experience during World War II, where as a member National War Labor Board, he worked to maintain industrial peace and production through the establishment of a stable industrial relations regime. After the war, Kerr, along with a number of labor economists, helped to develop a theory known as "industrial pluralism," which suggested that the growth of collective bargaining had transformed the U.S. economy, so recently in a period of crisis, into a relatively benign structure. In the 1950s, however, his career changed course. In 1952, he became the chancellor of the University of California at Berkeley, and in 1958, president of the University of California. Throughout the decade, moreover, he was engaged in a collaborative research project with three of the more prominent labor economists of his generation—John Dunlop, Frederick Harbison, and Charles Myers—that would redefine his intellectual objectives. Their research agenda took them far from the mainstay of industrial relations, the collective bargaining relationship, into subjects that Kerr would popularize in *The Uses of the University*—the "human resources" of managerial and scientific workers and the key role of knowledge in economic growth. By the time they published their global theory of economic development, *Industrialism and Industrial Man*, in 1960, they were convinced that education was "the handmaiden of industrialism."

This move from labor to education suggests that the career of Clark Kerr is marked by a turn toward the concept of "postcapitalism" that Howard Brick identifies in this volume.[4] Early on, Kerr had believed in the power of social institutions to shape economic reality. His work in labor economics reinforced this aspect of his thought, and provided him with a compelling model for economic harmony in the form of collective bargaining. This experience was pivotal for Kerr, as concepts derived from industrial relations influenced his work for the rest of his career. But in the 1950s, a new element entered Kerr's informal social philosophy, and altered his ameliorative agenda. The university, he now believed, had displaced mass-production industries at the center of the economy, and knowledge, rather than collective bargaining, would be the source of economic and social reform.

Kerr's intellectual trajectory, like that of a number of his colleagues, mirrored developments in capitalist democracies after the Second World War. Scientific research, managerial innovation, and the expansion of education were all central factors in the remarkable growth of the European and American economies in the early Cold War. Nowhere was this more the case than in the United States, which contributed a larger share of its GNP to research and development, and sent a far greater percentage of its population to college than comparable European countries. Within the U.S., California was in turn unique: by 1960, 55 percent of the state's high school graduates matriculated to postsecondary institutions, compared to a national average of 45 percent.[5] The growing economic significance of knowledge had a corresponding effect on the U.S. class structure, as Daniel Bell noted in 1958, since white collar workers surpassed blue collar workers as the largest sector of the labor force. In short, Kerr's career and scholarship were an obvious response to major socioeconomic trends.

Yet these secular changes in the economy also point to a more negligent aspect of Kerr's transition to the knowledge industry. As he moved beyond the more parochial concerns of industrial relations, Kerr became more and more invested in sectors of the economy where the labor movement was prevented from advancing. As Nelson Lichtenstein has argued, the provisions against supervisory unionism in the Taft-Hartley Act of 1947 and subsequent labor case-law made the unionization of a number of whitecollar industries "virtually impossible."[6]

From this perspective, Kerr did not so much move away from labor as abandon it. Yet he did not at the same time abandon his postcapitalist optimism. As he argued with Harbison, Dunlop, and Myers in 1960, the growing importance of knowledge production to the economy would encourage the business enterprise to become more like the university, where collaboration and consensus, rather than hierarchy and command, were the norm. This may sound preposterous in the face of the New Left image of Kerr as a technocrat, a charge that Mario Savio made famous on the Sproul Hall steps in the fall of 1964. Yet much of Kerr's work suggests an "optimism of the mind" (to draw on another incisive phrase of Howard Brick's) similar to that which animated the postindustrial hopes the early New Left.[7] Kerr's optimism, however, had contradictory effects. Undoubtedly, his enthusiasm for the future of an economy based on knowledge helped to create positive social change: witness the democratic expansion of higher education that occurred under Kerr's tenure as UC president. But the same enthusiasm also led Kerr to discount the importance of a labor movement to a just economic order. Casting aside the New Left critique of Kerr, then, only presents us with more difficult, but also more significant analytical problems. Their cogent presentation requires that we look past the 1960s to an earlier era of political upheaval, when Clark Kerr, a young graduate student in economics, first arrived at the university with which his name would be indelibly associated.

The Development of a Labor Economist

While an undergraduate at Swarthmore, Clark Kerr became a Quaker, and in 1932 he traveled to California with the American Friends Service Committee to raise interest in the League of Nations and international peace. He spent the following year at Stanford, but found little more than polite interest in his M.A. thesis on unemployed workers' cooperatives. When he heard that Paul Taylor, across the bay at Berkeley, was not only interested in the topic, but had already been conducting field research of his own, Kerr quickly transferred to Berkeley to pursue a Ph.D.[8]

Taylor, like many of the most important labor economists in the 1930s and 40s, had been a graduate student at the University of Wisconsin, where John Commons pioneered the institutional study of labor economics. Taylor's work, however, was eccentric in reference to the mainstream of labor economics. Many of Commons's students, like William Leiserson, Harry Millis, and Edwin Witte were influential in the development of New Deal labor law and welfare reform—Millis and Leiserson as chairmen of the NLRB, and Witte as the director of the committee that drafted the Social Security Act. While Taylor also worked for New Deal agencies, he studied more marginal groups in the American economy, from farmworkers in California to Mexican immigrants in Chicago. Taylor's methodology was, at times, equally eccentric. He claimed to be more interested in a direct encounter with social phenomena than their aggregate measurement, and this insistence on fieldwork transformed Commons's institutionalism into a unique form of economic ethnography.[9] Accordingly, Kerr's first assignment at Berkeley was not to review classics of political economy, but to head out to California's San Joaquin Valley to observe a burgeoning cotton-pickers strike.

Featuring the Communist-led Cannery and Agricultural Workers Industrial Union, recalcitrant growers, and vigilante murders of farmworkers, the strike was the largest of a series of agricultural upheavals that spread throughout California in the early years of the Depression.[10] Kerr and Taylor, who eventually published a detailed documentary report on the cotton-pickers strike, wrote a brief article describing the emergence of collective action among agricultural workers, "Uprisings on the Farms," for *Survey Graphic* in 1935. While they did not support the Communist leadership of agricultural unions, their sympathy for the farmworkers was evident: given "the rise of intensive agriculture," they asked, "is it a matter for surprise that the proletarians strike?" To Kerr and Taylor, the central question raised by the strike was whether or not farmers and the government would "use power intelligently and deal with causes." This was certainly reformist language, but it would guarantee that one made few friends among California growers.[11]

According to Kerr, the resolution of the cotton-pickers strike marked the beginning of his interest in labor mediation, but it was not until the early 1940s that he served as an arbitrator in a labor dispute. In the meantime, he employed the methods he had learned from Taylor in his dissertation, which he finished in 1939. A massive, four-volume study of unemployed workers' cooperatives during Depression, the bulk of the project was an historical documentation of California cooperatives based on extensive field research. While he used traditional methods of statistical measurement, Kerr's stated objective was not only the evaluation of cooperative organizations as a form of relief, but "the documentation of a social movement."[12]

After finishing his degree, Kerr made some significant changes in his career. While he continued to draw on Taylor's style of economic ethnography, he moved toward the mainstream of his profession. He taught briefly at Stanford before moving to Seattle to spend five years at the University of Washington. Like many labor economists, he spent the war years working for the government, primarily as the vice-chairman of the Twelfth Region of the National War Labor Board (NWLB) based in Seattle. Years later, Kerr argued that the wartime experience was pivotal for the development of industrial relations, since it forced scholars to become actual participants in industrial disputes, and therefore to "bring together theory and practice."[13]

The NWLB, at the national and regional levels, was composed of three equal groups of representatives, from management, labor, and the public. It was in this last role that Kerr and his labor economist colleagues served, and their position between two often discordant groups gave them a decisive efficacy. Because of the federal government's insistence on maintaining production throughout the war, moreover, the NWLB possessed an impressive authority. According to James Atleson, the board "largely determined the wartime terms of employment in American industry." Kerr, writing retrospectively, argued that the wartime experience also convinced labor economists that the "pure" labor market of neoclassical theory, regulated only by supply and demand, was mostly a myth. As this idea fell by the wayside, according to Kerr, "there was room for social policy to bring improvements." But a critique of the neoclassical labor market did not entail a strident critique of capitalism—to the contrary, Kerr suggested that the wartime experience caused "a rejection of ideology," whether Marxist or promanagement, as labor economists "became more unified in outlook and more neutrally professional in approach." For Kerr's later career, both as a labor arbitrator and university administrator, this experience of neutral efficacy was extremely significant.[14]

The NWLB's authority was only enhanced by the demands of a war economy, and in terms of membership growth, this was of great benefit to American unions. Full production required stable labor relations, and for most labor economists, collective bargaining was the best guarantee of industrial peace. A number of decisions mobilized the rhetoric of patriotism to legitimate the process of collective bargaining. For example, in an opinion supporting a decision of the Seattle Board to award union recognition to laundry workers in Eugene, Oregon, Kerr wrote,

> It is not sufficient to say, even if it could be proved, which is gravely doubted, that the community of Eugene, Oregon, is not engaged in the war effort, or that laundry service is not essential in time of war, because strikes or strike threats in any industry in any community have not only direct economic effects but also repercussions on morale and unity on both the home and foreign fronts.

Invoking the image of American soldiers abroad, he suggested that they would be distressed to feel "that their sacrifices are not only not being equaled but actually are being increased by the actions of other Americans."[15] From one perspective, Kerr's invocation of patriotism was decidedly beneficial to labor: anti-unionism, he implies, is anti-American. But Kerr's comments also point to the Faustian bargain at the heart of wartime unionization. The price for labor's gains in membership, as Nelson Lichtenstein has argued, was diminished autonomy and radicalism. Thus Kerr, writing in support of unionization, lambastes "strike threats," while at the national level, the federal government supported union security (in the form of maintenance-of-membership clauses) but also demanded a no-strike pledge and a crackdown on wildcat strikes.[16]

Despite its influence over the shape of collective bargaining agreements, the NWLB did not establish a precedent for governmental administration of collective bargaining in peacetime. To the contrary, as Atleson argues, it tended to serve as a forerunner of what came to be known in the postwar era as "industrial pluralism." As a philosophy of collective bargaining, industrial pluralism contained three key assumptions. First, following from their experience on the NWLB, industrial pluralists believed that strong and stable unions made for peaceful industrial relations. Second, they tended to assume that collective bargaining should occur with minimal or no government intervention. The NWLB, of course, which often created actual contract language for collective bargaining agreements, was unmistakably engaged in government intervention. But to a pluralist, the aim of such intervention was to establish a voluntarist process of bargaining between labor and management rather than a centralized form of labor administration directed by the state. The NWLB thus helped to pave the way from the corporatist environment of the war years to a more privatized system of collective bargaining in the postwar period. As Katherine Stone argues, governmental nonintervention was the dominant concept of postwar labor relations law, which envisioned the contract as creating a "self-contained mini-democracy" in the workplace, free from "the processes of the state." This view entailed a third fateful assumption on the part of pluralists: that there existed an "equality of power between management and labor" sufficient to guarantee democratic rule.[17]

In the short term, this collective bargaining system did achieve impressive results. Unionization grew robustly during the war, from 27.9 percent of the nonagricultural labor force in 1941 to 35.5 percent in 1945.[18] As a discipline, industrial relations grew alongside its principal object of study. A number of university centers devoted to the study of labor relations were founded in the early postwar years, including the Institute of Industrial Relations at the University of California, Berkeley. By now a recognized labor arbitrator and economist, Kerr returned to Berkeley in 1945 as the institute's first director. Established by the legislature at the request of Governor Earl Warren, the Berkeley Institute followed the logic of the NWLB in promoting itself as a representative of the "public interest" in the field of labor-management relations, a neutral third party in the conflict between capital and labor. The institute ran summer conferences for management and summer labor institutes for unions; likewise, its community advisory board included representatives from the AFL, the CIO, and local corporations. Moreover, initial members of the Institute staff, like Kerr, continued to work as labor arbitrators and mediators.[19]

Industrial relations scholars built on their greater public and academic prestige when they formed a new professional organization, the Industrial Relations Research Association (IRRA), in 1947.[20] Since it was founded in the same year as the Taft-Hartley Act, one might have expected the first meeting of the IRRA to be filled with somber remarks about the revision of New Deal labor law. But Edwin Witte, who gave the inaugural presidential address, was not too concerned about Taft-Hartley. Although he thought that the law was unfair to unions, Witte argued that "there was no reason why existing good relations could not be continued despite the Taft-Hartley Act." Citing a shibboleth of industrial pluralism, Witte argued that agreement between unions and management depended not on the law, but on "a process of give and take, carried on in the realization of common interests, despite differences." To Witte, any attempt by either management or unions to enlist the government on their side in labor disputes represented "perhaps the greatest of all dangers to free collective bargaining."[21]

Yet as recent scholars have argued, the theory of labor relations developed by Witte and his colleagues turned out to be much more dangerous to "free collective bargaining" than governmental intervention. Critics of industrial pluralism, while they admit the success of the NLRB and the NWLB in enabling union growth, suggest that the long-term consequences of a pluralist-inspired collective bargaining environment diminished union power. As Nelson Lichtenstein has shown, a pluralist insistence on strong national and international unions meant weak locals—in other words, union bureaucratization led to labor's deradicalization. An insistence on grievance and arbitration had a similar effect, as it channeled workplace dissent into procedural forms that prevented spontaneous resistance.[22] Even more perilous was the pluralist emphasis on a balance of group power in the workplace, which entailed that a managerial recognition of a union's right to bargain demanded a reciprocal recognition of the manager's "right to manage." In a representative essay, Kerr's colleague Charles Myers placed these two principles at the top of a list of "Causes of Industrial Peace."[23] But while this mutual recognition of rights may have meant harmony to Myers, to the mainstream of American business leaders, as Howell Harris has shown, it meant accommodating a union presence where necessary, while fiercely asserting managerial control over the workplace. As Katherine Stone has put it, the assumption of labor-capital equality at the heart of the pluralist image of the workplace actually prevented such equality from being achieved in practice.[24]

But the most fatal error of industrial pluralism may not have been its paradigm for collective bargaining, but the fact that most pluralists believed this paradigm produced equity and harmony in the industrial economy. Kerr was especially prone to such optimism—as he told the IRRA in his 1954 presidential address, *both* the Wagner Act (the National Labor Relations Act) and the Taft-Hartley Act were indicative of excessive governmental interference in the workplace: the first because it had served its purpose (to catalyze union growth); the second because the postwar strike wave had receded. Given the retrospective critiques of industrial pluralism, and the accelerating deunionization of the American economy over the last three decades, Kerr's optimism about the success of collective bargaining— it had been so successful that labor no longer need rely on the Wagner Act—certainly seems extravagant. Yet Kerr's vision was not entirely utopian: he did not think that collective bargaining would automatically produce economic equity, nor did his dismissal of the Wagner Act entail an economy completely free from governmental oversight. The role that he did imagine for government, however, was procedural rather than substantive. In pluralist fashion, Kerr saw a balance of group power as the linchpin of economic harmony. Strong associations would prevent state absolutism, just as a mature collective bargaining system no longer required direct state intervention. But "it is not enough to have power balancing power," Kerr argued; the state also had to ensure that there were "a substantial number of power centers" and that individuals could choose freely among them.[25]

The state, in other words, concerned with maintaining the process by which power was exercised, rather than intervening in that process itself, acted much like a mediator. This was but one instance of the mutability of industrial relations concepts in Kerr's thought. He thought of pluralism, for example, not only as paradigm for collective bargaining, but as the ideal structure for almost all forms of organization. The economy as a whole, he argued, should be composed of "multiple power centers," since decentralization provided the best guarantee of individual freedom. Mediation was an equally flexible concept. Taking the union-management-mediator relationship as a point of departure, he imagined the social order as composed of a multiplicity of resolvable conflicts. When describing the operation of centralized power, moreover, whether in the form of the state or a university president, he frequently compared its tasks to that of a labor mediator.[26]

Kerr, then, like many of his colleagues, arrived at one of the quintessential concepts of postwar social science, pluralism, as a solution to the problem of labor-capital conflict. This trajectory is in fact quite similar to those well-known postwar intellectuals who developed a realistic appreciation of the American political economy after becoming disillusioned with ideological radicalism. There was more than a conceptual harmony at work here: some of the most famous Cold War liberals were participants in many of the same intellectual circles as Kerr and other labor economists. Daniel Bell, for instance, who provided the best-known formulation of the "end of ideology" thesis in 1960, was the labor editor for *Fortune* in the 1950s and an early member of the Industrial Relations Research Association. Seymour Martin Lipset, to take the best example, wrote the final chapters of his *Political Man*, a key pluralist text, at the Berkeley Institute of Industrial Relations.[27] Kerr, on the other hand, who had honed his rhetorical skills at Swarthmore by debating Norman Thomas, never had much of a radical past to become disillusioned from. Yet his intellectual career did contain one key transition: In 1952, when he became the chancellor of UC Berkeley, Kerr brought his faith in pluralism and mediation from the industrial workplace to the college campus.

As Kerr acquired a new role at the University of California, he also began to develop a theory of the importance of knowledge to contemporary economies that would significantly affect his concept of pluralism. In this new theory, knowledge, rather than the mass-production industries, would be the "focal point of national growth." Knowledge production would also ensure a fair degree of economic justice, because intellectual workers, rather than industrial unions, would be the main force behind a pluralistic economic order. Kerr retained many of the concepts he used to describe the process of collective bargaining in his analysis of the knowledge economy. But this conceptual continuity doesn't elide the fact that for Kerr, the university, rather than the factory, was now the paramount institution in the modern economy.

Kerr Becomes a Chancellor

The late 1940s were not as kind to the University of California as they were to Kerr and his professional colleagues. While industrial relations scholars achieved public prominence in the postwar years, the University of California experienced a period of political and administrative crisis. On March 25, 1949, the UC Board of Regents, led by President Robert Sproul, instituted an anticommunist loyalty oath for the university faculty. Sproul acted in the context of an attempt by the California Senate's Un-American Activities Committee, chaired by Jack B. Tenney, to amend the state constitution in order to allow the legislature to determine the loyalty of university employees. Kerr would have a prominent role in the protracted oath controversy towards its close. As a member of the Academic Senate's Committee on Privileges and Tenure, he had to determine whether nonsigners of the oath were subject to dismissal. Kerr, who had signed the oath, argued that faculty members who offered an adequate explanation of their refusal to sign should be reinstated. As to those who refused to candidly discuss their political beliefs, Kerr and the committee endorsed their dismissal. Acting in a manner reminiscent of his wartime role at the NWLB, Kerr attempted to mediate between the conservative regents and radical elements on the faculty. But in the oath controversy mediation proved unsuccessful, as the regents, in a narrow vote, decided to fire all the nonsigners.[28]

The State Supreme Court eventually declared the oath null and void, though the decision was not exactly a victory for its opponents, as the faculty, by the terms of the 1950 Levering Act, were now required to sign a new oath mandated for all state employees.[29] Kerr's role in the controversy, however, brought him respect among the faculty, who soon nominated him as a candidate for chancellor of the Berkeley campus. Approved by Sproul and the Board of Regents, Kerr's 1952 appointment marked a significant turning point in the history of university governance. Previously a centralized institution dominated by the president and the Berkeley campus, the university in the 1950s and 60s would be transformed into a decentralized multicampus institution, with local authority vested in each campus administration. As both chancellor and university president, from 1958 to 1967, Kerr was a constant force behind this administrative reorganization.[30]

Just as his administrative appointment foreshadowed the future structure of the University of California, Kerr's inaugural address as chancellor pointed to the vision of instrumental reason Kerr would outline in *The Uses of the University*. "The university of today," Kerr argued,

is founded on the faith that man can consciously direct human progress. Without this faith society would not so liberally provide libraries, laboratories, land, and buildings, not afford faculty members such opportunities to work in their chosen fields, nor follow their work with such avid interest. . . . Our society does not afford freedom of thought and speech to the members of a university on an idle or casual basis. It affords these freedoms in the belief that they are part of a process by which men are able to discover truth and, through this truth, control their destiny.

In addition to this paean to the power of the intellect, Kerr offered a strong defense of academic freedom, likely meant to resolve the wounds of the oath controversy.[31] As he notes in his memoirs, Berkeley was something of a pariah in the world of academe circa 1952, and rumors abounded concerning its likely fall from the upper echelon of the nation's research universities. Under Kerr's tenure as chancellor and then as UC president, however, Berkeley did not decline but rather rose in stature. By 1960, it had become the most prominent public university in the nation. The devotion to knowledge evident in his chancellor's address proved to be a herald of Kerr's administrative success. But his argument for the power of knowledge did not merely foreshadow his work as an educator. As the decade progressed, Kerr also continued his scholarship in industrial relations, and here the chancellor's address would prove prophetic in another way. Throughout the 1950s, Kerr and likeminded associates developed a theory of industrialization that would support his claim that "ideas are the raw material of progress."[32]

From Labor to Education

The year 1952 was an auspicious one for Kerr. Not only did he become chancellor of the Berkeley campus, he was awarded, along with Frederick Harbison, John Dunlop, and Charles Myers, a small preliminary grant from the Ford Foundation for a comparative study of the "utilization of human resources." All four had been trained in labor economics in the 1930s and had gained practical experience in industrial relations during the late New Deal and the war. While Kerr was the most prominent figure of the group during the 1950s and 1960s, his public and academic career was rivaled by Dunlop, who wrote a foundational text for industrial relations in 1958 and served multiple administrations in Washington, including a stint as secretary of labor under President Gerald Ford.[33]

The working title of the group's research proposal was unwieldy, but supposedly germane to the Ford Foundation's directors, who had rejected a similar proposal in 1951 called "Labor Relations and Democratic Policy." This first precis had focused on a relatively traditional topic in the study of labor, the effect of the working class on national political structures. While Kerr and his colleagues eventually settled on a third and more modest title ("Labor Problems in Economic Development"), the shift in emphasis indicated by "utilization of human resources" remained and would become more pronounced over the course of the project. Their turn toward human capital fit nicely with the objectives of the Ford Foundation, which had made the enhancement of the American educational system one of its early priorities. Equally important, in terms of the larger aims of the foundation, was the international focus of Kerr's project, which would entail a diverse set of country-specific and comparative studies.[34]

Early on, Kerr and his coauthors made a key methodological decision to displace the labor movement from the center of their analysis. Earlier theories of labor, Kerr argued with Abraham Siegel in 1953, had accepted to varying degrees the premise that capitalism was "bad," and then focused on the worker's vision of "the 'good' and 'beautiful' state of affairs in which he can find fulfillment and secular salvation." This violation of the fact-value distinction, according to Kerr and Siegel, ruined any attempt at impartial analysis, and therefore any hope for informed normative judgment. The parochialism of traditional labor theory was equally liable to reproach, since "Western capitalism" was no longer "the dominant motif in the modern panorama." The twentieth century demanded a new theory, capable of comparing variant modes of industrialization, as opposed to traditional labor theory's normative critique of capitalism.[35]

The axis of comparison for this global analysis would still be the "labor organization," but Kerr understood labor organization not as a synonym for labor movement but "in the sense of the structuring of a web of rules relating the work force to the work process." In some cases of industrialization, as in Western capitalism, many of these rules would be influenced by workers' organizations, but in other cases of industrialization the employer or the state would be much more important in "the structuring of the labor force." The important analytical questions therefore revolved around "rule making." What were the rules? Who made them? How should they be evaluated?[36] This emphasis on the administrative context was an obvious legacy of Kerr's work for the NWLB, as well as the industrial pluralist conception of the collective bargaining relationship as an exercise in self-government.

Much subsequent work by Kerr, Harbison, Myers, and Dunlop was an elaboration of the framework presented in the Kerr-Siegel essay. In a 1955 article in the *International Labour Review*, the four authors argued that "traditional analyses of the labour problem . . . have concentrated too narrowly on labour movements." Scholars needed to look to the top, not the bottom, of the industrial hierarchy, since "the nature of business organisations and the elites that direct them is central to any full understanding of the labour problem in industrialisation."[37] Harbison and Myers extended this analysis of the corporate elite in their wide-ranging volume of 1959, *Management in the Industrial World: An International Analysis*, where they described the dominant role of "organization builders" in industrial development. Harbison and Myers argued that management was the most vital factor influencing increases in productivity, and they cited "the administrative genius of Alfred P. Sloan, Jr," as an exemplary case of management-driven economic growth.[38]

Management, however, was not only an "elite" and a "system of authority," it was also an "economic resource." Here, the authors referred not to "organization builders" like Alfred Sloan but to the large number of organization men in the middle and lower levels of the managerial hierarchy. As Kerr and his colleagues argued in 1955, these workers were "the scarcest components of the labour force," yet among the most essential to economic growth.[39] Where did they come from? Unlike the rare individuals who became "organization builders," middle managers and technical professionals were produced by a nation's educational system. The ability of a country to "finance and build on a sizable scale the particular kinds of educational institutions which an industrial society demands," therefore, was a key indicator of its potential for economic development.[40]

Industrialism and Industrial Man, published in 1960, reflected the growing importance of education to its authors' theory of industrialization. Higher education in particular, as Kerr would argue in *The Uses of the University*, had become essential to the development of industrial societies. However, not all types of higher education were equally valuable. Industrialism demanded increased attention to "the natural sciences, engineering, medicine, managerial training, whether private or public, and administrative law." A relatively weaker emphasis was placed on the humanities and arts, although the authors did suggest that industrialism would provide more leisure time for aesthetic appreciation. The social sciences, meanwhile, would focus on "the training of managerial groups and technicians for the enterprise and government." The problems of the "operation and administration of industrial society" were so important, in fact, that a new discipline, industrial relations, had to be formed to study "the relations of workers, managers, and governments."[41]

Industrialism and Industrial Man, however, was not primarily intended as a theory of the economic utility of education. Its ambitions were much larger. The book was no less than an attempt to theorize industrial development in all areas of the world. At the center of the argument was a typological analysis of the role of "industrializing elites" in economic development. The authors classified industrializing elites into a set of five "prime movers": a dynastic elite, the middle class, revolutionary intellectuals, colonial administrators, and nationalist leaders. Although the differentiation of elite groups gave the book a comparative element, the thrust of the argument was toward uniformity. In the end, "the elites all wear grey flannel suits," Kerr and his colleagues argued. The initial difference in the origins and ideologies of various industrial societies would be overcome by a realistic outlook required by the hazards of economic development. Thus while the introduction to the book argued that "the whole world cannot be like the United States or the Soviet Union, or India, and one should not be indignant about it," the concluding chapter suggested that industrializing societies would converge around a model of "pluralistic industrialism."[42]

This inversion of "industrial pluralism" was apposite. In their search for a global model, Kerr and his colleagues had moved beyond the narrow concerns of postwar industrial relations to larger questions of international economic development. They were less interested in explaining the back-and-forth process of collective bargaining than in developing a general theory for the "organisation of men in the course of the productive process." Yet they retained their faith in pluralism, even as the labor question became more marginal to their analysis. In the closing chapter of *Industrialism and Industrial Man*, the roots of the pluralist metaphor in a theory of labor-management relations were mostly ignored. Instead, one of the major factors behind the development of "pluralistic industrialism" was education, which now functioned not only as an economic resource but also as the cause and guarantor of economic justice. "As the skill level rises and jobs become more responsible," the authors argued, a regime was forced to consent to the interests of its workers, whose intelligence made the "discipline of the labor gang" impractical. Consensual control of the work process would originate in institutions of higher education and research, and then spread throughout the economy. "More and more," Kerr and his colleagues argued, "other industries take on some aspects of the university with its faculty. The university becomes more and more the model for the enterprise than the enterprise for the university."[43]

Thus instead of state-union-enterprise, the tripartite scheme of industrial pluralism, *Industrialism and Industrial Man* argued that "the occupational or professional association" would be the significant third locus of power between corporations and the government. As more and more workers in all sectors of the economy organized around occupation and skill, instead of by industry, "the day of ideological labor movements as we have known them will have passed." "Class warfare" would be replaced by the "bureaucratic contest of interest group against interest group." "The battles will be in the corridors instead of the streets," the authors wrote, and "memos will flow instead of blood."[44]

With these optimistic prophecies, which were of a piece with the pluralist agenda of mainstream social science, the research project had come full circle. It began as a departure from the "labor question" in all of its guises, including the framework of industrial pluralism. Kerr, Harbison, Dunlop, and Myers wanted to understand the industrialization of the world, not only the U.S. collective bargaining system. So they turned to management and the "structuring of the labor force" as the central feature of international economic development. Management led them to education, and now, in the closing passages of *Industrialism and Industrial Man*, education provided a solution to those old problems of the labor movement: democracy in industry and a more equitable distribution of wealth. Education turned the enterprise into a university, ensuring consensual governance of the economy. It promoted social mobility, and therefore a new economic and social equality "which has nothing to do with ideology." This was no utopia: industrialism remained a system of order and rules, and a necessary hierarchy of managers and managed would persist. But here too education had an ameliorative role, since it would encourage the pursuit of personal freedom in one's expanding leisure time, "the happy hunting ground for the independent spirit."[45]

The Uses of the University

Just as the commencement of the Ford Foundation project had coincided with Kerr's move from the Institute of Industrial Relations to the chancellor's office, the publication of *Industrialism and Industrial Man* occurred simultaneously with one of the more significant developments in the history of California higher education. In fact, it was for another collaborative document published in 1960, *A Master Plan for Higher Education in California*, that Kerr would acquire national recognition. Here Kerr's influence was mostly behind-the-scenes. He was not on the committee that drafted the plan, but as president of the University of California he had a definite impact on its recommendations. The plan was a compromise between the three segments of higher education in California—the state colleges, the junior colleges, and the University of California. A mix of populism and meritocracy, the master plan envisioned statewide "universal access" to higher education, but it also sought to preserve UC as the preeminent public research university in California. To Kerr, the master plan was also an object lesson in the importance of education to advanced industrial societies. In address to the California Labor Federation the year before the plan's adoption, Kerr focused on what would be a major theme in *Industrialism and Industrial Man*: since human resources were the central factor in economic growth, education was a requisite for "survival in the world." California needed to plan accordingly.[46]

Time put Kerr on its cover on October 17, 1960. Referring to Kerr as the "Master Planner," *Time* focused on the expansion of higher education in California, and said nothing about Kerr's scholarly work with Dunlop, Myers, and Harbison. *Time* did stress, however, Kerr's background as a labor arbitrator, referring to the master plan as "an academic armistice largely fashioned by Labor Mediator Kerr, who in 500 major labor negotiations developed the subtle skill that makes aides call him 'the Machiavellian Quaker.'"[47]

The Uses of the University would generalize this analogy between industrial relations and university administration. Extending the argument of *Industrialism and Industrial Man*, Kerr announced that the United States had entered the age of the "knowledge economy." In terms of the theoretical framework of *Industrialism and Industrial Man*, Kerr should have cast himself as a manager, structuring the labor force of the university to achieve maximum output of that "invisible product," knowledge. While there are statements in *The Uses of the University* to this effect, Kerr argued that the primary role of the university president was that of a "mediator." His most important tasks were to maintain institutional peace and progress. He did not actually require power, only a "consciousness of power." He had to see that power was distributed effectively among multiple power centers, and that moderates controlled each center, but his primary function was to persuade, not legislate. He was, in short, a third party to all perceivable conflicts.[48]

A fair explanation for the persistence of a strategy, mediation, drawn from industrial relations in Kerr's description of university relations is that both rest on a loosely structured theory of pluralism. Both insist on a decentralized administration of power, nonideological bargaining, and the intertwined objectives of harmony and progress. In Kerr's thought, however, industrial relations and university relations are also the respective origin and end of an intellectual trajectory. The fact that this trajectory goes unnoticed by those concerned with Kerr's work in higher education is testament to the significance of his role at the University of California. But it is also testament to the elision of the labor question that marked Kerr's intellectual development. As "high-talent manpower" became the central engine of economic development, the traditional concern of much labor theory—the importance of workers' organizations to achieving a just economic order—moved to the margins. This allowed Kerr, in a 1968 address titled "Industrial Relations and University Relations," to argue that "to the extent that industrial relations has been concerned with emergence and absorption of new social forces," it should now turn its attention to students and intellectual workers. The heyday of the working class was over; industrial laborers were "now largely assimilated."[49]

Why would Kerr draw such a strong distinction between the two major concerns of his career? An explanation might be found in a quality of his thought that persists across this analytic separation. While never given to excessive normative claims, Kerr remained a rather indefatigable optimist. Recall his 1954 address to the IRRA, where he suggested that the Wagner Act was no longer necessary since its object—union growth—had been achieved. A similar optimism informed his belief that by the 1960s, the labor question was no longer pivotal, since the working class had been "assimilated" and knowledge, rather than the mass-production industries, was at the center of the American economy. He was most optimistic, though, when describing the future society that a knowledge economy would help to create. The predictions of *Industrialism and Industrial Man* were in fact quite mild compared to a favorite speech of Kerr's entitled "1984 Revisited," in which he offered an alternative to Orwell's dystopia. Instead of Big Brother, Kerr argued, 1984 would see a four-day work week, a 50 percent gain in average income, and a more equitable distribution of wealth. These gains would be due primarily to investment in education and research, the main causes of higher rates of economic growth.[50]

The fact that these predictions proved wildly inaccurate indicates the excessiveness of Kerr's optimism. As was the case with the industrial pluralist assumption of union-management equality, Kerr's tenacious belief that social forces were working in a more harmonious direction arguably neglected a contrary reality. Yet such a critique shouldn't at the same time undermine the more resolute character of his prognostications. Industrial pluralists by no means wanted to encourage a decline in union growth, nor was Kerr's projected vision of 1984 the product of a technocrat's false consciousness. Kerr, it is worth recalling, had the courage of his convictions when it came to the future of the multiversity. Indeed, his dismissal as UC president in 1967 occurred in the face of his stubborn resistance to a budget cut and the first-ever imposition of student tuition, measures proposed by recently elected governor Ronald Reagan. In today's fiscal environment, where public universities have been forced to place a greater financial burden on their students, and to rely more on private capital in the absence of public funding, Kerr's final act as president seems all the more laudatory.[51]

Contemporary conditions also illuminate, however, the extent to which the advent of a knowledge economy has failed to resolve the classic problem of economic inequality once subsumed under the rubric of the "labor question." This question may have departed from Kerr's conceptual framework as he became more and more invested in the world of the university, but its relevance to the American political economy has remained. In the end, the work of Clark Kerr may not provide us with a framework for reassessing the labor question in the context of the knowledge economy, but it does present the necessity for such a reappraisal with acuity. Recasting his optimism in consideration of what it led him to neglect is a requisite task for both students of Kerr's career, and for those who continue to believe, as he did, in the power of knowledge and education to shape a more humane future.

John Kenneth Galbraith: Liberalism and the Politics of Cultural Critique

Kevin Mattson

Liberalism has become a bad word in the American political lexicon. The "L Word," as some call it today, symbolizes pie-in-the-sky dreams, bleeding heart sentimentalism, wimpy foreign policy, anything and everything that is out of touch with America's political realities. Ronald Reagan and George Bush, Sr. helped transform the word into something bad, by pinning it on their defeated enemies (most famously Walter Mondale and Michael Dukakis). But it's really been the punditocracy that's made the term something to be avoided at all cost. Take Ann Coulter, the blond bombshell pundit, who has equated liberalism with "treason" toward America. Even more sensible Generation X pundits today hammer out this interpretation of liberalism. For Michele Mitchell, a young journalist at the *New York Times,* her generation rejected the naïveté of 1960s liberalism, which she associated "with crumbling housing projects, holier-than-thou attitudes, and 'wouldn't it be great if' theories." Mitchell's assessment, echoed by many other Generation X pundits, symbolizes just how beaten up liberalism had become by the late 1990s. After all, if the 1960s stands as the heyday of American liberalism, the 1980s onward appear a time of conservatism, a time whose legitimacy depends upon excising liberalism from the American political language.[1]

Ironically, or perhaps not so, this is an inheritance from a strain of New Left political thought. Though many New Leftists saw their tradition as an extension of more radical variants of liberalism, others believed it was necessary to transcend the liberal tradition entirely. During the 1960s, this made sense to certain activists. The Kennedy administration, for instance, had pledged itself to a liberal vision but moved terribly slow in recognizing the moral imperative of the civil rights movement—reacting only to pressure of protestors and those willing to risk their lives in the deep South. Kennedy himself seemed hell-bent on continuing the Cold War internationally, and his major domestic policy was a tax cut that threatened the government's ability to attack poverty or accomplish wider public purposes. When the federal government did move in this direction, under President

Johnson's "Great Society" programs, it could never muster enough strength since the Vietnam War drained the public coffers. Vietnam—the bête noire of the New Left—was most certainly a war waged by liberal leaders. Even a partisan like Arthur Schlesinger admitted that "American liberalism certainly made its contribution to the mood that led us into Vietnam." Liberals had blood on their hands, as many angry student protestors believed. Some concluded that liberalism seemed little more than complicity with a power structure gone mad. The angry passion of that decade helped push liberalism off the map.[2]

In intellectual and historiographical terms, this is best captured in the concept of "corporate liberalism," a term that started getting play during the 1960s. The idea originated among young historians gathered around the New Left journal *Studies on the Left.* Long before the Vietnam War heated up, writers like James Weinstein, Martin Sklar, and Gabriel Kolko argued that "corporate liberalism" was a paltry reform tradition that originated during the Progressive Era, during which time, liberalism became little more than a rationalization for the centralizing tendencies in corporate capitalism. Sklar explained, "Twentieth century liberalism, insofar as it is not merely rhetorical, is a system of political ideas consciously developed to strengthen the system of large-scale corporate capitalism." Weinstein made the political consequences of this even clearer when he wrote in the pages of *Studies on the Left,* "'Victories' for reform within the system have never been more than partial and almost invariably have been intended to blunt the effect of, or break up, movements for serious social change." By this account, liberal reform seemed little more than a con game of cooptation and liberals little more than pawns of corporate power.[3]

This New Left characterization is unfair for numerous reasons. To a large extent, making liberalism the enemy of the left was something that could only have been done during the 1960s—a time when liberalism appeared ascendant in American politics. Scholars like Weinstein and Sklar believed there were left-leaning alternatives that could displace liberalism and that conservatism—that is, a hatred for regulatory economics—was thoroughly marginalized. In 1966, Weinstein and Sklar would argue that "liberalism will remain the dominant political ideology of the large corporations and the socially disruptive programs of the ultra-right will continue to be rejected." Such confidence appears anachronistic today, to say the least. Thanks to the work of younger scholars like Rick Perlstein and Lisa McGirr, we know that the right was much more vocal and effective during this period of time. It's much harder now to believe that there is anything like a "liberal consensus" reigning during the 1960s. Even if we continue to believe in such a thing, though, there was also something reductionist about the corporate liberalism thesis. It ignored the polyglot nature of postwar liberalism and especially a more radical and robust liberalism that had not reconciled itself to the status quo of corporate capitalism. I would suggest that today we need to do a better job at understanding liberalism's nuances and varieties—in part for scholarly reasons but also for political reasons. Quite simply, Sklar and Weinstein were wrong: the right has not been marginalized, and it would seem timely to rethink liberal alternatives for those not content with our conservative climate.[4]

A good start down this path is the social thought of John Kenneth Galbraith, a quintessential liberal during the supposed golden age of liberalism. That Galbraith played a significant role in postwar American intellectual life as related to capitalism and liberalism is incontestable. Galbraith was the quintessential public intellectual—discussing difficult economic matters for as wide an audience as possible. To write the classic *The Affluent Society* (1958), a book that questioned "growth" economics and chastised America's consumer culture, was a feat in itself, but Galbraith did much more. He was not simply a public intellectual but an *engaged* intellectual— one who moved ideas into the public sphere and the world of political decision making. During the 1930s, he did pioneering work in agricultural economics and worked for the Department of Agriculture and then the Farm Bureau, becoming immersed in New Deal reform (here he made clear his liberal bona fides, seeing as agricultural economics had, due to populist influences, reconciled itself to government intervention in the economy and shunned neoclassical economics). He then worked for the Office of Price Administration (OPA) during World War II, eventually being pushed out by angry businessmen upset with regulatory meddling. Afterward, he did a brief stint at the State Department and worked on the Strategic Bombing Survey, which examined the damage wrought by America in Europe and Japan. Proving his credentials as a "public intellectual," he wrote important articles for America's leading business magazine, *Fortune*, around the same time. While teaching at Harvard during the 1950s, he counseled Adlai Stevenson on economic issues, crafting numerous political speeches. Finally, he wound up serving as ambassador to India under JFK. After Kennedy's death, Galbraith gave advice to LBJ and then fell out with him over the Vietnam War. At that point, Galbraith managed to remain active within Americans for Democratic Action (ADA), pressing liberals to end their commitment to the Vietnam War. In all these ways, Galbraith managed to combine the act of thinking with the life of action and remained squarely within the postwar liberal tradition.[5]

If Galbraith teaches us anything at all about liberalism in the postwar era, it is that it was a conflicted worldview. Too often, the New Left critique built up a straw man of Cold War liberalism that was technocratic, top-down, and unified. In point of fact, Galbraith himself recognized that liberalism threatened to become too technocratic, thus encouraging an internal discussion *within* liberalism. Even as an ambassador for Kennedy, he chastised his fellow liberals. Just as Kennedy stepped into office and as Galbraith himself assumed ambassadorial power, he shot a memo over to Kennedy, arguing, "If my experience of the last two or three weeks is fair, I think the problem of the new Administration is going to be neither liberalism nor conservatism but caution. I am a little appalled at the eloquence of the explanations as to why things, neither radical nor reactionary but only wise, cannot be done." A little later, Galbraith was still worrying that the administration (his own) had become "too professional—too aware of criticism, too sensitive to what cannot be done. There are no political buccaneers with a fine enthusiasm for action—in the manner of Harold Ickes or Hugh Johnson." Nor did Galbraith embrace the limitations of postwar managed capitalism. Certainly he believed in Keynesianism (though he questioned its ability to tame inflation, as we will see later), but that did not allow him to ignore deeper problems within what he termed the "affluent society." Galbraith fails to measure up to the cookie-cutter notion of "corporate" or "growth liberalism," making him that much more important to analyze.[6]

To understand Galbraith's social thought better and to situate it within wider debates about capitalism in the postwar period, we must understand, if only briefly, the intellectual and political backdrop of liberal activism and ideas that formed his own. Galbraith straddled two different periods in American history—the Depression era of the 1930s and the affluent times of the Cold War. In many ways, he tried to think through some of the intellectual legacy (Keynesianism, regulatory capitalism, etc.) of the New Deal within a very different context. Galbraith had certain "tools" to think with, and it is necessary to understand those first before delving into his own intellectual development.

Contexts: From Veblen to Brain Trusters

There has always been a non-Marxian radical streak running through American economic thought. Populists, at the turn of the century, did more than just harangue banks and the gold standard; they articulated a rationale for nationalizing certain elements of America's economy and grounded their ideas in a conception of a moral economy guided by the ideals of equality and small production. The Socialist Party attempted to weld distinctly American ideals of democratic decentralization to communal ownership of certain industries. And closer to the time that Galbraith himself was coming to intellectual maturity, "radical" liberals like John Dewey and Alfred Bingham searched for an alternative to communism, laissez-faire capitalism, and the reforms of the New Deal. These different sets of ideas held in common a desire to move away from antistatist thought without succumbing to the overreaching and doctrinaire nature of state socialism or communism. Thinkers within this strain believed in what was sometimes referred to as a "mixed economy" and paid attention to problems of how labor was structured in a capitalist economy, never content with the capitalist status quo.[7]

The foundational thinker in this context was Thorstein Veblen. Veblen was neither a Marxist nor a professional (academic) economist of the neo-classical school. He paid attention to the role of culture in economic activities (most famously in *Theory of the Leisure Class*) and, more importantly, articulated a critique of capitalism that grew out of observations made about the internal operations of the American corporation. Here was his most significant and long-lasting legacy. To the typical list that an economist works with—land, labor, and capital—Veblen added technical knowledge. As corporate activities became more centralized, capitalists increasingly relied upon a new set of "engineers." This class of expert employees ensured the corporation was "more efficient on the whole." Nonetheless, they also prompted a conflict over the future of the corporation: "It is the industrial experts, not the businessmen, who have finally begun to criticize . . . businesslike mismanagement and neglect." Engineers took note of waste, recognizing that production for profit often conflicted with efficient productivity. They began seeing, so Veblen argued, the possibilities for production to move onto a new plane of efficiency and use-value, potentially in the interest of a wider community of consumers and producers, rather than the narrow interest of capitalists. Veblen believed that engineers within the managerial ranks of American corporations needed to carry out a revolt on behalf of more efficient production, moving economic activity away from the principle of private profit and toward a higher interest.[8]

Veblen was a notoriously crotchety individual prone to alienate followers more than build a social movement. Nonetheless, his impact was felt in liberal circles. During the 1930s, after Veblen had passed away, activist intellectuals like Stuart Chase took up Veblen's teachings to envision the "technician, not the businessman" as the person who could "usher in a functional economy of abundance." As the American economy sunk into depression, Chase articulated a "vision of a planned society" based on Veblen's social thought. Other intellectuals did the same, including Max Lerner who drew inspiration from Veblen in order to call for a "democratic collectivism." While Chase embraced the technocratic dimension in Veblen's social thought, Lerner tempered technocracy with his call to "humanism." With these differences in mind, both thinkers shared a vision of planning and redirecting the economy towards goals other than private profit. This constituted a radical and noncommunist wing of American social thought that correlated with the rise of the New Deal. And as certain historians point out, some elements of this radical vision made an impact on the admittedly more tepid reforms initiated by FDR.[9]

Max Lerner himself noted in 1935 that "there are New Dealers high in government councils who use not only [Veblen's] phrases but some of his ways of thought." He remembered that Veblen "was a godsend for the college instructors and other liberals who did not yet wear the stuffed shirts of capitalist apologists but who sought escape from the stridency of populism."

Lerner here was probably alluding to the "Brain Trust" operating behind the scenes of the New Deal—that is, the professors of social science and economics whom FDR called upon for help in crafting his political vision, if only briefly. Perhaps the best exemplar of this was Adolf Berle, a Brain Truster and coauthor of the monumental book *The Modern Corporation and Private Property*. In this work and its later shaping of politics and economic thought, we edge closer to ideas that had a direct impact not only on the New Deal but Galbraith himself. Indeed, Galbraith had deep respect and admiration for Berle, a man who would also wind up serving the Kennedy administration.[10]

Adolf Berle and his coauthor Gardiner Means (a Keynesian economist) essentially saw the same divide within the American corporation that Veblen noticed: managers, not the owners of capital, *ran* corporations. Berle also noted that corporations had become increasingly collectivized due to the public trading of stocks. In this way, corporations had transformed themselves from private entities into "quasi-public" actors. Thus, the laissez-faire world of Adam Smith had passed away, and corporations could not be treated like the small pin factories of Smith's era. As the historian Richard Pells explains Berle and Means's reasoning, "Since economic and social behavior had become thoroughly collectivized, there seemed little reason to preserve the antiquated forms of private property or the individualistic values on which they were based." Or as Berle and Means put it, the idea of "public benefit" could now serve as a means to judge the activities of corporations. Thus, from Veblen's teachings that ownership (capital) and management and "know how" (engineers) had become divorced within the modern corporation, Berle and Means justified state intervention in order to create a more just and rational economy. Not surprisingly, Berle wrote one of FDR's more radical speeches, one that called on Americans to embrace a "new individualism" that would displace the selfish individualism of yesteryear.[11]

Historians of the New Deal recognize that there was a diverse set of opinions that stood behind FDR's sometimes haphazard experiments with reform. Most also agree, though, that by the 1940s the diversity narrowed, leaving behind what some call "commercial Keynesianism," that is, a call for government not to regulate the economy directly but compensate for downturns via periodic fiscal stimulation. After the war, as Alan Brinkley points out, commercial Keynesianism "robbed the 'regulatory' reform ideas of the late 1930s of their urgency and gave credence instead to . . . ideas of indirect management of the economy." Thus, "sustained economic growth" became the key aim of America's policy leaders who wanted to "distribute income" and "enhance purchasing power" through mild welfare state reforms and fiscal stimulus. This set of moderate Keynesian ideas moved to the center of American politics and correlated with a weakening of the left-wing visions informing the New Deal. As John Morton Blum describes it:

"In the hope of eternal prosperity, built on eternal consumer spending, the adversary toughness of the 1930s disappeared." Now commercial Keynesian ideas would shape America's postwar prosperity.[12]

This transition from the 1930s to the postwar period is crucial to understanding John Kenneth Galbraith. It is striking to note that Galbraith seemed well aware of the shifts that historians like Blum and Brinkley took note of later. In 1958, Galbraith wrote a short piece for the *Financial Times* of England that was entitled "Keynesians in Washington." Here he declared what *Time* magazine would take seven more years to proclaim: "We are All Keynesians Now." Galbraith believed that almost all policy advisors in Washington agreed that "the Government must underwrite the level of aggregate demand and also that it can do so." But within this consensus, Galbraith saw an enormous divide between "liberal" and "conservative" Keynesians. "Conservative Keynesians are lining up on the side of a tax cut," he explained. Liberal Keynesians—Galbraith's own camp most obviously—believed the nation must focus its energy on "schools, slum clearance and urban renewal, roads, parks, resource development, and an infinity of other things," all of which demanded more public "spending." At another point, he pointed out that even President Eisenhower (a man prone to chastising the "creeping socialism" of the welfare state) accepted the principle of deficit spending in order to manage the economy through slumps, having learned to "have Keynes without liberalism." And as Galbraith put it in *The Affluent Society*, "It is the increase in output in recent decades, not the redistribution of income, which has brought the great material increase in the well-being of the average man." Galbraith thus recognized that mild Keynesian policies had alleviated the problems of Depression era America (his term "conservative Keynesianism" also seems a helpful term, maybe even better than "commercial Keynesianism").[13]

Unlike some liberals (Berle's coauthor Gardiner Means comes to mind), Galbraith did not accept that economic growth and fiscal stimulus would be enough to solve America's postwar problems. He made this painfully clear in a debate he had with Leon Keyserling, the same year he made the distinction between conservative and liberal Keynesians. Keyserling had served under President Truman on the Council of Economic Advisors and had been a chief proponent of growing the economy as a means of funding social welfare programs. He thought Galbraith's questioning of economic growth was odd and said so openly in the pages of the *New Republic*, prompting Galbraith to reply. Growth was essential to any liberal public policy, Keyserling argued, and to say otherwise struck him as sacrilege. Only continuous growth ensured Americans could solve the "two prime political problems of our times, . . . the vast impoverishment of millions or our citizens . . . and the vast impoverishment of our public services." Keyserling believed liberals needed to grow the economy, acquire public funds, and then put them to good use. But *first* grow the economy, Keyserling argued.

To a large extent, the heated debate that followed with Galbraith seemed really a matter of emphasis. For Galbraith believed in growth, but he thought liberals should stop putting this aim at the top of their agenda. He admitted in his response to Keyserling that this old New Dealer "does not minimize the importance of getting resources into public use, but he does continue to attach first importance to the rate of increase in total output." Growth, Galbraith pointed out, could simply generate more private wealth and consumerism and do nothing about addressing public squalor. Growth without any direct corrective, does "not improve proportionately our public position, at least in the absence of a powerful determination to the contrary." To generate more spending did not necessarily improve the quality of American life, Galbraith insisted.[14]

Galbraith was joined in this debate by the historian Arthur Schlesinger, Jr. Schlesinger had become not just a friend of Galbraith's but an ally in the cause of "qualitative liberalism." Both agreed that a prosperous economy demanded fresh thinking about liberal political ideas. And Galbraith did much to articulate this thinking in his own work on economics. Indeed, Galbraith dedicated much of his intellectual energy to understanding the new dynamics of corporate and managerial capitalism and the possibilities for reform that they generated. Three books—*American Capitalism* (1952), *The Affluent Society* (1958), and *The New Industrial State* (1967)—constituted something of a trilogy in which Galbraith dissected postwar capitalism. His intent was to highlight both the strengths and deficiencies existing within the economy. Understanding Galbraith's critique can shed light on postwar liberal social thought and its relation to contemporary questions surrounding capitalism.

Toward an Understanding and Critique of Postwar American Capitalism

Galbraith's starting point was that of Berle and Means: the large corporation had thoroughly centralized the American economy. As he pointed out in the opening pages of *American Capitalism*, a "small number of corporations" dominated economic production. Few could debate this point, especially with the massive centralization of the American economy during World War II. Galbraith, much like Veblen and Berle and Means before him, believed that economic centralization was a natural process, something that might be disliked but could not be stopped. He explained, "American liberals have for many years devoted far more time and energy to regretting big business than to learning how to live with it." Like Berle, Galbraith believed it silly to think that anything could be done to return to a day and age of smaller or more decentralized production.[15]

Economic centralization meant the free market of yore was no longer a reality. Galbraith saw the principle of planning coming not from the state but from corporations themselves. This was most evident in the consolidation of consumerism during the 1950s. *The Affluent Society* is well known for developing these themes, but it can already be recognized in *American Capitalism.* Here Galbraith noticed changes in American culture brought about by consumerism, captured best, he believed, in "redundant service stations, glossy packages, bread that is first denatured and then fortified, high pressure salesmanship, singing commercials and the concept of the captive audience." For Galbraith, any criticism of consumer culture had to recognize that it reflected an underlying shift in the American economy— the rise of overproduction and the need to channel and direct consumption. Consumerism was not a cultural phenomenon but an economic and functional necessity. It was a part of the conservative Keynesian worldview— the sort of society that Keyserling and others had a hard time calling into question. As with Veblen, Galbraith hated waste and ugliness and saw these values as inherent in the economic system itself. After all, corporations needed the stability of knowing that their products would be bought. In *The New Industrial State,* he summed up and made even clearer what had already recognized in *American Capitalism* and *The Affluent Society*: "The initiative in what is decided to be produced comes not from the sovereign consumer who, through the market, issues the instructions that bend the productive mechanism to his ultimate will. Rather it comes from the great producing organization which reaches forward to control the markets that it is presumed to serve and beyond, to bend the customer to its needs." The historian Loren Okroi has argued that Galbraith endowed corporations with too much control over the desires of ordinary consumers. Though a legitimate critique, it does not do away with Galbraith's central observation that corporations by the 1950s had recognized the need to ensure a steady pattern of consumption on the part of Americans. For Galbraith this meant that corporations, with the aid of the state's fiscal stimulus, were now planning economic activities and leaving behind the vagaries of smaller, free markets.[16]

A key role in all of this was played by a new class of people who had become increasingly important to the operations of the modern corporation, namely "men of diverse technological knowledge." Here again Galbraith tipped his hat to Veblen, while expanding his conception of a new class to include more than just engineers. The modern corporation relied upon large holdings of capital but also technology and knowledge—what Galbraith eventually termed the "technostructure." Thus, it drew upon the resources of an "educational and scientific estate" that possessed education, not capital. Here Galbraith was in line with a major strain of postwar social thought—namely, an emphasis on the "white collar" classes, as witnessed in the ideas of C. Wright Mills, David Riesman, and the popular sociology of William Whyte. Galbraith simply noted an exploding white collar class that was displacing blue collar workers as evidence of his claim.

And like Veblen, he believed this new class was creating changes that deserved notice (what he hoped this class would do will become clearer later).[17]

Galbraith's analysis of postwar capitalism thus relied upon prior thinkers.
Drawing upon Veblen, Berle, and Means and his own acute analysis of current economic trends, Galbraith argued that centralization and its concomitant ethic of planning had culminated within postwar capitalism. Like
Veblen, he denounced the waste that was inherent in capitalism. Building
on the conflictual model of the corporation he inherited from prior thinkers—those who saw different social groups (managers and owners of capital) vying for power—Galbraith stressed the new class's role in economic
production. Finally, he came up with his own political vision about what
could be done to make this system more humane and democratic.

The Politics of Cultural Critique

Though known for his cultural critique, Galbraith was foremost an economist, and one of his primary concerns was something that was not cultural
but economic in nature—namely, inflation. He believed inflation was a new
type of problem endemic to postwar economic prosperity. As wages went
up within an "affluent society," corporations raised prices. This "wage-price
spiral" was especially evident in the highly unionized sector of the American
economy (e.g., steel). Here too was another major wedge issue that made
Galbraith differ from "conservative Keynesians" and the political thought
of Leon Keyserling. Galbraith argued, "The preoccupation of Keynesian economics with depression has meant that inflation control has been handled
by improvisation." Indeed, Galbraith rejected the current tendency among
Keynesians to shy away from direct regulation of the economy by skulking
in the background and injecting stimulus only occasionally. Here he drew
upon his own career at the Office of Price Administration, arguing that a
return to price control was necessary to head off inflation. He illustrated
that when government stopped using price control mechanisms in the wake
of World War II, inflation shot up. Against more conservative critics, Galbraith asserted that price control could be used more flexibly than it was
during the war. Most importantly, he urged liberals to remain more open
toward direct interventions in the economy in order to address inflation as
well as other problems.[18]

Galbraith's interest in price control showed his willingness to embrace
the regulatory views of some earlier New Dealers. As Galbraith knew, he was
on the left wing of the postwar Keynesian spectrum. This became apparent
when he opposed JFK's tax cut. Kennedy took advice from his economic policy advisor Walter Heller (a friend of Galbraith's), who argued to cut taxes
early on within the presidency in order to stimulate corporate and consumer activity (the tax cut itself not being implemented until after Kennedy's
assassination). In *The Affluent Society*, written two years before JFK took office,

Galbraith had already warned that "the rational liberal, in the future, will resist tax reduction, even that which ostensibly favors the poor, if it is at the price of social balance." He continued this line of argument by making known his disagreement with Walter Heller and Kennedy, pointing out that tax cuts not only were sops to the wealthy but provided an excuse for conservatives to cut public spending in the future. In 1961, Galbraith wrote the president, "I am against a tax cut." In 1963, just as Kennedy had made the tax cut "must" legislation, Galbraith wrote the president again that he was "still not reconciled to tax reduction," being "alarmed at the applause" the proposal gained "from the wrong people" (in this case, corporate leaders and the wealthy). Galbraith rightfully believed the tax cut would prevent the president from doing something bigger, like supporting an "assistance program for families of unemployed" and providing "loans for public facilities in towns with serious unemployment" or even a "Youth Conservation Corps" that could assist "unemployed teenagers." In 1963, still protesting the tax cut, he would bundle these sorts of initiatives under the rubric "Civil Equality Drive," linking it to his wider support for the civil rights movement. Though he lost this particular battle, Galbraith prompted a debate among liberals about tax cuts and public spending (it should be pointed out that Galbraith *was* successful in calling on JFK to institute price control when the steel industry threatened to raise prices). Galbraith's primary motive was to preserve the government's capacity to play a stronger role in the economy.[19]

Though he debated him, Galbraith's political vision shared a great deal with Keyserling's and also with the social democratic vision of labor unions and leaders like Walter Reuther. To a certain extent, Galbraith hoped to move the American economy toward corporatist management. He called for a "public tribunal on which labor, management, and the public are represented." He believed such a managed economy could more easily avoid inflation and worried openly about a "recurrence of a speculative orgy" on Wall Street, arguing that the government had to be strong enough to avoid what happened in 1929. Opposing increased defense spending, Galbraith wanted more money for domestic initiatives and outlined the need for a stronger welfare state. He asked Kennedy to support a "supplementary assistance program for families of unemployed based on the number of children," aid for public housing, and numerous other public services. Galbraith's call to action allied with the social democratic vision that Reuther and others had championed earlier—a vision that both undergirded and went beyond LBJ's "Great Society."[20]

But Galbraith also went beyond the corporatism of Reuther. He wedded his corporatist views to a cultural critique of consumer capitalism. Of course, the 1950s was a decade known for criticisms of consumerism. C. Wright Mills, David Riesman, Paul Goodman, Vance Packard, and others dissected the ramifications of an economy based on planned obsolescence and the manufacture of consumer desire. Galbraith followed suit in *The Affluent Society*. Indeed, a paragraph from this book has become one of the most widely quoted examples of American social thought pertaining to the ramifications of consumer capitalism:

The family which takes its mauve and cerise, air-conditioned, power-steered, and power-braked automobile out for a tour passes through cities that are badly paved, made hideous by litter, blighted buildings, billboards, and posts for wires that should long since have been put underground. They pass on into a countryside that has been rendered largely invisible by commercial art. (The goods which the latter advertise have an absolute priority in our value system. Such aesthetic considerations as a view of the countryside accordingly come second. On such matters we are consistent.) They picnic on exquisitely packaged food from a portable icebox by a polluted stream and go on to spend the night at a park which is a menace to public health and morals. Just before dozing off on an air mattress, beneath a nylon tent, amid the stench of decaying refuse, they may reflect vaguely on the curious unevenness of their blessings. Is this, indeed, the American genius?

This quote is cited so often that it has almost lost its meaning. Therefore, it is important to stress that Galbraith saw the problem of consumerism not in terms of conformity or simply the manufacturing of false needs but as a more significant problem within the "affluent society"—that is how "private opulence" created "public squalor." Rampant consumerism was therefore not simply a cultural problem but a political one. This stood as a cornerstone in the political thought of qualitative liberalism. The central problem of a consumer culture for liberals was not just that it created an ugly social landscape but that it prioritized private satisfaction while denigrating public life.[21]

Galbraith knew it sounded odd for a liberal to question economic growth. "The goal of an expanding economy has," he explained, "become deeply embedded in the conventional wisdom of the American left." Indeed, economic growth undergirded liberal social policy during the 1960s (as his debate with Keyserling already made clear). Nonetheless, Galbraith believed it necessary to reject the mindless celebration of growth that marked the era. He argued, "The Russians want more because we have more. But we must ask ourselves *why* we want more." Growth was not the sort of principle that could provide an "enduring sense of national purpose." Galbraith suggested here that citizens needed more than the mantra of "more" to provide meaning in their lives. Indeed, he supported calls to public service, endorsing the Peace Corps heartily and suggesting that a teacher corps be started domestically (what would eventually become VISTA). He took seriously JFK's rhetoric in favor of civic and public sacrifice ("ask not what your country . . . ") precisely because economic abundance was such a paltry ideology.[22]

Galbraith was essentially searching for a deeper justification of public action. While New Dealers supported public work projects out of a sense of emergency, Galbraith developed a deeper defense of public spending and activity—the sort that could stand up to the new dynamics of an affluent society. He believed "public services" could help ensure "economic equity and social stability," but there were other, more important reasons for it. First, in his arguments for public service, Galbraith suggested that public sacrifice pulled people out of their own private worlds and nurtured their idealism, developing an almost Tocquevillian message, what some today call "civic liberalism." Secondly, he argued that "public services" were necessary if America was going to progress "toward a more civilized existence." In both ways, Galbraith articulated a need for public action that transcended mere emergency and Depression-era circumstances. Public work did not just put unemployed people back to work during a crisis, it promised to raise the level of civilization and provide a stronger sense of national purpose during a time of affluence when many would see no immediate need for it.[23]

Another reason for Galbraith to question economic growth was its unsustainability. Again, this critic of the 1950s seemed to foresee intellectual developments that some think came later. He condemned haphazard highway growth and the ugly billboards that dotted the 1950s suburban-urban landscape. He disliked, much in the vein of Veblen, the waste inherent in affluence, even suggesting the need to limit consumption in order to protect the environment. Galbraith reasoned not simply on pragmatic grounds (that we needed to conserve in order to protect resources). He had a deeper philosophical purpose behind his argument for limits—one that saw policy as a means to nurture and prompt discussion about public values. He justified the need to control consumption (via taxes and the bully pulpit, etc.) by calling on Americans to think more deeply about the meaning of freedom. "Those who argue that" freedom, Galbraith explained, "is identified with the greatest possible range of choice of consumers' goods are only confessing their exceedingly simple-minded and mechanical view of his liberties." He called this the "biggest supermarket theory of liberty" and argued that it failed to appreciate a richer, deeper, more mature and sustainable understanding of freedom as the need to control and limit our activities—the essence of self-government within an affluent society.[24]

Neoconservative historians like Fred Siegel have suggested these views expose Galbraith's elitism. A new class of people grown fat on prosperity, Siegel interpreted Galbraith as saying, would now create meaning in their lives by focusing on the quality of their civilization. This new class "could show their superiority to run-of-the-mill Americans . . . by rejecting consumption in the name of higher goals." Contemporaries of Galbraith had already pointed to the purportedly snobbish conclusions in his thought. When debating Galbraith and Schlesinger in the *New Republic*, Keyserling hinted that Galbraith and Schlesinger wanted "eggheads" to rule the world. Critics like Harold Rosenberg, the historian Richard Pells reminds us, had warned a number of years earlier that intellectuals themselves could be just as conformist as the faceless white collar employees they loved to condemn. Today, this criticism has been generalized to suggest that almost any critique of mass culture suggests elitism and little more. For instance, the historian Paul Gorman has written a book on the relationship between "left intellectuals and popular culture" during the twentieth century, in which he reduces critical ideas about the culture industry to snobbery. The critique of mass culture by New York intellectuals (contemporaries of Galbraith's), we are told, "grew out of a sophisticated philosophical rationale they created to support their tastes." The cultural studies maven Andrew Ross pioneered this critique of the mass culture critique by characterizing intellectuals' relation to popular culture as little more than "paternalism, containment, and even allergic reaction." Intellectuals, for Ross, were just jealous that they had lost cultural guardianship over their fellow citizens, as Americans took satisfaction in comic books and movies and not the ponderous writings of eggheads. Intellectuals just couldn't understand that people might actually like the things they were buying or watching on television. The political theorist Stephen Holmes, lampooning Christopher Lasch's social criticism, can't even imagine a critique of popular culture being anything but elitist and thus inherently "antiliberal."[25]

These criticisms merit attention but are generally unfair. In fact, Galbraith believed a critique of economic growth and consumer culture was necessary to buttress his liberal economic views. After all, he constantly pointed out, "public services" helped the poor more than the wealthy. It was the poor who needed public "parks and swimming pools," seeing as the rich already had their own. Therefore, he argued, "public services have . . . a strong redistributional effect." Growth in itself could not change inequality. "Economic growth," he would explain after the publication of *The New Industrial State,* "does little for those at the bottom of the economic pyramid. They lack the education, skills, work discipline, often the health, that allow them to participate effectively in the economy and therewith in the increasing income that growth provides." Galbraith also believed his critique of prosperity aimed itself mostly at the wealthy: "Overwhelmingly it is the production and consumption of the well-to-do and rich which cause the trouble. . . . They consume disproportionately to their numbers." Thus, a critique of growth and consumption was not elitist, precisely the opposite. As Galbraith quipped, "Growth is only for those who can take advantage of it."[26]

With this said, we should not downplay the aesthetic dimension of Galbraith's critique. In voicing aesthetic concerns, he was not just covering up economic views. He genuinely wanted to move "aesthetic experience" front and center to any critique of consumer capitalism. "Aesthetic goals contest the claims of power lines over landscape, of power development over natural streams or national parks," he wrote. Taking note of the ugliness of public architecture developed during the 1950s in Washington, D.C., for instance, he lambasted the narrow "utilitarian" demands American civilization placed on municipal development. Galbraith fumed, "In public housekeeping, the aim is not elegance but to get by." He believed that, within reason, the "pleasure" architecture "provides the community" is more important than economic cost. When he lambasted the "ghastly" nature of "the superhighway" he was, once again, standing on aesthetic ground. He believed highway development could be legitimately judged by ideals like "charm and beauty." In pursuing this sort of criticism, Galbraith renewed another long tradition within American social thought—one growing out of the arts and crafts movement at the turn of the last century and from "Young Americans" like Van Wyck Brooks and Randolph Bourne. This tradition criticized capitalism not only on the grounds that it was *exploitative* but also that it was *ugly*. Galbraith picked up on this tradition and argued that it was both legitimate and crucial for improving the status of public life within an affluent society.[27]

Galbraith was not alone in renewing this line of thought. During the 1950s, numerous intellectuals and activists articulated the need for a "qualitative liberalism." For instance, Galbraith's colleague and friend Arthur Schlesinger, Jr., believed postwar prosperity forced liberals to rethink politics and to emphasize qualitative rather than quantitative reforms. Take for instance the liberal fight for national parks as a means not only to conserve land and provide recreational opportunities but also to symbolize a deeper sense of national pride and purpose based not on economic growth but on limits (also seen in the larger "wilderness" movement of the time). Or look at how Schlesinger himself was setting out a "national cultural policy" (one that would include federal support for the arts and public television and that could address the low quality of American mass culture). Or notice how the liberal organization Americans for Democratic Action (ADA) contacted thinkers like Paul Goodman, the author of *Growing Up Absurd,* to learn more about his critique of alienated labor and consumerism within the postwar economy. John McDermott, the executive director of ADA, explained that the organization wanted to think about what was needed to "make leisure time humanizing rather than debilitating." He explained to Goodman, "We feel that not enough has been done to bring ideas and criticisms such as [yours] within broad political and social conceptions which serve to re-animate and re-direct progressive forces in this country." Essentially, McDermott and others wanted to emphasize a new reform agenda that would transcend the liberal emphasis on economic growth and redistribution. Rather, liberals now needed to address the "quality of civilization," to use Galbraith's term. What this general intellectual movement makes clear is that liberals—contra numerous New Left interpretations—had not grown complacent in the face of corporate and consumer capitalism. Nonetheless, within qualitative liberalism there appeared a new set of problems relating directly to Galbraith's critique of consumer capitalism.[28]

The Possibilities and Challenges of Qualitative Liberalism

Galbraith's qualitative liberalism drew out of his recognition that the regulatory state initiated by the New Deal had lost much of its passion and direction. As is clear already, he criticized the Kennedy administration's technocratic tendencies (this critique was echoed within the ranks of the ADA). But JFK's technocracy was only one symptom of a larger problem. Galbraith explained: "The regulation of economic activity is without doubt the most inelegant and unrewarding of public endeavors." Since this was the central focus of liberal activism up to his own time, his own political vision seemed to stand on weak grounds. Indeed, Galbraith explained how regulatory (i.e., New Deal) agencies were at first "aggressive," stoked by vision and passion. But "later," he pointed out, "they mellow, and in old age—after a matter of ten or fifteen years—they become, with some exceptions, either an arm of the industry they are regulating or senile." Liberalism therefore seemed *predestined* to a loss of passion. But if liberalism was to succeed in tackling problems like poverty and "public squalor" it was going to have to become what Galbraith called a "determined faith."[29]

Here was a central tension in Galbraith's social thought as it pertained to liberal activism. He seemed genuinely uncomfortable with bringing moralistic orientations to the world of modern politics. For instance, he had nothing nice to say about critics of Wall Street who, during the 1920s and 1930s, suspected that capitalism and stock trading might be inherently immoral. After all, Galbraith, as a liberal, was a modernist uncomfortable with purist or nostalgic moral judgments. In discussing critics of Wall Street, he sounded like Richard Hofstadter and the other authors collected together in *The Radical Right* (1955). The anti-intellectual and sermonizing tendencies within populist attacks on capitalist wealth frightened Hofstadter as it did Galbraith. In *The Great Crash*, a book written the same year *The Radical Right* was assembled and which dissected the politics of the 1930s, Galbraith wrote, "Our political tradition sets great store by the generalized symbol of evil. This is the wrongdoer whose wrongdoing will be taken by the public to be the secret propensity of a whole community or class." Galbraith eschewed such moralizing tendencies but knew, at the same time, that liberalism was in need of moral passion if it was to inspire activism and sacrifice. Here was a central liberal predicament.[30]

The predicament seemed all the more highlighted by the dynamics of an affluent society. If liberalism needed to address inequalities that affluence could not do away with in its own right, a new challenge emerged. Though Galbraith was far to the left of Adlai Stevenson (whom he tried to counsel on economic issues), he would certainly have agreed when Stevenson defined "liberalism" as "an emotional sympathy for the exploited." It was precisely that emotional sympathy that seemed so hard to strike up within the affluent society. This theme ran throughout *The Affluent Society*, a book that began as a treatise on modern poverty but that took a different direction when the author faced new evidence. As Galbraith put it in *The Affluent Society*, the poor lacked "political appeal" and voice, precisely because they were segregated within islands of poverty, that is, "rural and urban slums." This contrasted strikingly with the 1930s, when the poor (or the "people," as they were often referred to then) were omnipresent due not only to 25 percent unemployment but the documentary efforts of social realists and artists funded by the New Deal. How, amid affluence, could liberals hope to make the poor visible enough to mobilize political sentiments on their behalf? Poverty, Galbraith recognized, had become more invisible, thus posing difficulties for the "determined faith" he hoped to inspire. It should be noted that when Michael Harrington wrote *The Other America*—the book about poverty that helped generate the energy behind Johnson's "Great Society"—he tipped his hat to Galbraith. Though Harrington disagreed with Galbraith's belief in widespread prosperity, he pointed out that Galbraith "was one of the first to understand that there are enough poor people in the United States to constitute a subculture of misery, but not enough of them to challenge the conscience and the imagination of the nation."[31]

Here we must recall that Galbraith not only wanted to help the poor but wanted to move a critique of capitalism onto increasingly aesthetic grounds. He knew full well that this was dicey business. After all, aesthetic values are notoriously subjective and prone to debate. Take one of Galbraith's pet peeves: the declining quality of public architecture in America. He had little good to say about the public buildings found in America's postwar social landscape (he especially hated the U.S. State Department building on the National Mall). As contemporary cultural theorists would be quick to point out, Galbraith's complaints about the public square were based solely on his own set of opinions about aesthetics. Galbraith admitted so much: "Those who are unwilling to pay for beauty and some elegance, and those who profit from commercial squalor, will be quick to say that [my] standards are too subjective and Americans cannot be concerned with them." If we put this weakness alongside the fact that the poor—the raison d'être of a stronger liberal politics and its ethic of social justice—were increasingly invisible and marginal in contemporary political discussion, we can better understand why Galbraith might have felt it necessary to search for a firmer ground on which to place his political critique of corporate capitalism. It was in this search that we start to glimpse central tensions within Galbraith's social thought—tensions that unfortunately served to weaken his critique.[32]

When Galbraith was starting to get a handle on the dynamics of corporate capitalism in *American Capitalism*, he took the first step in putting his nascent political vision onto what he thought to be firmer ground. The subtitle included the two words that the book became most known for:

"countervailing power." This was not only a key theme of the book but also symbolized Galbraith's attempt to ground his critique. While writing about the centralization of corporate power during the 1950s, he recognized that classical political economists saw the competitive market as a means of checking economic power. Competition ensured that no businessman became too strong. But today that was no longer the case: "Competition which, at least since the time of Adam Smith, has been viewed as the autonomous regulation of economic activity and as the only available regulatory mechanism apart from the state, has, in fact, been superseded." The logical conclusion from this line of reasoning was that corporations now possessed a frightening type of absolute power. But Galbraith broke this logical train of thought and instead developed the concept of "countervailing power."[33]

This concept fit the wider intellectual interest in pluralism—the conflict of interest group against interest group—that dominated American political thought during the 1950s. As Galbraith saw it, struggles carried out in the past—especially those of farmers at the turn of the century and unions during the 1930s—had now been institutionalized as countervailing power. That is, the farm programs of the federal government and the legally sanctioned activities of labor unions now served to check the power of large corporations, much like business power was once checked by other competitive businesses. This account had a great deal of empirical weight behind it, witnessed in the growing power of labor unions in the postwar years for instance. But Galbraith went further than citing empirical evidence. He suggested there was almost a magical power internal to the dynamics of modern capitalism. He wrote in metaphysical terms: "Countervailing power is a self-generating force." Here is how he explained the rise of labor unions during the 1930s: "In the ultimate sense it was the power of the steel industry, not the organizing abilities of John L. Lewis and Philip Murray, that brought the United Steel Workers into being." Of course, today we would quickly accuse Galbraith of robbing ordinary people of their "agency" in passages like these. More to the point is that Galbraith believed he needed to delineate some sort of mythical power internal to capitalist development in order to ground his ideas. At other points, he admitted that countervailing power was contingent on *conscious* activity—for instance, on the federal government's initiative. But on the whole the concept of countervailing power seemed to suggest a new harmonious dynamic inbred in magical dynamics of the postwar American economy, a renewal of Adam Smith's "invisible hand" for a day and age of managed capitalism.[34]

This tendency to search for self-generating and corrective forces within corporate capitalism appeared again in Galbraith's writing on the new class. Here we see another inheritance from Thorstein Veblen. Galbraith's faith in the new class made a certain amount of sense. After all, this class was marked by increasing levels of education, and like most liberals, Galbraith believed education brought with it the critical insight inherent in any process of enlightenment. As the professional new class became more educated, Galbraith reasoned, it demanded more from life than just economic reward. This point might seem a reasonable one, but Galbraith took a further step, embracing a dialectical style of thought when writing about education's impact. In *The Affluent Society*, he hinted that America's growing educational system might "be expected to lessen the effectiveness of synthesis and emulation in the manufacture of new wants," since smarter people were less likely to fall prey to manipulation. He followed up this line of thought and wrote in more dialectical overtones when he wrote *The New Industrial State* towards the end of the 1960s: "The economy for its success requires organized bamboozlement. At the same time, it nurtures a growing class which feels itself superior to such bamboozlement and deplores it as intellectually corrupt." Thus, the politics that Galbraith hoped for— the sort that would emphasize nonutilitarian and aesthetic principles over profit-driven capitalism—seemed embedded in a class of people whose growth was inherent in the dynamics of modern capitalism. C. Wright Mills once pointed out that arguments on behalf of the new class (from Veblen to James Burnham) represented a sort of "Marx for the managerial classes," that is, an overvaluation of agency and revolutionary power on the part of mid-level bureaucrats. Oddly enough, Galbraith used a new class argument, replete with Marxian notions of class struggle, to justify his hope for a liberal politics. He tried to ground an idealistic, moral, and aesthetic set of values in a firmer, materialistic class analysis.[35]

Neoconservatives have argued that Galbraith's faith in the new class exposed his elitism. But instead of emphasizing elitism, it seems more appropriate to underscore the mythical line of reasoning Galbraith had to endorse in order to make his arguments. He had to take an odd leap of faith to get to his undeserved sense of hopefulness. Instead of seeing the *contingency* of his politics, he wanted to make his prescription for social change endemic to forces within the society he was criticizing. This was a problem for other postwar liberal thinkers who believed in, as the historian Howard Brick put it, "a kind of 'silent revolution' that promised the effective suppression of market automatism or subordination of economic affairs to social regulation." Galbraith made the serious intellectual error of elevating his political vision by giving it stronger ground than it deserved. His critique of capitalism's ugliness really was a value-laden critique, even if he didn't want to realize that. Today, the results of this wishful thinking seem all the more apparent. After all, the new class has *not* ensured that Galbraith's politics would become a reality. They have seemed quite willing to embrace materialism and even conservative politics at times. Nor has the countervailing power that Galbraith deemed inherent in modern capitalism persisted. Not only have unions declined (something he himself recognized), but the sort of values Galbraith hoped for have not been protected either inside or outside corporations, by the new class or anyone else for that matter. Indeed,

if anything, our political culture seems devastated precisely by a lack of countervailing power. Unfortunately, Galbraith's social thought cannot help
explain this situation.[36]

Conclusion

As Galbraith's social thought makes clear, postwar liberalism had not
grown entirely comfortable with the dynamics of corporate and consumer
capitalism. On this point, New Left historians painted a one-sided portrayal
of liberalism. There remained a more radical tendency among liberals—
even among those who believed in counseling the Kennedy administration
and felt comfortable in Cold War organizations like ADA. That critical tendency within liberal social thought is all the more relevant today. After all,
we are still faced with many of the same problems Galbraith outlined—
increasing income inequality that manifests itself in the fraying of civic and
social bonds, poverty that is both devastating and yet hidden from sight, a
consumerist ethic that sets no limits upon itself and engenders environmental destruction, and a weakening faith in public action. Take for instance
one of Galbraith's personal causes, what today we call suburban sprawl.
Can anyone deny that haphazard suburban highway development is even
more of a problem today then when Galbraith wrote *The Affluent Society*?
Galbraith believed that a public planning process was crucial in checking
such haphazard and ugly development. "We must explicitly assert the claims
of the community against those of economics," he wrote. Today, our collective support for planning has waned, but has anyone really offered a viable
alternative to it? Can suburban sprawl be checked by civic-minded devel-
opers taking a voluntary pledge or by a crafty voucher system of some sort?
No one seems to have offered any answers to this question, and the alternative to Galbraith's suggestion today seems increasingly to be found in
cities like Phoenix, Arizona and Atlanta, Georgia. It would not seem such
a bad thing to remind ourselves of the lessons that Galbraith taught his fellow citizens: that environmental and aesthetic concerns should matter as
much as profit, and that planning in the name of community control is a
noble task.[37]

Though we might be able to make use of Galbraith's social thought in
this manner—arguing that liberalism can assert the need for planning
while balancing that demand against support for individual rights and an
appropriate appreciation of market principles—there is much that we can
no longer draw upon. Galbraith lived during a time when political consensus seemed abundant. As mentioned above, he pointed out how the
Eisenhower administration stayed the Keynesian course. Galbraith seemed
assured that a vital center was going to hold in American politics. It is odd
to read passages such as this one, written in 1955: "Social welfare legislation is almost entirely noncontroversial." This statement of Galbraith feels

about as familiar today as writings done by the ancient Greeks. The vital center, quite simply, collapsed. To a certain extent, liberals like Galbraith failed to understand the power of ideas further to the right of their own. Galbraith also tried to provide his own political critique of capitalism, whether he talked about countervailing power or the civic sympathies of the new class, with an almost mystical grounding. Such political hopes seem about as quaint as laissez-faire capitalism seemed to Galbraith during the 1950s. And thus we are left with a political vision that is grounded in nothing more than conviction. That is not to say that it cannot win influence or votes in the future. But it must take note of how weak and fragile it has become.[38]

Therefore, the sort of liberal social thought that I am trying to revive here has an uphill battle in front of it. There are many other ideologies competing for an American public that has become more conservative over the years. Galbraith's most important lesson, however, remains the same: to show that a critique of consumer capitalism can be squared with an appreciation of liberal principles. Liberalism, though under attack by conservatives, is not mired in the same historical set of problems as communism or state socialism. Nor, as I hope that I have shown, is it mired in a craven willingness to accept the worst aspects of consumer capitalism. Galbraith's social thought illustrates that we can be both liberals and cultural critics at the same time. And just perhaps our politics can be enlivened by remembering this.

5

The Prophet of Post-Fordism: Peter Drucker and the Legitimation of the Corporation

Nils Gilman

> *What we need is not an ideology but a science—a new science of industrial peace.*
> *—Peter Drucker, 1946*

Given that most people consider running a business to be the very definition of a practical matter, it's a bit perplexing to consider how "management" emerged in the second half of the twentieth century as a discipline with intellectual aspirations as great as medicine or law. As late as the 1950s, there were only a few thousand graduate students of business administration anywhere in the world, and much of the senior management at large American companies had not been to college, much less to graduate school. By the end of the twentieth century, however, over 100,000 MBAs were being minted annually in the United States alone. The Leadership Initiative at Harvard Business School recently found that whereas 10 percent of the bosses and founders of large American companies in the 1960s had an MBA, by the 1990s almost 60 percent had a professional management degree.[1] Accompanying this professionalization of management has been the emergence of a vast literature, both popular and academic, on the art and science of management. Although much of this literature (especially the popular titles sold in airport bookstores) is schlocky, some of it has also aimed for and achieved significant theoretical and analytical rigor. It is high time that intellectual historians began to take seriously ideas about management and business.[2]

To begin unpacking the intellectual origins of this newest of modern professions, this chapter examines the early work of the founding father of modern management theory, Peter Ferdinand Drucker. Although "scientific" approaches to industrial operations trace back to the work of engineer Frederick Winslow Taylor at the beginning of the twentieth century, Drucker is, quite simply, the most important figure in the field. "In most areas of intellectual life nobody can quite decide who is the top dog," John Micklethwait and Adrian Wooldridge observe. "In the world of management gurus, however, there is no debate. Peter Drucker is the undisputed alpha male."[3] With over 30 published articles, Drucker is the most prolific individual contributor to the *Harvard Business Review,* the most influential publication on the theory and practice of management. Drucker was the first pro-capitalist to analyze workers as resources rather than costs, and he coined the term "knowledge workers" in 1959. He was the first to emphasize that capitalists create their customers, rather than merely responding to a priori markets. He conceived and evangelized the notion of "management by objectives," used by a great many American corporations today, whereby workers and management negotiate team and individual goals.[4] Business leaders such as Bill Gates of Microsoft, Jack Welch of GE, and Andy Grove of Intel—perhaps the three most admired American businessmen of the late twentieth century—cite Drucker as a key influence.[5] According to one commentator, "Nearly everyone in the business world is familiar with Drucker, either through his books or his columns in *The Wall Street Journal.* He is a household name among MBAs, corporate executives and business students. Drucker is the world's most sought-after business consultant."[6]

Moreover, Drucker's ideas have guided more than just businesses. For example, the Universities of Michigan, Minnesota, Iowa, and Michigan State in the late 1940s all reorganized according to the principles of administrative decentralization enunciated in Drucker's *Concept of the Corporation*

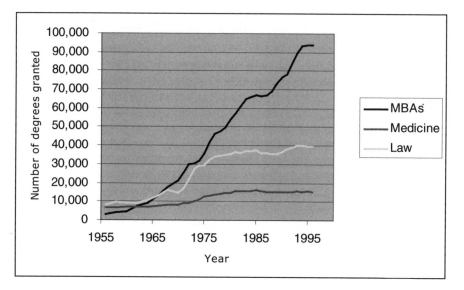

Figure 1. Professional degrees in the United States, 1955–1996. Source: U.S. Department of Education.

(1945). So did Cardinal Francis Spellman when reorganizing the Archdiocese of New York in the 1950s. Drucker has also exerted great influence in the political sphere. *Concept* was required reading for the first-year class of France's elite Ecole National d'Administration when that school opened in 1946. In the late fifties Drucker became the first to use the term "privatization" to describe the goal (which he advocated) of ending government management of industrial enterprises. Richard Nixon urged Drucker's ideas on government administrators; Newt Gingrich hailed Drucker as "the most influential writer of the twentieth century";[7] and George W. Bush awarded Drucker the Presidential Medal of Freedom. As his biographer concludes, "it is no exaggeration to say that Peter Drucker's name has become synonymous with the theory and practice of management."[8] By the 1980s, many of Drucker's ideas about management had reached the ultimate ideological apotheosis: they were so pervasive that people no longer recognized them as having originated with Drucker; they had simply become the only way to do business.

The Existentialist Roots of Modern Management

If Drucker's impact on management has been enormous, the origins of his ideas and his motives for developing them remain all but unexamined.[9] Like other mid-twentieth-century American intellectuals (including Clark Kerr, Talcott Parsons, and John Galbraith, all discussed in this book), Drucker was trying, as he put it in 1942, "to solve the universal problem of industrial society."[10] This chapter will argue that Drucker's later efforts as a management theorist spring from his efforts to prevent a recurrence of the crisis of liberal capitalism that defined his youth in the 1920s and 1930s. Despite the quantitative predominance of business and management in his writings of later years, Drucker's intellectual project is rooted in the fundamental political and religious perceptions formed in his Viennese upbringing and in the chilling political and spiritual climate of interwar Central Europe.[11]

Drucker was born in 1909 in Vienna to a Protestant family that had emigrated many generations earlier from the Netherlands. Drucker's father was a lawyer, economist and sometime Hapsburg civil servant; the selfless, disciplined ideals of civil service would remain the dominant model of leadership in Drucker's mind for the rest of his life. In his memoir, *Adventures of a Bystander*, Drucker writes movingly of how the Great War destroyed the Austria of his youth, though his own life in suburban Vienna remained relatively comfortable. Enveloped in the elite culture of Vienna, he had the chance to meet Sigmund Freud (whose theories he always rejected) and Thomas Mann (who bored him), and was a close friend of several members of the brilliant Polányi family. In 1927 he left Vienna for Frankfurt, where he took on various jobs as a banker and newspaper editor, while also taking a doctorate in public and international law at the University of Frankfurt. In Germany he would see Adolph Hitler speak at one rally, which confirmed for him that the anti-Semitism he had seen everywhere in the Austria of his youth appealed mainly to brutes.[12]

Drucker first came to minor prominence in the grim spring of 1933, at age twenty-three, when he wrote a pamphlet entitled "Friedrich Julius Stahl: Conservative Theory of the State and Historical Development."[13] Best known as a minor theorist of constitutional monarchy, Stahl, who happened to be a converted Jew, was a middleweight anti-Hegelian philosopher who after 1848 became the ideological spokesman for the cultural and political policies of Frederick William IV.[14] In his autobiography, Drucker mentions this essay mainly to highlight his own bravery and rectitude in celebrating the political theory of a Jew just as the Nazis were coming to power. (According to Drucker, "The book, I am happy to say, was understood by the Nazis exactly as I had intended; it was immediately banned and publicly burned. Of course it had no impact. I did not expect any. But it made it crystal-clear where I stood; and I knew I had to make sure for my own sake that I would be counted, even if no one else cared."[15]) However, many of the themes that would appear in Drucker's later arguments about business and management were already apparent in this youthful work.

For Drucker, Stahl was more than just an apologist for the post-1848 Prussian political regime. According to Drucker, Stahl's profound insight was to reject the hyperrationalism of the Hegelian dialectic "as a purely mechanistic and rationalist procedure," instead counterpoising an ideal of an undifferentiable "creative personality"—be that God or man. Stahl's originality lay in his effort to develop a "Conservative theory of the state" that would reconcile the reality of "history" (change and development) with "man's immutable nature" and concomitant desire for stability. Ventriloquizing through Stahl, Drucker argued "that state authority must lie with the rulers" and "the monarch is entitled to exercise supreme power completely and indivisibly." Although the principle of state authority was inviolable, Stahl emphasized that the monarch was duty-bound "to subordinate his interest to that of the state and to respect the rights of his subjects."[16]

Needless to say, such a view of the state's obligations to its citizens did not accord with Nazi doctrine, and Drucker made the wise choice of decamping to London, where he took up work as a banker. But he continued to mull over the problem of how to achieve social and political stability amid the rapid changes that capitalism's creative destruction created. In Drucker's view, the problem with both liberalism and socialism was that they defined men's social status in terms of their "mechanical" (economic) function, rather than any higher spiritual values. (From the Stahl essay on, the term "mechanical" recurs in Drucker's writing as a codeword for what is objectionable about modernity.) In a time of economic crisis, this conception meant that men without work were deprived not just of income but of their very social identities, resulting in a social crisis that opportunists like Hitler had been able to exploit as a means to seize political power. Drucker would conclude that for society to avoid the totalitarian temptation required a new understanding of capitalism, one that conceived of capitalist institutions as more than mere economic entities, but also organizations imbued with a duty of social integration.

The subject of Peter Drucker's first book in English, *The End of Economic Man* (1938), was the rise of Nazism. Drafted in England, this work was published in the United States two years after Drucker had emigrated from England to work as a journalist in the United States. According to Drucker, Nazism's opportunity for success was a result of the failure of both capitalism and (its spiritual mirror-image) socialism to address the social realities of industrialism. Drucker claimed that the origins of this crisis lay in the implosion of Christian accounts of social life and their replacement by soulless "mechanistic" notions of society: bourgeois capitalism and Marxist socialism. For Drucker, economic definitions of identity were of their nature existentially dissatisfying. Citing texts by Kierkegaard and Dostoevsky, Drucker claimed that the new economic concept of social identity meant that Western man

can no longer explain or understand his existence as rationally correlated and co-ordinated to the world in which he lives; nor can he co-ordinate the world and the social reality to his existence. The function of the individual in society has become entirely irrational and senseless. Man is isolated within a tremendous machine, the purpose and meaning of which he does not accept and cannot translate into terms of his experience. Society ceases to be a community of individuals bound together by a common purpose, and becomes a chaotic hubbub of purposeless isolated monads.

What had turned this grinding existential malaise into a full-blown social crisis, according to Drucker, was the coming of the Great Depression. The catastrophe of the Depression was not so much that there had been a decline in economic output—a result by itself not fatal in a society of abundance—but rather that an enormous percentage of society had lost its social and spiritual identity. This final straw, Drucker concluded, had deprived the individual of "his social order, and his world of its rational existence."[17]

Drucker's subsequent work on management cannot be understood apart from this existentialist core and his essential embrace of the left's view that it was the economic system itself that was in need of reform. Drucker acknowledged this in a 1992 introduction to what was in his own estimation his most outstanding article, "The Unfashionable Kierkegaard," written for *Sewanee Review* in 1949.[18] In that 1992 introduction, Drucker recounted that when he "stumbled across" Kierkegaard's *Fear and Trembling* in London shortly after leaving Germany, he did not quite understand what he had experienced, but in retrospect would realize that reading Kierkegaard had uncovered within himself "an existential dimension." In his 1949 essay

Drucker attacked Rousseau, Hegel, and Marx for denying the relevance of the individual (as opposed to social) experience. For Drucker, Kierkegaard was the only nineteenth-century thinker who had countered what he took to be Rousseau's freedom-denying portrayal of human identity as an exclusively social affair. In the finite, temporal world, only the social existed, subsuming the individual. But in the eternal, spiritual world, society did not exist, only the individual in his relationship with God. This tension between the unfolding of time, and the uniformity of eternity, Drucker explained, was the central paradox which defined religious experience, and which Kierkegaard insisted could not be undone or denied. Drucker's description of Kierkegaard's anti-Hegelian emphasis on the impossibility of reason to overcome the antinomies of existence dovetailed with his earlier celebration of Stahl's anti-Hegelian irrationalism.

With these Kierkegaardian thoughts coursing through him, Drucker argued in that liberalism's failure to overcome this existential crisis had opened the field for Nazism's new conception of man. Totalitarianism, Drucker argued, was "based on the affirmation of the meaninglessness of life and the nonexistence of the person . . . . As Kierkegaard foresaw a hundred years ago, an optimism that proclaims human existence as existence in society leads straight to despair. And this despair can lead only to totalitarianism."[19] For Drucker, Nazism was not the ultimate manifestation of capitalism (as Stalinists at the time argued), nor was it the culmination of systematic German philosophy (as fellow émigré scholars such as Hannah Arendt and Karl Popper would soon argue), nor was it just the reflex of Hitler's own extraordinary personality. Rather, the appeal of Nazism was its promise to deliver people "from the horror of a world that has lost its meaning."[20] Although intellectuals might be able to look unflinchingly into the modernist abyss, "the average individual cannot bear the utter atomization, the unreality and senselessness, the destruction of all order, of all society, of all rational individual existence through blind incalculable, senseless forces as a result of rationalization and mechanization."[21] For Drucker, "godless capitalism" was as much of a disaster as "godless Communism."

The goal of Nazism, Drucker said, was to find a solution to the crisis brought on by the mechanistic, economic conception of man by having the government sponsor a new set of credos and values based on communal belonging. Drucker noted how Nazi ideology and practice defined individuals' social identities not in terms of their economic role, but in terms of other social functions, notably their place in the Party, but also as leaders of youth troops, as mothers, and above as contributors to social mobilization for war. However, Drucker did not believe that Nazism represented a viable alternative to the economic definition of the individual in industrial society. According to Drucker, Nazism's obsessive persecution of Jews, the embodiment in the Nazi mind of "economic man," showed that the Nazi value system could only define itself in relation to its enemies. With a nod to Stahl's theory of social harmony, Drucker proposed that for a society to achieve stability it had to provide a "harmonious social basis" that did not require negative reference to an alternative value system. Drucker closed *The End of Economic Man* by declaring that although capitalism had failed, totalitarian alternatives were also doomed to failure.

Drucker published his next book, *The Future of Industrial Man*, four years later. In subtle ways, this book reflected his experience living in late Depression-era United States. Although skeptical of the New Deal's statism and critical of Franklin D. Roosevelt's factionalizing approach to governing, Drucker was deeply impressed by the country's energy, the focus on direct action, and the informality of its manners, which he used to advance his journalistic career by popping in on numerous senior editors at magazines and newspapers. What struck Drucker most was how the American people had reacted to the Depression. "Unlike Europe, where it was felt that 'the center cannot hold,'" Drucker later reflected, "the 'center' held in America. Society and community were sound, hale, indeed triumphant." Although Drucker did not paper over the country's class bitterness, its racism, or its pervasive anti-Semitism, what amazed him was that, unlike in Europe, the coming of the Depression had not caused these social fissures to erupt into open warfare. He credited Roosevelt for having turned the disaster of the Depression into "a celebration of community, of shared values, of the joy of life, and of common hope."[22] Unlike left-leaning immigrants to the United States from Europe in the 1930s, who often reacted with horror at the tawdriness of American mass culture and the country's willing embrace of capitalism, Drucker had from the outset a favorable reaction to the United States, a feeling shared by other Austrian conservatives who arrived during the interwar years, people like Ludwig von Mises, Joseph Schumpeter, and Friedrich von Hayek.

Despite Drucker's more optimistic sentiments, *The Future of Industrial Man* took up where his previous book had left off, arguing that the crisis of Western civilization that had led to Nazism stemmed from the disjuncture between the new mode of economic organization created by mechanical industrialism and the fact that Western society still was organized according to eighteenth-century social principles appropriate for a mercantile but not for an industrial society. This discordance of social organization and industrial technique created "a crisis of legitimacy" in the social institutions of Western life, which expressed itself in political terms. He claimed that, "No society can function as a society unless it gives the individual member social status and function, and unless the decisive social power is a legitimate power."[23] To understand social legitimacy, Drucker mobilized a new notion, namely that every stable society contains a metonymic social symbol, in relation to which the legitimacy of all other social institutions were defined. Drucker termed this the "socially constitutive" or "representative" institution. Drucker claimed that one could identify a society's representative

institution because its "values are the social values of a society, [its] rewards
the social rewards, [its] prestige the social prestige, and [its] ideals social
ideals."[24] In nineteenth- century England, for example, the idea of the gen-
tleman provided the basic social category around or against which other
social agents defined themselves. Drucker emphasized that the constitutive function of the gentlemanly ideal applied even to members of English
society who were themselves not gentlemen, and indeed even for those
who had nothing but disdain for gentlemen and gentlemanliness. In other
words, the socially constitutive sphere provided the benchmark values for
a society, against which any alternative value systems were always defined.

Having set the stage with this sociological concept, Drucker then asserted:
"The representative social phenomena of the industrial system of our time
are the mass-production plant and the corporation. The assembly line is
the representative material environment; the corporation is the representative social institution."[25] The question was, was the corporation "socially
legitimate"? If in a democracy sovereignty resided with the people and power
with the government, Drucker explained, then in a corporation sovereignty
resided with the stockholders and power with management. Legitimating
corporate power required a recognized and accepted way for those with
sovereignty to embrace and understand those wielding power. The problem for corporations was that no such mechanism existed. As a result, the
problem Western civilization faced was that "managerial power today is
illegitimate power."[26] Citing Adolf Berle and Gardiner Means's *The Modern
Corporation and Private Property* (1932) as evidence for the loss of shareholder
control over corporations, Drucker lamented that the power of management "is in the most literal sense unfounded, unjustified, uncontrolled and
irresponsible power."[27] Whereas democratic governments had formal procedures to establish legitimacy (such as elections), corporate management
lacked parallel mechanisms for establishing legitimacy. A solution to the
existential dilemma of modernity thus required finding ways to legitimate
of the representative social institutions of the industrial system, the mass-
production plant and the corporation. Returning to the notion of harmony
that he had first introduced in his essay on Stahl, Drucker argued the concept of harmony was the basic term of political action and judgment: the
goal of Drucker's analyses would be to "harmonize" the interests of management and workers, between individuals and industrial society.[28] Note
how these arguments nuanced Drucker's earlier claims: instead of saying
that economic definitions of social identity were *inherently* dissatisfying,
Drucker was now arguing that work-based definitions of social identity were
only dissatisfying *under the contemporary organization of industrialism.*

Drucker's focus on the socioeconomic roots of existential crisis of the
West in the 1930s was hardly unique. Drucker shared with other interwar
intellectuals—ranging from Talcott Parsons to Alexandre Kojève to Frankfurt Schoolers like Walter Benjamin, Theodor Adorno, or Erich Fromm

(whom Drucker would befriend when he joined the faculty at Bennington College in Vermont in 1942)—a concern that some essential failure of capitalism was responsible for the rise of antiliberal fascist or Stalinist movements. What was unusual, however, was for a self-described "conservative" to blame the current mode of economic organization for social alienation and its political consequences. Drucker accepted the left's argument that the fundamental source of the existential and political crisis of modernity stemmed from problems at the core of the economic system. At the same time, however, he rejected the left's idea that this social alienation stemmed from either economic stratification or the existence of private property. The gist of the New Deal, in Drucker's view, was an attempt to solve the problem of corporate illegitimacy by divesting corporate "management of its social and political power, and [transferring] these powers to the authorities claiming legitimacy on the basis of majority rule."[29] But contemporary "planners" and "technocrats" were mistaken in believing that legitimacy of the formal political sphere could be effortlessly transferred to the industrial sphere.[30] For Drucker, however, this solution would merely put people lacking relevant skills in charge of the industrial plant, without addressing the root cause of the social crisis of capitalism: worker's existential alienation from their work.[31] Legitimacy would only arrive when management and workers came to see themselves as part of a single harmonious organization, working toward mutually agreed upon, meaningful ends. Drucker's unique contribution would be to recognize and emphasize that conservatives had to develop a democratic theory of industrial organization if they wanted to save capitalism from existential implosion.

What this overview of Drucker's premanagement writings suggests is that his social and political commitments, and his recommendations to corporate management, emerged above all from his engagement with Kierkegaard and Stahl. If Drucker's learned philosophical and social diagnosis of the crisis of the West deemed capitalism a failure, it also represented the point of departure for Drucker's development of a new theory of capitalist management practices and goals, with the aim of providing the "capitalist machine" with social legitimacy and meaning. Though Drucker shared with fellow existentialists such as Jean-Paul Sartre a profound disdain for the soullessness of the contemporary capitalist order, instead of advocating revolution he would promote the less chiliastic (almost bathetic) goal of reshaping the management of corporations. According to Drucker, political revolution would in itself do nothing to overcome the alienating conditions inherent in the contemporary form of industrial organization. Resolute in his Kierkegaardian conservatism, Drucker insisted that attempts to mitigate alienation should never be allowed to mushroom into a desire for a secular, this-worldly utopian salvation. Drucker thus suggested a moderate, nuanced position: that one should attempt to mitigate alienation in this world by improving managerial techniques, while always keeping in mind that ultimate salvation could only come in the next world. The psychological trick Drucker called for was to retain the tension between existential pessimism and humility toward the infinite, on the one hand, and an action-oriented mindset aimed at improving the temporal finite world of its worst sins, on the other.[32] Much of the rest of Drucker's life would be spent questing for a proper basis for social harmony to mitigate the psychological pain of the existential dilemma.

Drucker's Critique of Fordism and Taylorism

This general analysis of the existential crisis of industrial society would become the point of theoretical departure for Drucker's epochal work, *Concept of the Corporation* (1946). Concluding that finding a basis of legitimacy for large corporations represented the most important task at hand for the postwar world, Drucker began in 1942 to cast about for a corporation that would allow him to examine its practices. He wrote letters to a variety of large corporations, but was everywhere met with suspicious refusals. (Who was this fellow with the funny accent who wanted to talk to about "management"?) Finally, quite by chance, the public relations department of General Motors telephoned him, inviting him to meet Donaldson Brown. A legend within GM, Brown had been chosen in 1922 by Pierre Du Pont (the largest stockholder in GM) to clean up the mess at GM that Billy Durant had created. (Durant was the brilliant entrepreneur who had put together the GM conglomerate, but his failure to rationalize the various parts had led the company into near-bankruptcy in the post-World War I recession.) It was Brown who had championed division chief Alfred Sloan's plan for creating separate corporate divisions to make and sell low- and high-priced cars to low- and high-income customers. After Du Pont made Sloan the new president of GM, Brown took on the job of designing financial controls for measuring and comparing the productivity of the different divisions. With Sloan leading the company, GM had proceeded to trounce the Ford Motor Company, which continued into the 1930s with a single-model approach to manufacturing and marketing. In the meanwhile, as a labor negotiator during the tumultuous 1930s, Brown had become increasingly interested in the social and human aspects of running a large corporation. It was in this context that Brown came across Drucker's *The Future of Industrial Man*. Meeting Drucker and suggesting that his rarified ideas might benefit from some hands-on experience of the actual operations of a large company, Brown offered to match Drucker's Bennington salary for a two-year study of GM. Drucker delightedly accepted.[33]

Having inveigled himself into the United States's largest and most successful corporation, Drucker would have unimpeded access to all aspects of GM's operations, including many meetings with the top management of the company. The result would be *Concept of the Corporation,* the foundational text of modern management theory, and the first systematic dissection of the virtues of administrative decentralization. What is striking as one reads *Concept*, however, is how tangential the particular concerns of GM are to the overall narrative thrust of the book. Drucker mentions GM only once in the first forty pages of the book, and then only to say that the book will treat GM as "a representative example of the American large corporation."[34] To understand the power of this book—as well as the annoyed reaction of GM's management and the incomprehension of most reviewers[35]—one must underscore that Drucker's interest in GM was but a means to solve a larger social problem. Framing the book with a call for the United States to demonstrate the viability of "capitalism in one country," Drucker's stated that the aim of the book was to show how "to make a free enterprise system work."[36] As we have seen, Drucker had argued in *The Future of Industrial Man* that the corporation was the socially constitutive institution of the capitalist West, and in *Concept* Drucker again predicted that as went the practice of big business in the United States, so would go the fate of capitalism generally. For capitalism to survive, the big business corporation had to "hold out the promise of adequately fulfilling the aspirations and beliefs of the American people."[37] Drucker wanted to show how American corporations could satisfy both their economic functions and fulfill the organic needs of society. *Concept* thus operated on two separate levels. On the one hand it provided concrete, basic, and subtle advice on the best management practices for large organizations. On the other hand it proposed a solution to the basic social and political crises of the previous decade. Its brilliance lay in making the former the basis for the latter. Its practical business advice, in other words, became the solution to the social crisis of capitalism.

The basic argument of *Concept* was that management should practice consistency of planning, establishing high-level goals while devolving authority for executing against those goals. Elucidating the principles of hierarchy and decentralization that Alfred Sloan had pioneered since the early 1920s, Drucker argued that rather than organize the entire company along functional lines (one finance department, one manufacturing department, one marketing department, etc.), it was better to organize a large corporation into smaller, functionally complete and separate divisions, each defined by its market goals. Decentralization and devolution would provide scope for flexibility and initiative throughout the organization, and avoid both managerial overload and bureaucratic stagnation. In contrast to contemporary literature on industrial management, which at the time mainly addressed finance and engineering questions, however, *Drucker's key methodological innovation was to conceive of the corporation as a social entity and to analyze its social function in political terms*. Drucker aimed not at addressing "the principles of industrial production" but at understanding "the social problems of the industrial enterprise."[38] For Drucker, the corporation was a metonym for society itself, and management for the government of that society. In attempting to develop a complete political theory of the modern corporation, Drucker would discuss not just how management treated labor, considered as a collective entity represented by union leaders, but also the relationship between the individual worker and the organization, between the individual worker and his or her work, and between people working together. By recasting the problem of management as a human problem, rather than merely a technical or mechanical problem, the book would launch the post-Taylorist, post-Fordist understanding of management.

The main targets of Drucker's critique of the "vision of the worker as an efficient, automatic, standardized machine" were Frederick Winslow Taylor's ideas about industrial efficiency, and Henry Ford's mass application of these ideas.[39] Taylor had claimed that what workers wanted most was high wages, whereas what managers wanted were low labor costs. Increasing productivity was thus required to satisfy both parties. To raise productivity and to undercut "soldiering" (slacking on the job), Taylor had concluded, required discovering "the one best way" to do a particular industrial task, and then to measure every worker's output against that gold standard. The result was Taylor's famous "time and motion" studies at Midvale Steel in Pennsylvania, which minutely scrutinized manufacturing processes to determine how to optimize the physical effort of workers to guarantee maximum output. For Drucker, Ford's massive River Rouge assembly plant, with raw coal, iron, wood, and rubber coming in one side, and finished cars rolling out the other side, was the maximal realization of Taylor's vision.[40] That the Rouge had become a well-known center of radical labor and disruptive industrial relations for Drucker proved the social inadequacy of Taylor's model.

In an article published in *Harper's* in 1947,[41] Drucker explained what was wrong with Ford's approach. Although the River Rouge plant was a "spotless mechanical perfection," Ford's problem was that "he made mechanical perfection an end in itself." Drucker gave due credit to Ford for having tried to "solve the social and political problems of an industrial civilization," in the form of the $5-a-day wage. But what Ford had solved with the daily wage was in fact the social and political problems of "the pre-Ford, the pre-mass-production industrial civilization": he had shown that industrial production could be "production *for* the masses," and not just for "the monopolist or banker." Unfortunately, Ford's single-minded focus on mechanical efficiency showed itself "a failure in its inability to produce the stable and happy society of which he dreamed." Like Taylor, Ford had never understood that managing employees was about more than simple wage rates. Drucker concluded that Ford's failure to develop an adequate solution to the labor problem "probably explains why Harry Bennett, starting as the plant's chief cop, rose to be the most powerful single individual in the Ford organization of the thirties." The inability to meet the social challenges of the industrial age, Drucker implied, led inexorably to the political organization of the factory becoming that of a police state.

Drucker's critique of Taylor was even more profound. Although Drucker would rank Taylor with Freud and Darwin as a "maker of the modern world,"[42] and would call Taylor's system "the most lasting contribution America has made to Western thought since the Federalist Papers,"[43] Drucker militated against Taylorism's limited view of humanity. Taylor's proposal to break down skilled jobs into a series of unskilled tasks, bereft of any opportunity for individual improvement or improvisation, had led to factory systems based on inflexible routine that destroyed initiative and self-reliance. As a result of the assembly line, "what has become automatic and mechanical is the worker," Drucker explained.[44] "Uniformity, absence of any personal relationship to the work, specialization on one unskilled manipulation, subdivision of the work into particles without comprehensible cohesion"[45]— Drucker argued that these Taylorist innovations in the name of efficiency treated workers not like sentient moral creatures but as if they were machines. Taylorism was a disaster because "the individual cease[s] to exist. The new technique demands standardized, freely interchangeable, atomic labor without status, without function, without individuality. It demands graded tools."[46] The worker in the contemporary Taylorist factory was "not a human being in society, but a freely replaceable cog in an inhumanly efficient machine."[47] As a social practice, in Drucker's view, Taylorism was dehumanizing.[48]

What was wrong with Taylor, Drucker stressed, was not his scientific approach to dissecting industrial processes but his approach to the human dimension of managing them. "Most of us," Drucker explained in *Concept*, "including a good many of people in industrial production itself, fail to understand that modern production . . . is not based on raw materials or gadgets but on principles of organization—organization not of machines but of human beings, i.e. on social organization. This misunderstanding . . . is to a considerable extent responsible for the labor problems of modern industry."[49] What workers really wanted, Drucker asserted, was not so much high wages as a sense of meaning in their work. Taylorism's single-minded focus on "one best way" exacerbated the spiritual crisis of capitalism by ensuring that workers felt no engagement by their work, and instead just felt like cogs in a machine. Drucker called for "a new theory of mass-production technology, more or less a complement to Frederick Taylor's famous studies but with the focus on the individual worker rather than on the individual manipulation."[50] Quietly drawing on Stahl's notion of personality,[51] Drucker insisted that men be considered and treated as integrated wholes, not just as an aggregate of traits. "We have yet to learn," Drucker lamented in 1950, "how to do the second half of the job of which Taylor and Gantt did the first half fifty years ago. They split up the [industrial] operation into its constituent motions; we shall have to put the motions back together again to produce an operation that is based both on the unskilled elementary motion and on the specifically human ability and need to coordinate."[52] Giving workers a chance to define the scope of their own work, and to see it in terms of the overall goals of the organization, would allow workers to find the meaning and happiness in their work.

To go beyond Taylorism's blinkered focus on mechanical technique, Drucker proposed expanding the scope of management from a science of technical efficiency to a liberal art that demanded both technical proficiency and a constant eye on the legitimacy of the corporation as a social institution. In this respect, *Concept* followed directly from the arguments of *The Future of Industrial Man*. Drucker had concluded that latter book by observing that to overcome the spiritual crisis of industrialism, "We shall have to prevent centralized bureaucratic despotism *by building a genuine local self-government in the industrial sphere. . . .* The plant must be made into a functioning self-governing social community. It must be made capable of serving industrial society in the same manner in which the village served the rural society and the market the mercantile society."[53] For Drucker, the first step was for management to clarify both for itself and for its employees the social importance of the work that employees do. And the answer that Drucker would propose, in *Concept,* was the "self governing plant community." What fell within the sphere of the self-governing plant community?

In *Concept* Drucker only began to sketch out what would fall within such a scope. "It must be possible," he argued,

to run such services as accident prevention, the cafeterias, the health services, or, in paces where women work, the day nurseries with the active participation of the worker, if not to entrust them entirely to committees of workers and foremen. This would provide an outlet for the desire of recognition among the workers which today finds satisfaction only in union activities, if at all. It would also give a good many workers managerial experience. It would also be a step toward making the plant a community in which people live a meaningful life, with a status and a function in their community.[54]

As we shall now see, Drucker would spend the better part of the 1940s developing this notion of the self-governing plant community.[55]

Workplace Federalism and the Self-Governing Plant Community

The underlying objective of *Concept of the Corporation,* indeed of all of Drucker's work, was to find a solution to the crisis of the liberal capitalist order. Drucker believed that unless the system underwent a fundamental reordering of the way workers related to their corporations, industrial strife (and possibly totalitarianism) was all but inevitable. What was striking for a conservative was that Drucker placed the majority of the onus for change on management. Calling on managements to overcome their "preconceived notion of the worker as an economic automaton,"[56] Drucker argued that workers felt justly aggrieved about being treated as mechanical objects, to be operated at the lowest possible cost. Optimistically claiming that the most important result of the war was that it made industrial management "conscious of the fact that the corporation is not only an economic tool but a social institution,"[57] Drucker proposed overcoming workers' existential alienation within the workplace by providing a sphere of worker "community" within the plant, clearly delimited from management's authority; by imbuing the work itself with more meaning; and by encouraging promotion into management and universalizing the "managerial attitude." Since workers would autonomously govern their separate plant community, they would be insulated from managerial arbitrariness and begin to learn the nature and problems of management itself, generating a sympathy to the perspective of management. The ultimate goal was to improve the democratic character of industrial society. To ensure that more democratic practices were put into place, Drucker would go so far as to propose that the government require that businesses engage an "independent audit of . . . executive-personnel policies and management organization," modeled after the financial auditing done of companies' accounts.[58] As radical as this may sound, however, Drucker's notion of democracy was a conservative, hierarchical one.

Between the publication of *The Future of Industrial Man* in 1942 and *The New Society* in 1950, Drucker worked ceaselessly to develop a federalist-communalist political analysis of the large business corporation, promoting the idea of the self-governing plant community as a cornerstone of legitimate "industrial citizenship." Rejecting corporate paternalism as undemocratic, Drucker called on management to "treat the worker as an adult and responsible citizen of the plant." Drucker argued that workers ought to be given control over, inter alia, "working rules and their change, safety, health, the firing of workers for infractions of the rules, the distribution of the burden of a layoff among the workers in the plant, the plant newspaper."[59] In connecting his political theory to his theory of management, however, Drucker revealed the nature of his democratic commitments:

The autonomous self-government of the plant community cannot be the governing organ of the enterprise. Its functions are not only limited; they are also strictly subordinate. Management must remain the governing organ of the enterprise, and economic performance its governing rationale. Indeed, the self-government of the plant community can only be justified if it strengthens management and makes it more capable of managing, and if it furthers the economic performance of the enterprise. But at the same time the self-government of the plant community has to have its own organs and officers. Its legitimacy lies not in approval by management but in election by the plant community. And in matters pertaining exclusively to the social life of the plant community, its authority must be original rather than derived—just as management enjoys original and autonomous authority over all matters pertaining to performance.[60]

In short, Drucker advocated an authoritarian politics of the workplace, but one legitimated by the *gemeinschaftliche* qualities of the plant. Drucker's desire for a worker's community, separate from (but ultimately subordinate to) management, sprang from his earlier insights about totalitarianism having effaced the difference between community and government. Since Drucker conceived of management as the "government" of a corporation, his desire for a self-governing plant community, whose sphere remained beyond the control of management, represented a way of avoiding workplace totalitarianism. For Drucker, both managers who wished to control workers (like Ford or Taylor), and union leaders who wished to have the workers control the management decisions of a company, were equally guilty of the totalitarian temptation.

To understand the importance of Drucker's antitotalitarian impulse in the formation of his theory of management, it is worth comparing his ideas to those of James Burnham, who just a year before Drucker issued *The Future of Industrial Man* had published the widely discussed *Managerial Revolution.*[61] A former Trotskyite in mid-ideological flight to neoconservatism (he would later become a founding editor of the *National Review*), Burnham also proposed a political theory of industrial management based on the notion that the technological imperatives of industrialism mandated a single form of managerial best practices. According to Burnham a new class of scientists, technicians, and bureaucrats had arisen that represented an inevitable, inexorable new form of power, and whether the overt political form was liberal, fascist, or communist was of little significance.[62] Like many other critics of Burnham, Drucker argued that to claim a moral equivalence of liberalism and totalitarianism was nothing but a cynical apology for bureaucratic despotism, "a denial of the reality of the moral issues at stake."[63] (In a review, George Orwell noted that *The Managerial Revolution* displayed an "unmistakable relish over the cruelty and wickedness of the processes that are being discussed."[64]) Drucker excoriated Burnham for believing that actual rule inevitably invented its own ideological justification.[65] For Drucker, managerialism might be inevitable, but the question was whether—or rather, how—it could be made more legitimate. Unlike Burnham, Drucker did not believe that a hierarchical society necessarily had to be an oppressive one.

For Drucker, the starting point for achieving a more legitimate industrial society was for management to stop looking at workers as just factors of production, and instead consider their human need for meaning. Peppering his writings from the late 1940s were numerous stories about managerial techniques for encouraging workers to take pride in their work by understanding its overall significance. For example, he recounted several versions of a story about a wartime GM plant that was making spare parts for bombers. The Air Force had proposed several times that a bomber and its crew visit the plant. The plant's management for some time had opposed to the meeting, seeing no useful purpose in diverting the workers from a day of work to meet with the pilots. When management at last agreed to the visit, the pilots had flown in, shown the workers the planes for which they were building parts, and socialized with the families of the workers. This encounter, according to Drucker, gave the workers a sense of the social meaningfulness of their work: building spare parts was no longer a simple mechanical exercise, workers now understood, but was intimately connected to the larger endeavor of winning the war. Although Drucker's main goal in telling this story was to improve the solidarity between management and workers (by having them understand that they shared a common set of objectives), he also made sure to appeal to management's immediate interests by noting that the increased morale led directly to an increase in productivity. The lesson, Drucker opined, "was that it is really not true that the worker is happy and content if he gets nothing out of his work except the pay check, or that he is not interested in his work or in his product."[66]

In addition to encouraging workers to understand the larger context of their work, Drucker recommended, in direct contradiction to Taylor, that workers be allowed to establish their own routines to achieve team goals. Letting workers establish their own work routines, Drucker argued, would liberate "that most precious of all creative assets, human inventiveness and imagination" in each employee,[67] leading to a more "flexible" approach than traditional assembly line work. According to Drucker, wartime production techniques had shown that the most efficient results did not always come from having engineers break down every industrial process into the most minute possible set of unskilled tasks; rather, it often worked best to allow workers to break down the tasks themselves and to work at their own pace. (Drucker credited the Soviet willingness to listen to line workers on how to improve industrial processes as the explanation for the extraordinary increases in Soviet industrial productivity during the 1920s and '30s.) The idea that workers would be less alienated if they established their own goals and means of achieving them was a signal idea that Drucker would develop into a cornerstone of his most lasting contribution to management theory, "management by objectives."

By emphasizing the productive benefit of giving workers a sense of recognition and meaning, Drucker was operating within a tradition of management thinking pioneered two decades earlier by Harvard Business School professor Elton Mayo (and before him by Mary Parker Follett). Drucker credited Mayo with being the first to emphasize that workers needed meaning and recognition. Drucker cited Mayo's famous "Hawthorne experiments" at the Western Electric Company in Illinois, where Mayo found that the mere act of showing employees that management cared about them spurred them to better job performance. Drucker used Mayo's findings as grist for his own mill: "These experiments showed clearly that it is not the character of the work which determines satisfaction but the importance attached to the worker. It is not routine and monotony which produce dissatisfaction but the absence of recognition, of meaning, of relation of one's own work to society."[68] If Drucker cited Mayo favorably, however, he also believed that Mayo's suggestion that management employ "listeners" was inadequate to solving management's legitimacy problems.[69] Whereas Mayo's analytical objective was more effective managerial control over workers, Drucker was seeking a more democratic workplace, rooted in a theory of the corporation's place within society. For example, when Mayo observed that informal groups within the work plant exercised strong control over the work habits and attitudes of the individual, he argued that these informal groups mainly inhibited productivity. By contrast, Drucker believed that by formally recognizing and validating these informal groups, their dynamics could be harnessed to foster productivity enhancement rather than restraint. For Drucker, the goal was not just to make workers *feel* included and empowered, but *to actually include and empower them,* albeit within a rigorously circumscribed ambit.[70]

Real empowerment and inclusion, for Drucker, meant creating opportunities for workers to advance into the ranks of management. Lamenting "the ever-growing tendency among plant managers to depend on outside sources rather than on the men in the plant for their supply of foremen and other junior executives,"[71] Drucker recommended that corporations recruit and develop management from within the ranks of line workers. Creating opportunities for advancement into management would align the interests of ambitious workers with the interests of the corporation. In phrasing this suggestion about improving the democratic character of the workplace, Drucker appealed to managerial self-interest: "Faced with an ever-growing need for executives and engaged in a technological and efficiency competition which is becoming fiercer all the time," Drucker explained, "the corporation simply cannot afford to deprive itself of the intelligence, imagination, and initiative of 90% of the people who work for it, that is, the workers."[72] Drucker here echoed fellow conservative Vilfredo Pareto's notion of the "circulation of elites": for rulers to stay in power, they had to admit recruits from below to ensure that the most talented men would always be at the top. Everyone needed to have a path of promotion within the corporation,[73] or else those with ambition would strike out on their own to create a separate power structure outside the corporation. (For Drucker, a major appeal of unions was that talented workers had no other opportunity for advancement and power.) Though he again appealed to the narrow self-interest of managements in their war for talent and their disdain for unions, Drucker's real motivation was to improve the democratic character of the workplace by proving that it was possible for any American to become CEO, just as in the political sphere it was possible for any American to become president.[74]

Making line workers a primary source for corporate management required building a "managerial attitude" throughout the workforce. This idea of instilling managerial values into everyone lay at the core of Drucker's vision for workplace democracy, and related intimately to his suggestion that management give workers an autonomous sphere within the plant for them to management themselves. As historian James Hoopes puts it, "running the cafeteria would teach 'the managerial vision,' which was the only path to power and dignity within the corporation."[75] Giving workers responsibility for managing what might today be called "noncore" services would "give the men on the machines some of the understanding of the functions, motives and problems of management on which a free enterprise depends and which is almost entirely absent today."[76] The goal was "to make the worker understand management's point of view and management's problems."[77] As biographer John Tarrant summarized Drucker's position, "In the new order, 'the managerial attitude' would be part of the intellectual equipment of even the lowliest worker. The managerial attitude would enable everyone in the organization to 'see his job, his work and his product the way the manager sees them, that is, in relation to the work of the group and the product of the whole.'"[78] Echoing Kierkegaard, "the management of the self" would remain an abiding theme throughout Drucker's long career.[79] The best way to short-circuit the authoritarian temptation on the part of (political or industrial) leaders was for the citizens (of society or of the plant) to universalize *self*-discipline and *self*-management.

Drucker imagined large enterprises mirroring within their organizational structure the federalism and communal independence that (to Drucker's mind) had proved so successful in the United States's formal political sphere. Like fellow conservative democrat Alexis de Tocqueville, Drucker regarded administrative centralization as a potential, indeed almost inevitable, instrument of despotism. Drucker's federalist vision of democracy motivated both his arguments about administrative decentralization of business units and his suggestions about the social organization of the workplace. By the late 1940s, Drucker would replace the term "decentralization" in favor of "federalism," noting that the latter term underlined the *political* nature of his argument, as opposed to the (misleading) spatial or geographic connotation of the term "decentralization."[80] Defending himself against a critic's claim that he was offering participation as a mere "psychological sop" to workers, Drucker explained that, "Federalism in the big-business enterprise attempts to establish decision-making at the lowest possible level; to make the decision as much 'situation-focussed' as possible; and to release human energy throughout the organization."[81] To some extent, Drucker's ideas about legitimacy also derived from his old hero Friedrich Julius Stahl: the central authority of the throne (management) should not be questioned, and yet at the same time the throne had a duty to the citizens (the self-governing plant communities and other stakeholders). Just as rulers in Stahl's theory had a duty to their citizens to subordinate their interests to that of the state and to respect the rights of their subjects, so managers had a duty to run a company responsibly and in the "balanced best interests" of all stakeholders. (It was only on arrival in the United States, Drucker would later note, that he realized that what Stahl had been "trying to do had actually been accomplished in the United States."[82])

Drucker found support for his views in another conservative political statesman from the 1840s, this one a homegrown version: John C. Calhoun. In a neglected essay, "A Key to American Politics: Calhoun's Pluralism," published in the *Review of Politics* in 1948 just as he was thinking hardest about the politics of workplace democracy,[83] Drucker argued that the "organizing principle of American politics" was Calhoun's "rule of the concurrent majority," namely "that every major interest in the country, whether regional, economic, or religious, is to possess a veto power on political decisions directly affecting it." This rule accounted for the admirably conservative, slow-moving nature of change in the American political system. It is worth considering Drucker's celebration of Calhoun in light of another 1948 essay on Calhoun, Richard Hofstadter's "Calhoun: The Marx of the Master Class."[84] In this essay, Hofstadter argued that Calhoun rejected the idea of "natural" individual rights, holding instead that the government determined what constituted a right, and then distributed those rights according to its own preferences. Following Drucker in viewing management as the "government" of a firm, and its stakeholders as its "citizens," one observes that the model for workplace democracy that Drucker was working toward in the late 1940s aimed at ideological uniformity across the entire set of stakeholders within an industrial society. In this respect Drucker resembled no one so much as social modernist consensus historians and "end of ideologists" who would emerge in the 1950s.

So what are we to make of this political philosophy? Even taken on Drucker's own existentialist terms, what seems most problematic about Drucker's political philosophy is its blindness to the psychology of *power*. Perhaps it was his existentialist belief that all humans were equally powerless before God that made Drucker fail to sufficiently appreciate the emotions caused by inequality in temporal power. This is odd when we consider the political context from which Drucker's ideas about management emerged. Was it just a coincidence that it was the humiliated Great Powers of World War I—the Russians and the Germans—and not the French or the English who turned to totalitarianism? In his early writing on management, he appeared to believe that merely having available a hypothetical path to advancement into management would be enough to make workers accept as legitimate the power of management over them. For Drucker, the CIO's efforts during World War II to broker a power-sharing deal whereby unions would have a say in basic production decisions was thus nothing more or less than a usurpation of management's role, an unwarranted fracturing of the social contract of the workplace. He could not accept that for some, the very idea of a hierarchy of power was outrageous and immoral—not just illegitimate, but *illegitimable*. In his unwillingness to recognize the humiliation and injustice inherent in unequal power, Drucker revealed a characteristic blindness of many conservatives. The Marx of the master class, indeed!

Conclusion

Reasons of space preclude a further discussion of the development of Peter Drucker's thought from the 1950s into the twenty-first century. However, the ideas delineated in this paper continued to guide the development of Drucker's thought: his abiding interest would remain to find a harmonious modality for industrial organization, a way of tempering the totalitarian temptation both within businesses and within society as a whole. Bit by bit, however, Drucker would concede that his proposals for workplace federalism and the self-governing plant community did not succeed in establishing a new basis for such harmony.[85] Both managements and unions rejected the idea, much to Drucker's chagrin. On the one hand, in industries of historic strength—especially in heavy manufacturing, public service, and transportation—unions would, in the main, continue to contest the legitimacy of management's exclusive authority over corporate strategy and objectives. The rising importance of a class of employees (and whole industries) dedicated to what Drucker would label "knowledge work" would undermine the centrality of manufacturing to the national identity, and erode the political capacities of organized labor. On the other hand, while management would eventually accept that there were certain areas of plant life they should not govern, they would seek to outsource these functions, rather than grant worker autonomy over these areas.

Drucker's initial response to the limited impact of his workplace federalism proposal was to proffer a much more modest idea known as "management by objectives" (MBOs).[86] Proposed in 1954, the result of four years Drucker spent consulting with Harold Smiddy at General Electric's Business Services Division, MBOs specified that management ought to collaborate with employees in setting business goals, and not micromanage the attainment of the agreed-upon goals.[87] MBOs represented a truncated version of Drucker's democratic vision for the workplace: instead of managers *imposing* goals on workers, they were to negotiate them discursively and intersubjectively, recognizing the ability of workers to define the content and meaning of their own work. Although many industries would accept MBOs as a pillar of employee management, this new mechanism also failed to create the social harmony that Drucker desired. By the 1980s, Drucker abandoned his earlier hopes for the reform of private enterprise, instead focusing on nonprofit "social organizations" such as churches, schools, and hospitals as the main vehicles for achieving his still bright hopes for social harmony.

Drucker's intellectual biography raises several important historiographical questions for this volume. The first is the social role of unions and the reasons for their decline. Drucker wanted to turn unions into cultural institutions rather than collective bargaining units. He did not propose company unions, always insisting that unions remain independent of managerial control. But at the same time, he wanted unions to aim at reconciling workers to the "tough choices" facing management. Instead of playing an oppugnant role "*against* management and *against* the enterprise,"[88] he would call for unions to serve as an educational and communications bridge between corporate management and local communities. But Drucker never accepted that unions ought to help set corporate goals, a function he arrogated exclusively to management. (Though Drucker never specified a concrete example of a positive union movement, he may have had in mind something along the lines of the Dutch trade union movement, with its accommodating brand of corporatism.) Given Drucker's suggestions for how unions could best serve what he called "a useful function," it is interesting to consider how much recent labor history has focused quite precisely on this issue of the role of union and the local labor hall in the civic life of working class American communities, and their role in facilitating the cultural assimilation process for immigrants, especially those from Southern and Eastern Europe. This role, at least, was undisputed by management, and perhaps remains unions' most lasting legacy in the twentieth century.

A second issue is Drucker's status as a "conservative." Although Drucker always called himself a conservative, and drew his inspiration from thinkers associated with conservatism, the intellectual and social problems he wrestled with—how to secure a just and stable society without a revolution—were more usually addressed in the middle of the twentieth century by liberals. At the same time, Peter Drucker's management theory represented an effort to put big business-friendly conservatism on a firm theoretical and political footing. Drucker wanted to show that for management (and capitalism) to produce social harmony did not require government control. At the same time, Drucker was never a simple-minded antigovernment sort of conservative. In time he supported various state-sponsored schemes often loathed by fellow conservatives. Not only did he support the Tennessee Valley Authority (a bête noir for many conservatives), he also advocated various government-sponsored wage stabilization schemes, and, as we have seen, even government-mandated auditing of corporate human relations practices. While he is credited with coining the term "privatization," his advocacy of small government was thus instinctual rather than doctrinaire. Finally, Drucker had no time for either nativism or racial segregation, only scorn for religiously motivated cultural intolerance, and little patience for libertarianism. Perhaps it is for this reason that Drucker's form of conservatism proved more influential on the form American capitalism would take than the more strident conservatism of contemporaries like James Burnham, Ayn Rand, or Friedrich von Hayek.

The question of Drucker's influence raises a final interesting point, namely his status as a harbinger of what scholars like David Harvey have called the "post-Fordist accumulation regime." As a prescient critic of Henry Ford, an ardent skeptic of unions, an early champion of outsourcing as a solution to labor strife, and a celebrator of "knowledge workers," Drucker prophesied of the idea of flexible production instead of fixed assembly lines, disaggregation of the centralized corporation, the devaluation of manual labor, and the marginalization of trade unions. Labor historians sometimes interpret post-Fordism as the latest form of worker disempowerment by management; but it is worth contemplating that part of the reason that flexible accumulation has proven so successful is not just because it allows transnational corporation to gain rents through cross-border wage arbitrage, but also because changing managerial practices mitigated the worst of the arbitrary management excesses of the first half of the twentieth century, at least in white collar industries. In this sense, although Drucker's individual proposals have had mixed success, his focus on the need of managers to lessen the alienating conditions of the workplace has undoubtedly helped to create an acceptance or at least acquiescence to capitalism on the part of the "individual contributors" who make up the bulk of workers in any economy. Indeed, some scholars see post-Fordism as a form of liberation. As industrial sociologists Horst Kern and Michael Schumann put it, "The project of liberated, fulfilling work, originally interpreted as an *anti*-capitalist project [is now] likely to be staged by capitalist management itself."[89] If this claim is anywhere close to correct, then Peter Drucker surely figures as one of the most influential intellectuals of the twentieth century. Put another way, Drucker's effort to make capitalist managers overturn the most alienating aspects of capitalist business practices may represent an untallied column in the accounts of why the United States won the Cold War.

Part III
A Critique from the Left

C. Wright Mills and American Social Science

Daniel Geary

On March 20, 1962, he died of a heart attack at the tragically young age of forty-five. The next day, the *New York Times* printed an obituary headlined "C. Wright Mills: A Sociologist." To many readers, this was not an apt description. After all, by 1962, Mills was best known, if not for his outspoken defense of the Cuban Revolution, as the social critic who offered a radical critique of American society in *White Collar* and *The Power Elite*. As Dan Wakefield recalled reading the obituary several years later, "If in the eyes of many of his academic colleagues Mills was less than that professional designation, he was also in the eyes of a great number of intelligent readers much more than simply 'A Sociologist.'"[1] Indeed, Mills has generally been celebrated (or dismissed) as a public intellectual whose insights gained power because he ventured outside of academic discourse. To admirers, he was the motorcycle-riding Texan maverick who famously dissented from the Cold War complacency of the 1950s, a "lone-wolf writer" who "excoriated the evils of American society" and hence became a hero to the New Left.[2]

According to this standard depiction, Mills was the antithesis of a mid-century academic social scientist. Yet we should take the *Times* obituary's designation more seriously. In order to understand the influential works of social criticism that Mills wrote in the 1950s, we must recognize that the roots of Mills's thought lay deep in the disciplinary matrix of professional sociology in the 1940s. By revising the captivating caricature of Mills as rebel iconoclast and academic outsider, we can construct a more complex understanding of his work. Rather than viewing Mills as standing in sharp contrast to the intellectual discourse of his day, Mills was actually a representative figure in several developments in midcentury American social science. I do not mean to suggest that we narrow our view of Mills to take into account only his social scientific engagements, nor should we ignore his important political writings, or forget that one of his significant virtues was his ability to address a nonprofessional audience. Yet, we cannot fully understand Mills unless we illuminate this essential yet often neglected aspect of his thought.

In this chapter, I examine three examples of how Mills's formative ideas in the 1940s were deeply embedded in the discourse of mid-century academic social science. As an undergraduate and graduate student, Mills's work in the developing field of the sociology of knowledge reflected a wide-spread concern within the sociological discipline to define the purposes and aims of social science. In addition, his call for the study of total social structures, influenced by the work of Max Weber, represented a new turn in the 1940s toward macroscopic social science. Finally, as a research associate at Columbia's Bureau of Applied Social Research (BASR) from 1945 to 1949, Mills participated in the growing prominence of social scientific research bureaus. It was in large part through these social scientific engagements that Mills developed his distinctive social thought.

Understanding Mills in this fashion asks us not only to reconsider his image, but to broaden our understanding of midcentury social science. If Mills owed more to academic social science than has been recognized, leading sociologists of his era were more embedded in the social and political discourse of their time than has generally been acknowledged. Yet, Howard Brick has persuasively argued that Talcott Parsons's left-liberal political views were a crucial component of his abstract social theory, and David Hollinger has recovered the antifascist political context of Robert Merton's early work. Rather than being ensconced within the ivory tower of academia, Parsons and Merton, like Mills, were deeply engaged with the public issues of their day.[3] Placing Mills in dialogue with these quintessential social scientific professionalizers, and even with their relentlessly quantifying colleague Paul Lazarsfeld, reveals a great deal about the range of possibilities inherent in midcentury American sociologists' attraction to theoretical and methodological reflection, macroscopic analysis of social structures, and bureau-driven research. Thus, I suggest not that we narrow our view of Mills as merely a social scientist, but that we widen our view of social science so that it includes Mills.

Mills's well-known commitments to left-wing politics did not preclude his engagement with professional social science. By the early 1940s, Mills identified himself as a "radical"; he spent the decade writing for left-wing magazines such as *politics* and developing connections with the American labor movement. To be sure, Mills's radicalism shaped his interaction with midcentury social science, but his radicalism emerged in part through his distinctive engagements with disciplinary trends of the 1940s. Thus, I conclude by examining how Mills's distinctive engagements with 1940s social science shaped his classic of 1950s radical social criticism, *White Collar.* In particular, examining Mills's roots in academic social science allows us to situate Mills in relation to the postcapitalist vision that Howard Brick has identified as prevalent in midcentury American social science.[4]

Methodological Consequences of the Sociology of Knowledge

C. Wright Mills was a remarkably precocious graduate student. In his early twenties, he became a leading American scholar in the cutting-edge field of the sociology of knowledge, and he participated in the methodological reflection characteristic of American sociology during this period. Mills's interest in the sociology of knowledge, in locating thought within a particular social and historical context, grew out of his early engagement with pragmatism. As an undergraduate and master's student in sociology and philosophy at the University of Texas in the late 1930s, Mills worked closely with the philosophers George Gentry and David Miller, and the economist C. E. Ayres, all of whom earned their Ph.D.s in philosophy at the seedbed of American pragmatism, the University of Chicago.

Though scholars have noted the influence of pragmatist thinkers such as John Dewey on Mills, they have not recognized that during his student years he was interested in pragmatism specifically as "methodology for the social sciences."[5] The pragmatist notion of science as inquiry and its conception of human action as deeply social in nature exerted a strong influence on Mills's methodological reflections on social science. Pragmatists viewed science not as a fixed body of ideas, but as a continuous, nondogmatic process in which knowledge was gained not by applying a formal system to a body of data, but by investigating a specific situation or problem. The young Mills assigned himself the ambitious task of making empirical inquiry into the social basis of knowledge more fruitful through methodological reflection. While pragmatism was a strong influence on Mills, he did not think the pragmatists presented an adequate methodology for social science. In his master's thesis, for instance, Mills complained that the overly general nature of Dewey's theories detracted from their usefulness in particular inquiries, especially with regard to social science, since Dewey drew his models uncritically from the natural sciences.[6]

In 1939, Mills accepted an offer from the University of Wisconsin for doctoral study in sociology. Sociology was a good match for a young, ambitious, and theoretically minded scholar such as Mills. The most general and least defined of the American social sciences throughout its history, sociology remained an especially open field of study in the late 1930s, particularly in contrast to philosophy, the other field Mills considered pursuing. By this time, sociology had become a highly professionalized and technical discipline. During the 1930s, the American Sociological Society (ASS) underwent a series of controversies about the nature of the discipline. Neither of the contending groups was successful in achieving disciplinary hegemony in the 1930s: not the objectivists, who sought to model sociology on physical science by confining it to the predominantly quantitative study of observable human behavior, nor the "Chicago school" sociologists, who advocated an ecological approach that investigated the interaction of individual and group using such qualitative techniques as ethnographic observation and life histories. By the end of the 1930s, sociology was divided and confused, but this very lack of disciplinary definition promoted the sort of methodological reflection that interested Mills.[7]

Though Mills was influenced by Chicago school sociology at Texas, by 1940, he identified with those theorists who were reevaluating the discipline's purpose and methods, seeing himself as aligned with "a few of the younger men in American sociology [who] are becoming tired of the paste-pot eclecticism and text-book tolerance which have characterized much of their tradition."[8] Indeed, Mills shared a sense of the requirements of sociological theory with a younger generation of sociologists, including Talcott Parsons, Robert Merton, and Mills's graduate advisor, Howard Becker. These theorists agreed that an adequate sociological theory would have to bear a close relationship with practice, would need to develop methods adequate for dealing with the distinct realm of social phenomenon, that concepts were necessary to lend facts meaning, and that social science needed to account for the values and meanings of its human subjects. Like these emerging leaders within sociology, Mills believed that American sociologists up to that point had largely failed to study society in a rigorous and systematic manner and that attention to sociological theory was necessary to move the discipline forward.

Indeed, Mills's methodological writings had much in common with the most significant work of American sociological theory of the period, Parsons's *Structure of Social Action*, a work that Parsons later described as a volley in "the 'war of independence' of the social sciences *vis a vis* the biological."[9] Like Parsons, Mills rejected positivist attempts to model social science on the natural sciences. "Nothing in its purely physical dimension interacts like persons," Mills argued.[10] Both were involved in a long-term trend in twentieth-century social science to develop a distinct approach to the understanding of the society that stressed that humans could not be adequately understood solely in terms of biological categories such as heredity and environment nor in terms of the rational actor theory drawn from economics.[11]

An exchange of letters between Mills and Robert Merton over Karl Mannheim's sociology of knowledge reveals that although the young Mills was engaged with the disciplinary discourse of sociological theory, he developed a methodological perspective with radical implications. In 1940, Mills sent Merton a draft of his article, "The Methodological Consequences of the Sociology of Knowledge," in which he defended Karl Mannheim's expansive program. The published translation of Mannheim's *Ideology and Utopia* in 1936 sparked a debate among American social scientists.[12] At the heart of the discussion was Mannheim's claim that all ideas were inseparable from the overall worldview and social position of its advocates. Hence, no truth was possible "independent of an historically and socially determined set of meanings."[13] All ideas, including those of the sociologist of knowledge himself, thus needed to be subjected to an ideological analysis that revealed their social embeddedness.

Most American social scientists, including Merton, were critical of Mannheim for the relativistic implications of his position. They adopted the influential neo-Kantian critique of Mannheim's German critic, Alexander von Schelting, who argued that Mannheim confused the motives of the thinker with the results of his work. To von Schelting and his American supporters, the validity of an idea had nothing to do with its origins.[14] Mills sought to defend Mannheim from this attack. As Mills wrote to Merton, despite Mannheim's flaws, "the guy has a very *suggestive* idea which . . . although blurred and loose and all becomes something really fine when one weds it to, interprets it not from the neo-Kantian view, but from the standpoint of American pragmatism."[15]

Mills agreed with Mannheim's critics that in a scientific system of verification the genesis of an idea did not affect its validity. However, he argued that it was naïve to assume that this settled the matter, for the "genesis" of ideas was deeply social and went beyond the simple matter of an individual's motivations for conducting research. To Mills, Mannheim's work was valuable because it offered a genuinely sociological account of knowledge first hinted at by pragmatist philosophers. Like Dewey, Mannheim "turned from traditional concerns and squabbles over the ubiquitous relation of thought in general to reality at large to a specific examination of the context, office, and outcome of a type of inquiry."[16] Mills concluded that criteria for determining truth claims, including scientific ones, were "legitimately open to social-historical relativization."[17] Relying on pragmatist notions, Mills thus suggested that ideas should not be viewed as passive reflections of an objective truth, but instead as tools that actively serve social purposes.

Robert Merton was unimpressed by Mills's arguments. Only a few years Mills's senior, Merton had already established a reputation as a promising young social theorist, and would soon become one of the most influential social scientists of his generation. Merton promoted Mannheim's sociology of knowledge as a program of substantive research into the social origins of ideas, but he rejected his expansive epistemological claims. Merton objected to Mills's defense of Mannheim's epistemology because it failed to provide an adequate basis for scientific knowledge. The implication of Mannheim's views, Merton wrote, was that it was "simply a matter of taste as to which criteria we adopt."[18] Indeed, given the Nazi advance across Europe, Merton saw this relativism as containing "an irreducible element of . . . nihilism."[19] The danger of Mannheim's epistemology to American sociologists like Merton was that it threatened scientific autonomy by treating social science like any other ideology. By questioning the special status of sociological knowledge, Mannheim undermined the scientific autonomy of the precarious discipline of sociology by blurring the lines between sociology and philosophy.

To Mills, however, Mannheim actually bolstered the significance of social science by stressing how deeply *social* the production of knowledge was. Like Mannheim, Mills was concerned that sociology would limit its scope by paying inordinate attention to its scientific status. Mills's early sociology of knowledge was distinguished by his willingness to subject social scientific knowledge to critical reflection. Because it was empirical and not speculative, the sociology of knowledge offered a means of methodological reflection that relied upon actual social inquiry and would thus avoid imposing an abstract and formalistic schema on the study of social science. Thus, Mills concluded "Methodological Consequences" with a call for the "detailed self-location of social science."[20] To Mills, the sociology of knowledge provided a means to critique the deepest presuppositions of contemporary social science. Indeed, because he advocated a sociology of sociology, which used social scientific tools for disciplinary self-criticism, Mills may be seen as an early proponent of the "reflexive sociology" later advanced by such figures as Alvin Gouldner and Pierre Bourdieu. In Gouldner's phrase, reflexive sociology offers a "distinctive awareness of the ideological implications and political resonance of sociological work."[21]

Mills's early methodological inquiries within the sociology of knowledge culminated in his 1943 study of social pathology textbooks, "The Professional Ideology of Social Pathologists." According to Mills, social pathology textbooks, which defined certain types of behavior as socially "maladjusted" in terms of a given normative structure, owed much to the homogenous social background of their authors. Mills argued that the concept of "adjustment" was used by social pathologists in neither a statistical nor a structural sense, but a normative one, since large groups, especially in urban areas, were described as "maladjusted." The rural and small-town background of the authors led them to define social norms in terms of primary groups of small, homogeneous communities characterized by face-to-face interaction. The concept of "adjustment," according to Mills, was thus little more than "a propaganda for conformity to those norms and traits ideally associated with small-town middle-class milieu."[22] Published after Mills had clearly affiliated himself with the political left, "Professional Ideology" was remarkable not only because of its attempt to turn sociological tools to a critical study of the discipline, but because of its political critique of professional social science. Mills argued that the sociological concepts exhibited in the professional discourse of social pathologists, while capable of supporting mild reforms, were not "usable in collective action which proceeds against, rather than well within, more or less tolerated channels."[23]

Despite the radical implications of the methodological consequences Mills drew from the sociology of knowledge, the differences between Mills and Merton should not be exaggerated. Indeed, Merton eventually called a truce to the argument by stressing their shared interest in promoting sound studies in the sociology of knowledge and suggesting that their differences might be mostly semantic.[24] Merton respected Mills's work enough to help Mills get jobs at the University of Maryland in 1941 and Columbia University in 1945. In 1945, Merton hoped that Mills would join him in metaphorically placing "a small time-bomb . . . under the complacent, chair-sitting rear ends of our more traditional colleagues in the field of sociology."[25] And Merton was no defender of the political status quo against Mills's radical attack: indeed even Merton's defense of the autonomy of science can be seen as a strategy for spreading left-liberal values in a capitalist society.[26] Thus, Mills's distinctive methodological ideas were situated within, not outside, the discourse of academic social science.

Mills, Gerth, Parsons: The Turn to Social Structure and the Reception of Weber

"The Professional Ideology of Social Pathologists" revealed Mills's distinctive use of the sociology of knowledge for disciplinary self-critique, but it also indicated his inclusion in another important trend of 1940s social science. In arguing that the methods of American sociology were inadequate and needed to be revised by a theoretically informed viewpoint, Mills found himself in agreement with many of the discipline's emerging leaders. In particular, they agreed with one of Mills's central criticisms of social pathologists: that due to their "low level of abstraction" they failed "to consider total social structures."[27] Functionalism, which became increasingly prominent in the 1940s, sought to exchange the atomistic analysis Mills criticized in "The Professional Ideology of Social Pathologists" for a structural approach that examined the interrelated features of large-scale societies. While earlier American sociologists had generally investigated smaller communities, this new macroscopic approach took national societies or even modernity itself as its subject. "Social structure" became a buzzword of American sociology in the 1940s; for example, the title of Robert Merton's influential 1949 collection of essays was *Social Theory and Social Structure.*[28]

This greater effort to understand total social structures owed much to the appropriation of European sociological theory and to the influence of Max Weber in particular. In the 1940s, this trend toward the study of total social structures was best represented by the increasing prominence of Talcott Parsons, who made his reputation on the basis of a textual study of European sociologists and whose theories were used to understand modern societies. Like Parsons, Mills played an important role in introducing Weber's work to Americans. Yet, under the influence of German émigré Hans H. Gerth, Mills developed an interpretation of Weber's work substantially at odds with that put forth by Parsons and others. Thus, while participating in the disciplinary trend toward macroscopic study, Mills once again gave it his own distinctive radical twist.

German émigré social scientists played an important role in introducing American sociologists to a more structural and macroscopic approach. For Mills, the influence of Gerth proved decisive. Gerth, who studied under Mannheim, was firmly within the Weberian tradition of German social science: seeking to understand social structures by utilizing a comparative and historical method. A lifelong socialist, Gerth developed a post-Marxist interpretation of Weber's work, attempting to combine Marx's materialist interpretation of history, shorn of dialectical hopes for an immanent historical goal, with Weber's respect for the complexity of social structure and the significance of noneconomic social spheres.[29] After Gerth arrived at Wisconsin as a professor of sociology in 1940, he and Mills became fast friends and collaborators. Under Gerth's influence, the significance of the German sociological tradition on Mills's intellectual development was so crucial that, by 1944, he claimed that he had "never had occasion to take very seriously much of American sociology as such" and that his "main impulse has been taken from German developments, especially the traditions stemming from Max Weber and, to a lesser degree, Karl Mannheim."[30]

In 1941, Gerth and Mills began work on *Character and Social Structure*, a social psychology textbook that would stress a concern with total social structures, eventually published in 1953.[31] A genuine social psychology, the authors argued in an August 1941 book outline, would move beyond the problems inherent in the orthodox Freudian approach, which made unwarranted "suprahistorical" assumptions regarding human nature. More significantly, it would challenge the "behavioralist" approach dominant in the American human sciences, which, despite its valuable empirical approach and "readiness to observe changability of man" was "rather sterile and limited to small field analyses, with the fields not connected." The problem was that American social psychologists lacked a tradition of "*structural* sociology." Gerth and Mills criticized American "milieu sociology," which ignored the significance of large-scale institutions and the connections between different aspects of the social structure. They proposed a comparative and historical approach for their book that would utilize the Weberian method of ideal types to provide a general yet flexible framework to analyze "specific roles in their structural setting" without losing sight of the psychology of the individual human actor.[32]

In a draft introduction to the book, Gerth and Mills made it clear that their approach to social psychology was a larger critique of a "narrowing of attention" in social science that had led to "the loss of any larger focus upon the structural and historical features of societies." In terms that recalled Mills's debt to pragmatist notions of science, they criticized the "idea that 'science' is so narrow that its minimum ideals of disinterested naturalism must be sacrificed in order to deal with the big problems of man and society." Yet Gerth and Mills described their work not as an isolated effort, but as part of a new trend in American social science. They believed that two things had contributed to the newfound attention to total social structures. The first was a "theoretical renaissance . . . in American sociology during the last ten years . . . fertilized by a renewal of contact with German sociology and economics of the 19th and early 20th centuries." The second was a concern to understand the "rise of totalitarian social structures" that had led to World War II.[33]

Talcott Parsons was clearly representative both of the theoretical renaissance and the attempt to understand totalitarian social structures. A leading advocate of European theory in the U.S. throughout the 1930s who came to increasing prominence in the postwar period, Parsons became one of the most influential social theorists of the twentieth century. According to the standard image, Mills and Parsons offered opposite visions of social science. After all, in his 1959 book *The Sociological Imagination* Mills pilloried Parsonian "Grand Theory" as jargon-ridden, overly abstract and formalistic. And Parsons was a leading critic of Mills's *The Power Elite*.[34] Yet, Mills and Parsons each were part of a shift to the study of total social structures, which was a significant departure from earlier traditions of American sociology: both the ethnographic "milieu" sociology associated with the Chicago school and the tradition of statistical sociology.

Likewise, both Mills and Parsons were interested in applying sociological theory to the understanding of contemporary modern social structures. Both drew especially on the work of Max Weber in their efforts. And both played key roles in securing Weber's influence on postwar sociology by providing translations of his work—Mills by assisting Hans Gerth in publishing the first English translation collection of Weber's essays, *From Max Weber* (1946).[35] During World War II, in an attempt to understand the rise of fascism, Parsons's work underwent a subtle shift from abstract sociological theory to an analysis of specific national social structures. An examination of Parsons's use of Weber indicates this shift. In *The Structure of Social Action*, Parsons was primarily interested in Weber as a sociologist of religion and as a methodologist. In the 1940s, however, he applied Weber's theories in an attempt to understand the "contemporary political crisis." In a series of essays on Nazi Germany, Parsons analyzed fascism as a charismatic anti-modernist movement that emerged from the structural dynamics of modernization. In contrast to his later, more optimistic rendering of modernity, Parsons here depicted modern society based on rational-legal authority and impersonal, universalistic norms as a fragile social structure since its process of rationalization threatened to create a widespread psychological anxiety and insecurity upon which fascism could feed.[36] The attempt to understand modern social structures through the lens of social psychology was a task adopted not only by Parsons here, and by Mills and Gerth in *Character and Social Structure*, but by many American social scientists during World War II seeking to understand the rise of totalitarianism.[37]

While Mills's attempt to understand total social structures was much closer to that of Parsons than he later acknowledged, there were nevertheless important differences in their approaches, as reflected in their interpretations of Max Weber. The differences were both methodological and political. Mills persuaded Gerth that their arrangement of Weber's pieces should stress Weber's "multi-perspectivism . . . as against Parsons etc with their for-malized SYSTEMS of every goddamned thing anybody tried to do anything with."[38] If Parsons valued Weber for his incomplete attempt to develop a systematic theoretical framework, Mills praised him for his substantive his-torical and comparative investigations. Parsons's "Grand Theory" was not always as abstract as Mills later portrayed it. Nevertheless, as against Parsons, Mills emphasized the significance of specific social and historical contexts for social action, a particularizing, historicist approach that he had stressed in his early 1940s methodological works and continued to balance against his ambition to tackle the big questions. This stance set Mills's macroscopic, structural approach to social science apart from a postwar trend exempli-fied in Parsons's work toward constructing generalized theoretical frame-works applicable to all societies.[39]

As Mills bragged to Dwight Macdonald, "The son of a bitch [Parsons] has translated it [Weber] so as to take all the guts, the radical guts, out, whereas our translation doesn't do that."[40] In describing modern society as characterized by an inexorable trend toward rational-legal authority and bureaucratic organization, Mills and Parsons drew upon Weber. However, they presented opposite evaluations of the trends that Weber described. Particularly during the postwar period, Parsons gave an optimistic render-ing of Weberian modernity that stressed that a society governed by imper-sonal, universalistic standards of rational-legal authority and bureaucratic organization was free of "rigidly fixed traditionalism" and allowed for more efficient organization, as well as equality of opportunity and equality before the law.[41]

Rather than stressing the positive effects of rationalization in the mod-ern world, Gerth and Mills described its adverse effects on "personal free-dom." While Parsons highlighted Durkheimian elements of Weber stressing the significance of social cohesion, Gerth and Mills highlighted Marxist elements of Weber's thought, stressing the compulsive character of large-scale economic, military, and political institutions. Against Parsons's ideal-ist interpretation of Weber that concentrated on the significance of shared values, Gerth and Mills put forth a materialist interpretation stressing that Weber's work should "be seen as an attempt to 'round out' Marx's eco-nomic materialism by a political and military materialism."[42] According to Gerth and Mills, though Weber rejected Marxian economic determinism, he nevertheless stressed the ultimate significance of the distribution of power and resources on the social structure. Weber, a nostalgic liberal pes-simist, rather than rejecting Marx's conclusions, showed them to be par-ticular cases in a more fundamental trend of bureaucratization—a trend that alienated not only proletarians, but nearly all modern men.

If Parsons used Weber's description of modernity to present a relatively optimistic vision of a postcapitalist world, for Gerth and Mills, Weber was sig-nificant because of his readiness to criticize modernity "as a configuration of institutions, which by the logic of their own requirements increasingly narrow the range of effective choices open to men."[43] Yet, if their evaluations of modernity differed, their descriptions of it were similar. Not only were Parsons and Mills eager to examine total social structures, but they also described modernity in Weberian terms of bureaucratization and rationalization, rather than stressing the economic processes of capitalism. As I will later demonstrate, the social criticism that Mills became famous for in such works as *White Collar* and *The Power Elite* owed much to his reading of Weber, as he concentrated his attention less on class conflict and exploitation than on the social causes of alienation and the individual's feeling of powerlessness when confronted with large-scale organizations dominated by elites.

Mills at the Bureau of Applied Social Research

In the 1940s, Mills engaged not only the macroscopic turn toward the study of total societies, but also the microscopic methods of bureau research that became increasingly prominent during that decade. In 1945, Mills left his post at the University of Maryland to take a job as a research associate at Columbia University's Bureau of Applied Social Research (BASR), a position he held until 1949. Mills was hired to conduct a study of personal influence in Decatur, Illinois, but over the next few years a conflict over the interpretation of this data erupted between Mills and the bureau's director, Paul Lazarsfeld, that ultimately contributed to Mills's marginalization from professional sociology in the 1950s. In retrospect, especially after Mills's damning portrait of Lazarsfeld as an "abstracted empiricist" in *The Sociological Imagination*, it is easy to see why the conflict arose. Mills's theoretical scope, radical politics, and valorization of the autonomous intellectual seemed uniquely unsuited to bureau research.[44]

Such a retrospective view, however, neglects the fact that Mills was eager to join the BASR in 1945. Indeed, Mills was so excited after being offered the job over dinner by Lazarsfeld and Robert Merton (the bureau's associate director), he "wandered into another restaurant and ate another huge meal!"[45] Mills was energized by more than just the opportunity to leave a deteriorating situation at Maryland for New York City. For Mills, the new techniques of bureau research held out the promise of a better understanding of social stratification and of social psychology, and could be utilized for critical rather than commercial ends. Even though this promise soured for Mills and his relationship with Lazarsfeld deteriorated, Mills's work at the bureau helped shape the two books that established his national reputation: *The New Men of Power* and *White Collar*.

Lazarsfeld had sought to establish a permanent social research bureau since emigrating to the U.S. from Austria in 1933. He finally succeeded when Columbia University formalized its commitment to the BASR in 1945.

The expansion of bureau-driven research in the 1940s reflected the growing desire of social scientists to utilize the most advanced and rigorous techniques of quantitative social research. Research bureaus such as the BASR, as well as the National Opinion Research Center (at Chicago) and the Survey Research Center (at Michigan) allowed social scientists to generate their own data. The BASR pioneered a variety of methods of survey research new to American social science, including the panel survey, which involved reinterviewing a sample of individuals over time in order to gauge how they made decisions, and sociometric surveys, which linked subjects to their social networks.[46]

Columbia's failure to provide a greater subsidy for the BASR meant that its formalized relationship with the university amounted to little more than "a license to hunt for outside support of projects." During Mills's tenure, the bureau received most of its funding from business contracts, though it also received significant funding from foundations and nonprofit organizations.[47] Yet, as he explained to his radical friends among the New York intellectuals, Mills felt that he could make bureau research serve critical ends. For one thing, the BASR offered Mills the skills and resources to conduct his own research; as Mills wrote Dwight Macdonald, the position "gives me the means of big research staff with assistants etc, also from what I understand a good deal of autonomy in what I'll research on and how I'll do it."[48] Moreover, as Mills wrote Daniel Bell, he could not "see how in the hell any such study as they have in mind can possible [*sic*] be properly designed without finding out a great deal about class and status solidarity," concluding that there were "legitimate points of coincidence between commercial and radical research."[49] For Mills, bureau research techniques were promising tools of social analysis that the radical social critic could utilize just as the businessman could. Indeed, Mills was irritated by left-wing social scientists who believed that such empirical techniques held an inherently conservative bias. As he wrote in a reader's report for the Oxford University Press on Frankfurt School theorist Max Horkheimer's *Twilight of Reason*, "For God's sake get the author to cut out these adolescent barbs at 'statistics,' 'questionnaires,' and 'polls' . . . In trying to understand the world, we may use any method we can lay our hands on."[50]

Indeed, in Austria, Lazarsfeld himself first became attracted to bureau research through a commitment to left-wing political transformation. A socialist raised in the household of Marxist theorist Rudolf Hilferding, Lazarsfeld wanted to study voting behavior. As such study was discouraged for political reasons, he turned instead to commercial research, believing in the "methodological equivalence of socialist voting and the buying of soap."[51] Even though he had largely given up his commitment to left-wing political transformation by the time Mills joined the BASR (in later years, he referred to himself as a "Marxist on holiday"), Lazarsfeld's research did contain insights into social stratification and social psychology of interest to left-wing sociologists such as Mills. For instance, Lazarsfeld's pioneering study in radio research in the late 1930s concluded that audiences for radio programs self-selected largely according to class.[52]

Mills had his greatest success at the BASR when he was able to put bureau resources and techniques to use on his own projects. For instance, in 1946, Mills persuaded Lazarsfeld to establish the Labor Research Division, with Mills as its head. Mills convinced Lazarsfeld to establish the division by explaining that it could bring in more outside contracts (and perhaps by playing on Lazarsfeld's lingering prolabor sympathies).[53] For Mills, the LRD was an experiment to see if bureau techniques could be used to serve his political goal of supporting the labor movement. As Mills wrote, research techniques such as those developed at the BASR, were being "monopolized" by "a handful of businessmen," but the LRD was a means for putting these "new skills and visions" to use for labor.[54] In order to communicate his research expertise to those in the labor movement, Mills and his research associates published a regular feature, "What the People Think," in the liberal-labor magazine, *Labor and Nation*, analyzing the accuracy and significance of labor polls. He also used the BASR to conduct a poll for the United Automobile Workers (UAW) and a poll for *politics* magazine subscribers. In 1946, Mills conducted a mail survey of American labor leaders that constituted the significant statistical portion of his first book, *The New Men of Power: America's Labor Leaders*, which was jointly funded by the BASR and the organization that published *Labor and Nation*, the Inter-Union Institute for Labor and Democracy.[55] To be sure, helping the labor movement through bureau research was a modest goal for a radical, and Mills never fully integrated his statistical analysis of American labor leaders with his larger political arguments in *The New Men of Power*. Nevertheless, with the Labor Research Division, Mills was able to use the new research techniques and bureau resources to advance his own political and scholarly goals.

In the Decatur study that he was hired to conduct, however, Mills was unable to bend bureau research to his purposes. The Decatur study was designed to test the Bureau's theory of "two-step flow of communication" by investigating how individuals influenced the decisions of others in the areas of consumption of household goods, fashion, movie going, and politics. The two-step theory, first developed in the bureau's study on voting behavior, *The People's Choice*, held that influence resulted from the flow of ideas from the mass media to "opinion leaders" who persuaded others in their primary groups. In the summer of 1945, Mills and his team gathered a "snowball sample" by interviewing all those whom the initial respondents listed as having influenced them in their decision making, conducting nearly 3,000 interviews for the project.[56]

From these data, Mills dutifully sought to trace the paths of interpersonal influence through statistical analysis. However, he also tried to use the data to answer his own concerns. In his draft report, Mills ambitiously sought to combine Lazarsfeldian research methods with a left-wing concern to uncover the sources of power in American society. As Mills put it in a 1946 speech, unlike the "microscopic" research associated with Lazarsfeld, "macroscopic" research (such as that conducted in Robert and Helen Lynds' influential *Middletown* studies) sought to determine a "chain of leaders" in order to "grasp the power and influence structure." Mills suggested that integrating a concern with hierarchies of social power could improve upon the methods previously developed at the BASR. The Decatur study was promising to Mills because the technique of snowball sampling it developed could be used as "a bridge between macroscopic and microscopic conceptions of research." By tracing the flow of influence from one individual to another, researchers could learn not only about the process of influence, but also about structures of power. By doing so, empirical research could shed light on the nature of modern American society.[57]

In this instance, Mills's attempt to adapt bureau techniques for his own ends brought him into conflict with Lazarsfeld. The conflict centered around three basic issues: social scientific methodology, political ideology, and intellectual autonomy. In his continuing attempt to understand the total structure of American society, Mills interpreted the Decatur survey data to determine whether the United States was a classic liberal society in which face-to-face intervention was the crucial influence or a totalitarian mass society in which the mass media, concentrated as property in the hands of a small elite, was the dominant influence. Mills's attempt to use the data to shed light on epochal modern social trends was rejected by Lazarsfeld, who believed that such theories could not be proved by rigorous empirical methods. To Lazarsfeld, to speculate on such trends was simply not "social science." Mills came into conflict with Lazarsfeld not because Mills was more of a social critic than a social scientist, but instead because Mills had a far more expansive sense of the tasks of social science. Indeed, Mills later remembered Lazarsfeld in these terms: "I have never known a more dogmatic man," he wrote, "I suppose because he wasn't dogmatic about any set of beliefs but about the limits of reason itself."[58]

Though Lazarsfeld did not share Mills's macroscopic concern with total societies, the Decatur study was intended to prove a particular theory of the two-step model of personal influence. Though Lazarsfeld insisted that this theory merely described interpersonal influence and not modern society as a whole, the implication of the two-step model was that the U.S. was a relatively democratic society where decisions were made not by elites, but by widely dispersed "opinion leaders." Moreover, by equating political decisions with decisions about what to wear and what movie to see, Lazarsfeld implicitly endorsed a consumerist version of democracy.[59] If Lazarsfeld was unwilling to draw the ideological implications of his theory, the study's sponsor, MacFadden Publishers, showed no such restraint. "We must sell things—but also ideas—American ideas," they claimed, "and get those ideas spread faster and more effectively than before! If this report makes any effective selling, and idea spreading, however, small, it will have fulfilled the aims of its sponsor."[60] Through interpreting the Decatur data, Mills developed a more nuanced portrait of American society than he presented in his subsequent political analysis, synthesizing his belief that the U.S. was in part an elite-dominated mass society with the insights into interpersonal influence suggested by Lazarsfeld's research. For Mills, however, unlike for Lazarsfeld, any adequate theory of modern American society had to account for the influence exercised by elites and a normative commitment to a more expansive notion of democratic participation.[61]

The final element of the conflict involved Mills's role at the bureau. From the beginning, Mills saw himself as a near equal with Lazarsfeld, writing Gerth when he took the job that he, Lazarsfeld, and Merton were "supposed to be the logicians and theoreticians: the idea people."[62] While Mills did in fact possess autonomy in his labor projects, since the Decatur study was designed to test a pet theory of Lazarsfeld's, it was particularly difficult for Mills to push his own interpretation of the data. Here, Lazarsfeld acted as Mills's boss in a hierarchically structured bureaucracy, insisting that the study be completed to his specifications. Mills's conflict with Lazarsfeld was hardly unique: many others at the BASR complained that Lazarsfeld wanted them to work as extensions of himself, not to develop their own ideas.[63] Indeed, no fewer than five sociologists (including Mills) were asked by Lazarsfeld to write the Decatur report and found wanting.[64] Yet, in Mills's case, the dispute was particularly bitter because of the value Mills placed on his intellectual autonomy and the far-reaching methodological and political implications of their conflict. As late as 1951, Mills expected to publish the report under his name. However, Lazarsfeld completed the study with Elihu Katz. Published in 1954 and reflecting Lazarsfeld's vision of empirical social research, *Personal Influence* became known as a paradigmatic text of postwar media studies.[65]

The conflict over the Decatur report precipitated Mills's alienation from professional sociology in the 1950s. Because of Mills's failure to complete the report to Lazarsfeld's satisfaction, the sociology department delayed Mills's promotion to associate professor in 1947.[66] After Mills quit the BASR in 1949, he retreated to Columbia College, the undergraduate wing of Columbia, and he therefore never advised any graduate students. Mills had become disillusioned not only with bureau research but also with academic social science. Indeed, in the postwar period, the discipline of sociology as a whole gained a clearer definition, but at the expense of openness to alternative voices such as Mills's. Concluding that it was no longer possible for him to exercise his sociological imagination from within the profession, he developed a distinctive style that mixed analytic social science with hortatory social criticism, earning him a mass audience for such works as *White Collar* and *The Power Elite.*

White Collar and American Social Science

Indeed, Mills became famous not as a social scientist during the 1940s, but as a radical social critic in the 1950s. Yet, his work cannot be understood as it too often is: as simply a lonely and compelling protest against the complacency of Cold War America. Indeed, his mature thought was influenced in important respects by his engagement with professional social science in the 1940s, which was evident in the work that cemented his reputation as a radical social critic, *White Collar* (1951). Today *White Collar* is rightly recognized as a classic work of social analysis—even a recent critic of the book has called it "the most important book we have about the American middle classes."[67] A complete interpretation of *White Collar* would need to take into account all of the many ambitious projects Mills undertook with this book: a work of "sociological poetry" written to reach a mass audience, a contribution to the rethinking of left-wing ideas in the wake of political defeats suffered in the 1940s, a celebration of the critical intellectual as one of the few remaining social types capable of defending the values of rationality and freedom, and a total damnation of American society by a man who at the end of the 1940s found himself isolated from all groups pursuing intellectual or political alternatives. Here, I would like to emphasize the aspect of *White Collar* that has been most neglected—its origins as a work of social science.[68] By examining the significance that bureau-driven research, the study of total societies, and the sociology of knowledge had for the development of *White Collar*, it becomes clear that Mills's influential social criticism of the 1950s was deeply indebted to his prior engagements with professional social science.

In 1944, Mills wrote to friends about his project on the "social psychology of the middle class," and in that year he applied for (and received) a Guggenheim grant to conduct research on white-collar workers.[69] While employed at the BASR, Mills conducted research on the project. The bureau afforded him the skills and resources needed to document statistically a momentous occupational shift in the U.S. from a property-owning old middle class to a salaried new middle class. More important, Mills utilized bureau techniques to study the social psychology of white collar workers. In a BASR-funded study on "Everyday Life in America," Mills achieved one goal for his project: to "exploit fully . . . the newer [research] technique[s], especially the intensive interview."[70] Like his work in the Labor Research Division, the Everyday Life study was a successful instance of Mills adapting bureau resources and techniques for his own purposes.

In the fall of 1946, Mills supervised 128 intensive interviews of white collar workers in New York City.[71] While the BASR is generally depicted as solely concerned with quantitative survey research, it also developed qualitative techniques designed for a deeper understanding of individual psychology. A particular model for the Everyday Life study was Robert Merton's 1944 study of a marathon radio broadcast by celebrity Kate Smith to sell war bonds, published in 1946 as *Mass Persuasion*. Employing the technique of the open-ended "focused interview," *Mass Persuasion* proved that bureau research could offer a deeper, more qualitative examination of social psychology. Though the study is now best remembered for pioneering the widely used market research tool of the "focus group," *Mass Persuasion* revealed that bureau research could offer critical insights into American society. Merton argued that the reactions of the broadcast's listeners could only be understood by placing them in the context of a "manipulative society" in which the value of salesmanship was pervasive.[72]

Like Merton's study, the Everyday Life project employed open-ended interviews. Though interviewers had a set list of 74 questions to ask, Mills encouraged them to ask "probe questions . . . to allow the individual's experience to enter fully into the answers given."[73] The interviews were intended not to learn just about the subjects' work lives, but to glimpse their everyday lives—to get a complete picture of each individual. Although the responses could be tabulated statistically, Mills encouraged interviewers to develop a qualitative sense of the psychology of the individual white collar worker interviewed. In particular, Mills sought to capture the "dream life" of white collar workers—their deepest thoughts and feelings. As he instructed his interviewers: "You've found out what he is most concerned with when he is awake; now you want to know what he dreams of when he goes to sleep. What is the focus of his life, if he has one? What purpose does he feel he serves, if any?"[74] The interviews were designed with a critical purpose in mind, to develop what Mills called a "deep radical slant" on the psychology of white collar workers.[75] Mills instructed the interviewers to uncover the various conscious and unconscious ways in which modern men and women were alienated from modern society and the questionnaire contained a series of questions on "political apathy" designed to uncover "the roots of political indifference."[76]

Mills made only partial use of the Everyday Life material in *White Collar*, using them "only as a source of quotations and an informal limit to psychological statements," claiming that the results of the study would be reported in a "later volume on qualitative method" that never appeared.[77] This choice, which occurred after Mills's fallout with Lazarsfeld over the Decatur study soured him on the uses of bureau research, had unfortunate consequences for *White Collar*. The interviews would have offered more evidence for Mills's depiction of white collar alienation and anxiety, and greater inclusion of these voices in the text might have moderated Mills's caustic description of white collar workers, making them seem more human.

Most intriguingly, the interviews might have led Mills to deal more explicitly with the gendered dimension of white collar work, mostly neglected in the text.[78] Even though *White Collar* may have benefited had Mills made more use of the interviews, they remained a critical part of *White Collar*'s development, making the book more than just the impressionistic account of an iconoclastic social critic.[79] Though underutilized, the interviews nevertheless offered a key source of empirical material for Mills's imaginative depiction and critique of white collar worlds and styles of life.

Mills decided to make less use of the Everyday Life interviews because he had his sights set on a more ambitious, and not entirely compatible, task. As Mills wrote in the introduction to *White Collar*, "By understanding these diverse white-collar worlds we can also understand better the shape and meaning of modern society as a whole."[80] As I have demonstrated, the hope of understanding "modern society as a whole" was characteristic of American social science in the 1940s. In the postwar period, owing much to Parsonian theory, this trend toward macroscopic social science was evident in the growth of modernization theory during the postwar period, which attempted to understand developing third world societies.[81]

Not only was Mills's project similar to that of Parsons, their depictions of modern society had elements in common. Howard Brick has argued that Parsons was only one of many prominent "postcapitalist" thinkers in mid-century American social thought who believed that American society was undergoing an important transition beyond traditional forms of capitalism.[82] In *White Collar*, though Mills employed the term "capitalism" on a few occasions, he preferred the term "modern society," suggesting that like postcapitalist theorists, Mills found the term "capitalism" no longer an adequate description for "the outlines of a new society."[83] Moreover, Mills believed that modern society needed to be understood "in more psychological terms," an idea he shared with postcapitalist thinkers such as Parsons who sought to develop a noneconomic conception of civil society.[84] Indeed, Mills's concept of "status anxiety" in *White Collar* anticipated some of the social psychological insights of postcapitalist thinkers and leading liberal social scientists, including Parsons, Daniel Bell, Richard Hofstadter, and David Riesman.[85]

It is possible to situate Mills in relationship to postcapitalist social theorists such as Parsons by examining how his particular interpretation of Weber affected *White Collar*.[86] If Mills's portrayal of modern society owed much to his use of Weber, characteristic of contemporary American social scientists, it was also indebted to his distinctive reading of Weber. Mills's interpretation of Weber as a post-Marxist materialist led him to concentrate on the powerful role played by large-scale institutions in modern society. Mills's Weberian approach to social psychology, developed in *Character and Social Structures*, emphasized the role of hierarchical institutions in shaping individual persons. Unlike Parsons, Mills saw society as bound together not by common values but by "big chains of authority."[87] Hence, Mills never lost sight of the importance of inequalities of political and economic power. In *White Collar*, Mills specifically rejected the "managerial" thesis of Adolph Berle and Gardiner Means (as well as James Burnham), who suggested that the power of property had declined in modern society as corporations were increasingly run by managers rather than owners. In contrast, Mills argued that while the power of property had been bureaucratized, "the executives of the modern corporation in America form an utterly reliable committee for managing the affairs and pushing for the common interests of the big-property class."[88] In fact, according to Mills, the power of property had increased in modern American society, due to a shift from more widely dispersed "entrepreneurial property" to "class property" concentrated in the nation's largest corporations. Relying upon a post-Marxist interpretation of Weber that emphasized the significance of property relations in modern society, *White Collar* continued traditional left-wing critiques of capitalist society.

On the other hand, Mills, like postcapitalist theorists, often downplayed the significance of property relations in modern society. Also drawing upon Weber, Mills suggested that such trends as bureaucratization, rationalization, and centralization were fundamental for understanding modern society and required a serious revision of traditional notions of "capitalism." Thus, Mills contended, "The world market, of which Marx spoke of as the alien power over men, has in many areas been replaced by the bureaucratized enterprise."[89] To Mills, bureaucratic manipulation had replaced free market mechanisms in "the more managed integration of a corporate-like society."[90] In Mills's dystopian vision of a world in which freedom and rationality had been expropriated from men by gigantic rationalized organizations, it was uncertain that it mattered whether those organizations were privately or collectively owned. Thus, as Brick suggests, Mills might be understood as offering a pessimistic version of the postcapitalist vision optimistically expounded by Parsons and others.[91]

Indeed, thinking of Mills as espousing a qualified version of postcapitalist theory allows us to get beyond the hackneyed analysis that portrays Mills as a lone social critic of the postwar period. For as Brick and other contributors to this volume argue, there was indeed the potential for social criticism within postwar liberalism.[92] This was evident in Riesman's enormously popular *The Lonely Crowd* (written with Nathan Glazer and Reuel Denney), which appeared one year before *White Collar*. Like *White Collar*, *The Lonely Crowd* had an origin in the Everyday Life study that Mills conducted at the BASR. Mills shared his data with both Riesman and Glazer at an early stage in their project.[93] Riesman's famous portrait of the "other-directed" personality type who seemed to be emerging in postcapitalist society was similar to Mills's critique of the "new little men" in *White Collar*. For Riesman as for Mills, a new person was arising in the midst of a momentous shift from production-oriented to consumption-oriented society. Riesman agreed with Mills that the major problems faced by modern men were increasingly psychological rather than material. Though middle-class Americans benefited from living in a society of increasing affluence and leisure, Riesman wrote, "They pay for these changes . . . by finding themselves in a centralized and bureaucratized society."[94] In describing the psychological problems created by a "society increasingly dependent on the manipulation of people," Riesman's critique of the "false personalization" of the other-directed type unable to develop an individuated personality was similar to Mills's portrait of the alienated white collar worker.[95]

Thus, Mills's postwar social criticism was in key respects consistent with the work of liberal social scientists such as Riesman. However, Mills did offer a radical version of that critique. Riesman ultimately located his hopes for developing what he called "autonomous" personality types within the postwar social order itself, in the "effort to develop a society which accepts rather than rejects new potentialities for leisure, human sympathy, and abundance."[96] Riesman focused on the realm of leisure and consumption, offering a more complex analysis of mass culture and middle-class leisure activities than did Mills. Yet, unlike Mills, Riesman often lacked a sense of the social and political obstacles that would prevent the development of autonomous character types. Not only did Riesman largely ignore issues of work, and concentrate his focus almost solely on individuals, he often blunted his call for more autonomous personalities at leisure by reducing it to a mere call for more sophisticated consumers.

A similar dynamic was evident in the works of Talcott Parsons and other liberal postwar social theorists. By the 1950s Parsons's critique of individualist society had lost its edge. The Harvard sociologist now thought American society had superseded competitive individualism, failing to recognize the political steps necessary to realize the values he assumed were now part of the fabric of American life.[97] Though Mills's pessimistic radicalism exaggerated the bleakness of postwar American society, it nevertheless protected him from the wishful thinking of postwar liberals. In his next book after *White Collar, The Power Elite,* Mills would resoundingly debunk Riesman's notion, shared by other postwar liberals, that the United States no longer suffered from "the power hierarchy of a ruling class."[98]

The influence of Mills's early works in the sociology of knowledge on his mature social thought are less tangible, but nevertheless important, initiating a life-long concern with the relationship between knowledge and society. As Mills later wrote, "It's been said in criticism that I am too much fascinated by power . . . [but] It is intellect I have been most fascinated by, and power primarily in connection with that."[99] A concern with the social role of knowledge was in many ways characteristic of midcentury social science. Theorists often posited the emergence of a "knowledge economy," a trend that seemed confirmed by the unprecedented level of prestige social science enjoyed in the postwar period. It was on the question of knowledge and power that Mills most sharply distinguished himself from postwar liberals. Rather than praising the possibilities of a knowledge-based postindustrial economy, Mills offered a moralistic damnation of intellectuals for failing to join him in criticizing the established political order. One of the most powerful chapters of *White Collar* was "Brains, Inc.," a withering critique of the bureaucratization of knowledge and the political withdrawal of contemporary intellectuals.

In *White Collar*, Mills did not just harp on the treason of these intellectuals. He wanted to explain it, and to that end he turned to the reflexive sociology he had developed in his earlier work in the sociology of knowledge. Mills argued that the intellectual was a special case of the bureaucratic trends identified elsewhere in the book. According to Mills, the rise of massive bureaucratic organizations controlling the means of communication inhibited the intellectual from relating to a broader public. Though Mills's contrast of the present era with a romanticized age of the "free intellectual" (in which pamphleteers like Thomas Paine could easily reach a mass audience) lacked empirical rigor, his depiction of contemporary social scientists more nearly hit its mark. Exacting his revenge on Lazarsfeld's BASR, Mills criticized the effects of government and private funding of social research and bureau-driven social science. Mills persuasively argued that the obsession of social scientific experts with technique accepted "as given the big framework and the political meaning of his operation within it."[100] By challenging social scientists not to hide behind their self-images as objective social observers but to question their political role in society, Mills's critique emerged from his reflexive sociology.

Mills's radical critique of American society was also more subtly, yet perhaps more fundamentally, influenced by his early work in the sociology of knowledge. His willingness to subject the deepest presuppositions of social science to analysis and critique had most distinguished his position from that of Merton. Well before he conceived of himself as a political radical, Mills was a radical in the classical sense—his analysis went to the root of the matter. Part of the appeal to Mills of a radical political perspective must have been similar to the appeal of an expansive conception of the sociology of knowledge. Each allowed him to get outside of the object studied and bring into question its fundamental values. In an important sense, Mills's radicalism emerged not from extradisciplinary political commitment, but from within the disciplinary matrix of American social science.

Mills extended the themes of "Brains, Inc." in his 1959 book, *The Sociological Imagination*, a full-scale attack on academic social science, in which he singled out Parsons and Lazarsfeld for critique. In 1951, Mills anticipated the main theme of this book, writing in a letter that sociology "is now split into statistical stuff and heavy duty theoretical bullshit."[101] It was precisely because Mills believed in the potential of social science so deeply that his attack on those who seemed to betray it was so vitriolic. In the first chapter of *The Sociological Imagination*, Mills described "the promise" of social science as allowing people the ability to understand the large social forces that shape their lives.[102] While Mills drew a sharp distinction in *The Sociological Imagination* between his social science and that which prevailed in the academy, his approach was deeply embedded in the disciplinary trends of midcentury sociology. Rather than abandoning the social scientific enterprise in the 1950s, in his famous works Mills laid out an alternative conception of social science that owed much to his distinctive engagement with earlier disciplinary trends. By the 1960s, Mills's vision of social science inspired younger academic social scientists associated with the New Left to reexamine the potential uses of their most characteristically professional techniques.

C. L. R. James and the Theory of State Capitalism

Christopher Phelps

C. L. R. James, the Afro-Caribbean writer best known for *The Black Jacobins*, his 1938 history of the San Domingo slave revolution led by Touissant L'Overture, is the subject of a vast secondary literature treating him largely as a cultural thinker. Whole volumes are devoted to James and cricket, James and the Caribbean, James and race, and James and philosophy, leaving vivid impressions of a figure whose life arched from the West Indies to London and Los Angeles, who examined comic strips and gangster films as avidly as Thackeray and Shakespeare, and who took Hollywood movies and radio soap operas as seriously as Pan-Africanism and Hegelian dialectics.[1]

This cultural James, so well etched, deserves supplementation. When specifying the signal result of his American sojourn between 1938 and 1953 in one late life interview, James did not refer to his now celebrated reflections on black liberation, the novels of Herman Melville, or American civilization.[2] "What was important about my work in the United States," he said, "was this: I insisted on analyzing the capitalist society of the age in which we live."[3] The esteem that James himself felt for his assessment of modern capitalism makes it all the more stunning that scholars have devoted so little attention to the concept of state capitalism running through his oeuvre.[4] Largely unpursued is Robin D. G. Kelley's tantalizing insight that James's significance lies in the connection he drew between issues of identity and culture and "political economy, labor, and the state."[5]

Inattention to James's theory of state capitalism has multiple causes: the rise of cultural studies, for whose practitioners James's enthusiasm for popular culture holds greater appeal than his social, political, and economic theory; the decline of the socialist movement and the consequent thinning of the ranks of those inclined to follow the intricacies of Marxist argument; prejudice against anti-Stalinist revolutionary radicalism as sectarian, leading to dismissal of its theoretical preoccupations; and the intrinsic denseness of James's theoretical writings, steeped in Hegel, Marx, Lenin, and the insular debates of the far left. Since the collapse of Communism in 1989–1991, debate over the structure of Soviet-type societies—a crucial point of reference for James's state capitalist theory—has come to seem obscure, esoteric, or antiquarian. It requires an imaginative leap to recapture the once commonplace feeling that it matters, profoundly, how one characterizes the Soviet Union and similarly patterned societies. That is precisely the leap that must be made in order to comprehend the intellectual universe that C. L. R. James inhabited and his distinctive contribution to social theory at midcentury.

The Workers' State, the Left Opposition, and the Russian Question

When James arrived in the United States in October 1938, he was in his late thirties, having undergone several earlier phases of intellectual development. Born in 1901 on the island of Trinidad in the British West Indies, he spent a youth centered upon English literature and cricket, and then developed affinities for Trinidadian nationalism. His commitment to revolutionary socialism came uncommonly late, after his 1932 emigration from the Caribbean to England. The conditions of Europe—the slump, the rise of fascism, and increased worker militancy—prompted James to read Karl Marx and Vladimir Ilych Lenin for the first time, initiating his lifelong study of their writings. Even as he covered cricket for the *Manchester Guardian*, James, persuaded by Leon Trotsky's *History of the Russian Revolution*, helped in 1934 to form one British faction of the revolutionary socialist opposition movement that Trotsky had inspired.[6]

Trotsky, the foremost leader of the Russian October Revolution of 1917 alongside Lenin, had led a Left Opposition in the Soviet Union to resist its bureaucratic course after Lenin's death in 1924. By the end of the decade, the Left Opposition had lost out and Trotsky was banished to exile as Joseph Stalin outmaneuvered all rivals and consolidated his exclusive hold on state power. The Left Opposition hewed to the belief that it, not Stalin, was the genuine heir to Lenin's revolutionary tradition. It attracted small clusters of adherents among dissenting Communists around the world, all devoted to upholding the revolutionary socialism and internationalism that were the hallmark of the Bolshevik Party and early Communist International.[7] The late 1930s in Britain were for James a period of simultaneous Trotskyist and Pan-Africanist activism. He edited both *International African Opinion* (organ of the International African Service Bureau) and *Fight* (organ of the Marxist Group, later the Revolutionary Socialist League), wrote a play about Touissant L'Overture that starred Paul Robeson, and published *World Revolution* (1937), *The Black Jacobins* (1938), and *A History of Negro Revolt* (1938).

James's conception of state capitalism arose as one response to the Russian Question, a field of political and theoretical inquiry that, for obvious reasons, preoccupied the Left Opposition. Why had the Bolshevik Revolution deteriorated from its early foundation on soviets, or workers' councils, into a monstrous bureaucratic state despotism under Stalin? For the small revolutionary socialist groups that were the locus of James's activity from the moment of his radicalization in Britain during the crash throughout his stay in the United States, this was a practical—indeed, decisive—matter. In actuality, the Russian Question was a constellation of questions. If the Soviet Union under Stalin's ruthless bureaucratic dictatorship was not socialist or egalitarian, what exactly *was* it? What were its characteristic property forms and social relations? Was it a transitional regime between capitalism and socialism, or a new kind of class society unanticipated by classical theory? Why had bureaucratic decay set in? What could prevent its recurrence in a future revolutionary scenario? Should the Soviet Union be defended or repudiated? And what was the import of Stalinism for the doctrine of historical materialism, which had traditionally posited that capitalism would be succeeded by socialism, not some other productive system?

Trotsky's influential analysis in *The Revolution Betrayed* (1937) and other writings was that the October Revolution's supplanting of private ownership heralded a progressive advance, a social revolution that established a "workers' state" beyond capitalism. However, as a result of unpropitious conditions—underdevelopment, the First World War, civil war, boycott, and encirclement by hostile powers—the Bolshevik Revolution degenerated, succumbing to a reactionary ruling bureaucracy that controlled the state and society through its ironclad control of the party. Since it did not own property, the bureaucracy was not a new ruling class. Rather, it was a parasitical caste. No matter how retrograde the bureaucracy and its measures, nationalized property represented an advance over capitalism and private property. The arrested revolution in the Soviet Union faced two possibilities: restoration of capitalism or advancement toward socialism. Therefore, socialists should defend the Soviet Union against external imperialist threats while criticizing Stalinist corruption untiringly, promoting a Fourth International to replace the degenerated Third International, and advocating a new workers' movement to restore proletarian rule to the Soviet Union in a political revolution that would preserve the social basis of the workers' state.[8]

Initially, James shared this analysis unreservedly. *World Revolution*, his most comprehensive attempt to address Soviet history and politics during the late 1930s, was a compendium of Left Opposition complaints against Stalinism. It followed Trotsky's framework, although it was far more critical of Stalin's USSR. Several of James's remarks deriving from Trotsky's suspicion that the bureaucracy might restore private property to the Soviet Union were delivered with such enthusiasm, in fact, that they might be seen as prefigurations of his theory of state capitalism. James argued that because Stalin is "first and foremost a bureaucrat," he therefore "believes in the bourgeoisie far more than he believes in the proletariat." And in the great intraparty struggles of the 1920s, James alleged, "behind the party bureaucracy was the State bureaucracy, and behind these were the capitalist elements in the Soviet Union."[9] The bureaucracy's rapprochement with capitalism and lack of confidence in the working class in James's account explained most of Stalin's catastrophic international and domestic policies: the ill-fated alliance with the Kuomintang that all but destroyed the Chinese Communist movement in 1927 and the class-collaborationist Popular Fronts in France and Spain, as well as the decimation of the Old Bolsheviks, persecution of Left and Right Oppositions, and the Moscow Trials, all suppressions of independent resistance to bureaucratic privilege. "They wish to live on good terms with the bourgeoisie, if allowed," James wrote of the Soviet bureaucrats, "but the revolutionaries are enemies of their prestige, privileges, and perquisites."[10]

Yet James did not, at this time, subscribe to anything approaching a full-fledged theory of state capitalism. To hold that the party apparatus leaned toward capitalism and threatened to undermine the proletarian state was not the same as claiming that the Soviet Union was itself capitalist, from which would flow a position of total revolutionary opposition to the regime, a stance that Trotsky would never countenance. Trotsky persisted in defining the Soviet Union as a "workers' state"—albeit a degenerated one—on the basis of its collectivized property. Left Oppositionists, in deference to October and in defiance of Stalin's slander that they were in league with British imperialism and the fascist powers, positioned themselves as better defenders of the Soviet Union than the brutal bureaucratic tyrants at its helm. For a time, James dutifully followed suit. "If the Soviet Union goes down," he concluded, "then Socialism receives a blow which will cripple it for a generation."[11] In the newspaper *Fight*, James editorialized for "Defence of the U.S.S.R.!"[12]

James's theory of Soviet state capitalism, first declared in 1941, was not merely a repudiation of Stalinism, thus, but a rupture with Trotsky's intellectual system. Against Trotsky's call to defend the Soviet Union as a degenerated workers' state, James would instead posit that the Soviet Union under Stalin had become a new type of exploitative class society. Despite pervasive state ownership, he held, the Soviet Union operated on the capitalist mode of production and was not a progressive step toward socialism. Nationalized property did not prevent the state from functioning as the extractor of surplus value produced by the proletariat, nor did a state lacking workers' decision making warrant the designation "workers' state." James's theory of state capitalism was unusual, however, in that he considered state capitalism a worldwide phenomenon, characteristic of advanced capitalism as well as Soviet-type regimes. A review of the relationship of state and capital in prior social thought, especially Marxism, is necessary to make sense of James's self-congratulatory but earnest reference in 1950 to "the theory of state capitalism, Marxism of *our* period."[13]

State and Capital in Marxist Theory

Marx never used the term "state capitalist," for to him it would have been redundant. As a class system, capitalism had a state. The function of the capitalist state was to defend the interests of capital. *The Communist Manifesto* famously characterized the executive of the modern representative state as "but a committee for managing the common affairs of the whole bourgeoisie."[14] Writers like James, seeking to anchor their theories of state capitalism in the authority of classical texts, were nevertheless undaunted. They returned again and again to a passage in *Anti-Dühring* (1879), by Friedrich Engels:

The modern state, no matter what its form, is essentially a capitalist machine, the state of the capitalists, the ideal personification of the total national capital. The more it proceeds to the taking over of productive forces, the more does it actually become the national capitalist, the more citizens does it exploit. The workers remain wage-workers—proletarians. The capitalist relation is not done away with. It is rather brought to a head. But, brought to a head, it topples over. State ownership of the productive forces is not the solution of the conflict, but concealed within it are the technical conditions that form the elements of that solution.[15]

This attained particular force when combined with such statements as Marx's, in *Capital* (1867), that the tendency toward concentration might well unite capital "in the hands of either a single capitalist or a single capitalist company."[16] Marx and Engels, it seemed, had allowed for the possibility that the state could "become the national capitalist" in the process of a total concentration of capital.

At the dawn of the twentieth century, a number of writers began to note the increasing interpenetration of public and private, state and capital, under advanced capitalism. The social-democratic "Austro-Marxists" Rudolf Hilferding, Karl Renner, and Otto Bauer began to argue that the classical free enterprise system with its corresponding laissez-faire liberal state had by the twentieth century given way to a new stage of capitalism. The most important of their works, Hilferding's *Finance Capital* (1910), held that the centralization of industrial capital observed by Marx was enhanced by sophisticated banking systems which turned monetary capital into finance capital by investing it in industry. As capital grew ever more concentrated into nationwide monopolies, trusts, and cartels, the state no longer was merely a broker of separate competitive interests, but a regulator and facilitator of "organized capitalism."[17] The Austro-Marxists were given to statements like the following of Renner's in 1916: "We are in the epoch of organized private enterprise economy which is determined by the state and has become a thoroughly state-dominated organization."[18] The political implication of organized capitalism was that the labor movement through its parliamentary representatives could make *itself* the organizer, displacing finance capital from control of the republic and attaining socialism by peaceful, gradual, electoral methods.

This theory was interpolated by Nikolai Bukharin, a Russian Marxist, in *Imperialism and World Economy* (completed 1915, published 1918). Bukharin, a leading Bolshevik in exile from czarism who studied under Hilferding in Vienna, judged capital considerably more concentrated than when Hilferding had written. Every advanced capitalist economy had become, in effect, a "combined enterprise with an organizational connection between all the branches of production." The relentless combination of industrial, bank, and state industries was rendering each economy (with Germany the archetype) into a giant trust. The modern, interventionist, regulative state, according to Bukharin, acted to arrange economic, imperialist, and military endeavors on behalf of capital. In what may well be the first literal mention of the phrase, Bukharin called this integrated system "state capitalism." He considered it portentous, writing that "the future belongs to economic forms that are close to state capitalism." In this analysis, the state was exactly as Marx had thought—a class instrument operating on behalf of a powerful bourgeoisie—and not a neutral vehicle susceptible to gradual transformation by the labor movement. Nor did elaborate administration and organization render the society stable, for Bukharin thought state capitalism had increased "competition between state capitalist trusts" seeking profits, markets, and outlets for investment. The consequence was war, out of whose devastation would come revolution as workers came to recognize capitalism for what it was.[19]

Lenin and State Capitalism

When, as if in fulfillment of Bukharin's analysis, the Bolshevik Revolution of 1917 erupted in Russia in response to the destruction and carnage of the First World War, a new set of interpretive problems arose for historical materialist theory, namely, how to comprehend the postrevolutionary social structure and internal class relations of an overwhelmingly peasant nation that had been pushed by a militant working-class minority into a socialist revolution. The most influential Bolshevik meditations on this contradictory social process were by Lenin. While Lenin referred often to "state monopoly capitalism" in his writings on imperialism (borrowed in part from Bukharin), his most germane references to state capitalism concerned the functioning of post-insurrectionary Russia. Lenin recognized that revolution was a prolonged process, and that Soviet society would long contain admixtures of capitalism despite its aim of socialism. To chart a course consistent with Marx's method, Lenin lamented, was difficult, because it "did not occur even to Marx to write a single word on this subject."[20]

In 1918, hectored by Left Bolshevik critics (including Bukharin) who charged that the new order was creating "state capitalism," Lenin began to make surprisingly positive references to state capitalism. The Soviet Union would do well, he insisted, to emulate "the organized state capitalism of technically well-equipped Germany."[21] To Lenin, the transitional, composite Soviet economy contained an intermingling of economic structures: precapitalist subsistence peasant farming, small commodity production, private capitalism, state capitalism, and socialism. Each of these stages comprised an advance over the former, so furtherance of state capitalism would help the Soviet Union to transcend feudal agrarian relations and petty or proprietary capitalism. State capitalism, according to Lenin in 1918, would be "a step forward" toward socialism, bringing with it nationwide centralization, accounting, control, and socialization.[22] There was, he wrote, a "present *correlation* of state capitalism and socialism."[23]

These themes faded in Lenin's thought for several years, displaced by "war communism," but resurfaced during the concessions to market incentives made in the New Economic Policy (NEP) of 1921–23. Lenin characterized the NEP as a retreat necessitated by the devastation of war, revolution, and civil war. Often referring back to his 1918 writings, Lenin wrote that the NEP would resort to both private capitalism (encouragement of commodity exchange in agriculture) and state capitalism (governmental concessions to capital, namely the leasing of mines, forests, and oilfields to foreign business without denationalizing such properties). This, he anticipated, would enhance the development of productive forces, improve knowledge of advanced methods of production, raise living standards, and uproot old feudal structures.[24] According to Lenin, because the workers' state controlled foreign trade and owned the land, power output, railways, transport, and most large-scale industry, state capitalism was strictly circumscribed:

> To a certain extent, we are recreating capitalism. We are doing this quite openly. It is state capitalism. But state capitalism in a society where power belongs to capital, and state capitalism in a proletarian state, are two different concepts. In a capitalist state, state capitalism means that it is recognized by the state and controlled by it for the benefit of the bourgeoisie, and to the detriment of the proletariat. In the proletarian state, the same thing is done for the benefit of the working class, for the purpose of withstanding the as yet strong bourgeoisie, and of fighting it.[25]

Lenin understood well that to foster "state capitalism in a proletarian state"[26] was to play with fire, but he did not confront that contradiction in detail. Glaringly absent from his writings on the topic is any sustained investigation of the paradox or predicament of workers exploited in the industries and properties leased out to foreign capital by the putative workers' state.

Lenin's writings on state capitalism were of paramount importance for C. L. R. James, who revered Lenin to the point of religiosity. However, Lenin's usage differed substantially from James's. As a head of state improvising in strenuous circumstances, Lenin used the term to describe either policies (state concessions to peasant commodity production and to foreign investors) or a specific sector of the economy (those means of production controlled by the state but organized capitalistically for extraction of private profit). For him, state capitalism did not characterize the entire system, the Soviet economy. It was but one element in a hybrid, heterogeneous, transitional mode of production that revolutionaries were attempting to steer toward communism. Because it existed under proletarian surveillance, Lenin believed, it was harnessed in the service of socialist objectives. For James, by contrast, state capitalism described the Soviet Union's mode of production, not a mere policy or sector. Nor was it a transitional form on the way to communism or a practice checked by the Soviet state. Rather, it was a totalitarian abnegation of socialist aims that workers could not manipulate to their advantage. James's application of the designation "state capitalism" to the Soviet Union under Stalin differed utterly from Lenin's of twenty years before. Nevertheless, James would claim fidelity to Lenin and claim to be vindicated by his references to Soviet state capitalism. This idiosyncrasy was characteristic of James across his life. A daring and creative revolutionary thinker, James preferred to wrap his heresies in orthodox capes.[27]

State Capitalism as Criticism and Analysis of Stalinism

By the late 1930s, when James was living in the United States and struggling toward his distinctive set of ideas, the question of whether the Soviet system should be called "state capitalism" was a live proposition on the international left and among American intellectuals. As Communist parties gained credence in Western countries during the antifascist Popular Front, the Soviet Union itself descended into a maelstrom of forced collectivization, purges, frame-up trials, and the Hitler-Stalin pact. This lent the term "state capitalism" a moral, as distinct from a technical or clinical, quality. Critics of the Soviet regime, eager to lay bare the treachery and barbarism under Stalin, found in the phrase a useful retort to Stalin's claim that the Soviet Union had achieved socialism. Although the state capitalist interpretation was rare in comparison to more conventional liberal and radical understandings of the Soviet Union, a thinker who read as widely as James could easily recognize its existence on the continuum of interpretive possibilities.

References to Soviet state capitalism in the 1920s and 1930s are striking for their abundance and sheer political variety.[28] *State Capitalism in Russia*, published by the liberal Foreign Policy Association in 1926, justified its title by Soviet industry's use of "business methods."[29] In 1935, the anarchist Emma Goldman wrote in H. L. Mencken's *American Mercury* that while "it would be fantastic to consider it in any sense Communistic," the Soviet system "may be called state capitalism."[30] Conservative Democratic representative Martin Dies of Texas, founder of the House Committee on Un-American Activities (HUAC), alleged in 1940 that Communists sought to "substitute bureaucratic state Capitalism for our present political and social system."[31] The moderate American socialist leader Norman Thomas warned in 1944 that "the Russian type of totalitarianism will remain a bureaucratic state capitalism, undemocratic, ruthless and Machiavellian."[32]

These were provocations, epithets confined to a single phrase, rather than sociological theories. More sophisticated perspectives were voiced in European Marxist circles, a probable influence on James. In Germany, a breakaway faction of the Communist leadership in the late 1920s—allies of the ousted Comintern leader Grigori Zinoviev—advocated a state capitalist appraisal of Stalin's Soviet Union as elaborated in Arthur Rosenberg's *A History of Bolshevism* (1934).[33] In France (which James visited in the 1930s to research the Haitian revolution and take part in Fourth International meetings), Boris Souvarine, a onetime Communist expelled in the mid-1920s for "Trotskyism," described the Soviet Union in 1929 as "progressive state capitalism." By the time of his biography *Stalin* (1939), translated into English by James, Souvarine disavowed the theory of state capitalism, however, on the grounds that Soviet "methods of production are not exactly capitalist, a term which in any case is indefinable." Instead, he suggested more harshly, "the system deserves rather the name of slavery" or "a sort of bureaucratic feudalism under which the proletariat and the peasantry, debased by officialdom and the mandarinate, have been reduced to a kind of serfdom."[34]

Even as Souvarine backed away from the hypothesis of state capitalism, another Continental radical based in Paris, the Croation Ante Ciliga, began to argue for it adamantly. Ciliga had joined the Yugoslavian Communist Party in 1920 and became a Comintern official in the Soviet Union in 1926 before being expelled from the Soviet party in 1929 and imprisoned from 1930 to 1935 for sympathies with the Left Opposition. In the political "isolator" at Verkhne-Uralsk, he engaged in debates with a wide variety of revolutionary prisoners, some of whom had concluded that the Soviet Union, lacking workers' control of production or multiparty workers' democracy, was state capitalist. Freed, Ciliga escaped the Soviet Union and collaborated briefly with Trotsky before breaking with him in 1936. In *Au pays du grand mensonge* (1938; published in English as *The Russian Enigma*, 1940), Ciliga argued that both Stalin and Trotsky "wanted to pass off the State as being the proletariat, the bureaucratic dictatorship over the proletariat as the proletarian dictatorship, the victory of state capitalism over both private capitalism and socialism as the victory of the latter." The Soviet Union, he maintained, "had preserved all the essential characteristics of capitalism: production of goods, wages, exchange markets, money, profits, and even partial sharing out of profits among bureaucrats in the form of high salaries, privileges, and so on."[35]

A substantial state capitalist analysis came from R. L. Worrall, a former Trotskyist in England who was an acquaintance of James's. In an article on the Soviet Union first published in the British periodical *Left* and reprinted in two American left-wing magazines in 1939, Worrall argued that while private ownership "*has been* a basic principle of capitalism, it is neither specific to capitalism nor "*essential to that mode of production in every phase of its development.*" Means of production, he continued, remain capital even if under the control of the state, so long as wage labor and commodity production persist—and thus accumulation of capital continues. In this manner, state ownership and capitalist production are compatible. While the structure of the Soviet bureaucracy differed from that of the bourgeoisie, their larger function remained the same:

This primary function of accumulating capital, which a bureaucracy now performs in its entirety for the first time in history, is not combined with working-class control of that bureaucracy, through soviets or other forms of industrial organization of the proletariat. And precisely that fact makes the Russian State a capitalist instead of a workers' State. A new type of capitalist State, it is true, since the principle of private property still lies in the dust, but a capitalist State for all that, since the State, minus workers' democracy, pursues the aim and compelling motive of capitalism in general.

The proletarian revolution of 1917, Worrall concluded, had been destroyed by a counterrevolution of purges, censorship, and bureaucracy, ending workers' control and eventuating in a state capitalist regime that nevertheless represented a progressive advance over conventional capitalism.[36]

Among American intellectuals as well, the question of state capitalism was open to consideration as the Moscow Trials and 1939 Molotov-Ribbentrop pact led to melancholy over the fate of the Bolshevik Revolution. When V. F. Calverton, the eclectic radical editor of the *Modern Quarterly*, organized a symposium on the Soviet Union in 1938–1939, the questions he posed included these: "Can a proletarian State arise on the basis of the wage system, managed by a Party-State? What constitutes the abolition of capitalism?" Most respondents presumed that Calverton was asking whether the Soviet Union was capitalist, and several hinted that it was, as when Liston Oak wrote that "socialism can be realized only when both private and State capitalism are abolished, when the wage system, along with profits, prices, etc., are ended, and democratic control established." Others denied the value of the suggestion, defining capitalism as private ownership of the means of production. Somewhat unique was the response of journalist Benjamin Stolberg, who replied that he could not "imagine any transition to socialism, which would not in the beginning have state-capitalist features."[37]

Johnson-Forest and the Theory of State Capitalism

The theory of state capitalism espoused by C. L. R. James represented a coalescence of two divergent streams in the history of ideas: the analysis of advanced capitalism as typified by Bukharin, and the interrogation of the

Soviet Union's bureaucratic regime under Stalin. Atypically, James's usage extended to *both* advanced capitalist and Soviet-type societies. Initially, however, his theory arose straight out of the Russian Question.

After arriving in the United States in November 1938, James toured the country for months on behalf of the Socialist Workers Party (SWP), the largest Trotskyist grouping in the world at several thousand members. Trotsky had relocated to Mexico, and James traveled there in March 1939 to meet with him, discussing the status and politics of African Americans. After returning to New York City, James could not escape the raucus internal debate that erupted within the SWP over how to address the onrush of events in Europe in 1939–1940. Finding himself in agreement with those calling for reconsideration of the long-established policy of unconditional defense of the Soviet Union, James was forced to break with Trotsky.

Even in the face of unending new Stalinist horrors, Trotsky held firm to his defensist position. Those like Souvarine, Ciliga, and Worrall who saw a class society in the Soviet Union had succumbed to "ultraleft"—syndicalist and anarchist—influences, he charged. They had failed to adhere to Marx's view that the state bureaucracy never exists as an autonomous social class, only in the service of other, more fundamental classes. The state was not capital; bureaucracy could not sell or bequeath it.[38] James, however, concluded that unconditional defense of Stalin's Soviet Union made little sense if it meant giving carte blanche to Stalin's maneuvers to align the Soviet Union with various imperialist powers (first the French and British, then the Nazis) or to the Red Army occupations of Estonia, Latvia, Lithuania, Poland, and Finland. West Indian and Pan-African activism made him an anticolonial and anti-imperialist revolutionary at his core, and to him the Soviet military conquests were a disaster that imposed on Eastern Europe a social order dedicated to the ruthless destruction of all independent working-class movements.[39] Now James faced a question that every Left Oppositionist unable to stomach the critical defense of the Stalinist system had to confront: what theory ought to replace Trotsky's?[40]

As the movement sundered, James joined the substantial minority of defectors from the SWP who created a new Workers Party (WP), led by Max Shachtman. The SWP majority was led by James P. Cannon and sustained by ferocious polemics from the pen of Trotsky. It interpreted the Soviet territorial expansions as the extension of a progressive, if deformed, social order. Trotsky in his final writings had allowed for the possibility that the Soviet Union might turn out to be a bureaucratic class society, but this intimation did not prevent his adherents, particularly after his death in 1940, from sticking hard and fast to his original formulations. Those who broke with Shachtman to form the Workers Party were more variegated in outlook. A small number, James included, continued to hold to the conventional thesis of the USSR as a degenerated workers' state requiring defense if invaded from without, but did not believe that the wartime conquests were defensible. A much larger number came to espouse a theory formulated in 1937 by Joseph Carter but eventually labeled "Shachtmanite" as the new party's leader adopted it. This theory held that the Soviet Union was "bureaucratic collectivism," a society with state ownership of the means of production ruled by a new bureaucratic class neither capitalist nor proletarian in character. Some Workers Party veterans, including Hal Draper and those writing for Phyllis and Julius Jacobson's journal *New Politics*, continued to combine this interpretation with a left-wing democratic socialist outlook until the end of the twentieth century, but as Shachtman himself drifted ever further to the right in the 1950s and 1960s his analysis of Soviet state despotism had a long-range echo in theories of totalitarianism counseling acquiescence in the West, including neoconservative calls for a renewed Cold War in the 1970s and 1980s.[41]

James's theory of state capitalism was shaped in response to both the degenerated workers' state and bureaucratic collectivist theses. Since James had never intended to remain in the United States for an extended period, his immigration status lapsed into a dubious state and he ceased to write under his own name, instead adopting a number of pseudonyms, mostly "J. R. Johnson." He led a faction formed within the WP at its September 1941 convention to advocate the state capitalist position. This insular political circle, known as the "Johnsonites," comprised James's mode of Marxist intellectual production while in the United States for fifteen years. His admirers typically paid his way. James barely ever worked for remuneration, and he wrote for limited audiences on the small-group left, no longer for London publishers. His foremost cothinker was Raya Dunayevskaya (party name "F. Forest"), a Russian Jewish immigrant who briefly served as Trotsky's secretary in Mexico, and their grouping became known as the Johnson-Forest Tendency by the late 1940s.[42] A third integral leader was Grace Lee, a Chinese American with a doctorate in philosophy from Bryn Mawr. This tight-knit coterie, never much larger than seventy people and often smaller, operated within the WP until 1947, then rejoined the SWP in 1948, and finally broke from organized Trotskyism altogether in 1951, forming the independent organization Correspondence Committees, which disintegrated by the 1960s after James's deportation to Britain in 1953.[43] Ironically, James's theory of a crisis-prone and class-divided state capitalism, which more accurately anticipated the self-implosion of the Eastern European regimes than State Department and Reaganite theories of a formidable totalitarianism, would not make many inroads among American intellectuals who were later attracted to James more for his cultural contributions than his political economy, and who often harbored illusions about the progressive nature of the Soviet system.

Even to Johnsonites, the Tendency's writings, overlaid with Hegelianisms, could seem arcane. Constance Webb, a Californian model who later married James, recollects that in the Workers Party debates over the Russian

Question in the early 1940s, "I kept my mouth shut with all sides, not only because I didn't really know what they were talking about but because I failed to see why it was of primary concern in our struggle as revolutionaries."[44] To James, however, the debates were vital. Against orthodox Trotskyists who held that the Soviet bureaucracy comprised a caste, not a class, he and his cothinkers held that the bureaucracy was a ruling class controlling national capital. Against the Workers Party majority and its theory of "bureaucratic collectivism," James and his cothinkers argued that the Soviet Union still followed the laws of motion laid down in Marx's *Capital*.[45] Neither a workers' state nor a new kind of class society, the Soviet Union was state capitalist, subject to class struggles and economic crises. For James, this entailed moving beyond both Trotsky's position of unconditional defense of the Soviet Union and his own 1939–40 position of conditional defense, and toward a position of principled opposition to the states and social orders of both East and West. In a stream of articles, pamphlets, and mimeographed documents—particularly *State Capitalism and World Revolution* (1950), whose title paid homage to Lenin's *State and Revolution* (1917)—the Johnson-Forest Tendency elaborated its theory of state capitalism.[46]

According to Johnson-Forest, "capitalism, though in its classic form an economy of private property, can reach a stage where the capitalist class can plan the economy as a whole."[47] The imperatives of global competition after 1929 produced a struggle for world mastery between national states, leading to a basic tendency toward "state-capitalism or statification of production," "centralization on a world scale."[48] Built up during the Second World War, the U.S. state was by the late 1940s organizing world agricultural production, sending arms and aid worldwide, fighting off revolutionary movements in Turkey, Iran, and Greece, and intervening in Europe through the Marshall Plan. The U.S. government was a "state-trust," a "collective capitalist on a hitherto undreamt-of scale."[49] This assessment of state capitalism as a product of the imperatives of capital centralization, worldwide competition, and imperialism recalled Bukharin's theory. "The state," wrote Johnson-Forest, "takes over the economy, both in preparation for resisting other economies and for allying itself to the other mass of capital to which it is attracted or repelled. National capital must deal with national capital."[50]

At the same time, the Johnson-Forest analysis spoke to the Russian Question by describing the Soviet Union as a variant of capitalism, a class society that revolutionaries should challenge fundamentally. According to Johnson-Forest, the October Revolution had established workers' control of production, but from the phase of war communism through Stalin, the Soviet Union became ruled by functionaries rather than workers.[51] The social order over which these functionaries presided manifested all the categories of Marx's *Capital*: money, wage labor, commodity production, class distinctions, and the law of value. The persistence of such practices and structures required Soviet political economists to explain them away by revising Marxist theory.[52] Stalinism's labor regime, charged Johnson-Forest, owed much to Taylorism and Fordism, the speed-up techniques of American capital.[53]

As the Cold War dawned in 1947, James held that "the world proletariat . . . must make no distinction whatever between Russian state-capitalism and American imperialism as enemies of the proletariat and the chief torturers and oppressors and deceivers of hundreds of millions of workers and peasants."[54] This abstention from the Cold War camps attributed a reciprocity to the rival systems that passed beyond theorists of state-capital interpenetration (like the Austro-Marxists or Bukharin) and likeminded socialist critics of the Soviet Union as state capitalist (such as Ciliga or Worrall). "If Stalinist Russia is a vast state-capitalist and military trust," Johnson-Forest wrote, "American imperialism is a vast state-capitalist and military syndicate."[55] Centralized capital under state guidance existed in American capitalism, Nazi Germany, and Stalinist Russia alike. "The plan, the party, the state are totally capitalistic," Johnson-Forest wrote of Germany and Russia. "Nazi or Stalinist, they represent capital."[56] (In this, James's theory overlapped somewhat with that of Frankfurt School theorist Friedrich Pollack, who described Nazism as "state capitalism" because under it the plan held sway over the market. Pollack, however, did not extend the term to the Soviet Union.[57])

This theory of state capitalism abutted a number of mainstream theories of the Soviet bloc and Western societies popular in the 1940s and 1950s, two of which provide an especially important comparative contrast: the theory of totalitarianism and convergence theory. The theory of totalitarianism posited an identity of Nazi and Stalinist systems and complete thought control over their subjects by elimination of dissent.[58] James was given to references to "the totalitarian madness which swept the world first as Nazism and now as Soviet Communism," but he perceived an unfolding worldwide system not limited to Nazism and Stalinism alone.[59] An equally powerful trend toward bureaucratic domination, managerial command, and state organization existed in the West, he believed. Furthermore, James did not subscribe to the disposition that total state control threatened to accomplish total mind control, reducing citizens to Orwellian "proles."[60] On the contrary, James held that the Stalinist terror was rooted in production and the need for control over workers, leading him to see it as a perverse measure of worker assertiveness, which was temporarily suppressed and driven from view but was certain to lead to future explosions. In marked contrast to the totalitarian school, the theory of state capitalism implied no level of organization, propaganda, or repression sufficient to diminish or eliminate social crises. Class conflict, James believed, was exacerbated rather than resolved by state capitalism. Statification, planning, and regulation only intensified the fundamental antagonisms of capitalist production, which even in state capitalist form could not avoid the tendency of the rate of profit to fall as identified in *Capital*.[61] "Historical viability they have none," he wrote, "for state-ownership multiplies every contradiction of capitalism."[62]

The second contrasting school of thought, convergence theory, held that differences between Western and Soviet systems were attenuating or disappearing because both were mature industrial societies dependent upon the same managerial, scientific, and technocratic rationalism. While this view was promoted by a wide range of thinkers drawing very different practical conclusions from their work, it often went hand in hand with modernization theory and functional sociology.[63] Johnson-Forest protested—implausibly, given their emphatic declaration of state capitalism as a worldwide phenomenon—that their theory did not imply convergence: "We have never said that the economy of the United States is the *same* as the economy of Russia. What we have said is that, however great the differences, the fundamental laws of capitalism operate."[64] All the same, the Johnson-Forest theory of state capitalism may be seen as something of a far-left variant of convergence theory, so long as we allow for several important qualifications. Technical features and industrialism were never axiomatic for James, because for him capitalism and its economic laws were the rub. Nor did James see a diminution of inter-imperialist rivalries in international relations, since state capitalism pitted great blocs of national capital in irreconcilable conflict.

James's postulates set him in revolutionary political opposition not just to Stalinism, Nazism, and corporate capitalism, but to the reformism of liberal intellectuals and the trade union officialdom. As the militant sit-down strikes that built the Congress of Industrial Organizations in the late 1930s gave way to trade union leadership's acquiescence in a no-strike pledge supported by the Communist Party in the 1940s, James saw in shopfloor discontent and wildcat strikes an irrepressible proletarian striving against the labor bureaucracy and Stalinist left. From the Johnson-Forest vantage, social democracy and progressive liberalism extended the regulatory and welfare state against their bête noire, private capital, but in so doing were merely vanguards of state capitalism. The reformist left, held Johnson-Forest, misguidedly emphasized the realm of consumption (wages, benefits, provision) over relations of production. To supersede capitalism would require workers' power, not mere conversion of private property into state property. For revolutionaries, they wrote, the issue is "not the fruits of toil but the toil itself."[65] Revolution requires workers to be subjects, not mere objects, and capitalism, state or private, could never satisfy this criterion. Communists and social democrats in the United States and Western Europe were devoted to challenging private property but not to advancing workers' power, and consequently were merely "the political form corresponding to the final form of capitalism, state capitalism."[66]

This represented a bold extension of the concept of state capitalism, transforming it into a radical critique of prevailing radical practice. It explains

James's rejection of self-constituted vanguards as state capitalist bureaucracies in embryo, and his view of union bureaucrats as administrators of capitalism.[67] For James, the working class itself in its own activity—and not its purported representatives—was the vehicle for an "invading socialist society" preparing the revolutions of tomorrow. A careful observer could discern this immanent resistance within quotidian experience and popular consciousness. Trade unions, Stalinism, and reformism were to Johnson-Forest not opponents of capitalism but bureaucratic counterparts to it: "State-property and total planning are nothing but the complete subordination of the proletariat to capital."[68] All of this is to emphasize that for Johnson-Forest the political corollary of the theory of state capitalism was an affirmation of the enduring revolutionary potentiality of the working class, East and West: "What we call the theory of state-capitalism is the theory of the proletariat as a class directed against capital and any agent of capital, in this case the bureaucracy."[69]

Conclusion: C. L. R. James and the Theory of State Capitalism

For James, the theory of state capitalism implied nothing less than a recasting of the whole of social theory. Even today the Johnson-Forest proposition is striking for its audacity. In the epoch of conservatism and neoliberalism, when nationalization and expropriation are forbidden in the public imagination, a radicalism unsatisfied by "mere confiscation" is something to behold.[70] Time and again, James asserted the revolutionary potential of the working class, believing that workers have an instinctual desire for free and creative labor. Liberation was to be found neither in the extension of the welfare state nor in Communist-bureaucratic regimes, but in "the creative power of the modern worker relieved from the status of proletarian."[71]

This revolutionary optimism inoculated James against resignation and defeatism. It also occluded sober appraisal of the conservatism that can run deep in working classes, an important subject for Marxist theory to face squarely. A danger of mysticism lurked in James's imagined worker, perpetually militant, always on the edge of spontaneous rebellion. The rank and file has often showed an interest in wages, benefits, and other economistic ambitions that are a reflection of their desire for security, not merely the preoccupation of the labor bureaucracy.[72] Furthermore, labor movements have often made demands upon the state. Resistance, rebellion, revolution, reformism, acquiescence, and even conservatism are *all* characteristics of working-class movements. Johnson-Forest mistook the revolutionary *potential* of the working class for its *essence*.

James's theory of state capitalism had grave analytical defects. The Johnson-Forest characterization of the Soviet Union alleged a capitalism without capitalists, a theory as counterintuitive as Trotsky's theory of a workers' state without worker control. Johnson-Forest downplayed important systemic differences between Nazism, Stalinism, and the United States, creating the impression that liberal and dictatorial states were, if not identical, more alike than different. They conflated systems in which capitalists dominated based on private property ownership with systems in which a bureaucracy controlled a state. When to this amalgam were added isomorphic phenomena such as trade union bureaucracies, "state capitalism" threatened to become a term directed against any top-down social structure opposed by revolutionaries. The Johnson-Forest claim that Stalinists in the U.S. and Western Europe were "deadly enemies of private property capitalism" did not jibe with the claim that state capitalism already existed in the West, for if state capitalism were already an established fact why would Communists need to challenge it?[73] These sorts of problems were magnified by the habitual Johnson-Forest resort to airy philosophical allusiveness whenever hard evidence and plain reasoning were warranted.

All the same, James's state capitalist theory had strengths. It placed labor, production, and work life at the center of social thought. It dispelled free-market and individualist mythologies by underscoring the role of the state in capitalist development. Dialectically, it unsettled many superficial antinomies—market and state, capital and regulation, economics and politics—still presumed today. If it was dubious when attached to Stalin's Soviet Union, "state capitalism" is more readily applicable to China today, where social explosions of the kind James imagined may be waiting just over the horizon. It may also hold insights into the present-day United States, where an individualist-competitive economy has been replaced by planned, coordinated conglomerates with a regulatory apparatus under business control, extensive links between state and private power, and policies by which profit is private while cost and risk are socialized—a system Noam Chomsky calls "state capitalist."[74]

Furthermore, James's insistence on direct producer democracy and his refusal to settle for any lesser vision of socialism preserved his revolutionary focus, sustaining his militancy across the 1940s and 1950s and making him a spiritual forerunner of 1960s radicalism. His emphasis on "self-emancipation"—self-directed activity from below—rendered him fully prepared for the uprisings in Hungary in 1956, France in 1968, and Poland in 1980–1981.[75] In each case, he observed, a militant working class exploded in revolutionary class struggle. Not only did it do so without the tutelage of a revolutionary party, but these mobilizations consciously repudiated the party form, instead creating workplace-based democratic councils or pluralistic revolutionary movements analogous to the original Russian soviets of 1905 and 1917. In this manner, James's opposition to Stalinism, liberalism, and social democracy in preference for more radically democratic approaches anticipated the antibureaucratic New Left. James's theory of state capitalism, sometimes seen as sheerly economic or about the "commanding heights," was in fact a perspective that led him and his disciples to approach society from the bottom up, keeping their ears open for rumblings of alienation and resistance in popular consciousness, leaving no sphere of culture or society unexamined, an approach that helped to transform social history and cultural criticism.[76]

This brings us back full circle to the matter of culture. James's theory of state capitalism, "Marxism of *our* period," was crucial to the entirety of his thought. While detained on Ellis Island prior to his 1953 deportation to Britain at the height of the McCarthy era, James wrote a small book on Herman Melville, a novelist he considered nonpareil. Only by recourse to his theory of state capitalism can we make sense of James's interpretation of Melville's *Moby Dick* (1851). Captain Ahab, he wrote, is the "embodiment of the totalitarian type," representative of the class of "administrators, executives, organizers, labor leaders, intellectuals" whose "purpose is to plan." Ahab in James's rendering was Hitlerian, a hierarchically fixated figure seeking a degree of control and domination leading inexorably to isolation, distrustfulness, and ultimate destructiveness. In obsessing over the White Whale, Ahab forsook easier prey that would have brought better market returns, and he put the ship at risk, revealing his contempt for the ship's owners and private property. Ahab's folly meets with resistance (though not rebellion) from the "meanest" mariners, renegades, and castaways, the lowly harpooners and crew, the workers whose life is grounded in the warmth, humor, community, and sanity of labor. Many—not by accident— were islanders and people of color. This, according to James, is what made Melville a writer far in advance of his time. In the contrast between Ahab's madness and his heroic subaltern crew, Melville anticipated the basic choice of modernity: "The voyage of the Pequod is the voyage of modern civilization seeking its destiny."[77] For C. L. R. James, civilization and culture were inseparable from production, class, and work life. For him, the Russian Question was an American Question, the American Question was a world question, and the most fertile answers to these questions could be expressed in shorthand as "state capitalism."

Oliver C. Cox and the Roots of World Systems Theory

Christopher A. McAuley

Although Oliver C. Cox never claimed to be a Marxist, he never denied being a socialist.[1] In many respects, the distinction he drew between Marxist and non-Marxist socialism was true to his own intellectual inclinations; he wanted the freedom to borrow from orthodox Marxism what he found useful and to modify it when and where its insights on unforeseen developments were limited. Cox's movement toward and away from Marxism largely followed the major political-economic developments of the period beginning with the Great Depression and continuing through the height of the Cold War. In that period, Cox's thinking on the sources of socialism underwent a profound transformation: no longer did he expect the working classes of the capitalist leader nations, as he called them, to inaugurate the charge, but rather that their counterparts in the former colonial world would do so. This shift was supported by the findings of his three-volume foray into what is now known as world systems theory: since imperialism has always been a mainstay of capitalism, the leading anticapitalists will continue to be drawn from the colonial or neocolonial world.

Background and Political Evolution

Oliver Cromwell Cox (1901–1974), the often-ignored sociologist who authored, among other works, *Caste, Class, and Race* (1948) and *The Foundations of Capitalism* (1959), was born into a lower-middle-class family in the then English colony of Trinidad. Cox's place of birth and its place in the British empire had a direct bearing on how he conceived of the capitalist world economy in the 1950s and 1960s, the subject of this essay. Although his father's income afforded him the privilege of attending primary school, Cox did not earn the grades necessary to continue on to St. Mary's College, the top Catholic school in the island. After a couple of years of taking odd jobs and attending an agricultural school, Cox's father decided to send the young Cox to the United States in 1919 to join two of his older brothers and to improve his future prospects.

Cox intended to take a law degree and return to Trinidad. After completing high school in Chicago, where his brothers had settled earlier, and attending Crane Junior College, Cox was accepted into Northwestern University, where he earned a bachelor of science in law degree in 1928. As far as we know, he intended to take his law degree from the same institution.

Then personal tragedy struck. In the year of the Great Depression, Cox was stricken with polio. For the rest of his life he moved with the aid of crutches. Aside from the loss of normal mobility, dashed too were his plans to become a lawyer and to return to Trinidad. Instead, he decided to remain in this country, where he would receive better health care, and to become an academic, a profession, he believed, that would require less physical movement than a legal career.[2] Toward this end, Cox enrolled in the economics department at the University of Chicago.

His initial field of study reflected one of the unintended consequences of his illness: the recognition that impersonal forces can shape a person's success or failure in larger measure than individual effort. In short, Cox was ridding himself of the middle-class individualism on which he was nursed in Trinidad, and he began looking to structural explanations of socioeconomic status. Of course, it is likely that the Depression alone would have forced him to re- or unthink what he had assumed to be "common sense" up to that point. Although his inchoate political ideas were not yet left-leaning, they were critical enough to compel him to leave the University of Chicago's economics department on the grounds that its faculty was unable to explain the causes of the Depression.[3]

If or why Cox thought that the study of sociology would have supplied him the answers he sought, he never said. In any event, based on the dates of publication of a significant portion of the works cited in *Caste, Class, and Race*, it is clear that Cox began reading leftist literature as a graduate student in the University of Chicago's sociology department. If we had to give Cox's political beliefs a name, New Deal/Popular Front socialist would be fitting. He was one for whom socialism is primarily the state direction or state ownership of key sectors of the economy, and fascism, capitalist rule stripped of its liberal trappings. Cox's long admiration of Franklin Delano Roosevelt and of the Soviet Union reflected this worldview.[4]

While in graduate school in the mid-1930s Cox began to contest the manner in which his professors interpreted race relations in the United States generally and in the American South specifically. In the opinion of the University of Chicago's then best-known sociologist, Robert Park, Southern race relations were little different from the caste system as he believed it to operate in India. For Park and other subscribers to the "caste school" of Southern race relations, the primary markers of caste relations were the severe sanctions (de jure and de facto) against intermarriage between members of different races and against their taking meals together. Park's ideas on Southern race relations were largely formed during the "seven winters" between 1905 and 1912 that he spent "partly at Tuskegee, but partly roaming about the South, getting acquainted with the life, the customs, and the condition of the Negro people."[5] Aside from the work he did as Booker T. Washington's ghostwriter, Park admitted that the experience fed his

interest in the Negro in the South and in the curious and intricate system which had grown up to define his relations with white folk. I was interested, most of all, in studying the details of the process by which the Negro was making and has made his slow but steady advance. I became convinced, finally, that I was observing the historical process by which civilization, not merely here but elsewhere, has evolved, drawing into the circle of influence an ever widening circle of races and peoples.[6]

Although younger scholars may have shared neither Park's vision nor his optimism, his articles on race relations in general and Southern race relations in particular in the 1910s, '20s, and '30s inspired their own contributions a decade or two later. The most notable of these works are Charles S. Johnson's *Shadow of the Plantation* (1934), John Dollard's *Caste and Class in a Southern Town* (1937), Hortense Powdermaker's *After Freedom* (1939), and Allison Davis and Burleigh and Mary Gardner's *Deep South* (1941). Cox also found these and related works indispensable to the study of Southern race relations.[7]

He objected, nonetheless, to the use of the term "caste" to characterize Southern race relations, on the grounds that the system of social stratification in India is based on other variables besides sanctions on exogamy and commensality. From his study of the Indian caste system, his recollections of how that system continued to operate in the Indian communities of his native Trinidad,[8] and his conversations with members of these communities and other Trinidadians,[9] Cox concluded that the variable that distinguishes the caste system from other forms of social stratification is its foundation in the sacred. "Caste relationships," he wrote in *Caste, Class, and Race*, "are not only right but also sacred—and sacred to all Hindus, regardless of caste position."[10] Elsewhere, he remarked: "Not by accident are men unequal, not by luck or by variations in personal effort, not because of differences in race or defeat in war, but because of the Divine Plan in the creation of the social order."[11] Nevertheless, individual behavior influences even the "Divine Plan," for it is one's conduct in past lives that determines one's current caste standing. Thus, "birth in a given caste is no accident. The individual, on the basis of his works in a former life, merits his status. Indeed, it may be said that he so lived, then, that he consciously selected his present natal caste."[12]

Although neither Park nor any other caste school member went so far as to claim that Southern race relations were grounded in the sacred, Park himself naturalized them by explaining their origins as the "products of migration and conquest," as "true of the ancient world" as it is "of the modern."[13] Elsewhere he asserted that race relations exist in "all those situations in which some relatively stable equilibrium between competing races has been achieved and in which the resulting social order has become fixed in custom and tradition."[14] In Cox's mind, these assertions suggested not only that the "beginnings of modern race prejudice may be traced to the immemorial periods of human associations,"[15] but that Southern Blacks in particular had largely accepted their social subordination in Southern society. As Cox saw it, although one could draw this last conclusion from the public face that Southern Blacks customarily wore, it did not explore their inner feelings behind the stoic mask. On this score, he remarked that the "caste interpretation of race relations in the South cannot see that the intermarriage restriction laws are a social affront to Negroes, it cannot perceive that Negroes are smarting under the Jim Crow laws; and it may not recognize the overwhelming aspiration among Negroes for equality of social opportunity."[16]

When one takes these feelings into account, one necessarily ceases to describe a caste system, for they are proof that the subordinate population rejects the ideological justification of its social position. Park's obtuseness on the ideological underpinnings of the caste system allowed him to make the following claim without any recognition of its internal contradiction: "On the whole . . . race prejudice in the Southern states is caste prejudice. If the Negro were content to remain in a subordinate position to which the white man's prejudices . . . assigned him, racial animosities would probably not exist."[17]

However, what Cox found most troubling about the caste interpretation of Southern race relations were its political implications. Two of these are most relevant for our discussion: the minimization of racial violence and the promotion of the belief that the perpetrators of racial violence are the primary shapers of Southern race relations.

One searches in vain in Park's writings for a presentation of Southern racial violence that is more than episodic when it is mentioned at all. Cox found this underestimation of racial violence not merely an apology for its occurrence, but a case of mythmaking, since by it one skirts the fact that the "Southern racial system 'lives, moves, and has its being' in a thick matrix of organized violence."[18] The cruelest form of this violence is lynching, a subject to which Cox devoted a thorough analysis in *Caste, Class, and Race.*[19] Of course, Park's omission of racial violence is understandable in light of the challenges its consideration poses to a caste interpretation of Southern race relations: violence is only needed when "tradition" fails to circumscribe behavior. For this reason Cox concluded that the caste school "seeks to explain a 'normal society' in the South. In short, it has made peace with the hybrid society that has not secured harmony for itself; and in so far as this is true, its work is fictitious."[20]

The matter of racial violence raises Cox's second political objection to the caste interpretation of Southern race relations. According to its adherents, the rank and file of a lynch mob forces affluent whites to agree with the "verdict" that the former reached. Thus, as the caste school imagined the social scenario, the lowest class of the white caste—poor whites—harbors the greatest resentment of ambitious blacks. Cox thought that this reading of Southern racism was an inversion of the truth. In his assessment of the situation, affluent Southern whites have the most to gain from the continuation of the racial division between working-class blacks and whites since it keeps wages low and virtually nullifies working-class collective action. "We may take it as axiomatic," Cox declared with some irony, "that never in the history of the world have poor people set and maintained dominant social policy in a society."[21]

Cox made these views public only after he had left graduate school, particularly in his 1948 classic, *Caste, Class, and Race*. In graduate school, he "lay low" and submitted an uncharacteristically apolitical 1938 doctoral dissertation, "Factors Affecting the Marital Status of Negroes in the United States." After having published a number of articles drawn from his dissertation, Cox followed these with another set critiquing those scholars who likened Southern race relations to the Indian caste system. The manner in which he argued his points, however, earned him the Marxist label in a staunchly anti-Marxist era.

For Cox, race relations are the product of a capitalist division of labor in which physically or culturally distinct populations by and large occupy specific class positions. Born in the expropriation of Amerindian lands and the enslavement of African peoples by European colonizers, this social order has been justified ideologically by capitalist elites as reflecting the intellectual or physical capacities of the populations so stratified. Accordingly, Cox defined racism as the "socio-attitudinal matrix supporting a calculated and determined effort of a white ruling class to keep some people or peoples of color and their resources exploitable. . . . Thus race prejudice may be thought of as having its genesis in the propagandistic and legal contrivances of the white ruling class for securing mass support of its interest."[22] Moreover, Cox asserted that racial identification and membership depend on the relative populations of the dominant and subordinate groups in a given capitalist society. In the Americas, whenever the population of European descent is less than 10 percent of the national total, mixed-race people constitute a separate racial category and thereby act as the stabilizer of the two racial poles. Cox called this "situation" of race relations the ruling-class one, familiar to him from his upbringing in Trinidad. By contrast, in what Cox called the bipartite situation of race relations, where the subordinate groups of color comprise more than 10 percent of the national total, mixed-race people enjoy few if any privileges for their lighter complexion and are identified by the dominant racial group as members of the subordinate group. The United States was Cox's model of the bipartite situation of race relations.[23] Among other practical results, racial categories maintain social divisions between subordinate populations whose combined efforts could literally shake the foundations of the capitalist social hierarchy. Consequently, Cox concluded that capitalist elites were not only the founders of racial distinctions, but the principal perpetuators of racism as well.

The tone and the pointed anticapitalist remarks in *Caste, Class, and Race* indicate that Cox could not see capitalism surviving long past the close of World War II. Convinced that the lessons learned about the capitalist system by the Western working class during the Depression and the global war against fascism would provoke it to fulfill the historic role Marx had prescribed for it, Cox believed that capitalism's days were numbered. However, when it became clear to him by midcentury that the working-class revolution was not going to materialize anytime soon, he was forced to make a choice: to continue to adhere to a Marxist understanding of the nature of capitalism and the social conditions which lend themselves to the transition to socialism or to formulate an alternative approach that would better explain capitalism's staying power. As we know, Cox opted for the latter, and some see in the fruits of his efforts—*The Foundations of Capitalism* (1959), *Capitalism and American Leadership* (1962), and *Capitalism as a System* (1964)—the elements of what would later be called "world systems theory," or in Cox's own description of his project, "a system or network of national and territorial units bound together by commercial and exploitative relationships . . . weighted in favor of the most powerful nations."[24] However, in order to understand how he came to this new outlook on the capitalist world economy, we must address two influences in Cox's life in the 1950s: Harry Truman and Henri Pirenne.

The Making of a World Systems Perspective

In *Caste, Class, and Race*, Cox detailed the ideological attacks that political conservatives leveled at everyone from liberals to leftists to stem the tide of what they understood to be "communism" in the 1930s and 1940s. One instance took place at the University of Chicago while Cox was a graduate student there. In the fall semester of 1934, the millionaire drugstore chain owner Charles Walgreen withdrew his eighteen-year-old niece from the university when he learned that she was being exposed to leftist ideas in her social science classes. Sensationalized by the local press, the Illinois State Senate launched an investigation into Walgreen's allegations. Subpoenaed to testify were faculty members and university president Robert Maynard Hutchins. Apparently, this instance of red baiting failed to garner public support, for the matter was quickly dropped. Cox, nevertheless, drew the following conclusions from what had transpired:

The value of these witch hunts is to elicit a public denial of any communistic tendencies on the part of the faculty and to condition it to shy away from any investigation of vital social problems unless it is apparent that its conclusions will be in glorification or in resigned acceptance of the status quo. It is fairly certain that the social sciences, having experienced such panic and warning, will thereafter tend toward scholastic ruminations and statistical refinements of inconsequential details.[25]

Characteristically, Cox refused to heed his own warnings and proceeded to expose the American capitalist elite's role in the creation of social problems and in the reproduction of social divisions. As a result, he briefly feared being called before the House Un-American Activities Committee. Yet, this, the most infamous of all the "red scares" since the Bolshevik Revolution, began, as Cox duly noted, in the realm of foreign policy before it boomeranged home. In Cox's mind, at the center of this maelstrom was Harry Truman.

As Cox reports in his second volume on the capitalist world economy, *Capitalism and American Leadership*, when Truman assumed the presidency in April 1945 he took pains to reassure the American public that he would not deviate from the policies of the recently deceased Franklin Delano Roosevelt. Like his predecessor, Truman railed against "'big business,' the 'concentration of wealth and power,' 'the money changers,' 'organized selfish interests,' "the hatred of a 'special class' for the 'welfare of the people' . . . the 'reactionaries who fear that their profits would be reduced,' and a host of other anti-capitalist allusions and suggestions."[26]

However, Truman limited this rhetoric to domestic politics. In foreign affairs, Truman and likeminded public officials labeled communist those movements, parties, or governments which made the same critique of domestic and transnational capital. Whereas the Fair Deal president offered his constituents left-liberal rhetoric on domestic issues, he categorically rejected attempts on the part of weaker nations to put those ideas into practice by alternately winning them over with the carrot of aid and investment (the Marshall Plan, etc.) or threatening them with the stick of military intervention (the Truman Doctrine). As Cox underscored, Truman was long unaware of how his indiscriminate anticommunist charge could be used by his political opponent to undermine his Fair Deal at home. Their argument was simple: if only "communist" forces seek to curtail corporate enterprise abroad, then the same must be true at home. Thus, Cox remarked, "In foreign relations the President became the mouthpiece of his own powerful domestic adversaries."[27] Still, there was a way of unifying these ostensibly opposed political positions: through defense spending.

As Cox saw it, when Truman moved to reduce the defense budget as part of the normal reconversion to a peace economy, he discovered that the unemployment rate actually increased rather than declining or remaining unchanged. According to the figures Cox referenced, the "total monthly average of unemployed workers increased from 670,000 in 1944 to 3,395,000 in 1949, and the number was still rising in the first half of 1950. In other words, an acute recession was apparently under way."[28] It was only in the opening year of the Korean War that "unemployment fell to 1,879,000."[29] The cause of the reduction was lost on neither Truman nor the American business community: only warfare or war preparedness could at once reduce unemployment and stimulate economic growth. "What seemed to be needed," remarked Cox, "was a continually rising military outlay commensurate with the rise in gross national product."[30] However, since the formal decision to go to war and even the informal one to prepare for the possibility is not made by private enterprise, only the federal government has the authority to set this economic process in motion by awarding contracts to armament firms. Accordingly, Cox understood the Cold War and its domestic counterpart, the Red Scare, as a two-front economic plan: an effective marketing campaign for the institutionalization of the military-industrial complex, a mélange of the New Deal and a simulated wartime economy. Cox summarized this development like this:

Since . . . up to 1949 no anti-depression substitute for war expenditure had been worked out, the business community itself began seriously to analyze the trend and apparently reached the consensus that to ensure economic stability by sufficient Government spending for security purposes a continuous state of emergency would be necessary. . . . Government spending for military purposes, then—usually referred to as security or defense—became the principal and most critical reliance in support of the capitalistic system.[31]

Like other commentators of the era, Cox recognized the added political benefit of defense spending: the winning over of the wallets and minds of formerly militant workers.[32] With this and other examples in mind, he would later conclude that the capitulation to capital is typical of working classes in economically advanced countries.

While Cox was taking stock of the post-World War II American scene and theorizing about the world capitalist economy under its leadership, he was also exploring the origins of capitalism in the European past. In this endeavor, the work of the renowned Belgian historian Henri Pirenne were as central to Cox's thoughts as Truman's actions were to his ideas on Cold War America. With this claim, I do not mean to reduce Cox's intellectual inspiration on the roots of capitalism to a single thinker (a mere glance at the bibliography of *The Foundations of Capitalism* shows that his references were vast and varied), but to suggest that one of the main sources of his description of medieval Europe in *Caste, Class, and Race* was also instrumental to his later thoughts on the subject.

Virtually all of Cox's references to Pirenne's work in *Caste, Class, and Race*, appear in the eighth and ninth chapters, "Estates" and "From Estate to Social Class." Among other objectives, Cox sought to show that the pre-French Revolution system of estates (which he defined as a "number of persons forming a social-status stratum more or less clearly defined from other strata in customary or statutory law . . . [and] having expressed or implied legal claims to some degree of importance in the government") was static because it was legally reinforced and "correlates directly with the extent of landowner-ship."[33] Furthermore, in a world where "production was largely localized and in a number of virtually self-sufficient units," Cox saw little possibility of capitalism or some other alternative social system emerging from and overtaking the estate system."[34] "There were great commercial cities," he continued on the theme, "but the agricultural communities were very much greater still and they always dominated the society."[35] For such reasons Cox could not date the origins of capitalism before the Industrial and French Revolutions or until capitalism "gained complete ascendancy over the 'nat-ural economy' based upon land" as a result of the former, and "shatter[ed]" the estates system and launched the "ascendance of individualism" as a result of the latter.[36] Nevertheless, we should note that in the 1940s Cox was rather indifferent to the dating of capitalism's origins, remarking that, "We do not know, of course, when capitalism originated; some form of com-mercial capitalism—buying and selling rationally for profit—has probably always been known in market places."[37] However, soon after these words were published, what was a source of indifference became a decade-long preoccupation.

It was only after Cox had concluded in the early 1950s that the anticipated working-class upheaval in the industrialized West would not materialize, that he felt compelled to rethink both his ideas about capitalism and the social forces that would undermine it. On the first of these matters, Pirenne was undoubtedly helpful. For not only did he forcefully argue in (among other works) *Economic and Social History of Medieval Europe* that commercial capitalism is integral to industrial capitalism, he also showed that its roots can be traced to medieval Europe. In the 1940s, Cox resisted these claims. However, in revisiting Pirenne in the following decade, he may have been struck by the following passage:

Strange though it may seem, medieval commerce developed from the beginning under the influence not of local but of export trade. It was this alone which gave birth to that class of professional merchants which was the chief instrument of the economic revival of the eleventh and twelfth centuries. In both parts of Europe where it started, Northern Italy and the Low Countries, the story is the same. The impetus was given by long-distance trade. This is clear directly when we examine the nature of the goods carried, for all were of foreign origin, and indeed early medieval commerce bears a certain resemblance to colonial trade.[38]

One of these commodities, Cox would later discover, was sugar cane, and the Venetian plantation colonies of Crete and Cyprus, in Immanuel Waller-stein's words, "played the same role vis-à-vis Venice that the Indies would later play vis-à-vis Spain, then England."[39] To a scholar from the Caribbean these historical similarities must have struck a chord, and perhaps drove him to the conclusion that Venice is the birthplace of capitalism.

Both examples revealed other elements that Cox thought essential to capitalism. One of these is fairly obvious: the reduction of many social formations to mere suppliers of raw materials for the commercial and consumptive needs of the capitalist leaders. Of course, colonies like Crete and Trinidad were, by design, just this. However, even politically independent societies frequently became neocolonies of Venice. In marketing their goods throughout the Mediterranean, Venetian merchants indirectly strengthened the political power of those sectors of the producer nations that supplied them. In this manner, Venetian traders sometimes created, and always emboldened foreign allies whose political-economic interests coincided with their own.

Venice's imperialistic relationship with its Mediterranean colonies also illustrates another characteristic of capitalistic international relations: the capitalist leaders' objective to "export the products of foreign peoples and to supply them with goods from abroad."[40] This type of commercial intervention between social formations Cox termed "provisioning," by which the Venetians were able to factor into the prices of the commodities they distributed a considerable charge for their services. Thus Cox concluded that "One of the characteristics of leadership . . . is that the capitalist nation thus situated controls the most demanded and consequently indispensable articles of world trade."[41]

Of course, all of this commercial activity required the development of the city's primary transportation industry, shipbuilding. "It was in the shipbuilding industry," Cox underscored in his discussion of the Venetian case, "that Venice evinced most clearly the strains of capitalist industrial enterprise. Here emerged large-scale organization for efficient factory production with specialization of skills, under the direction of both private and State enterprise."[42] The most visible proof of the Venetian commitment to shipbuilding was its Arsenal, the shipbuilding and ship-repairing complex that "gradually became the world's largest industrial organization, employing thousands of workers and spreading over sixty acres of 'ground and water.'"[43]

Still, what is important to note in this brief sketch of the trading world in which Cox saw the "foundations of capitalism," was the Venetian Republic's ability to structure the incipient capitalist "world" economy such that it supplied surrounding polities with the most important of their service and commodity requirements. To these social formations, Cox gave the names *subsidiaries, progressives, dependents,* and *passives.* In this hierarchical schema, the Hanseatic League and perhaps Genoa rated as subsidiaries of Venice since of the three only Venice was "least subject to the economic restraints and plans of other nations, while it [was] most influential in altering the affairs of others in its own interests."[44] Into the category of the progressives, Cox placed the urban republics of Florence and Amalfi, for "each [had] . . . ambitions and capabilities for development somewhat similar to those" of Venice. The various kingdoms, principalities, duchies, and even caliphates with which the Venetians conducted trade, he considered the dependents and passives of the system. While the former exhibited "little self-initiative in foreign commerce and [were] subject to the immediate, self-interested, economic calculations of the great powers," the latter were "regarded by the leading powers as having no international rights . . . and their resources were organized directly with a view to the enhancement of the economic welfare of any active capitalist nations that was able to establish and maintain control."[45]

Finally, we should mention Venice's political structure and what role Cox thought that it played in ensuring the city-state's economic success. Unlike the duchies, principalities, and kingdoms that surrounded it, Venice was a republic. The closest that it came to having a monarch was in the person of the doge (duke), but the title was neither hereditary nor unhindered by a number of formal restrictions imposed by three representative bodies, the general assembly (Concio or Arengo) and the Ducal and Great Councils. Cox believed that this political arrangement enabled Venice to avoid falling prey to the neocolonialist designs of its rivals, given that monarchs and other autocrats are wont to enter into commercial contracts with foreign merchants to secure sorely needed money or coveted commodities in exchange for trade concessions. "Capitalist foreign traders," Cox asserted on the theme, "in their drive for commercial privileges, have from earliest times to the present day made strategic use of gifts to autocrats. The giving of presents, that seducer of unwary chieftains, has been good business. . . . It was in this peaceful way that a bare handful of capitalist merchants succeeded in striking off the heads of some of the most powerful backward states."[46] Thus, to the degree that one-person rule lends itself to the disregard of economic nationalism, shared governance typically promotes it. Little wonder, then, that nonleader nations have frequently been ruled by autocrats when they are not outright colonies of capitalist leader nations.

Although Venice was the leading pole of capitalism in medieval Europe and the city-state to which Cox devoted the most pages in *The Foundations of Capitalism*, it was not the only one. What the Venetians were able to do first in the Aegean and then in the Mediterranean, the Hanseatic League was able to do in the Baltic. Nevertheless, "powerful as they were in the north," Cox was sure to comment, "they were still pupils among the Venetians."[47]

The Hanseatic League or Community was a coalition of German-speaking merchants that dominated Baltic Sea trade in the late medieval/early modern eras and at its height could boast of representatives from over 150 cities. The Hansards drew on two inspirations: the seafaring warrior-trader tradition of the Vikings and what we may call the northern crusade, equal in intensity and ferocity as that waged against the Moors in the Levant. Thus the Hanseatic conquest was by both land and by sea.

Apart from those instances of outright military conquest, the Hansards won their position in the Baltic arena through a combination of tactics: the transshipment of western Baltic goods to the eastern Baltic and vice versa; the provision of loans to insolvent monarchs; and the ability to effectively boycott any trade partner that expressed economic nationalism or class contentiousness. The effectiveness of these measures relied, of course, on the strength of the Hansards' shipping industries.

We can be sure, once again, that Cox took note of the parallels between Trinidad's economic relationship with an imperial England and a younger England's economic relationship with the Hansards. Both situations were founded on contracts between colonial or indigenous elites and foreign merchants by whose terms the host territories agreed to supply agricultural and/or mineral raw materials to the foreign merchants who coordinated both the processing or manufacture of those materials and their distribution throughout the Baltic and Atlantic arenas.

In the case of England, what the Hansards sought was wool. Superior in quality to most other grades, English wool fed the fine woolens industries of Flanders and northern Italy. Before the eleventh century, English pastures supplied a national woolens industry that had achieved international renown. However, with the growth of production in Flanders after that date, English wool farmers, thinking more in monetary than nationalistic terms, did not hesitate to supply Flanders woolens manufacturers by way of foreign merchants, some of whom became Hansards. This incipient neo-colonial relationship between the Hanseatic League and the English crown had reached maturity in the fourteenth century when Edward III awarded a select group of English wool merchants (who became the Fellowship or Company of the Staple) not only the exclusive right to export English wool, but also an exclusive site (Calais) where foreign buyers could purchase English wool. Thus, without a shipping industry to rival Hanseatic and Italian carriers, every increase in England's raw wool production was, in effect, a greater net gain for the Hanseatic and Italian carrying trades than it was for English producers.

The important economic point to be drawn from this scenario is that as long as the Hansard arrangement with the English crown endured, England remained both a supplier of raw wool, and later even of woolens to the Baltic economy, and not a distributor of its own products. The English economy was only able to come "out from underdevelopment," to borrow James Mittelman's clever title, after the crown in the fifteenth century chartered the Company of Merchant Adventurers to rival the Hanseatic League; closed the Hansard's London kontor at the end of the sixteenth; outlawed the "export of English wool in 1614";[48] and assigned England's extra-European colonies the task of supplying agricultural and mineral raw materials to be processed by English manufacturers and distributed by English merchants. In other words, it was at the moment that English merchants, like the Hansards before them, secured "among foreigners all the commercial advantages it denied them,"[49] that the process of England's economic development began. This perspective explains Cox's contention that "the Germans thus served as the immediate, though unwilling, instructors of the English in the capitalist practices and organizations."[50]

From this synopsis of Cox's treatment of the two sites where he believed capitalism originated in late medieval Europe, we can isolate at least five elements essential to its development and reproduction. One, that the capitalist world economy is composed of *leaders, subsidiaries, progressives, dependents,* and *passives,* structured such that the first two supply the rest with the most important of their service and commodity requirements. Two, that provisioning or "securing the consumptive needs of a [foreign] people,"[51] is an essential role of a capitalist power. Three, that transportation industries must be the leading sectors of all a capitalist power's industries. Four, that colonial or neocolonial trade relations with commercially weaker social formations are the bases of a capitalist power's economic strength. And finally, that in a capitalist society, business interests, if not business people themselves, must dominate the sites of political power.

This is hardly an exhaustive list, but it captures Cox's contention that leaders, subsidiaries, and progressives have been those nations most able to make as many other societies as possible into their colonies or neocolonies; the leader is simply the nation-state with the greatest number of them. By Cox's definition, colonies and neocolonies are societies whose products (ideally in their raw state) and the services necessary for their exchange (transportation, financing, wholesaling, etc.) are owned by firms in leader, subsidiary, or progressive nations. These are the economic terms of the political arrangements made between the ruling strata of colonial and neocolonial societies and the representatives of colonizing and neocolonizing interests.

Of course, such a conceptualization of the pillars of the capitalist system was the result not only of Cox's academic meditations on the history of late medieval Europe, but also of his lived experiences as a British colonial subject and an immigrant in the United States. In short, Cox formulated a model of capitalism drawn from Europe's imperial history in the African, Amerindian, and Asian worlds beginning in the sixteenth century. In the course of plumbing that history, Cox apparently uncovered even earlier examples of similar political-economic processes within Europe itself. In his estimation, European merchants merely applied to a wider world the techniques perfected by their predecessors in the Mediterranean and Baltic arenas in the late medieval era. Cox's theory, then, on the origins and maintenance of the capitalist world economy was simultaneously a "third" and "first" world perspective at least a decade before world systems theory burst on to the academic scene.[52]

It is also important to note how Cox's theory of the origins and structure of capitalism differs from others. Unlike those which locate capitalism's origins in the emergence of a class conflict between landlords, tenant farm-ers, and dispossessed laborers (à la Marx) or of profit-seeking exchange between rational actors within and between societies (à la Weber), Cox's begins with the premise that imperialism "provide[s] its very base, its broad structural underpinning."[53] For Cox, however, imperialism did not mean what it meant to J. A. Hobson and Vladimir Lenin. Whereas these last mainly thought of imperialism as mid- to late nineteenth-century British and French territorial acquisition in, financial domination of, and capital exportation to Africa and Asia, Cox maintained that the "prime object of imperialism is the monopolization of the major productive capacity and the foreign trade of weaker countries."[54] Moreover, like other scholars from the Caribbean, Cox could not see limiting imperialism to the nineteenth century; after all, its roots in the region date from the early sixteenth cen-tury. Imperialism "is not, as sometimes thought," he declared, "a late nine-teenth century development; rather, it has gone hand and hand with the rise of the capitalist system as a necessary component."[55]

Finally, Cox insisted that capitalism be understood as a system, to borrow one of his own titles, not as a mode of production in a single country. Cox located the origins of capitalism in thirteenth-century Venice precisely be-cause the maritime republic had created an international system based on the political-economic vulnerabilities first of neighboring Aegean countires and then of far-flung Mediterranean polities. From the Venetian example and those of subsequent capitalist leader nations, Cox drew the conclusion that the "wealth of a leading capitalist nation is not entirely, or sometimes even mainly, accumulated from the exploitation of domestic workers," but is "based significantly on economic relations with backward countries."[56] Here, in short, is the secret of capitalism's staying power and the reason for its ability to withstand the challenges of the Great Depression and World War II in the twentieth century.

In the 1959 preface of *The Foundations of Capitalism*, the first volume of his trilogy on the world capitalist economy, Cox offered three tentative, almost hypothetical motives for such an undertaking: to provide a scholarly sketch of capitalism's "characteristics," such as he felt lacking in the avail-able literature on the subject; to elaborate on the contention that "race relations are a feature exclusively of capitalism," one of the main themes of *Caste, Class, and Race*; and finally, to map capitalism's "cyclical movements" over time.[57] Ultimately, Cox addressed only the first and third of these objectives in the trilogy, devoting a mere twenty pages to the explicit dis-cussion of race relations in *Capitalism and American Leadership*, the second volume.[58] But Cox's public rationale for having undertaken the project did not entirely reflect his private, personal motivations, which were fare more political. With the decline of working-class militancy in the capitalist leader nation in the 1950s before the combined might of the Red Scare and the Cold War, and the resilience of the capitalist system to withstand the blows of the Great Depression and World War II, Cox sought to locate a replacement for the industrial working class to spur the transition to socialism. By his last volume of the trilogy, *Capitalism as a System*, he found one in the working classes of what he termed the "backward" nations of the world capitalist economy.

It is not hard to discern how Cox arrived at this conclusion. In light of imperialism's pivotal role in the creation and maintenance of capitalism, Cox drew two related conclusions: that "in leading capitalist nations . . . workers tend to become participants in foreign exploitation";[59] and that the "backward peoples are the real exploited and exploitable proletariat of the system."[60] More important, however, than even these structural observations were the political ideologies to which the working classes of the two types of nations named above adhered. In the first case, Cox asserted:

The working class in a leading nation . . . has sufficient reason to walk arm in arm with its oligarchy against the world. On imperialistic questions, we should ordinarily expect this class to be nationalistic, because a threat to the imperial position of the nation tends to become a threat to its own welfare. The class struggle thus goes on at home . . . for a larger share of the national income. But it is a struggle that tends to stop at the water's edge where antagonisms with rival imperialists and exploited backward peoples begin. The working people of a leading capitalist nation are likely to rise up in wrath against those of their fellows who disclaim the imperialist actions of the government, regarding them as traitors.[61]

In other words, with more to gain from demanding a larger share of the capitalist pie than from following a new social recipe altogether, the working classes of leading capitalist nations "have been essentially reformists from the beginning," and have remained, along with their employers, imperialistic in economic and political outlook.[62] By contrast, the working classes of what Cox calls the "backward" nations of the capitalist world economy tend to be more revolution- or socialist-prone because unlike their wealthier counterparts, "they have no valuable exploitative claims abroad to relinquish."[63] Lacking colonies or neocolonies from which to draw profits, the "social situation in the major backward countries is such that revolution is not only indicated, but also feasible and largely profitable. Hence revolutionary solidarity seems far more easily attainable among them. Their successes will bring not only a change in the economic orientation and organization of the advanced capitalist nations, but also a new perspective on the benefits of planned economies to workers everywhere."[64]

Cox's departure from Marx's early designation that the English working class would spearhead the revolutionary overthrow of capitalism, is reminiscent of Marx's own abandonment of this formulation in his later years. Observing the reformism of Victorian-era British labor, Marx also set his sights on other potentially revolutionary social formations.[65] Although their reasoning differed, Cox and Marx agreed that Russia and countries like it were possible sites of socialist revolutions. Neither one, however, tackled the difficult issue of how socialist accumulation can occur in societies characterized by huge agricultural populations, miniscule industrial sectors, and equally small commercial classes. Still their willingness to modify their earlier political convictions in order to engage with new social realities is nothing less than commendable.

From the time of his political awaking in the 1930s to the year of his death in 1974, Cox held firmly to the belief that a socialist world would be more democratic and materially satisfying for the majority of its inhabitants than our current capitalist one. But as we have seen in this chapter, when a socialist revolution failed to materialize in the industrialized West, either during the Great Depression or just after World War II, Cox led a generation of fellow leftists, during the 1950s and afterward, to search for new sites of revolutionary engagement. In many respects, then, his trilogy on the capitalist world economy can be considered an empirical and theoretical grounding for the idea of a revolutionary "third world" so popular within the late New Left. And it bears repeating that Cox centered his theory on what we may call capitalist imperialism, or the monopolization by leader and subsidiary nations of what economists blandly refer to as "services" (transportation, wholesaling, banking, insurance, etc.) of the most important commodities in the world economy.

In other words, it is in the distribution rather than in the actual production of commodities that the lion's share of capitalist profit is realized. Accordingly, workers in these industries will not undermine the sources of their livelihood when discontent over wages, duties, or benefits arises. At most, they want to have their grievances met in an incremental, reformist fashion. Cox therefore concluded that only those workers, largely in agriculture and extractive industries, who labored in dependent and passive nations could initiate truly transformative revolutionary movements, designed in part to win control of the exchange of national exports and imports. In this regard, socialist revolutions in the third world were also nationalist revolutions that could transform a world system dominated by a set of imperialist countries whose own nationalist self-interest denied real self-determination to the vast majority of the planet's population.

Feminism, Women's History, and American Social Thought at Midcentury

Daniel Horowitz

The development of women's history between 1956 and 1969 reflected and helped reshape postwar American social thought. The links that historians have recently made between union activity and the Old Left in the 1940s and second wave feminism in the 1960s are apparent in key writings about women's history.[1] The debt four major figures—Carl Degler, Eleanor Flexner, Aileen Kraditor, and Gerda Lerner—owed to the Marxist feminism they learned early in their lives helps us understand many of the questions they asked and the answers they offered on a whole range of issues, including the relationship between capitalism and women's lives.

This chapter charts the first phase of the reemergence of women's history, before the arrival of a younger generation of historians that took its bearings from the revival of feminism in the late 1960s. Central to the work of these four more senior historians was the connection between what they experienced in the Old Left and the feminism of the 1960s. Early in their careers, these four writers saw capitalism as a force that oppressed women in ways that only socialism could remedy. By the 1960s they paid much less attention to the power of economic forces and focused instead on gender, patriarchy, and race.

The encounters of Degler, Flexner, Kraditor, and Lerner with anti-fascism and Marxism in the 1930s and 1940s shaped their careers and writings. What they read early in their lives gave capitalism a central role in their vision of the forces that both oppressed and liberated women. Beginning as early as the mid-1950s, however, as they reconsidered their commitment to a Marxist critique of capitalism, they rethought their assumptions about the relationship of economic forces and social justice. Ideological consistency over decades is not necessarily a virtue, especially given revelations of the horrors of Stalinism in the Soviet Union, the dramatic recovery of the American economy in the postwar years, and changes in the lives of African Americans and women. The careers of these four historians illuminate the complicated personal and ideological factors that caused them, especially after the late 1960s, to take different paths—sometimes dramatically different ones. Above all, this chapter explores one of the reasons gender gained importance in American social thought, to a considerable extent displacing capitalism from the predominant position it had held in the 1940s.

The Development of Feminist Consciousness, 1935–1955

These four writers had much in common, but a number of factors differentiated Eleanor Flexner (1908–1995) from the others: she was the oldest of them, the one who grew up in the most privileged circumstances, and the one whose participation in the Old Left generally and the Communist Party specifically was the most sustained. Early in the Depression, soon after she graduated college, she was horrified by the suffering of others she witnessed in Manhattan but was personally protected by her parents' wealth. Joining the Communist Party in 1935, from the early 1930s until the mid-1950s Flexner participated in a wide range of radical causes, focusing on social justice for African Americans, the working class, trade unionists, and women. The party drafted her to serve, from 1946 to 1948, as executive secretary for the Congress of American Women (CAW), the Popular Front feminist organization driven out of existence in 1950 soon after the Justice Department placed it on its list of subversive organizations. From 1950 to 1954, using pseudonyms that were more obviously Jewish than her own (her father was born Jewish; her mother was from a Protestant background), she wrote and taught on women's issues and women's history in publications and at the Communist Party's Jefferson School of Social Science in New York. In 1953–54 she offered a course there, relying on *The Woman Question: Selections from the Writings of Karl Marx, Frederick Engels, V. I. Lenin, Joseph Stalin* (1951). Her activism exposed her to the sexual discrimination against working women, including what she personally experienced from both employers and male activists on the left; it was one of the many factors that caused her to leave the party in 1956. In the mid-1950s, Flexner began to work on a book on the history of women in the United States that that would make the lives of African American and working-class women central to the stories of conflict she dramatized. In 1957, with Helen Terry, her "beloved companion" of thirty years, Flexner moved to Northampton so she could do research in the Sophia Smith Collection at Smith College.[2]

Carl Neumann Degler (1921-), born in Orange, New Jersey and raised by American-born Lutheran parents of German and Swiss ancestry, differed from others under consideration in several ways, including the fact that he was a man and never joined the party. Degler became politicized in the early 1940s during his last two years at Upsala College. Many of his closest friends were Jews whom he later affectionately called "semi-Commies," identifying himself as an anti-fascist who was "pretty close" to the party. His friends persuaded him to read Marxist-socialist literature, including August Bebel's immensely popular book on women and socialism, originally published in

1879. Degler developed an interest in African American history and led a campus protest against racial discrimination. After a stint in the military during World War II, Degler earned his Ph.D. in 1952 from Columbia under Richard Morris. Although Degler remained politically active during graduate school, picketing the anti-union Senator Robert Taft and passing out copies of the *Daily Worker*, like many vets on the GI Bill he focused mainly on launching his career.[3]

In his dissertation, "Labor in the Economy and Politics of New York City, 1850–1860," Degler both drew on and distanced himself from his Marxist past. He chronicled the struggles of workers who challenged industrialism. He saw their protests as coming out of a desire for "dignity" and "independence," not from the wellsprings of solidarity or class consciousness.[4] He used the word "industrialism," with "capitalism" making its appearance only when he was quoting an original source. Included in the thesis was a chapter on "A New Role for Women" in which he charted the "opposition by workingmen's groups to women's competition," the extent of women's participation in the paid work force, and the "often appalling" conditions women faced when they did out-sourced work in their homes or labored in factories, at times turning to prostitution to make ends meet. Though he concluded that working women "mainly" accepted "their lot" because their family situations (as widows, sole income earners in a household, or young girls) made it necessary for them to reconcile themselves to their "fate and status," he nonetheless noted the occasional attempts of women workers to organize. He acknowledged how women's jobs were often "only a short step from" traditional domestic activities, but saw factory work involving a move for women along the path from household drudgery to fulfilling employment.[5]

When he joined the faculty at Vassar College in 1952, Degler, married and with two young children, focused on building a career and a family. He did not take an active role in campus politics or speak up on national political issues. However, in the classroom, he was, according to historian Marilyn B. Young who first encountered Degler in the fall of 1953, "a classic, passionate liberal: equal rights for women and minorities was an early and total conviction and commitment and one he passed on to his students." Several factors intensified his interest in women's history. He developed a special pride in Vassar as a women's college. He was in a department with a tradition of strong, accomplished, and supportive female colleagues—including two of the founders of the Berkshire Conference of Women Historians. Teaching at a women's college and committed to a present-minded approach to history, he searched for historical sources that might interest his students.[6]

If Gerda Lerner (1920–) shares with the others an early engagement with the Old Left, her experience under Nazism and then as an émigré gave her life a distinctive cast. She spent her first nineteen years in Vienna in an upper middle-class, assimilated Jewish household. Her interest in politics and a career as a writer began in her teens—with poverty, class, socialism, Marxism, anti-fascism, and anti-Semitism providing the issues that sharpened her social consciousness. In 1938, the Gestapo jailed her and her mother for five weeks and under brutal conditions. The family left Vienna in 1938, and Lerner migrated by herself to New York in 1939. In that year, she read Friedrich Engels's *Origin of the Family, Private Property, and the State* and was, she later recalled, "especially carried away" by it. Her early years in the United States were difficult, characterized by poverty and anxiety about the fate of her parents who had remained in Europe and whom she was powerless to help. By 1940, she began to build a new life, marrying Carl Lerner, a theater writer, with whom she moved to Los Angeles and started a family. Carl, a member of the Communist Party, introduced her to American history. Around 1942, she continued her education when she took her first course in that field from John Howard Lawson (later one of the Hollywood Ten), who focused on African Americans and women. Yet her fear that her politics might jeopardize her application for citizenship caused her to avoid joining organizations or signing petitions. After she became a citizen of the United States in 1943, she increasingly aligned herself with Popular Front organizations, gained more steady employment, and began to have success as a professional writer and translator. She joined the Communist Party in 1946 and participated in the Popular Front tradition that emphasized local issues and connected progressivism with Americanism.[7]

In the 1940s, Lerner focused on women's issues. Wartime conditions intensified her interest in child care and women's work. In 1948, she was a founding member of the Los Angeles chapter of the CAW and soon joined its national board. Looking back on her life in her 2002 memoir, she dated her fascination with American women's history and her interest in having a career as an historian to her activity in CAW. As was true for Flexner, Lerner's involvement with Popular Front feminism sharpened her sense of the shortcomings of the Old Left on women's issues.

In 1949, the Lerners moved to New York, because the graylisting of Carl threatened his ability to make a living in the movie industry. The move coincided with the government's suppression of CAW, an event that, along with the attacks on Hollywood friends, reinvoked for Lerner the memory of the Nazi attacks on the left and civil liberties in Vienna. She lived the 1950s in fear, not revealing her Old Left past until she published her autobiography in 2002, something Flexner did not allow to happen until her papers opened after her death. Throughout the 1950s, Lerner was active in progressive causes on the local level—especially on issues of race, peace, child care, and education. She continued her work as a writer, in 1950 coauthoring, with Eve Merriam, a dramatic pageant on the history of women. By the late 1950s, she left the party and over the ensuing years, according to her own account, thought her way out of Marxist theory as well. In 1958, fearing she was at a dead end as a writer, Lerner tried her hand at new genres. She entered the New School for Social Research, earning her B.A. in 1963; while still an undergraduate she taught a course on women's history. Aware that she needed training as a historian to write historical fiction, she went on to study history at Columbia, where she earned her Ph.D. in 1966 with a thesis on the Grimké sisters under the supervision of Eric McKitrick and Robert Cross.[8]

Aileen Kraditor's career followed a trajectory both similar to and dramatically different from that of others under consideration here. Born in Brooklyn in 1928 into a middle-class Jewish family, she joined the Communist Party in the late 1940s when she began to read Marxist literature, including Engels's essay and the compilation *The Woman Question* that Flexner had relied on. After graduating from Brooklyn College, Kraditor entered the labor force, first as a factory worker and then in her family's law and accounting office. Around 1958, she left the party and began a long process of rethinking her commitment to Marxism. In the late 1950s she turned to history as a way of studying social philosophy, earning her Ph.D. from Columbia in 1963 with a thesis written under William Leuchtenburg. From 1962 until her retirement in 1980, she held a series of academic positions. Unlike Lerner and Flexner, she believed that as a woman she had experienced only minor examples of discrimination.[9]

As these four historians read Marxist literature in the 1940s and early 1950s, they developed their views of the relationship between capitalism and women's lives. In Flexner's case there is abundant evidence of how she interpreted key Marxist feminists texts. "In primitive communal society," she noted in her 1953–54 syllabus at the Jefferson School, women had "equal status" to that of men. By forcing women into a subordinate position, slavery and feudalism changed their status. The "emergence of exploitative class society" reduced "women to an inferior status in the home and community." Then under the heading "WORKING WOMEN AND CAPITALIST EXPLOITATION," Flexner pointed to "How the capitalist class makes enormous super-profits out of the labor of women." She highlighted "the greater intensity and different quality of oppression of Negro women" as well as the "special abilities" they brought to the working-class movement. She emphasized how capitalism imposed new kinds of oppression of women. Among these forces was "male supremacist ideology," a belief system that was "part of the social superstructure," with both "its origin and role in the class struggle." The result was that "typical bourgeois ideas" about women's inferiority strengthened "capitalist exploitation." Only under socialism, most evident in the Soviet Union, were women liberated from capitalist exploitation, especially by "the extensive and unparalleled provisions for the protection of mothers and children."[10]

Flexner highlighted women's struggle for a better position under capitalism. She emphasized the important roles women played in the fight against slavery and for union power and the vote. Prefiguring consciousness raising among a later generation of women, she asked women in her course to talk about the way "male supremacist ideology" oppressed them at home and work, and in community, unions, and radical organizations. She insisted that fights against the special oppression of women were inextricably connected with the struggle for peace and social justice, as well as the battle against fascism. She made clear the key role that labor unions, progressive organizations, and African American women played. Calling on women to fight on both the ideological level and in concrete ways, she insisted that the battles against the oppression of women were necessary to move forward the interests of the working class.[11]

In addition, Flexner picked up on the strand of Marxist thought that stressed how capitalism helped liberate women. In 1950 she noted the central tension in capitalism's impact: that it both oppressed women and, in its search for cheap labor, drew millions of them into industry, in the process creating "the conditions out of which equality for woman can begin to develop." Writing in the *Daily Worker* in the early 1950s, she said that though women encountered "super-exploitation" when they entered factories, industrial work "set in motion the process of their eventual liberation." In the course she taught, she suggested that "the development of capitalism advance[d] the status of women." In a pamphlet written for the Jefferson School in 1953, she argued that, by drawing women out of the home, capitalism made it possible for them to become more self-sufficient economically, offered settings in which they could fight for social justice, and "provided the technological foundation (realizable only under socialism) for the eventual liberation of women from household drudgery."[12]

Flexner's rendition of Marxist theory differed from and resembled Engels's in a number of ways. His writing was more complicated, historical, and theoretically sophisticated than what Flexner conveyed on her syllabus. She explored connections to contemporary situations, emphasizing trade unions, the unique position of African American women, male chauvinism, and the glories of the Soviet Union in ways he did not or could not. For our purposes the most interesting similarity was on the issue of whether capitalism liberated or oppressed women. Engels had asserted that under capitalism women were caught between the impossible-to-reconcile claims of "public production" and "the private service of her family." He wrote that "the emancipation of women will only be possible when woman can take part in production on a large, social scale, and domestic work no longer claims anything but an insignificant amount of her time."[13]

Engels's essay shaped the world view of Lerner and Kraditor. In *Singing of Women*, her 1950 drama, Lerner offered a feminist critique, placed her work within the framework of a Marxist treatment of the woman question, and emphasized the resistance by African American and union women. She stressed how factory work, even with its unequal pay and harsh conditions, liberated women from the confines of the household. "We understood women's oppression," she commented later, "to come from capitalism ('the boss'), from the remnants of sexism in otherwise supportive males, and, above all, we presented a glorious vision of male-female, black and white cooperation in the greater cause of unionism and peace."[14] When Kraditor read Engels's essay around 1950, she carefully highlighted passages in which he explained historical materialism and explored the ways economic forces shaped the relationships between men and women.[15]

If Engels's essay was important in the education of the three women, in college Degler cut his teeth on Bebel's book, which gave him a distinctive perspective on class relationships and on the power of capitalism to liberate women. Engels focused mostly on proletarian women, though at one moment he had remarked that the elite women, placed on a pedestal and not doing authentic work, had a lower social position than did the productive women of an earlier time. Bebel explored the condition of upper middle-class women and class dynamics among women, noting that women of "privileged social standing" saw the insurgency of their working-class counterparts as dangerous. Though he acknowledged the "class-antagonism" among women, he thought the "hostile sisters" could cooperate: "although marching separately," they could "strike jointly."[16]

For our purposes the most important difference between Engels and Bebel (and correspondingly between how the educations of Flexner, Kraditor, and Lerner differed from Degler's) came on the issue of the liberating power of capitalism. Bebel wrote extensively and rhapsodically of how modern capitalism enhanced the lives of women by socializing household work. Public production of food and clothing, along with public provision of utilities, had produced what he called "a great revolution . . . within our family life" that made "antiquated conditions" the exception in modern nations such as Germany. America, he noted, had gone even farther since it lacked "old European prejudices" and "institutions that have survived their day." Women in advanced societies, "freer, more independent," had more time for public life, with bourgeois women starting organizations, establishing publications, and calling conventions at the same time that working-class ones met in unions halls and joined men's organizations. Wealthy women could take advantage of cooperative kitchens, hotels, central heating, electrical lighting—which if extended more broadly would dramatically improve the living conditions of more women. Though he acknowledged that "capitalist society evokes no benificent [*sic*] phenomenon unaccompanied with a dark side," he believed nothing could hold back the advance of technological change. "Bourgeois society, having conjured" it "into life, Degler read in Bebel's book, "has the historic mission of also carrying the revolution to perfection, and to promote on all fields the budding of the germs for radical transformations, *which a social order, built on new foundations, would only have to generalize on a large scale, and make common property.*"[17]

The Reemergence of Women's History, 1956–1969

Beginning in 1956, Degler, Flexner, Kraditor, and Lerner offered broad and ambitious renderings of women's history in which they pondered the balance of forces that oppressed and liberated women. In his 1956 article on Charlotte Perkins Gilman and his 1959 *Out of Our Past: The Forces That Shaped Modern America*, Degler explored the tensions women experienced as they struggled to balance careers and family life, what it meant to think of women as members of a minority group, and what he saw as the unique conditions of the new nation that opened up opportunities for women. Flexner suggested the dynamics of the relationship between working-class, middle-class, and African American women during a century of struggle. Gerda Lerner concentrated on the contribution of white women to the fight against slavery and reminded her readers of the relationship between middle-class and working-class women, crediting ladies with the creation of women's rights and mill girls with living it. Kraditor explored the tensions between means and ends in American social movements that engaged the energies of women. These writers concentrated on the role of working-class and African American women. They explored the relationship between social and economic forces, ideas, organizational strategies, and reform movements. They found their heroes not only in those who campaigned for the vote but also among those who worked for a wide range of social reforms. When they focused on women's history, Degler, Flexner, Kraditor, and Lerner worked against what they saw as the dominant narrative, one that emphasized the fights over suffrage. Despite the efforts of Mary Beard to promote a different approach and of many women historians to focus broadly on social and cultural history, in the popular mind the dominant narrative focused on the campaigns to secure the vote, with historians concentrating on the stories of white, middle-class reformers.[18]

Degler's 1956 article on Gilman was the first scholarly work of women's history to emerge from these authors in their post-Popular Front phases. He shifted his attention from the emphasis on working-class women in his thesis, even as, consistent with his debt to Bebel, he ascribed liberating powers to industrialization. His article appeared at a time when few scholars were aware of, let alone paid any attention to Gilman. Degler hailed her as someone who offered "truly thought-provoking analyses of woman's position in a man's world." Though he found her thought "hopelessly tinged with utopianism," he recovered many of the most important aspects of Gilman's feminism, including her emphasis on the distorting power of women's sexuality, her call for women's economic independence in a world where men suppressed their search for freedom and dignity, and her focus on the way the professionalization of household activities would strengthen marriages and enhance women's freedom. When he turned to the relevance of Gilman's writings for contemporary Americans, he noted the dramatic increase in the percentage of women who worked outside the home. He hastened to note that there was still a gap between reality and what Gilman had hoped for. He was well aware that women who worked full time outside of the house bore the burden for housework. He ended on an optimistic note, crediting Gilman with heralding modern marriages that enabled women to combine career and family. As he wrote in the article's final sentence, she focused on the way women's work and talents served to "enlarge the pool of human energy and to enhance human happiness."[19]

Much of what Gilman had stressed Degler neglected or minimized. By making Gilman someone who showed college-educated women of the 1950s the road to personal fulfillment, he paid little attention to the way *Women and Economics* provided a socialist critique. He mentioned neither Gilman's discussion of class relationships among women nor how she looked at women through imperialist and racist lenses. Even though he understood the way Gilman highlighted the power of specialization and professionalization in transforming housework, he incorrectly asserted that she "pointed to no other social engine for the accomplishment of such a mighty domestic revolution other than its desirability." Nor did Degler show any inclination to use Bebel's analysis to draw out what was often vague or implicit in Gilman's work, the notion that especially in the United States affluence and women's entry into industry was increasingly underwriting their liberation from household drudgery. Degler remedied the inattention to the argument that the industrial revolution made the women's movement possible when, ten years after he published the article, at the urging of Kraditor he wrote an introduction to a new edition of Gilman's book.[20]

Degler's *Out of Our Past* incorporated women's history within a framework shaped by the Cold War. Rejecting the approach of Charles Beard, Degler made it clear that he preferred to emphasize the power of ideas rather than economic forces. Steering his way between "arraignment" and "panegyric," Degler stood in awe of what Americans had accomplished and emphasized the nation's uniqueness. Though he was unusual in his frequent use of the word "capitalism," in many ways he joined in the powerful ideological consensus of the 1950s. He emphasized the fluidity of class lines, the infertility of American soil for socialism, the conservatism of the union movement, and the lower social costs of economic development.[21]

Degler linked women's relatively substantial role in his narrative with his emphasis on the uniqueness of the American experience. Following what Mary Beard had written in *Woman as a Force in History* (1946), he wrote that because middle-class women were not subordinate, they did not need to be emancipated; rather, they successfully took advantage of new opportunities afforded them. Indeed, Degler found in early American history "A Paradise for Women," with forces, especially demographic ones, giving women their "special place" throughout the nation's life. Compared with their European counterparts, poor women in America worked less, young women enjoyed more freedom, middle-class women exercised more legal power, and urban women had more opportunity to work outside the home.[22]

When he turned to the nineteenth and early twentieth centuries, he again stressed the relatively privileged position of white women, especially compared to that of African Americans. His familiarity with Marxist literature (Bebel especially) and his appreciation of the power of Gilman's arguments impelled him to ascribe to industrialization and urbanization women's achievement of greater independence, an approach that undercut his insistence on the primacy of ideas over material forces. Although he recognized the "deadening drudgery" of women's factory work, he emphasized how from the 1840s on industrialization led to women's increased workforce participation and weakened their dependence on their fathers. For middle-class women living in cities at the turn of the century who did not work for a living, the shrinking of the size of the home and the commercial provision of goods and services opened up new opportunities for leisure and civic participation. Emphasizing the importance of economic independence and the "peculiar creative talents of women," Degler hailed Florence Kelley, Mary Simkhovitch, and Vida Scudder as exemplars of the fuller participation of women in the fight to improve society. He paid particular attention to the question of how to think of American women as a minority group. While he acknowledged subordination and discrimination, he insisted that middle-class and elite women "have shared in the rewards and perquisites of power, prestige, and wealth as no other 'oppressed' group ever has," an assertion that stood in stark contrast with the bleak picture of the lot of working-class women he had portrayed in his thesis seven years earlier.[23]

A number of factors help explain the characteristics of Degler's discussion of women, especially his emphasis on their privilege and opportunities. He had reckoned with Bebel's book in the early 1940s. He participated in the Cold War consensus. He wanted his book to appeal to a broad audience. Above all, it was his view that, comparatively speaking, African Americans suffered greatly more than white women, an idea that grew out of his Popular Front commitments and his maleness. Degler believed that racism, a word he used, preceded slavery and suffused the history of blacks, at least until segregation came under attack beginning in the 1950s. These factors gave his work its distinctive cast.

In *Out of Our Past*, Degler noted that there was "no satisfactory history of the woman's movement of the late nineteenth and early twentieth century." Eleanor Flexner remedied that situation in late summer of 1959, when her *Century of Struggle: The Woman's Rights Movement in the United States* appeared as the first history of women in the United States that covered a century's sweep, relied on archival materials, and met rigorous professional standards. The book was pathbreaking in its joining of social, legal, educational, labor, and political history; in its focus on the history of working-class and African

American women; and in its deployment of struggle as the theme that bound the narrative together.[24]

With this book, Flexner both drew on and distanced herself from her past, in the process avoiding an excessively schematic approach. Minimizing any emphasis on class conflict, she carefully linked struggles of middle- and working-class women. She highlighted Elizabeth Cady Stanton's "derogatory references to 'Sambo,'" Chinese Americans, and "'ignorant foreigners'" and emphasized how what we would call the racist beliefs among whites spurred African American women on. However, much less so than would be true of a later generation, she paid relatively little attention to the racism of white women reformers and suffragists. Moreover, she treated as largely separate the efforts of white women to improve the conditions of African Americans and of African Americans themselves to better their lives. Throughout her book there were remarkably few villainous people or institutions. There were a few greedy capitalists, whose pursuit of profits kept women in poverty, and no corporations or economic system responsible for women's plight; indeed at a key point, she used the passive voice to describe the need of "giant enterprises" for "cheap tractable labor." She did mention "male prejudice" as a factor in prompting women to organize separate temperance societies, described a handful of chauvinist men who systematically suppressed women's aspirations, and referred to a few men in labor unions who opposed women's organizing. More typically, when she described resistance women faced, she did not make it explicit that it was from men. Instead, clearly preferring cooperation with supportive men rather than separatism (an approach she learned in the Popular Front), she offered frequent examples of husbands and reformers who supported women's struggle. She emphasized how changes in religion, public opinion, and belief systems shaped the lives of women but she only vaguely asserted the connections of these factors to the role of larger social and economic forces. Indeed what drove the narrative were the heroic women from varied backgrounds who were willing to combine disciplined militancy with strong organizational skills to achieve a broad range of goals, rather than just the vote. She appreciated the cross-fertilization between the efforts of well-to-do and working-class leaders as, for example, in the interrelated battles for suffrage and unions in the early twentieth century.[25]

Flexner thus retreated considerably from the version of Popular Front women's history she developed earlier in the 1950s, with its emphasis on how capitalists and male supremacists exploited women. The book contained only hints of the force of economic determinism and the evils of capitalism. However muted, much remained from her Old Left experiences. She still stressed the centrality of struggle, appreciated disciplined militancy and organization, and suggested that business interests stood behind the fight against suffrage. She continued to focus on working-class and African American women, emphasize cross-class and cross-gender (but not cross-race) cooperation, avoid issues of sexuality, and insist on the importance of an agenda that went beyond the franchise to include ambitious campaigns for social justice. In the end, one can only speculate about what motivated her to mute her Old Left heritage. She wanted to reach a larger audience and needed to hide her past during the period of McCarthyism. In addition, her own political shifts—her departure from the Communist Party in 1956 and her later separation of herself from her Marxist past—helps account for the way she had gone from an outspoken Marxist in the mid-1950s to a muted leftist a few years later.[26]

In the late 1960s, Gerda Lerner published important studies in women's history, in which she pondered the implications of economic transformations for women. In *The Grimké Sisters from South Carolina: Pioneers for Woman's Rights and Abolition* (1967), she drew on her skills as a novelist and script writer to tell the dramatic story of how economic and biographical factors transformed the sisters from Southern ladies into fighters for women's rights and the abolition of slavery. Their lives illustrated the emergence of American feminism well before Seneca Falls in 1848. She emphasized how the discrimination the Grimké sisters faced as girls impelled them to understand the oppression slaves experienced. Linking race, class, and gender, she stressed the sisters' consciousness of sisterhood; their sensitivity to the costs of adversity built on race and class discrimination; and the ways the shifting economic and personal situations of their lives fueled their politics. Lerner focused on how they developed as leaders—the skills they honed and the courage they mustered in face of male and conservative opposition. The moral of her story was that it was dangerous for feminists to narrow their vision by emphasizing middle-class reforms to the exclusion of issues affecting working-class and African American women. What drove the narrative was the progression of the Grimké sisters from privileged Southern ladies in a slaveholding family with sharply defined separate spheres to women who, "no longer sheltered by wealth, privilege or spinsterhood," worked hard as reformers and grew sensitive to the low wages and terrible working conditions for women in Northern industries. Over the long haul, these experiences enabled them to understand "the basic problem that was to haunt the average woman for the next century": how after a day of domestic labors they had enough energy "to concern" themselves "with issues outside the home or to do anything about them." Lerner offered a hint of the argument Bebel, Degler, Kraditor, and Flexner adopted: "The problems posed by the multiple roles of women," she remarked, "were made infinitely easier and more possible of solution by technological and social changes," as well as by the gains "the woman's rights movement won."[27]

The book on the Grimké sisters echoed Lerner's own life. She told the stories of young women who gained a political education under an oppressive social system with which they refused to compromise and then went into exile. She charted how they emerged as writers, organizers, and orators.

She focused on the means, ends, and tactics they used to fight for what they believed in, including free speech. She celebrated the courage of women who worked for social justice. Then, as she would later write of herself, she told of how they believed that saving the world "gives one a sense of purpose and the satisfaction of contributing to a greater good."[28]

In "The Lady and the Mill Girl: Changes in the Status of Women in the Age of Jackson" (1969), Lerner continued her lifelong fascination with the intersection of economic forces, class, race, and gender. From Engels, she had learned that "the lady of civilization, surrounded by false homage and estranged from all real work" had "an infinitely lower social position than the hard-working woman" characteristic of a more matriarchal time. In her book on the Grimké sisters, Lerner contrasted the "false protection of chivalry" afforded ladies with the low wages factory women earned for hard work. In the 1969 article, she contrasted the colonial period, which like Degler she described as a time when women did respected work inside and outside the home and had "relative social freedom," with the way their situation had deteriorated dramatically by the 1830s. While democracy and opportunity increased for men, women were now denied the benefits of political participation. Changes in demography, ideology, and technology led to a bifurcation in the lives of women across class lines. On the one hand, the "genteel lady of fashion had become a model of American femininity," albeit one for whom the proper sphere of activity was increasingly confined. Lerner saw this operating most dramatically in the way professionalization increasingly marginalized women. On the other hand, working-class women faced difficulties when they entered factories, especially as unions were defeated and technology deskilled labor. For them "the changes brought by industrialization were actually advantageous, offering income and advancement opportunities, however limited, and a chance for participation in the ranks of organized labor." If the lives of women differed dramatically, both groups "were equally disfranchised and isolated from the vital centers of power." By the 1840s, frustrated by the thwarting of rising expectations, middle-class and elite women launched the women's rights movement, which confined its focus to legal and property issues. Not until the beginning of a new century, Lerner concluded, would the lady and the mill girl learn "to cooperate, each for her own separate interests."[29]

What was remarkable about this article was Lerner's ability to demonstrate that changes accompanying "industrialization" shaped two phenomena seen at the time as distinct—the conditions of mill girls that involved both immiseration and opportunity contrasted with the leisure that enabled some ladies to engage in political activity, even while the scope of the lives of many elite women grew more confined. In this essay, more than any of the others under consideration here, Lerner emphasized class, race, and gender, as well as the power of intersecting ideological and industrial forces. As she did so, she drew on her earlier Popular Front education even as she complicated and muted what she had learned in the 1940s. She demonstrated that in some instances, for working-class women more than for privileged ones, industrialization served as a liberating force.[30] In this essay, and in her book on the Grimké sisters, the results of Lerner's Popular Front education were abundantly clear. She understood how race, class, and gender were interconnected. She pondered how economic forces shaped political consciousness. She explored how social movements fostered leadership. She emphasized the importance of understanding alliances that crossed the lines of class and race.

Like Lerner and others, in the 1960s Kraditor wrote on the connections between race, gender, and political activism. What Kraditor said during the 1960s on the history of women in social movements in many ways reflected her engagement with Marxism in the 1950s, though absent to a considerable extent was the assertion that capitalism oppressed women. Her first work, *The Ideas of the Woman Suffrage Movement, 1890–1920* (1965), bears comparison with Flexner's 1959 book. Despite the title, Kraditor used the battles over the vote to explore a wide range of reform movements and to emphasize how the fight for the vote was, at its core, a struggle over democracy and social welfare. As was true of Flexner, Kraditor did not portray men as villains, hinted that she sided with the militants, and expressed great appreciation for those middle-class women who aligned themselves with the struggles of working women. She showed how as victory neared, suffragists "cultivated a rapport with working women and foreign-born voters," albeit not with African Americans. The differences between the two books were important. Much more than Flexner, Kraditor emphasized the way suffragists and antisuffragists both had deep-seated prejudices against workers, African Americans, Indians, and immigrants. More so than Flexner, she emphasized the chasm that separated the activism of middle- and working-class women. If Flexner focused on the nuts and bolts of organizations, Kraditor concentrated on the relationship between ends and means, justice and expediency, ideology and tactics. For our purposes the most significant difference had to do with the explanation of the relationship between capitalism and the condition of women. If Flexner had vaguely linked material conditions and ideas, Kraditor worked out a more explicit cause-and-effect relation. She made clear how changing economic conditions led to shifts in ideas. She wrote in ways that echoed what Bebel and Degler had argued and offered few hints at the ways capitalism oppressed women. "Industrialization" undermined the ideology that had created barriers between separate spheres, fostered women's suffrage by freeing middle-class women from domestic obligations, and gave them enough leisure to enter the public sphere as reformers.[31]

Kraditor finished her book on women's suffrage in the summer of 1964, when feminism's revival was only beginning and when President Lyndon Johnson was still poised between the Great Society and a greatly expanded war in Vietnam. Her edited book *Up From the Pedestal* (1968) and her *Means and Ends in American Abolitionism* (1969) appeared at a dramatically different time, when feminism and radicalism were in the ascendancy. Kraditor remained committed to the left until 1968, when she completed work on *Means and Ends*. In her introduction to *Up From the Pedestal*, she rephrased what she had said in her first book about what she now saw as how "the Industrial Revolution was the soil in which feminism grew." She wrote that she selected documents that illustrated "racism and xenophobia" that suffragists relied on. At the end of the essay she argued that the family as an institution stood in the way of women's equality. Middle-class feminists had to challenge the family unless they wanted to fall into the tragic trap of the "urge toward individual autonomy." In *Means and Ends*, Kraditor's radicalism came through in a number of ways. In *Means and Ends*, she drew analogies between Garrisonians and antifascists in the 1930s and Black Power advocates in the late 1960s. She focused on William Lloyd Garrison and his followers, again emphasizing the issues that inspired her life's work: the relationships between tactics and ideology, means and ends. Now she had a topic—slavery—that demanded a different approach than did the fact that middle-class women could not vote. Kraditor aligned herself wholeheartedly with the radical abolitionists, letting them off the hook when they gave a higher priority to emancipation of slavery than women's rights or even the rights of workers. She applauded their abilities as agitators who fought for basic change in the "institutional structure and ideology" of an American society that was "fundamentally immoral." A revolution, she remarked, was "not necessarily . . . a violent overthrow" of a society but a "change in the fundamentals" that a radical had to wrestle with when confronted with an immoral society.[32]

Kraditor's work of the 1960s reflected issues with which she had long dealt, commitments now intensified by events of the late 1960s: social justice for women and African Americans, the relationship between means and ends, the role of the agitator, the shoals of compromise, the importance of disciplined organization, and the place of middle-class people in other people's struggles. Nonetheless, what is striking is how much she had rejected from her reading of Engels's *Origin*. Her book on abolitionism had virtually nothing to say on the relationship between slavery, capitalism, anti-slavery agitation, and women. In her first book and her introductory essay to *Up From the Pedestal*, she suggested a positive relationship between changes in the means of production and women's liberation, focusing on how "industrialization" or "industrialism" (not capitalism) liberated middle-class women.

The Legacies of Midcentury Feminism After 1969

Beginning in the late 1960s, Degler, Flexner, Lerner, and Kraditor embarked on divergent paths. Degler sustained a mainline and distinguished career as a historian. Though political activism did not generally tempt him, he accepted Betty Friedan's invitation to be one of the founders of the National Organization for Women. As a scholar, he continued to focus on the history of women and African Americans, topics central to others whose education began in the Old Left. He did, however, move from a not fully formed Popular Front politics in the 1940s to liberalism in the ensuing years.[33]

After the publication of her book in 1959, Flexner remained on the left and committed to a career as a writer. After converting to Catholicism in 1960, she spoke out on issues surrounding Vatican II, race, the environment, poverty, and sexuality in the diocesan and local newspapers and in the Northampton Democratic Party. Despite her continuing commitment to progressive causes, over time she distanced herself from second wave feminism, for whose participants *Century of Struggle* had provided a history. In the late 1960s, she did not identify with the new generation and called, at times angrily, on its advocates to balance liberation with responsibility. From the mid-1960s on, Flexner felt that key people—including young feminists, women's historians, and faculty members at Smith College—did not adequately acknowledge her contribution. At one point, she delivered what she thought of as a "non-feminist speech," in which she asserted that feminists exaggerated the extent to which men could lead trouble-free lives. What undergirded the turns in her religion and politics until her death in 1995 was a sense of tragedy that stemmed largely from personal causes.[34]

If the development of women's liberation and academic feminism embittered Flexner because she was an outsider, these changes were tremendously positive for Lerner. By the late 1960s Lerner had begun a career that would soon lead to her emergence as one of the nation's leading historians of women. More than any of those under consideration here, continuity marks her writings. From the 1930s on, the heritage of Popular Front shaped her writing and activism. As a scholar and organizer, she focused on issues where women, class, and race intersected. In important ways, her major contribution to feminist thought, the two-volume *Women and History* (1986 and 1993), continued and transformed the project Engels had begun of explaining, in bold strokes, the history of women in a patriarchal world.

What set Kraditor off from Degler, Lerner, and Flexner was her sharp turn to the right after the late 1960s. Soon after the publication of *Means and Ends*, she distanced herself from both women's history and the women's movement. In two books she published in the 1980s, she was critical of Old Left activists she had known before 1958 and of New Left scholars who reshaped the writing of history beginning in the 1960s. When she wrote a new preface to her book on women's suffrage in 1979, she acknowledged that she wished she could have eliminated her expression of a "Marxist bias" from her earlier work. She criticized the rising generation of women's historians for being motivated "by the desire to provide current feminists with a heritage of oppression-plus-achievement." In much of her later writing, women were more acted upon than active. Her career reminds us of others who broke new scholarly and political ground in the 1960s and then turned to the right, all the while struggling with the legacy of their Marxist pasts. Her story was that of a one-time feminist who confronted a God that failed, something abundantly clear in her 1988 article "Unbecoming a Communist" in which she charted how she went from communism to a Maoist version of Marxist-Leninism, to "independent" Marxism, before at last giving up Marxism altogether. Too much is unclear from the published record to know what factors shaped her embrace of radicalism as well as her rejection of it. Although she did not elaborate on what she meant, she did assert that both her decisions to accept and reject the Marxism had to be explained not in terms of external events but of "the individual psyche and personal history of the radical."[35]

In their Popular Front years, these historians believed in the inextricable connections between capitalism, women, African Americans, and patriarchy. All of them wrestled with the question of whether capitalism oppressed or liberated. Relying on Engels, they asserted that capitalism exploited even as it contained the seeds of liberation—first under a doomed economic system and then in full flower under a transformed one. Degler, a man influenced by Bebel rather than Engels, was more delicately poised between the opposite poles of exploitation and liberation. In what they all wrote on women's history between 1956 and 1969, they both departed from and drew on what they had earlier believed. From the days that she read Engels's *Origin* to the late 1960s, Kraditor lowered her estimate of the power of corporations to oppress women and placed greater emphasis on the power of industrialization to liberate them. As she moved away from the Communist Party and wrote *Century of Struggle*, Flexner turned away from a belief in the tension between capitalism as oppressive and liberating and expressed little sense that men or the social system degraded women. Lerner showed the most persistence in her position, continually emphasizing the intersection of the economic system, class, race, and gender. During the 1950s, Degler shifted his focus from working-class women to middle-class ones, as well as from Marxism to Cold War consensus. However, he continually focused on the tension between work and family and on the ways that capitalism (or industrialization), along with distinctive American conditions, helped liberate women—a position that Bebel had articulated.

After 1969, none of them in their key writings on women focused on whether capitalism oppressed or liberated women. In her 1971 pamphlet *Women's Rights—Unfinished Business*, Flexner argued that women—especially working-class and African American ones—suffered from the terrible effects of discrimination. Labor unions and public policy could mitigate this damage, but they hardly eliminated the tragic consequences of sex discrimination. However, when she came to explain why all this was so, she was vague. She raised questions about the persistence of deeply imbedded traditions but avoided any assertion that capitalism or sexism was responsible. Thus, compared with what she had taught in the mid-1950s or in 1959, Flexner minimized any sense that social structures impeded women's advancement. In *At Odds: Women and the Family in America from the Revolution to the Present* (1980), Degler concentrated on the tension women faced between family obligations and the pursuit of equality through careers, a question that reverberated with what Engels had written in *Origin*, an issue that Flexner focused on in 1971, and topic about which Degler was more pessimistic of a successful resolution than he has been in the 1950s. In her antiradical writings of the 1980s, Kraditor, rather than seeing workers as victims of an oppressive "system," saw them as participants in a more open society shaped by religion, ethnicity, community, culture, and a complex intersection of public and private worlds. In *The Creation of Feminist Consciousness: From the Middle Ages to Eighteen-Seventy* (1993), the second volume of her sweeping work *Women and History*, Lerner made clear that "crucial to the development of feminist consciousness are societal changes which allow substantial numbers of women to live in economic independence," an idea Engels and Bebel had earlier developed. Although she acknowledged the power of the economic base to shape a social, ideological, and cultural superstructure, Lerner nonetheless concentrated on the liberating power of women's networks, friendships, and organizations. For Degler, Kraditor, and Flexner, the non-Marxian superstructure had somehow emerged as autonomous. Lerner stressed the formidable power of women to create feminism, although she placed capitalism more in the background than Engels had done.[36]

The careers of these four historians remind us that the Old Left spurred interest not only in class but also in race and gender. As historians nurtured in the left, they pioneered in writing history that focused on the struggles of women, workers, and African Americans for social justice. If especially after the late 1960s they went in different, sometimes dramatically different directions, Degler, Flexner, Kraditor, and Lerner all remained committed to a worldview where politics, social structures and ideas were intertwined— even as they shifted from capitalism to women, families, beliefs, and culture as the relevant forces. Whatever the variety of their personal experiences and their political trajectories, throughout their careers their common cast of mind led them to see the struggles of women in conjunction with, and not in isolation from, other social groups—including men and African Americans.

Gender and the relationship to the Communist Party played a role in shaping their approaches to women's history. Degler was the only one for whom women's issues were not always at the center. The three women, involved in the party rather than, like Degler, vaguely sympathetic to it, gravitated to the role of women in the abolitionist movement because that is where women found their voices in a supposedly egalitarian movement.

They felt compelled to develop some way of thinking about cross-class and cross-race efforts, especially of how middle-class educated women could reach out to others. In that crucible women had found their voices, just as these three historians tried to find their voices in the CP. In the nineteenth-century movements they studied and the twentieth-century ones they joined, they took their clues from fighters for social justice who had to face hostility of conservatives. Their experiences in the party undergirded their fascination with issue of tactics, discipline, means and ends, the heroic life, and the role of the middle class in other people's revolutions.

Why over time (least so with Lerner) did these four historians focus on the role of women in history in ways that involved diminished attention to the power of capitalism? In the 1940s, fights against corporate greed and in favor of social justice for African Americans, women, and workers were closely connected. Eventually, the intertwined vision shaped in the Popular Front unraveled. As a result, to a greater or lesser extent these historians shifted their focus from capitalist exploitation to issues surrounding the history of African Americans and women. Whatever the personal causes of such a change, political, social, ideological, and economic factors prompted reconsiderations that resulted in a change of focus from the economy to gender and race. McCarthyism made language about the costs of capitalist development dangerous, while information about the impact of Stalinism in the USSR made it more problematic. If the Depression of the 1930s made the end of capitalism seem possible, the sustained prosperity of the American economy that began with World War II made its demise seem less likely. Changed conditions—including the growth of the suburbs, the steady increase in women's workforce participation, the weakened position of labor unions, the struggle for civil rights for African Americans—transformed the terms of the debate over the nation's future. In many quarters, issues surrounding psychological well-being and group identity emerged as compelling ways for social scientists and activists to view the world. The ideological constructs that replaced Marxist-feminism, with its emphasis on capitalism, involved gender, the family, and the organizations that connected private and public life.

Part IV
The Rise of the Right

The Road Less Traveled: Reconsidering the Political Writings of Friedrich von Hayek

Juliet Williams

In the latter part of the twentieth century, Anglo-American liberal political thought was dominated by debates about where to draw the line between public power and private rights. Spurred by the effort to implement the New Deal in the United States and the subsequent growth and development of the welfare state apparatus, liberal theorists became entangled in fierce disagreements over just how much government is too much. Of course, ever since John Locke, thinkers in the liberal tradition have been centrally concerned with delimiting the appropriate scope and reach of governmental power. But in recent decades in the United States, this long-standing philosophical inquiry has assumed a degree of political urgency, as the regulatory and redistributive capacity of the federal government has expanded in historically unprecedented ways, propelled by forces ranging from the social to the technological. As the modern welfare state has expanded, two main camps of opinion have emerged among liberal theorists on the question of its legitimacy. On the one side are those thinkers who assert that government can and should play a central role in maintaining the underlying social and economic conditions necessary for individuals to enjoy their liberties. These theorists, known variously as redistributionists or welfarist liberals, characteristically contend that respect for individual liberty entails positive obligations on the part of government to enable persons to enjoy their liberties. On the other side of the debate are self-described classical liberals, often referred to as libertarians, who insist that a proper respect for liberty can be maintained only with the most minimal intervention by the state. For thinkers assuming the latter pose, it is agreed that a liberal government should adopt a laissez-faire posture toward the regulation of both the economy and other aspects of social and personal life, limiting interventions to a few circumscribed tasks, typically those having to do with law and order and national security.

In the wake of several decades of intramural debate, the political philosopher John Rawls is now generally regarded as the exemplar of the welfarist liberalism. Rawls today is widely hailed as the most significant liberal thinker of the twentieth century, having achieved the rare distinction of becoming a canonical figure in his own time. While liberalism historically has been associated with an attitude of wariness toward state power, in Rawls's rendering of the liberal ideal, the emphasis shifts from constraining coercion to justifying it. Dispensing with the attitude of tortured ambivalence long characteristic of liberal reflections on the "necessary evil" of government, Rawls famously contends that minimalist liberalism must yield to a version of the ideal which creates a significant role for government in regulating the processes through which resources are distributed. In this way, Rawls accentuates the critical distinction between opposing big government and supporting limited government, a distinction that historically has been elided in liberal discourses on government.

Among liberal theorists in the U.S. academy, welfarist liberalism now represents the consensus position, and those on the libertarian side of the spectrum struggle not simply for legitimacy but for mere recognition, even during eras, such as the 1990s, when libertarian ideologies enjoyed a swell of popularity in mainstream political discourse.[1] In this regard, the career of Friedrich von Hayek is illustrative, for though it is Rawls who has won the hearts and minds of the vast majority of U.S. academics, it is Hayek who ultimately achieved greater popular recognition in the United States, Great Britain, and in many of the former eastern bloc countries as well.[2] Born in Austria in 1899, Hayek's intellectual trajectory was established while he was still a student at the University of Vienna. It was there that he first encountered the theories associated with the Austrian School of Economics, a brand of economic thought with origins in the writings of Carl Menger and strongly associated with antisocialist, anticollectivist, and proliberal capitalist economics and politics.[3] After completing a brief stint as a civil servant, Hayek left Austria for England in 1931 and spent the next two decades at the London School of Economics. There he solidified his reputation as one of the leading economic theorists of the day, gaining notoriety for publicly sparring with Keynes and his Cambridge colleagues.[4] Hayek's tenure in England was capped by the publication, in 1944, of *The Road to Serfdom*. In that now (in)famous volume, Hayek declared war on socialism, arguing that it would be only a matter of time before the apparently benevolent welfare state devolved into a tyrannous "total state." *The Road to Serfdom* launched Hayek's career as a public intellectual, cementing his reputation as an antiwelfare "classical liberal," but forever crippling his reputation as a serious academic. After World War II, Hayek moved to the University of Chicago, though not without serious resistance from many faculty precincts, and he continued to produce scholarship until well beyond his eightieth year. When he died in 1992, Hayek left a legacy of scholarly writing in an array of fields, including economics, law, philosophy, and social theory, but in the eyes of most observers, his reputation never advanced beyond *The Road to Serfdom*.

In later works, including *The Constitution of Liberty* and the *Law, Legislation, and Liberty* trilogy, Hayek offers substantially expanded and, in important ways, refined discussions of the liberal tradition and its implications for modern public policy, but throughout his career he remained unwavering in his opposition to the "planning" mentality.[5]

Among political theorists today, Hayek generally is treated as little more than a Cold War crank—that is, when he is given consideration at all. Viewed more as an ideologue than a serious thinker, Hayek is regarded as a libertarian extremist, one who exalts the ideal of liberty but ignores the role that the free market plays in undermining individuals' ability to enjoy their vaunted freedom. Contemporary liberal theorists have dismissed Hayek variously as a "laissez-faire extremist,"[6] an "anti-egalitarian,"[7] and one of the "zealots of laissez-faire liberalism."[8] Political theorist Stephen Holmes is typical in depicting Hayek as a hard-core minimalist, one who, in Holmes's words, believes that "liberalism is wholly incompatible with positive programs of public provision, all of which require confiscatory taxation."[9] Having chosen the losing side in the battle between welfarist liberalism and the laissez-faire alternative, political theorists seem to have consigned Hayek to the dust heap of irrelevance. In what follows, however, I argue for a critical reconsideration of the political writings of Hayek. By reading Hayek through the lens of the welfarist/libertarian debate, acolytes and antagonists alike have seriously misunderstood his contribution to liberal theory. Although Hayek has been portrayed as a libertarian fundamentalist, throughout his career he adopted a far more nuanced and far less severe position than most commentators appreciate. Indeed, if Hayek was dogmatic about anything, it was his dislike of dogmatism itself—libertarian or otherwise. Regrettably, critics largely have failed to appreciate Hayek's willingness to consider alternatives to laissez-faire policies, assuming that in his philosophical writings Hayek sought to justify his political preferences. But Hayek did no such thing, recognizing that liberal principles themselves entail little by way of constraints on the scope of legislative discretion. Thus, although Hayek sharply criticized redistributionist social policies on grounds of efficiency, he willingly acknowledged that there was no principled reason to prohibit them. Indeed, Hayek steadfastly refused to advocate for categorical bans against welfarist and redistributionist initiatives, for in Hayek's view, liberalism neither requires nor rejects laissez-faire economics.

In suggesting that Hayek has been miscast as a libertarian dogmatist, my intent is not to redeem him in the eyes of the mainstream academy. Rather, I reconsider Hayek in particular with the broader aim of seeking to clarify where liberal political thought finds itself in the wake of the battle between welfarists and libertarians. Twentieth-century liberalism began as the story of a search for first principles which could supply a decisive resolution to long-raging debates among liberals over the limits of the legitimate use of state power. In the end, however, the quest for a philosophical resolution to a fundamentally political question led liberals, including Hayek, to the conclusion that liberal principles can provide no final settlement to the most basic political, social, and economic controversies of our time.

Liberalism Against Democracy

Although it is virtually an article of public faith in the United States that free markets and democratic self-government are mutually supportive, throughout his career Hayek insisted that democratic government poses a grave threat to freedom, both for markets and for individuals. In *The Constitution of Liberty* (1960), which stands as his most significant contribution to political philosophy, Hayek offered perhaps his most spirited defense of the democratic ideal, but only to counter what he saw as a potentially dangerous rising tide of conservative elitism. Here, Hayek went out of his way to make it clear that he had "no sympathy with the anti-democratic strain of conservatism."[10] At the same time, however, he reminded his readers, "I do not regard majority rule as an end but merely as a means, or perhaps even as the least evil of those forms of government from which we have to choose." Hayek gave democracy his most sustained—and most damning—treatment in *The Political Order of a Free People* (1979), the culminating volume of the three-part *Law, Legislation, and Liberty* series he first published in the 1970s to detail and develop the abstract ideal of a liberal political order he had originally sketched in *The Constitution of Liberty* (1960). In *The Political Order of a Free People*, Hayek again defends democracy, but this time only by likening it to "sanitary precautions against the plague," a necessary evil whose chief merit is to ward off the potential for something worse.[11] With this tepid endorsement, Hayek goes on to provide a scathing critique of democracy as we know it, charging that "under the prevailing system it is not the common opinion of a majority that decides on common issues, but a majority that owes its existence and power to the gratifying of the special interests of numerous small groups, which the representatives cannot refuse to grant if they are to remain a majority."[12] He goes on to say that "we have under the false name of democracy created a machinery in which not the majority decides, but each member of the majority has to consent to many bribes to get majority support for his own special demands."[13] While certainly worth preserving, he concluded, democracy "is far from being the highest political value, and an unlimited democracy may well be worse than limited government of a different kind."

Hayek's grave distrust of democratic decision-making bodies, especially representative legislatures, might be mistaken as an argument for minimalist government. However, in *The Political Order of a Free People*, Hayek cautions against the impression

that we regard the enforcement of the law and the defense against external enemies as the only legitimate functions of government. . . . Far from advocating such
a "minimal state," we find it unquestionable that in an advanced society government ought to use its power of raising funds by taxation to provide a number of
services which for various reasons cannot be provided, or cannot be provided adequately, by the market.[14]

Hayek goes on to endorse state provision of roads and publicly financed
education,[15] as well as

building regulations, pure food laws, the certification of certain professions, the
restrictions on the sale of certain dangerous goods (such as arms, explosives, poisons
and drugs), as well as some safety and health regulations for the processes of production and the provision of such public institutions as theatres, sports grounds, etc.[16]

Given statements such as these, one wonders how it could be that Hayek
is so widely regarded as a libertarian extremist. The confusion is attribut-
able, as I will explain, to a gap that Hayek himself was never able to bridge
between his philosophy and his politics. Too often, it simply has been
assumed that Hayek's philosophy provides the justification for his policy preferences, but this is not the case. However enticing the promise of
absolute prohibitions against coercive acts of government may have been
to a thinker with libertarian leanings, Hayek did not believe there was a
philosophical basis for categorical bans on governmental intervention in
the market. Rather, as a liberal Hayek felt compelled to acknowledge the
potential legitimacy of all sorts of public policies he nonetheless believed
ill-considered; in this way, Hayek recognized a distinction between illiberal
policies and unwise ones. As far as Hayek was concerned, foolish policies
should be dismissed simply because they are foolish, and in most cases, there
would be neither cause nor need to invoke higher-order liberal principles.
This crucial point has been lost in the critical conversation surrounding
Hayek's work, as more mainstream liberal commentators such as those
mentioned above, including Bruce Ackerman, Benjamin Barber, Stephen
Holmes, and Cass Sunstein, have ignored Hayek's own, explicit warning
against the temptation to invoke principles as a way to preempt policy debate. Throughout his long career, Hayek never diverged from the idea that
"the habitual appeal to the principle of non-interference in the fight against
ill-considered or harmful measures [has] had the effect of blurring the fundamental distinction between the kinds of measures which are and those
which are not compatible with a free system."[17] Despite his protestation to
the contrary, ever since *The Road to Serfdom* Hayek has been portrayed not
just as a political but as a philosophical proponent of laissez-faire policies,
though this depiction badly distorts both our understanding of his work,
and more broadly, our view of the meaning and limits of liberalism as a
theory of politics.

Limited Government in the Hayekian Regime

Hayek's plan for limiting government rests on the proposition that to be legitimate, a law must be framed as a "general, abstract [rule], equally applicable to all."[18] As he explained most succinctly in *The Road to Serfdom,* "Government confines itself to fixing rules determining the conditions under which the available resources may be used, leaving to the individuals the decision for what ends they are to be used." [19] As Hayek explains, "the general, abstract rules, which are laws in the substantive sense, are . . . essentially long-term measures, referring to yet unknown cases and containing *no references to particular persons, places, or objects*" (emphasis added).[20] The insistence that all legislation be general and abstract lies at the core of Hayek's rule-of-law ideal—the rule of law requires that only legislation that conforms to this requirement be accorded the status of law.

Why does Hayek adopt a formal theory of limited government, one which establishes constraints on the kinds of laws that can be passed but which does not explicitly prohibit any measures in particular? The reason has to do with Hayek's understanding of the meaning of liberalism itself. Specifically, Hayek believed that a liberal state should remain neutral on questions about which reasonable disagreement is possible, such as the question of which rights are to be regarded as fundamental (and hence, which kinds of laws are held to violate these fundamental rights). This obligation to neutrality, however, poses a dilemma for liberals: to limit government we must specify which rights are fundamental, but in doing so we privilege the worldviews of some over others. Consider, for example, the question of whether members of a liberal democracy have a right to a social minimum or, alternatively, whether we have a right to be free from taxes to fund social programs we oppose. The determination of the meaning and extent of rights ranging from free speech to reproduction inevitably takes sides in matters of significant social controversy. But for Hayek, as for all liberals, the stakes of overcoming the dilemma of neutrality are high. In the absence of a consensus on first principles, the discourse of limited government becomes little more than a rhetorical ploy, masking the triumph of some people's values over others, undermining the very goal toward which limited government aims in the first place. Does Hayek's formal theory of the rule of law, which avoids taking a position on the controversial question of fundamental rights, accomplish the end of limiting government?

Hayek's approach has been roundly criticized by thinkers spanning the liberal spectrum of welfarists to libertarians. The critical consensus is that the Hayekian rule of law is hopelessly ambiguous and, hence, unable to guarantee that government will remain minimal. Notably—and somewhat confoundingly for those familiar with Hayek's reputation as a rabid free-marketeer—libertarian observers have been among the harshest critics of Hayek's rule-of-law conception.[21] The problem, from a libertarian perspective, is that so many laws could meet the formal requirements of the rule of law—that is, they might be general, abstract, and prospective—and nonetheless, highly invasive of individual liberty. In short, a regime might satisfy the criteria of the Hayekian rule of law and yet be illiberal. As Chandran Kukathas, whose *Hayek and Modern Liberalism* (1989) remains among the most thoroughgoing and insightful treatments of Hayek's philosophical legacy to date, opines: "it is not clear that the abstract and general rules which conform to the ideal of the rule of law will always occur with principles which Hayek, and liberals generally, would find morally acceptable—unless those other principles are explicitly endorsed."[22] Ronald Hamowy, a longtime libertarian commentator, goes even further, suggesting that Hayek's theory might actually be used as a justification for illiberal laws:

Hayek's proposed framework . . . offers a rationale for what clearly are coercive acts of the state, e.g. conscription, interference in the economy (under the principle that it is attempting to minimize personal coercion) and alteration by fiat of the social structure of personal relationships which have developed spontaneously and undirected over the course of centuries.[23]

Libertarian commentators are not alone in concluding that Hayek fails to deliver a prescription for a minimalist government. In *Legal Reasoning and Political Conflict*, Cass Sunstein contends that "the rule of law, standing by itself, does not provide [the] theory" that could enable us to distinguish "arbitrary state intervention in the free market from acceptable forms of regulation," and Sunstein goes on to fault Hayek for assuming a relationship between the rule of law and the free market, noting that given the vagueness of Hayekian constraints, a socialist regime could be as compatible with Hayek's version of the rule of law as a free-market regime would be.[24] In a similar vein, Andrew Gamble observes that "since Hayek believes that the state must retain some coercive powers, the question of the scope of these powers is left indeterminate. It is a practical question to be decided case-by-case. Hayek assumes that the legislators in his ideal constitution will embrace a liberal political philosophy. But he offers no reason why they should."[25] Or as Richard Bellamy puts it, "the trouble with this criterion is that it is so weak that with a little ingenuity numerous injunctions totally incompatible with individual liberty in either the positive or negative sense can be made to pass it."[26]

The critical consensus about Hayek, then, is that he fails because he assumes that conformity to the rule of law will guarantee liberal outcomes, when in practice his rule-of-law requirements are too weak and ambiguous to produce the desired result. I suggest, however, that critics have made an error in assuming that, as John Gray puts it, Hayek "expects" the rule of law to have "classical liberal implications."[27] In fact, Hayek himself was well aware of the indeterminacy of his rule-of-law prescriptions. Ignoring this acknowledgment, however, critics have preferred to present their revelations of the indeterminacy of the rule of law as a critical coup, rather than merely a reiteration of Hayek's own ideas.

Though Hayek acknowledged that "no entirely satisfactory criterion has been found that would always tell us what kind of classification is compatible with equality before the law," he cautions against the conclusion that the rule of law is therefore a "meaningless" constraint.[28] Instead, Hayek offers a series of tests to guide deliberations about the legitimacy of proposed legislation. For example, he suggests that in considering legislation, we ask ourselves whether "those inside any group singled out acknowledge the legitimacy of the distinction as well as those outside it."[29] Admittedly, this still leaves ample room for discretion, but this is not, in Hayek's view, a fatal weakness. For as important as limited government is, Hayek is equally concerned that government not be hamstrung by categorical limits on the exercise of power, for he insists that there are situations in which intervention is warranted. The problem with absolute prohibitions, as Hayek sees it, is that they do not allow sufficient room for a society to respond to contingency. Thus, Hayek insists on a conception of the rule of law that will provide "ample scope for experimentation and improvement within the permanent legal framework which makes it possible for a free society to operate most efficiently. . . . The continuous growth of wealth and technological knowledge which such a system makes possible will constantly suggest new ways in which government might render services to its citizens and bring such possibilities within the range of the practicable."[30]

The critical emphasis placed on Hayek's rhetoric has crowded out attention to the extent of his attention to the details of public policy, an interest that clearly demonstrates his preference for "case-by-case" decision making over categorical pronouncements. Realizing that liberal principles only go so far in proscribing the scope of political power, throughout his career Hayek offered detailed discussions of such issues as housing, health care, and education. Unfortunately, critics outside the field of economics typically have ignored this dimension of his work. This is especially true with respect to treatments of *The Constitution of Liberty* by political theorists, who generally have neglected the entire second half of the book, presumably on the assumption that the policy chapters are little more than a tedious and mechanical effort to apply the general principle of the rule of law as stated in the first half. But this is not the case: though Hayek insists that nuts-and-bolts policy discussions must assume a background commitment to the rule of law, this contention marks the beginning, rather than the end, of his treatment of policy questions. Consider, for example, Hayek's discussion of what he refers to as "the crisis of social security" in the U.S. in the early 1960s. Hayek distances himself from doctrinaire opponents of statist welfare programs that provide a social minimum, recognizing the value of such programs despite the fact that they necessarily "involve some redistribution of income."[31] In seeking to draw a line between the use of public policy to provide for those in need and the use of public policy to achieve what some may consider a more just distribution of wealth, Hayek defends means testing for services rather than a regime of universal entitlements. Similarly, in his discussion of education, housing, and monetary policy, to cite just some examples, Hayek concedes a role for the state and seeks to identify the appropriate level of intervention based on a consideration not simply of principles but of the likely outcomes of various measures. In essence, then, for Hayek policy analysis picks up where philosophy leaves off. Though liberal principles may "provide the criterion which enables us to distinguish between those measures which are and those which are not compatible with a free system," Hayek is emphatic that "those that are may be examined further on the grounds of expediency. Many such measures will, of course, still be undesirable or even harmful."[32] The problem with most governmental measures in Hayek's view, then, is not that they violate the rule of law (which they do not, given how open-ended the standard is), but rather that "the great majority of governmental measures which have been advocated in [the field of economic policy] are, in fact, inexpedient, either because they will fail or because their costs will outweigh the advantages. This means that, so long as they are compatible with the rule of law, they cannot be rejected out of hand as government intervention but must be examined in each instance from the viewpoint of expediency."[33]

But what does Hayek mean by "expediency"? Is a reliance on judgments of expediency a way of sneaking principled foundations back in under the cover of objective policy analysis? Though Hayek does, in places, leave himself open to charges of covert foundationalism, one should avoid the temptation to draw such a conclusion. To illustrate, consider the following well-known passage from *The Constitution of Liberty*, where Hayek describes a hypothetical situation

in which somebody has acquired control of the whole water supply of an oasis and used this position to exact unusual performances from those whose life depends on access to that water. Other instances of the same kind would be the only doctor available to perform an urgent life-saving operation and similar cases of rescue in an emergency where special unforeseeable circumstances have placed into a single hand the power of rescue from grave danger. They are all instances where I should wish that those in whose hands the life of another is placed should be under a moral and legal obligation to render the help in their power even if they cannot expect any remuneration—though they should of course be entitled to normal remuneration if it is in the power of the rescued. It is because these services are regarded as rights to be counted upon that a refusal to render them except on unusual terms is justly regarded as a harmful alteration of the environment and therefore as coercion.[34]

Statements like this have been rallied as evidence that Hayek relies on an implicit theory of rights, despite his avowed commitment to neutrality. But the above passage should be read not as a claim about what liberalism *requires*, but rather as a policy recommendation based on an interpretation of what liberal principles *allow*. Hayek implies only that it would be consistent with liberalism for government to constrain the market in the way he describes above, but he does not claim that liberal principles *require* such constraints. He says that he "should wish" that there would be moral and legal obligations in force to encourage the delivery of services, but he does not say that liberal commitments entail such obligations. Furthermore, he stresses that the obligation to deliver services exist because "these services *are regarded* as rights," placing the emphasis on social agreement, not on the dictate of principle.

My portrait of Hayek as one who recognizes the limits of liberal principle, rather than one who insists that liberalism entails a commitment to particular policy orientations such as laissez-faire economics, helps to make sense of Hayek's otherwise mysterious endorsement, late in his career, of the writings of none other than John Rawls. In the preface to *The Mirage of Social Justice* (1976), Hayek goes out of his way to say that he has "no basic quarrel" with the position Rawls defends, concluding that the differences dividing them are "more verbal than substantial." Hayek's assessment is surprising, to say the least—how could the author of *The Road to Serfdom* endorse the writings of a man whose project has been described as "the most comprehensive effort in modern philosophy to justify a socialist ethic"?[35] Hayek's enthusiasm seems to derive from his approval for Rawls's view that "the task of selecting specific systems or distributions of desired things as just must be 'abandoned as mistaken in principle, and it is, in any case, not capable of a definite answer'."[36] Hayek recognizes that Rawls refrains from prescribing this or that particular allocation of resources; rather, Rawls defines a just allocation as the pattern of distribution that emerges when individuals take actions within a social structure that itself is fundamentally just. According to Rawls, the "primary subject" of social justice is the arrangement of the basic social and political institutions, and justice does not require— indeed, it forbids—government from dictating particular outcomes at the level of allocations. Though Rawls is sometimes treated as if he were a proponent of redistribution, it is important to understand, as Hayek certainly did, that Rawls seeks to achieve a more equitable allocation of resources by indirect means, arranging the basic institutions of society such that a just distribution will result without specifying in advance just what this distribution is. In this way, Hayek sees Rawls as an ally in the campaign against the planned economy—and Hayek reveals that his antipathy to the welfare state is rooted in an opposition to planning, not to economic equality per se.

Still, in fairness to the critics it should be noted that Hayek's own rhetoric invites precisely the kind of hasty dismissal that has obscured the subtlety of his account of limited government for so long. As John Maynard Keynes once noted, Hayek himself eclipsed the nuance and complexity of his account by indulging in rhetoric that misrepresented his own theorizing, such as his well-known warning that "so soon as one moves an inch in the planned direction you are necessarily launched on the slippery path which will lead you in due course over the precipice."[37] In the end, Hayek seemed torn between his philosophy and his politics, hoping, perhaps, that powerful rhetoric might make the case that liberal principles surely could not. Throughout his career, Hayek took stands on public policy issues—from opposition to public housing to rent control to agricultural subsidies to conservationism to public funding for academic research—that marked him as a conservative, but Hayek never claimed that his policy positions were justified by consideration of liberal principle alone. Indeed, while sharing with conservatives an opposition to many, if not most welfare state policies, Hayek distinguished himself from "true conservatives" on the grounds that he was not opposed in principle to change, only to the specific changes in the size and scope of government associated with the development of the welfare state.[38] Nonetheless, the stridency of his tone has made it all too easy for conservative acolytes to appropriate Hayek as a champion of their cause.

Dethroning Politics?

One suspects that it was Hayek's own recognition of the modesty of his proposed rule-of-law constraints on government that propelled him later in life to explore the possibility that institutional limits might serve as an additional bulwark against excessive coercion. In *The Political Order of a Free People* (1979), Hayek laid out an ambitious program of institutional reforms, including a planned redesign of the legislature, judiciary, and executive branches, as well as several important changes in voting rules and citizenship eligibility. Unfortunately, in exaggerating the significance of rule-of-law constraints in Hayek's ideal regime, commentators have failed to seriously engage Hayek's proposed institutional innovations, treating these later writings as little more than the indulgent musings of a thinker sadly past his prime. That said, Hayek himself did much to invite this dismissiveness, offering a plan for institutional reform that does seem, at least on its face, rather eccentric. And then there is the fact of the irony—if not outright hypocrisy—of Hayek's turn to the task of institutional design in the first place. Though Hayek is remembered as a staunch enemy of the planned economy, at the end of his career he becomes an advocate for what we might think of as "planned politics." Hayek's institutional turn is especially surprising given his skepticism about such undertakings. In *The Constitution of Liberty*, Hayek makes a point of denying credit even to the framers of the U.S. Constitution. He opines:

Much is sometimes made of the fact that the American constitution is the product of design and that, for the first time in modern history, a people deliberately constructed the kind of government under which they wished to live. . . . This attitude

. . . was more justified here than in many similar instances, yet still essentially mistaken. It is remarkable how different from any clearly foreseen structure is the frame of government which ultimately emerged, how much of the outcome was due to historical accident or the application of inherited principles to a new situation. What new discoveries the federal Constitution contained either resulted from the application of traditional principles to particular problems or emerged as only dimly perceived consequences of general ideas.[39]

Nonetheless, Hayek treads into the uncertain territory of constitutional design. The most dramatic change he proposes concerns the distribution of legislative power. First, Hayek advocates for a Legislative Assembly to be charged solely with the determination of general rules of just conduct.[40] His unusual proposals for the election of members to these offices reflects a desire to shield legislators from the crude play of power politics. As he explains, "it would seem wise to rely on the old experience that a man's contemporaries are his fairest judges and to ask each group of people of the same age once in their lives, say in the calendar year in which they reached the age of 45, to select from their midst representatives to serve for fifteen years."[41] In what is generally considered to be among the most risible passages Hayek ever penned, he goes on to suggest that, in the interest of promoting more responsible decision making, members of each class should mix throughout their adult life in local political clubs which, Hayek explains, "would possibly be more attractive if men of one age group were brought together with women two years or so younger."[42] Hayek next proposes the creation of a second legislative body, the Governmental Assembly, which is to be charged with administering the general rules established by the Legislative Assembly. Hayek suggests that the former be modeled according to present-day parliaments; the difference in outcome would be an effect of its being limited by the upper house.[43] Additionally, he argues for the creation of a constitutional court to settle disagreements between the two assemblies and to make changes in the constitution as deemed necessary.[44]

There is good reason to be skeptical that such a scheme would be capable of actualization, given the evident difficulties entailed in distinguishing general rule making from administration and application. Hamowy points out that Hayek's proposal is politically naïve, since "the effect of such a division of powers would be (and, indeed, was) to place in the hands of the lower house all substantive power to govern; for, while it could pick and choose which rules of conduct enacted by the upper house it wished to enforce, it could further enforce its own rules via the taxing power."[45] In other words, Hayek shuffles power around, but in the end he does nothing to contain it. Hamowy's verdict is unequivocal: "Despite his elaborate and complex schema of government, in the end Hayek returns to his original restrictions on the formal qualities of the rules of conduct that he first laid down in his *Constitution of Liberty* as the only protection against arbitrary government."[46]

While a libertarian critic like Hamowy contends that Hayek's proposals fail to provide sufficient checks on the potential for democratic excess, political theorist William Scheuerman draws the opposite conclusion, suggesting that Hayek in effect trades democracy for authoritarianism. A more mainstream thinker than Hamowy, Scheuerman ardently defends the possibility of preserving the rule of law in a welfare state capitalist democracy From Scheuerman's perspective, the risk posed to individual liberty in the Hayekian regime emanates not in majority tyranny, as Hamowy suggests, but rather in a tendency toward authoritarian rule.[47] At first glance, such a claim seems implausible, even absurd: how could one of the twentieth century's most ardent defenders of limited government possibly be vulnerable to a charge of enabling too much governmental coercion? Scheuerman claims that Hayek inadvertently buys into authoritarianism rule by uncritically appropriating Carl Schmitt's critique of the welfare state. It is well known that Hayek found much that was compelling in Schmitt's case against the effort to marry liberalism and democracy, and Scheuerman insists that "having chosen to play by the rules of Schmitt's intellectual universe, Hayek proves unable to escape from all of its dangers."[48] Explaining that Schmitt's embrace of authoritarianism is based on the assumption that dictators are less likely to fall prey to interest group politicking, Scheuerman suggests that the main distinction between Schmitt and Hayek is simply that Schmitt openly embraces "decisionistic" lawmaking whereas Hayek ducks the issue of how choices will be made in his ideal regime. Scheuerman observes: "Some versions of Hayek's definition of general law suggest that virtually any form of state intervention is incompatible with general law, whereas others provide at least some room for welfare state-type activities." Scheuerman's suggestion is that Hayek exploits the ambiguity of the generality requirement of the rule of law, bending its meaning "so as to accord with the immediate imperatives of the political struggle against defenders of the welfare state."[49] In other words, Hayek insists on a rigorous definition of generality when he wants to argue against a particular measure, but softens its meaning when a policy he considers innocuous or expedient is under consideration.

Scheuerman's charges might be dismissed out of hand were Hayek the principled minimalist so many have assumed him to be. But as I have suggested above, this line of defense rests on a mistaken view. Given that Hayek does allow for a host of state interventions in the market and private life, there can be no dodging the question of *how* such decisions are to be made in his ideal regime. Scheuerman's contention is that since we know Hayek distrusts democracy, he must intend for decisions to be made by an authoritarian actor. To bolster his claim, Scheuerman recalls Hayek's proposal that the Legislative Assembly be elected by a one-time vote by a single age cohort, suggesting that this policy is tantamount to de facto disenfranchisement, a system that "would undoubtedly result in a vast reduction of existing possibilities for democratic participation."[50] Pointedly, Scheuerman wonders whether Hayek's proposed scheme even deserves "to be considered compatible with the basic ideals of modern liberal democracy?"

While Hayek is undeniably critical of much that passes for democratic decision-making, Scheuerman goes too far in suggesting that Hayek's proposed reforms of the democratic process are intended to dismantle democracy altogether. Indeed, in light of the evident failures of the democratic process in the contemporary U.S., perhaps we should question the commitment to democracy of those like Scheuerman who seek to defend the status quo! Though Hayek's proposal to curtail voting rights certainly gives one pause, we only do a disservice to the democratic ideal in suggesting, as Scheuerman does, that voting rights are the ultimate measure of a citizen's capacity for "democratic participation." Whatever objections one might have to Hayek's specific proposals, his intent is to shift from a conception of democratic citizenship that exalts occasional voting to a system based on sustained and intimate connections in a community context. Even if one thinks Hayek's favored reforms inadequate or misdirected, one nevertheless may welcome his willingness to broach the taboo subject of the embarrassing failure of U.S. democracy to live up to its potential. In equating criticism of current democratic practice with advocacy for authoritarianism, Scheuerman only contributes to the suppression of the kind of productive dissent necessary to chart a course toward democratic reform.

In the end, Hayek is best viewed not as a closet authoritarian, but rather as a reluctant democrat, for his true failure lies in an unwillingness to embrace the depth of his own commitment to the project of self-rule. Recognizing the limits of liberal principles to pre-settle fundamental questions about the scope and reach of government—including the issue of the legitimacy of redistributionist social and economic policies—Hayek believes that such decisions must be made in the political process. And though Hayek is wary of democratically elected decision makers, in the end he defends a legislative structure that retains a foundation in the principle of self-governance, if only because of his unsentimental judgment that democracy in some form is the surest protection against the devolution into tyranny. In the end, then, Hayekian liberalism proves itself to have but a contingent relationship with capitalism, while being married—for better and for worse—to the democratic ideal.

What is true for Hayek holds more generally for liberal theorists at the dawn of the millennium. It is time to shift from a debate about the nature of prepolitical principles to a consideration of the state of democratic political practices in liberal societies. Though liberals have construed the question of limited government as a matter of liberal principle constraining democratic majorities, this way of framing the problem obscures the critical role that politics plays in a liberal regime as a site for debate and decision about the scope and reach of government. Rather than asking whether government is doing too much, then, liberal theorists might begin to consider whether the people are doing too little. In a liberal regime, the fate of rights is in the hands of those who participate in politics, for it is in the political process itself that the meaning and extent of rights is determined.

11

The Politics of Rich and Rich:
Postwar Investigations of Foundations
and the Rise of the Philanthropic Right

Alice O'Connor

In July 1953, Representative B. Carroll Reece (R-Tenn.) made an announcement on the floor of the U.S. House of Representatives pitched for maximum shock appeal. He had evidence of a "diabolical conspiracy" to promote "the furtherance of socialism in the United States," and he was seeking congressional approval to lead a special investigation into its nefarious workings. The target of investigation would be the nation's biggest tax-exempt foundations and the putatively educational organizations they were funding. Under the cover of philanthropic beneficence, Reece contended, foundations like Rockefeller, Carnegie, Ford, and Russell Sage were using their vast fortunes for "un-American and subversive activities" and "for purposes other than the purposes for which they were established."[1] In a betrayal of the very principles of free enterprise underlying its accumulated wealth, big philanthropy had become the chief financier of a plot to undermine capitalism. That plot, as later elaborated in Reece's investigation, involved a systematic program of indoctrination by a cadre of government bureaucrats, policy intellectuals, university professors, and educators bent on making New Deal collectivism—along with a cascading array of "isms" that came to include internationalism, cultural relativism, racial integrationism, and social scientific empiricism—the reigning philosophy in American life.[2] Knowingly or not, the captains of industry behind the nation's biggest foundations had allowed their fortunes to be conscripted into capitalism's demise.

Much to his disappointment, Reece's dramatic accusations fell far short of the intended effect. The investigations were approved, but with a bare majority of the Republican-dominated House, and with a committee membership set up to keep Reece, as designated chairman and self-appointed dragon slayer, in check. Reece's efforts as official Red hunter also fell short: several months of investigation generated a ridiculously expansive list of red by innuendo and association, but failed to uncover any plausible evidence of communist infiltration within foundation ranks. Nor did the Reece investigation produce added regulation beyond the prohibitions on political activity that Congress had already legislated in the Revenue Act of 1950. In fact, as fellow committee member Wayne L. Hays (D-Oh.) eviscerated the parade of foundation-unfriendly witnesses one by one, the widely covered Reece committee hearings—held in the wake of the Army-McCarthy hearings in summer 1954—made it embarrassingly clear to all but his die-hard supporters that the congressman from Tennessee had gone too far. Having caught the McCarthyite wave when the political tides were finally turning against it, Reece abruptly ended the hearings without giving the foundations a chance to defend themselves in public.

Of course, Reece's allegations have a certain contemporary resonance, as charges of conspiratorial liberal indoctrination—or, for that matter, of a foundation-financed right-wing coup—get replayed in current-day "culture wars." But the two can also be connected as part of a continuous, albeit evolving right-wing critique of the "collectivist" drift of postwar capitalism and of the role of major cultural institutions in bringing it about. The big foundations, situated as they are at very nexus of capitalism and its culture, proved especially apt targets for this emerging critique—not, as it were, for the socialist conspiracies they were harboring but for the changes in postwar political economy and political culture they had come to represent. Moreover, it was in this capacity that, from the early 1950s through the late 1960s, philanthropy in general—and a handful of the nation's leading foundations in particular—came under an unprecedented degree of public scrutiny from various quarters, including Congress, the Treasury Department, and political activists on the left as well as the right. As others have pointed out, this period of scrutiny and investigation culminated in some important changes in the way foundations do business, largely instituted in response to the regulations of the Tax Reform Act of 1969.[3] But more significant for purposes of this discussion, it also reflected important changes in the politics of postwar capitalism, in two related ways.

First, the postwar investigations spotlighted important shifts in the political and ideological alignments of concentrated philanthropic wealth. When first subject to congressional investigation during the Progressive Era, foundations were charged with furthering the monopolistic schemes of corporate capitalism. By the postwar decades big foundations like Carnegie, Rockefeller, and the newly created Ford Foundation were under attack for the nominally neutral, research-based reformism they had come to embrace and for their role in facilitating an ongoing accommodation between a more softened, heavily managerial brand of corporate capitalism and an expanding, increasingly bureaucratized postwar state. Elsewhere heralded as a sign of "consensus," to critics such accommodation—and the role of big philanthropy in it—reflected the growing ideological hegemony of a narrowly constituted, big corporate/big government and, increasingly, big university elite.[4] By the 1960s, much of this criticism was coming from the left—in a new, nearly decade-long set of congressional investigations launched in 1961 by Texas populist Wright Patman, in the rising furor over revelations of foundation collusion with the CIA, and in scholarly critiques of the role of foundations in promoting imperialistic schemes of modernization and development in the third world.[5] But it was the right that made big philanthropy its particular and persistent target throughout the postwar decades, consistently attacking prominent foundations on political and ideological grounds.

From the narrow standpoint of partisan politics, these foundations proved useful targets for right-wing Republicans as emblems of the growing power of an increasingly liberal establishment—and of the complicity of Republican moderates in its rise. Foundations were also apt targets on a broader ideological front, as bellwethers of the "collectivist" drift of postwar government and political economy, and of the role of intellectuals and professional bureaucrats in bringing it about. Whether for narrow partisan or broader ideological purposes, an attack on big philanthropy could be used to mobilize various strands of discontent—anticommunist, anti-intellectual, isolationist, racist—in efforts to regain ascendancy for the right. It also proved something of a rehearsal for a now familiar movement-defining narrative, with a coddled, unaccountable class of professional "philanthropoids" playing the part later assigned to the "new class": diverting the fruits of capitalist enterprise to promote a radical agenda of economic planning, welfare statism, internationalism, and racial integration.[6]

Second, the right-wing attack on the big foundations underscores the degree to which postwar battles over capitalism were being fought on cultural as well as political and economic grounds. For all the hysterics in Reece's charges, they were grounded in a crude awareness that the cultural underpinnings of old-fashioned, individualistic, "free enterprise" capitalism were under threat; that foundations, or, really, the concentration of cultural and intellectual capital they had come to represent, were somehow implicated in its demise; and that restoring "free enterprise" capitalism to a position of dominance would require recapturing control over cultural just as much as economic production. Thus, while Texas populist Wright Patman went after gigantic foundation fortunes as the nexus of economic monopoly, critics on the right honed in on the cultural monopoly they exercised, especially through their hold on education, social science, and government— notably, the very segments of postwar society that, in the eyes of Clark Kerr, Daniel Bell, John Kenneth Galbraith, and others discussed in this volume, were making the old struggles of industrial capitalism obsolete. In this instance, we can see that the right-wing move to make culture the issue— even when conservatives sidestepped or elided the traditional categories of class, capital, and labor—was not so much an abandonment of the old struggles as an attempt to fight them on other grounds. By the same token, the right's attack on the big foundations illuminates an aspect of recent-day "culture wars" that is often overlooked: their grounding in a revolt against the vaguely pluralist, empiricist, putatively "value-free" tradition of social science underlying liberal "consensus" politics and political culture.[7]

Unlikely though it may have seemed at the time, the right proved highly effective at mobilizing its cultural critique into lasting political action—far more effective than its left or its liberal center counterparts. Thus, even as the mainstream philanthropic establishment was reorganizing in response to reform legislation passed in 1969, the conservative right was laying the groundwork for an alternative philanthropic network that would aim to provide the cultural, intellectual, and ideological capital for the triumphant return of laissez-faire capitalism—heralded, as it were, by the escalating erosion of the New Deal welfare state and progressive taxation, as well as the deregulation of labor markets and of corporate and individual wealth. This in turn helped to set the stage for the consolidation of what Sidney Blumenthal aptly refers to as a conservative "counter-establishment" of philanthropoids, social scientists, and policy intellectuals—for it was very much with an eye toward countering the work of liberal foundations and their grantees that conservative philanthropy developed its own radical agenda for political, economic, and cultural reform.[8]

Congress and the Foundations: From Capitalist Tools to Cultural Subversives

It was in a much different context, of labor radicalism and rising resistance to enormous concentrations of capitalist wealth, that Progressive-era reformers began to take official notice of the large philanthropic trusts and to portray them as powerful instruments of cultural and ideological indoctrination as well as political influence. They were spurred in this direction by a number of factors, not least of them the broader effort to rein in the "money trust." And would-be reformers were responding to the massive spate of philanthropic institution-building that reached its climax during the first decade and a half of the twentieth century. These were the years that saw the creation of the gigantic general purpose foundations that would dominate the field for decades to come: the Russell Sage Foundation (1907), the Carnegie Corporation (1911), and the Rockefeller Foundation (1913).

While hardly the first time great industrial fortunes would be channeled into tax-free charitable trusts, to a host of critics the arrival of big general-purpose philanthropy had all the markings of a dual-purpose capitalist plot: to forestall public regulation of industrial monopoly by bathing it in benevolence; and to extend the already considerable monopoly private wealth held over production and labor to the education and "general welfare" of the nation as a whole.[9] Significantly, some of the sharpest criticisms came from within the very social work/social welfare circles that, assisted by philanthropic dollars, were becoming an increasingly effective network linking social research, social documentary, journalism, and reform.[10] Writing in the network's house organ *The Survey*, editor Edward T. Devine (former director of the New York School of Philanthropy) warned of "the brutal power of concentrated wealth, even when embodied in a philanthropic foundation." Devine argued that foundations should be subject to taxation as well as limitations on their life spans, lest "'the dead hand'" of capitalism be allowed to impede "human progress."[11] Taft administration officials were similarly skeptical that such "indefinite scheme[s] for perpetuating vast wealth" could be construed to be consistent with "the public interest," as opposed to the decidedly private interest of preserving the great trusts.[12] And when Congress got wind of an arrangement between the Department of Agriculture and Rockefeller's General Education Board to channel philanthropic dollars into USDA demonstration farming projects, charges of a "dark plot" to undermine the very "fabric of government" made national headlines.[13]

Such suspicions were only heightened by a sequence of what hardly looked like coincidences involving Rockefeller philanthropy and the fate of the Standard Oil Company.[14] In 1910, John D. Rockefeller had his lawyers petition Congress for a federal charter of incorporation for what would become the Rockefeller Foundation—just days before Standard Oil Company lawyers filed a last-resort appeal to the Supreme Court to avoid the breakup of the Standard Oil monopoly. After three years of protracted debate, Rockefeller dropped the congressional petition and incorporated in New York, but his foundation soon became the target of an incendiary investigation by the congressionally chartered Commission on Industrial Relations as part of its mandate to study the conditions underlying the rise of labor radicalism and industrial violence. The commission had been authorized in 1912, nominally as a response to the 1910 bombing of the *Los Angeles Times* by radical labor activists. But by the time the public phase of its work got underway in 1914, the commission's focus had shifted to the violence of capital against labor. The catalyst was the infamous Ludlow Massacre, where national guardsmen deployed at the behest of the Rockefeller-owned Colorado Fuel and Iron Company engaged in pitched battle against striking miners and their families—leaving women and children among the dead. Commission chair Frank P. Walsh expanded the investigations to include new general purpose foundations when he learned that John D. Rockefeller, Jr., had used his philanthropic reach to commission an alternative industrial relations study from Canadian labor minister (and later prime minister) Mackenzie King. Declaring it "a menace to the welfare of society," Walsh denounced Rockefeller's entire philanthropic enterprise as an exercise in public relations, an attempt "to present to the world, as handsome and admirable, an economic and industrial regime that draws its substance from the sweat and blood and tears of exploited and dispossessed humanity."[15] The Commission's final report went considerably further, charging that the industrial "domination" of the corporate giants was "being rapidly extended to control the education and social service of the Nation." As the instruments of that domination, the report concluded, the huge general purpose foundations should be abolished, their wealth appropriated by the state for unemployment relief, as just compensation for all the "laborers who really contributed to the funds."[16]

These, along with other Walsh Commission proposals, went unheeded, as did most of the contemporary proposals for regulating the large general purpose philanthropic trusts.[17] Nevertheless, the investigations—and the reform period they embodied—at once signaled and helped set off the very changes within organized philanthropy that would later draw Reece's fire and that, for the time being, would make it less overtly an instrument of "creeping capitalism." Most importantly, the Walsh investigations drew the big general purpose foundations into the fiercest battles of industrial capitalism, not simply as individual trusts, but as part of the larger, newly expanded and institutionalized presence of private philanthropy in public life. In response, organized philanthropy did not so much collude with capital as establish alternative, ostensibly less political spaces for engaging and defusing those battles—nonprofit space, as it were, inhabited by academics, policy intellectuals, social workers, and civil servants, albeit space demarcated far more by the concerns and interests of capital than of labor.[18] In the process, the big foundations put varying degrees of separation between themselves and the fiercely partisan, competitive capitalism that had initially produced their fortunes—by funding studies of industrial conditions, creating ostensibly neutral policy institutes, putting foundation management in the hands of professional staffers, and even, albeit selectively, by investing in expert-driven, "scientifically" proven programs of reform.[19] In these ways, organized philanthropy sought to set itself off as somehow above politics, partisanship, and the vast inequities reflected in its own concentrated wealth: inequities not long ago embraced and justified as necessities in Andrew Carnegie's gospel of wealth would now be studied, objectified, and explained in foundation-funded studies to ameliorate their effects. At the same time, organized philanthropy operated to delimit and contain the acceptable parameters of reformism so as not to betray its own commitment to capitalism. It was here, in that limited engagement with reformism, that B. Carroll Reece would find the "diabolical conspiracy" he was looking for.

The Reece investigations were actually the second of two inquiries designated to rout out communist subversives from foundation ranks. In late 1951 Representative Eugene E. Cox (D-Ga.) announced his intention to submit a resolution for the creation of a special committee to conduct a "full and complete investigation" of tax-exempt foundations "to determine which such foundations and organizations are using their resources for un-American and subversive activities or for purposes not in the interest or tradition of the United States."[20] Approved in a vote that split moderates from anti-Fair Deal conservatives in both parties, Cox's committee launched the most extensive public inquiry into foundation funds and practices since the Walsh Commission. The irony of the situation was not lost on the Cox Committee, which in its own final report made reference to the warning from the earlier inquiry, "that the foundations would prove the instruments of vested wealth, privilege, and reaction." Now, the committee report noted, the question driving congressional investigation was whether foundations had become "the enemy of the capitalistic system."[21]

Equally significant was the development acknowledged by the hearings themselves: the further expansion of big philanthropy as part of an increasingly organized, not quite public but not entirely private sector, hand in hand with the comparably enormous growth of the federal government. Since the early twentieth-century founding of the Russell Sage, Rockefeller, and Carnegie Foundations, philanthropy had grown bigger in every way: in numbers; in assets (close to $5 billion); and in ambition as a self-appointed steward of the "general welfare."[22] While relatively modest in comparison to corporate wealth, government spending, GNP, or even overall individual giving (foundation expert F. Emerson Andrews wrote that "Americans exhale in tobacco smoke every year more than the accumulated wealth of all the foundations"), the big foundations were nevertheless increasingly self-conscious about justifying their tax-free funds as "venture capital" for social betterment.[23]

Nowhere was this more in evidence than in the gigantic newcomer the Ford Foundation, which just three years earlier had announced its intention to devote its some $500,000,000 in assets to a breathtakingly ambitious agenda designed to promote international peace, world economic development, democratic governance, and scientific understanding of human behavior.[24] But Ford's arrival also signaled other, more qualitative changes that were making the big foundations a lightning rod for the right. Although very much a product of dynastic industrial fortune, the Ford Foundation made little pretense of being under the direct control of its major benefactor, Henry Ford, II. From the start, this was to be philanthropy by expert committee: the Gaither Committee, to be exact, headed by no less an exemplar of the institutionalization of expertise than RAND corporation board chairman G. Rowan Gaither. Gaither, in turn, made sure that Ford's philanthropic enterprise would be based on an unprecedented degree of consultation with academics, policy intellectuals, and experienced philanthropoids. The earliest staff appointments featured such leading lights of the industry-government-university establishment as ex-Marshall Plan administrator and Studebaker CEO Paul Hoffman and University of Chicago president Robert Maynard Hutchins. What's more, this philanthropic newcomer fancied itself a maverick in the field, willing to look beyond major issues of war and human need "to help man achieve his entire well-being—to satisfy his mental, emotional, and spiritual needs as well as his physical wants."[25] In a world of philanthropic "venture capitalists," the Ford Foundation would go one better, to provide, as Henry Ford himself put it, the "venture capital of philanthropy."[26]

As the first of a series of postwar investigations that the leading foundations would alternately treat as a major threat and a minor annoyance, the Cox Committee put the foundations on notice that their wealth, with the tax exemption it enjoyed, was not a birthright but a privilege granted at congressional discretion. It also brought charges that would remain at the core of the decades-long campaign to label mainstream philanthropy the agent of a politically and culturally subversive left-leaning elite.

The Cox Committee organized its investigation around a set of 12 allegations—said to have come from "persons, groups and organizations of widely different backgrounds and all parts of the country"—but that in actuality reflected the anti-New/Fair Deal, McCarthyite, anti-internationalist, and vaguely conspiratorial convictions of the coalition of Southern Democrats and right-wing Republicans that instigated the probe. Three of the allegations, posed as questions, had to do with foundation subsidy for Communists, Communist sympathizers, and/or "Marxist socialism" through hiring and grant making; two with foundation support for "internationalism"; and the others with various charges of financial malfeasance, ranging from tax evasion and undue secrecy to control by "interlocking directorates composed primarily of individuals residing in the North and Middle-Atlantic states."[27]

Although it was couched largely as a loyalty inquiry, insiders were aware that Cox and his allies had a much greater store of political payback and personal animosity to tap. Thus, Cox was widely rumored to be targeting the Carnegie and Rosenwald Foundations, and through them the NAACP, for their race relations work in the South. Cox also tapped into the considerable anti-internationalist contingent, in Congress and more broadly on the right, who were coming together behind Senator John Bricker's proposed amendment to limit presidential treaty-making powers. Their sentiments were captured in a widely circulated pamphlet by conservative *Chicago Tribune* columnist William Fulton, who charged the big foundations with diverting great philanthropic fortunes into "propaganda for globalism, including international communism."[28] The investigations were also caught up in election-year politics: strongly supportive of the Cox resolution were right-wing Republican partisans of Robert A. Taft, who were particularly irked at the prominent support offered by the Rockefellers, Fords, and Ford Foundation president Paul Hoffman, among other representatives of the "eastern establishment," for Eisenhower over Taft in the upcoming 1952 presidential race.[29] Added to all this was an evidently deep stock of animosity for Robert Maynard Hutchins. Summing up the list of "enthusiasts" brought together behind the Cox investigation, reporter Helen Hill Miller included "those who wanted to get rid of the United Nations, those who wanted to get rid of Eisenhower, and those who wanted to get rid of Hutchins."[30] Fearing a witch hunt or an attack on civil rights activists, liberals in both parties had tried to block the investigation, but had managed only to get moderates such as Brooks Hays (D-Ark.) and Angier Goodwin (R-Mass.) appointed to the committee. In assessing the situation for Henry Ford and the still very new Ford Foundation leadership, political consultants raised gravest concerns about whether these more moderate members of the committee would be able to rein Cox in.[31]

But to the extent that conservative critics put much hope in the Cox Committee investigations, they were hugely disappointed by the final report, issued several months later and after Cox's untimely death, which not only exonerated foundations of the charges, but found them praiseworthy in some respects. Indeed, in sharp contrast to Cox's initial charges, the report itself was about as measured as it could be, given the animus that motivated it in the first place. Noting that there had been incidences of communist "infiltration," the report nevertheless concluded that "on balance the record of the foundations is good," that they were "aware of the ever present danger," and guilty primarily of "gullibility" in having let red influence slip through.[32] The report even exonerated foundations on charges of internationalism, finding them "chiefly motivated by consideration of the welfare of the American people and as such . . . entirely praiseworthy." Calling for greater internal scrutiny and public accountability, the Cox Committee report let the foundations off the hook.[33]

Hardly satisfied with the outcome, right-wing partisans used the Cox Committee report to mobilize support for further inquiry. The *American Legion Magazine* later denounced the hearings as "superficial and timid," raising the suspicion that the whole operation had been undermined by the machinations of the "apparently leftist dupes" running the Rockefeller, Carnegie, and Ford Foundations.[34] Setting aside the conspiratorial rhetoric, they were not entirely off base. Deeply concerned about the hearings, foundation officials had courted allies in Congress, and came especially to rely on committee member Brooks Hays –a member of the Committee on Foreign Relations and later acting chair of the Cox Committee—to keep the attacks on internationalism in check. Their meetings with Treasury Department officials brought assurances of the agency's generally favorable disposition toward foundations, and through the intercession of the New York law firm White and Case, the presidents of several leading foundations met with the committee's general counsel, they said, in the interest of assuring proper conduct of the inquiry.[35] If need be, of course, the foundations had friends—and board members—in high places in the Truman and Eisenhower administrations. Such connections would merely confirm the right's suspicion that the foundations were operating as a kind of shadow government run by the internationalist eastern establishment elite.

B. Carroll Reece counted himself among the skeptics, despite having served on the exculpatory Cox Committee. While drawing on much the same mix of political motives that had come together behind the Cox investigation (earlier pushed out as chairman of the Republican National Committee, Reece was a leading Taft partisan), he reserved a special animus for the Ford Foundation, which, he claimed, had not been adequately scrutinized the first time around. Chief among his bill of particulars was the civil liberties defense organization the foundation had established just two years earlier, the Fund for the Republic—a fund, Reece declared (not entirely inaccurately), set up to "investigate the investigators" and otherwise to discredit the McCarthyite onslaught. Much to the bewilderment of its sponsors, Reece also cited the foundation's support for a booklet produced by the Advertising Council entitled *The Miracle of America,* a publication lauding the achievements of American capitalism that had originated, according to Advertising Council president Theodore Repplier, in the conviction "that the country was in grave danger of losing the propaganda wars." A paean to American ingenuity, productivity, and economic freedom, the booklet nevertheless drew Reece's ire as "a restatement of the principles of American society" drawn from the "British-Labor-Socialist Party Platform"—likely, assuming he'd read it, for its praiseful references to a labor-management-government accord.[36] More than any single grant or allegedly subversive program officer, however, Reece singled out Robert Maynard Hutchins as the mastermind behind the Ford Foundation's subversive activities. By then, Hutchins had become a favorite target in the right-wing press, as one of those "shrewd foundation brains" who made sure that, as *American Legion Magazine* put it, "the real Foundation story had not been told."[37]

What the Cox Committee lacked in antifoundation invective, the Reece investigations more than made up for during the hearings and in its 416-page staff report. This sprawling, often hysterical report was prepared for the committee by staff member Norman Dodd and prefaced by the committee's self-described "professional anti-Communist" legal counsel, New York tax lawyer Renee Wormser.[38] As was soon apparent even to impartial observers, the hearings and Dodd's report were little more than extensive elaborations on Reece's original charges, delivered by "experts" drawn from the ranks of professional red baiters and disgruntled college professors, based on strings of quotations from foundation-supported projects taken out of context, and aimed at proving the existence of a plot against capitalism, financed by the foundations, and carried out through the "triangle" linking them to education and government. Included in the piles of "evidence" brought to bear on the charges were FDR's "Four Freedoms," everything ever associated with the National Resource Planning Board, programs to support international education, and the fact that the Carnegie Corporation-funded *American Dilemma* was written by Gunnar Myrdal, a foreigner who just so happened to be a "very left-wing socialist."[39] For all such hints of far-left sympathizing, the most damning of Dodd's allegations placed the foundations squarely within the New Deal orbit.

This, then, was the sum total of the "diabolical conspiracy" with which Reece had launched his investigations and subsequently laid out in the Dodd report: the startling revelation that the New Deal was a deliberately plotted "revolution" hatched in the halls of what were coming to be known as "the big three" foundations (Carnegie, Rockefeller, and, despite the fact that it hadn't gotten started until the late 1940s, Ford). Claiming to work in "the public interest," the foundations were in fact operating through an inter-locking network of educational and research organizations to *redefine* the public interest around the ideas of planning, internationalism, and govern-ment responsibility for the welfare of its people. This revolution, moreover, had taken place under the auspices of "typically American fortune-created foundations" that had been diverted from their original purposes by schem-ing intellectuals and federal government officials. What's more, it had largely been carried out under cover of empirical social science, unattached to and thus subversive of the fundamental principles of American individualism. In place of those principles, and out of a "zeal for a radically new social order in the United States," the conspirators had insinuated a new set of cul-tural values, based on collectivism, interdependence, relativism, and, Dodd's report hinted by indirection, racial egalitarianism.[40]

As this last set of claims indicates, what most preoccupied Reece's band of investigators about the foundations was their vast and far-reaching cul-tural influence. Nowhere was this more evident to Reece than in growing foundation support for "what are called the social sciences," and through them for the transformation of American education into an instrument of social change.[41] It was through this infiltration—truly, the plot within the plot—that the foundations and the intellectuals they funded had secretly laid the essential groundwork for the New Deal revolution, a revolution that "could not have occurred peacefully, or with the consent of the majority unless education in the United States had prepared in advance to endorse it."[42] The campaign of indoctrination encompassed all the major learned societies, universities, research institutions, and prominent educational asso-ciations, and counted as especially pernicious "accessories" the American Council of Learned Societies, the American Historical Association, the Social Science Research Council, the John Dewey Society, and the Parent-Teachers Association. Together, these organizations had done the essential, cultural work of revolution, on the one hand by eroding the values underlying laissez-faire capitalism, and on the other by introducing a dangerous "excess of empiricism" into American education and public life. Empiricism, whether in the form of Alfred Kinsey's research on human sexuality or Myrdal's on race relations, was simply a cover for social scientists bent on eroding all sorts of "American" principles and morals. More ominous, empiricism was based on the fallacy that human behavior could be scientifically controlled.

Indeed, having achieved its greatest triumph in the coming of the New Deal, empiricism was now paving the way for the reign of the social engineers.[43]

To the extent that Reece's rather sloppy charges ever had much chance of political traction, they were undermined by the hearings themselves, which turned into a circus of partisan wrangling, pitting the recently elected Representative and committee member Wayne L. Hays (D-Oh.) against Reece and his appointed witnesses in often personalized, and on one occasion televised, exchange. Hays, who took to interrupting Reece's friendly witnesses with factual questions and demands for evidence, proved for the foundations a reliable but sometimes problematic ally. At one point the exchange became so vituperative that the hearings were suspended, after Hays attacked fellow committee member (and holdover from the Cox Committee) Angier Goodwin for "taking one position in public with pious speeches" while secretly admitting to reservations about the conduct of the inquiry. "Why can't you act like a man?" Hays asked—and then proceeded to denounce the "Alice in Wonderland investigation which came out with the verdict before it heard the evidence."[44] Not long after Hays's show stopper, Reece and the other Republicans on the committee adjourned the hearings without allowing foundation representatives to testify in response to the charges against them—a strategy that eventually backfired, by drawing considerable anti-Reece editorial opinion in the press.[45] (Several foundations subsequently submitted written replies for the record.) As editorial opinion turned against Reece's efforts, anticommunist stalwart Senator Pat McCarran introduced an amendment to an impending tax bill revoking tax-exempt standing from any organization making grants to "Communist and Communist front organizations and individuals." Recognizing the threat it entailed, the big foundations moved quickly, and successfully, to keep it from passing.[46] The Reece committee, meantime, issued its report with supporting signatures (one with caveats) from its three Republican members, dissents from the two Democrats, and with no substantive reform recommendations.

While the Cox and Reece investigations produced no legislation, they did take their toll on the big foundations. Having approached the postwar future with greater resources, and a sense that they stood incontrovertibly for the common good, by the mid-1950s the leading philanthropies had been relentlessly reminded that—fairly or not—they were not above reproach. Complying with the investigations had proved enormously time-consuming and costly, requiring responses to detailed, repetitive questionnaires about their activities, internal practices, and especially about their procedures for screening out subversives on their staffs and among prospective grantees. Parsing the response to the charges became a major preoccupation at all the "big three" foundations, leading to what amounted to a retrospective ideological monitoring at Carnegie, and absorbing nearly full-time attention from Ford Foundation presidential assistant Waldemar Nielsen for much of 1954. Nielsen estimated the total money costs at $325,000, including the substantial fees paid to an outside public affairs firm brought in to safeguard the foundation's image.[47] There was also no small degree of personal cost associated with the investigations, especially to the staff members and grant recipients targeted by red-baiters in the hope of uncovering another Alger Hiss in foundation ranks.[48]

Despite claims to the contrary, the investigations also had a definite chilling effect on the kinds of projects the foundations were willing to take on. In response to pressure from red-baiters in Congress and the press, many found themselves providing personal information about particular staff members, engaging in futile efforts to placate right-wing columnists and American legionnaires, instituting stepped-up antisubversive screening processes and background checks, and acquiescing in blacklisting organizations on the Attorney General's list of "known subversives."[49] The Ford Foundation, biggest and presumably boldest of the big three, was doing its best to temper or put a distance between itself and its most controversial projects. Projects promoting racial integration, let alone civil rights, were widely understood to be off limits for direct foundation funding. Its initially ambitious behavioral sciences program was terminated, albeit as much due to internal drift as to external scrutiny. Even the Fund for the Republic felt it necessary continually to "balance" its civil liberties program with such projects as an extensive bibliography on communism and subversive activity in the U.S.[50] In 1955, worried about the bad publicity from the Reece hearings and mindful of the flyers telling Ford Motor customers that they were unwarily subsidizing a communist plot, the foundation made a huge, utterly uncharacteristic series of public relations grants to hospitals and universities covering nearly all congressional districts in the country, in a barely disguised attempt to purchase public good will.[51]

Equally important, the investigations confronted the philanthropoids with the fundamentally political and necessarily ideological nature of their work. For all their efforts to keep a distance, the Cox and Reece hearings had drawn the foundations into a dynamic in partisan politics that, playing out gradually over the next several years, would leave them vulnerable to continued attack. Targeted by the conservative anticommunist right in its efforts to gain control of the Republican Party, the big foundations were also vilified by racist Southern Democrats for even their cautious pro-integrationist stance. Nor were they likely to find natural allies among Democrats more generally: foundation trustees, as political consultant James Newmyer pointed out, were "generally associated with [Eisenhower] Republicans." Given calls for still further investigation, he warned, "foundations find themselves in the position of being a potential political football regardless of the Party in power. They stand of good chance of joining the oil companies and the utilities as perpetual candidates for politically-motivated investigations"—a likelihood the foundations could avoid only through concerted effort to cultivate supporters on Capitol Hill.[52]

Even more starkly evident was the ideological battle to which foundations were party through their work, especially when it involved such presumably unassailable objectives as promoting international peace or scientific inquiry. Their response to the Dodd report is especially revealing in this regard. Faced with such a bold and accusing rendition of their ideological project, the foundations reacted with what would be a similarly pattern-setting response: denying, rather than formulating and defending, the ideological dimensions of their work. Accustomed to presenting themselves as somehow above or at least able to transcend partisan politics and ideology, they staked their claim to legitimacy on strategies that would later make it more difficult to respond to an even more concerted challenge from the conservative right. One was to insist that, save for such universalistic values as world peace, theirs was an investment in building and applying scientific knowledge rather than in promoting *ideas*. The other was to claim what William H. Whyte, Jr., referred to as "neutralism," and which he faulted, along with the foundation penchant for "projectitis," as "false objectivity at best and, at worst, ineffective middle-of-the-roadism."[53] Similarly telling was the way foundations and their defenders responded to charges that they had plotted the New Deal: by treating the "revolution" in governance and political economy not as a triumph or even a conscious shift in ideology, but as a series of pragmatic responses to Depression, World War II, and the Communist threat. This, in some sense, played into Reece's point: the triumph had been so thorough, the indoctrination so complete, that few save the stalwart free-market conservatives would even think to question the New Deal order as anything but the natural course of events.

Meanwhile, although generally acquitted of the most outrageous charges of subversive activities, the foundations did not exactly emerge unsullied in the public eye. For all the pains they took to appear open and cooperative with the investigations, foundations as a rule were hardly forthcoming about how they shaped their programs or made funding decisions—let alone who got to apply. To most, including elected legislators, they remained remote and somewhat mysterious institutions—a subject for frequent lament but little action on the part of the foundations themselves. The hearings and public debate had also revealed a considerable disconnect between the self-image cultivated within enclosed philanthropic circles and the broader public view. Where the philanthropoids and their boards saw high-minded humanitarian resources, legislators especially saw great concentrations of tax-free wealth—and wondered why it was not more publicly accountable. And while the biggest foundations had created a wall of staff and programs to separate their good works from the great capitalist fortunes that made them possible, critics were quick to point out that huge tax breaks rather than generosity were the real motivation behind the trusts.

Most of all, if not part of a vast communist conspiracy, the big foundations were undeniably part of a fairly insulated, at least moderately liberal, heavily Ivy League, and, yes, interlocking corporate-government-university elite. Even sympathetic observers were inclined to point this out. The "median trustee," Whyte wrote in *Fortune*, "is a banker or a corporation president who went to Harvard, is about sixty, and lives in New York City."[54] Professional staff members, with a younger but similar profile, came more through university and government than corporate channels. Along with this pedigree, which was also overwhelmingly white, male, and upper middle class, came a reputation for arrogance that the philanthropoids, in their dismissive attitudes toward their chief accusers, did very little to dispel. And as philanthropy became more professionalized, it was these prototypically "new class" middlemen who drew fiercest animosity from the right, for using the *fruits* of free enterprise—other people's money, as it were—to betray the very *spirit* of free enterprise.

For the time being, though, the big foundations felt vindicated, bolstered by the mostly sympathetic press they had gotten in the episode and by Reece's ultimate retreat. The congressional right, too, relinquished its crusade against philanthropy, having played the red card beyond its limits. And yet, if little else, Reece's witch hunt had produced the basic outlines of what would prove a remarkably enduring account of big philanthropy's "true" ideological objectives and interlocking machinations, an account that hard-line conservatives would echo with striking consistency in books such as Rene Wormser's *Foundations: Their Power and Influence* (1958), in grassroots broadsides, and in the pages of the right-wing press. Two decades later, that account would reemerge as part of a full-blown narrative in which a handful of conservative stalwarts, frozen out by the conspiratorial liberal elite, would be called upon to rise to the defense of free-market capitalism and its underlying values by taking part in a massive countermobilization led by a newly energized philanthropic right.

Shifting Foundation Fortunes and the "Great Foundation Debate"

By the time that countermobilization was getting underway in the 1970s, the big foundations had already lost much of their credibility, following a period of still further public scrutiny and growing disaffection with establishment politics. Thus, in the far differently motivated congressional investigations that spanned the 1960s and sparked what the *National Review* called the "great foundation debate," right-wing critics found an unlikely opening to expand and capitalize on their long-standing case against foundations, and of the overreaching liberal establishment they emblemized.

The first of the investigations would bring the big foundations up against Congressman Wright Patman. Unlike his immediate predecessors, Patman was determined to take on the tax exempt foundations primarily as vast accumulations of money that were being used to perpetuate the privileges of concentrated wealth—including, he charged (invoking Theodore Roosevelt), the ongoing monopoly power of the Rockefellers and Standard

Oil.[55] A populist Democrat from rural Texas with more than thirty years service in the House, Patman had remained one of the few standard-bearers of anti-monopoly regulation following the New Deal, and he had earned a reputation as a tough, persistent reformer in his efforts to defend small business against the encroachments of chain stores and multinational corporations. He was also a persistent critic of the Federal Reserve.[56] And unlike his predecessors, Patman came to the investigations with concrete regulatory stance and in the name of a constituency—the (white) working-class "little guy"—a combination that, over the course of an extraordinarily volatile decade, tapped into a well of popular frustration that took the foundations, and the establishment liberalism they had come to represent, by surprise.

Patman announced his intention to take what would turn out to be an eight-year "fresh look" at tax-exempt foundations in 1961, just as organized philanthropy was beginning to enjoy what its leaders thought would be a "beautiful running time," as Ford program officer Paul Ylvisaker put it, smoothed by having JFK in office, the New Frontier ahead, friends and allies in positions of influence in government, and, of course, the liberal establishment at its height of self-confidence.[57] With Cox, Reece, McCarran, and McCarthy well behind them, the time and setting seemed ripe to launch such ambitious projects as educational television, community action, public interest law, and an increasingly assertive stance on civil rights and minority empowerment strategies. Foundations, in the familiar lingo, should be willing to act as "change agents" in increasingly obvious ways. Once again the Ford Foundation, still largest and most visible in the field, embodied the broader change, culminating in the appointment of the ultimate establishment figure, Kennedy/Johnson national security adviser McGeorge Bundy, as president in 1966.[58]

From the start Patman positioned himself as a lone crusader in a series of House speeches pointing to the "disproportionately rapid" growth in the number and size of tax-exempt foundations since the late 1940s, a growth he attributed chiefly to the desire to avoid potentially huge tax liabilities and to keep family control of wealth. Under pressure from colleagues who wanted to keep the investigations in check, he agreed to formalize the inquiry under the auspices of the Committee on Small Business, and launched an exhaustive survey of some 575 foundations, focusing on their financial holdings and spending patterns in great detail. Keeping tight control over the investigation and related proceedings, Patman began to release his findings in somewhat sporadic hearings and in a voluminous series of reports compiled annually through 1967. His overriding charge was that tax-exempt foundations were dangerous, unaccountable, economically distorting accumulations of wealth that both drained the treasury of needed resources and allowed the wealthy to exert economic control over key markets. His more specific charges involved a compendium of clear-cut abuses —only some of them illegal—uncovered during the course of investigation:

large accumulations of untaxed, and unspent, capital gains; the use of foundations to maintain (tax-free) control of major corporations through stock ownership; profitable business enterprises run under the guise of charitable activity; and incidences of foundation "self-dealing" through loans or outright grants to board members. While his critics argued that most such abuses could be handled with stepped-up enforcement of existing law, Patman used the admittedly shocking evidence he was uncovering—including a tax-exempt organization called Americans Building Constitutionally, set up to show wealthy clients how to form a foundation to avoid paying taxes—to call for measures ranging from a complete moratorium on tax exemption to a twenty-five-year legal limit on the life of foundations. Near the end of his inquiry he called on foundations to donate all of their grant money to the federal government to pay the escalating costs of the war in Vietnam.[59]

Damning and often colorful as Patman's findings were (among other things, the investigation uncovered evidence of CIA collusion with the J. M. Kaplan Foundation, and brought the political activities of Texas oilman H. L. Hunt's Lifeline Foundation to light), they had yet to produce any significant legislation by the late 1960s. But Patman did tap into the kind of economic populism that right-wing conservatives were eager to exploit for their own, quite distinct purposes. Writing about the hearings in the *National Review*, Jeffrey Hart applauded Patman for uncovering the shady financial dealings of the taxpayer-subsidized institutions. Condescending though he was in his depiction of Patman's "rotund, benign, almost elfin presence," Hart claimed to be impressed by his toughness against the big money. The real issue, though, was less in the financial abuses than in "the role of foundations as a kind of shadow government, disposing of vast social and political power, and using that power, in fact, in highly questionable ways." This was of particular concern for conservatives, Hart continued, for the most powerful foundations were liberal, and while there were indeed a few big foundations willing to fund conservatives, they were "less aggressive in the political and social spheres and have less over-all impact." The liberal foundations, in contrast, operated as "a kind of farm club or taxi squad for the executive branch of the Federal Government"; they held the key to the old liberal establishment interlock. And despite legal restrictions on their political activities, they were carrying out a decidedly "aggressive" political and social agenda. Clearly, Hart concluded, conservatives had to become more vigilant lest the foundations succeed in carrying out the "social revolution" their grants had helped to instigate.[60]

But beyond the association with "big government," with all its echoes of the anti-communist past, Hart also used the occasion of Patman's investigation to broaden and sharpen the right-wing case against liberal establishment philanthropy in politically effective ways. In particular, and especially in light of the very recently emboldened foundation support for civil rights activism, he played on growing white middle- and working-class resentment over civil rights, black power, welfare, and urban revolt. The wealthy liberal foundations were not only "attempting to carry out a social revolution" with support for black "militants" and open housing, they were doing so "at the expense of the middle and lower-classes—who, it is safe to say, won't put up with it, and don't have to."[61] Moreover, he claimed with a nod back to Patman's economic populism, foundation support for the "social revolution" was actually a strategy of cooptation, in order to maintain the liberal establishment's essentially corporate status quo.

It was in such a heavily loaded atmosphere that the foundation issue came before Wilbur Mills's House Ways and Means Committee in its own efforts to crack down on tax loopholes for the wealthy, and in the process to forestall a looming taxpayer "revolt."[62] Charitable foundations, the IRS revealed, had allowed a number of millionaires to avoid paying taxes at all. But what would at first glance appear to be a return to the early-century politics of capitalist regulation soon turned into an attack on the liberal establishment. With the die cast against the foundations as symbols of concentrated wealth, Mills's Ways and Means Committee took up the question of tougher regulation in its first set of hearings on the tax reform bill in 1969. Making things far more difficult for the foundations was a series of contemporaneous revelations about their more overt political ties, which only fed into the more generalized resentment of liberal "social engineering," "welfarism," and racial "favoritism" that had been curried in the 1968 presidential elections. Just a week before the hearings, at which McGeorge Bundy was scheduled to appear, the *New York Times* reported on the "study grants" the Ford Foundation had made to several members of Senator Robert F. Kennedy's staff after his assassination. Also resurrected for scrutiny was Ford's support for the voter registration drive that helped to elect an African American, Carl Stokes, mayor of Cleveland in 1967, as well as its role in launching the hugely controversial school decentralization experiments in New York City. These grants, among others, had been the basis of an American Conservative Union pamphlet entitled *The Financiers of Revolution*, charging Ford with deliberately fomenting unrest among students, the poor, and black extremists, and against the patriotic white working and middle classes. To make matters worse, Bundy himself appeared condescending and arrogant, clearly offending the committee with his insistence that Ford's grants were not partisan but "educational."[63] The foundations, observers argued in retrospect, were the scapegoats for a broader cultural and political reaction against the liberal establishment.[64]

Reclaiming Philanthropy for Capitalism: Tax Reform and Its Aftermath

The Tax Reform Act of 1969 combined much-needed restrictions on flagrant self-dealing, hoarding of assets, and nondisclosure with blatantly punitive measures to keep the liberal "change agents" in check. In addition to new excise taxes and payout requirements, foundations now faced new restrictions on allowable voter education grants.[65] That these and other regulations were aimed at curbing support for black activism and grassroots civil rights seemed clear to Urban League president Whitney Young, who publicly took note of the fact that Congress was changing the rules of grant making only after civil rights groups started getting substantial grants.[66] By then, these had become known in press accounts as the "McGeorge Bundy" amendments. Still, after an initial bout of panic, the major foundations began to adopt the far more extensive administrative and legal procedures they would need to comply with the new rules.

But while many of the changes could be absorbed with administrative and legal measures, it would take much more for the philanthropoids to recover from what many experienced as a severe psychological and political blow. At a conference convened shortly after the law went into effect, spokesmen professed shock at the level of hostility and mistrust aimed at their foundations and wondered why they remained "unappreciated, misunderstood, criticized."[67] Feeling bewildered and vulnerable, key executives did what foundations are wont to do in difficult circumstances: they established an elaborate study commission, meant as much to signal a kind of collective soul-searching as to stave off further efforts at regulation. The commission, headed by insurance executive John Filer and organized by John D. Rockefeller, III, issued a report that sought to smooth ruffled feathers on all sides—by reaffirming the value of philanthropy, calling for pluralism in the field, and establishing an organization known as Independent Sector to represent the interests of nonprofit organizations.

Yet even as the decidedly chastened philanthropic mainstream was repositioning itself as more pluralistic, accountable, less insular, and more responsive to public concerns, the philanthropic right was beginning a concerted countermobilization around a narrow, unpluralistic set of conservative ideas and ideological convictions. Important among the catalysts for this countermobilization was the decision by the mainstream trade organization, the Council on Foundations, to adopt a code of ethics in 1983. Made up of eleven principles meant to set a kind of industry standard, its eighth clause—committing members to affirmative action in their own hiring and grant making practices—proved the last straw for a self-identified group of conservative renegades. Led by the Milwaukee-based Bradley Foundation, this breakaway faction formed the Capital Research Center and the Philanthropy Roundtable in 1984, as strategy-setting and watchdog groups.

By then, representatives from the Bradley, Olin, Sarah Scaife, Smith-Richardson, Adolf Coors, and other conservative foundations had already been coming together around a strategy anticipated by Irving Kristol in *Wall Street Journal* editorials and in an influential memorandum prepared for the U.S. Chamber of Commerce by soon-to-be Supreme Court Justice Lewis Powell. But the strategy was most fully laid out in William E. Simon's post-Treasury Department broadside against what he characterized as the reigning Washington-Ivy League-government-friendly corporate elite, *A Time for Truth* (1978).[68] There, picking up themes harbored on the right since the Dodd report, Simon wrote of a "society ruled by a small band of moral and economic despots who, as Kristol says, *are* our universities and *are* our foundations and *are* our media and *are* our bureaucracies."[69] These despots, with an ideological lineage dating back to the New Deal, had orchestrated a hidden revolution in values as well as political economy, in the process sending the country "careening with frightening speed toward collectivism and away from individual sovereignty, toward coercive centralized planning and away from free individual choices, toward a statist-dictatorial system and away from a nation in which individual liberty is sacred."[70] What was needed, Simon concluded, was a "powerful counterintelligentsia" to challenge and ultimately to overthrow the liberal dictatorship. Its elements were there—to be found in the University of Chicago economics department, the newly emergent band of New York neoconservative intellectuals, and the free-market business elite. What they awaited was a galvanizing force: "Foundations imbued with the philosophy of freedom . . . to funnel desperately needed funds to scholars, social scientists, writers and journalists who understand the relationship between political and economic liberty."[71] Foundations, that is, like the recently reenergized Olin Foundation, soon to be presided over by William E. Simon himself.

Even more than their common commitment to free-market individualism, the conservative network of funders Simon appealed to shared an intense animosity to what liberal philanthropy had wrought. The mainstream foundations, in this sense, set the template for conservative philanthropic activism: public interest law; environmentalism; and welfare became the chief targets of the movement to "defund the left."[72] Equally important, in creating an institutional infrastructure of conservative think tanks, advocacy groups, law firms, and academic "beachheads," conservative foundations put themselves in the business less of funding research than of funding ideas—here again distinguishing themselves from the philanthropic culture of social scientific empiricism the Reece committee had singled out for attack. And, although entirely willing to use the state as an instrument of change, they cultivated a dramatically privatized—more recently "faith-based"—vision of civil society with which to counter the old state-centered liberal "interlock."

Revisiting the twists and turns of "the great foundation debate" of 1969, contemporary foundation watchers cannot help but be struck by how much the political tides have turned. The same language, albeit more likely to be found in the pages of the *Nation* or *American Prospect* than the *National Review*, can be used to describe the interlock and the assertiveness of a handful of conservative foundations, as they provide the essential capital for revolution—and as their more liberal counterparts stand passively aside.[73] Just as in the aftermath of the McCarthy-era hearings, when confronted with their own fundamentally political nature, the big foundations have since the Tax Reform Act gone into retreat: not only from overt support for social movements, but from the prospect of wielding political power at all. But they have also failed to confront the increasingly uncomfortable fact of their existence, for which Patman, in his own way, had attempted to hold them accountable: the fact that, as social and economic institutions, they did rely on—and since the 1980s, have profited immensely from—vast inequalities in the distribution and favorable tax treatment of wealth. That conservative philanthropy has been able to exploit this contradiction in promoting its own, more explicit brand of economic privilege is but one of the ironies of its success. The other is that conservative foundations succeeded, at least in part, through what they imagined the liberal establishment to have been up to all along: a conscious program of ideological reorientation that sees American capitalism as a cultural as well as a political and economic project.

American Counterrevolutionary: Lemuel Ricketts Boulware and General Electric, 1950–1960

Kimberly Phillips-Fein

The decade of the 1950s has long been seen as an epoch of consensus, especially regarding questions of political economy. As historian Godfrey Hodgson puts it, during the postwar period, "to dissent from the broad axioms" of agreement upon a liberal capitalism was "to proclaim oneself irresponsible or ignorant."[1] During the postwar period, the argument goes, economic growth replaced class conflict. Serious ideological dissension gave way to interest-group pluralism mediated by a broker state. Corporate leaders accepted the power of labor unions, provided that they respected certain managerial prerogatives, while workers gave up their radical ambitions and acknowledged management's legitimate power.[2] Allied against the common threat of the Soviet Union, Cold War liberals and "modern Republicans" alike could agree on the basic principles of the welfare state, anti-Communist unionism and Keynesian economics.[3]

This vision of consensus on economic questions does capture some elements of 1950s political culture, but it is incomplete. Economic growth and the Cold War did not eliminate conflict over matters of political economy. During the Eisenhower years a small but increasingly influential group of conservative businessmen, and their allies among intellectuals, economists and politicians, mobilized against what most thought to be well-accepted tenets of New Deal liberalism. Seeing the economic order of the postwar period—with its powerful unions and strong public sector—as a substantial threat to their power, these business leaders sought to demonize and weaken labor and the state, by fighting unions within their own companies, funding free-market intellectual organizations like the American Enterprise Association and the Mont Pelerin Society, and supporting political causes like right-to-work campaigns and Barry Goldwater's bid for the presidency. Even as Daniel Bell mourned the "end of ideology," this group in the business community, its vision legitimated by free-market thinkers like Friedrich von Hayek, Ludwig von Mises, and Milton Friedman, was attempting to develop a fiercely ideological, self-consciously radical economic agenda that would roll back the New Deal, end the welfare state, and restrict the power of labor. While these business conservatives were in the minority during the 1950s, their efforts would help create the institutional and personal infrastructure of the modern American right.

Many companies that took a leading role in fighting unions and opposing the welfare state were large corporations that had not been organized by national unions during the 1930s and 1940s (like Eastman Kodak, Du Pont, and Sears Roebuck), and mid-sized privately owned firms, both union and nonunion (such as Thompson Products, Kohler Company, Perfect Circle, Lone Star Steel), also played an important part.[4] But foremost among American corporations in developing a highly politicized antiunionism during the decade was General Electric, under the leadership of Vice-President for Employee and Community Relations Lemuel Ricketts Boulware. During the 1950s, GE was the fourth largest publicly held industrial in the United States, having grown fifteen times over the previous twenty years, and it was the third largest employer in the nation, with 136 factories in 28 states.[5] GE produced many of the durable goods that were most closely associated with the "age of abundance"—televisions and radios, refrigerators and washing machines—as well as military equipment and goods for heavy industry. Unlike Du Pont or Sears, GE had been unionized during the 1930s by one of the largest, most radical mass production unions in the United States, the United Electrical Workers. Yet while the company flourished economically during the postwar years, during the 1950s, executives at GE articulated a free-market vision of capitalism, and sought to organize other corporate leaders to defend an economic order they believed was in grave danger. As Boulware wrote, "The 'American Consensus"—as a political party dogma—is on its way to being one of the biggest busts of our time."[6]

They were driven in part by a simple economic logic: GE executives were frightened that labor militancy, so well demonstrated in the industry-wide strike of 1946, would erode corporate power and management prerogatives. To a great extent, GE officials succeeded in limiting the union's strength. Workers at GE did not win a union shop during the decade, wages and benefits for the company's workforce lagged behind those of workers in the auto and steel industries, and the company was able to shutter scores of factories and shift much production to the South without facing substantial resistance from either its workforce or the political officeholders who represented GE communities.[7]

Yet labor relations at GE went beyond an internal struggle over the corporation's bottom line. Boulware, a salesman extraordinaire (one subordinate claimed that his passionate speeches moved spectators to tears), saw himself as a warrior in a deep struggle over the future of the country, which he believed was lurching toward the welfare state and socialism (the two, for him, being more or less the same).[8] Businessmen, he believed, were the only leaders who could bring the country back from the brink of disaster. Charming, clever, and an entrepreneurial peddler of ideology—to quote *Fortune*, "a jovial, fast-talking man, [who] combines the folksiness of a Kentucky farm background with the fervor of a washing machine salesman"— Boulware successfully demonstrated to the American business community that it was possible to beat back unions.[9] GE's conservative activism had long shadows in the late 1960s. Virgil Day, Boulware's successor, helped organize the Labor Law Study Group, a predecessor of the Business Roundtable.[10] Herbert Northrup, another Boulware protégé, founded the Research Advisory Group at the Wharton School of Business, which provided research for antiunion campaigns and encouragement for companies like Phelps Dodge during the 1983 copper strike (in which the union was crushed).[11] And Ronald Reagan, who worked at the company during the 1950s, remained in supportive contact with Boulware until the 1980s.

Historians in recent years have started to challenge the idea of the postwar liberal consensus, describing the public relations campaigns companies ran to dissuade workers from supporting unions, the antiunion strategies of businessmen, the political roots of the Goldwater campaign and of popular anti-Communism, and challenging the idea of a labor-management accord.[12] GE and "Boulwarism," the unique philosophy and practice of labor relations developed by Lemuel Boulware, have generally received little more than a few lines of commentary in these studies. Yet GE's political activity is important not only for its considerable impact on the conservative movement of the 1950s and beyond, but also because it served as an example for other corporations and so contributed to the growing mobilization of business throughout the rest of the twentieth century. While liberals dallied about the Vital Center, Boulware and his conservative allies were busy writing, speaking, and building a conservative movement—working to weaken the labor unions that once provided liberalism's mass base. In both its enthusiastic embrace of political conflict and its quasi-utopian free market ideology, this vanguard movement of right-wing businessmen rejected the faith of the disappointed 1950s liberals that class conflict was dead and political ideology a relic from a radical past.

The 1946 Strike

Although General Electric's leaders always saw themselves as corporate statesmen, before the 1950s they were not associated with antiunionism. As a manufacturer of goods that were emblems of modernity, GE had been deeply concerned with corporate image and public relations ever since the company began to produce for the consumer market. During the 1920s, Owen Young, the chairman of the board, and Gerard Swope, president, hired Bruce Barton and the advertising firm B. B. & O. to portray the company as the bearer of "electrical consciousness," liberating people (especially women) from meaningless drudgery, brightening the path to a better, freer world. The company spent time and money developing its logo, seeking to make it, in the words of one advertising campaign, "the initials of a friend."[13] Swope and Young were professionals who saw themselves as sensitive and cultured (Swope's wife had worked with Jane Addams at Hull House). They wanted their company to be the same way.[14] During the Depression, while companies like Maytag, Emerson, and RCA did open battle with the electrical workers' union, GE signed a nationwide contract in 1937—based on the existing employee handbook—with the United Electrical Workers (UE) without a strike.[15]

The most important factor in the company's political transformation was the growth of the electrical workers' union during World War II. At the beginning of the war, the UE was a local organization, representing workers at each plant. During the war, however, the UE won more than 800 union representation elections, becoming the third-largest union in the CIO (at its peak, it represented 600,000 workers).[16] With its new power, the union was able to fight the company's practice of paying lower wages in areas where unions were weak and the discriminatory pay scales for women (especially important because the proportion of women in GE's workforce rose from 20 percent in 1940 to 40 percent in 1944).[17] And at the end of the war, the UE was ready to strike on a national level to guarantee that electrical workers would be able to share in the fruits of renewed civilian production.[18]

The electrical workers' strike in early 1946, part of the largest nation-wide strike wave in the country's history, was a watershed for GE management. The basic demand was a raise of $2 a day (about 25 percent a year). Two hundred thousand UE members struck GE, Westinghouse and General Motors simultaneously, starting on January 14, 1946.[19] On the very first day of picketing, hundreds of workers massed at the gates of one plant (in Erie, Pennsylvania), before 6 A.M., when picketing was officially supposed to begin, building fires against the cold.[20] In Bridgeport, Connecticut, where nearly 11,000 workers were striking, GE offered strikers one of its buildings as a rest hall for picketers in subfreezing weather; the union refused.[21] Restaurants delivered hot punch to the strikers.[22] College students came down to walk the picket lines.[23] City governments endorsed the aims of the strikers, and fifty-five senators and representatives signed a public statement supporting the strike.[24] In Bloomsfield, New Jersey, where there were both Westinghouse and GE plants, 5,000 picketers marched to the center of the town, carrying signs like "Our Fight Is Your Fight," "GI Versus GE," and "We're Not Dumb Clucks—We Want Two Bucks." The rally was led by seven supportive policemen and by picketers on horseback. The local American Legion post supported the strikers, and its band joined in the parade. The mayor of the town opened the rally with a prayer: "Help us so that when we pray each day, 'Give us this day our daily bread,' the 'us' will include all people." One policeman quoted in the *New York Times* said, "I can't talk officially, but any working man would be for the strike."[25] Children of strikers at a Westinghouse plant in Essington, Pennsylvania, ranging in age from four to twelve, marched on the picket lines, bearing signs reading "I'm Backing My Daddy," and "More Money Buys More Shoes."[26]

For much of the strike, workers controlled plant access. Hundreds marched in mass picket lines, refusing to allow even white-collar and management workers in, only permitting a few maintenance men to go through. Charles Wilson, GE's president, described the situation in Schenectady, New York, in a congressional hearing:

The picketing in the larger plants was literally hundreds of people, actually joining hands and going around in an ellipse in front of the plant so that nobody could get through. . . . They had their hands joined and kept going around and around in this elliptical formation. And nobody was going to try to buck that line and try to get through.[27]

The strike was settled in early March. The employees won an 18½ cent increase—well over what the company had been offering. For the General Electric management, the strike was traumatic and shocking. In 1944, employee compensation amounted to 36 percent of sales, but in 1946 it jumped to 50 percent.[28] Wilson testified before Congress, "These bitter conditions . . . have never been obvious in our own relationship with our people before they were unionized, or after they were unionized. I mean we haven't had bitter and bad controversies between the management and the unions."[29] Wilson couldn't believe that he would not be allowed to enter his own plants. "To me it is the height of stupidity that we, as a corporation, should not be allowed to get into our plants, people who are not members of the union," he said (he actually granted that the workers had the right to keep strikebreakers and scabs out of the plant, appealing only to the right of management and supervisory personnel).[30] "I don't think that the corporation should have to go with its hat in hand to a union and ask for permission to bring its engineers and so on into a plant."[31] But as frightening as the sudden intransigence of the workers was the feeling GE officials had that they were alone. Local mayors, clergy, teachers, small businesses, town residents, politicians—all seemed to be on the union's side, all seemed to believe that GE was in the wrong.[32]

To remake labor relations at GE after the strike, Charles Wilson hired a balding, middle-aged man—Lemuel Ricketts Boulware. Boulware, the son of a banker, was born in Springfield, Kentucky, in 1895. He had attended the University of Wisconsin, and his background was in sales and marketing. His early employers quickly recognized him as a talented young man.[33] During the 1920s, he worked as sales manager for the Syracuse [Easy] Washing Machine Corporation, where he was responsible for training the sales staff. He helped to found the Marketing Executives Society and wrote articles on sales and advertising as ways to resolve price competition in the

Depression. Boulware met Ralph Cordiner and Charles E. Wilson (future and current presidents of GE) while all three were working at the War Production Board during World War II. After the war, Wilson hired Boulware and put him in charge of labor relations at the "affiliated companies," subsidiary companies owned by GE that bargained with unions separately. None of the employees at these companies joined in the 1946 strike, although they were also represented by the UE, and after the strike, Wilson asked Boulware to expand the labor relations program he had pioneered there, which had been shaped by his long background in marketing and public relations.[34]

Boulwarism

From his first days at GE, Boulware's entire career was predicated on the idea that business was losing in a massive political struggle, and it needed to fight back. As he wrote in one of his first memos at GE, circulated even before the 1946 strike,

Management is in a *sales* campaign to determine *who* will run business and the country,—and to determine if business and the country will be run *right*. Union leaders and left wingers are out calling on the "customers," finding out what the customers want and doing something about it, meanwhile vigorously, courageously, imaginatively, brutally and effectively attacking management as incompetent and crooked.

Unions sought to transform society. In contrast, businessmen saw themselves as apolitical technocrats, for whom politics was a distraction from the more pressing matters of production and budgets.

Management, on the other hand, is "staying home" and remaining silent—the most negative possible sales procedure. Who has been winning this sales competition for 13 years, and who still is, is all too evident in elections, labor laws, the attitude of all public servants, and the convictions held by workmen and the public about management.[35]

Boulware's philosophy of labor relations combined paternalism with a utopian view of the free market. The market allowed each individual actor to pursue his or her own ends, magically optimizing outcomes for all. Unions threatened the free market, and therefore were necessarily opposed to the interests of those they claimed to represent. "The union official," he said in a speech to GE managers, "simply represents the most familiar symbol of the socialist opposition to maximizing the free market that is workable, to giving business the freedom it may otherwise prove it deserves, and to progressing toward that better material and spiritual America where decisions are decentralized to the individual citizen to the maximum degree possible."[36] Since the conflict between unions and management was a battle between the tyrannical forces of collectivism and the liberating promise of the free market, Boulware believed that the relationship between labor and management at GE was a vital part of a much larger struggle. No contract negotiation could ever be viewed as a simple, self-contained, and particular discussion over terms, in which both sides came together, exchanged views, and arrived at a fair solution. Rather, every negotiation was, in his view, a chance to demonstrate the power of the corporation and the weakness of the union. "In one sense," he proclaimed,

There is never a beginning and never an end to preparing for bargaining. What happens in the periodic sessions at the bargaining table is merely an accounting— a more or less formal tallying up—of what happens in the daily relations that go on year in and year out between General Electric managers and their associates in the plants and in the communities.[37]

As he had learned during the strike of 1946, no conflict with the union— no negotiations, no demonstrations, and certainly no strikes—could ever be viewed simply as an economic event. The particulars were never really at stake. Rather, the union was a political threat, challenging the ability of management to make decisions unfettered, to decide what was right, and to exercise its power. As he put it in a memo regarding a strike threat in 1954, "This threat is more than mere window dressing. It is the real show-down for power over employees, management, our communities and all others concerned. What is at stake is not just our current profits, but our whole right to run the business in the balanced best interests of all, and our ability to have GE grow, serve, prosper and even survive."[38]

During the 1950s, "Boulwarism" (Boulware himself always rejected the term, saying that his program was nothing "new or unorthodox or even experimental") was best known as a contract negotiating strategy.[39] When a contract came up for negotiation at GE, the company would generally refuse to engage in active negotiating sessions. Managers would speak little during the meetings with the union. But on the last day of negotiations, they would present their contract offer publicly to the entire community—as though they were advertising a new model of washing machine or a special brand of refrigerator. The company would then say that since its offer expressed structural economic realities as perfectly as any fixed contract could reflect the ceaseless ebb and flow of the marketplace, it would not change the offer, no matter what the union did. As Boulware said, a strike "obviously should not be any factor at all in determining whether an offer or settle-ment is to represent more or less than what's right." GE would then put the proposal into effect for all nonunion workers (and any workers in different unions who might accept it). It would set a date for the union to accept the contract, and refuse to give retroactive wage increases past that deadline.

The primary theory behind Boulwarism as a contract strategy was that the union should never be shown to win anything for the employees. The union was an interloper; real industrial democracy lay in the connection between the employer and the employees.

Management determined wages, benefits, and work rules based on market conditions. Perhaps it might take a few casual recommendations from the union. But the union could never force management to do anything that management did not genuinely believe was in the best interest of the company, based on its superior understanding of the free market. In a sense, not even the employer was responsible for the matters it bargained over with the union: the market set wages and determined working conditions, not the employer. "Governments, unions and shareholders have no way to protect permanently the employee of one business against the employee of another, more efficient business—or against the customer who refuses to pay."[40] The internal planned economy of the corporation dissolved into the infinite market interactions that made it up. In a speech to employee relations managers in preparation (eight months early) for the 1960 negotiations, Boulware said,

We must . . . tell the truth about productivity, how much it is, how many people make how many kinds of contributions to it, how the fruits are distributed by market action alone even when inflationary and discriminatory pay increases have been forced on some leading businesses and when there have been other harmful distortions of the free market process.[41]

But while Boulwarism became famous as a contract bargaining strategy, it also described a state of affairs within the plant between negotiations. Boulware envisioned a constant stream of propaganda aimed at workers, designed to cement their loyalties to the company. Just as union organizers sought to build a network of relationships within the company that would bolster the power of workers, Boulware imagined a network of relationships between workers and supervisors that would guarantee employee solidarity with GE. Boulware called this strategy "job marketing." As though the job was another product made by the company, the job would be "sold" to the worker. "We . . . take the initiative in doing right voluntarily and . . . respond as far as feasible, to what our job customers [tell] us [are] the material and emotional needs and aspirations which they would like us to try our best to satisfy in return for an honest day's work," he mused in one 1956 division managers' meeting.[42]

The grounds on which Boulware sought to "sell" GE went far beyond a defense of the company's virtues, emphasizing the ideology of the free market. For example, the *Works News* (a weekly publication that Boulware used to communicate with employees) contained regular features such as a question column called "The Grapevine," where workers could ask about difficulties or disagreements—or, as the paper put it, where "rumors" could be answered with "facts." In early 1955, one worker inquired: "I have heard that Christmas bonuses are granted by many employers who possess less wealth than the General Electric Company. Why then does not the GE Company prove beyond doubt its sincere good will in this matter also?" The company responded, "General Electric prefers a program of enduring value, one which may not be dramatized in flash acts. . . . Mostly, however, we feel that every time the state, an employer, or anyone else takes over one of our individual responsibilities completely, we are one step farther along the road to socialism and a halt to progress."[43] At about the same time, as anxiety about job loss, plant closures and automation began to spread in cities like Schenectady, the *Works News* printed a copy of an old handbill opposing the railroad, with the headline, "The Fearful Always Attempt to Halt Progress."[44] A few years later, the paper ran an article, "Foreign Competition and American Investors"—about how American investors were putting their money into foreign countries. "Put yourself in the investor's shoes. Where would you invest your money if you had reason to believe American production costs were headed higher, and American profits lower?"[45] In a dramatic effort to teach all its workers about economics, the company conducted a course (using materials developed by Du Pont) on company time entitled "How Our Business System Operates." According to Boulware, all 190,000 GE employees took part in it; he claimed that the company spent more than $2 million in lost time for workers to take the class.[46]

The centerpiece of Boulware's vision of labor relations was the creation of a network of organizers—whom he called "job salesmen," or supervisors, in other words—on behalf of the corporation and the free market, which could rival the structure of the union in the plant. Management should consciously strive to create a dense web of affective relationships that could supplant those created by the union. A job, Boulware suggested, was "an intimate relationship between two people—the employee and his boss."[47] The supervisor, he hoped, was to be "Mr. General Electric—or, better still, as nearly as humanly possible . . . Mr. Everything" on matters related to the job.[48] Starting in 1947, each of the company's supervisors was given a lengthy handbook of "scripts" explaining at great length good answers to difficult questions that workers might ask. These responses were almost always couched in the most general, abstract, and philosophical terms, seeking to encourage a market logic and vision of the company rather than respond to particular concerns at GE. For example, workers might fear that big business was "greedy and unprincipled," and that its growth came at the expense of workers and small business. The supervisor's response:

The size of a business is determined by the amount of goods it sells. In the absence of monopoly, the amount of goods it sells is determined all over again every day by the votes of individuals in that most free and democratic of processes, the "plebiscite of the marketplace."[49]

Free-market ideology was intended to politicize GE's managers as much as tame its workers. Boulware's background in public relations strongly influenced his view of political action. Society, for him, was simultaneously highly decentralized and extremely hierarchical. It was a collection of small social orders, in which people were divided into leaders and followers. "Thought-leaders" were people who exercised a disproportionate amount of power over other people's lives and opinions, and they needed to be located, contacted, and persuaded to believe in the free market and GE: "there [i]s a thought-leader for every 8, 10, or 12 people, whether these people made up a baseball team, a football team, an army squad, a company president and his top officers, a U.S. president and his cabinet, or a little group in the corner of a shop or office or community."[50] The basic problem facing American society was that a small number of union leaders had managed to seize a disproportionate amount of power over American workers by establishing themselves as "thought-leaders." To combat the broad political force of the labor movement, businessmen needed to use their power over their employees to attack the labor movement and to preach a stringent market economics: they needed to become thought-leaders themselves.

To this end, GE recommended readings to managers, supervisors, and "many other concerned thought-leaders in and out of plants and offices," including publications by William Roepke (*Economics of the Free Society*), Lawrence Fertig (*Prosperity Through Freedom*), writers affiliated with the Foundation for Economic Education, and several works by conservative journalist Henry Hazlett.[51] Obviously Austrian economists did not set labor relations policy at GE. But Boulware's vision of liberal domination inexorably leading to control of the market and hence to socialist totalitarianism was heavily influenced by writers like Hazlett, Roepke, Hayek, and Ludvig von Mises, whose books he owned.[52] He sprinkled his speeches with quotes by Edmund Burke and Milton Friedman.[53] Boulware himself wrote a free-market text, which was revised and published under the name of economics journalist Lewis Haney, that the company distributed (Boulware had originally wanted to commission Austrian economist von Mises to write an economic "catechism," but von Mises declined) to managers and workers; supervisors and workers were encouraged to organize study groups to talk about the book.[54] GE suggested that "concerned thought-leaders" regularly read the *Wall Street Journal* editorial page, Henry Hazlett and Lawrence Fertig's columns, William Buckley's editorials, the *National Review*, and the *Freeman Magazine*. *The Road Ahead*, a short, nightmarish work of social criticism by conservative writer John Flynn depicting an imminent socialist dystopia, was distributed to all managers.[55] The work of thinkers like Hayek, von Mises, and Flynn helped to legitimate GE's antiunionism, by recasting it from old-fashioned reaction to a blow struck for freedom against tyrannical control of the market.

Boulware thought it was essential that GE communicate to the broader community, influencing the broader culture in which plant relationships took place. "The five to 50 neighbors per employee—adding up to as many as 50 thousand in a community where we had a thousand employees—had to be offered the same initial and corrective information as was offered to the employee," Boulware wrote.[56] In one of his first memos at GE, he suggested a "children's chorus," advertising in national magazines, including "racial and religious" ones, plant tours for everyone from the Kiwanis and Rotary clubs to milk delivery men, and "leadership in all heart-warming local activities, such as crippled children, injured veterans, and perhaps Community Chest, Red Cross, etc."[57] The company developed a series of "Planned Community Advertising" programs, which used "all the techniques of modern two-way communication." The "Program for Clergy," for example, described a program for meeting with and organizing clergymen to be more supportive of business causes. (Late in his life, Boulware would remember, "The clergymen were the worst. They were always against us."[58]) After they were asked to participate in planning the event, local clergymen would meet at the plant and take a factory tour. "A very important psychological approach was used in this first step by taking this selected group of local clergymen into confidence in the planning." From the company's standpoint, the communications program was highly successful.

All you need to do is look at the difficult periods of 1950, 1951, 1952, and the early part of 1953, with their union strife—and compare them with the earlier periods. A few plants did strike, but in those communities we found public sentiment in our favor. But here was the real pay-off. Unlike 1946, *there were no clergymen in the picket lines.*[59]

While top management always supported Boulware's policies, they took a while to catch on throughout the middle ranks. At first, many managers resented the new power of the labor relations department. Boulware's ascendancy took place at the same time as CEO Ralph Cordiner (whose nicknames within the company were "the Undertaker" and "Razor Ralph") sought to decentralize the company and make management at all levels more aware of competition. Executive earnings began to be indexed to profits, so that managers were asked to bear a higher level of risk. Some were asked to leave their old towns to go to new factories.[60] Managerial assistants, whom Cordiner believed were nothing but "prop[s] for a manager who can't get his own work done," were fired.[61] In this context, as one plant manager in Schenectady remembered, "a lot of the old-timers thought Boulware was for the birds." In particular, they did not share his stark opinion on the opposition of the company and its workers: "He was far more aware of a sharp different of feeling between management and labor than I felt, or than we felt, in Schenectady."[62]

But over the course of the 1950s, Boulware's authority actually expanded. Cordiner, who was extremely enthusiastic about Boulware's policies, insisted that all divisions of GE make labor relations a priority. Many old-time managers quit GE, angry at the disruption the company's policies had caused in their careers.[63] The company began to recruit heavily on college campuses, to the point that a degree became a prerequisite for a managerial job. At the same time, GE established its own business school, the General Electric Management Research and Development Institute, in Crotonville, New York. The result was that Boulware supervised a staff of employee relations managers who were mostly college graduates, carefully trained by the corporation, which gave him a power base within the firm independent of the older supervisors. The new white collar managers had little personal experience at all of solidarity with the unions or with production workers.[64]

At the same time, GE sought to hire at least some people with expressly conservative politics for leadership positions. For example, early in 1957 John McCarty of the Plant Community Relations Services Department wrote to Boulware to suggest that the company hire Peter Steele, then director of education for the Associated Industries of Missouri. Steele's main claim to fame was his authorship of a pamphlet entitled *Blueprint for World Revolt,* which GE had circulated widely to its managers and executives. McCarty wanted Steele to contact and work with leaders of national liberal organizations, in the hopes of converting them to the GE program: "Just like in war, someone has to go in and individually contact the enemy."[65] Steele was thrilled to go work for GE. As he wrote to his brother, Boulware was "without a peer among businessmen who speak up for what they believe and the General Electric Company is way out ahead of others in the realization of what needs to be done and its willingness to take up the lead in doing it."[66] Steele urged GE to support the American Economics Association and the Remnant (an attempt to mobilize conservative clergymen). He ultimately left GE to campaign for Barry Goldwater. The hiring of Steele on the basis of his conservative ideology and writing shows how far the company had gone towards conceiving of its political program in terms that resembled those of a giant think tank.

Class Politics

Yet even as GE proselytized to its employees about the glories of the free market, the company was teaching another lesson about power in the marketplace. During the mid-1950s, GE moved production from the older plants (located in a ten-state belt of Massachusetts, Rhode Island, Connecticut, New York, New Jersey, Pennsylvania, Ohio, Indiana, Illinois, and Michigan) to newer facilities, such as the company's gigantic Appliance Park in Louisville, Kentucky, which had been a war plant during World War II. Employment at the Bridgeport, Connecticut, plant, which made consumer appliances such as toasters and electric blankets, dropped from 6,500 in 1947 to 2,888 in 1955 (even though the market for these goods was rising)—jobs moved to Allentown, Pennsylvania; Syracuse and Brockport, New York; and Ashboro,

North Carolina. The Schenectady Works plant, which made producer goods such as turbines, saw employment fall from 20,000 in 1954 (it had peaked at 40,000 during World War II) to 8,500 in 1965. The production was shifted to Roanoke, Waynesboro, and Lynchburg, Virginia; Shelbyville, Indiana; Baltimore, Maryland; Johnson City, New York; and towns in Vermont and California.[67]

The company explicitly favored opening new plants in right-to-work states.[68] In one case, a West Virginia management consultant who had been working with Boulware and Wilson in 1954 signed an affidavit in which he said that his efforts to bring the company to Clarksburg, West Virginia, foundered when Boulware recalled being grilled in a congressional hearing in the late 1940s by a West Virginia representative. (The plant went to Kentucky instead.)[69] In a speech given in Arizona, Boulware announced that "a very important factor" in the company's decision to invest in computer factories in the state was "the fact that you do have a right-to-work law, and the fact that a growing majority of the citizens are so obviously coming to appreciate and support voluntarism as opposed to compulsion in union membership."[70] Boulware helped develop a "Better Business Climate" survey, measuring how friendly a town was to industry (he even got the U.S. Chamber of Commerce to establish a committee on Getting and Keeping Good Employers and make him the chair).[71] Even once the plants had opened, the company continued to use the specter of competition to discipline workers. One union leader told of a plant that had relocated from Bloomsfield, New Jersey, to Tyler, Texas, where wages were 30 to 35 cents an hour lower and benefits less generous: "when our Tyler local asked the company for a wage increase it was told that GE could not afford it because it was not competitive in Tyler! Exactly the same story was told to people in Bloomsfield."[72]

GE publicly justified its decision to transfer jobs and speed up production in terms of the company's competitive position. But inside the company Boulware discussed it in terms of disciplining the workforce. At the Schenectady Works plant, for example, where thousands of skilled machinists (in addition to line workers) made generators, turbines, and other industrial equipment, management announced in 1954 a plan to double the plant's production and profits over ten years—without hiring any additional employees. Several lines of production—Industrial Controls, Industrial Heating, Porcelain Division, and Cables—were moved out of Schenectady to Southern shops. Within the plant, the company embarked on a program of automation and speed-up. Grievances piled up as foremen refused to deal with stewards during the workday. As a result, workers began to engage in stoppages, especially in departments such as the Turbine Department, where there were concentrations of machinists with strong union consciousness and craft solidarity.[73] Such wildcat strikes, however, only intensified company's determination to move the jobs. In a memo dated September 1956, Boulware warned:

Schenectady in general and the Turbine shop in particular have a problem. It is that the pay is too high for the value of work done, that the employees are unresponsive to guidance and in the matters of cooperation, that the supervision is frustrated and even doubtful as to the soundness and ethics of our plans unknown, and that the situation is getting worse rather than better with the inevitable result that more and more of the other operations must be taken out of such a high-cost atmosphere, and that as much as possible of the Turbine business must be drained off to be taken to other places where it is more possible to operate within the prices people can and will pay.

Boulware was aware that this would devastate Schenectady, but he saw moving the jobs as discipline for workers who had grown accustomed to organization and power.

This is not a question of General Electric profits. This is a question of pay for schoolteachers, the number of ads in the newspapers, the amount of collections in the church boxes, and whether people's homes are going to be worth anything or not in Schenectady. Underlying all of this is that we have grown so large in Schenectady that we have created a seller's market on labor there. It is up to Schenectady to prove that it can go contrary to most all other human experience, and that is that it can discipline itself morally and economically not to take the short-term course of abusing the future through trying to cash in exorbitantly on the present sellers' market.[74]

The fact of the company's decision to move production out of its industrial base, combined with its rhetoric about the wisdom of the free market, made the threat of job loss a potent factor in negotiations. Especially during the recession of the late 1950s, Boulware frequently referred to capital flight and to GE's competition with low-cost companies abroad (and in the South) during negotiations, suggesting that if the workers did not cooperate with whatever the company wanted to do, their jobs might be the next to go. The miracle of social harmony through the free market could as easily turn violent, closing factories and destroying cities with impersonal cruelty. Preparing for negotiations in 1960, Boulware warned workers about the "new and pressing realities of the 1960 problem." Low-cost foreign competition was forcing prices down, leaving companies to face "the customer strike, or slow-down, or sit-down, which can be permanent—as empty factories with broken windows in many older industrial areas so vividly dramatize."[75] The Japanese had supposedly captured 60 percent of the market in Christmas tree lights. Domestically there was also increased competition: "New communities, eager for industrial growth, are taking business away from older communities by challenging the values produced in many of the long-established communities." Inexorable competition left the company no choice. While workers were preparing for a strike vote in 1960, the *Works News* queried:

If there is a strike, how long would it take the company to regain its market position once it has settled? How many jobs will be lost before the company could regain the business it would lose during a strike? Would my job be one of those that would be lost? Would the loss be temporary or permanent?[76]

But perhaps the most important aspect of Boulwarism—and the way in which it differed most deeply from the technocratic liberalism of the postwar era—was its relentless politicizing of the economy. GE took a hard-line stance against Communist workers, who were an important group in the company's factories and in the UE leadership. The company cooperated with Senator Joseph McCarthy in identifying suspected Communists for HUAC hearings, which were at times conducted directly prior to union elections in which the anti-Communist International Union of Electrical, Radio, and Machine Workers (IUE) faced off against the radical UE, and workers who took the Fifth Amendment were fired.[77]

Still, for Boulware, unions—regardless of their political affiliation—were the real opponent, not the Communist Party. Unlike the Cold War liberals and the moderate Republicans of the Eisenhower administration, Boulware did not view the Soviet Union as the greatest political threat facing the United States. Far more dangerous was the welfare state and the power of labor. In a speech to the National Canners' Association, he proclaimed, "We are in deep trouble—and not from Russian brilliance or force but from our own ignorance and weakness among us low and high alike."[78] In 1948, as the Cold War in the CIO intensified, GE put out an advertisement in the plants: "We honestly believe that the top leaders on both sides in UE are consciously or unconsciously working in a direction opposite to our better understanding of our free system and to our better use of that system."[79] Boulware testified in Senate hearings on Communist unions in May 1952 that there was no way of telling, from activities in the plant, "which unions were Communist-dominated and which were not."[80] "Let's face it," he said in a speech he delivered to many audiences in the late 1940s and early 1950s, "Our real danger is that, while we are scared to death of communism, too many of us seemingly haven't come to fear socialism at all."[81]

Boulware and GE supported the right-to-work campaigns of the late 1950s (the company even gave financial support to the campaign for right-to-work Proposition 18 in California during Republican senator William F. Knowland's disastrous gubernatorial campaign).[82] Winning the campaigns mattered less to Boulware than using them as an educational tool. As he wrote to a supporter, "The discussion and promotion of right-to-work measures in the various states—even though most of these measures do not pass on the first trial—is the best process I know of so far by which employers and other thoughtful people in the public can . . . bring to employees and the public the damage which compulsory unionism does to employees and citizens."[83] The company also donated money to business organizations like the National Association of Manufacturers, the Business Advisory Council, and the Committee on Economic Development.[84]

But most important, Boulware urged other businessmen to become active in electoral politics. After delivering a speech to the Phoenix Chamber of Commerce entitled "Politics: The Businessman's Biggest Job in 1958," he received fan mail: "I hope you are sending this speech to every businessman in the country," wrote Fred G. Clark of the American Economics Foundation. Boulware responded that he had already sent out about 160,000 copies of the speech to all GE supervisors, to "our plant community lists made up of clergymen, teachers, heads of women's organizations and other thought leaders," to all congressional representatives ,and to "all the remaining names in Poor's Directory of Directors not otherwise covered." The Phoenix Chamber distributed 800 copies, one newspaper ran the whole text, Senator Barry Goldwater put the speech in the Congressional Record, and "requests are now coming in for one dozen to 400 or 500 each."[85] Around the country, businessmen were paying attention to Boulware's program. *Fortune* magazine ran an editorial arguing that corporations were "rediscovering" politics, which focused on GE, and the *Wall Street Journal* ran a similar piece on business and politics ("Business and Elections: One Aim: To Counter Unions"), which featured GE as well.[86] As one James Collins of the Fidelity Union Life Insurance Company wrote to Boulware, "We need more companies to take the same positive attitude that GE is taking."[87]

The company's executives, including Boulware, gave money and time to conservative causes.[88] In 1964, Ralph Cordiner—who had recently stepped down as GE's CEO—took on the job of leading the fund-raising campaign for Barry Goldwater in the months leading up to the election, while Boulware himself (also recently retired) contributed about $10,000 to the Goldwater campaign.[89] Later in life, Goldwater would remember Boulware as a key supporter, rhapsodizing about "the great inspiration that you provided for me as you so stubbornly, rightly and forcefully fought with the union that was trying to take over your company. I wish we had more like you around. The woods are full of softies, not many tough ones left."[90] Less directly, though perhaps more important over the long run, in the 1950s the company employed Ronald Reagan, then a failed movie actor reduced to doing gigs in Las Vegas. Reagan introduced the company's television program and traveled around the country, speaking to audiences of workers and giving the famous GE speech. Earl Dunckel, the man who trained Reagan, remembered that when Reagan came to GE,

His politics were in the process of change. He had been a New Deal Democrat. He didn't like the way things were going, the trend of things. I was, am, and always will be an arch conservative . . . I was drumbeating this at him all the time. Whenever he tried to defend New Dealism, or what was passing for it at the time, we would have some rather spirited arguments. I think this helped him to realize, as he put it later, that he didn't desert the Democratic party; the Democratic party deserted him.[91]

Boulware offered financial support to Reagan throughout his political career, and Reagan remembered him over his entire time in politics. In 1966, after Reagan declared for governor of California, Boulware contributed to the campaign. Reagan wrote back thanking him and expressing anxiety: "somehow making the actual declaration was like stepping off the high dive and realizing you were on the way to the water and it might be cold."[92] Ten years later, Reagan wrote again: "I promise you I'll be trying to stir up the business world, including the exhortation to fight back against government's increasing lust for power over free enterprise."[93] And once he'd attained the presidency, Reagan sent Boulware autographed golf balls and a personal note: "Dear Lem—in case I do something wrong—hit one of these with a 9 iron or a 'wedge' and I'll feel it."[94]

More important than Boulware's financial donations, though, was the role he played in instilling the sense in a part of the business community that ideological and political engagement was an appropriate, legitimate, and absolutely essential part of being a businessman. Businessmen needed to fight on behalf of the free market, against the monopolistic threat of unions and the welfare state that threatened to exercise illegitimate power over the state. The idea of businessmen as crusaders on behalf of the free market—the weak and powerless rebels against the omnipotent forces of labor—was the Boulware's real legacy. Businessmen had to bear the burden of politics. As he put it, "No one else seems to be willing to go through the agony of trying to put what we think is right and what we instinctively know is right into language that is intelligible and convincing to the great mass of citizens who at the moment are being lied to by their government and by their unions."[95] Exhorting businessmen to "inner regeneration" and admonishing them that they must "literally be born again" in the fight for the free market, he concluded: "Let us businessmen stop being Nervous Nellies about this! There is no such thing as a humiliating defeat in a just cause. And, anyhow, let's go at this job fearlessly—recognizing that mightier than armies is the power of a righteous idea whose time has come."[96]

The direct impact of Boulwarism on GE's unions is difficult to separate from the larger political context in which his strategies were developed—the repressive culture of fear created by anticommunism, and the slow turn away from the left in the postwar era. GE's unions were weakened by McCarthyism and by the internecine warfare that the national political shift to the right caused within the labor movement. The CIO expelled the UE in November 1949, on the charge that it was a Communist-dominated union, and Philip Murray granted a charter to the IUE specifically in order to create an anti-Communist CIO union in the electrical industry. The UE and the IUE spent much of the 1950s attacking each other, and the UE leadership claimed with good reason that the division within the labor movement debilitated the union more than GE's strategies.[97] Still, despite the damage done to the labor movement by internal political conflicts,

Boulwarism did weaken the unions at GE. This was most evident in the disastrous 1960 IUE strike, described by a *New York Times* labor reporter as "the worst setback any union has received in a nationwide strike since World War II."[98]

The recession of the late 1950s saw a general resurgence of antilabor activism: right-to-work campaigns in states like Kansas, Indiana and California, the McClellan Committee hearings on corruption in the labor movement, an increase in unfair labor practices during organizing drives, and a hardening bargaining position in industries such as steel (prompting the lengthy 1959 steel strike), focused primarily on issues relating to work rules.[99] It was not the optimal time for a challenge to Boulwarism. But during the recession, the electrical workers' unions were becoming increasingly aware of the negative impact of GE's management decisions on the rights and living standards of union members. Managers were using "decentralization" to avoid settling grievances. The new plants in the South were starting to lay people off. The issues the IUE sought to raise in negotiations in 1958 and 1960 (the IUE had signed a five-year contract in 1955, the best one in the decade, with an agreement to renegotiate wages in 1958) spoke to the basic conflicts of the postwar economy—an end to regional and sexual wage differentials, the establishment of joint committees to handle the problem of automation, protection of seniority in plant relocations. GE refused to deal seriously with any of them.[100] The union relinquished most of its demands in 1958, but it began to prepare in earnest for a national strike in 1960—holding local meetings, bringing an IUE "caravan" across the country to each plant, broadcasting television messages, conducting surveys for bargaining.[101]

The company was preparing for a strike as well, as it had been in one way or another ever since 1946. Not only did it seek to evade the union's demands regarding employment security, but it also wanted to eliminate the cost-of-living provision that had been negotiated in 1955. By 1958, the company was already saying that the 1955 contract had been "too generous," and by 1960, it was adamant that the "business situation" necessitated that "any offer the Company made . . . would have to be far less generous than the 1955 offer."[102]

For months leading up to the strike, GE made it clear to workers and to the general public that it planned to keep its plants operating if workers struck. Jack Parker (Boulware's successor—Boulware had retired in 1957, but continued to consult the company and was heavily involved in planning the 1960 strike strategy) told meetings of management employees, "The Company will take a long strike rather than accede to demands that are detrimental to the future of the business or that infringe on the basic individual rights of employees."[103] He elaborated, "General Electric will make every effort to see that the plants remain open and will do all possible to encourage proper law enforcement to maintain this condition should there be a strike this fall." At the plant gates in Louisville, Kentucky, after the start of the strike, management hung a sign: "The plant is open and all employees are urged to report for work as usual."[104]

Yet the first days of the strike looked very much like 1946. In Philadelphia, hundreds of picketers shut down the switchgear plant entirely. Nearly all workers were out on strike in Fort Wayne, Indiana. The huge Appliance Park in Louisville, Kentucky was virtually idled—although picketers had to walk past the giant sign saying the plant was open, one company spokesman said he didn't know if there were enough workers in any one department to sustain "what you would call production." The Syracuse local had initially voted against striking, but when the strike began it shut down the plant.[105] Almost all hourly employees were out on strike at the plant in Pittsfield, Massachusetts.[106] There were substantial pickets in Lynn, Massachusetts, where supervisors had to be conducted by police through picket lines, and after the first week of the strike 3,500 workers showed up for a single shift of picket duty in Schenectady, even though the local had been divided about striking and had initially voted against it.[107]

For Boulware, even though there was little real violence during the strike, the picket lines seemed a perfect expression of the union's implicit force. The reluctance of the police to break up picket lines demonstrated their collusion with the illicit power of the unions. "Are you now in the grip of a SUPER-GOVERNMENT of LAW-BREAKERS?" read one draft of a company pamphlet. "Can or do this super-dictatorship's imported or local goons damage at will your person, your family, your car, your neighbor's savings, your city's property and future?"[108] In Pittsfield, the company prepared a public response to the strike:

Your mayor is murdering Pittsfield. These law breakers are preventing citizens from coming in to the GE plant and doing work they want to do. Your mayor's police, when asked for protection in going through the brutal picket line, are answering, "Don't be foolish. We are not strike breakers." Well, they and the mayor may not be strike breakers but they are Pittsfield breakers. Your cowed mayor—and his cowed police—are stupidly driving out not only GE but any other employers out of this town. This conduct will put a black eye on Pittsfield that will last for generations. Grass will and should grow in Pittsfield streets—if your mayor does not stop instantly his dishonorable abandoning of his sacred oath to enforce the law.[109]

A few days before the strike deadline, managers sent personal letters to the workers' homes, painting the leadership as out of touch. "The union officials should be the servants and not the masters of the members," one letter read. "It is thus now up to you to decide where your own interest lies. We hope your decision—in your own and the common interest—will be to come into work Monday morning after having told your local union officials and the local law enforcement officials that you do not want any fooling about your being able to exercise your rights or about your being protected against unlawful interference with the exercise of those rights."[110] After the strike started, Boulware and Parker began to direct managers to urge workers to cross the picket lines, "not through ultimatums or organized 'back to work' movements, but through patient persuasion of individuals and groups of employees that it is in their own best interests to return to work now." The plan encouraged managers and supervisors to maintain "close contact" with people crossing the picket lines, for "they represent a channel by which management can learn more of the feelings and desires of all employees with respect to the question of returning to work." Supervisors were instructed to keep in phone contact with their employees, and to pay home visits; the company provided them with scripts of arguments to persuade strikers to cross the picket lines. Certain workers should be targeted—"key individuals or small groups of employees whose return is particularly important, perhaps because of defense work . . . or whose judgment is particularly respected by other employees." The supervisors were told to keep in touch with community leaders aware of "the lasting damage . . . a long and hopeless strike could have upon job security and the community," and to encourage them to talk to other people.[111]

The company took out full-page ads in the *New York Times*, the *Wall Street Journal*, and local publications, attacking James Carey (the IUE president) and denouncing the picketers. Letters were sent to shareholders, reminding them that in addition to their direct interest in GE they were also consumers and businessmen who were "adversely affected" by inflation and high wages, and by the "union's restriction of output and insistence on destroying property and otherwise breaking the law when they call a strike."[112] GE even encouraged secretaries and women employees to pose as the wives of strikers and call into radio talk shows, angry with the union for what it was doing to their families.[113]

The Cold War divisions within the labor movement proved the perfect backdrop for Boulware's strategies. While the IUE was striking, most of the other unions at GE were settling contracts with the company. The UAW and the IAM accepted the contract, and by October 20, more than sixty of the unions at GE had taken the offer.[114] Without support from the other unions, it was difficult to sustain the strike, and IUE workers began to cross the picket lines. The strike fell apart completely after two weeks, when the Schenectady local voted to go back to work. The union accepted the very contract it had originally struck to reject.

But while the weakness of the unions at GE may have been the real secret of Boulware's success, from the standpoint of management around the country the breaking of the strike seemed like a turning point—a sign that management no longer simply had to accept labor's power. Boulwarism was widely credited with the company's victory in the strike. Maurice Franks, president of the conservative National Labor-Management Foundation, wrote, "Congratulations! I believe the settlement of the GE strike is the beginning of a new era in industrial relations. The era when management will no longer cowtow to the whims of the selfish, incompetent or radical labor leader."[115] Businessmen across the country wrote to Boulware to congratulate him on the company's victory in the strike. A Detroit lawyer named Raymond Dykema wrote, "It appears to me that the failure of the strike is one of the noteworthy events of 1960. Probably it is a milestone in labor relations. Undoubtedly it arises from what you call management's 'homework.' I think America owes you a debt of gratitude."[116] Maxwell Goodwin wrote, "Your crowning glory—Carey bites the dust! The recognition being given you is grand and you must love Carey now that he stuck his neck out and gave you the chance to prove your policy. Now perfect it for politics and USA will be saved."[117] Another business friend wrote, "All this week I have meant to write and tell you what a helluva good job you did for GE—and the malicious malignancy forthcoming from your sparring-partner through the press makes your victory all the more pleasing to some of us. Bless you for it."[118] Arthur Rosenbaum, the director of economic research for Sears, wrote with congratulations and to ask to see the material GE had distributed to its workers.[119] A major part of Boulware's approach, of course, was to never stop working. In an executive office meeting memo shortly after the strike, Cordiner asked each manager to "appraise . . . what had been learned of management-labor relations" at each plant, and to offer "suggestions of what could be done to place the company in an even stronger position three years hence."[120]

Conclusion

In 1964, the National Labor Relations Board ruled that Boulwarism violated the obligation of the company to bargain with the union.[121] In 1969, the IUE and the UE transcended their Cold War history to join forces for a lengthy and far more successful strike that partially diminished the memories of 1960.[122] Yet despite these setbacks for the corporation, at the very moment when labor seemed to be winning at GE once again, the kinds of strategies that GE had pioneered began to spread throughout the rest of American industry. Under the new pressures generated by the recession and political upheaval of the 1970s, the free-market politics the company had long championed started to emerge as a unifying force throughout the entire business community. "His ideas were thought reactionary at the time, but Lemuel Boulware has lived to see many of them accepted," a *Forbes* journalist wrote in 1989.[123]

What can we learn from General Electric and Boulwarism? First, the case of GE suggests that the liberal consensus in the 1950s on matters of political economy was far more strained than the historiography has suggested. For corporate leaders like Ralph Cordiner and Lemuel Boulware, the power of labor unions upheld the entire structure of postwar liberalism, which—despite its many limitations, regardless of its political timidity—was and remained a real restriction on corporate power. Accordingly, they pursued an aggressive antilabor, antiwelfare state politics, joining businessmen together in a defense of capitalism and the free market. Memories of the 1946 strike wave and of the potential power of organized workers haunted GE's leaders throughout the seemingly placid days of the 1950s boom. The liberal and social-democratic elements of the New Deal order seemed as great a threat to management power as the Communists and the Soviet Union. Nor were they alone in this way of thinking: The intellectual work of theorists like Hayek and von Mises legitimated the free-market project, as did an increasingly vocal group of think tanks and organizations committed to recasting the idea of the market and rolling back the welfare state. For these business leaders and their allies in the intellectual world, prosperity did not quell class conflict.

The story of Boulwarism also suggests that in the late 1950s there was a real shift in the world of conservative politics. Corporate management was starting to see labor relations as political, and to believe that political engagement was key to maintaining control—not only over the firm, but also in American society more generally. For Boulware, the key was to build a conservative grassroots movement from the top down, encouraging supervisors and management to see themselves as organizers for conservative economic politics. Superficially this resembled—and consciously borrowed from—the organizing project and tactics of the union, but the power dynamics that drove it were fundamentally different. The free-market movement would later present itself as a populist movement. But it had its origins in the efforts of companies like GE to find ways to combat the liberal order at the end of World War II. The idea of the market—an anarchic space of desire and individual achievement, in which even the mammoth GE was reduced to an insignificant cipher—provided them with an elegant theory that they could use to justify and explain their power. The roots of this market vision and the politics that followed from it lay not in the dissatisfied longings of populist Americans, but in the political orientations and ambitions of the top strata of American society.

13

Godless Capitalism: Ayn Rand and the Conservative Movement

Jennifer Burns

In 1954 New York, two titans of the twentieth-century American right came face to face. Fiery procapitalist ideologue Ayn Rand, author of the best-selling novel *The Fountainhead* (1943), met a young William F. Buckley, Jr., fresh off the notoriety and success of his *God and Man at Yale* (1950). As Buckley recalled in later years, upon meeting him, Rand declared in her imperious Russian accent, "You arrh too eentelligent to bihleef in Gott!"[1] It was, to say the least, an inauspicious beginning to an acquaintanceship that would span many decades. The pious Buckley never quite recovered from his immediate dislike of Rand, while she never lost her sense that Buckley's religiosity ruined an otherwise valuable fellow traveler. Beyond the clash of two proud and ambitious personalities, the first Rand-Buckley encounter encapsulates many of the dynamics of right-wing thought in the twentieth century. In Buckley, Rand saw the first glimmers of a religious conservatism that would soon coopt the antistatist ideals she had been promoting for her entire career. What Buckley encountered in the person of Rand was a nearly pure incarnation of the putative Old Right, for Rand had formed her positions in the ideological matrix of the 1930s and 1940s. Yet Rand was far from a dusty relic of the past, as her continued appeal over the century would demonstrate. Buckley himself quickly grasped that in Rand he faced a formidable competitor for the loyalty of the antistatist forces in America. And there was no question of collaboration, for Buckley was convinced that as an atheist, Rand missed the central truth his conservatism had to offer: that religion was the only viable foundation for victory over the collectivist madness of Stalin's terror. But neither could Rand simply be dismissed, for her works of radical individualism advanced controversial arguments about the moral status of capitalism, thus touching upon a core issue of conservative identity. In 1957, Buckley declared open warfare on Rand in the pages of his journal *National Review*, publishing a scathing review of her second novel, *Atlas Shrugged* (1957). Yet this rebuttal proved insufficient, and *National Review* returned to the subject of Rand and her relevancy to conservatism with two articles in 1961 and a cover story in 1967. When it came to dealing with Rand, Buckley wheeled out the big guns, enlisting conservative luminaries such as Whittaker Chambers, Garry Wills, and M. Stanton Evans to deliver their judgments. As distasteful as the outspoken Rand might be to Buckley, it was clear that she could not be safely ignored.

Debates over Ayn Rand remained contentious for conservatives throughout the 1960s because her promarket ideology, and its popularity, exposed the fault lines upon which modern American conservatism rested. The publication of *Atlas Shrugged,* her magnum opus, brought to the surface uncertainties about how capitalism—and justifications for it—fit into the conservative program. Responding to Rand compelled conservatives to wrestle with a profound set of dilemmas about the nature and meaning of the market economy. Was capitalism a fundamental part of the conservative program or simply a necessary evil? The answer might be a delicate blend of both, but Rand's intoxicating novels threatened to overwhelm such subtleties with polemical sophistries. Furthermore, Rand's vast popularity meant she could conceivably eclipse conservatives in the public eye. Therefore, managing Rand and containing her influence were critical projects if the editors at *National Review* were to retain any control over the movement they were so carefully nurturing into maturity. The process by which conservatives attempted to repudiate the atheistic Rand was an inverse of the larger process whereby antigovernment, individualistic, procapitalist ("libertarian," if you will) thought allied itself with an aggressive Christian outlook and tried to disown its secular roots. While conservatives might try to reject Rand root and branch, in many cases they ended up echoing her arguments and conclusions, albeit in a more modulated voice. An examination of Rand's career, and conservative relations with her, shows how the conservative movement as a whole managed to absorb Rand's embrace of the market while preserving the primacy of Christian ethics. Consideration of Rand also reestablishes the significance of the 1930s and 1940s to conservatism broadly considered. To date, historians have generally portrayed the ideas which Rand represented as of little concern to Buckley and the movement he embodied.[2] Recent scholarship on the right reinforces this impression by focusing extensively on the 1960s. Yet conservatism had deeper roots than this, and the legacy of these early origins was manifest throughout the century.[3]

Conservatism, as assembled under the flag of Buckley's *National Review,* was a rather hybrid creed.[4] When he founded the magazine in 1955, Buckley deliberately sought to weld the established libertarian, anti-New Deal critique with a renewed appreciation for Christian tradition. Yet this accord did not come easily, and debates raged wildly about the issue of "fusionism," or the desirability and practicality of joining Christian advocacy with a defense of capitalism. While all could agree with anticommunism, traditionalists like Russell Kirk disliked the libertarian emphasis on the free market and individual liberty. Libertarians fought back fiercely, refusing to cede any ground to traditionalists and their talk of "virtue." Buckley and one of his editors, Frank Meyer, struggled to keep the peace and to convince everyone that they belonged in one alliance.[5]

Into this debate, Rand came like an ideological time capsule from the libertarian fringe of the 1930s. Her unreconstructed defense of capitalism and business made no concessions to religion or to the post-New Deal, welfare state consensus that had emerged. *Atlas Shrugged* explicitly endorsed capitalism and promoted a comprehensive system of promarket ethics in a way that Rand's previous blockbuster, *The Fountainhead* (1943), had not. It articulated a set of values that conservatives wanted desperately to disavow, combining antigovernment rhetoric, staunch procapitalism, and atheism into a particularly noxious mixture. Yet if Rand had so clearly misconstrued conservatism, then why spill so much ink? Beyond the articles he published, throughout the 1960s, Buckley took potshots at Rand during his public appearances. In 1967, he sneered to an audience at the New School for Social Research, "Ayn Rand . . . is there anyone more boring?"[6]

Buckley's jab at Rand contains a clue to this puzzle, for he clearly expected his audience to know who she was and what she stood for, thereby implicitly acknowledging her public stature. It is difficult to exaggerate Rand's popularity or her ubiquity in 1960s popular culture. Sales figures for her novels tell part of the story. Within five years of publication, *The Fountainhead* had sold 400,000 copies, and it broke the million mark soon thereafter. *Atlas Shrugged* was even more popular, quickly surging into the million-copy range. And neither book's success was ephemeral, for decades after publication both continued to sell over 100,000 copies annually, making Rand's novels the stuff of publishing lore.[7] Moreover, Rand was not simply a novelist, but she was also a popular guest on national TV shows and radio programs, a favorite of political cartoonists, a syndicated columnist, a frequent lecturer at college campuses, and, as of 1962, the publisher of her own periodical, *The Objectivist Newsletter*. Her fictional characters quickly passed into conversational parlance and her political slogans surfaced in magazines and newspapers across the land. For the staff of a magazine that struggled to break into the 50,000 circulation range, Rand's capacity to draw an audience had to be a bit aggravating.[8]

Yet it was not just popularity that the Buckleyites craved; they aspired to respectability as well. Here, Rand's successes hit another sore spot. Given the media's interest in the "New Conservatism," and Rand's considerable cultural presence, it was quite possible that she might be anointed by liberals as a spokesperson for conservatism, and then be used to discredit their entire program. Such dangers had arisen before in the early 1950s, when liberals such as Arthur Schlesinger, Jr., eagerly took upon themselves the task of defining who was and who was not a true "conservative."[9] Buckley and his writers had bridled at this interposition on their own ideological formations, and had fought long and hard to present a united, coherent front to their liberal adversaries. But even as they pilloried liberals, they clearly wished to be taken as worthy opponents, and even as they mocked professors, their desire for intellectual respectability was clear.[10] It was obvious that Rand would be of no help in this effort, for popular as she was, her overwrought literary style ensured that she would never be respectable among the country's intelligentsia. Even worse, she might confirm the liberal stereotype that conservatism was nothing more than an ideological cover for the naked class interests of the haves. But the most important reason to reject Rand was her hostility to religion, because it meant she had fundamentally misunderstood what conservatism was all about.

Nonetheless, the task of disowning Rand was formidable, because she had been a significant presence on the right-wing scene since long before Buckley entered Yale. Many leading conservatives, particularly those of a libertarian bent, had been profoundly inspired by her early work and continued to find her a valuable ally in the struggle against statism. Furthermore, while her strident atheism set her apart from many on the right, key features of Rand's thought mimicked the dynamics of conservative ideology and ensured that her work would have continued relevance in the years ahead. Like the Catholic conservatives of *National Review*, Rand advanced a vituperative critique of liberalism, depicted a world consisting of moral absolutes, and touted the wisdom of the people against an overweening elite. While her advocacy of pure laissez-faire might owe much to the nineteenth century, she presented her arguments in a twentieth-century form that dovetailed easily with the rhetoric of the burgeoning conservative movement.

This symmetry, and Rand's contribution to the broader development of right-wing thought, can be seen most easily in the way her anticommunist attitudes shaded imperceptibly into procapitalism. In her early work, Rand focused on establishing the moral depravity of communism, drawing heavily on her own experience in Russia. Later she shifted into portraying the positive aspects of the American system, focusing on what she identified as the intrinsic moral nature of capitalism. Rand advanced both these ideas under the rubric of "individualism versus collectivism," which allowed her to construct a series of theoretical arguments about the good society that were not religious in nature. Rand was not the first to develop this binary of individualism versus collectivism, which was widespread at the popular level in the 1940s, but she did much to popularize and shape its form.[11] Rand was also one of the first to argue against communism and in favor of capitalism on purely ethical grounds. Long before the evils of communism were widely known, Rand maintained its ideals were fundamentally corrupt, and she likewise insisted upon the beneficence of capitalism when such attitudes were far out of the mainstream. In large part, her career was shaped by the penalties she paid for being an early advocate of unpopular ideas that would later pass into conventional wisdom. In order to understand why *National Review* reacted to Rand with such vehemence, it is necessary to see how deeply embedded she was in the prewar conservative world, and how her work embodied core themes of conservative ideology. Rand was particularly vexing because she was only partially wrong. In many ways she looked like a friend to conservatism, which made establishing a clear policy on her ideas all the more imperative.

In 1936, long before there was a Cold War, Rand established herself as a cold warrior with the publication of her first novel, *We the Living*, a bitter indictment of life in Soviet Russia. In contrast to later anticommunist writers, Rand, a lifelong atheist, did not base her arguments on religion.[12] Instead, she fictionalized her own history to depict the hopelessness and despair of life under collectivism. Rand, who had emigrated from Russia in 1926, knew from firsthand experience what cost revolution could exact. Her father's business had been nationalized in the first wave of communist reforms, plunging the family into dire poverty. This experience instilled in Rand a deep suspicion of government and a passionate desire to tell the truth about what communism was—to her, a corrupt system built entirely upon theft. She wrote to her agent: "No one has ever come out of Soviet Russia to tell it to the world. That was my job."[13] *We the Living* follows the fate of three young Russians who struggle against the injustices and violence of totalitarianism. Ultimately, Rand argues it is impossible to lead a life of integrity or meaning in a society that demands man must live for the state. While the novel is concerned with communism on the surface, its deeper theme invokes the problem of the individual against the collective. With these baseline ethics, Rand attacked communism because of its very principles. As one character tells a Communist Party member, "I loathe your ideals."[14] Because the basic unit of value for Rand was the individual, she argued forcefully that any system which prioritized the common good over the lives of individuals was ethically bankrupt. Rand's systemic critique of communism laid the groundwork for her later dismissal of liberalism, which she would argue fundamentally shared the ideals of communism. This early recognition of communism's evils gave Rand considerable credibility and moral stature on the right.

By 1940, Rand's fealty to the ideals of individualism led her to Wendell Willkie's presidential campaign, where she imbibed a strong dose of traditional American laissez-faire, the hoary creed of William Graham Sumner and Andrew Carnegie that was fast becoming radicalized by the ascendancy of the Roosevelt administration.[15] The Willkie campaign provided a gathering place for the slowly germinating conservative movement that stood opposed to the New Deal. Rand was drawn into a network of unregenerate individualists, including the economist Friedrich von Hayek and the writers Albert J. Nock, Isabel Paterson, and Rose Wilder Lane. The political atmosphere of the New Deal transformed these thinkers, causing them to fear that any accommodation with government could result in the dangerous state expansion typified by Roosevelt's programs. Under the pressures of the New Deal, what would earlier have been no more than a traditional affection for limited government was fast becoming a deeply felt antistatism. This dislike of big government was linked to a keen appreciation of capitalism or, as the more politic among them had it, "free enterprise." The banner year for this circle was 1943–44, which brought the publication of Rand's *The Fountainhead*, Hayek's *The Road to Serfdom*, Paterson's *God of the Machine*, Lane's *The Discovery of Freedom*, and Nock's *Memoirs of a Superfluous Man*. Although Rand's and Hayek's books were the only ones to attain immediate success, the others went on to become sleeper classics that heavily influenced midcentury conservatives.[16] Rand would carry on the legacy of these earlier thinkers, albeit with her own innovations. While she shared their basic political orientation, she disagreed with Lane and Paterson's friendliness towards religion and went on to celebrate what Nock attacked as "economism."[17] Hayek she regarded with suspicion because he supported limited planning. Nonetheless, these relationships broadened Rand's perspective on the United States and helped form her political judgments. In this period she also dipped into more mainstream economic theory, profiting greatly from Carl Snyder's *Capitalism the Creator: The Economic Foundations of Modern Industrial Society* (1940).[18] Snyder, a well-known economist and statistician at the Federal Reserve Bank, argued in this book that capitalism was the chief mechanism by which societies moved from "barbarism and poverty to affluence and culture."[19] His vision of creative and beneficent capitalism would soon find its way into Rand's fiction. The laissez-faire doctrine she absorbed from Snyder, her libertarian friends, and general newspaper reading was also reinforced by her own biography, for Rand's career embodied the Horatio Alger story. Like countless self-made men, Rand came to believe fervently in the gospel of success.

These ideas and influences were manifest in Rand's wildly popular second novel *The Fountainhead*, which established her as a towering figure among her political associates. In a time of right-wing ascendancy, it is difficult to envision just how enervated the movement was in the 1940s: there was no Buckley, no Ronald Reagan, no Barry Goldwater, no *National Review*. People who identified as conservatives lacked any discernable program or institutional base. But there was Ayn Rand, and her best-selling novel of unmistakable political import, *The Fountainhead*. In this book, Rand celebrated the freedoms of American capitalism while also warning that there were diabolical forces afoot that threatened liberty. The novel follows the career of the brilliant architect Howard Roark, who embodies Rand's idea of the heroic individual. Unlike the characters in *We the Living*, Roark finds ample room for his genius in America. Perceiving his work to be fundamentally representative of his soul and character, Roark refuses to modify his radical, avant-garde designs to gain popularity. He suffers early professional setbacks but emerges triumphant by the end of the novel because he has never compromised his own individuality. *The Fountainhead* parts ways from Rand's first novel because it is clearly a didactic parable, rather than an attempt to portray life under totalitarianism. Each character symbolizes a certain range of human characteristics that is then linked to a specific political position. Rand took special care to skewer liberals throughout the novel. As she wrote to a friend just after its release, "When you read it, you'll see what an indictment of the New Deal it is, what it does to the 'humanitarians' and what effect it could have on the next election—although I never mentioned the New Deal by name."[20] Rand even modeled her arch-villain Ellsworth Toohey on the British socialist Harold Laski, thereby situating her tale of the individual versus the collective within current politics.[21]

In the dramatic climax of the novel, Roark gives voice to Rand's antistatism when he dynamites a government-funded housing project that has been built based on his adulterated architectural plans. He remains unrepentant about the destruction and insists that the entire project was morally flawed because it set a collectivity against an individual. Defending himself in court, Roark rejects the idea of any social obligation to the poor. While he is speaking specifically of the housing project he designed, his sentiments encode a general rejection of progressive taxation or government welfare projects. Roark argues: "It is believed that the poverty of the future tenants gave them a right to my work. That their need constituted a claim upon my life. That it was my duty to contribute anything demanded of me. This is the second-hander's credo now swallowing the world. I came here to say that I do not recognize anyone's right to one minute of my life. Nor to any part of my energy. Nor to any achievement of mine. No matter who makes the claim, how large their number or how great their need."[22] Luckily for Roark, a jury composed of virtuous American everymen agrees with his defense, and he is acquitted of any crime. The carefully selected jury demonstrates Rand's faith in the level-headed common sense of the average American: it is composed of two executives of industrial concerns, two engineers, a mathematician, a truck driver, a brick layer, an electrician, a gardener, and three factory workers. Although her novel centered on the esoteric profession of architecture, with the jury Rand extended her conception of work as spiritual craft to any individual who took pride in his or her profession, no matter how humble. With its suspicion of government projects, resolute belief in populist wisdom as superior to the counsel of Machiavellian experts, and reflexive patriotism, Rand's novel adumbrated many basic themes of right-wing thought. It proved a heady brew indeed for those who chafed at the policies of the Roosevelt years.

While *The Fountainhead*'s success established Rand as a considerable intellectual force on the right, its popularity also pulled her out of the rapidly expanding conservative political orbit. After moving back to Hollywood in 1945 to help with the screen adaptation of *The Fountainhead*, Rand fell out of contact with many of her Willkie-era friends (although she became active in California right-wing politics).[23] Soon after, *The Fountainhead*'s emotive power attracted her a unique constituency in the form of Nathaniel and Barbara Branden, two college students who were avid admirers of her fiction. The Brandens, who would go on to be her primary intellectual collaborators in the years ahead, fell quickly under Rand's sway and did little to challenge her opinions.[24] From 1950 until the publication of *Atlas Shrugged*, Rand isolated herself from wider society, socializing predominantly with the Brandens and their relatives. She was thus largely absent from the critical discussions about the nature and meaning of conservatism that dominated the early and mid-1950s. As conservatives struggled to extract moral meanings from totalitarianism, and to bolster religion in a society they believed had gone fundamentally astray, Rand focused exclusively on her own fictional world. After all, she had long ago made up her mind about the evils of totalitarianism and what must be done to combat it. Her opinions sprang from experience, not theology. And experience had taught her that America was the promised land because it allowed unprecedented political and economic freedom, not because it enjoyed divine favor. This freedom had made possible her meteoric rise from impoverished immigrant to literary sensation. Rand, wealthy now from sales of *The Fountainhead*, knew firsthand the blessings of the market. With the same sense of mission that had inspired *We the Living*, she turned to the political and economic ideologies of her new homeland.

Atlas Shrugged, much more so than *The Fountainhead*, was essentially a vindication and defense of American capitalism. During its composition, she wrote that the novel's theme was "those who are antibusiness are antilife."[25] Like its predecessor, *Atlas Shrugged* offered a dystopian vision of a world on the brink of ruin, due to years of liberal policy making and leadership. The aggrandizing state has run amok and collectivism has triumphed across the globe. Facing exploitative tax burdens and unbearable regulation, the creative minds of America have gone "on strike" and throughout the course of the story, all competent individuals in every profession disappear. The man masterminding this strike, John Galt, appears halfway through the 1,084-page novel. He faces off against—and falls in love with—one of Rand's dynamic female characters, Dagny Taggert, the gorgeous and brilliant head of Taggert Transcontinental Railroad. Besides melodrama and dime store romance, the novel is studded with nuggets of politically instructive detail. Some are sheer capitalist fantasy: upon arriving at Galt's secret hideaway, Dagny learns that all the money she has paid in taxes over her working lifetime has been collected into a secret bank account and will now be returned to her. Others are more cutting, such as her caustic descriptions of Washington insiders and a young man with "an odor of public payroll."[26] Galt's vision of the future United States, to be restored after the corrupt liberal government falls under its own weight, represents a flat-out rebuttal of every major policy initiative of the twentieth century. Galt's band will abolish income taxes, foreign aid, social welfare programs, and will return currency to the gold standard.

Rand's depiction of capitalism in *Atlas Shrugged* is simultaneously nostalgic and visionary. When the competent go on strike, they retreat to Galt's Gulch, a refuge nestled deep in the mountains of Colorado, where they recreate a nineteenth-century world. Residents of the valley are on a first name basis with each other, and attend Chautauqua-type lectures at night.[27] The former head of Sanders Aircraft is a hog farmer, while a federal court judge supplies the eggs and butter. This affectionate picture of small town America rests side by side with Rand's definition of capitalism as the ultimate cerebral achievement, a social system that calls for constant innovation, learning, and a commitment to rationality. In a manner remarkably apropos to the late twentieth-century knowledge economy, Rand conceptualized money as mind made manifest: "Wealth is the product of man's capacity to think," claims one of her characters.[28] Many of Rand's protagonists have an entrepreneurial bent and accumulate wealth through an ingenious invention or by making a scientific breakthrough. Even Dagny, whose railroad is the emblematic old-economy business, is successful because she has an outstanding conceptual grasp of the marketplace and is the only executive who understands the potential of new technologies to improve her operations. Reprising the Protestant work ethic, Rand also suggests that money has a direct relation to values: "Money is the product of virtue, but it will not give you virtue, and it will not redeem your vices."[29] For Rand, the market not only rewarded virtue, but regulated vice. Without the interference of the government, the market would evenly distribute its rewards to those who were deserving and punish those who did not make use of their talents. For this reason, Rand dismissed the dangers of inherited wealth. If an heir was not worthy, he or she would soon be stripped of all financial advantage. Because it operated on pure reason and rewarded only objective achievement, Rand saw capitalism as inherently self-regulating.

As in *The Fountainhead*, the ethics of *Atlas Shrugged* posit self-interest as the highest good, and explicitly reject sacrifice or obligation. Entrants to Galt's Gulch take the following oath, reminiscent of Roark's courtroom speech: "I swear by my life and my love of it that I will never live for the sake of another man, nor ask another man to live for mine."[30] Rand's heroes are a diverse band of "producers," including industrialists, artists, and scientists, whom she intends to embody moral truths. These producers lead moral lives because they do not extract resources from others, but rather depend on their own talents and ingenuity to advance. Although all their actions are guided by selfishness, there is room in Rand's world for self-interest that accrues goods to the commons, as exemplified by Rearden Metal. Henry Rearden, owner of several steel mills, is the only man able to bring to market a new material that will make trains safer and provide inestimable boons to industrial society as a whole. Through Rearden, Rand advances her belief that innovation and progress will happen in the private sector, and only be inhibited by government. If the greater good of Rearden metal does somewhat undercut her emphasis on selfishness, Rand is careful to emphasize that any social benefits capitalism creates are secondary effects, and rightly so. Social welfare should never be a goal of private enterprise, but rather the profit motive should be acknowledged and celebrated as a spur to creativity. If the profit motive is considered selfish, then so be it: Rand gladly celebrates selfishness as humanity's highest moral calling.

As she elaborated these already controversial ideas in *Atlas Shrugged*, Rand was often deliberately provocative, even inflammatory. Beyond simply presenting capitalism as a moral system, she seemed to take an adolescent delight at sending up traditional conventions and mores. One of her admirable characters proudly assumes the nickname "Midas" Mulligan. Another declares Robin Hood to be the most contemptible symbol known to man, and makes a practice of stealing humanitarian aid intended for poor countries, giving it instead to the productive rich. A third discourses upon "money, the root of all good."[31] Moreover, in her efforts to portray the ideals of selfishness, Rand often ended up glorifying singularly unappealing characters. Radical individualism might look noble in the case of Howard Roark, a single male professional. But it did not come off quite the same in the married Henry Rearden. When Rearden's mother worries what will befall the family if he is sentenced to jail, Rearden tells her, "I don't know and I don't care," and then walks out on Thanksgiving dinner to visit his mistress. That same evening, he tells his feckless brother, "Whatever affection I might have felt for you once, is gone. I haven't the slightest interest in you, your fate or your future."[32] While Rand implies that Rearden's family deserves the treatment they receive, what remains is Rearden's cold manner and Rand's depiction of this as a proper course of action.

Rand called her literary style "romantic realism" and maintained that the goal of her fiction was to portray life as it could be, not as it was. To this end, she developed a series of sharp polarities between her characters. Her heroes are always fair of form and strong in jaw line, while her villains are correspondingly flabby and shifty-eyed. Since Rand meant to demonstrate on both a personal and social level the result of faulty ideals, she was often merciless with her characters, depicting their sufferings and failings with relish. In one noteworthy and repellent scene, she describes in savory detail the personal flaws of passengers doomed to perish in a violent railroad crash, openly suggesting their deaths are warranted by their ideological errors.[33] The spoofing of liberals in *The Fountainhead* was positively gentle compared to the vicious caricatures of *Atlas Shrugged*.

Rand eagerly awaited the reviews in 1957, but she was to be sorely disappointed. While virtually no one had seen her coming in 1943, now it seemed legions were prepared. The *New York Times Book Review*, which had generously praised *The Fountainhead*, featured a scathing review of *Atlas*

Shrugged by ex-Communist Granville Hicks, who declared, "loudly as Miss Rand proclaims her love of life, it seems clear that the book is written out of hate."[34] For the most part, reviewers did not primarily object to Rand's political or moral views, or even her adulation of the superior man. What they focused on instead was the tone and style of the book as a whole. Echoing Hicks's comment, the *Saturday Review* wrote, "the book is shot through with hatred."[35] Other frequent complaints were Rand's repetition and her habit of overdrawing the contrasts between good and evil characters. In many cases, Rand inspired a particularly visceral reaction. Reviews were often savage and mocking commentaries, rather than literary assessments. As *Time* asked, "Is it a novel? Is it a nightmare?"[36] Such spleen may have been due to Rand's own renunciation of charity as a moral obligation. After all, she had voluntarily opted out of the traditional expectations of politeness or courtesy. Or, it may have been due to the book's prodigious length, which taxed even the most enthusiastic commentators. Occasional reviewers doled out grudging praise for Rand's dramatic flair, but found such strengths overshadowed by her hectoring tone. Most glumly agreed that whatever its faults or merits, the novel was likely to outsell even *The Fountainhead.*

Over at *National Review*, Whittaker Chambers went for the jugular. In an article entitled "Big Sister Is Watching You," Chambers deemed *Atlas Shrugged* "a remarkably silly book" and announced that "the news about this book seems to me to be that any ordinarily sensible head could possibly take it seriously."[37] He noted Rand's popularity and her promotion of conservative ideals such as anticommunism and limited government, but argued that because she was an atheist, her underlying message was faulty and dangerous. The book began by "rejecting God, religion, original sin, etc. etc.," and in so doing created "a materialism of the Right" that differed little from "a materialism of the Left." According to Chambers, Rand was foolish to think that collectivism, an essentially godless philosophy, could be defeated by anything other than religion. Without the guidance of religion, Chambers believed, societies would be led astray into the hubris of socialism and dictatorship. Rand's work, in fact, foreshadowed this outcome, for it was marked by strong fascist elements and ultimately pointed to rule by a "technocratic elite."

But it was not just this criticism which marked the review: far more striking was the article's vituperative tone. The insults came thick and fast. Rand's writing was "dictatorial" and had a tone of "overriding arrogance"; she was certainly not sufficiently feminine, hinted Chambers, speculating that "children probably irk the author and may make her uneasy." And in a stunning line that must have been particularly galling to the Jewish Rand, Chambers intoned, "from almost any page of *Atlas Shrugged*, a voice can be heard, from painful necessity, commanding: 'To a gas chamber—go!'" At base, it was a clash of two radically different versions of human nature. Rand's worldview was fundamentally optimistic, and her novel showed mankind, guided by rationality alone, achieving heroic deeds. Chambers, fresh from the traumas of the Hiss trial, saw rational man as a doomed and helpless creature trapped in dangerous utopian fantasies of his own creation.

Yet there was another source of the viciousness. Chambers was fully conscious that Rand's ideas put conservatism, as Buckley was trying to promote it, under grinding strain. This current of thought ran just below the surface of the review. In his article, Chambers argued that Rand's book was materialist not simply because she was an atheist, but because she was a capitalist. He wrote that if Rand's fictional world ever became real, the only value would be hedonism, leading to cultural degradation and a "general softening of the fibers of will, intelligence, spirit." This would happen because "a free enterprise system . . . [is] in practice materialist (whatever else it claims or supposes itself to be)." The observation came in passing, but it cut to the heart of the conservative problem with Rand. By spinning out the logic of capitalism to its ultimate conclusion, she highlighted all the contradictions that had lately caused such ferocious infighting among conservatives. Her novel showcased the paradox of defending free-market capitalism while at the same time advocating Christianity. But it was just this combination which made conservatism distinctive and which, Buckley and his allies believed, was both morally defensible and politically expedient. Books like Rand's, however, might undermine or redirect the whole venture. If this was what capitalism meant, how could a Christian possibly support it? Chambers, long a student of dialectics, grasped these contradictions in an instant. He sensed immediately that Rand's ideas had to be quarantined if conservatism was to maintain its careful balancing act between capitalism and Christianity.

Chambers's evisceration of Rand reflected both the new importance religion had assumed for conservatives in the 1950s and the tension they felt over the issue of capitalism. Communism was by now always and everywhere "Godless," making the presence of a strident atheist intrinsically problematic. But godless capitalism was, potentially, even worse. While postwar conservatives promoted laissez-faire capitalism as superior to the liberal welfare state, they did not wish to glorify the pursuit of wealth, or fall into what Nock had termed "economism."[38] To *National Review* conservatives, Rand represented a dangerous departure from the libertarian tradition, which had simultaneously bemoaned the rise of government and the degradation of a society oriented solely to commercial concerns. By contrast, Rand argued that economic life was the highest good, that in the striving and struggling to forge a career and make a living mankind achieved his highest potential existence. She sought to free capitalism of the stigma it had acquired during the Depression and to protect it from the disdain of intellectuals and religious believers alike. Her capitalism was a market infused with spirit that came complete with its own laudable moral code, not a cold system of exploitation. While this idea might seem ridiculous to book reviewers, it would prove to be a compelling vision to millions of Americans.

As it turned out, this vision even had its attractions for Chambers. In 1959, two years after he had attacked Rand, Chambers had nearly crossed to her side of the fence. Starkly, he told Buckley: "I am not a conservative." In a series of remarkable letters to Buckley, Chambers attempted to clarify his position vis-à-vis *National Review* and its assorted agendas. He wrote: "I am a man of the Right. I am a man of the Right because I mean to uphold capitalism in its American version. But I claim that capitalism is not, and by its essential nature cannot conceivably be, conservative."[39] Although Chambers, a Quaker, retained a deep sense of personal religious belief, in the political realm he chose to endorse capitalism, giving in to his fundamentally historicist sense that in capitalism lay the future. If such was the case, it was futile to fight and impossible to maintain a position that was both procapitalist and truly conservative. For this reason, Chambers wished to separate himself from the program that Buckley was developing. In his review of Rand, Chambers's comments had focused mainly on the materialism of capitalism, and how that stood in opposition to religion. Now, he tried to explain to Buckley how capitalism's intrinsic dynamism posed a challenge to those who sought to preserve the past. And he evinced a Rand-like appreciation for the market's innate flux: "Conservatism is alien to the very nature of capitalism whose love of life and growth is perpetual change." Although he was fascinated with the transformative power of capitalism, Chambers's valuation of the market was tinged with ambiguity. In a passage replete with Spenglerian undertones, he told Buckley, "I am procapitalist; I would only retard for an instant, seek to break the fearful impacts of change, hold back lest the rush of development (in a multitude of frightful forms) carry us to catastrophe, as, in fact, seems almost inevitable."[40] Yet if capitalism might carry us to catastrophe, Chambers, an ex-Communist, was sure that the alternatives were worse. It was capitalism that must be defended, against its enemies both conservative and liberal. Only a few years earlier, these ideas and insights had lain dormant beneath his attack on Rand. Now fully manifest, later in 1959 they led him to resign from *National Review*, much to Buckley's dismay.[41]

Although Buckley viewed Chambers's review as the party line on Rand, it was far from the last word on the topic.[42] The attention-grabbing article set off reverberations across the right-wing community. Many libertarians, in particular, were incensed. Supporters of laissez-faire had fought for years to be on equal footing with the Catholics of *National Review*, and these debates were still contentious in 1957. John Chamberlain, who had reviewed *Atlas Shrugged* favorably in *Freeman*, was one high-profile defender.[43] But he and other libertarians were disappointed in Rand, too, for if the conservatives had needlessly attacked her, it was also true that she had failed to make any accommodations to them. In a letter to *National Review*, Chamberlain lamented, "if Miss Rand had chosen to admit just one vocal and practicing Christian in her Fellowship of the Competent . . . there would have been no outcry against *Atlas Shrugged*." He praised her "magnificent" exposition of freedom and averred that he would continue "the lugubrious task of persuading people to read it in spite of themselves."[44] Although a number of readers canceled their subscriptions in outrage, the controversial article was invigorating for *National Review*. Chambers's bold pronouncements helped the magazine stake its claim as the arbiter of the conservative mainstream. Buckley professed that conservatism was free of any formal litmus tests for membership, but the *Atlas Shrugged* review signaled that definitive boundaries would nonetheless be drawn.

Despite this attempt at excommunication, Rand retained a considerable following among the *National Review* audience. In 1960, Buckley accepted an article on Rand written by poet and anticollectivist polemicist E. Merrill Root, an English professor at Earlham College and the author of *Collectivism on Campus* (1956) and *Brainwashing in the High Schools* (1958). At *National Review*, Root was considered something of a second string writer. But Buckley needed to keep stalwart foot soldiers like Root happy and engaged, and letting him write on Rand was the perfect solution. In his article, "What About Ayn Rand?" Root openly challenged *National Review*'s policy on Rand and lauded her heroic vision of life and her celebration of man as creator. He was copious in his praise, calling her "a life-giving sun among her planets" and "our most original artist-philosopher."[45] He praised Rand for "her brilliant skinning alive of all the phonies of the earth," noting that she and the conservatives held many common enemies: "cheapjack existentialists," relativists, behaviorists, positivists. Root's article then descended into improbable assertions that Rand was an "unconscious" Christian and that her novels showed the deep imprint of theism. Like Chambers, Root was troubled by Rand's irreligion, but he chose to wish it away, rather than directly attack it. Unlike Chambers, he proved unable to conceptualize the contradictions that lay under the surface.

Root's article drew an almost immediate response from Garry Wills, who represented the more cosmopolitan and sophisticated new guard at *National Review*. The Jesuit-educated Wills missed entirely the populist appeal of Rand, and found Root's review "painful" to read, he wrote Buckley privately. He begged to be given space for a response. It seems that neither Buckley nor Wills had read either of Rand's novels, although they had looked at John Galt's famous 57-page speech in *Atlas Shrugged* as a précis of her thought (Rand herself identified this as the most important part of the book).[46] But even if they weren't familiar with her oeuvre, Wills and Buckley both knew enough to see that Rand needed to be restrained. Wills wrote to Buckley: "I read the speech you referred me to, hard as it is to wade through gibberish. This is something too serious, it seems to me, to take a soft stand on. I know you always have a lunatic fringe to placate; and on the economics level that is all right, [but] allowing any connection to be established, in any one's mind, between National Review and Ayn Rand is a betrayal of National Review's stance and past record."[47] Buckley replied, "I cannot agree with you more, that one cannot afford to confuse our two theses."[48] While Buckley was willing to give limited editorial space to defenders of Rand, it was clear where his sympathies lay.

Root and Wills's divergent opinions of Rand reflected continuing divides among conservatives. Partially, these differences were matters of culture and style. Root's tastes ran more to the proletarian than those of the Jesuit-educated Wills. Thus he admired Rand's literary expression whereas Wills thought her writing was simply "gibberish." Root spoke for *National Review* readers who approached conservatism from a less intellectual angle. Many of Rand's most ardent admirers were small businessmen from the Midwest, who were untroubled by Rand's atheism or her style and saw her as an inspiration.[49] But their different assessments were also tied to ideology, for Root was clearly more to the libertarian side of the conservative spectrum. He was a writer for *Freeman,* a publication of the Freedom for Economic Education which maintained a vigorous promarket stance. While *National Review* and *Freeman* shared a number of writers, on the issue of capitalism the differences between the two camps emerged starkly.

Responding to Root's article in February 1960, Wills demolished Root's facile argumentation, and then honed in on the more important issue at stake. "The simple equation of capitalism with conservatism is not only naive, it is fatal," Wills wrote. He argued "it is *treason,* betrayal from within, for conservatives to endorse any fanatic who agrees with certain methods which conservatives must use to implement their view of man."[50] Here was exactly what Rand would have disagreed with: the idea that "certain methods" (i.e., free markets or capitalism) must be used, whatever their underlying morality or implications if fully elaborated. Whereas Rand saw capitalism as the ultimate fulfillment of human nature, Wills had a much more limited appreciation of its function. According to Wills, "political and economic freedom" were the basic grounds on which man must come to know himself, but they were no route to "beatitude." Wills denied that capitalism was the true foundation of conservatism, promoting "history" instead as "the first principle of conservatism." But if the two were not identical, they were hardly incompatible. Capitalism was simply a handy tool that American conservatives would use to shape the world according to their view of man, which was deeply informed by Catholic conceptions of original sin.[51] Even so, it was an imperfect method that certainly did not deserve the turgid praise Rand bestowed upon it. According to Wills, the true conservative "knows a 'captain of industry' can be as ruthless as the leader of a commune." He finished with a call to duty. Root was wrong, Rand and her ilk must be resisted: "The narrow fixations of Miss Rand, the logorrhea of Mr. Root, should meet with more strenuous opposition from conservatives than from any other group of thinkers, especially when such chaos takes to itself the unearned title of conservatism. The conservative's job is to see complexity, to continue standards, to learn from history." While Rand was odious in Wills's sight, she had unknowingly provided a useful service to conservatism. Due to her presence, a consensus was gathering. Whatever conservatism's relationship to capitalism, it was not to be the answer Rand proposed. Yet neither was it to be the one that Chambers ultimately found, for Wills seemed confident that capitalism and conservatism could be complementary to one another. More so than the others, Wills spelled out the reasoning behind this conclusion. And if the exact relationship couldn't be pinpointed, Rand could always be kept at bay by sheer invective.

For her part, Rand was happy to return the insults. In December 1960, she gave a lecture at Princeton University entitled "Conservatism: An Obituary." She scorned the label conservative, preferring to be called a "radical for capitalism." Much of her criticism was sheer anger at compromisers. Rand insisted that the only effective defense of capitalism was a wholehearted one. Unlike Chambers, she found conservatives not unclear or confused about their ultimate stance toward capitalism, but rather full of cowardice: "The moral treason of the 'conservative' leaders lies in the fact that they . . . do not have the courage to admit that the *American* way of life was *capitalism*, that *that* was the politico-economic system born and established in the United States, the system which, in one brief century, achieved a level of freedom, of progress, of prosperity, of human happiness, unmatched in all the other systems and centuries combined."[52] Any compromising ceded both moral and rhetorical ground to liberals: "collectivism, the ancient, frozen, status society is offered to us in the name of *progress*—while capitalism, the only free, dynamic, creative, society ever devised, is defended in the name of *stagnation*."[53] Cowardice led conservatives to misrepresent the essence of capitalism, which impeded their ability to defend it. If capitalism were only celebrated for its true merits, as her fiction attempted to do, its defense would be simple. According to Rand, it was the very genius of capitalism that it stood opposed to all traditional morality. But conservatives "are paralyzed by the profound conflict between capitalism and the moral code which dominates our culture: the morality of altruism. . . . Capitalism and altruism are incompatible; they are philosophical opposites; they cannot co-exist in the same man or in the same society."[54] What Rand called "altruism" was essentially indistinguishable from Christian ethics. Hence, like Chambers, Rand understood that capitalism opposed conservatism on two main grounds. Conservatism supported established tradition while the market demanded change; and conservatism called for Christianity, whereas such ethics were fundamentally crippling to capitalism. Although they differed in their estimation of religion, Rand and Chambers concurred on these fundamental points.

As Rand's popularity surged in the 1960s, she became impossible to ignore. In the wake of *Atlas Shrugged*, she became a media sensation and a star of the college lecture circuit, appearing to capacity crowds and attendant campus controversy. Her original fan base had been business people, but as the decade wore on, Rand drew to her banner increasing numbers of libertarians, anarcho-capitalists, and so-called "hippies of the right." The dogmatism and moral certainty of her novels proved especially appealing to adolescents, many of whom were marked lifelong by this early encounter. Although conservatives repudiated her atheistic philosophy, in so doing they allowed Rand to carve out a vital niche as spokesperson for the secular right. Secular and Jewish right-wing youth who were put off by Christian inflected conservative rhetoric flocked to her lectures and the trademarked courses on "Objectivism" offered by the Nathaniel Branden Institute.[55] Rand labeled her philosophy Objectivism because she taught that values were absolute and could be rationally, objectively determined. Accordingly, Objectivism promoted capitalism as a system that grew naturally out of the self-interested ethics her novels depicted. Through her periodical *The Objectivist* (1962–1971), Rand kept readers appraised of her views on current events and literature, providing a forum for the real world application of her philosophical ideas.[56] On most issues, she took a fairly predictable right-wing line, although her justifications for such positions were often idiosyncratic and linked to her larger agenda of promoting rationality. Once again, Rand was headed in the same direction as the conservatives, but for very different reasons. She stood in solid opposition to what she called "today's intellectual trend," including relativism, behaviorism, civil rights, and the welfare state. Rand was also a vigorous opponent of campus political activism and lifestyle experimentation. The former she opposed for being a distraction to the intellectual mission of the university, the latter because drugs and sexual promiscuity encouraged irrational thought and impulsive behavior.[57] By contrast, Rand taught her students that reason was the only means to the good. She insisted that all her political stances flowed directly from the ideas she had expressed in her fiction, and that she had created a fully integrated philosophical system free of contradictions or error. If ideology was dead on the left, Rand had certainly resurrected it on the right.

National Review was not blind to these developments, and returned to Rand yet again in 1967, a year which marked the zenith of her national fame. This time, Buckley tapped M. Stanton Evans to write the review. Evans, a protégé of Buckley's who had graduated from Yale in 1955, was a respected young activist who had been instrumental in the founding of Young Americans for Freedom (YAF), an organization of young conservatives that was sponsored by Buckley but heavily influenced by Rand.[58] At the time of the review, he was an editor at the *Indianapolis News*. Buckley wrote to Evans that he wanted a "definitive" piece on Ayn Rand which would "demonstrate to people of commonsense that her ideological and philosophical presumptions make her an inadequate mentor."[59] The magazine's cover in October featured a portrait of Rand rendered as a stained glass window, surrounded with dollar signs, along with the headline "The Movement to Canonize Ayn Rand." (In point of fact, the dollar sign was Rand's personal totem, and she wore a gold dollar sign pin for many of her public appearances.)

This prominent *National Review* story covered many of the themes Wills had raised six years earlier, but it granted Rand a far greater measure of praise and authority. It also, paradoxically, revealed how many of Rand's beliefs had been absorbed by *National Review* conservatives even as she remained, officially, persona non grata. Evans clearly shared some of the instinctive like for Rand felt by young conservatives in the 1960s. He was untroubled by her defense of capitalism and her attack upon government regulation, accepting it as conventional wisdom. She had, Evans wrote, "an excellent grasp of the way capitalism is supposed to work, the efficiencies of free enterprise, the central role of private property and the profit motive, the social and political costs of welfare schemes which seek to compel a false benevolence."[60] He also admired her polemical fire and consistency, and defended her against Chambers's accusation she was an unconscious Nazi. Evans's review reflected the more relaxed attitude of *National Review* in its maturity. It also indicated how capitalism had become less of a charged topic for conservatives as the arguments surrounding fusionism faded into the background. Partially, this reflected the libertarian's success at redefining capitalism as a moral economic system, specifically when contrasted to communism or socialism. Rand herself had been harping on this theme for decades, and by the late 1960s, her arguments had been picked up by numerous politicians, businesspeople, students, and journalists.[61] This openness to capitalism also reflected the experience of a new generation who had grown up in the flush prosperity of the 1950s.

Evans went on to argue that despite these features, Rand remained a dangerous figure for conservatives because she mixed her good qualities up with the bad: namely, atheism. Rand's work raised several "central dilemmas of the era," such as "Can faith in God be reconciled with liberty for man? Is Christian belief compatible with libertarian attachment? Is Capitalism anti-Christian?" These questions were no longer deeply problematic, and failed to exercise Evans the way they had Chambers and Wills. Evans seemed confident that a general consensus on each had already been reached. The only hitch was that Rand answered all of these questions incorrectly. Evans urged that conservatives make judicious use of Rand, all the while being careful not to swallow her argument whole. Now that a strident defense of capitalism was considered fairly standard by conservatives, her atheism, which had been the original ground of Buckley's dislike for her, remained the fundamental problem. Chamberlain's lament about the missing Christian in *Atlas Shrugged* seemed ever more prescient. These developments aside, whatever critical issues Rand raised would soon be theoretical in nature, for her career went into rapid eclipse soon after. In 1968, the

Objectivist movement imploded in a series of personal schisms and Stalin-esque purges.[62] Rand fell into a deep depression and ceased most public activities and publishing. Yet if Rand was no longer an institutional pres-ence, she remained a powerful ideological influence, and in the 1970s echoes of her thought could be heard throughout the Nixon and Ford administrations.[63] But as far as *National Review* was concerned, Rand had come to the sorry end she deserved.

Almost fifty years after the Chambers review, Buckley still relished his self-declared victory over her. In 2003, he published a work of historical fiction, *Getting It Right*, which was significantly oriented to Rand and Objec-tivism. In this novel, set in the 1960s, Buckley's secular Jewish protagonist, Lenora Goldstein, is an ardent Objectivist. She is romantically involved with another misguided young conservative, Woodroe Raynor, who works for the John Birch Society. Over the course of the book, both Lenora and Wood-roe recant their ideological foolishness, deciding to forsake their extremist positions and work instead for mainstream, *National Review*-style conserva-tism. At the novel's conclusion the two are engaged and, to boot, Lenora is planning her conversion to Catholicism.[64] Buckley's novel intends to narrow the circle of acceptable conservatism, but at the same time under-scores its diverse and unwieldy origins. Although *National Review* is the clear winner in this battle, it is Objectivism and the John Birch Society that inspire the young recruits and bring them into the right-wing scene. Significantly, Buckley does not probe the ideological tensions that separate *National Review*, the John Birch Society, and the Objectivists. Rather, it is sexual deviance which alerts both youth to the error of their ways. Leonora leaves Objectivism when she learns of Rand's extramarital affair with Nathaniel Branden, and Woody's disillusionment begins with intimations of homosexuality that surround General Edwin A. Walker, a John Birch favorite. For Buckley, right-wing politics are still not enough: only the Cath-olic Church can keep youth from falling into profound error.

The novel covers much the same territory as Chambers's, Wills's, and Evans's discussions of Rand, but excises any mention of capitalism, the most contentious issue historically. At the dawn of the twenty-first century, capi-talism has almost faded from view, and is taken for granted not simply as a conservative ideal, but as a generalized desideratum of the postcommunist world.[65] As examination of conservative reaction to Rand demonstrates, however, it was not always so. Because Rand represents such a forthright procapitalist position, her career highlights the shifting fortunes of capi-talism on the right. In the 1940s, she was an inspiration to those who strug-gled against the New Deal and hoped to bring about a new, market friendly political order. As a second generation of conservatives built upon these sen-timents and attempted to tie them to a defense of Christian tradition, Rand's status began to erode. Because she clung so tenaciously to her atheism and her heroic vision of capitalism, she was soon a liability to conservatism as envisioned by the newly powerful *National Review.* In 1957, Chambers set the terms of the debate with his controversial review of *Atlas Shrugged.* The fulcrum then swung the other way with the populist effusions of Root's pro-Rand article, which drew Wills' wrath. Finally, conservative opinion settled into a kind of stasis with Evans's 1967 article and Rand's subsequent personal disintegration.

This resolution, however, did not come without cost. It is notable that tension over the issue of capitalism propelled two of conservatism's brightest intellectual stars, Garry Wills and Whittaker Chambers, right out of the movement. In the early 1970s, like Chambers had done earlier, Wills distanced himself from Buckley and *National Review,* partially because he believed its advocacy of capitalism to be incompatible with Catholic social ethics.[66] When confronted with Rand's work, both men understood immediately that while she might appear to be simply a lightweight popularizer, her work touched upon the deepest structures of conservative thought. Rand forced both writers to consider how a creed oriented to transcendence would respond to the mundane realities and potentially devastating outcomes of the marketplace. While they might mock her style, Chambers and Wills recognized that Rand gave powerful voice to ideas that threatened to overwhelm their own allegiances. Eventually, the two major architects of conservative policy on Rand became disenchanted with their own formulations. If conservatism in the 1950s had not tied itself firmly enough to capitalism for Chambers's taste, by the 1970s its identification with the market was deep enough to repel Wills. Although they differed in their reasons for leaving the conservative fold, Wills's and Chambers's encounter with Rand was part of a larger process whereby both men concluded it was untenable to rest on an intellectual program so rife with contradictions.

In *Getting It Right,* the eventual drawing of Leonora into the fold symbolizes conservative success at neutralizing Rand, while relying on the ardor she inspired. Her fictional conversion points to a real world similarity between the dogmatism of Objectivist and Catholic ethics, which both lay claim to absolute truth.[67] This progression also mimics the broader success conservatives had in integrating capitalism into their larger agenda of revitalizing Christian values and tradition. At first, such a combination seemed impossibly jarring, but repetition would help the problem fade. And as a newly modified, state regulated capitalism showered the country with riches and a grateful religious revival swept the land, the two seemed more compatible than theoreticians might argue. Moreover, conservative success at managing Rand and denying her full membership benefits of the coalition helped pave the way for later celebrations of the market. If capitalism could be modulated, or its ultimate logic inhibited by the strictures of Christianity, then it could fit right in with motherhood, apple pie, and other emblems of the American way.

Notes

Introduction: Social Theory and Capitalist Reality in the American Century

1. Daniel Bell, *The End of Ideology: On the Exhaustion of Political Ideas in the Fifties* (Cambridge, Mass.: Harvard University Press, 1960), 404.

2. Francis Fukuyama, "The End of History," *National Interest* (Spring 1989): 14–15. Fukuyama's essay and his subsequent books have already generated a considerable historiography. See, for example, Philip Abbott, "'Big' Theories and Policy Counsel: James Burnham, Francis Fukuyama, and the Cold War," *Journal of Policy History* 14 (Fall 2002): 417–30. And in this vein see also Michael Mandelbaum, *The Ideas That Conquered the World: Peace, Democracy, and Free Markets in the Twenty-First Century* (New York: Public Affairs, 2002), 277–93.

3. Michael Lewis, "Why You?" *New York Times Magazine*, September 23, 2001, 70–71.

4. Michael Cox, "American Power Before and After 11 September: Dizzy with Success?" *International Affairs* 78, 2 (2002): 289–91.

5. Godfrey Hodgson, *The World Turned Right Side Up: A History of the Conservative Ascendancy in America* (Boston: Houghton Mifflin, 1996), 186–215; Robert Kuttner, *Everything for Sale: The Virtues and Limits of Markets* (New York: Knopf, 1997), 68–109; Thomas Edsall and Mary Edsall, *Chain Reaction: the Impact of Race, Rights, and Taxes on American Politics* (New York: W.W. Norton, 1991), 154–97.

6. David Pilling, "Japanese Companies: How Could a Corporate Sector That Dominated the World a Decade Ago Have Become So Unproductive?" *Financial Times*, April 21, 2003, 9; Paul Krugman, *The Return of Depression Economics* (New York: W.W. Norton, 1999) The once-vaunted "four tigers"—South Korea, Hong Kong, Taiwan, and Singapore—also had their troubles, but south China, whose labor relations and regulatory regime resembles that of nineteenth-century Pittsburgh, has roared ahead. It is fast becoming the workshop of the world.

7. Paul O'Neill quoted in Geoffrey Nunberg, *Going Nucular: Language, Politics, and Culture in Confrontational Times* (New York: Public Affairs, 2004), 202.

8. Howard Brick makes this point in Chapter 2 of *Beyond the Bourgeoisie: The Postcapitalist Vision and American Social Liberalism in the Twentieth Century* (Ithaca, N.Y.: Cornell University Press, 2006). For a quite different but provocative reading of the way European intellectuals thought about the market, see Jerry Z. Muller, *The Mind and the Market: Capitalism in Modern European Thought* (New York: Knopf, 2002), esp. 229–57, 288–316.

9. John L. Thomas, *Alternative America: Henry George, Edward Bellamy, Henry Demarest Lloyd, and the Adversary Tradition* (Cambridge, Mass.: Harvard University Press, 1983),

354–66; Jeffrey Sklansky, *The Soul's Economy: Market Society and Selfhood in American Thought, 1820–1920* (Chapel Hill: University of North Carolina Press, 2002), 225–32.

10. Daniel T. Rodgers, *Atlantic Crossings: Social Politics in a Progressive Age* (Cambridge, Mass.: Harvard University Press, 1998), 52–75; Alan Dawley, *Changing the World: American Progressives in War and Revolution* (Princeton, N.J.: Princeton University Press, 2003), 41–72; Robert Johnson, *The Radical Middle Class: Populist Democracy and the Question of Capitalism in Progressive Era Portland, Oregon* (Princeton, N.J.: Princeton University Press, 2003).

11. Rodgers, *Atlantic Crossings*, 276.

12. JFK quoted in Allen J. Matusow, *The Unraveling of America: A History of Liberalism in the 1960s* (New York: Harper and Row, 1984), 50–51.

13. Andrew Ross, *No Respect: Intellectuals and Popular Culture* (New York: Routledge, 1989); Daniel Horowitz, *The Anxieties of Affluence: Critiques of American Consumer Culture, 1939–1979* (Amherst: University of Massachusetts Press, 2004).

14. Walter A. Jackson, *Gunnar Myrdal and America's Conscience: Social Engineering and Racial Liberalism, 1938–1987* (Chapel Hill: University of North Carolina Press, 1990); Daniel Horowitz, *Betty Friedan and the Feminine Mystique: The American Left, the Cold War, and Modern Feminism* (Amherst: University of Massachusetts Press, 1998).

15. Eric Hobsbawm, *The Age of Extremes: A History of the World, 1914–1991* (New York: Pantheon, 1994), 257–63.

16. John T. Dunlop, Frederick H. Harbison, Clark Kerr, and Charles A. Myers, *Industrialism and Industrial Man: The Problems of Labor and Management in Economic Growth* (Cambridge, Mass: Harvard University Press, 1960), 10, 293. One can gain an even more expansive sense of Clark Kerr's worldview from his collection of 1950s essays, *Labor and Management in Industrial Society* (Garden City, N.Y.: Doubleday, 1964).

17. Public Broadcasting Service interview with Arnold Harberger, October 3, 2000, *Commanding Heights* interview show, transcript at *www.PBS.org/wgbh/commandingheights*.

18. Harold Meyerson, "Worker Friendly Politicians, Unite," *American Prospect Online Edition*, February 2, 2005; Thomas Frank, "What's the Matter with Liberals?" *New York Review of Books*, May 12, 2005.

Chapter 1. The Postcapitalist Vision in Twentieth-Century American Social Thought

1. On the post-Cold War "triumph" of capitalism, see Robert Heilbroner, "The Triumph of Capitalism," *New Yorker*, January 23, 1989, 98; Radek Sikorski, "The Coming Crack-Up of Communism: Decline or Fall?" *National Review* 41 (January 27, 1989), 28–30; Jerry Z. Muller, *Commentary*, December 1997, quoted in Alexander Cockburn, "Who's Burying Whom?" *Nation*, February 20, 1989, 222. On the heritage of the term capitalism, see Fernand Braudel, *Civilization and Capitalism, 15th–18th Century*, vol. 2, *The Wheels of Commerce*, trans. Siân Reynolds (New York: Harper and Row, 1982), 232–38, 388, 624n48; the French original, *Civilisation matérielle, économie et capitalisme: XVe–XVIIIe siècle*, vol. 2, *Les jeux de l'échange*, appeared in 1979. For typical nineteenth-century dismissals of the term, see William Graham Sumner, *What Social Classes Owe to Each Other* (1883; Caldwell, Ida.: Caxton, 1952), 56, and "Capital," *Encyclopedia Britannica*, 11th ed., new form, vols. 5 and 6, 278.

2. The key texts, of course, were Sombart's *Der moderne Kapitalismus* (1902) and Weber's "Die protestantische Ethik und der Geist des Kapitalismus," in the *Archiv für Sozialwissenschaft und Sozialpolitik* (1904–5). On Sombart's somewhat scandalous break from the conservative reformers of German historical economics to take seriously Marx's work and the impact of the Socialist (Second) International, see

Arthur Mitzman, *Sociology and Estrangement: Three Sociologists of Imperial Germany* (New York: Knopf, 1973), 151, 192n, 217. For other landmarks in the increasingly academic uses of "capitalism," see Henri Pirenne, "Les périodes de l'histoire sociale du capitalisme," *Bulletin de l'Académie Royale de Belgique, Classe des Lettres* (Bruxelles: Académie Royale, 1914); trans. in *American Historical Review* 19 (1914): 494–515, and *Les périodes de l'histoire sociale du capitalisme* (Brussels: Librairie du Peuple, 1922); John A. Hobson, *The Evolution of Modern Capitalism: A Study of Machine Production*, rev. ed. (New York: Scribner's, 1910); Henri Sée, *Modern Capitalism: Its Origin and Evolution*, trans. Homer B. Vanderblue and Georges F. Doriot (New York: Adelphi, 1928); R. H. Tawney, *Religion and the Rise of Capitalism: A Historical Study* (New York: Harcourt Brace Jovanovich, 1926).

3. James Warren Prothro, *The Dollar Decade: Business Ideas in the 1920s* (Baton Rouge: Louisiana State University Press, 1954), 219, 225–25, 232.

4. Prothro, *The Dollar Decade*, xiv–xv, 216; Francis X. Sutton et al., *The American Business Creed* (Cambridge, Mass.: Harvard University Press, 1956), 28, 32, 46. For the continuation of references to "capitalism" on the hard right of the Republican Party, see Lisa McGirr, *Suburban Warriors: The Origins of the New American Right* (Princeton, N.J.: Princeton University Press, 2001), 99, 224.

5. The slogan "Forbes: capitalist tool" appeared in occasional double-page ads in the magazine starting January 1967, aimed at boosting advertising revenue by comparing the education, income, high-status purchases, managerial positions, and stock ownership of its readers to that of other business magazine readers. The slogan assumed new prominence in the mid to late 1970s. Starting November 1, 1976, "Forbes: capitalist tool" appeared in almost every issue of the magazine, marking the monthly classified page and printed on novelty items advertised in the magazine, such as the $20 "Capitalist Tool umbrella" and $10 "Capitalist Tool neckties." The slogan began appearing regularly as a self-advertisement to subscribers ("Do you know anybody who is somebody in business who does not read *Forbes* Magazine?"), on the magazine's index page, March 5, 1979, and by February 1980 appeared as a registered trademark.

6. Anthony Crosland, *The Future of Socialism* (London: J. Cape, 1956); Ralf Dahrendorf, *Class and Class Conflict in Industrial Society* (Stanford, Calif.: Stanford University Press, 1959); Talcott Parsons, *The System of Modern Societies* (Englewood Cliffs, N.J.: Prentice-Hall, 1971); Howard Brick, "Optimism of the Mind: Imagining Postindustrial Society in the 1960s and 1970s," *American Quarterly* 44 (September 1992): 345–80.

7. Donald Sassoon, *One Hundred Years of Socialism: The West European Left in the Twentieth Century* (New York: New Press, 1996), 244–45; Geoffrey Foote, *The Labour Party's Political Thought: A History* (New York: St. Martin's Press, 1997), 201–28; G. L. Arnold, "Britain: The New Reasoners," in *Revisionism: Essays on the History of Marxist Ideas*, ed. Leopold Labedz (New York: Praeger, 1962), 300.

8. Anthony Crosland, "The Transition from Capitalism," in *New Fabian Essays*, ed. R. H. Crossman (London: Turnstile Press, 1951), 42; see also Crosland, *The Future of Socialism.*

9. See, for example, Stephen Marglin and Juliet Schor, eds., *The Golden Age of Capitalism: Reinterpreting the Postwar Experience* (New York: Oxford University Press, 1990); Elizabeth Fones-Wolf, *Selling Free Enterprise: The Business Assault on Labor and Liberalism, 1945–60* (Urbana: University of Illinois Press, 1994).

10. Thomas Mann, "The Making of *The Magic Mountain*," *Atlantic Monthly*, January 1953, reprinted in Mann, *The Magic Mountain*, trans. H. T. Lowe-Porter (New York: Vintage, 1969), 719.

11. Talcott Parsons, "'Capitalism' in Recent German Literature: Sombart and

Weber," *Journal of Political Economy* 36 (1928): 641–44, and "'Capitalism' in Recent German Literature: Sombart and Weber—Concluded," *Journal of Political Economy* 37 (1929): 31–51.

12. See Talcott Parsons, "On Building Social System Theory: A Personal History," *Daedalus* 99 (Fall 1970): 838, 852, 858.

13. For a focus on "economic individualism," see Tawney, *Religion and the Rise of Capitalism.* On the centrality of market expansion, Henri Pirenne, in his *Medieval Cities: The Origins and the Revival of Trade* (Princeton, N.J.: Princeton University Press, 1925) set the standard. See the critique of Pirenne's "commercialization model" by Ellen Meiksins Wood, *The Origin of Capitalism* (New York: Monthly Review Press, 1999), 11–25. Karl Polanyi's *The Great Transformation* (1944; Boston: Beacon Press, 1957) tends to identify capitalism with the policy push toward unregulated markets, while the more recent work of Fernand Braudel strictly identifies "capitalism" with the upper layer of trade, dominated by an elite of "big merchants," financiers, or the "moneyed bourgeoisie," whose keynote is flexibility and adaptation in moving financial resources freely between different branches of commerce or production. While this represents "the commanding heights of society," Braudel refused to identify capitalism with market economy in general or with society as a whole, insisting on "the essential pluralism" of societies: it was just as mistaken to define modern society as "capitalist" as it was to identify medieval society with "feudalism," which properly applied "only to the fief and things pertaining to it, and to nothing else." Nonetheless, he judged "the word *capitalism*" to be "an *essential* model, applicable to several centuries" in understanding the development of early-modern and modern economy and society (Braudel, *Civilization and Capitalism*, vol. 2, *Wheels of Commerce*, 228–29, 374–76, 433, 464, 466, 504, 619; see also vol. 1, *The Structures of Everyday Life*, 23–29, 415, 477, 514, 561). Braudel's concept of capitalism is neatly summarized by Giovanni Arrighi in *The Long Twentieth Century: Money, Power, and the Origins of Our Times* (London: Verso, 1994), 8. Marx's model is the one that isolated the peculiar mechanism of accumulation (perpetual reinvestment of profits for the sake of self-expanding private wealth) associated with *capital* as such and most fully realized first in modern industrial production, based on the generalization of wage labor, beginning in Britain. On the *geistige* construction of capitalism, of course, see Weber, "Die protestantische Ethik und der Geist des Kapitalismus," and Sombart, *Der moderne Kapitalismus.*

14. Note, for instance, the passing remark by Columbia University sociologist William J. Goode on "the capitalist use (for the modern scene, read 'industrial use') of machinery"—as if the limited case of capitalism no longer sufficed as a target of social criticism. William J. Goode, *World Revolution and Family Patterns* (Glencoe, Ill.: Free Press, 1963), 16.

15. See Marquis Childs, *Sweden: The Middle Way* (New Haven, Conn.: Yale University Press, 1936); E. F. M. Durbin, *The Politics of Democratic Socialism* (London: Labour Book Service, 1940); and Lewis Corey, *The Unfinished Task: Economic Reconstruction for Democracy* (New York: Viking, 1942) on the notion of a "socialist mixed economy."

16. Raymond Aron, *The Century of Total War* (London: Verschoyle, 1954), 355, quoted in Crosland, *The Future of Socialism*, 63.

17. Kenneth Young, "Asia's Disequilibrium and American Strategies," in *The United States and Communist China*, ed. W. W. Lockwood (Princeton, N.J.: Haskins Press, 1965), 51–52. See also David Engerman, "To Moscow and Back: American Social Sciences and the Concept of Convergence," in this volume.

18. George Lichtheim, *The New Europe: Today—and Tomorrow* (New York: Praeger, 1963), 193–94.

19. Sociologist Judith Stacey has remarked on a degree of "uncertainty, an insecurity,

a doubt" that lay at the heart of the "postmodern" sensibility in assessing social structure and change, but the same may be said of any formulation in social diagnosis that begins with the open-ended prefix, "post-." Even the boldest advocate of an explicit "postcapitalist" interpretation, Anthony Crosland, seemed on occasion to undercut his own claims: as the British Laborite reviewed the tasks of socialist politics in the 1950s, he noted that "since [the 1930s], alas, the mischievous enemy [capitalism] has retreated, and gone into disguise as well." Was it part of "postcapitalist" theory to assert that capitalism had both surrendered to a successor regime—some kind of state-directed or social economy—*and* still held the stage in a "disguised" form? It was as if contemporary social structure, for the postcapitalist theorist, was a kind of shape-shifter, appearing at one moment as an updated form of modern capitalism and at another as a newfangled order where private property, markets, business cycles, bourgeois prestige, class inequality, and the like had lost their determinant force in social relations. See Judith Stacey, *Brave New Families: Stories of Domestic Upheaval in Late Twentieth Century America* (New York: Basic Books, 1990), 17; Crosland, *The Future of Socialism*, 5.

20. Eduard Bernstein, *Evolutionary Socialism: A Criticism and Affirmation*, trans. Edith C. Harvey (New York: Schocken, 1961); Peter Gay, *The Dilemma of Democratic Socialism: Eduard Bernstein's Challenge to Marx* (New York: Columbia University Press, 1952), 145–47.

21. Jean Jaurès, quoted in Daniel T. Rodgers, *Atlantic Crossings: Social Politics in a Progressive Age* (Cambridge, Mass.: Harvard University Press, 1998), 18.

22. Herbert Marcuse's notion of "one-dimensional society" carried forth Horkheimer and Adorno's pessimistic view into the radical 1960s, though Marcuse remained Marxist in the sense of regarding one-dimensional society as only apparently devoid of conflict, particularly due to a depoliticized public life, while he continued to recognize its essential character as a *capitalist* regime. Nonetheless, and as a telling indicator of his times, Marcuse very largely avoided citing the category of "capitalism" throughout the text of *One-Dimensional Man*. A franker Marxism gained more exposure in his 1970 *Essay on Liberation*.

23. Personal correspondence, Daniel Bell to Howard Brick, June 11, 2001.

24. Kevin Mattson, *Intellectuals in Action: The Origins of the New Left and Radical Liberalism, 1945–1970* (University Park: Pennsylvania State University Press, 2002), 73.

25. C. Wright Mills, quoted in Mattson, *Intellectuals in Action*, 91, 80. See also Daniel Geary, "C. Wright Mills and American Social Science in the 1940s," in this volume.

26. Paul Potter, quoted in Jim Miller, *"Democracy Is in the Streets": From Port Huron to the Siege of Chicago* (New York: Simon and Schuster, 1987), 232.

27. Paul Potter, quoted in Kirkpatrick Sale, *SDS* (New York: Random House, 1973), 187–88.

28. C. L. R. James, *State Capitalism and World Revolution* (Detroit: Facing Reality, 1969).

29. Parsons's 1940s thesis on the obsolescence of "the capitalism/socialism dichotomy," for instance, continued to guide him in his analysis of contemporary society in the 1960s. In what he then called "the system of modern society," the key trends of social development toward freedom, egalitarianism, belonging in a broad national community, and social rights to welfare cut across "the ideological dilemma of capitalism versus socialism," he wrote. See Parsons, *The System of Modern Societies* (Englewood Cliffs, N.J.: Prentice-Hall, 1971), 96–98. The proximity of this kind of social thought, and the consciousness of reformers in the 1960s, is indicated by Martin Luther King, Jr.'s remarks on his goals in 1967: "The good and just society is neither the thesis of capitalism nor the antithesis of communism, but a socially conscious democracy which reconciles the truth of individualism and collectivism." Martin

Luther King, Jr., *A Testament of Hope*, ed. James Melvin Washington (San Francisco: HarperSanFrancisco, 1991), 630.

30. Andrew Jamison and Ron Eyerman, *Seeds of the Sixties* (Berkeley: University of California Press, 1994), for instance, holds to this dominant perspective even while striving to uncover the exceptional few who dissented from the postwar conservative mold and thus prefigured characteristic dispositions of the New Left.

31. Mike Davis, *City of Quartz: Excavating the Future in Los Angeles* (New York: Vintage, 1992), 302.

32. Ideas of a "new order" or "new era" were initially closely linked to left-liberal visions of reform, before they were attached to a conservative vision of "new era" capitalism under Herbert Hoover. At *The Dial* in 1918, Thorstein Veblen, John Dewey, and editor Helen Marot collaborated on offering a "Reconstruction Programme," to be elucidated on a regular editorial page entitled (at Veblen's urging) "The Old Order and the New." Soon Veblen began his own series of articles entitled "The Modern Point of View and the New Order." The British radical J. A. Hobson began his book, *Incentives in the New Industrial Order* (London: Leonard Parsons, 1922), published in what his publisher called "The New Era Series," with the declaration that "a New Industrial Order is struggling into life, displacing piece by piece the old system of private capitalism." In 1928, the young Talcott Parsons persisted in using this rhetoric as he discussed reforms "more nearly approaching an ideal society": "In the transition from capitalism to a different social system surely many elements of the present would be built into the new order." Parsons, "'Capitalism' in Recent German Literature: Sombart and Weber," *Journal of Political Economy* 36 (December 1928): 652–53, 658–59.

33. Marx, *Capital* 3, chaps. 23 and 27, quoted in T. B. Bottomore, *Theories of Modern Capitalism* (London: Allen and Unwin, 1985), 17–18; *Grundrisse*, Martin Nicolaus translation (New York: Vintage, 1973), 705.

34. Friedrich Engels formulated the key contradiction of capitalist development as that between increasingly socialized production and private accumulation, in his pamphlet, *Socialism: Utopian and Scientific* (1880), in *The Marx-Engels Reader*, ed. Robert C. Tucker, 2nd ed. (New York: W.W. Norton, 1978), 716.

35. Rudolf Hilferding, *Finance Capital: A Study in the Latest Phase of Capitalist Development*, trans. Morris Watnick and Sam Gordon, ed. Tom Bottomore (London: Routledge and Kegan Paul, 1981); on Hilferding's notion of "organized capitalism," see William Smaldone, *Rudolf Hilferding: The Tragedy of a German Social Democrat* (DeKalb: Northern Illinois University Press, 1998), 69–72, 96, 101, 104–6, 117, and Tom Bottomore and Patrick Goode, eds., *Austro-Marxism* (Oxford: Oxford University Press, 1978).

36. See chap. 18, "Origin, Rise and Withering Away of Political Economy," in Ernest Mandel, *Marxist Economic Theory*, vol. 2, trans. Brian Pearce (New York: Monthly Review Press, 1968), 690–733; Martin J. Sklar, "On the Proletarian Revolution and the End of Political-Economic Society," *Radical America* 3 (May-June 1969): 1–41.

37. John Dewey, quoted in Robert B. Westbrook, *John Dewey and American Democracy* (Ithaca, N.Y.: Cornell University Press, 1991), 227.

38. Dorothy Ross, *The Origins of American Social Science* (New York: Cambridge University Press, 1991), 303–6, 319–20.

39. Reinhold Niebuhr, "The Church and the Industrial Crisis," *Biblical World*, November 1920, 590.

40. Arthur R. Burns, *American Diary* (Arthur R. Burns papers, Rare Books and Manuscripts, Columbia University Archives), July 25, August 4, 1928.

41. Walter Lippmann, *Drift and Mastery: An Attempt to Diagnose the Current Unrest* (New York: Mitchell Kennerley, 1914), 36, 51, 57–58.

42. Lippmann, 292–93.

43. Rexford Guy Tugwell, ed., *The Trend of Economics* (New York: Knopf, 1924), 18–19, 26, 21, 148, 150, 464.

44. Tugwell, review of *Communism*, by Harold Laski, *New Republic*, February 22, 1928.

45. Adolf A. Berle and Gardiner C. Means, *The Modern Corporation and Private Property*, rev. ed. (New York: Harcourt Brace and World, 1968), 305, 116, 306, 46. Interestingly, the same phrase was used right after World War I by the famed German business reformer Walter Rathenau, who noted that "large enterprises [had] developed into 'social institutions' [*Anstalten*]," which spelled "the 'disappearance of the private' in the sphere of social labor." See Jürgen Habermas, *The Structural Transformation of the Public Sphere: An Inquiry into a Category of Bourgeois Society* (Cambridge, Mass.: MIT Press, 1989), 153.

46. Berle and Means, *Modern Corporation*, 297, 116, 309, 312.

47. Berle and Means, *Modern Corporation*, quoted in James Burnham, "Comment," *The Symposium* 4 (1933): 273.

48. Berle and Means, quoted in Burnham, 271–72.

49. Tugwell, ed., *The Trend of Economics*, 360, 367 (emphasis added).

50. Bronislaw Malinowski, *Argonauts of the Western Pacific: An Account of Native Enterprise and Adventure in the Archipelagoes of Melanesian New Guinea* (New York: E.P. Dutton, 1961).

51. Marcel Mauss, *The Gift: The Form and Reason for Exchange in Archaic Societies*, trans. W. D. Halls, foreword by Mary Douglas (New York: W.W. Norton, 1990).

52. Raymond Williams, *Culture and Society, 1780–1950* (1958; New York: Columbia University Press, 1983).

53. See letters, Margaret Mead to John Dollard, February 15, 1934, February 25, 1935; John Dollard to Margaret Mead, February 20, 1935, May 2, 1935, box C2, Margaret Mead papers, Library of Congress, Washington, D.C.

54. Karen Horney, *The Neurotic Personality of Our Time* (New York: W.W. Norton, 1937), 188, 192, 278–79, 284–85; John Dollard, *Caste and Class in a Southern Town*, 3rd ed. (1937; New York: Doubleday, 1949, 1957), 58, 72–79, 438, 440–43; Erich Fromm, *Escape from Freedom* (New York: Holt, Rinehart and Winston, 1941). On Fromm's early Freudian-Marxist development, see Martin Jay, *The Dialectical Imagination: A History of the Frankfurt School and the Institute of Social Research, 1923–1950* (Boston: Little, Brown, 1973).

55. Ralph Linton, *The Study of Man: An Introduction* (New York: Appleton-Century, 1936). Fred Matthews, *Quest for an American Sociology: Robert E. Park and the Chicago School* (Montreal: McGill-Queen's University Press, 1977), 131, referred to *The Study of Man* as "one of those synoptic volumes which mark a plateau, a staging-area, in the movement of thought within a discipline," one that "would set new limits of knowledge for many in the generation of the 1940s and 1950s." On the rise of anthropological functionalism, see George Stocking, "Ideas and Institutions in American Anthropology: Thoughts Toward a History of the Interwar Years," in *Selected Papers from the American Anthropologist, 1921–1945*, ed. George W. Stocking, Jr. (Washington, D.C.: American Anthropological Association, 1976), 1–53. On Linton, see Clyde Kluckhohn, "Ralph Linton," *Biographical Memoirs* (New York: National Academy of Sciences, Columbia University Press, 1958); Adelin Linton and Charles Wagley, *Ralph Linton* (New York: Columbia University Press, 1971), 1–78.

56. Isaac Kramnick and Barry Sheerman, *Harold Laski: A Life on the Left* (New York: Penguin, 1993), pp. 88–150.

57. In the opening pages of *The Structure of Social Action*, Parsons declared, "Spencer is dead," and added, "Is it not possible that the future holds in store something

other than 'bigger and better' industrialism . . . that instead of this, contemporary society is at or near a turning point . . . [?]" Talcott Parsons, *The Structure of Social Action* (1937; New York: Free Press, 1968), 3–4. See also Howard Brick, "The Reformist Dimension of Talcott Parsons's Early Social Theory," in *The Culture of the Market: Historical Essays*, ed. Thomas L. Haskell and Richard F. Teichgraeber III (Cambridge: Cambridge University Press, 1993).

58. See Howard Brick, "Talcott Parsons's 'Shift Away from Economics,' 1937–1946," *Journal of American History* 87 (September 2000): 490–514.

59. The teaching of social science in the core program of the University of Chicago assumed this form. See David E. Orlinsky, "Chicago General Education in Social Sciences, 1931–92: The Case of Soc 2," in *General Education in the Social Sciences: Centennial Reflections on the College of the University of Chicago*, ed. John J. MacAloon (Chicago: University of Chicago Press, 1992), 120. One of several sequences of courses first taught in the 1930s, Social Science 2, or Soc 2, moved through several permutations, and was reconstituted in 1947 as Personality and Culture, then Character and Society in 1966 and Self, Culture, and Society in 1968. In a 1966 memo, Richard Flacks defined the fields covered in the course as "sociology, psychology, anthropology, and social psychology." Quoted in Michael Schudson, "A Ruminating Retrospect on the Liberal Arts, the Social Sciences, and Soc 2," in MacAloon, 137. Note also David Riesman's comment that in 1947, when the course was called Personality and Culture, "happily, the line especially at Chicago between sociology and anthropology was not sharply drawn" (in MacAloon, 190). As another example of this paradigm, Howard Becker at the University of Wisconsin later wrote an introductory textbook along similar lines, *Man in Reciprocity: Introductory Lectures on Culture, Society and Personality* (New York: Praeger, 1956).

60. Cf. Robert Berkhofer, *A Behavioral Approach to Historical Analysis* (New York: Free Press, 1969); also see William Buxton, *Talcott Parsons and the Capitalist Nation-State: Political Sociology as a Strategic Vocation* (Toronto: University of Toronto Press, 1985), 144, 167–81. This sense of a "behavioral" turn is not to be confused with the behavior*ism* of John B. Watson and B. F. Skinner, against which Parsons had always polemicized.

61. For a brief discussion of this point, see Perry Anderson, *Considerations on Western Marxism* (London: NLB, 1979), 75, 79–80, 92–93.

62. This phrase was suggested to me by Jeffrey C. Alexander.

63. Talcott Parsons and Neil Smelser, *Economy and Society: A Study in the Integration of Economic and Social Theory* (New York: Free Press, 1956), 22–24, 29, 57, 75, 92–93, 139, 143, 281–85.

64. Karl Polányi, *The Great Transformation* (1944; Boston: Beacon, 1957), 252–54; quoted in István Mészáros, *Beyond Capital: Toward a Theory of Transition* (London: Merlin, 1995), 777.

65. Arthur M. Schlesinger, Jr., , quoted in Nelson Lichtenstein, *State of the Union: A Century of American Labor* (Princeton, N.J.: Princeton University Press, 2002), 151–52.

66. G. Bromley Oxnam, *The Church and Contemporary Change*, part 1, quoted in Robert Wuthnow, *The Restructuring of American Religion* (Princeton, N.J.: Princeton University Press, 1988), 38.

67. Daniel Bell echoed Lippmann as well as Berle and Means as he wrote that "private productive property, especially in the United States, is largely a fiction," and that "two 'silent' revolutions . . . seem to be in process" accompanying the rise of managerial authority: "One is a change in the *mode of access* to power insofar as inheritance alone is no longer all-determining; the other is a change in the *nature of power-holding itself* insofar as technical skill rather than property, and political

position rather than wealth, have become the basis on which power is wielded." *The End of Ideology: On the Exhaustion of Political Ideas in the Fifties*, rev. ed. (New York: Free Press, 1960), 44–45.

68. Andrew Shonfield, quoted in William Leuchtenberg, *The FDR Years: On Roosevelt and His Legacy* (New York: Columbia University Press, 1995), 305.

69. David Riesman, "A Personal Memoir: My Political Journey," in *Conflict and Consensus: A Festschrift in Honor of Lewis A. Coser*, ed. Walter W. Powell and Richard Robbins (New York: Free Press, 1984), 327–64; David Riesman, "My Education in Soc 2 and My Efforts to Adapt It in the Harvard Setting," in MacAloon, *General Education in the Social Sciences*, 178–216; Riesman to Mead, July 12, 1948, Mead Papers, box C19, Correspondence 1948 R.

70. David Riesman with Nathan Glazer, *Faces in the Crowd: Individual Studies in Character and Politics* (New Haven, Conn.: Yale University Press, 1952), 37–38.

71. See Eugene Lunn, "Beyond 'Mass Culture': *The Lonely Crowd*, the Uses of Literacy, and the Postwar Era," *Theory and Society* 19 (1990): 63–86.

72. For a reading of Riesman as exponent of an individualist revival, aimed against an overorganized society, see Wilfred McClay; *The Masterless: Self and Society in Modern America* (Chapel Hill: University of North Carolina Press, 1994), 226–57.

73. Robert A. Dahl, "Socialist Programs and Democratic Politics: An Analysis" (Ph.D. dissertation, Yale University, 1940).

74. Robert A. Dahl and Charles E. Lindblom, *Politics, Economics, and Welfare: Planning and Politico-Economic Systems Resolved into Basic Social Processes* (New York: Harper, 1953), 4–5, 7, 16, 46.

75. Howard Brick, "Optimism of the Mind: Imagining Postindustrial Society in the 1960s and 1970s," *American Quarterly* 44 (September 1992): 348–80.

76. Daniel Bell, "The Post-Industrial Society," in *Technology and Social Change*, ed. Eli Ginzberg (New York: Columbia University Press, 1964), 44–59.

77. Berle, "Property, Production, and Revolution, a Preface to the Revised Edition," in Berle and Means, *Modern Corporation*, xxvi (emphasis added). Tellingly, Berle relied on the old socialist slogan (in italics) to define the direction of contemporary social change.

78. Amitai Etzioni, *The Active Society: A Theory of Societal and Political Processes* (New York: Free Press, 1968), 198, 211, 516, 528. Although his reformist confidence waned in the following decades, Etzioni continue to argue that economic reasoning ought to be subsumed by moral values, expressed in policies enacted by a state that represented the common interests of civil society. Whereas Etzioni's vision of the active society stemmed from a revitalization of social norms spurred by mass movements such as civil rights, his later communitarianism—in some sense, a latter-day reduction of the postcapitalist vision—rested on the state's presumptive role as agent of moral first principles. See Etzioni, *The Moral Dimension: Toward a New Economics* (New York: Free Press, 1988), and Etzioni, ed., *The Essential Communitarian Reader* (Lanham, Md.: Rowman and Littlefield, 1998. See also the critique of Etzioni's communitarianism in Samuel Farber, *Social Decay and Transformation: A View from the Left* (Lanham, Md.: Lexington Books, 2000), esp. 11–14.

79. Richard Lannoy, *The Speaking Tree: A Study of Indian Culture and Society* (London: Oxford University Press, 1971), 426–27.

80. Howard Brick, *Daniel Bell and the Decline of Intellectual Radicalism: Social Theory and Political Reconciliation in the 1940s* (Madison: University of Wisconsin Press, 1986), 199–210.

81. Such trouble was evident already when Bell drafted his books in 1969, amidst political turmoil and new signs, following the dollar crisis of 1968, of profound

economic distortions in the postwar growth engine. See Robert Collins, "The Economic Crisis of 1968 and the Waning of the 'American Century,'"*American Historical Review* 101 (April 1996): 396–422.

82. A good contemporary indication of the return of free-market theories (as well as "radical political economy") in the wake of the 1970s economic crisis is Daniel Bell and Irving Kristol, eds., *The Crisis of Economic Theory* (New York: Basic Books, 1981). See also Michael A. Bernstein, *A Perilous Progress: Economists and Public Purpose in Twentieth-Century America* (Princeton, N.J.: Princeton University Press, 2001), 148–84. On the general revival of Marxism in the 1970s, see Bertell Ollman and Edward Vernoff, eds., *The Left Academy: Marxist Scholarship on American Campuses* (New York: McGraw-Hill, 1982).

83. Parsons, *The System of Modern Societies*, 11–14.

84. See *The American Societal Community*, Parsons Papers, Harvard University Archives.

85. Braudel, *Civilization and Capitalism*, vol. 3, *The Perspective of the World*, trans. Siân Reynolds (Berkeley: University of California Press, 1984) (French, *Le temps du monde*, 1979), 619.

86. Braudel, *Civilization and Capitalism*, vol. 2, *The Wheels of Commerce*, 231.

87. Milton Friedman, *Capitalism and Freedom*, rev. ed. (Chicago: University of Chicago Press, 1982); Michael Novak, *The Spirit of Democratic Capitalism* (New York: Simon and Schuster, 1982); Irving Kristol, *Two Cheers for Capitalism* (New York: Basic Books, 1978); Ernest Mandel, *Late Capitalism*, trans. Joris De Bres (London: NLB, 1975); Immanuel Wallerstein, *The Capitalist World-Economy* (Cambridge: Cambridge University Press, 1979); Giovanni Arrighi, *The Long Twentieth Century: Money, Power, and the Origins of Our Times* (London: Verso, 1994); Robert Brenner, "Agrarian Class Structure and Economic Development in Pre-Industrial Europe," *Past and Present* 70 (February 1976), reprinted in, *The Brenner Debate*, ed. T. H. Aston and C. H. E. Philpin (Cambridge: Cambridge University Press, 1985); Robert Brenner, "The Origins of Capitalist Development: A Critique of Neo-Smithian Marxism," *New Left Review* 104 (July–August 1977): 25–92; J. Rogers Hollingsworth and Robert Boyer, eds., *Contemporary Capitalism: The Embeddedness of Institutions* (Cambridge: Cambridge University Press, 1997); Gøsta Esping-Andersen, *The Three Worlds of Welfare Capitalism* (Princeton, N.J.: Princeton University Press, 1990).

88. Braudel, *Civilization and Capitalism*, vol. 3, *The Perspective of the World*, 619–32.

89. Charles S. Maier, *Recasting Bourgeois Europe: Stabilization in France, Germany, and Italy in the Decade after World War I* (Princeton, N.J.: Princeton University Press, 1975, 1988), 43, 3, 82, 9, 594.

90. Maier, 12–13.

91. Maier, 594.

92. Historian Arno Mayer captured the historical circumstances and political pedigree of these ideas aptly: "There is something comforting about taking partisan wishes for historical reality. Beginning in the mid-1950s, in the wake of European reconstruction and restabilization, Western intellectuals of the progressive-liberal and democratic socialist persuasion prophesied first the advent of postcapitalism, then the end of ideology and eventually the coming of postindustrial society." Arno Mayer, "Europe After the Great Thaw," *Nation*, April 9, 1990, 492.

93. Martin J. Sklar, "The Corporate Reconstruction of American Capitalism: A Note on the Capitalism-Socialism Mix in U.S. and World Development," in *The United States as a Developing Country* (New York: Cambridge University Press, 1992); James Livingston, *Pragmatism and the Political Economy of Cultural Revolution, 1850–1940* (Chapel Hill: University of North Carolina Press, 1994); Fred L. Block, *Postindustrial Possibilities: A Critique of Economic Discourse* (Berkeley: University of California

Press, 1990) and "Rethinking 'Capitalism,'" in *Economic Sociology*, ed. Nicole Woolsey Biggart (Cambridge: Blackwell, 2002).

Chapter 2. To Moscow and Back: American Social Scientists and the Concept of Convergence

Thanks to Nils Gilman, John Summers, and Bernie Yack for informative discussions of these themes, and to Ethan Pollock for a close reading. The first version was presented at a conference, Capitalism and Culture (University of California, Santa Barbara, February 2003); Robert Brenner offered a spirited commentary there, and comments and discussion with the audience were also helpful. Special thanks to Nelson Lichtenstein for the opportunity to present the paper as well as helpful criticisms and suggestions. All archival materials are from the Harvard University Archives.

1. [John Gardner,] "Russian Studies," July 14, 1947 and Clyde Kluckhohn to Gardner, July 23, 1947, both in Russian Research Center Correspondence, series UAV 759.10, box 1. For a critical history of the Center, see Charles Thomas O'Connell, "Social Structure and Science: Soviet Studies at Harvard" (Ph.D. dissertation, University of California, Los Angeles, 1990); also Betty Abrahamsen Dessants, "The American Academic Community and United States-Soviet Union Relations: The Research and Analysis Branch and Its Legacy, 1941–1947" (Ph.D. dissertation, University of California, Berkeley, 1995).

2. For overviews of American views of the USSR in this era, see Eduard Mark, "October or Thermidor? Intepretations of Stalinism and the Perception of Soviet Foreign Policy in the United States, 1927–1947," *American Historical Review* 94, 3 (October 1989): 937–62; David S. Foglesong, "Roots of 'Liberation': American Images of the Future of Russia in the Early Cold War, 1948–1953," *International History Review* 21, 1 (March 1999): 57–79.

3. The connections between DSR and RRC were so numerous, in fact, that some DSR members feared their department would lose its distinctiveness by focusing too much on Soviet topics. Kluckhohn, "Notes on Discussion of Social Relations Research in Connection with the Russian Research Center," June 3, 1948, RRC Correspondence, series UAV 759.10, box 1.

4. Seminar Notes, February 6, 1948, RRC Seminar Notes, series UAV 759.8, box 1.

5. Howard Brick, "The Reformist Dimension of Talcott Parsons's Early Social Theory," in eds., *The Culture of the Market: Historical Essays*, ed. Thomas L. Haskell and Richard F. Teichgraeber, III (New York: Cambridge University Press, 1993), 366.

6. Critic Alvin Gouldner (discussed at the conclusion of this essay) noted that even on those occasions that Parsons "himself does not deal directly with every important theoretical problem, he brings us to its threshold." Gouldner, *The Coming Crisis of Western Sociology* (New York: Basic Books, 1970), 168–69. The number of biographies of Parsons is only one other indicator of his significance; I have been especially guided by two sympathetic analyses—Guy Rocher, *Talcott Parsons and American Sociology* (New York: Barnes and Noble, 1975) and Roland Robertson and Bryan S. Turner, eds., *Talcott Parsons: Theorist of Modernity* (London: Sage, 1991)—and by Howard Brick's articles "Reformist Dimension" and "Talcott Parsons's 'Shift Away from Economics,' 1937–1946," *Journal of American History* 87, 2 (September 2000): 490–514.

7. On the Americanization of the social sciences, see Dorothy Ross, *The Origins of American Social Science* (Cambridge: Cambridge University Press, 1991); Edward A. Purcell, Jr., *The Crisis of Democratic Theory: Scientific Naturalism and the Problem of*

Value (Lexington: University Press of Kentucky, 1973); Roland A. Robertson and Bryan S. Turner, "An Introduction to Talcott Parsons," in Robertson and Turner, eds., *Talcott Parsons*, 17.

8. Parsons, *The Structure of Social Action: A Study in Social Theory with Special Reference to a Group of Recent European Writers* (New York: McGraw-Hill, 1937), 505–6, 150–51, 3–4. See also Brick, "Reformist Dimension," 373–79.

9. Parsons, "The Professions and Social Structure" (1939), in Parsons, *Essays in Social Theory*, rev. ed. (Glencoe, Ill.: Free Press, 1954); N. S. Timasheff, "Business and the Professions in Liberal, Fascist, and Communist Society," *American Journal of Sociology* 45, 6 (May 1940): 863–69.

10. Parsons, "On Building Social System Theory: A Personal History," *Daedalus* 99, 4 (Fall 1970): 840–41; Brick, "Talcott Parsons's 'Shift Away from Economics.'"

11. Parsons, "The Department and Laboratory of Social Relations: The First Decade" (1956), Harvard University Archives, HUF 801.4156.2; Ron Robin, *The Making of the Cold War Enemy: Culture and Politics in the Military-Intellectual Complex* (Princeton, N.J.: Princeton University Press, 2001); Ellen Herman, *The Romance of American Psychology: Political Culture in an Age of Experts* (Berkeley: University of California Press, 1995).

12. Parsons, *The Social System* (Glencoe, Ill.: Free Press, 1951).

13. Talcott Parsons, Edward Shils, et al., eds., *Toward a General Theory of Action* (Cambridge, Mass.: Harvard University Press, 1951). On the hoped-for role of this book, see Patrick L. Schmidt, "Towards a History of the Department of Social Relations, Harvard University, 1946–1972" (Honors thesis, Harvard University, 1978), 64. See also Parsons, "A Short Account of My Intellectual Development," *Alpha Delta Kappan* 29 (1959): 11–12.

14. Parsons, "On Building Social System Theory," 842; Parsons, "The Superego and the Theory of Social Systems" (*Psychiatry*, 1952), in Parsons, *Social Structure and Personality* (New York: Free Press, 1964); and Parsons, "Psychoanalysis and Social Science with Special Reference to the Oedipus Problem," in *Twenty Years of Psychoanalysis*, ed. Franz Alexander and Helen Ross (New York: W.W. Norton, 1952).

15. Seminar Notes, March 5, 1948, series UAV 759.8, box 1.

16. Parsons, "Some Reflections on the Institutional Framework of Economic Development" (1958), in Parsons, *Structure and Process in Modern Societies* (Glencoe, Ill.: Free Press, 1960), 100, 116–17.

17. Parsons, *Social Structure*, 187–88, 193, 526–33 (quote 532); Barrington Moore, Jr., *Soviet Politics, the Dilemma of Power: The Role of Ideas in Social Change* (Cambridge, Mass.: Harvard University Press, 1950); Alex Inkeles, "Social Stratification and Mobility in the Soviet Union, 1940–1950," *American Sociological Review* 15 (August 1950): 465–79. On the appointments of Inkeles and Moore to Harvard's RRC and (eventually) DSR, see Morton Keller and Phyllis Keller, *Making Harvard Modern: The Rise of America's University* (Oxford: Oxford University Press, 2001), 94–95.

18. For examples of economists' alarums to nonspecialist audiences, see Abram Bergson, "Russia Turns to Economic Competition," *Challenge* 6 (February 1958), 50–54; Gregory Grossman, "The Soviet Economy and World Power," in *International Stability and Progress: U.S. Interests and Instruments: Final Report* (New York: American Assembly, 1957).

19. Merle Fainsod, *How Russia Is Ruled* (Cambridge, Mass.: Harvard University Press, 1953), ix, 499. Political scientist Andrew C. Janos blames American assimilation of Weber's theory of power for promoting interpretations of the USSR "that provided insights into the origins, but not the dynamics, of Soviet power": Janos, "Social Science, Communism, and the Dynamics of Political Change," *World Politics*

44, 1 (October 1991): 81–89. Abbott Gleason, *Totalitarianism: The Inner History of the Cold War* (Oxford: Oxford University Press, 1995), chap. 7; Carl J. Friedrich, "The Unique Character of Totalitarian Society," in *Totalitarianism*, ed. Friedrich (Cambridge, Mass.: Harvard University Press, 1954).

20. George W. Breslauer, "In Defense of Sovietology," *Post-Soviet Affairs* 8, 3 (1992): 197–238. The incorporation of the USSR into social science peaked in the late 1960s and 1970s; see Jerry F. Hough, *The Soviet Union and Social Science Theory* (Cambridge, Mass.: Harvard University Press, 1977); Frederic J. Fleron, Jr., ed., *Communist Studies and the Social Sciences: Essays on Methodology and Empirical Theory* (Chicago: Rand McNally, 1969).

21. This corresponds with the chronology suggested by political scientist (and RRC affiliate) Alfred Meyer. Meyer, "Theories of Convergence," in Chalmers Johnson, ed., *Change in Communist Systems*, ed. Chalmers Johnson (Stanford, Calif.: Stanford University Press, 1970), 320.

22. Black wanted to call the volume, "The *Modernization* of Russian Society," but economic historian Alexander Gerschenkron protested vehemently against that term; "the Soviet Union," he wrote Black, "is being modernized in some respects and thrown back to a remote period in her history in others." Gerschenkron to Black, December 13, 1955, Gerschenkron Papers, series HUG(FP) 45.10, box 2; for more on Gerschenkron, see David C. Engerman, "Modernization from the Other Shore: American Observers and the Costs of Soviet Economic Development," *American Historical Review* 105, 2 (April 2000): 411–14.

23. Parsons, "Some Principal Characteristics of Industrial Societies," in *The Transformation of Russian Society: Aspects of Social Change since 1861*, ed. Cyril Black (Cambridge, Mass.: Harvard University Press, 1960), 13.

24. Parsons, "Some Principal Characteristics," 14–16, 22–23; Parsons, *Social System*, chap. 2.

25. Parsons, "Some Principal Characteristics." He parallels arguments by Harvard colleague Alexander Gerschenkron; see especially Gerschenkron, "Economic Backwardness in Historical Perspective" (1952) and the other essays in Gerschenkron, *Economic Backwardness in Historical Perspective: A Book of Essays* (Cambridge, Mass.: Harvard University Press, 1962).

26. Parsons, "Some Principal Characteristics," 19–20.

27. Parsons, *Structure of Social Action*, 488–95; Parsons, "Social Sciences and Modern Industrial Society" (c. 1955), in Parsons Papers, series HUG(FP) 42.41, box 6. The archival materials offer no explanation of this paper's original purpose or the reason it remained unpublished.

28. This insight was also central to the writings of Michel Foucault, a point made by Robertson and Turner, "How to Read Parsons," *Talcott Parsons*, 257.

29. Parsons, "From the Point of View of the Author," in *The Social Theories of Talcott Parsons: A Critical Examination*, ed. Max Black (Englewood Cliffs, N.J.: Prentice-Hall, 1961), 361–62; Parsons, "Social Sciences," 7–8, 14.

30. Parsons, "Social Sciences," 15.

31. Parsons's coauthor Edward Shils and fellow sociologist Daniel Bell famously described these concerns in the 1950s; Parsons too wrote about the relationship between ideology and development. Edward Shils, "The End of Ideology?" *Encounter* 5 (1955), 52–58; Daniel Bell, "The End of Ideology in the West," in Bell, *The End of Ideology: On the Exhaustion of Political Ideas in the 1950s* (New York: Free Press, 1960). See also the discussion in Nils Gilman, *Mandarins of the Future: Modernization Theory in Cold War America* (Baltimore: Johns Hopkins University Press, 2004).

32. Parsons, "Social Sciences," 14–15.

33. Parsons, "Communism and the West: The Sociology of the Conflict" (n.d.), Parsons Papers, series HUG(FP) 42.41, box 6.

34. Parsons, "Polarization and the Problem of International Order," *Berkeley Journal of Sociology* 6 (1961): 131–32.

35. Bruno Rizzi, *The Bureaucratization of the World; The USSR: Bureaucratic Collectivism*, trans. Adam Westoby (1939; London: Tavistock, 1985). Burnham, *The Managerial Revolution: What Is Happening in the World* (New York: John Day, 1941). John P. Diggins, *Up from Communism: Conservative Odysseys in American Intellectual* History (New York: Harper, 1975), 186–98. For some insights into the accusations of plagiarism, see Adam Westoby's introduction to the Rizzi volume; also Daniel Bell, *The Coming of Post-Industrial Society: A Venture in Social Forecasting* (New York: Basic Books, 1973), 96–97n69; Bell, "The Strange Tale of Bruno R.," *New Leader* 42 (September 28, 1959): 19–20.

36. Friedrich A. von Hayek, *The Road to Serfdom* (Chicago: University of Chicago Press, 1944).

37. Herbert Marcuse, "Recent Literature on Communism," *World Politics* 6, 4 (July 1954): 525; Marcuse, *Soviet Marxism: A Critical Analysis* (1958; New York: Vintage, 1961), 243, 191, 66.

38. Marcuse, *One-Dimensional Man: Studies in the Ideology of Advanced Industrial Society* (Boston: Beacon, 1964), 17, xv; Alfred G. Meyer, review of Marcuse, *Soviet Marxism, American Slavic and East European Review* 18, 2 (April 1959): 250. See also Morton Schoolman, *The Imaginary Witness: The Critical Theory of Herbert Marcuse* (New York: Free Press, 1980), 150–59; Barry Katz, *Herbert Marcuse and the Art of Liberation: An Intellectual Biography* (London: Verso, 1982).

39. C. Wright Mills, *The Causes of World War Three* (1958; Westport, Conn.: Greenwood Press, 1976), 17–18.

40. Mills, "Culture and Politics" (1959), "The Decline of the Left" (1959), and "The Problem of Industrial Development" (1959), all in Mills, *Power, Politics and People: The Collected Essays of C. Wright Mills*, ed. Irving Louis Horowitz (Oxford: Oxford University Press, 1963), 241, 227, 155, 152.

41. Irving Howe, review of C. Wright Mills, *The Causes of World War Three, Dissent* 6 (Spring 1959): 191–96; Mills and Howe, "The Intellectuals and Russia," *Dissent* 6 (Summer 1959), 297–98; Gerald Sorin, *Irving Howe: A Life of Passionate Dissent* (New York: New York University Press, 2002), 170–71.

42. W. W. Rostow, *Stages of Economic Growth: A Non-Communist Manifesto* (Cambridge: Cambridge University Press, 1960), 103–4; Walt Whitman, "One Thought Ever at the Fore" (1891), quoted in Max F. Millikan and W. W. Rostow, *A Proposal: Key to an Effective Foreign Policy* (New York: Harper and Brothers, 1958), 151; Nils Gilman, "Modernization Theory: The Highest Stage of American Intellectual History," in *Staging Growth: Modernization, Development, and the Global Cold War*, ed. David C. Engerman, Nils Gilman, and Mark H. Haefele (Amherst: University of Massachusetts Press, 2003).

43. Cyril Black, *The Dynamics of Modernization: A Study in Comparative History* (New York: Harper, 1966), 172–74.

44. Marion Levy, *Modernization and the Structure of Societies: A Setting for International Affairs*, 2 vols. (Princeton, N.J.: Princeton University Press, 1966).

45. Economist Joseph Berliner, another participant in the Interview Project, agreed that one of the most important findings of the project was that "in most respects Soviet society reflected the characteristics of a class society of the Western industrial kind." Berliner, Foreword to *Politics, Work, and Daily Life in the USSR: A Survey of Former Soviet Citizens*, ed. James R. Millar (Cambridge: Cambridge University Press, 1987), x.

46. Alex Inkeles and Raymond A. Bauer, *The Soviet Citizen: Daily Life in a Totalitarian*

Society (Cambridge, Mass.: Harvard University Press, 1959), chap. 16 (emphasis in original).

47. Raymond A. Bauer, Alex Inkeles, and Clyde Kluckhohn, *How the Soviet System Works: Cultural, Psychological, and Social Themes* (1956; New York: Vintage, 1960), 250–51, 256, 262, 279–83. On the death of Stalin, see Inkeles, *Public Opinion* (1950; Cambridge, Mass.: Harvard University Press, 1960), 325; "Addendum: 1950–1960?" added in 1958.

48. Inkeles, "Models and Issues in the Analysis of Soviet Society" (1966), in Inkeles, *Social Change in Soviet Russia* (1968; New York: Simon and Schuster, 1971).

49. Inkeles and Peter Rossi, "National Comparisons of Occupational Prestige" (1956), in Inkeles, *Social Change.*

50. Inkeles and David H. Smith, *Becoming Modern: Individual Change in Six Developing Countries* (Cambridge, Mass.: Harvard University Press, 1974); Inkeles, *One World Emerging? Convergence and Divergence in Industrial Societies* (Boulder, Colo.: Westview Press, 1998), 26.

51. See, for instance, Parsons diary, May 9, 1964 and Parsons, "Report of Cultural Exchange Visit to the Soviet Union, May 5–22, 1964," both in Parsons Papers, series HUG(FP) 15.4, box 19.

52. George Fischer, *Science and Politics: The New Sociology in the Soviet Union* (Ithaca, N.Y.: Cornell University Center for International Studies, 1964); Parsons also cited a report by Merton and Henry W. Reicken published by the National Institute of Social and Behavioral Science. For more context on Soviet sociology, see G. Osipov and M. Yovchuk, "Some Principles of Theory, Problems, and Methods of Research in Sociology in the USSR," *American Sociological Review* 28, 4 (August 1963): 620–23; and the series of articles on the development of the social sciences appearing in *Vestnik Akademii Nauk SSSR* and *Voprosy filosofii* in 1962 and 1963.

53. Parsons, "Social Sciences"; Fischer, *Science and Politics*, 19.

54. Parsons, "An American Impression of Sociology in the Soviet Union," *American Sociological Review* 30, 1 (February 1965): 123.

55. Untitled handwritten notes, opening with "General idea: Close parallel of Communism to Calvinism," Parsons Papers, series HUG(FP) 15.4, box 19.

56. See Ethan M. Pollock, "The Politics of Knowledge: Party Ideology and Soviet Science, 1945–1953" (Ph.D. dissertation, University of California, Berkeley, 2000), chap. 1; Allen Kassof, "American Sociology Through Soviet Eyes," *American Sociological Review* 30, 1 (February 1965): 114–19; Leopold Labdez, "Sociology as a Vocation," *Survey* 48 (July 1963), 57–65. This latter article was part of a symposium on sociology in the USSR.

57. Parsons, "Evolutionary Universals in Society," *American Sociological Review* 29, 3 (June 1964): 339–57.

58. Parsons, "Evolutionary Universals in Society," 149–53, 349, 356–57.

59. Parsons, "Evolutionary Universals in Society," 356–57. This prediction of Soviet democratization led two somewhat defensive analysts of Parsons to acknowledge this weakness in his argument. His "confident assumption that the lack of a political democracy would generate instabilities in the soviet system has not so far proved accurate," they wrote in 1986, shortly after Mikhail Gorbachev's ascension to power. Robert J. Holton and Bryan S. Turner, "Against Nostalgia: Talcott Parsons and a Sociology for the Modern World," in Holton and Turner, *Talcott Parsons on Economy and Society* (London: Routledge and Kegan Paul, 1986), 224.

60. See the correspondence between Inkeles, Parsons, and Prentice-Hall staff, 1964–1965, in Parsons Papers, series HUG(FP) 15.4, box 9.

61. Parsons, *The System of Modern Societies* (Englewood Cliffs, N.J.: Prentice-Hall, 1971), chaps. 4–5.

62. Parsons, *The System of Modern Societies*, 128, chap. 6.

63. Parsons, *The System of Modern Societies*, 127, chap 7.

64. Parsons to Helen Parsons, 11 October 1967, Parsons Papers, series HUG(FP) 15.10, box 3; Fischer, *Science and Politics*; A. G. Zdravomyslov, *Sotsiologiia rossiiskogo krizisa* (Moscow: Nauka, 1999), part 3; Alexander Vucinich, "Marx and Parsons in Soviet Sociology," *Russian Review* 33, 1 (January 1974), 1–19.

65. Parsons to Joseph Slater, October 27, 1967, Parsons Papers, series HUG(FP), 15.60, box 3.

66. Matthew Evangelista, *Unarmed Forces: The Transnational Movement to End the Cold War* (Ithaca, N.Y.: Cornell University Press, 1999), 210–11. For information on the trip, see the handwritten notes, the letter to Carl Kaysen (November 22, 1967), and the lists of those present (December 28, 1967 and January 3, 1968), all in Parsons Papers, series HUG(FP) 15.60, box 3.

67. Parsons to [Ambassador] L. E. Thompson, January 18, 1968, Parsons Papers, series HUG(FP) 15.60, box 3.

68. Parsons to Rostow, January 16, 1968, Parsons Papers, series HUG(FP) 15.60, box 3.

69. Gouldner, *Coming Crisis*, 11, 452, 466–67; see also the unsympathetic contributions to two symposia on *Coming Crisis*: *American Sociological Review* 36, 2 (April 1971): 317–28; *American Journal of Sociology* 77, 2 (September 1971): 312–23.

70. Gouldner, *Coming Crisis*, 473, 474.

71. Gouldner, *Coming Crisis*, 9–10; Brick, "Talcott Parsons's 'Turn Away from Economics.'"

72. Clifford Geertz from oral discussion of the Parsons autobiographical essay, in Parsons, "On Building Social Systems Theory," 870.

73. This argument had been in Western social-scientific though since the mid-nineteenth century. See Hugh J. Dawson, "E. B. Tylor's Theory of Survivals and Veblen's Social Criticism," *Journal of the History of Ideas*, 54, 3 (July 1993): 489–504 and William F. Ogburn, *Social Change with Respect to Culture and Original Nature* (New York: B.W. Huebsch, 1923).

Chapter 3. Clark Kerr: From the Industrial to the Knowledge Economy

1. Clark Kerr, *The Uses of the University* (Cambridge, Mass.: Harvard University Press, 1995), 78. The book was originally presented as the Godkin Lectures at Harvard University in 1963. *The Uses of the University* reached its fifth edition in 2001.

2. This is even true of Kerr's own recent memoirs, which are focused on his role at the UC. See *The Gold and the Blue: A Personal Memoir of the University of California, 1949–1967*, 2 vols (Berkeley: University of Press, 2001, 2003). There is no full-length published biography of Kerr, and much commentary on his career is located in studies focused either on the Free Speech Movement or the research university. See for instance W. J. Rorabaugh, *Berkeley at War: The 1960s* (New York: Oxford University Press, 1989) and Mark Kitchell's influential documentary *Berkeley in the Sixties* (New York: First-Run Features, 1990), as well as the recent collection, Robert Cohen and Reginald E. Zelnik, eds., *The Free Speech Movement: Reflections on Berkeley in the 1960s* (Berkeley: University of California Press, 2002). For commentary focusing on Kerr's career in higher education, see, in addition to the works by Douglass and Geiger cited later in this essay, Mary Soo and Cathryn Carson, "Managing the Research University: Clark Kerr and the University of California," *Minerva* 42, 3 (September 2004): 215–36.

3. Clark Kerr, *The Gold and the Blue*, vol. 1, *Academic Triumphs*, 14.

4. In addition, see Howard Brick, "Talcott Parson's 'Shift Away from Economics,' 1937–1946" *Journal of American History* 87, 2 (September 2000): 490–515.

5. In 1964, U.S. expenditures on research and development as a percentage of GNP were 3.4 percent, UK 2.3 percent, France 1.6 percent, Sweden and Japan 1.5 percent, Germany 1.4 percent. OECD Directorate for Scientific Affairs, *Reviews of National Science Policy: The United States* (Paris: OECD, 1968), Table 2, 32; see Table 15, 51, for school enrollment rates, which follow a similar pattern. See also Herman Van der Wee, *Prosperity and Upheaval: The World Economy, 1945–1980* (New York: Viking, 1986), chaps. 4 and 5. For California numbers, see John Aubrey Douglass, *The California Idea and American Higher Education 1850 to the 1960 Master Plan* (Stanford, Calif.: Stanford University Press, 2000), 1. A sense of the postwar growth in higher education can be seen in change in the percent of the population aged eighteen to twenty-four enrolled in college. In 1946 it was 12.5 percent, in 1960, 22.2 percent, in 1970, 32.1 percent. *Historical Statistics of the United States: From Colonial Times to 1970*, vol. 2, 383, Series H 700–715. A number of economists began to write about "human capital" in relation to education in the late 1950s and early 1960s, including Theodore Schultz, Gary Becker, and Fritz Machlup. For a review of this literature, see Paul J. McNulty, *The Origins and Development of Labor Economics: A Chapter in the History of Social Thought* (Cambridge, Mass.: MIT Press, 1980), 192–97. See also David A. Hollinger, *Science, Jews, and Secular Culture* (Princeton, N.J.: Princeton University Press, 1996), especially chapter 8, "Science as a Weapon," for an incisive portrait of the liberal attraction to science and education in this period.

6. Daniel Bell, "Labor," *Fortune*, April 1958, 215–18. See also Bell, "The Capitalism of the Proletariat: A Theory of American Trade-Unioinism," in *The End of Ideology* (1960; New York: Collier, 1962), 211–26; Nelson Lichtenstein, *State of the Union: A Century of American Labor* (Princeton, N.J.: Princeton University Press, 2002), 118–21, 176–77.

7. Howard Brick, "Optimism of the Mind: Imagining Postindustrial Society in the 1960s and 1970s," *American Quarterly* 44, 3 (September 1992): 348–80.

8. Kerr, *The Gold and the Blue*, 1: 3–15.

9. Another of Kerr's mentors, the labor historian Ira B. Cross, was also a student of Commons. For background on the development of labor economics in the U.S., see McNulty, *The Origin and Development of Labor Economics*. For Taylor's ethnographic bent, see, for example, Paul Taylor, "Nonstatistical Notes from the Field," in Paul Taylor, *On the Ground in the Thirties* (Salt Lake City: Peregrine Smith Books, 1983), 233, and his documentary work with Dorothea Lange, *An American Exodus: A Record of Human Erosion* (New York: Reynal and Hitchcock, 1939).

10. "Beyond question," Carey McWilliams wrote in 1939, "the strikes of these years are without precedent in the history of labor in the United States. Never before had farm laborers organized on any such scale and never before had they conducted strikes of such magnitude and such far reaching social significance." Carey McWilliams, *Factories in the Field: The Story of Migratory Farm Labor in California* (Boston: Little, Brown, 1939), 211. According to Kerr and Taylor, over 10,000 workers were involved in the cotton-pickers strike. The strike was eventually resolved when both sides submitted to an agreement worked out by a fact-finding committee chaired by Ira B. Cross. "Documentary History of the Strike of the Cotton Pickers in California 1933," in Taylor, *On the Ground in the Thirties*, 17–158, 19, 99–117.

11. Clark Kerr and Paul Taylor, "Uprisings on the Farms," *Survey Graphic* 24, 1 (January 1935): 19–22, 44. Other examples of Kerr's work with Taylor include "Whither Self-Help?" *Survey Graphic* 23, 7 (July 1934): 328–31, 348 and "Putting the Unemployed at Productive Labor," *Annals of the American Academy of Political and Social Science* 176 (1934): 104–11. The full version of Kerr and Taylor's report on

the strike, "Documentary History of the Strike of the Cotton Pickers," unpublished until 1940, was an excellent example of Taylor's "nonstatistical notes from the field." Containing only a bare skeleton of narrative structure, the report was a montage of interviews, press clippings, and brief commentary. The full report was first published by the LaFollette Committee in the Senate, as part of a series of investigations into the "Violations of Free Speech and Rights of Labor."

12. Clark Kerr, "Productive Enterprises of the Unemployed, 1931–1938," 4 vols. (Ph.D. dissertation, University of California, Berkeley, 1939), 1: v. California contained by far the largest number of worker cooperatives throughout the depression (see 1: 24, 31, 33). For a study of the California cooperatives based primarily on Kerr's dissertation, see Derek C. Jones and Donald J. Schneider, "Self-Help Production Cooperatives: Government-Administered Cooperatives During the Depression," in *Worker's Cooperatives in America*, ed. Robert Jackall and Harry Levin (Berkeley: University of California Press, 1984), 57–84.

13. George Bernard Noble, "Twelfth Regional War Labor Board, Seattle Washington. Termination Report." *Termination Report of the N.W.L.B.* (Washington, D.C.: Government Printing Office, 1947), 2: 80. According to Kerr, governmental work during the war led to later scholarly prominence— "Only a few others, without comparable wartime experience, made major contributions in the immediate postwar period." Clark Kerr, *The Balkanization of Labor Markets and Other Essays* (Berkeley: University of California Press, 1977), 1.

14. James B. Atleson, *Labor and the Wartime State: Labor Relations and Law During World War II* (Urbana: University of Illinois Press, 1998), 46; Kerr, *Balkanization of Labor Markets*, 3

15. "Opinion," "In the Matter of New Service Laundries, Inc., Eugene, Oregon and Laundry Workers International Union, Local #206, AFL," Case No. 111-1536-D, U.S. National War Labor Board, Region 12, *Directive Order[s]*, vol. 3 (Seattle:, 1942–45; located in Main Library, University of California, Berkeley). Kerr has a few other opinions scattered throughout these volumes, which record the actions of the board on a series of cases. For more patriotic rhetoric, see his opinion on the board's decision, "In the Matter of Pacific Northwest Foundry Operators, Washington and Oregon, and International Molders and Foundry Workers' Union of North America" Case No. 12-5819, vol. 3. See also Atleson, *Labor and the Wartime State*, 113, for another example.

16. See Nelson Lichtenstein, *Labor's War at Home: The CIO in World War II* (Cambridge: Cambridge University Press, 1982), esp. chap. 10 and Atleson, *Labor and the Wartime State*, chapter 6.

17. Atleson, *Labor and the Wartime State*, chap. 4. A similar voluntarist philosophy, Christopher Tomlins has shown, animated the work of William Leiserson at the National Labor Relations Board before the war. Tomlins, *The State and the Unions: Labor Relations, Law, and the Organized Labor Movement in America, 1880–1960.* (Cambridge: Cambridge University Press, 1985), esp. chap. 6; Katherine Van Wezel Stone, "The Post-War Paradigm in American Labor Law," *Yale Law Journal* 90, 7 (June 1981): 1511–80, 1515. On the declension from corporatism, see Nelson's Lichtenstein's classic "From Corporatism to Collective Bargaining: Organized Labor and the Eclipse of Social Democracy in the Postwar Era," in *The Rise and Fall of the New Deal Order*, ed. Steve Fraser and Gary Gerstle (Princeton, N.J.: Princeton University Press, 1989), 122–52. See also Reuel Schiller, "From Group Rights to Individual Liberties: Post-War Labor Law, Liberalism, and the Waning of Union Strength," *Berkeley Journal of Employment and Labor Law* 20 (Summer 1999), for an especially good overview of how the assumption of unions as a "countervailing power" to management informed postwar labor case law, and Katherine Van Wezel Stone, "The Legacy of Industrial Pluralism:

The Tension Between Individual Employment Rights and the New Deal Collective Bargaining System," *University of Chicago Law Review* 59, 2 (Spring 1992): 575–644.

18. Numbers from Michael Goldfield, *The Decline of Organized Labor in the United States* (Chicago: University of Chicago Press, 1987), 10.

19. A sister institute was established at Los Angeles by the same act of the California Legislature. The New York Legislature had established a School of Industrial Relations at Cornell in 1944; in the same year Yale founded a Labor and Management Center. Besides the institutes at Berkeley and Los Angeles, three other industrial relations centers were established in 1945, at the Universities of Chicago, Illinois, and Minnesota; at least seven more were founded in the next three years. Adding to this number the five centers organized before the war produces a formidable institutional presence of industrial relations among America's major research universities. Except for an institute at North Carolina (est. 1947), these research centers were scattered throughout the Northeast, the Midwest, and the Pacific Coast, thus following the geographical distribution of the labor movement. Robert Lancelot Clewett, "Industrial Relations Research Centers in American Universities," M.A. thesis, University of California, Berkeley, 1949; see also Milton Derber, *Research in Labor Problems in the United States* (New York: Random House, 1967), 8–9. For the research and policy agenda of the Berkeley Institute, see University of California, Institute of Industrial Relations, *Institute of Industrial Relations, 1946* and *A Progress Report of the Institute of Industrial Relations, 1945–1952* (both at Bancroft Library, University of California, Berkeley).

20. The first annual meeting of the IRRA occurred the following year. Kerr was a member of the IRRA Organizing Committee, which included some of the more renowned labor economists of the 1930s, like Edwin Witte, Sumner Slichter, and George W. Taylor. Also on the committee were younger students of labor, like Kerr's colleague Frederick Harbison, and C. Wright Mills (vice-president of the IRRA for 1948; Mills seems to have left the association shortly thereafter). See Milton Derber and William H. McPherson, "The Formation and Development of the IRRA," Industrial Relations Research Association, *Proceedings of the First Annual Meeting*, 1947, 2–4. The IRRA was formed as an interdisciplinary association, but while it drew members from many social science fields, economists and industrial relations scholars were in the clear majority. The 1954 Membership Directory lists 307 "Academic" members affiliated with "Economics and Commerce" and 128 with "Industrial Relations" but only 23 law professors, 11 political scientists, 26 psychologists, and 23 sociologists. Industrial Relations Research Association, *Membership Directory*, 1954. On the interdisciplinary character of industrial relations, see McNulty, *Origin and Development of Labor Economics*, 197–200.

21. Edwin Witte, "Where We Are in Industrial Relations," IRRA, *Proceedings of the First Annual Meeting*, 1947, 6–20.

22. Lichtenstein, *Labor's War at Home: The CIO in World War II* (Cambridge: Cambridge University Press, 1982), esp. chap. 10; Atleson, *Labor and the Wartime State*, chap. 6. On the pitfalls of arbitration, see Atleson, chap. 4; Stone, "The Post-War Paradigm"; and Nelson Lichtenstein, "Great Expectations: The Promise of Industrial Jurisprudence and Its Demise, 1930–1960," in *Industrial Democracy in America: The Ambiguous Promise*, ed. Nelson Lichtenstein and Howell John Harris (Cambridge: Cambridge University Press, 1993), 118–41.

23. Myers wrote, "1. There is full acceptance by management of the collective bargaining process and unionism as an institution. The company considers a strong union an asset to management. 2. The union fully accepts private ownership and operation of the industry; it recognizes that the welfare of its members depends upon the successful operation of the business." Kerr, Harbison, Myers, and Dunlop

all participated in this study, sponsored by the National Planning Association, which ran from 1947 to 1953 and consisted of a series of case studies of relatively harmonious union-management relationships. Summaries of each case, plus a final report, were collected as *Causes of Industrial Peace Under Collective Bargaining*, ed. Clinton Golden and Virginia D. Parker (New York: Harper, 1955). See Myers, "Conclusions and Implications," 46–54.

24. Stone, "The Post-War Paradigm," 1513–14. According to Howell John Harris, the progressive managerial attitude described in *Causes of Industrial Peace* "simply failed to win the support of most nationally important firms." Howell John Harris, *The Right to Manage: Industrial Relations Policies of American Business in the 1940s* (Madison: University of Wisconsin Press, 1982), 138–39. See also Ronald Schatz, "From Commons to Dunlop: Rethinking the Theory and Field of Industrial Relations," in Lichtenstein and Harris, *Industrial Democracy in America*, 87–112.

25. Clark Kerr, "Industrial Relations and the Liberal Pluralist"; IRRA, *Proceedings of the Seventh Annual Meeting*, 1954, 10, 12–13.

26. "From one point of view," Kerr argued, "society is a huge mediation mechanism, a means for settling disagreements between rival claimants—taxpayers and recipients of benefits, buyers and sellers, proponents of opposing political ideologies—so that people may live together in some state of mutual tolerance. . . . Society in the large is the mediation machinery for industrial as well as other forms of conflict." Clark Kerr, "Industrial Conflict and its Mediation," *American Journal of Sociology* 60, 3 (November 1954): 243. See also Kerr, "An Effective and Democratic Organization of the Economy," in President's Commission on National Goals," *Goals for Americans* (Englewood Cliffs, N.J.: Prentice-Hall, 1960), 149–61.

27. See Seymour Martin Lipset, *Political Man: The Social Bases of Politics* (New York: Doubleday, 1959), 12–13. For a more extensive discussion of the relationship between pluralism and industrial pluralism, see Lichtenstein, *State of the Union*, 148–56.

28. For a narrative of the oath controversy, see David P. Gardner, *The California Oath Controversy* (Berkeley: University of California Press, 1967). The dispute between the faculty and the Board of Regents was concerned not only with whether or not nonsigners should be reinstated, but whether or not the Committee on Privileges and Tenure even had the authority to determine the tenure rights of the nonsigners. Thus the dismissal of the nonsigners was also a demonstration of the regents' supremacy. Kerr thought such this course of action rash; he attempted to persuade the Board to seek an alternative solution (for Kerr's interchange with John Francis Neylan at a pivotal meeting of the Board, see Gardner, 188–89). Kerr's role in the controversy as an embattled mediator would become even more familiar in the 1950s and 1960s, as he contended with right-wing politicians in California, from Hugh Burns (Jack Tenney's successor on the Senate Un-American Activities Committee) to Ronald Reagan, while attempting to fend off the charges of radical students and faculty at the same time. This is the self-portrait he sketches in his memoirs, especially in vol. 2, which is focused on "political turmoil" on the UC campus (see vol. 2, chap. 2 for his narrative of the oath controversy, and chap. 3 for his encounters with the anticommunist right wing). Kerr argues that the oath controversy had a strong influence on the political culture of the University of California throughout the 1950s; the negative heritage of the controversy, he suggests, was not fully cast aside until, with his backing, the Regents formally approved lifetime tenure for all UC faculty in 1958. As it turned out, Kerr, who was fired as UC president in the winter of 1967, but retained his academic appointment, would become one of the first beneficiaries of the new tenure provision (*The Gold and the Blue*, vol. 1, chap. 9).

29. In 1952, the Levering Act oath was incorporated into the state constitution, an action that Kerr, in league with other Quakers, publicly opposed. See *The Gold*

and the Blue, 1: 130. While it did not specifically mention "communism," the Levering oath, Gardner argues, was "more offensive than the one they [the nonsigners] had fought earlier" (*California Oath Controversy*, 250). For more on the court's decision and the Levering Act, see Gardner, chaps. 7 and 8.

30. Kerr was in fact the first chancellor ever appointed at a UC campus (Raymond Allen was appointed chancellor of UCLA in 1952 as well). As chancellor, however, his impact was restrained by the Sproul administration; Kerr characterizes his position as something more like an Academic Provost, with significant power over academic matters, but very little control over external administrative decisions (*The Gold and the Blue*, 1: 29). For a survey of Kerr's administrative agenda, see Douglass, *The California Idea and American Higher Education*, chap. 9, and Roger L. Geiger, *Research and Relevant Knowledge: American Research Universities Since World War II* (New York: Oxford University Press, 1993), 73–82.

31. Clark Kerr, "The University in a Progressive Society," *Pacific Spectator* 7, 3 (Summer 1953): 268–77, 268, 276–77.

32. Kerr, "The University in a Progressive Society," 268.

33. For a brief biography of Dunlop, see the obituary in the *New York Times*, October 4, 2003. Dunlop's 1958 book, *Industrial Relations Systems* (New York: Henry Holt, 1958), drew on a Parsonian inspired methodology—the state, management, and labor as the three principal "actors" in an industrial relations system—and emphasized, as did Dunlop's work with Kerr et al., the importance of a "web of rules" that these actors created to regulate the work process.

34. See James L. Cochrane, *Industrialism and Industrial Man in Retrospect: A Critical View of the Ford Foundation's Support for the Inter-University Study of Labor* (Ann Arbor, Mich.: University Microfilms International, 1979), especially chapter 4. For the continuing emphasis on human resources, see also notes 41 and 42 below. The foundation's devotion to American education was evident in the establishment of the Fund for the Advancement of Education and the Fund for Adult Education in 1951 and the expenditure of close to $33 million on education by 1953. Thomas C. Reeves, *Freedom and the Foundation: The Fund for the Republic in the Era of McCarthyism* (New York: Knopf, 1969), chap. 1. The foundation also supported a long term project at Columbia, the National Manpower Council, which produced a series of books concerning education and scientific manpower in the contemporary United States. See National Manpower Council, *Manpower Policies for a Democratic Society* (New York: Columbia University Press, 1965). For the Ford Foundation's support of international studies, see Robert A. McCaughey, *International Studies and Academic Enterprise: A Chapter in the Enclosure of American Learning* (New York: Columbia University Press, 1984), chap. 6. See also Edward H. Berman, *The Ideology of Philanthropy* (Albany: State University of New York Press, 1983), chap. 4. Here I focus on the major theoretical work of Kerr et al.'s project, *Industrialism and Industrial Man*, and mainly in the context of Kerr's shift from labor to education. There is much more to be said about the international dimension of the group's research agenda. A sense of the scope of the project can be seen in the bibliographies in Cochrane and in Kerr, Dunlop, Harbison, and Myers, *Industrialism and Industrial Man Reconsidered* (Princeton, N.J.: Inter-University Study of Human Resources in National Development, 1975). By 1975, foundation funding had supported the research behind 36 books and 43 articles. At one time or another, 95 scholars, in the U.S. and abroad, were affiliated with the study .

35. Clark Kerr with Abraham J. Siegel, "The Structuring of the Labor Force in Industrial Society: New Dimensions and New Questions," in Kerr, *Labor and Management in Industrial Society* (New York: Anchor Books, 1964), 304, 316, 327. This essay was originally published in *Industrial and Labor Relations Review* in January 1955. Cochrane notes that Kerr and Siegel first presented the essay as a paper at a Cornell University Conference in 1953.

36. Kerr with Siegel "The Structuring of the Labor Force," 321. Kerr and Siegel, as they noted at the beginning of their essay, were clearly borrowing from the social sciences in order to develop their interpretation of industrialization. Their debt to sociology especially was evident in the language of the essay, which was rife with abstractions like "structuring of the labor force," "organized instrumentality," the "strategies and tactics" of "contending groups" in a given "environmental context." This move towards social science was reflected in the Berkeley Institute as well. In 1946, the research staff included Kerr, Lloyd Fisher, and three research assistants. By 1953, when E. T. Grether took over as director of the institute, the research staff had expanded to twenty-four members. While still dominated by labor economists, the staff included the sociologists Reinhard Bendix and Philip Selznick (soon to be joined by Seymour Martin Lipset), three psychologists, and two political scientists. *A Progress Report of the Institute of Industrial Relations, 1945–1952,* 48–49.

37. Clark Kerr, Frederick H. Harbison, John T. Dunlop, and Charles A. Myers, "The Labour Problem in Economic Development: A Framework for a Reappraisal,". *International Labour Review* 71, 3 (March 1955): 223–35, quotes 227, 231–32.

38. Frederick H. Harbison and Charles A. Myers, *Management in the Industrial World: An International Analysis* (New York: McGraw-Hill, 1959), 16. This appreciation of management, however, didn't prevent Harbison and Myers from criticizing American business elites for their resistance to union representation and growth (see 376).

39. Kerr et al., "The Labour Problem in Economic Development," 231.

40. Harbison and Myers, *Management in the Industrial World,* 121. Much of the argument about the importance of education was anticipated in J. Douglas Brown and Frederick Harbison, *High-Talent Manpower for Science and Industry: An Appraisal of Policy at Home and Abroad* (Princeton, N.J.: Industrial Relations Section, 1957). Harbison and Myers would spend much of the remainder of their careers writing about the function of education in economic development. Their subsequent publications included Frederick H. Harbison and Charles A. Myers, *Education, Manpower, and Economic Growth: Strategies of Human Resource Development* (New York: McGraw-Hill, 1964); Harbison and Myers, eds., *Manpower and Education: Country Studies in Economic Development* (New York: McGraw-Hill, 1965). Harbison published independently *Educational Planning and Human Resource Development* (Paris: UNESCO, 1967) and *Human Resources as the Wealth of Nations* (Oxford: UNESCO, 1973).

41. John T. Dunlop, Frederick H. Harbison, Clark Kerr, and Charles A. Myers, *Industrialism and Industrial Man: The Problems of Labor and Management in Economic Growth* (Cambridge, Mass: Harvard University Press, 1960), 36–37. The significance of education was also reflected in two subsequent grants received by Kerr and his colleagues. In 1960, they accepted $200,000 from the Carnegie Corporation to study the "role of education and high-level manpower in the modernization process," and in 1961 they received a terminal grant from the Ford Foundation ($250,000) under the title "human resources in industrializing countries." The group had received one other small grant in 1955 ($50,000) to finance research by Harbison in the Middle East. The total of all grants received, then, was $1,050,000 (Cochrane, *Industrialism and Industrial Man in Retrospect,* 2). On the change of the title, and the turn towards human resources and education, see also Dunlop, Harbison, Kerr, and Myers, *Industrialism and Industrial Man Reconsidered,* 1–5. The study ended up supporting a number of books focused on higher education in the United States and abroad, including the work of Harbison and Myers, a few books by the labor economist E. Wright Bakke and a comparative study by Seymour Martin Lipset.

42. Dunlop et al., *Industrialism and Industrial Man,* 10, 288.

43. Dunlop et al., *Industrialism and Industrial Man,* 289.

44. Dunlop et al., *Industrialism and Industrial Man*, 292–93.

45. Dunlop et al., *Industrialism and Industrial Man*, 286, 295.

46. Clark Kerr, "Education for a Free Society: The California Experience," in *Writings and Addresses*, vol. 3 (Bancroft Library). The dual nature of the plan—to provide universal access and preserve meritocracy—is obvious in the planned freshman acceptance rates of each segment of the system: UC, top 12.5 percent of high school graduates; state colleges, 33.33 percent; junior colleges, 100 percent. See *A Master Plan for Higher Education in California* (Sacramento: California State Department of Education, 1960), chaps. 4 and 5. The story of the master plan is best told in Douglass, *The California Idea and American Higher Education*, chaps. 9–11. For a more critical view see Nicholas Lemann, *The Big Test: The Secret History of the American Meritocracy* (New York: Farrar, Straus and Giroux, 1999) chaps. 10, 11, 14. A good examination of the strains experienced by the Plan in operation is Neil J. Smelser, "Growth, Structural Change, and Conflict in California Higher Education, 1950–1970," in *Public Higher Education in California*, ed. Gabriel Almond and Neil J. Smelser (Berkeley: University of California Press, 1974).

47. "Master Planner," *Time*, October 17, 1960, 58–69; 59.

48. *The Uses of the University*, 22–30.

49. Clark Kerr, "Industrial Relations and University Relations," IRRA, *Proceedings of the Twenty-First Annual Winter Meeting*, 1968, 18.

50. Clark Kerr, "1984 Revisited," Commencement Address, Albright College, Reading, Pennsylvania, June 5, 1960, *Writings and Addresses*, vol. 6.

51. For contemporary coverage of the Kerr's battle with Reagan, see *Time*, January 20, 1967, 64, and January 27, 1967, 60, as well as *Los Angeles Times*, January 19, 20, 21, 22 1967. See also Kerr's version in *The Gold and the Blue*, vol. 2, chaps. 15 and 16. On the state of the public university today, see, e.g., David Hollinger, "Money and Academic Freedom a Half-Century After McCarthyism: Universities amid the Force Fields of Capital," in *Unfettered Expression: Freedom in American Intellectual Life*, ed. Peggie J. Hollingsworth (Ann Arbor: University of Michigan Press, 2000), 161–84; Eyal Press and Jennifer Washburn, "The Kept University," *Atlantic Monthly* (March 2000): 39–54; Peter Schrag, *Paradise Lost: California's Experience, America's Future* (New York: New Press, 1998), 87–93.

Chapter 4. John Kenneth Galbraith: Liberalism and the Politics of Cultural Critique

1. Michele Mitchell, *A New Kind of Party Animal: How the Young Are Tearing Up the American Political Landscape* (New York: Simon and Schuster, 1998), 34; Ann Coulter, *Treason: Liberal Treachery from the Cold War to the War on Terrorism* (New York: Crown Forum, 2003). For more on Mitchell and young pundits who are critical of liberalism, see Kevin Mattson, *Engaging Youth: Combating the Apathy of Young Americans Towards Politics* (New York: Century Foundation Press, 2003), chap. 4. On the tie between liberalism's sagging reputation and the punditocracy, see Eric Alterman, *Sound and Fury: The Making of the Punditocracy* (Ithaca, N.Y.: Cornell University Press, 1999), 123–4.

2. Arthur Schlesinger, Jr., *The Crisis of Confidence* (Boston: Houghton Mifflin, 1969), 125. Recently, liberals have been taken to task for their silence on civil rights; see Carol Polsgrove, *Divided Minds: Intellectuals and the Civil Rights Movement* (New York: W.W. Norton, 2001); David Chappell, "Niebuhrisms and Myrdaleries: The Intellectual Roots of the Civil Rights Movement Reconsidered," in *The Role of Ideas in the Civil Rights South*, ed. Ted Ownby (Jackson: University of Mississippi Press, 2002), 4; and Tony Badger, "Fatalism, Not Gradualism: Race and the Crisis of Southern Liberalism, 1945–1965," and Walter Jackson, "White Liberal Intellectuals, Civil

Rights, and Gradualism, 1954–1960," both in *The Making of Martin Luther King and the Civil Rights Movement,* ed. Brian Ward and Tony Badger (New York: New York University Press, 1996). Liberals' anticommunism has been pilloried in Frances Stonor Saunders, *The Cultural Cold War* (New York: New Press, 2000). For the New Left strain of thought more in line with liberalism, see my own *Intellectuals in Action* (University Park: Pennsylvania State Press, 2002).

3. Quotes can be found in Kevin Mattson, "Between Despair and Hope: Revisiting Studies on the Left," in *The New Left Revisited,* ed. John McMillian and Paul Buhle (Philadelphia: Temple University Press, 2003), 34. Martin Sklar has gone on to develop the "corporate liberalism" thesis in greater detail in his *The Corporate Reconstruction of American Capitalism, 1890–1916* (Cambridge: Cambridge University Press, 1988). Here he still sees corporate liberalism as a justification for corporate restructuring of the economy; see, e.g., 173.

4. Sklar and Weinstein quoted in Kevin Mattson, "Between Despair and Hope," 37; Rick Perlstein, *Before the Storm: Barry Goldwater and the Unmaking of the American Consensus* (New York: Hill and Wang, 2001); and Lisa McGirr, *Suburban Warriors: The Origins of the New American Right* (Princeton, N.J.: Princeton University Press, 2001).

5. For details on Galbraith's life, I rely upon John Kenneth Galbraith, *A Life in Our Times: Memoirs* (Boston: Houghton Mifflin, 1981). For more on his departure from OPA, see also Helen Sasson, ed., *Between Friends: Perspectives on John Kenneth Galbraith* (Boston: Houghton Mifflin, 1999), 33. Galbraith himself noted that he was a "public intellectual" in his interesting rejoinder to a critical review: see "Professor Gordon on 'The Close of the Galbraithian System,'" *Journal of Political Economy* 77 (1969): 494–95. As this article went to press, Richard Parker's comprehensive biography about Galbraith appeared: *John Kenneth Galbraith: His Life, His Politics, His Economics* (New York: Farrar, Straus, and Giroux, 2005). See also my review of this biography, *Wilson Quarterly* 29, 2 (Spring 2005): 126–27.

6. John Kenneth Galbraith to President Kennedy, February 2, 1961, memo in Galbraith Archives, John F. Kennedy Library, Boston, box 77; *Ambassador's Journal* (Boston: Houghton Mifflin, 1969), 23. For a fine description of "growth liberalism," see David Farber, *The Age of Great Dreams: America in the 1960s* (New York: Hill and Wang, 1994), 104–5; and Robert Collins, *More: The Politics of Economic Growth in Postwar America* (New York: Oxford University Press, 2000). This is not the right place to focus on Galbraith's views on foreign policy. But here too, Galbraith was not a typical Cold Warrior; he had a very nuanced appreciation of foreign policy (in part because he was ambassador to a country that tried to *stay out* of the Cold War). He opposed JFK's Bay of Pigs action and early involvement in Vietnam. He stressed economic aid, not military action, as a means to battle the Cold War.

7. Here I rely upon numerous works including Lawrence Goodwyn, *The Populist Moment* (New York: Oxford University Press, 1978); Bruce Palmer, *"Man over Money": The Southern Populist Critique of American Capitalism* (Chapel Hill: University of North Carolina Press, 1980); John L. Thomas, Alternative America: Henry George, Edward Bellamy, Henry Demarest Lloyd, and the Adversary Tradition (Cambridge, Mass.: Belknap Press, 1983); Nick Salvatore, *Eugene Debs: Citizen and Socialist* (Urbana: University of Illinois Press, 1982); Donald Miller, *The New American Radicalism: Alfred M. Bingham and Non-Marxian Insurgency in the New Deal Era* (Port Washington, N.Y.: Kennikat, 1979).

8. Thorstein Veblen, *The Engineers and the Price System* (New York: Viking, 1921), 30, 44.

9. Robert Westbrook, "Tribune of the Technostructure: The Popular Economics of Stuart Chase," *American Quarterly* 32 (1980): 397, 399; Max Lerner, *It Is Later Than You Think: The Need for a Militant Democracy* (New York: Viking, 1938), 243–44; Sanford

Lakoff, *Max Lerner: Pilgrim in the Promised Land* (Chicago: University of Chicago Press, 1998), 34 on the influence of Veblen and 99–100 for his views on democratic collectivism. For more on the radical influence on the New Deal, see Robert McElvaine, *The Great Depression* (New York: Times Books, 1984).

10. Max Lerner, "What Is Usable in Veblen?" (1935), reprinted in *Ideas Are Weapons: The History and Uses of Ideas* (New York: Viking, 1939), 129, 132.

11. Adolf A. Berle and Gardiner C. Means, *The Modern Corporation and Private Property* (New York: Commerce Clearing House, 1932), 4; Richard Pells, *Radical Visions and American Dreams: Culture and Social Thought in the Depression Years* (New York: HarperTorchbooks, 1973), 70; Berle and Means, *The Modern Corporation*, 353; Jordan Schwarz, *Liberal: Adolf Berle and the Vision of an American Era* (New York: Free Press, 1987), 78–79.

12. Alan Brinkley, "The New Deal and the Idea of the State," in *The Rise and Fall of the New Deal Order*, ed. Steve Fraser and Gary Gerstle (Princeton, N.J.: Princeton University Press, 1989), 109; John Morton Blum, *V Was for Victory: Politics and American Culture During World War II* (New York: Harcourt Brace Jovanovich, 1976), 327. See also Theodore Rosenof's remarks on the career of Gardiner Means in *Economics in the Long Run: New Deal Theorists and Their Legacies, 1933–1993* (Chapel Hill: University of North Carolina Press, 1997), 117.

13. Galbraith, "Keynesians in Washington," *Financial Times*, March 19, 1958, 7; "An Agenda for American Liberals," *Commentary*, June 1966, 29; *How Keynes Came to America* (Boston: Houghton Mifflin, 1965), 17; *The Affluent Society* (Boston: Houghton Mifflin, 1958), 96. *Time* magazine's announcement is mentioned in Allen Matusow, *The Unraveling of America: A History of Liberalism in the 1960s* (New York: Harper and Row, 1984), 57 (Matusow's chapter on Keynesianism is a very helpful guide to economic thought at this time).

14. Leon Keyserling, "Eggheads and Politics," *New Republic*, October 27, 1958, 15; "Galbraith and Schlesinger Reply to Leon Keyserling," *New Republic*, November 10, 1958, 14; on Keyserling, see W. Robert Brazelton, "Retrospectives: The Economics of Leon Hirsch Keyserling," *Journal of Economic Perspectives* 11 (1997): 189–97. It is interesting to note that Galbraith and Keyserling were friends, as can be seen in their correspondence in the Galbraith Archives.

15. Galbraith, *American Capitalism* (1952; New York: Houghton Mifflin, 1962), 7, and 33–36 on the natural process of centralization; *The Liberal Hour* (Boston: Houghton Mifflin, 1960), 131. On World War II's centralization of the economy, see Blum, *V Was for Victory*, 123.

16. Galbraith, *American Capitalism*, 95; Galbraith, *The New Industrial State* (Boston: Houghton Mifflin, 1967), 6; see also *The Affluent Society*, 131. For more on the earlier variation of this argument, see Galbraith, "The Unseemly Economics of Opulence," *Harper's*, January 1952, 58–63. Loren J. Okroi argues that Galbraith overestimates the power of corporations in determining people's choices: *Galbraith, Harrington, Heilbroner: Economics and Dissent in an Age of Optimism* (Princeton, N.J. : Princeton University Press, 1988), 87.

17. Galbraith, *The New Industrial State*, 59, 293. See 267 for the statistics that Galbraith cites on white collar growth. Galbraith already recognized the role of the new class in *The Affluent Society*, 261–64.

18. Galbraith, "Are Living Costs Out of Control?" *Atlantic Monthly*, February 1957, 38 (wage-price spiral); "Will Managed Capitalism Pull Us Through?" *Commentary*, August, 1951, 131; *A Theory of Price Control* (Cambridge, Mass.: Harvard University Press, 1952), 57, 42. On inflation, see also *American Capitalism*, 200–201 and *The Affluent Society*, 189.

19. Galbraith, *The Affluent Society*, 314; *Ambassador's Journal*, 42, 381. Galbraith to

Kennedy, March 25, 1961, reprinted in *Letters to Kennedy*, ed. James Goodman (Cambridge, Mass.: Harvard University Press, 1998), 39; Galbraith to Kennedy, January 29, 1963, Galbraith Archives, box 76; *Letters to Kennedy*, 42; Galbraith in memo to Attorney General Kennedy, June 11, 1963, found in Arthur Schlesinger Archives (John F. Kennedy Library, Boston), box WH-11. For the setting of Kennedy's tax cut, see Matusow, *The Unraveling of America*, chap. 2.

20. Galbraith, *The Affluent Society*, 229; "The Strategy of Limited Control," *Fortune*, March 1951, 66–67; *The Great Crash, 1929* (Boston: Houghton-Mifflin, 1955), 194; "Some Unfinished Business for Liberals," *New Republic*, February 9, 1957, 7; *Letters to Kennedy*, 42. Galbraith was also, early on, favorable about the public works programs of the New Deal: John Kenneth Galbraith and G. G. Johnson, *The Economic Effects of the Federal Public Works Expenditure 1933–1938* (Washington, D.C.: Government Printing Office, 1940). On Reuther's political vision, see Nelson Lichtenstein, *The Most Dangerous Man in Detroit: Walter Reuther and the Fate of American Labor* (New York: Basic Books, 1995), 155 and Kevin Boyle, *The UAW and the Heyday of American Liberalism* (Ithaca, N.Y.: Cornell University Press, 1995).

21. Galbraith, *The Affluent Society*, 253, 256–57.

22. Galbraith, *The Affluent Society*, 80; *The Liberal Hour*, 10–11. For Galbraith's support of the Peace Corps, see Elizabeth Cobbs Hoffman, *All You Need Is Love: The Peace Corps and the Spirit of the 1960s* (Cambridge, Mass.: Harvard University Press, 1998), 190.

23. Galbraith, "Let Us Begin: An Invitation to Action on Poverty," *Harper's*, March, 1964, 18; "An Agenda for American Liberals," 29. For more on civic liberalism, see Mickey Kaus, *The End of Equality* (New York: Basic Books, 1992).

24. Galbraith, "How Much Should a Country Consume?" in *Perspectives on Conservation: Essays on America's Natural Resources*, ed. Henry Jarrett (Baltimore: Johns Hopkins University Press, 1958), 96.

25. Frederick Siegel, *Troubled Journey: From Pearl Harbor to Ronald Reagan* (New York: Hill and Wang, 1984), 115; Richard Pells, *The Liberal Mind in a Conservative Age* (Middletown, Conn.: Wesleyan University Press, 1989), 223; Paul Gorman, *Left Intellectuals and Popular Culture in Twentieth Century America* (Chapel Hill: University of North Carolina Press, 1996), 138; Andrew Ross, *No Respect: Intellectuals and Popular Culture* (New York: Routledge, 1989), 227; Stephen Holmes, *The Anatomy of Antiliberalism* (Cambridge, Mass.: Harvard University Press, 1993), 260.

26. Galbraith, "Let Us Begin," 23, 24, 16; "Galbraith Answers Crosland," *New Statesman*, January 22, 1971, 101. See also Galbraith, "The Starvation of the Cities" (1966), reprinted in *A View from the Stands: Of People, Politics, Military Power, and the Arts*, ed. Andrea D. Williams (Boston: Houghton Mifflin, 1986).

27. Galbraith, *The New Industrial State*, 348; "For Public and Potent Building," *New York Times Magazine*, October 9, 1960, 34, 64, 68, 70; *Liberal Hour*, 11. For the arts and crafts movement, see Eileen Boris, *Art and Labor: Ruskin, Morris, and the Craftsman Ideal in America* (Philadelphia: Temple University Press, 1986); and on the Young Americans, Casey Blake, *Beloved Community: The Cultural Criticism of Randolph Bourne, Van Wyck Brooks, Waldo Frank, and Lewis Mumford* (Chapel Hill: University of North Carolina Press, 1990).

28. John McDermott quoted in Kevin Mattson, *Intellectuals in Action: The Origins of the New Left and Radical Liberalism, 1945–1970* (University Park: Pennsylvania State Press, 2002), 131. On Schlesinger's "qualitative liberalism," see Stephen Depoe, *Arthur M. Schlesinger, Jr. and the Ideological History of American Liberalism* (Tuscaloosa: University of Alabama Press, 1994), 40; and Carrol Englehardt, "Man in the Middle: Arthur M. Schlesinger, Jr. and Postwar American Liberalism," *South Atlantic Quarterly* 80 (1981): 133. See also Kevin Mattson, *When America Was Great: The Fighting Faith of Postwar Liberalism* (New York: Routledge, 2004).

29. Galbraith, *The Great Crash*, 31, 171; "Let Us Begin," 18. See also Galbraith, "The Big Defense Firms Are Really Public Firms and Should be Nationalized," *New York Times Magazine*, November 16, 1969, 162.

30. Galbraith, *The Great Crash*, 159. To a certain extent, this was the predicament that Lionel Trilling recognized in his classic work *The Liberal Imagination* (Garden City, N.Y.: Anchor Books, 1950).

31. Adlai Stevenson quoted in Jean Baker, *The Stevensons: A Biography of an American Family* (New York: W.W. Norton, 1996), 363; Galbraith, *The Affluent Society*, 324–27; Michael Harrington, *The Other America: Poverty in the United States* (1962; Baltimore: Penguin, 1969), 12. See also Maurice Isserman, *The Other American: The Life of Michael Harrington* (New York: Public Affairs, 2000), chap. 7.

32. Galbraith, "Some Reflections on Public Buildings and Public Works" (undated), Galbraith Archives, box 102; see also Galbraith's recognition of the subjective dimension of aesthetic discussion, see the comments made in "For Public and Potent Building," 70.

33. Galbraith, *American Capitalism*, 112.

34. Galbraith, *American Capitalism*, 113, 115.

35. Galbraith, *The Affluent Society*, 279; *The New Industrial State*, 293. For more on Galbraith's relation to new class theory, see Okroi, *Galbraith, Harrington, Heilbroner*, 88–94. For Mills's critique, see "A Marx for the Managers," reprinted in *Power Politics and People: The Collected Essays of C. Wright Mills*, ed. Irving Louis Horowitz (New York: Oxford University Press, 1963).

36. Howard Brick, "Talcott Parsons's 'Shift Away from Economics,' 1937–1946," *Journal of American History* 87 (2000): 511. On new class politics, we would seem better off embracing Alvin Gouldner's argument that the new class was both "emancipatory and elitist." See his *The Future of the Intellectuals and the Rise of the New Class* (New York: Seabury, 1979), 84. At the least, the new class, like any other class, is contradictory.

37. Galbraith, *A View from the Stands: Of People, Politics, Military Power, and the Arts* (Boston: Houghton Mifflin, 1986), 24. To a certain extent the new urbanist school of design has recognized this. See, for instance, the work of James Howard Kunstler and others.

38. Galbraith, *Economics and Public Controversy* (New Brunswick, N.J.: Rutgers University Press, 1955), 81.

Chapter 5. The Prophet of Post-Fordism: Peter Drucker and the Legitimation of the Corporation

Epigraph: Peter F. Drucker, "The Way to Industrial Peace," *Harper's Magazine* 193, 1146 (November 1946): 386.

1. "But Can You Teach It?" *Economist*, May 20, 2004. Prior to World War II, business schools had not concerned themselves with *management* per se, but rather with techniques for specific operational areas such as accounting, salesmanship, advertising, factory organization, or industrial engineering. That the 1950s were the key decade for the professionalization and intellectualization of "management" finds further support in the establishment date of several important journals of management scholarship: *Management Science* (1954), *Administrative Science Quarterly* (1957) and *Academy of Management Journal* (1958).

Although this essay periodizes the emergence of "management" to the postwar period, World War I was also an important watershed. The success of the War

Industries Board, under the leadership of banker Bernard Baruch, in organizing American industrial production for wartime purposes generated awareness of the power of organization to increase industrial production. The decade after the Great War saw the first sprouts of professionalized interest in something called "management." *Management Review* was founded in 1918, and consultancies such as Arthur D. Little and McKinsey and Company began to offer advice on organization and management as one of their services. Both of these organizations, which had experienced linear growth through the 1920s, '30s, and '40s, experienced exponential growth starting in the late 1940s. For a history of McKinsey see Elizabeth H. Edersheim, *McKinsey's Marvin Bower: Vision, Leadership, and the Creation of Management Consulting* (New York: John Wiley, 2004); for a more skeptical view, see Nicholas Lemann, "The Kids in the Conference Room," *New Yorker,* October 18, 1999.

2. Despite the vast sums being spent on "management education," a persistent chorus continues to doubt whether managerial ability can be defined in terms of generic skills or analytical abilities, as opposed to situated knowledge. McGill business school professor Henry Mintzberg has been a particular gadfly of management education, arguing that the most important dimension of management is "leadership," and that leadership is unlearnable in a classroom. See Mintzberg, *Managers Not MBAs: A Hard Look at the Soft Practice of Managing and Management Development* (San Francisco: Berrett-Koehler, 2004).

3. John Micklethwait and Adrian Wooldridge, *The Witch Doctors: Making Sense of the Management Gurus* (New York: Random House, 1996), 63.

4. In December 2002 CNBC ran a documentary on Drucker: *Peter F. Drucker: An Intellectual Journey.* Although the film suffers from its lack of any critical distance from its subject, director Ken Witty is quite right to suggest that Drucker "brings a communitarian philosophy to his consulting. . . . He said that what he's all about is this search for community, the search for where people and organizations find community for noneconomic satisfaction" (http://www.businessweek.com/bwdaily/dnflash/dec2002/nf20021224_6814.htm).

5. John E. Flaherty, *Peter F. Drucker: Shaping the Managerial Mind* (San Francisco: Jossey-Bass, 1999), 2.

6. Mark Skousen, "The Other Austrian," *Forecasts and Strategies* (January 29, 2000).

7. Newt Gingrich, "When Peter F. Drucker Speaks," *Inc. Magazine* (March 1998).

8. Flaherty, *Peter F. Drucker*, 3.

9. Although Drucker receives enormous amounts of fawning attention from business writers, and while business historians dutifully cite his large oeuvre, there have been few systematic efforts to understand Drucker historically. Journalist Jack Beatty's hagiography, *The World According to Peter F. Drucker* (New York: Free Press, 1998), traces the origins of Drucker's ideas to the interwar Austrian economists Drucker had known as a child and young man. Other biographies include John J. Tarrant, *Peter F. Drucker: The Man Who Invented Corporate Society* (Boston: Cahner's Books, 1976) and Flaherty, *Peter F. Drucker.* Useful chapters on Drucker appear in Andrea Gabor, *The Capitalist Philosophers: The Geniuses of Modern Business—Their Lives, Times, and Ideas* (New York: Three Rivers Press, 2000); and James Hoopes, *False Prophets: The Gurus Who Created Modern Management and Why Their Ideas Are Bad for Business* (Cambridge, Mass.: Perseus, 2003). Although this essay will argue that Drucker deserves more attention from historians, this is not to affirm his Rodney-Dangerfield-esque attitude toward the academy.

10. Drucker, *The Future of Industrial Man* (1942; New Brunswick, N.J.: Transaction Publishers, 1995), 23 (Hereafter *FIM*).

11. As Drucker explained to his Japanese translator, "Because my starting point was not business and not management but the collapse of Western society and

Western civilization in the First World War, the twenties and the thirties, I have seen management and the business enterprises as much as social, and indeed, as spiritual phenomena as I have seen them economic phenomena. Yes, the purpose of a business is to create a customer, to produce wealth, to generate jobs. But it can do this only if it creates a community, if it gives the individual meaning, status and function, if, in other words, it is as much a social, as an economic organ" (http://www.iot.ac.jp/manu/ueda/interview/e08.html).

12. In 1936 he would publish a pamphlet pleading for religious tolerance, *Die Judenfrage in Deutschland.*

13. Available in translation at http://www.peterdrucker.at/en/texts/p_drucker_stahl_en.pdf. The essay was published by J. C. B. Mohr.

14. John Toews, "The Immanent Genesis and Transcendent Goal of Law: Savigny, Stahl, and the Ideology of the Christian German State," *American Journal of Comparative Law* 37, 1 (1989): 139–69. Toews emphasizes the centrality of "personality" to Stahl's theories, a term that also recurs repeatedly in Drucker's work. Two collections of Stahl's essays have appeared in English: *The Present-Day Parties of the Church and State* (State College, Pa.: Blenheim Publishing House, 1976) and *What Is the Revolution?* (State College, Pa.: Blenheim Publishing House, 1977).

15. Drucker, *Adventures of a Bystander* (New York: Wiley, 1977), 161.

16. According to Drucker's epilogue to *The Ecological Vision: Reflections on the American Condition* (New Brunswick, N.J.: Transaction Books, 1992), the Stahl essay was originally conceived as part of a large work of political theory which was to have had three chapters, one on Stahl, a second on Wilhelm von Humboldt, and a third on Joseph von Radowitz. These three thinkers attracted Drucker because they all had sought a balance between continuity (political conservatism) and change (a requirement of capitalism).

17. Drucker, *The End of Economic Man* (1938; New Brunswick, N.J.: Transaction Publishers, 1994), 55 (Hereafter *EEM*).

18. Drucker, "Unfashionable Kierkegaard" (1949), reprinted in *The Ecological Vision: Reflections on the American Condition* (New Brunswick, N.J.: Transaction Publishers, 1993).

19. Drucker, "Unfashionable Kierkegaard," 435.

20. *EEM*, 86.

21. *EEM*, 67.

22. Drucker, *Adventures of a Bystander*, 302.

23. *FIM*, 28.

24. *FIM*, 115.

25. *FIM*, 60. Drucker's vision aligns seamlessly with the Calvinist view of a person's spiritual (and thus social) identity as divinable from the work they do. His understanding of employment harkened the etymological derivation of the word from the Latin *implicare*, "to fold into something" or "to make part of something." For Drucker, employment was what integrated a person into society. The disaster of unemployment was thus that it deprived the worker not just of his income but of his social identity. In emphasizing that full employment was the most important requirement for achieving social stability, Drucker was in the mainstream of economic thinking during the1940s. The specter of a return to the mass unemployment of the Great Depression hung over Drucker's work, as it did so much contemporary writing.

26. *FIM*, 75.

27. *FIM*, 64.

28. A point underscored emphatically in Peter F. Drucker, *Concept of the Corporation* (1946; New Brunswick, N.J.: Transaction Publishers, 1993), 16 (Hereafter *CC*).

29. *FIM*, 95

30. Reviewers of *The Future of Industrial Man* argued that Drucker set himself up directly against "the public control of competing interests within a framework of democratically defined general good." These critics expressed the dominant liberal temper when they asserted that such public control was "a safer and more practical road to social harmony." Tagging Drucker as a modern-day George Fitzhugh, some criticized Drucker for promoting a philosophy "pre-industrial in spirit, vague in describing actual controls, and optimistic in assuming the motives which are to secure harmony." Arnaud B. Leavelle and Thomas I. Cook, "George Fitzhugh and the Theory of American Conservatism," *Journal of Politics* 7, 2 (1945): 165.

31. "State-ownership or state-management of industry would in no way result in a realization of equal opportunities or of self-fulfillment for worker or foreman," Drucker would explain in *Concept*. "The problems to be solved are not problems of ownership or of political control. They are problems of the social organization of modern technology" (*CC*, 204).

32. George Cotkin, *Existential America* (Baltimore: Johns Hopkins University Press, 2003) argues that the characteristic American take on existentialism was to use the focus on anguish and uncertainty as a spur to action and commitment. At the same time, Cotkin for the most part reads Kierkegaard out of his narrative, claiming that reading Kierkegaard "led to passivity and conservatism" (87) For Cotkin, Drucker's essay on Kierkegaard fits this pattern, painting a picture of life as consisting of "rules and regulations, a holding pattern maintained until death lifted the individual into the realm of the infinite" (61). But this is not quite right. If Drucker rejected optimism, his engagement with worldly pursuits also led him to reject the fatalism and quietism so conspicuous in many Kierkegaardians; resigning himself to "imagining Sisyphus happy" would never do for Drucker. Considering Drucker's comments on Kierkegaard in light of his wider oeuvre on management makes it clear that Drucker fits nicely into Cotkin's larger interpretation about the action-oriented nature of American existentialism, while undermining Cotkin's argument that Kierkegaard's influence was exclusively morbid.

33. For a more detailed account of Drucker's time at GM, see Hoopes, *False Prophets*, 242–48.

34. *CC*, 11.

35. Alfred Sloan saw no reason why he should concern himself with things like education, health care, or politics—much less "social integration." GM's business, as Sloan saw it, was building and selling cars. Drucker reports that for years *Concept* was treated at GM as a "nonbook." Drucker inaccurately claims that Sloan's own account of his tenure at GM, *My Years with General Motors* (1964; New York: Currency, 1996), was written as a "refutation" of *Concept*.

36. *CC*, 1.

37. *CC*, 14.

38. *CC*, 22.

39. *FIM*, 79.

40. Two helpful books on Taylor include Daniel Nelson, *Frederick W. Taylor and the Rise of Scientific Management* (Madison: University of Wisconsin Press, 1980) and Robert Kanigel, *The One Best Way: Frederick Winslow Taylor and the Enigma of Efficiency* (New York: Viking, 1997).

41. Drucker, "Henry Ford: Success and Failure," *Harper's* 195, 1166 (October 1947): 1–8.

42. Quoted in Scott Heller, "Taking Taylor's Measure: Book Weighs Cultural Impact of Efficiency Expert's Ideas," *Chronicle of Higher Education*, July 21, 1993, A8. Drucker's characteristic modesty was on display when he noted that those who attacked Taylor "as making no more sense that those who belittle Newton because he

did not anticipate quantum mechanics"—a comparison which suggests that Drucker considers himself the Einstein (or perhaps Heisenberg) of management (quote in Tarrant, *Peter F. Drucker*, 17).

43. Quoted in Hoopes, *False Prophets*, 253.

44. *FIM*, 102.

45. *FIM*, 79.

46. *FIM*, 84.

47. *FIM*, 85.

48. Drucker would continue after the war in the same vein: "The unthinking use of the human being as if he were a machine tool designed for one purpose only . . . is a gross abuse, or misuse, of that wonderful multipurpose tool, the human being. . . . Traditional mass production—as in the Ford assembly line . . . is simply a piece of poor engineering judged by the standards of human relations, as well as by those of productive efficiency and output" ("The Way to Industrial Peace," 189–90).

49. *CC*, 21–22. Drucker reiterated this point: "To understand that the modern large corporation is the representative institution of our society; that it is above all an institution, that is, a human organization and not just a complex of inanimate machines; that it is based upon a concept of order rather than upon gadgets; and that all of us as consumers, as workers, as savers, and as citizens have an equal stake in its prosperity, these are important lessons we have to learn" (201).

50. *CC*, 192.

51. Drucker's holistic view "personality" explains his hostility toward psychological testing for determining managerial aptitude: "Such tests never measure the important thing, the integration of specific traits and skills into a personality" (CC 181).

52. Drucker, *The New Society: Anatomy of an Industrial Order* (1950; New Brunswick, N.J.: Transaction Publishers, 2002), 173. Hereafter *NS*.

53. *FIM*, 203, 205–6.

54. *CC*, 198–99.

55. Drucker made a number of other policy suggestions (*CC*, 284–88). Arguing that the state's main economic policy objective should be to guarantee full employment, he recommended that businesses be allowed to set up tax-exempt "employment funds" to offset losses or for employment-creating capital investments. He also recommended policies to protect farmers, antitrust action, and environmental protection. Generally, however, Drucker advocated a "small government" philosophy. The government's main intellectual task was to determine "those spheres in which the survival interest of society demands political rather individual economic action" and to pursue vigorous policies in those areas.

56. "The Way to Industrial Peace," 514.

57. *CC*, 208.

58. *NS*, 276

59. "The Way to Industrial Peace," 519.

60. *NS*, 283.

61. James Burnham, *The Managerial Revolution: What Is Happening in the World* (New York: John Day, 1941).

62. Virtually all extended writing on Burnham has been celebratory, including the recent Samuel Francis, *James Burnham* (London: Claridge Press, 1999), which paints Burnham as a "paleoconservative"; and Daniel Kelly, *James Burnham and the Struggle for the World* (Wilmington, Del.: ISI Press, 2002), which depicts him as a "proto-neoconservative." Useful shorter overviews include Francis P. Sempa, "The First Cold Warrior," *American Diplomacy* 5, 4 (2000) and John Patrick Diggins, *Up from Communism: Conservative Odysseys in American Intellectual History* (New York: Harper and Row, 1975).

63. *CC*, 9.

64. George Orwell, "James Burnham and the Managerial Revolution," *New English Weekly*, May 1946, http://www.unc.edu/depts/diplomat/AD_issues/amdipl_17/articles/sempa_burnham1.html.

65. Ironically, Burnham's amoral view of management would echo in the work of postwar liberals like Clark Kerr, who also argued that modern society was destined to be ruled by managers, and that Communism and liberal capitalism were converging on a single set of managerial and administrative practices that would attenuate Cold War tensions. For details on the convergence hypothesis, see David Engerman's paper in this volume, as well as the conclusion to chapter 3 of my *Mandarins of the Future: Modernization Theory and Cold War America* (Baltimore: Johns Hopkins University Press, 2003).

66. *CC*, 187.

67. *CC*, 190.

68. *CC*, 157.

69. "The Way to Industrial Peace," 513. Drucker's desire for an appointment at Harvard may also have contributed to soft-pedaling his criticism of Mayo. Even the criticism as it stood was apparently too much for Mayo, however. When Drucker gave a kind keynote address at Mayo's retirement in 1947, Mayo responded by literally thumbing his nose at Drucker, "pretending that he intended the rude gesture only as an example of worker's attitude toward top-down management" (Hoopes, *False Prophets*, 252).

70. In this sense, Drucker's most obvious intellectual antecedent is Mary Parker Follett. As Andrea Gabor observes, "While Mayo and Company thought it was important to make workers *feel* important, Follett was one of the first theorists who thought they *were* important" (*Capitalist Philosophers*, 59). In the introduction to a recent collection of Follett's essays, Drucker says that he did not discover Follett until the early 1950s, though he duly credits her with having prefigured several of his ideas. Pauline Graham, ed., *Mary Parker Follett: Prophet of Management*, intro. Peter F. Drucker (Cambridge, Mass.: Harvard Business School Press, 1995).

71. *CC*, 178.

72. *CC*, 206.

73. This logic would lead Drucker at the end of life to advocate that companies "should outsource everything for which there is no career track that could lead into senior management" (interview by Brent Schlender, "Peter Drucker Sets Us Straight," *Fortune*, January 19, 2004). In other words, outsource everything that is not immediately relevant to the central objectives of the organization. Such is in fact the corporate policy of many organizations operating in the high end of the service sector today: receptionists, cleaners, food services, physical plant, information technology, and many "human resources" functions are contracted from outside firms—firms that may (or may not) pursue similar policies.

74. Corporate America understood its need for greater managerial talent. But the response would not be to promote more from the ranks. Rather, it would be to professionalize management—hence the fantastic growth of business education, especially graduate business education, as catalogued in the opening paragraph of this chapter. But if corporate America eschewed Drucker's recommendations about promoting from the ranks, it would embrace his ideas about generalizing the managerial mentality in its employees.

75. Hoopes, *False Prophets*, 254.

76. *CC*, 207.

77. "The Way to Industrial Peace," 514.

78. Tarrant, *Peter F. Drucker*, 57.

79. See, for example, Peter F. Drucker, "Managing Oneself," *Harvard Business Review* 77, 2 (1999): 64–74; Peter F. Drucker, "Managing Knowledge Means Managing Oneself," *Leader to Leader* 16 (Spring 2000): 8–10.

80. *NS*, 267–68.

81. Drucker, "The Development of a Theory of Democratic Administration: Replies and Comments," *American Political Science Review* 46, 2 (1952): 499–500. The critic was Ralph Waldo.

82. Drucker went on to claim that the U.S. Constitution was the "first and so far practically alone among written constitutions, contains explicit provisions how to be changed. This probably explains more than anything else why, alone of all written constitutions, the American Constitution is still in force and a living document. Even less did they realize the importance of the Supreme Court as the institution which basically represents both conservation and continuity, and innovation and change and balances the two" (*The Ecological Vision*), 444.

83. Republished in *The Ecological Mind* (1993).

84. In Richard Hofstadter, *The American Political Tradition and the Men Who Made It* (New York: Knopf, 1948).

85. The definitive concession appears in Peter F. Drucker, "Civilizing the City," *Leader to Leader* 7 (Winter 1998), http://pfdf.org/leaderbooks/121/winter98/drucker.html

86. Drucker, *The Practice of Management* (New York: Harper and Row, 1954).

87. Ronald G. Greenwood, "Management by Objectives: As Developed by Peter F. Drucker, Assisted by Harold Smiddy," *Academy of Management Review* 6, 2 (1981): 225–30.

88. *NS*, 310–11.

89. Quoted in Steven Vallas, "Rethinking Post-Fordism: The Meaning of Workplace Flexibility," *Sociological Theory* 17, 1 (1999): 68.

Chapter 6. C. Wright Mills and American Social Science

1. Dan Wakefield, "Taking it Big: A Memoir of C. Wright Mills," *Atlantic Monthly*, September 1971, 65.

2. Jim Miller, "Democracy and the Intellectual: C. Wright Mills Reconsidered," *Salmagundi* 70–71 (1986): 83, 85.

3. Howard Brick, "The Reformist Dimension of Talcott Parsons' Early Social Theory," in *The Culture of the Market: Historical Essays*, ed. Thomas L. Haskell and Richard F. Teichgraeber, III (New York: Cambridge University Press, 1993), 357–95; Howard Brick, "Talcott Parsons' 'Shift Away From Economics,' 1937–1946," *Journal of American History* 87 (September 2000): 490–514; David A. Hollinger, "The Defense of Democracy and Robert K. Merton's Formulation of the Scientific Ethos," in *Science, Jews, and Secular Culture: Studies in Mid-Twentieth-Century American Intellectual History* (Princeton, N.J.: Princeton University Press, 1996), 80–96.

4. Howard Brick, "The Postcapitalist Vision in Twentieth-Century American Social Thought," this volume.

5. C. Wright Mills, "Reflection, Behavior, and Culture" (MA thesis, University of Texas, 1939). On the general influence of pragmatism on Mills, see Rick Tilman, *C. Wright Mills: A Native Radical and His American Intellectual Roots* (University Park: Pennsylvania State Press, 1984); Cornel West, *The American Evasion of Philosophy: A Genealogy of Pragmatism* (Madison: University of Wisconsin Press, 1989), 124–38. One account that does explore Mills's pragmatist approach to social scientific methodology is Robert Paul Jones, "The Fixing of Social Belief: The Sociology of C. Wright Mills" (Ph.D. dissertation, University of Missouri, 1977).

6. Thus, Mills was more attracted to the methodological reflections of practicing social scientists, such as that provided in the introduction to the classic work of Chicago School sociology, William I. Thomas and Florian Znaniecki *The Polish Peasant in Europe and America* (New York: Knopf, 1927). As Mills wrote, "I do believe . . . that the ninety-page 'Methodological Note' to the research job of Thomas and Znaniecki is concretely and directively worth more to the sociologists than any thousand pages of Dewey's writing; for it arose out of a set of researches under way, and the formulations and canons it contains have gone back in advisory capacity, into a dozen further researches" ("Reflection, Behavior, and Culture," 76).

7. Robert A. Bannister, *Sociology and Scientism: The American Quest for Objectivity, 1880–1940* (Chapel Hill: University of North Carolina Press, 1987), 188–238; Henrika Kuklick, "'A Scientific Revolution': Sociological Theory in the United States, 1930–1945," *Sociological Inquiry* 43: 3–22. Kuklick's argument that sociology underwent a Kuhnian "paradigm shift" in the late 1930 not only places the shift toward functionalist predominance too early, it illustrates the perils of applying a theory drawn from the study of physical science to the social sciences, where a tight disciplinary consensus is far more difficult to achieve.

8. Mills, "The Language and Ideas of Ancient China," unpublished graduate paper, 1940, reprinted in *Power, Politics, and People: The Collected Essays of C. Wright Mills*, ed. Irving Louis Horowitz (New York: Oxford University Press, 1963), 463.

9. Talcott Parsons, *The Structure of Social Action* (New York: Free Press, 1937). The quote is from Charles Camic, "Structure After 50 Years: The Anatomy of a Charter," *American Journal of Sociology* 95, 1 (July 1989): 44.

10. This quote comes from Mills's unpublished review of George Lundberg's *Foundations of Sociology* (1940), "Sociological Methods and Philosophies of Science," Charles Wright Mills Papers, Center for American History, University of Texas (henceforth UT), box 4B 362. Mills claimed that this piece was plagiarized by Becker. Becker published a review of the same book in the July 1941 *Journal of Social Philosophy* that shared many arguments with Mills's piece. That Becker was perhaps willing to steal Mills's ideas suggests that the two rejected Lundberg's positivism for similar reasons.

11. Howard Brick, "Society," in *Encyclopedia of the United States in the Twentieth Century*, vol. 2, ed. Stanley Kutler, Robert Dallek, David Hollinger, and Thomas McGraw (New York: Scribner's, 1996), 917–39.

12. David Kettler and Volker Meja, *Karl Mannheim and the Crisis of Liberalism* (New Brunswick, N.J.: Transaction Publishers, 1995), 193–245.

13. Karl Mannheim, *Ideology and Utopia*, trans. Louis Wirth and Edward Shils (New York: Harcourt Brace, 1936), 80.

14. For example, Parsons endorsed von Schelting's position and stressed it as a necessary corrective to a possible American adoption of Mannheim's ideas on pragmatist principles. See Talcott Parsons, review of Alexander von Schelting, *Max Webers Wissensoziologie*, *American Sociological Review* 1, 4 (August 1936): 681–82.

15. Mills to Merton, November 12, 1940, UT, box 4B 339.

16. Mills, "The Methodological Consequences of the Sociology of Knowledge," *American Journal of Sociology* 46, 3 (November 1940): 319.

17. "The Methodological Consequences," 318.

18. Merton to Mills, April 16, 1940, UT, box 4B 339. For Merton's interpretation of Mannheim see Robert Merton, "The Sociology of Knowledge," *Isis* (November 1937): 493–503; "Karl Mannheim's Sociology of Knowledge," *Journal of Liberal Religion* (Winter 1941): 425–47.

19. Merton to Mills, November 6, 1940, UT, box 4B 339.

20. Mills, "Methodological Consequences," 330.

21. Alvin Gouldner, *The Coming Crisis of Western Sociology* (New York: Basic Books, 1970), 481–512, esp. 499; Pierre Bourdieu and Loic J. D. Wacquant, *Invitation to Reflexive Sociology* (Chicago: University of Chicago Press, 1992). Bourdieu's reflexive sociology differs from that of Gouldner in important respects. While Gouldner focuses his attention on the moral responsibilities of the individual social scientist, Bourdieu undertakes a more expansive exploration of the ways in which the basic presuppositions of social science, in objectifying the social world, structures its conclusions. Mills's stress on the moral and political responsibility of the sociologist approximates Gouldner's position, but his call for the "detailed self-location of social science" in "Methodological Consequences," though not fully developed, anticipates Bourdieu in certain respects.

22. Mills, "The Professional Ideology of Social Pathologists," *American Journal of Sociology* 49, 2 (September 1943): 179.

23. Mills, "The Professional Ideology," 168–69.

24. Merton to Mills, April 5, 1941, UT, box 4B 339.

25. Merton to Kingsley Davis, December 4, 1944, letter in author's possession.

26. Andrew Jewett, "Retrenchment for Progress: Robert K. Merton's Early Sociology of Science," paper for conference, Capitalism and Its Culture, University of California, Santa Barbara, March 1, 2003.

27. Mills, "The Professional Ideology," 166.

28. Robert Merton, *Social Theory and Social Structure* (Glencoe, Ill.: Free Press, 1949).

29. Hans Gerth, "'As in the book of fairy tales: all alone . . . ' (a conversation with Jeffrey Herf)," in Gerth, *Politics, Character, and Culture: Perspectives from Hans Gerth*, ed. Joseph Bensman, Arthur J. Vidich, and Nobuko Gerth (Westport, Conn.: Greenwood, 1982), 14–49; and Bensman, "Hans Gerth's Contribution to American Sociology," 221–74.

30. "Guggenheim Application," in C. Wright Mills, *Letters and Autobiographical Writings*, ed. Kathryn Mills with Pamela Mills (Berkeley: University of California Press, 2000), 79.

31. Hans Gerth and C. Wright Mills, *Character and Social Structure: The Psychology of Social Institutions* (New York: Harcourt, Brace, 1953).

32. "Emendation and Augmentation of Outlining Done in Madison by Gerth & Mills, August 18–19, 1941," UT, box 4B 339.

33. "Preface" (written August 1942, revised October 1943), UT, box 4B 339.

34. The chapter of *The Sociological Imagination* in which Mills criticized Parsonian "Grand Theory" was originally written as an (unpublished) book review of Parsons's *The Social System* (1951) for the *New York Times*. Thus, in describing Parsons's work, Mills was dealing with his most abstruse and abstract book, which even many students of Parsons admitted did not render concepts useful for actual social research. See Review of Talcott Parsons, *The Social System*, UT, box 4B 389. It is also worth noting that Parsons misunderstood Mills's *The Power Elite* in his "The Distribution of Power in American Society," in *Structure and Process in Modern Societies* (New York: Free Press, 1960.) Parsons claimed that Mills held a zero-sum notion of power as exploitation and failed to grasp that power could serve a positive function as a "resource" for solving the problems of society. In fact, Mills did believe that power should be exercised collectively and rationally as a social resource (drawing on older Progressive ideas of "social control"), and Mills condemned the power elite not only for their hoarding of power, but for their irresponsible use of it.

35. The question of credit for *From Max Weber* remains controversial, since Gerth later protested that Mills claimed an unfair share of intellectual credit for the work.

The preface stated that Gerth was responsible for the selections and the translations from German and Mills was responsible for the formulation of the English text, while the book as a whole represented their "mutual work." This explanation left open the question of credit for the introductory essay. Clearly, Gerth had developed the general outlines of the interpretation put forth. But Mills certainly believed that he deserved some credit for the introduction, and a careful reading of the correspondence indicates that Mills made important suggestions (such as adding more about the Marx/Weber comparison). In addition, Mills was more aware than Gerth of the implications their interpretation of Weber held for American social scientists. The controversy over credit for this work (as well as for *Character and Social Structure*) has recently been taken up in Guy Oakes and Arthur J. Vidich, *Colloboration, Reputation, and Ethics in American Life: Hans H. Gerth and C. Wright Mills* (Urbana: University of Illinois Press, 1999). However, rather than clarifying the issue, this book merely feeds the flames of controversy. Despite their tone of objectivity, the authors (one of whom was a student of Gerth's and fails to mention this fact) are intent on making an unsustainable case that Mills was an intellectual fraud who shamelessly took credit for Gerth's work. In his review of this work, "False Indignation," *New Left Review* 2 (March/April 2000): 154–59, Russell Jacoby convincingly reveals Oakes and Vidich's perspective to be biased and offers a persuasive judgment that Mills acted in a "reasonable, if not saintly, manner" in his dealings with Gerth regarding credit for their joint work.

36. Talcott Parsons, "Max Weber and the Contemporary Political Crisis," *Review of Politics* 4 (1941): 61–76, 155–72 ; "Some Sociological Aspects of the Fascist Movements," *Social Forces* 21 (1942): 138–47. Parsons's attention to the particular historical situation in Germany made this work less vulnerable to the charge that Mills would later levy against him: that his generalized theoretical analysis was too abstract to be of use in understanding concrete historical developments.

37. See Ellen Herman, *The Romance of American Psychology: Political Culture in the Age of Experts, 1940–1970* (Berkeley: University of California Press, 1995), 17–81.

38. Mills to Gerth, n.d. (June or July 1944), copy of letter in author's possession.

39. See Ron Robin, *The Making of the Cold War Enemy: Culture and Politics in the Military-Industrial Complex* (Princeton, N.J.: Princeton University Press, 2001).

40. Mills to Macdonald, *Letters and Autobiographical Writings*, 53.

41. See, for instance, Talcott Parsons, "Introduction," to Max Weber, *The Theory of Social and Economic Organization*, trans. A. M. Henderson and Talcott Parsons, ed. Talcott Parsons (New York: Oxford University Press, 1947).

42. Hans Gerth and C. Wright Mills, "Introduction" to Max Weber, *From Max Weber: Essays in Sociology*, ed. Gerth and Mills (New York: Oxford University Press, 1946), 47.

43. Gerth and Mills, "Introduction," 65.

44. The conflict between Mills and Lazarsfeld is portrayed as virtually inevitable in Richard Gillam, "C. Wright Mills: An Intellectual Biography, 1916–1948" (Ph.D. dissertation, Stanford University, 1971), 299–301.

45. Mills to Mother and Dad, January 1945, *Letters and Autobiographical Writings*, 84.

46. Jean M. Converse, *Survey Research in the United States: Roots and Emergence, 1890–1960* (Berkeley: University of California Press, 1987), 213–32, 267–304; Allan Barton, "Paul Lazarsfeld and the Invention of the University Institution for Social Research," in *Organizing for Social Research*, ed. Burkhart Holzner and Jiri Nehnevajsa (Cambridge, Mass.: Schenckman, 1982), 17–83; Paul Lazarsfeld, "An Episode in the History of Social Research: A Memoir," in *The Intellectual Migration: Europe and America, 1930–1960*, ed. Donald Fleming and Bernard Bailyn (Cambridge, Mass.: Harvard University Press, 1969), 270–337.

47. Barton, "Paul Lazarsfeld," 27.

48. Mills to Macdonald, February 5, 1945, Dwight Macdonald Papers, Rare Books and Manuscripts Division, Yale University, folder 855, box 34.

49. Mills to Bell, January 30, 1945, letter in author's possession.

50. "Confidential Reader's Memorandum Regarding Horkheimer's *Twilight of Reason*," UT, box 4B 389.

51. Lazarsfeld, "An Episode," 279. In fact, Lazarsfeld's major study in Austria was of proletarian adolescents and unemployment.

52. Paul Lazarsfeld, *Radio and the Printed Page* (New York: Duell, Sloan, and Pearce, 1940).

53. Only 20 of the 200 major American unions had research divisions of their own, Mills informed Lazarsfeld, and the rest would need an outside agency such as the BASR to conduct their research. See Mills, Memo to Lazarsfeld, November 29, 1945, UT, box 4B 368.

54. Mills, "The Politics of Skill," *Labor and Nation*, June-July 1946, 35. On Mills's hopes for labor-based social transformation during the immediate postwar period, see Daniel Geary, "The 'Union of the Power and the Intellect': C. Wright Mills and the Labor Movement," *Labor History* 42 (November 2001): 327–45.

55. Mills, *The New Men of Power: America's Labor Leaders* (New York: Harcourt, Brace, 1948).

56. "Script for Slide Film Report on Opinion Leadership," Bureau of Applied Social Research Papers, Columbia University Rare Books and Manuscripts (henceforth BASR), box 9; Elihu Katz and Paul Lazarsfeld, *Personal Influence: The Part Played by People in the Flow of Mass Communications* (Glencoe, Ill.: Free Press, 1955).

57. Mills, "The Influence Study: Some Conceptions and Procedures of Research," Address to the American Association for the Advancement of Science, Boston, December 29, 1946)," BASR, box 9.

58. Mills, *The Cultural Apparatus*, note 4, UT, box 4B 368.

59. See Todd Gitlin, "Media Sociology: The Dominant Paradigm," *Theory and Society* 6 (September 1978): 205–53.

60. Macfadden Publishers, "Script for Slide Film Report on Opinion Leadership," BASR, box 9.

61. Mills's interpretation of the Decatur data can be found in "The Sociology of Mass Media and Public Opinion," written in 1950 and intended for publication in the Department of State's Russian language publication *Amerika*, but censored by Soviet authorities. It is reprinted in Horowitz, *Power, Politics, and People*, 577–98.

62. Mills to Gerth, January 1945, copy in author's possession.

63. See James Coleman, "Columbia in the 1950s," in *Authors of Their Own Lives: Intellectual Autobiographies by Twenty American Sociologists*, ed. Bennett M. Berger (Berkeley: University of California Press, 1990), 85–89.

64. Barton, "Paul Lazarsfeld," 46.

65. See Gitlin, "Media Sociology."

66. Merton to Theodor Abel, November 19, 1947, letter in author's possesion.

67. Robert Johnston, *The Radical Middle Class: Populist Democracy and the Question of Radicalism in Progressive Era Portland* (Princeton, N.J.: Princeton University Press, 2003), 4.

68. An excellent account of the origins of *White Collar* is provided by Richard Gillam, "*White Collar* from Start to Finish: C. Wright Mills in Transition," *Theory and Society* 10 (1981): 1–30. However, Gillam underestimates its origins as a work of social science.

69. Mills to Cochran, n.d., 1944, UT, box 4B 265.

70. Mills to Gerth, May 8, 1945, letter in author's possession.

71. *White Collar* (New York: Oxford University Press, 1951), 356. The BASR

interviews conducted by Mills were used not only in *White Collar* but also in *The Lonely Crowd*: Riesman's collaborator Nathan Glazer worked at BASR and Mills made the data available to both of them. Indeed, according to Glazer, Mills taught him the newer techniques of social survey research, which Glazer then imparted to Riesman. See Glazer, "From Socialism to Sociology," in *Authors of Their Own Lives*, 199, 202.

72. Robert K. Merton with Marjorie Fiske and Alberta Curtis, *Mass Persuasion: The Social Psychology of a War Bond Drive* (New York: Harper and Brothers, 1946), 10; Robert K. Merton and Patricia L. Kendally, "The Focused Interview," *American Journal of Sociology* 51 (May 1946): 541–57.

73. "General Instructions for the 'Everyday Life in America' Guide: *White Collar Study*," UT, box 4B 401, 1.

74. "General Instructions," 4.

75. Mills to Gerth, November 26, 1946, copy in author's possession.

76. "General Instructions," 4.

77. *White Collar*, 356.

78. "Sexual Exploitation in White Collar Employment," unpublished notes, UT, box 4B 347. The Everyday Life project contained a series of questions for women about domestic versus career ambitions and the prevalence of sexual propositioning in the workplace. In a planned chapter not included in the final manuscript, Mills was to discuss "Sexual Exploitation in White-Collar Employment." Though Mills was no feminist, in his notes he described the white collar world as a "commercialized patriarchy" in which young women served older men. Interestingly enough, in a recent review essay on the development of scholarship since *White Collar*, Nelson Lichtenstein has convincingly shown that feminist scholars of white collar work have been able to build on many of the insights of *White Collar*. Lichtenstein, "Class, Collars, and the Continuing Relevance of C. Wright Mills," Labor 1, 3 (September 2004): 109–23.

79. This characterization of *White Collar* comes from Gillam, "*White Collar* from Start to Finish."

80. *White Collar*, xv.

81. Nils Gilman, *Mandarins of the Future: Modernization Theory in Cold War America* (Baltimore: Johns Hopkins University Press, 2003). In addition to Parsons, Edward Shils, who was known primarily as a translator of works of German social science in the 1930s and 1940s (both Mannheim and Weber), became a leading modernization theorist in the postwar period.

82. See Brick, "The Postcapitalist Vision."

83. *White Collar*, xx.

84. *White Collar*, xx. On the general rise of psychological explanations during this period, see Herman, *The Romance of American Psychology*.

85. See the essays of Bell, Parsons, Reisman, and Hofstadter in *The New American Right*, ed. Daniel Bell (New York: Criterion, 1955). There was a crucial difference, however, in Mills's use of the idea that the uncertainties of modern society created a status anxiety. While *New American Right* authors applied it to a minority of Americans (particularly the followers of Joseph McCarthy), Mills believed it characterized the American middle class as a whole.

86. "The technical vocabulary used, and hence in many ways the general perspective of the volume, is derived from Max Weber" (*White Collar*, 357). Mills also acknowledged his debt to writings in the Marxist tradition (in which he included Weber).

87. *White Collar*, xvii.

88. *White Collar*, 105.

89. *White Collar*, 226.

90. *White Collar,* 77, 78.

91. Brick, "The Postcapitalist Vision."

92. See also the chapters by David Engerman and Paddy Riley.

93. David Riesman, "A Suggestion for Coding the Intensive White Collar Interviews," February 5, 1948, UT, box 4B 350. See also Riesman, *The Lonely Crowd* (New Haven, Conn.: Yale University Press, 1950), 47–48; Nathan Glazer, "From Socialism to Sociology," in Berger, *Authors of Their Own Lives,* 199, 202. On the basis of these transcripts, Riesman suggested that the respondents be classified into three types—the Protestant ethic, marketing ethic, and rational ethic—and suggested that the country was in the midst of a transition from the protestant ethic to the marketing ethic. These categories were clearly forerunners of the categories of inner-directed, other-directed, and autonomous, employed in *The Lonely Crowd*

94. Riesman, *The Lonely Crowd,* 18.

95. Riesman, *The Lonely Crowd,* 132.

96. Riesman, *The Lonely Crowd,* 160.

97. Jeffrey Alexander, *Twenty Lectures: Sociological Theory Since World War II* (New York: Columbia University Press, 1987).

98. Riesman, *The Lonely Crowd,* 235.

99. Mills "A Personal Note to the Reader," UT, box 4B 378. Indeed, Mills's concern with power arose initially from his work in the sociology of knowledge. It was in an unpublished portion of "The Professional Ideology of Social Pathologists" that Mills first used the term "power elite," writing that sociologists of knowledge needed to be aware that ideas were often "the social weapons of the power elites."

100. *White Collar,* 160.

101. Mills to Phillip Vaudrin, September 17, 1951, in *Letters and Autobiographical Writings,* 155.

102. Mills, *The Sociological Imagination* (New York: Oxford University Press, 1959).

Chapter 7. C. L. R. James and the Theory of State Capitalism

The author would like to express gratitude to Nelson Lichtenstein, Howard Brick, and Scott McLemee for their astute comments on various drafts, as well to Judith Stein, commentator on a panel at the annual meeting of the Organization of American Historians in Boston in March 2004, and to the participants in an exchange about these ideas at the Interdisciplinary Humanities Center, University of California, Santa Barbara, on January 10, 2005.

1. Studies placing culture at the center of James scholarship include Darrell E. Levi, "C. L. R. James: A Radical West Indian Vision of American Studies," *American Quarterly* 43 (September 1991): 486–501; Cynthia Hamilton, "A Way of Seeing: Culture as Political Expression in the Works of C. L. R. James," *Journal of Black Studies* 22 (March 1992): 429–43; Paget Henry and Paul Buhle, eds., *C. L. R. James's Caribbean* (Durham, N.C.: Duke University Press, 1992); Grant Farred, ed., *Rethinking C. L. R. James* (Cambridge: Blackwell, 1996); Aldon Lynn Nielsen, *C. L. R. James: A Critical Introduction* (Jackson: University of Mississippi Press, 1997); Anthony Bogues, *Caliban's Freedom: The Early Political Thought of C. L. R. James* (London: Pluto, 1997); Paget Henry, *Caliban's Reason: Introducing Afro-Caribbean Philosophy* (New York: Routledge, 2000); Anuradha Dingwaney Needham, *Using the Master's Tools: Resistance and the Literature of the African and South-Asian Diasporas* (New York: St. Martin's, 2000); Nicole King, *C. L. R. James and Creolization: Circles of Influence* (Jackson: University Press of Mississippi, 2001); Grant Farred, *What's My Name? Black Vernacular*

Intellectuals (Minneapolis: University of Minnesota Press, 2003); James, *Letters from London: Seven Essays by C. L. R. James,* ed. Nicolas Laughlin (Maraval, Port of Spain, Trinidad and Tobago: Prospect Press, 2003).

2. James, *C. L. R. James on the "Negro Question",* ed. Scott McLemee (Jackson: University Press of Mississippi, 1996); C. L. R. James et al., *Fighting Racism in World War II* (New York: Monad, 1980); C. L. R. James, *Mariners, Renegades, and Castaways: The Story of Herman Melville and the World We Live In* (New York: C. L. R. James, 1953); C. L. R. James, *American Civilization* (Cambridge: Blackwell, 1993).

3. Interview with C. L. R. James, in *Visions of History* by MARHO, the Radical Historians Organization (New York: Pantheon, 1984), 271.

4. Two notable exceptions to this lacuna, though almost wholly descriptive, are Marty Glaberman, "The Marxism of C. L. R. James," in *C. L. R. James: His Intellectual Legacies,* ed. Selwyn R. Cudjoe and William E. Cain (Amherst: University of Massachusetts Press, 1995), 304–13, and Kent Worcester, "C. L. R. James and the American Century," ibid., 180–81.

5. Robin D. G. Kelley, "The World the Diaspora Made: C. L. R. James and the Politics of History," in Farred, ed., *Rethinking,* 104. One work that does examine James as a Marxist thinker in this holistic sense, though without great attention to the concept of state capitalism, is Cedric J. Robinson, *Black Marxism: The Making of the Black Radical Tradition* (1983; Chapel Hill: University of North Carolina Press, 2000), 241–86.

6. For the life of James, consult Kent Worcester, *C. L. R. James: A Political Biography* (Albany: State University of New York Press, 1996) and Paul Buhle, *C. L. R. James: The Artist as Revolutionary* (London: Verso, 1988). Also indispensable is the special issue of *Urgent Tasks* 12 (1981), ed. Paul Buhle, later published as *C. L. R. James: His Life and Work* (London: Allison and Busby, 1986).

7. For a concise explanation of the origination of Trotskyism, see Robert V. Daniels, "The Left Opposition as an Alternative to Stalinism," *Slavic Review* 50 (Summer 1991): 277–85.

8. Leon Trotsky, *The Revolution Betrayed* (Garden City, N.Y.: Doubleday, Doran, 1937).

9. James, *World Revolution, 1917–1936: The Rise and Fall of the Communist International* (1937; Atlantic Highlands, N.J.: Humanities Press, 1993), 267, 149, 156.

10. James, *World Revolution,* 336.

11. James, *World Revolution,* 418–19.

12. See, for example, C. L. R. James, "Revolutionary Socialist League," *Fight* (April 1938): 3.

13. James, *State Capitalism and World Revolution* (1950; Chicago: Kerr, 1986), 32.

14. Karl Marx and Friedrich Engels, *The Communist Manifesto* (New York: Monthly Review Press, 1998), 5.

15. Karl Marx and Friedrich Engels, *Collected Works,* vol. 25 (New York: International, 1987), 266.

16. Karl Marx, *Capital,* vol. 1 (New York: Vintage, 1977), 779.

17. Rudolph Hilferding, *Finance Capital: A Study of the Latest Phase of Capitalist Development* (1910; London: Routledge and Kegan Paul, 1981).

18. Karl Renner, "Problems of Marxism," in *Austro-Marxism,* ed. and trans. Tom Bottomore and Patrick Goode (Oxford: Clarendon Press, 1978), 98.

19. Stephen Cohen, *Bukharin and the Bolshevik Revolution: A Political Biography, 1888–1938* (1973; Oxford: Oxford University Press, 1980), 25–34.

20. Lenin, *Collected Works* (Moscow: Progress, 1965), 33: 278.

21. Lenin, *Collected Works,* 27: 22.

22. Lenin, *Collected Works,* 27: 293.

23. Lenin, *Collected Works*, 27: 338.

24. Lenin, *Collected Works*, 32: 458

25. Lenin, *Collected Works*, 32: 491.

26. Lenin, *Collected Works*, 32: 491.

27. James continually reinterpreted Lenin so eclectically as to render him almost unrecognizable, not merely on the matter of state capitalism. After repudiating the vanguard party, James insisted that the revolutionary party mattered *not at all* for Lenin, only the working class. Near the end of his life, James claimed that Lenin had *condemned* the USSR in his final years. No other thinker corroborates these opinions. C. L. R. James, "Lenin and the Vanguard Party" (1963), in *The C. L. R. James Reader*, ed. Anna Grimshaw (Oxford: Blackwell, 1992), 327–30; and C. L. R. James, "Fully and Absolutely Assured: Author's Foreword to New Edition" (1984), *State Capitalism and World Revolution* (Chicago: Kerr, 1986), viii–ix.

28. For overviews, see W. Jerome and A. Buick, "Soviet State Capitalism? The History of an Idea," *Survey* 62 (January 1967): 58–71; Daniel Bell, "The Post-Industrial Society: The Evolution of an Idea," *Survey* 17 (Spring 1971): 102–47; Erich Farl, "The State Capitalist Genealogy," *International* 2 (Spring 1973): 18–23; and J. E. King and M. C. Howard, "'State Capitalism' in the Soviet Union," *History of Economics Review* 34 (Summer 2001): 110–26.

29. Savel Zimand, *State Capitalism in Russia: The Soviet Economic System in Operation, 1917–1926* (New York: Foreign Policy Association, 1926).

30. Emma Goldman, "There Is No Communism in Russia," in *Red Emma Speaks: An Emma Goldman Reader*, ed. Alix Kates Shulman (New York: Schocken, 1983), 407.

31. Quoted in Gary Gerstle, *American Crucible: Race and Nation in the Twentieth Century* (Princeton, N.J.: Princeton University Press, 2001), 159.

32. Norman Thomas, quoted in Eduard Mark, "October or Thermidor? Interpretations of Stalinism and the Perception of Soviet Foreign Policy in the United States, 1927–1947," *American Historical Review* 94 (October 1989): 937–62.

33. This faction included Ruth Fischer and Arkadi Maslov. See Isaac Deutscher, *The Prophet Outcast: Trotsky, 1929–1940* (London: Oxford University Press, 1963), 53; Arthur Rosenberg, *A History of Bolshevism* (London: Oxford University Press, 1934); Ruth Fischer, *Stalin and German Communism: A Study in the Origins of the State Party* (Cambridge, Mass.: Harvard University Press, 1948).

34. In France, the Union Communiste that Henri Chazé launched in 1933 published a periodical, *L'Internationale*, that briefly espoused a theory of state capitalism, as well. See Boris Souvarine, *Stalin* (New York: Longmans, 1939), 674; Deutscher, *The Prophet Outcast*, 45–47; Al Richardson, "Introduction to the Paperback Edition," in James, *World Revolution*, xi–xxiii; Robert J. Alexander, *International Trotskyism, 1929–1985* (Durham, N.C.: Duke University Press, 1991), 502.

35. Quoted in Jerome and Buick, "Soviet State Capitalism," 61; see also Ante Ciliga, *The Russian Enigma* (London: Labour Book Service, 1940) and the extremely informative article by Michael S. Fox, "Ante Ciliga, Trotskii, and State Capitalism: Theory, Tactics, and Reevaluation During the Purge Era, 1935–1939," *Slavic Review* 50 (Spring 1991): 127–43.

36. Professor Bryan Palmer of Trent University in Canada owns a book of James's inscribed to Worrall. Worrall retained a great deal of Trotsky's framework. He held that despite its state capitalism, the USSR required defense against a hostile imperialism, because Stalin's Soviet Union was capitalist but not imperialist: it had not reached the point of seeking to export capital and seize colonies. Because of its national ownership of property, the Soviet Union represented "a transitional stage to socialism—a transition stage in which the principle of private property has been abolished, and the means of production are withheld from proletarian control only

by a precariously placed bureaucracy." Thus, Worrall temporally and politically lay between Trotsky's theory and James's later theory. Worrall visited Russia after the Soviet Revolution as a correspondent for the Australian Labour Party's daily newspaper, and, impressed by what he saw, joined the British Communist Party, having moved to England. He was expelled from the CP in 1929, then turned to Trotskyism briefly before lapsing from the organized left, while maintaining a political interest and writing several books on science. Bryan Palmer, letter to author, January 13, 2005; see also R. L. Worrall, "U.S.S.R.: Proletarian or Capitalist State?" *Socialist Review* (November-December 1939): 12–14; R. L. Worrall, "U.S.S.R.: Proletarian or Capitalist State?" *Modern Quarterly* (Winter 1939): 5–19; Sam Bornstein and Al Richardson, *Against the Stream: A History of the Trotskyist Movement in Britain, 1924–1938* (London: Socialist Platform, 1986), 31–33. Intriguingly, Worrall's position was rebutted by none other than Rudolf Hilferding in an article first published in 1940 arguing that the Soviet Union was "totalitarian," not state capitalist: "State Capitalism or Totalitarian State Economy?" *Modern Review* (June 1947): 266–71.

37. "Was the Bolshevik Revolution a Failure?" *Modern Quarterly* (Fall 1938): 7–28.

38. These arguments are advanced in Trotsky's abusive work *In Defense of Marxism* (New York: Pathfinder, 1943).

39. J. R. Johnson, "The Defense of the USSR and the Present Imperialist War," *Internal Bulletin* (Socialist Workers Party) 2, 1 (October 10, 1939): 23–28; J. R. Johnson, "The Roots of the Party Crisis," mimeographed document (1940).

40. Many of James's most searching meditations on this wrenching process are found in his 1948 document *Notes on Dialectics* (Westport, Conn.: Lawrence Hill, 1980).

41. Ernest Haberkern and Arthur Lipow, eds., *Neither Capitalism Nor Socialism: Theories of Bureaucratic Collectivism* (Atlantic Highlands, N.J.: Humanities Press, 1996); Sean Matgamna, ed., *The Fate of the Russian Revolution* (London: Phoenix Press, 1998); Max Shachtman, *The Bureaucratic Revolution: The Rise of the Stalinist State* (New York: Donald Press, 1962); Peter Drucker, *Max Shachtman and His Left: A Socialist's Odyssey Through the "American Century"* (Atlantic Highlands, N.J.: Humanities Press, 1994).

42. There is dispute over whether James persuaded Dunayevskaya or vice versa of the theory of state capitalism. Paul Buhle writes, "Even before she met James, [Dunayevskaya] had fixed her ideas about Stalin's society as a form of state capitalism—no mere 'bureaucratic society' as liberals, socialists and former Trotskyists had begun to argue—subject to the class conflict and economic crisis characteristic of capitalism. . . . Dunayevskaya convinced James that such a position helped make sense of capitalism's shifts in the West, toward a more bureaucratic society inside the labour movement and outside. Together, she and James would work out the ramifications." However, Buhle supplies no evidence for his claim. Meanwhile, Dunayevskaya's followers have written that James "had independently also come to a state-capitalist position." This seems most plausible, given that James was the exclusive author of the first major article the tendency produced on the question. Paul M. Buhle, *C. L. R. James: The Artist as Revolutionary* (London: Verso, 1988), 74; Peter Hudis, "Introduction" to Raya Dunayevskaya, *The Marxist-Humanist Theory of State Capitalism* (Chicago: News and Letters, 1992), xi.

43. The best rooting of James in revolutionary socialist organization is Scott McLemee and Paul Le Blanc, *C. L. R. James and Revolutionary Marxism* (Atlantic Highlands, N.J.: Humanities Press, 1994). For useful reminiscences of the Johnson-Forest Tendency, see Grace Lee Boggs, *Living for Change: An Autobiography* (Minneapolis: University of Minnesota Press, 1998), and Constance Webb, *Not Without Love: Memoirs* (Hanover, N.H.: Dartmouth College, 2003).

44. Webb, *Not Without Love*, 83.

45. James and Raya Dunayevskaya would later claim that because the theory of

bureaucratic collectivism "posed the question of a third alternative"—that is, a social system neither capitalist nor socialist—it "represented the greater deviation from Marxism." This view that the alternatives were simply capitalism or socialism spoke to the dogmatism and sectarianism of the James circle, since obviously historical materialism had explained other modes of production (slavery, feudalism) and could well imagine future modes of production unanticipated by Marx. However, their belief that Shachtman and his circle were deviating from Marxism might also be seen as an anticipation of the eventual reconciliation of Shachtman to the American state as a supporter of the Bay of Pigs invasion of Cuba and the Vietnam War. Probably not too much should be made of this, however, since the nature of intra-group polemic in the 1940s was such that all disputants in any political difference would accuse one another of incipient abandonment of the one true creed. See J. R. Johnson and F. Forest, "A Letter to the Membership," *Internal Bulletin* (Workers Party) 9, 4 (June 1947): 15–24.

46. The ensuing analysis concentrates on the collaborative works *The Invading Socialist Society* (New York: The Johnson-Forest Tendency, 1947) and *State Capitalism and World Revolution* (1950), the Johnson-Forest Tendency's fullest expressions of its theory of state capitalism. *The Invading Socialist Society* was written by James, Lee, and Dunayevskaya and issued by the Johnson-Forest Tendency while en route from the Workers Party back into the Socialist Workers Party. *State Capitalism and World Revolution* was a contribution to debates in the Fourth International and was signed "Johnson-Forest" when originally published in the Socialist Workers Party's *Discussion Bulletin* 4 (September 1950). In several later interviews, James referred to it as "my masterpiece." When reissued in small printings in 1956, 1968, and 1986, all editions credited C. L. R. James. The last credited Raya Dunayevskaya and Grace Lee, as well, though only the names Johnson and Forest, not Ria Stone, Lee's party name, appeared on the original. The edition used here is the 1986 Kerr edition (Chicago), probably the most widely available. See also J. R. Johnson, "Russia—A Fascist State," *New International* 7 (April 1941): 54–58; J. R. Johnson, "Russia and Marxism," *New International* 7 (September 1941): 213–16; Raya Dunayevskaya, "An Analysis of Russian Economy," *New International* 8 (December 1942): 327–32; 9 (January 1943): 17–22; Raya Dunayevskaya, "The Nature of Russian Economy," *New International* 12 (December 1946): 313–17; 13 (January 1947): 27–30.

47. *State Capitalism*, 22.

48. *State Capitalism*, 62, 64.

49. *Invading*, 30.

50. *State Capitalism*, 64.

51. *State Capitalism*, 44–45.

52. See, for example, *State Capitalism*, 11–12. This point was initially made by Dunayevskaya, in a mid-1940s *American Economic Review* debate with fellow-traveler economists. See "Teaching of Economics in the Soviet Union," trans. Raya Dunayevskaya, *American Economic Review* 34 (September 1934): 501–30; Raya Dunayevskaya, "A New Revision of Marxian Economics," *American Economic Review* 34 (September 1944): 531–37; Paul A. Baran, "New Trends in Russian Economic Thinking?" *American Economic Review* 34 (December 1944): 862–71; Leo Rogin, "Marx and Engels on Distribution in a Socialist Society," *American Economic Review* 35 (March 1945): 137–43; Oscar Lange, "Marxian Economics in the Soviet Union," *American Economic Review* 35 (March 1945): 127–33; Raya Dunayevskaya, "Revision or Reaffirmation of Marxism? A Rejoinder," *American Economic Review* 35 (September 1945): 660–64; M. M. Bober, "Marx and Economic Calculation," *American Economic Review* 36 (June 1946): 344–57; Alfred Zauberman, "Economic Thought in the Soviet Union," *American Economic Review* 16 (1948–1949): 1–12.

53. Several passages make this point: "The subsequent history of the labor process of Russia, is the telescopic reenactment of the stages of production of the United States; and added to this, the special degradation imposed upon it by the totalitarian control of the bureaucracy and the plan" (*State Capitalism*, 44). "Ford's regime before unionization is the prototype of production relations in fascist Germany and Stalinist Russia" (40).

54. *Invading*, 57.

55. *Invading*, 30. For an alternate formulation, see *State Capitalism*, 43, where the authors write, "The Stalinist bureaucracy is the American bureaucracy carried to its ultimate and logical conclusion, both of them products of capitalist production in the epoch of state-capitalism."

56. *State Capitalism*, 50, 69.

57. Frederick Pollack, "State Capitalism: Its Possibilities and Limitations," *Studies in Philosophy and Social Science* 9 (1941): 200–225; Frederick Pollack, "Is National Socialism a New Order?" *Studies in Philosophy and Social Science* 9 (1941): 440–45. See also Franz Neumann, *Behemoth* (New York: Oxford University Press, 1942).

58. George Orwell, *1984* (New York: Milestone, 1949); Hannah Arendt, *The Origins of Totalitarianism* (New York: Harcourt, Brace, 1951); Les K. Adler and Thomas G. Paterson, "Red Fascism: The Merger of Nazi Germany and Soviet Russia in the American Image of Totalitarianism, 1930's-1950's," *American Historical Review* 75 (April 1970): 1046–64.

59. *Mariners, Renegades, and Castaways*, unpaginated introduction.

60. *Animal Farm* (1945) and *1984* (1948) associate Orwell with the standard totalitarian thesis, but in his earlier work *Homage to Catalonia* (1938) he momentarily speculated about Stalinist-supported "state capitalism" supplanting the worker and peasant revolution from below in Spain; as quoted in King and Howard, "'State Capitalism' in the Soviet Union," 114.

61. *State Capitalism*, 29–30. Again: "For us, production in Russia is subject to the laws of the capitalist world-market. The bureaucracy is subjected to the basic laws of capitalism as is any capitalist class. All the monstrosities of Stalinist society are rooted in the laws of the capital-labor relation which reach their highest expression in Russia" (*Invading*, 27).

62. *State Capitalism*, 7. Alternately: "The achievement of state-capitalism is at the same time the beginning of the disintegration of capitalism as a social system" (*Invading*, 25).

63. The list could include James Burnham, Pitirim Sorokim, Talcott Parsons, Raymond Aron, Clark Kerr, Peter Drucker, John Kenneth Galbraith, Jacques Ellul, C. Wright Mills, and Herbert Marcuse. For overviews, see Jan S. Prybyla, "The Convergence of Western and Communist Economic Systems: A Critical Estimate," *Russian Review* 23 (January 1964): 3–17; Ian Weinberg, "The Problem of the Convergence of Industrial Societies: A Critical Look at the State of a Theory," *Comparative Studies in Society and History* 11 (January 1969): 1–15; Donald Kelley, "The Soviet Debate on the Convergence of the American and Soviet Systems," *Polity* 6 (Winter 1973): 174–96; Reinhard John Skinner, "Technological Determinism: A Critique of Convergence Theory," *Comparative Studies in Society and History* 18 (January 1976): 2–27.

64. *State Capitalism*, 49.

65. *State Capitalism*, 114.

66. *Invading*, 17. This was connected to a theory of Communist parties in Western society. Stalinists, they wrote, aspire to power and are "deadly enemies of private property capitalism" but not proletarian revolutionists, for they seek to "reorganize the means of production without releasing the proletariat from wage slavery" (*State Capitalism*, 7). Johnson-Forest held that the problem of Stalinism was "only superficially

a Stalinist bureaucratic corruption"; fundamentally, "It is a class corruption, corruption by the petty-bourgeoisie": "These petty-bourgeois elements, revolutionized, are ready to expropriate the national bourgeoisie, and 'plan the economy.' But their conception of planning is the administration by themselves of the productive forces, including the proletariat." Far from radical, wrote Johnson-Forest, "State-property and total planning are nothing but the complete subordination of the proletariat to capital. The prejudices and fears of intermediate classes have been used by frightened leaders in every revolution to corrupt and demoralize the vanguard and strengthen the rearguard against it. Nothing but the revolutionary movement of the revolutionary masses will draw the petty-bourgeoisie to it, genuinely revolutionize it and leave thousands of bureaucrats without a medium for corruption" (*Invading*, 18).

67. C. L. R. James, *Lenin, Trotsky, and the Vanguard Party: A Contemporary View* (Detroit: Facing Reality, 1964); and *Visions of History*, 273–74.

68. *State Capitalism*, 51.

69. *State Capitalism*, 32.

70. *State Capitalism*, 37.

71. *Invading*, 57.

72. For considerable evidence that this was precisely what animated the great upsurge of the 1930s, see Nelson Lichtenstein, *State of the Union: A Century of American Labor* (Princeton, N.J.: Princeton University Press, 2002), 20–53.

73. *State Capitalism*, 7.

74. Noam Chomsky, *Class Warfare* (Monroe, Me.: Common Courage, 1996), 147; Noam Chomsky to author, February 3, 2003.

75. See, for example, Grace C. Lee, Pierre Chaulieu, and J. R. Johnson, *Facing Reality* (Detroit: Correspondence, 1958).

76. An early example of the approach is the Johnson-Forest pamphlet by Paul Romano and Ria Stone, *The American Worker* (New York: n.p., 1947). Quite a list of subsequent permutations and influences could be compiled. Martin Glaberman, for many years James's most loyal American disciple, authored *Wartime Strikes* (Detroit: Bewick Editions, 1980) and *Punching Out* (Chicago: Kerr, 2002). *The American Revolution* (New York: Monthly Review Press, 1963) and *Racism and the Class Struggle* (New York: Monthly Review Press, 1970) by James Boggs, a onetime Correspondence member, continued some of the methods while rejecting James's Marxism. As editor of *Radical America*, Paul Buhle devoted an entire issue to James's writings (May 1970), introducing James to a younger generation, and Buhle has continued to write labor history in his vein. George P. Rawick, a historian of labor and slavery, was a member with Glaberman of the last Jamesian organization, Facing Reality, and visited him in London, affecting his conceptualizations in *From Sunup to Sundown: The Making of the Black Community* (Westport, Conn.: Greenwood, 1972). David Roediger, Rawick's student, has developed a working-class cultural history of great sophistication, most prominently *The Wages of Whiteness: Race and the Making of the American Working Class* (London: Verso, 1991). Scott McLemee, editor of two books of James's writings published in the 1990s, is one of the best book and culture critics writing for the national press.

77. *Mariners, Renegades, and Castaways*, 12–13, 18.

Chapter 8. Oliver C. Cox and the Roots of World Systems Theory

1. In his contribution to *Monthly Review*'s twenty-fifth anniversary issue on the theme of "Marxism: Looking Backward and Forward," Cox remarked: "I asked the

editors of this symposium not to categorize me as a 'Marxist-Leninist' because, although I am not an 'anti-Marxist-Leninist,' I see my orientation to the study of the emergent socialist world as distinct enough to avoid such an identification." *Monthly Review* 26 (June 1974): 53. Years earlier, in the preface of *Caste, Class, and Race,* Cox had similarly stated that, "If . . . parts of this study seem Marxian, it is not because we have taken the ideas of this justly famous writer as gospel, but because we have not discovered any other that could explain the facts so consistently." Oliver C. Cox, *Caste, Class, and Race: A Study in Social Dynamics* (1948; New York: Monthly Review Press, 1970), xi.

2. This is what Cox wrote to Northwestern University Law School dean John H. Wigmore in a letter dated January 3, 1931. Northwestern University Archives, John H. Wigmore Papers, series 17/20: General and Subject Correspondence Files, box 40, folder 9. I have reproduced the entire letter in my *The Mind of Oliver C. Cox* (Notre Dame, Ind.: University of Notre Dame Press, 2004), 34.

3. Elmer P. Martin, "The Sociology of Oliver C. Cox: A Systematic Inquiry" (Master's thesis, Department of Sociology, Atlanta University, May 1971), 12 as cited in Herbert M. Hunter, "The Life and Work of Oliver C. Cox" (Ph.D. dissertation, Department of Sociology, Boston University, 1981), 23.

4. See *Caste,* 245–82 and McAuley, *The Mind of Oliver C. Cox,* 41–50.

5. Robert Ezra Park, "An Autobiographical Note," in *Race and Culture: Essays in the Sociology of Contemporary Man* (New York: Free Press, 1950), vii.

6. "An Autobiographical Note," vii–viii.

7. *Caste,* xvi.

8. The Trinidad of Cox's youth was home to over 100,000 East Indians (one-third of the island's total) over half of whom had been born in India. More than 8,000 of these mainly agricultural workers lived in Montserrat Ward, where the Cox family had a small cocoa estate. According to Cox's niece Juliet Uibopuu, Cox's mother, Virginia Blake, learned basic Urdu in order to better communicate with the East Indians who worked for the Coxes. Personal communication, Miami, February 27, 2004. For the population figures, see Eric Williams, *Inward Hunger: The Education of a Prime Minister* (Chicago: University of Chicago Press, 1971), 19 and Walton Look Lai, *Indentured Labor, Caribbean Sugar: Chinese and Indian Migrants to the British West Indies* (Baltimore: Johns Hopkins University Press, 1993), 280, Table 11.

9. See *Caste,* xvii.

10. *Caste,* 42.

11. *Caste,* 23–24.

12. *Caste,* 41.

13. Robert Ezra Park, "The Nature of Race Relations," in *Race Relations and the Race Problem: A Definition and an Analysis,* ed. Edgar T. Thompson (Durham, N.C.: Duke University Press, 1939), 31.

14. Park, "The Nature of Race Relations," 4.

15. *Caste,* 474.

16. *Caste,* 495–96.

17. Park, "The Bases of Race Prejudice," in *Race and Culture,* 236.

18. *Caste,* 472.

19. See *Caste,* 548–64.

20. *Caste,* 504.

21. *Caste,* 575–76.

22. *Caste,* 475.

23. For Cox's descriptions of these and other situations of race relations, see *Caste,* 353–91. I discuss three of them at some length in *The Mind of Oliver C. Cox,* 69–95.

24. Cox, *The Foundations of Capitalism* (New York: Philosophical Library, 1959), 15.

25. *Caste*, 266.

26. Cox, *Capitalism and American Leadership* (New York: Philosophical Library, 1962), 186–87.

27. *Caste*, 188.

28. *Caste*, 105.

29. *Caste*, 105.

30. *Caste*, 107.

31. *Caste*, 103, 104.

32. See, for example, Paul A. Baran and Paul M. Sweezy, *Monopoly Capital: An Essay on the American Economic and Social Order* (New York: Monthly Review Press, 1966), 210.

33. *Caste*, 123.

34. *Caste*, 144.

35. *Caste*, 144.

36. *Caste*, 144, 147.

37. *Caste*, 144–45.

38. Henri Pirenne, *Economic and Social History of Medieval Europe* (San Diego: Harcourt, Brace, 1937), 140–41.

39. Immanuel Wallerstein, "Three Paths to National Development in Sixteenth-Century Europe," in *The Capitalist World-Economy: Essays by Immanuel Wallerstein* (Cambridge: Cambridge University Press, 1979), 42.

40. *Foundations*, 356.

41. Cox, *Capitalism and American Leadership*, 63.

42. *Foundations*, 76.

43. *Foundations*, 77.

44. Cox, *Capitalism as a System* (New York: Monthly Review Press, 1964), 4.

45. *Capitalism as a System*, 5, 6.

46. *Capitalism as a System*, 144, 143.

47. *Foundations*, 94.

48. Maurice Dobb, *Studies in the Development of Capitalism* (New York: International Publishers, 1963), 113.

49. *Foundations*, 196.

50. *Foundations*, 191.

51. *Foundations*, 72.

52. Immanuel Wallerstein, who many regard as the founder of world systems theory, has only recently acknowledged Cox's role in the development of that school of thought: "Oliver Cox expounded in the 1950s and 1960s virtually all the basic ideas of world-systems analysis. He is a founding father, albeit one who is hardly recognized as such and is widely neglected, even today." "Oliver C. Cox as World-Systems Analyst," in *The Sociology of Oliver C. Cox: New Perspectives*, ed. Herbert M. Hunter (Stamford, Conn: JAI Press, 2000), 174. Wallerstein was apparently moved to admit this only after Paul Sweezy, late editor of *Monthly Review* and Cox supporter, asserted that "Both chronologically and logically, Oliver Cox deserves to be considered not only a forerunner but a founding father" of world systems theory. "Foreword" to *Race, Class, and the World System: The Sociology of Oliver C. Cox*, ed. Herbert M. Hunter and Sameer Y. Abraham (New York: Monthly Review Press, 1987), x.

53. *Capitalism as a System*, 138.

54. *Capitalism as a System*, 150.

55. *Capitalism as a System*, 136.

56. *Capitalism as a System*, 190, 195.

57. *Capitalism as a System*, 1.

58. See Cox, *Capitalism and American Leadership*, 242–61.

59. *Capitalism as a System*, 190–91.

60. *Capitalism as a System,* 195.
61. *Capitalism as a System,* 194.
62. *Capitalism as a System,* 197.
63. *Capitalism as a System,* 195.
64. *Capitalism as a System,* 198.
65. See Isaiah Berlin, *Karl Marx* (1939; New York: Oxford University Press, 1996), 193–201 and Robert Bidelux, *Communism and Development* (London: Methuen, 1985), 1–28.

Chapter 9. Feminism, Women's History, and American Social Thought at Midcentury

In working on this chapter, I have benefited from the responses of Robert H. Abzug, Darcy Buerkle, George Cotkin, Carl Degler, Ellen C. DuBois, Lynn Dumenil, David Engerman, Michael Fellman, Helen Lefkowitz Horowitz, Nelson Lichtenstein, Linda Nicholson, and Mark Van Wienen. I delivered an earlier and very different version on April 22, 1999 at the meeting of the Organization of American Historians in Toronto. What follows is hardly a comprehensive analysis of how women's history emerged by the early 1970s; to cite just one omission, it does not cover Anne Firor Scott's *The Southern Lady: From Pedestal to Politics, 1830–1930* (Chicago: University of Chicago Press, 1970).

1. See especially Kate Weigand, *Red Feminism: American Communism and the Making of Women's Liberation* (Baltimore: Johns Hopkins University Press, 2001); Daniel Horowitz, *Betty Friedan and the Making of* The Feminine Mystique*: The American Left, the Cold War, and Modern Feminism* (Amherst: University of Massachusetts Press, 1998); Dorothy Sue Cobble, *The Other Women's Movement: Workplace Justice and Social Rights in Modern American* (Princeton, N.J.: Princeton University Press, 2004).
2. Eleanor Flexner, diary entry, August 23, [1983], carton 1, folder 5, Eleanor Flexner Papers, Schlesinger Library, Radcliffe Institute for Advanced Study, Harvard University (EF-SLRI). For biographical data, see Ellen Fitzpatrick, "Foreword" to the Enlarged Edition of Eleanor Flexner and Ellen Fitzpatrick, *Century of Struggle: The Woman's Rights Movement in the United States* (Cambridge, Mass.: Harvard University Press, 1996), ix–xxvii, and Daniel Horowitz, "Eleanor Flexner," in *Notable American Women: A Biographical Dictionary Completing the Twentieth Century,* ed. Susan Ware (Cambridge, Mass.: Harvard University Press, 2004), 213–14. For her writings, see Irene Epstein [Eleanor Flexner], "Woman Under the Double Standard," *Jewish Life* 4 (October 1950): 8–12; [Eleanor Flexner and Doxie Wilkerson], syllabus for "The Woman Question," Jefferson School of Social Science [1953–54], carton 1, folder 29, EF-SLRI. Flexner and Wilkerson relied on *The Woman Question: Selections from the Writings of Karl Marx, Frederick Engels, V. I. Lenin, Joseph Stalin* (New York: International, 1951); Grace Hutchins, *Women Who Work* (New York: International, 1952); [Betty Goldstein Friedan], *UE Fights for Women Workers* (New York: United Electrical Workers, 1952); Betty Millard, "Woman Against Myth," *New Masses* 66 (December 30, 1947): 7–10 and "Woman Against Myth: II" (January 6, 1948): 7–10.
3. Carl Degler, interview by Daniel Horowitz, Stanford, California, November 19, 2002. For biographical information, I am drawing on "Carl Neumann Degler," *Directory of American Scholars* (Lancaster, Pa.: Science Press, 2002), 130 and the Degler interview. August Bebel, *Woman Under Socialism,* trans. from the 33rd ed. by Daniel De Leon (New York: Labor News Press, 1904). For a discussion of the book's importance, see Lise Vogel, *Marxism and the Oppression of Women: Toward a Unitary Theory* (New Brunswick, N.J.: Rutgers University Press, 1983), 96–103. On the larger issues

surrounding the discussions of feminism, see Ann Taylor Allen, "Feminism, Social Science, and the Meanings of Modernity: The Debate on the Origin of the Family in Europe and the United States, 1860–1914," *American Historical Review* 104 (October 1999): 1085–113.

4. Carl N. Degler, "Labor in the Economy and Politics of New York City, 1850–1860: A Study of the Impact of Early Industrialism" (Ph.D. dissertation, Columbia University, 1952), 264.

5. For instances of the use of the word "capitalist" when quoting a 1850s source, see Degler, "Labor," 265 and 266. The word "industrialism" appeared in the title of the thesis; "industrialism," industrialization," "industrial society," "industrial system," "industry," and "factory economy" appeared frequently in the text: Degler, "Labor," ii, 96, 100, 124, 258, 259, 262, 264, 266. The other quotes come from Degler, "Labor,"106, 109, 110, 113.

6. The quote is from Marilyn B. Young, email to Daniel Horowitz, December 30, 2002; the other information comes from Clyde Griffith and Sally Griffith, telephone interview by Daniel Horowitz, November 1, 2002 (reference to two founders of the Berkshire Conference—Evelyn Clark and Mildred Campbell); Marilyn B. Young, telephone interview by Daniel Horowitz, December 22, 2002.

7. The quote is from Gerda Lerner, *Fireweed: A Political Autobiography* (Philadelphia: Temple University Press, 2002), 71. For biographical information, see "Gerda Lerner," in *Complete Marquis Who's Who* (Farmington Hills, Mich.: Gale Group, 2004); "Gerda Lerner," in *Contemporary Authors Online* (Detroit: Gale Group, 2002); and Lerner, *Fireweed*.

8. For her realization of the problems with Marxism, see Gerda Lerner, interview, *Chronicle of Higher Education*, May 3, 2002, A14; Lerner, *Fireweed*, 351. In her first year at Columbia, she took a seminar with Degler.

9. Biographical data come from "Kraditor, Aileen," in *Directory of American Scholars: History* (New York: Bowker, 1982), 419; Aileen S. Kraditor, "Unbecoming a Communist," *Continuity* 12 (1988): 97–102; Aileen S. Kraditor, biographical note, probably mid-1970s, Gloria Steinem Papers, box 166, folder 7, Sophia Smith Collection, Smith College. I am grateful to Amanda Izzo for bringing this document to my attention. In addition, there are scattered references to her experience in the CP and to her political development in Aileen S. Kraditor, *"Jimmy Higgins": The Mental World of the American Rank-and-File Communist, 1930–1958* (Westport, Conn.: Greenwood Press, 1988). For her reconsideration, see Aileen S. Kraditor, "On the History of American Reform Movements and Its Legacy Today," *Continuity* 1 (Fall 1980): 37–59. In my possession is Kraditor's copy of Frederick Engels, *The Origin of the Family, Private Property, and the State* (New York: International, 1942). She inscribed it with the address of her parents' home in Brooklyn, where she lived until about 1951: Aileen Kraditor, interview by Daniel Horowitz, August 29, 2003, Westboro, Massachusetts. In the interview Kraditor said she also read Lenin on the woman question, but I assume she meant the widely available 1951 compilation *The Woman Question*, with Lenin among the contributors. When she began to work on her dissertation, she went to Northampton to see Eleanor Flexner. When Flexner met her at the door, she realized this was the Eleanor F. she knew in Manhattan in Communist Party circles: Flexner interview. It is reasonable to assume that that Flexner and Lerner encountered one another at CAW meetings in New York.

10. Flexner and Wilkerson, "Woman Question," 1–6. What might be the key documents of the 1950s for Lerner's view of women in the 1940s and 1950s are not in her papers at the Schlesinger Library; see, however, her extensive notes for a 1942 course on American literature that explored the nature of "Americanism" but paid relatively little attention to women: Gerda Lerner Papers, series 3, subset A, folder 5.7, GL-SLRI.

11. Flexner and Wilkerson, "Woman Question," 1–6.

12. Epstein [Flexner], "Woman Under the Double Standard," 9; Betty Feldman [Eleanor Flexner], "Pay Inequalities Rob Women of $5.5 Billion a Year," [*Daily Worker*, ca. 1952], clipping, carton 1, folder 29, EF-SLRI; Flexner and Wilkerson, "Woman Question," 3; Irene Epstein [Eleanor Flexner] and Doxie A. Wilkerson, eds., *Questions and Answers on the Woman Question* (New York: Jefferson School of Social Science, 1953), carton 1, folder 29, EF-SLRI. In this pamphlet, Flexner cited Bebel's work, as well as those by Lenin, Stalin, and Engels: Epstein and Wilkerson, *Questions*, bibliography following p. 14. One Popular Front feminist asserted that the emancipation Engels ascribed to modern industry, even under capitalism, came only when women fought on the picket line, in legislative halls, and in the home to turn possibility into actuality: Millard, "Women Against Myth: II," January 6, 1948, 8.

13. Engels, *Origin*, 65, 148.

14. Lerner, *Fireweed*, 323; Gerda Lerner and Eve Merriam, *Singing of Women: A Dramatic Review* (New York: New York Council on the Arts, Sciences and Professions, 1950).

15. Kraditor's markings in her copy of Engels, *Origin*, copy in author's possession.

16. Engels, *Origin*, 43; Bebel, *Woman Under Socialism*, 4–5. Unless otherwise noted, for specific passages and quotations, I am relying on De Leon's edition, most likely the one Degler read.

17. Bebel, *Woman Under Socialism*, 184, 187, 186 (emphasis his); see also 340–42.

18. Alma Lutz was the key figure in this older tradition. Loyal to the National Woman's Party, she offered a series of widely read books that kept alive the story of the heroic struggle for the vote. Julie Des Jardins, *Women and the Historical Enterprise in America: Gender, Race, and the Politics of Memory, 1880–1945* (Chapel Hill: University of North Carolina Press, 2003), 177–213 focuses on the writing of the history of suffrage but makes a larger point about the variety of approaches; see also Ellen F. Fitzpatrick, *History's Memory: Writing America's Past, 1880–1980* (Cambridge, Mass.: Harvard University Press, 2002). For works by Alma Lutz, see *Challenging Years: The Memoirs of Harriet Stanton Blatch* (New York: Putnam, 1940); *Created Equal: A Biography of Elizabeth Cady Stanton, 1815–1902* (New York: John Day, 1940); *Susan B. Anthony: Rebel, Crusader, Humanitarian* (Boston: Beacon Press, 1959).

19. Carl N. Degler, "Charlotte Perkins Gilman on the Theory and Practice of Feminism," *American Quarterly* 8 (Spring 1956): 21, 38, 39. When Gilman met Bebel in 1896 at a Socialist and Labor Congress in London, she knew who he was. Charlotte Perkins Gilman, *The Diaries of Charlotte Perkins Gilman*, ed. Denise D. Knight (Charlottesville: University Press of Virginia, 1994), 2: 631–32. When Gilman was writing *Women and Economics*, which first appeared in 1898, an American edition of Bebel's work was recently available. The first edition in English was published in London in 1885; an 1897 edition published in London and an edition published in San Francisco in the same year both contained a version of the key passages: see August Bebel, *Woman in the Past, Present and Future*, trans. H. B. Adams Walther (London: William Reeves, 1897), 114–17; and August Bebel, *Woman in the Past, Present and Future* (San Francisco: G.G. Benham, 1897), 86–88. On the publishing history, see Anne Lopes and Gary Roth, *Men's Feminism: August Bebel and the German Socialist Movement* (Amherst, N.Y.: Humanity Books, 2000), 22. On Gilman's relation to Marxism, Bebel, Engels, populism, and Edward Bellamy's nationalism, see Mark W. Van Wienen, "A Rose by Any Other Name: Charlotte Perkins Stetson (Gilman) and the Case for American Reform Socialism," *American Quarterly* 55 (December 2003): 603–34. On Mary Beard, see Nancy F. Cott, "Putting Women on the Record: Mary Ritter Beard's Accomplishment," in Beard, *A Woman Making History: Mary Ritter Beard Through Her Letters*, ed. Nancy F. Cott (New Haven, Conn.: Yale University Press, 1991), 1–62.

20. Degler, "Gilman," 38; Carl N. Degler, "Introduction to the Torchbook Edition," in Charlotte Perkins Gilman, *Women and Economics: A Study of the Economic Relation Between Men and Women as a Factor in Social Evolution,* ed. Carl N. Degler (New York: Harper and Row, 1966), esp. xxv. For Kraditor's role in its publication, see Degler, interview.

21. Carl N. Degler, *Out of Our Past: The Forces That Shaped Modern America* (New York: Harper and Brothers, 1959), xiv; for his use of "capitalism" and "industrialization," see Degler, *Our Past,* 262, 357. Degler was not the only man who made contributions to women's history in the period: see also Andrew Sinclair, *The Better Half: The Emancipation of the American Woman* (New York: Harper and Row, 1965); William R. Taylor, *Cavalier and Yankee: The Old South and American National Character* (New York: Braziller, 1961); David M. Kennedy, *Birth Control in America: The Career of Margaret Sanger* (New Haven, Conn.: Yale University Press, 1970); Christopher Lasch, *The New Radicalism in America, 1889–1963: The Intellectual as a Social Type* (New York: Knopf, 1965); David M. Potter, "American Women and The American Character" (presented as a lecture in 1959; first published in 1962), in David M. Potter, *History and American Society: Essays of David M. Potter,* ed. Don E. Fehrenbacher (New York: Oxford University Press, 1973), 278–303. For a feminist critique of Potter's views of women, see Linda Gordon, Persis Hunt, Elizabeth Pleck, Rochelle Goldberg Ruthchild, and Marcia Scott, "Historical Phallacies: Sexism in American Historical Writing," in *Liberating Women's History: Theoretical and Critical Essays,* ed. Berenice A. Carroll (Urbana: University of Illinois Press, 1976), 55–74; reprinted, with revisions, from *Women's Studies* 1 (1972). For important reviews, see Jacob Cohen, *Nation* 188 (June 6, 1959): 519–20 and David M. Potter, *Saturday Review* 42 (February 7, 1959): 18.

22. The quote is from Degler, *Our Past,* 57; other information comes from Mary R. Beard, *Woman as a Force in History: A Study of Traditions and Realities* (New York: Macmillan, 1946); Degler, *Our Past,* 57, see also 358–59. Degler hardly infused the book with women's history. Women dropped out of sight in the narrative for sustained periods of time. In many sections, for example in his discussion of slavery and of the labor movement, he missed the opportunity to bring them into the story, let alone underscore how women's situation illustrated the limits of freedom and equality.

23. The quotes are from Degler, *Our Past,* 352, 362, 357. Though he did mention the Seneca Falls convention of 1848, neither the name of Susan B. Anthony nor the Nineteenth Amendment appeared in the book's index; moreover, he paid virtually no attention to how women won the vote. He credited Gilman with understanding "the radiating effects of the emergence of women" from the home into reform efforts: Degler, *Our Past,* 361. The article on comparative privilege that influenced Degler was Helen Mayer Hacker, "Women as a Minority Group," *Social Forces* 30 (October 1951): 60–69; Hacker, an important Popular Front feminist, explored the differences and similarities in the experiences of women and African Americans. Degler's reading of Hacker's 1951 article provided him with a comparative framework for the discussion of women's condition: Degler interview

24. Degler, *Our Past,* 453.

25. Eleanor Flexner, *A Century of Struggle: The Woman's Rights Movement in the United States* (Cambridge, Mass.: Harvard University Press, 1959), 50, 51, 55, 61, 80, 112, 117, 141, 144, 181, 187, 193, 204–5, 212, 243, 247, 259, 263, 287. For one of her least veiled attacks on women of privilege, see 296. At one point, she ascribed the distinctive nature of organizational life among African American women not to "the fact that by and large they were largely excluded from white women's groups" but rather to "the totally dissimilar circumstances of their lives" (186). The major

exception to her general neglect of groups against whom women struggled came when Flexner focused on the opposition to women's suffrage. Behind the liquor interests, Southern racists, and political machines were representatives of large corporations who opposed granting women the vote because it would unleash pressure for democratic reforms that would delimit the freedom and power of industrialists (294–305). In emphasizing the economic sources of opposition, Flexner tended to minimize the role of the Catholic Church (271, 299). For one example of where she emphasized ideas when she might also have focused on conditions, see 203. For essays on Flexner, see Carol Lasser, "Century of Struggle, Decades of Revision: A Retrospective on Eleanor Flexner's Suffrage History," *Reviews in American History* 15 (June 1987): 344–54; Fitzpatrick, "Foreword," ix–xxvii; Ellen C. DuBois, "Eleanor Flexner and the History of American Feminism," *Gender and History* 3 (Spring 1991): 81–90; for her definition of Flexner as a "left feminist," see 84.

26. For a hint of her deradicalization, see Eleanor Flexner to Pat King, May 13, 1983, Schlesinger Library, office correspondence, RG XVIII, Ser. 2.1, Box 49, Flexner folder, SLRI.

27. Gerda Lerner, *The Grimké Sisters from South Carolina: Pioneers for Woman's Rights and Abolition* (Boston: Houghton Mifflin, 1967), 292–93, 326; see also 21, 24, 34, 48, 59, 65, 86, 132, 173, 193, 326, 334. For reasons that are hard to understand, Kraditor did not refer to Lerner's work on the Grimké sisters. In the 1979 preface to *Ideas of Woman Suffrage,* she took issue with Lerner's 1969 statement that she (and Flexner) focused too much on women's fight for the ballot: Aileen S. Kraditor, "Preface to the Norton Edition," *The Ideas of the Woman Suffrage Movement, 1890–1920* (New York: W.W. Norton, 1981), v.

28. Lerner, *Fireweed,* 292.

29. Engels, *Origin,* 43; Lerner, *Grimké,* 193; Gerda Lerner, "The Lady and the Mill Girl: Changes in the Status of Women in the Age of Jackson," *Midcontinent American Studies Journal* 10 (Spring 1969): 6, 7, 13, 12, 14.

30. Lerner, "Lady and the Mill Girl," 7.

31. Aileen S. Kraditor, *The Ideas of the Woman Suffrage Movement, 1890–1920* (New York: Columbia University Press, 1965), xiv, xv; see also 2, 5–6, 8, 21, 43, 67, 71, 96, 127, 148–49, 156, 161, 282; Aileen S. Kraditor, "Introduction," *Up from the Pedestal: Selected Writings in the History of American Feminism* (Chicago: Quadrangle Books, 1968); Aileen S. Kraditor, *Means and Ends in American Abolitionism: Garrison and His Critics on Strategy and Tactics, 1834–1850* (New York: Pantheon, 1969). On the reaction to immigrants, labor, blacks, see Kraditor, *Ideas,* 123–62; on race, also see 163–218. For her use of the word racism, see 78; for her positive appraisal of Jane Addams, see 142. Unlike Flexner, she avoided focusing on the "ulterior motives" of the business interest that opposed the vote for women (15 n 2).

32. Kraditor, *Up from the Pedestal,* vii and "Introduction," 14, 24; *Means,* 8, 21, 135, 276, see also 3. She later said that "radicalism ceased being the framework of my perceptions (starting around 1968)": Aileen S. Kraditor, *The Radical Persuasion, 1890–1917: Aspects of the Intellectual History and Historiography of Three American Radical Organizations* (Baton Rouge: Louisiana State University Press, 1981), 1.

33. For his later writings on women, see Degler, "Introduction" to Gilman, *Women and Economics,* vi–xxxv; Carl Degler, *Is There a History of Women? An Inaugural Lecture Delivered Before the University of Oxford on 14 March 1974* (Oxford: Clarendon Press, 1974); Carl N. Degler, *At Odds: Women and the Family in America from the Revolution to the Present* (New York: Oxford University Press, 1980).

34. Eleanor Flexner, interview by Jacqueline Van Voris, 1977, 1982, 1983, carton 1, folder 6, EF-SLRI (quote p. 47 of January 15, 1977 version); Eleanor Flexner, *Mary Wollstonecraft: A Biography* (New York: Coward, McCann, and Geoghegan, 1972), 266; Eleanor Flexner, "Preface to the Atheneum Edition," *Century of Struggle* (New

York: Atheneum, 1968), ix; Eleanor Flexner, *Women's Rights—Unfinished Business* (New York: Public Affairs Pamphlet 469, 1971), 28; Ann Shanahan, "Northampton Author Eleanor Flexner: Works Quietly at Her Craft," *Daily Hampshire Gazette*, December 7, 1972; box 2, folder 5, EF-SLRI contains her diaries of 1971–83, which contain her discussion of local politics. In 1986 Flexner sold her Northampton house and moved to a retirement community in Westboro. She died in Worcester on March 25, 1995.

35. Kraditor, "Preface to the Norton Edition" of *Ideas*, vii, viii; Kraditor, "Unbecoming," 97–98. In this article Kraditor distinguished between the process of radicalization, which she ascribed to personal dynamics, and the choice of a specific vehicle, such as the Communist Party, which she explained in terms of friendship networks. Among the issues that remain unclear are the exact timing of the changes in her politics and to what extent as a member of the party she engaged in discussions about the women's issues. In Aileen Kraditor, "American Radical Historians on Their Heritage," *Past and Present* 56 (August 1972): 136–53, she signaled her rethinking, an article in which she foreshadowed many of the themes of her later work: that Old and New Left historians had misinterpreted the past because of their presentist political concerns, that Americans society was more open than radicals assumed, and that the ideologies of historically important radicals and reformers were problematic and contradictory. In "Preface to the Norton Edition," vi–viii she remarked that she considered as "barbarisms" words such as "chairperson." She acknowledged that she would now take antisuffragists more seriously, seeing them as offering not an "ideology" but "a comprehensive belief system" that was "far more complex" than she had earlier imagined. Although in *"Jimmy Higgins"* she mentioned individual women, she did not really focus on women's issues. On the discussion of how radicals viewed women, see Kraditor, *Radical Persuasion*, 154–204. In the early 1960s, Kraditor acknowledged her friendship with Eugene D. Genovese, whose own political trajectory—from member of the Communist Party to conservative—to some extent parallels her own. For evidence of her friendship with him, see Kraditor, *Ideas*, 1965 ed., xii.

36. Flexner, *Women's Rights*; Degler, *At Odds*, 132, 181, 375–84, 391–99, 411, 416–35, 453, 463, 471–73; Engels, *Origin*, 65; Kraditor, *Radical Persuasion*, 51, 61, 76–77, 89, 226, 227. Gerda Lerner, *The Creation of Feminist Consciousness: From the Middle Ages to Eighteen-Seventy*, Women and History 2 (New York: Oxford University Press, 1993), 276; the first volume of this series is *The Creation of Patriarchy* (New York: Oxford University Press, 1986). See also Kraditor, *"Jimmy Higgins"*. Already in Kraditor's writings during the 1960s it is possible to identify a commitment to intellectual history so at odds with much of both Old and New Left historians; an appreciation of the genuineness of religion as a central part of human experience; and a penchant for irony and contradiction more in tune with consensus intellectuals than with hard-line Party members.

Chapter 10. The Road Less Traveled:
Reconsidering the Political Writings of Friedrich Hayek

1. For an insightful account of the rise of libertarian thinking in the U.S. during the twentieth century, see Stephen Newman, *Liberalism at Wits' End: The Libertarian Revolt Against the Modern State* (Ithaca, N.Y.: Cornell University Press, 1984).

2. See Hilary Wainright, *Arguments for a New Right: Answering the Free Market Right* (London: Blackwell, 1994) for an in-depth discussion of the popularization of Hayek's thought in the 1980s.

3. See Andrew Gamble, *Hayek* (New York: HarperCollins, 1996), 13–16. For a

comprehensive intellectual biography of Hayek, see Alan Ebenstein, *Hayek's Journey: The Mind of Friedrich Hayek* (New York: Palgrave Macmillan, 2003).

4. See Gamble, *Hayek*, 150–76.

5. Throughout this chapter, I will focus largely on the political writings Hayek published in the years following *The Road to Serfdom*. These more mature works provide, for the most part, a much less strident and much more complex articulation of the central ideas he first presented in *The Road to Serfdom*, and for this reason strike me as more appropriate—and interesting—works to engage.

6. Bruce Ackerman, "The Political Case for Constitutional Courts," in *Liberalism Without Illusions: Essays on Liberal Theory and the Political vision of Judith N. Shklar*, ed. Bernard Yack (Chicago: University of Chicago Press, 1996), 214.

7. Jeremy Waldron, *Liberal Rights: Collected Papers, 1981–1991* (New York: Cambridge University Press, 1993), 29.

8. Benjamin Barber, *The Conquest of Politics: Liberal Philosophical in Democratic Times* (Princeton, N.J.: Princeton University Press, 1998), 105.

9. Stephen Holmes, *Passions and Constraint: On the Theory of Liberal Democracy* (Chicago: University of Chicago Press, 1995), 238.

10. Friedrich A. von Hayek, *The Constitution of Liberty* (Chicago: University of Chicago Press, 1960), 403 (henceforth *CL*).

11. Hayek, *Law, Legislation, and Liberty*, vol. 3, *The Political Order of a Free People* (Chicago: University of Chicago Press, 1979), 5 (henceforth *PO*). (Vols. 1 and 2 are *Rules and Order* and *The Mirage of Social Justice*.)

12. *PO*, 134.

13. *PO*, 138.

14. *PO*, 41.

15. *PO*, 44, 61.

16. *PO*, 62.

17. *CL*, 221.

18. *CL*, 154.

19. Hayek, *The Road to Serfdom* (1944; Chicago: University of Chicago Press, 1976), 73.

20. *CL*, 208.

21. See the discussion of Chandran Kukathas and Ronald Hamowy below. The author of a book-length treatise on Hayek as well as *The Liberal Archipelago: A Theory of Diversity and Freedom* (Oxford: Oxford University Press, 2003), Kukathas today is among the most prominent and well-respected theorists writing with a libertarian orientation. Ronald Hamowy, professor emeritus of history at the University of Alberta, is a well-known libertarian who has published widely in libertarian journals.

22. Chandran Kukathas, *Hayek and Modern Liberalism* (London: Oxford University Press, 1990), 157–58.

23. Ronald Hamowy, "Hayek's Concept of Freedom: A Critique," *New Individualist Review* 1 (1961): 31.

24. Cass Sunstein, *Legal Reasoning and Moral Conflict* (New York: Oxford University Press, 1996), 118.

25. Gamble, *Hayek*, 10.

26. Richard Bellamy, *Liberalism and Modern Society* (University Park: Pennsylvania State University Press, 1992), 225.

27. John Gray, "F. A. Hayek and the Rebirth of Classical Liberalism," *Literature of Liberty* 5 (1982): 51.

28. Bellamy, *Liberalism and Modern Society*, 209.

29. Bellamy, *Liberalism and Modern Society*, 154.

30. Bellamy, *Liberalism and Modern Society*, 231.

31. *CL*, 303.

32. *CL*, 222.

33. *CL*, 221.

34. *CL*, 28–29.

35. Daniel Bell, quoted in Hayek, *Law, Legislation and Liberty*, vol. 2, *The Mirage of Social Justice* (Chicago, University of Chicago Press, 1976), 183 (hereafter *MSJ*)

36. *MSJ*, 100.

37. Quoted in Gamble, *Hayek*, 160.

38. *CL*, 397–411.

39. *CL*, 183–84.

40. *MSJ*, 112–18.

41. *MSJ*, 113.

42. *MSJ*, 117.

43. *MSJ*, 119–20.

44. *MSJ*, 120–22.

45. Hamowy, "Hayek's Concept of Freedom," 138.

46. Hamowy, "Hayek's Concept of Freedom," 141.

47. William Scheuerman, "The Unholy Alliance of Carl Schmitt and Friedrich A. Hayek," *Constellations* 4 (1997).

48. Scheuerman, "The Unholy Alliance," 180.

49. Scheuerman, "The Unholy Alliance," 179.

50. Scheuerman, "The Unholy Alliance," 182.

Chapter 11. The Politics of Rich and Rich:
Postwar Investigations of Foundations and the Rise of the Philanthropic Right

Earlier versions of this essay were presented at the UCSB Conference on Capitalism and Its Cultures, and at the Columbia University Workshop on Twentieth Century American Politics and Society, both in Winter 2003. My thanks to Nelson Lichtenstein at UCSB and to Alan Brinkley and Ira Katznelson at Columbia for providing the opportunity to present work in progress. Thanks as well to Nelson Lichtenstein, George Cotkin, Mary Furner, Michael Kazin, Alice Kessler-Harris, Robert C. Lieberman, Rick Perlstein, and Ron Schatz for comments on earlier drafts. This essay draws on research funded by a travel grant from the Rockefeller Archives Center. I am also grateful to the Ford Foundation for permission to quote from its archival holdings.

1. B. Carroll Reece, Congressional Record, U.S. House of Representatives, 83rd Congress, 1st sess., vol. 99, July 27, 1953, 10015–16.

2. William Fulton, "Foundations Wander into Field of Isms," reprint of columns published in the *Chicago Tribune*, October 15–21, 1951.

3. Eleanor L. Brilliant, *Private Charity and Public Inquiry: A History of the Filer and Peterson Commissions* (Bloomington: Indiana University Press, 2000); Peter Frumkin, "Private Foundations as Public Institutions: Regulation, Professionalization, and the Redefinition of Organized Philanthropy," in *Philanthropic Foundations: New Scholarship, New Possibilities*, ed. Ellen Condliffe Lagemann (Bloomington: Indiana University Press, 1999), 69–98.

4. Notably, for much of the postwar period neither "big labor" nor the civil rights movement was especially included in the interlocking directorates the big foundations maintained. Not until the 1970s did they begin—and then only

sparingly, particularly in the case of labor—to include representatives from these groups.

5. See, for example, Robert F. Arnove, ed., *Philanthropy and Cultural Imperialism: The Foundations at Home and Abroad* (Boston: G.K. Hall, 1980).

6. Dwight Macdonald put the insiders' term "philanthropoids" into general circulation in his often biting journalistic account of the Ford Foundation, published in 1956. He attributes the term to president of the Carnegie Corporation Frederick Keppel. *The Ford Foundation: The Men and the Millions* (New York: Reynal, 1956), 95–96.

7. The "culture wars" in knowledge have recently begun to draw more attention, much of it focused on the role of think tanks. See, for example, Andrew Rich, *Think Tanks, Public Policy, and the Politics of Expertise* (New York: Cambridge University Press, 2004).

8. Sidney Blumenthal, *The Rise of the Counter Establishment: From Conservative Ideology to Political Power* (New York: HarperCollins, 1988).

9. For an earlier, particularly instructive example of the use of charitable trusts for political purposes, see Stephen Pimpare, *The New Victorians: Poverty, Politics, and Propaganda in Two Gilded Ages* (New York: Free Press, 2004).

10. On the reform networks, see Robyn Muncy, *Creating a Female Dominion in American Reform, 1890–1935* (New York: Oxford University Press, 1991).

11. Devine, quoted in John Lankford, *Congress and the Foundations in the Twentieth Century* (River Falls: Wisconsin State University, 1964), 13–14.

12. Attorney General George W. Wickersham, quoted in Lankford, *Congress and the Foundations*, 16.

13. Lankford, *Congress and the Foundations*, 21–25.

14. More detailed accounts of these episodes can be found in Judith Sealander, *Private Wealth and Public Life: Foundation Philanthropy and the Reshaping of American Social Policy from the Progressive Era to the New Deal* (Baltimore: Johns Hopkins University Press, 1997), 218–234; Lankford, *Congress and the Foundations*, 9–32; and Waldemar Nielsen, *The Big Foundations* (New York: Twentieth Century Fund, 1972), 50–54. While acknowledging the appearance of ulterior motives, Sealander and Nielsen treat the coincidences as signs of political naïveté more than conscious efforts to manipulate public opinion on the part of the Rockefellers. On the Walsh Commission, see Mary O. Furner, "Knowing Capitalism," in *The State and Economic Knowledge: The British and American Experiences*, ed. Mary O. Furner and Barry Supple (New York: Cambridge University Press, 1990), 274–84; and Leon Fink, *Progressive Intellectuals and the Dilemmas of Democratic Commitment* (Cambridge, Mass.: Harvard University Press, 1998), 80–114.

15. Walsh quoted in Sealander, *Private Wealth and Public Life*, 224.

16. Commission report quoted in Lankford, *Congress and Foundations*, 30–31.

17. Additional Walsh Commission proposals called for regulations on foundation accumulations and expenditures, a special commission to investigate foundations, and expanded government expenditure in education and social service to counter the influence of private wealth.

18. For an especially enlightening study of the politics of the role of foundations and policy think tanks in labor/capital relations during this period, see G. Mark Hendrickson, "Labor Knowledge and the Building of Modern Industrial Relations, 1918–1929" (Ph.D. dissertation, University of California, Santa Barbara, 2004).

19. Sealander, *Private Wealth and Public Life*; Ellen Lagemann, *The Politics of Knowledge: The Carnegie Corporation, Philanthropy, and Public Policy* (Chicago: University of Chicago Press, 1992); Guy Alchon, "Mary van Kleeck and Social-Economic Planning," *Journal of Policy History* 3, 1 (1991): 1–23.

20. Hearings Before the Select Committee to Investigate Tax-Exempt Foundations

and Comparable Organizations, U.S. House of Representatives, 82nd Congress, 2nd sess. (Washington, D.C.: Government Printing Office, 1953), 1.

21. *Final Report of the Select Committee to Investigate Foundations and Other Organizations.* (Cox Committee Report). U.S. House of Representatives, 82nd Congress, 2nd sess., Report No. 2514 (Washington, D.C.: Government Printing Office, 1953), 21.

22. Foundations were notoriously hard to keep track of before 1950, when the Revenue Act required that they file publicly available statements of assets and grant expenditures to the IRS. The best estimates at the time of the Reece hearings indicate that the number of foundations had grown to nearly 5,000, as compared to just under 30 in 1915. F. Emerson Andrews, *Philanthropic Foundations* (New York: Russell Sage Foundation, 1956), 13–14.

23. Andrews, *Philanthropic Foundations,* 17, 19.

24. H. Rowan Gaither, ed., *Report of the Study for the Ford Foundation on Policy and Program* (Detroit: Ford Foundation, 1949).

25. Gaither report, quoted in Andrews, *Philanthropic Foundations,* 20–21.

26. Henry Ford, III, quoted in Robert Bendiner, "Report on the Ford Foundation," *New York Times Magazine* February 1, 1953, 12.

27. Cox Committee report, 10–11.

28. Fulton, "Foundations Wander into Field of Isms," 1.

29. Thomas C. Reeves, *Foundations Under Fire* (Ithaca, N.Y.: Cornell University Press, 1970), 18.

30. Helen Hill Miller, "Investigating the Foundations," *Reporter,* November 24, 1953, from Rockefeller Archives Center (RAC), Tarrytown, New York, RG 3.2 (Rockefeller Foundation Collection), series 900, box 14, folder 85, 2. See also Harold M. Keele, "Foundations Under Investigation: A Review and Evaluation of Cox, Reece and Patman," unpublished proceedings of New York University's Ninth Biennial Conference on Charitable Foundations, RAC, RG IV4B5 (Council on Foundations Collection), box 7, folder 61.

31. Confidential memoranda from Gerald J. Lynch to Henry Ford, II, April 9, 1952 and May 1, 1952; Arthur Newmyer to Earl Newsom, May 7, 1952, Office Files of H. Rowan Gaither, box 11, folder 129, all in Ford Foundation Archives (FFA), New York.

32. Cox Committee report, 17–18.

33. Cox Committee report, 27.

34. Harold Lord Varney, "Are the Foundations Untouchable?" *American Legion Magazine,* June 1955.

35. Joseph M. Hartfield to Paul Hoffman, August 26, 1952, FFA, Gaither Office Files, box 11, folder 129.

36. Reece's allegations, made in a lengthy extension of his original July 1953 call for renewed investigations, were recorded in a special issue of the *American Foundation News Service,* August 11, 1953, Carnegie Corporation Archives, Columbia University, Rare Book and Manuscript Collections, Butler Library, box 7, folder 5. *The Miracle of America* and the Advertising Council response to Reece's allegations are in FFA, Office Files of Waldemar Nielsen, series I, box 4, folder 38.

37. Varney, "Are the Foundations Untouchable?" 18.

38. Wormser later published an extended missive based on his Reece Committee experience, that came to be highly regarded within the conservative movement and that has recently been reprinted by Radio Liberty. Renee Wormser, *Foundations: Their Power and Influence* (New York: Devon Adair, 1958).

39. Reece Committee hearings quoted in Wormser, *Foundations,* 114.

40. Norman Dodd, "Report to the Special Committee to Investigate Tax Exempt Foundations" (Dodd report), FFA, Nielsen Office Files, box 3, folder 54.

41. Statement by B. Carroll Reece at the opening of the Reece Committee hearings, May 10, 1954.

42. Dodd report, p. 11.

43. Hearings Before the Special Committee to Investigate Tax-Exempt Foundations and Comparable Organizations, 83rd Congress, 2nd sess. (Washington, D.C.: Government Printing Office, 1954); Dodd report, 27–28.

44. Reece Committee Hearings, 1: 864. The exchange is excerpted at length in Lankford, *Congress and the Foundations*, 81–82.

45. One headline sums it up: "Another Stupid Inquiry," *New York Times*, July 5, 1954. The hearings and report also drew a strong rejoinder from economist Sumner H. Slichter in the *Atlantic* and a cutting critique from Dwight Macdonald in his book on the Ford Foundation. Slichter, "Undermining the Foundations," *Atlantic* (September 1954): 50–54; Macdonald, *The Ford Foundation*, 29–35.

46. William McPeak to Rowan Gaither, July 20, 1954, Gaither Office Files, FFA, box 11, folder 139.

47. Among the extensive "briefs" prepared by Carnegie staff members in anticipation of the Reece hearings was a series of "Question and Answer" memoranda based on aspects of grants that might be flagged as subversive. For example, "Memorandum for Council: Questions and Answers re: The Negro in America," Carnegie Corporation Archives, Columbia University, box 6, folder 9. Nielsen to Ford Foundation Trustees, September 8, 1954, Nielsen Office Files, box 5 folder 58.

48. Hiss, as conservatives rarely failed to mention, had been president of the Carnegie Endowment for Peace. A case in point was one-time Ford employee Bernard Gladieux, a veteran of government service in the War Production Board, Budget Bureau, and the Commerce Department who had already been smeared as a "Henry Wallace protege" and who left the foundation while the Reece hearings were underway.

49. Colin Stam to Gaither, October 20, 1954, and reply, "report on luncheon with foundation presidents and American Legion leadership."

50. The most extensive study of the Fund for the Republic is Thomas C. Reeves, *Freedom and the Foundation: The Fund for the Republic in the Era of McCarthyism* (New York: Knopf, 1969). The bibliography, like many Fund projects designed to assuage critics, backfired, bringing a torrent of criticism on the Fund for having missed crucial items in a deliberate effort to minimize the communist threat.

51. The flyers were circulated by a number of groups, including one calling itself the Constitutional Education League, which charged Ford with plotting with the American Bar Association against McCarthyism as well as for communism. Gaither Office Files, box 12, folder 145.

52. James Newmyer to Waldemar Nielsen, December 22, 1954, Nielsen Office Files, box 4, folder 42.

53. William H. Whyte, Jr., "Where the Foundations Fall Down," *Fortune*, November 1955, 219–20.

54. William H. Whyte, Jr., "What Are the Foundations Up To?" *Fortune*, October 1955: 110–13.

55. *Tax-Exempt Foundations and Charitable Trusts: Their Impact on Our Economy. Chairman's Report to the Select Committee on Small Business* (first installment), U.S. House of Representatives, 87th Congress, 1st sess., December 31, 1962 (Washington, D.C.: Government Printing Office, 1962).

56. Nancy Beck Young, *Wright Patman: Populism, Liberalism, and the American Dream* (Dallas: Southern Methodist University Press, 2000).

57. Paul Ylvisaker, Oral History, FFA, 28. For more on foundation/government relationships in the 1960s, see Alice O'Connor, "The Ford Foundation and Philanthropic

Activism in the 1960s," in *Philanthropic Foundations: New Scholarship, New Possibilities*, ed. Ellen Condliffe Lagemann (Bloomington: Indiana University Press, 1999), 169–94; and Ellen Condliffe Lagemann, *The Politics of Knowledge: The Carnegie Corporation, Philanthropy, and Public Policy* (Middletown, Conn.: Wesleyan University Press, 1989), 216–52.

58. For a discussion of Bundy's tenure at the Ford Foundation, see Kai Bird, *The Color of Truth: McGeorge Bundy and William Bundy, Brothers in Arms* (New York: Simon and Schuster, 1998), 376–95.

59. Patman's charges and recommendations are laid out in his Chairman's Report to the Select Committee on Small Business, issued in five installments from 1962–1967. For a detailed discussion of the legal issues, see John E. Reicker, "Foundations and the Patman Committee Report," *Michigan Law Review* 63, 1 (November 1964): 95–140.

60. Jeffrey Hart, "The New Class War," *National Review*, September 9, 1969, 898–99.

61. Hart, "New Class War," 901.

62. Julian E. Zelizer, *Taxing America: Wilbur D. Mills, Congress, and the State, 1945–1975* (New York: Cambridge University Press, 1998), 298–311.

63. For a lively description of the hearings and the atmosphere around them, see Nielsen, *The Big Foundations*, 7–17.

64. Significantly, some also felt they had been used as scapegoats for resentment against concentrated wealth, as a ploy by oil interests to draw attention away from controversy over the oil depletion allowance. Nielson, *The Big Foundations*, 14; Ben Whitaker, *The Foundations: An Anatomy of Philanthropy and Society* (London: Eyre Methuen, 1970), 113.

65. The major changes the big foundations had to contend with were a 4% excise tax on earnings (later reduced to 2%), a "pay-out" requirement of 6%, limits on stock ownership in any single company, and various restrictions on activities such as funding for voter registration.

66. Nielsen, *The Big Foundations*, 18–19.

67. Merrimon Cuninggim, "Broader Significance of the Law," in *Foundations and the Tax Reform Act of 1969: Proceedings of Conferences Held on February 17, 1970 at Kansas City and February 23, 1970 at New York City* (New York: Foundation Center, 1970), 37.

68. On the Powell memo, see David A. Hollinger, "Money and Academic Freedom a Half-Century After McCarthyism: Universities amid the Force Fields of Capital," in *Unfettered Expression: Freedom in American Intellectual Life*, ed. Peggie J. Hollingsworth (Ann Arbor: University of Michigan Press, 161–84); and Oliver A. Houck, "With Charity for All," *Yale Law Journal* 93, 8 (July 1984): 1457–60.

69. William E. Simon, *A Time for Truth* (New York: Reader's Digest Press, 1978), 216, emphasis in original.

70. Simon, *A Time for Truth*, 222.

71. Simon, *A Time for Truth*, 230.

72. David Callahan, "$1 Billion for Ideas: Conservative Think Tanks in the 1990s" (Washington, D.C.: National Center for Responsive Philanthropy, 1999); Sally Covington, "Moving a Public Policy Agenda: The Strategic Philanthropy of Conservative Foundations" (Washington, D.C.: NCRP, 1997); Richard Delgado, Jean Stefancic, and Marck Tushnet, *No Mercy: How Conservative Think Tanks and Foundations Changed America's Social Agenda* (Philadelphia: Temple University Press, 1996); Karen Paget, "The Big Chill: Foundations and Political Passion," *American Prospect* 10, 44 (May–June 1999).

73. See, for example, David Callahan, "Liberal Policy's Weak Foundations," *Nation*, November 13, 1995; Paget, "The Big Chill."

Chapter 12. American Counterrevolutionary:
Lemuel Ricketts Boulware and General Electric, 1950–1960

I would like to thank Greg Vargo for his comments on drafts of this chapter. I would also like to thank Nelson Lichtenstein and the Tamiment Library Labor History Seminar.

1. Godfrey Hodgson, *America in Our Time* (New York: Vintage Books, 1978), 67. Also see James Patterson, *Grand Expectations: The United States, 1945–1974* (New York: Oxford University Press, 1996).

2. For examples of the diverse historiography shaped by the vision of the liberal consensus, see Alan Brinkley, *The End of Reform: New Deal Liberalism in Recession and War* (New York: Knopf, 1994); Robert Collins, *More: The Politics of Economic Growth in Postwar America* (New York: Oxford, 2000); and Theodore Lowi, *The End of Liberalism: The Second Republic of the United States* (New York: W.W. Norton, 1979).

3. Arthur Larson, *A Republican Looks at His Party* (New York: Harper and Brothers, 1956) provides a description of the Eisenhower administration's attitude toward labor and social welfare programs, written by Eisenhower's undersecretary of labor.

4. Sanford Jacoby, *Modern Manors: Welfare Capitalism Since the New Deal* (Princeton, N.J.: Princeton University Press, 1997) discusses antiunion policies at Eastman Kodak, Sears and Thompson Products (later TRW). David Anderson, "The Battle for Main Street, United States of America: Welfare Capitalism, Boosterism and Labor Militancy in the Industrial Heartland, 1895–1963" (Ph.D. dissertation, University of North Carolina at Chapel Hill, 2002), looks at Indiana's Perfect Circle. David Stebenne, *Arthur J. Goldberg: New Deal Liberal* (New York: Oxford University Press, 1996) examines Eugene Germany's Texas-based Lone Star Steel. Rick Perlstein, *Before the Storm: Barry Goldwater and the Unmaking of the American Consensus* (New York: Hill and Wang, 2001) describes the Kohler conflict. Also see Kimberly Phillips-Fein, "Top-Down Revolution: Businessmen, Intellectuals and Politicians Against the New Deal, 1945–1964" (Ph.D. dissertation, Columbia University, 2005).

5. William B. Harris, "The Overhaul of General Electric," *Fortune*, December 1955.

6. Lemuel Boulware Papers, MS Collection 52, Rare Books and Manuscripts Collection at Van Pelt Library, University of Pennsylvania (LBP), box 12, folder 255, Background Memo: "The Myth and Deceit of the 'American Consensus'."

7. For the union shop, see Lemuel Bouware to John Moxon, June 13, 1958, LBP, box 45, folder 1307. Workers at GE had dues check-off provisions and maintenance of membership for the life of the contract, but they did not have a full-fledged union shop. Also see Salvatore Joseph Bella, "Boulwarism and Collective Bargaining at General Electric: A Study in Union-Management Relations" (Ph.D. dissertation, Cornell University, 1962), for more detailed analysis of labor conditions at GE. For the comparison with the auto and steel industries, see Ronald F. Filipelli and Mark D. McColloch, *Cold War in the Working Class: The Rise and Decline of the United Electrical Workers* (Albany: State University of New York Press, 1995), 166.

8. Gerald Zahavi, Interview with A. C. Stevens, Oral History Project: Schenectady General Electric in the Twentieth Century, 29, IUE/UE Local 301 Collection, series 3, box 3, M. E. Grenander Department of Special Collections and Archives, State University of New York at Albany.

9. "Carey vs. Boulware," *Fortune*, October 1952.

10. James Gross, *Broken Promises: The Subversion of U.S. Labor Policy, 1947–1994* (Philadelphia: Temple University Press, 1995), 200–204.

11. Jonathan D. Rosenblum, *Copper Crucible: How the Arizona Miners' Strike of 1983 Recast Labor-Management Relations in America* (Ithaca, N.Y.: ILR Press, 1995), 44, 61–63.

12. See, for example, Elizabeth Fones-Wolf, *Selling Free Enterprise: The Business Assault*

on Labor and Liberalism, 1945–1960 (Urbana: University of Illinois Press, 1994); Howell John Harris, *The Right to Manage: Industrial Relations Policies of American Business in the 1940s* (Madison: University of Wisconsin Press, 1982); Jack Metzgar, *Striking Steel: Solidarity Remembered* (Philadelphia: Temple University Press, 2000); Perlstein, *Before the Storm*; Lisa McGirr, *Suburban Warriors: The Origins of the New American Right* (Princeton, N.J.: Princeton University Press, 2001); Matthew Dallek, *The Right Moment: Ronald Reagan's First Victory and the Decisive Turning Point in American Politics* (New York: Free Press, 2000); Nelson Lichtenstein, *State of the Union: A Century of American Labor* (Princeton, N.J.: Princeton University Press, 2002), esp. chap. 3.

13. Roland Marchand, *Creating the Corporate Soul: The Rise of Public Relations and Corporate Imagery in American Big Business* (Berkeley: University of California Press, 1998), 151–55.

14. David Loth, *Swope of GE: The Story of Gerard Swope and General Electric in American Business* (New York: Simon and Schuster, 1958), 31–34.

15. James Matles and James Higgins, *Them and Us: Struggles of a Rank-and-File Union* (Englewood Cliffs, N.J.: Prentice-Hall, 1974), 78–88. Ronald Schatz, *The Electrical Workers: A History of Labor at General Electric and Westinghouse, 1923–1960* (Urbana: University of Illinois Press, 1983), 70–74. Also see Ronald Schatz, "The End of Corporate Liberalism: Class Struggle in the Electrical Manufacturing Industry," *Radical America* 9 (July–August 1975), for an analysis of the 1946 strike that emphasizes the unique economic position of GE. Nor did this liberalism entirely disappear in the late 1940s, after the emergence of labor conflict at GE—Charles E. Wilson ("Electric Charlie") headed President Harry Truman's commission on civil rights in 1947, which called for the desegregation of the military and for federal action on behalf of civil rights.

16. Schatz, "The End of Corporate Liberalism," 194.

17. Schatz, "The End of Corporate Liberalism," 195.

18. Matles and Higgins, *Them and Us*, 138–39.

19. Schatz, "The End of Corporate Liberalism," 199.

20. Matles and Higgins, *Them and Us*, 142.

21. A. H. Raskin, "200,000 Quit in 16 States, Mass Picketing Is Started, Electrical Workers Swell Ranks of Nation's Strikers," *New York Times*, January 16, 1946.

22. Matles and Higgins, *Them and Us*, 144.

23. "Getting First-Hand Strike Information," Associated Press Wirephoto, *New York Times*, January 20, 1946. Students from Mount Holyoke joined a Westinghouse picket line, carrying signs reading "Salary Workers Need $2 a Day Too!"

24. Matles and Higgins, *Them and Us*, 144. The statement read, "UE workers deserve full moral and financial support in their grim struggle for a substantial wage increase and for a decent American standard of living."

25. Lucy Greenbaum, "Townfolk in Bloomsfield Support Strike of Its Electrical Workers," *New York Times*, January 16, 1946.

26. Associated Press Wirephoto, "A Juvenile Picket Line on the March at Westinghouse Electric Plant," *New York Times*, February 23, 1946.

27. U.S. Congress, Senate, Committee on Education and Labor. Hearings . . . on S. 1661, A Bill to Provide for the Appointment of Fact-Finding Boards to Investigate Labor Disputes, 79th Congress, 1st and 2nd sess., Part 1, 644.

28. Schatz, *The Electrical Workers*, 145.

29. Senate Hearings, Part I, 1945–1946, 647.

30. Senate Hearings, 645.

31. Senate Hearings, 652.

32. See Herbert Northrup, *Boulwarism* (Ann Arbor: University of Michigan Press, 1964), 21, for more on the company's mindset following the strike.

33. Paul Warner to the Goodyear Company January 19, 1920. LBP, box 8, folder 22.

34. Northrup, *Boulwarism*, 25–26 Warner to the Goodyear Company, January 19, 1920.

35. "Proposed Program of Industrial and Community Relations," August 1, 1945. Charles E. Wilson, the chief executive at GE, wrote at the top of the memo, "Mr. Boulware: A splendid contribution, I think. Give it wide distribution." LBP, box 8, folder 154.

36. LBP, box 9, folder 181.

37. Memo dated April 2, 1955. LBP, box 8, folder 166.

38. Division Managers Meeting memo, dated November 17, 1954. LBP, box 8, folder 170.

39. Stephen K. Galpin, "Boulwareism: C.I.O. Cries Foul as 'Tough but Fair' Wage Policy Spreads," *Wall Street Journal*, November 3, 1954, 1.

40. Memo, July 1, 1960. LBP, box 10, folder 196.

41. Boulware, "A Job of Two Magnitudes," speech to employee relations managers, December 8, 1959. LBP, box 80, folder 1619.

42. Directors' meeting notes, December 17, 1954. LBP, box 8, folder 170.

43. *GE Schenectady News*, January 14, 1955. Library, State University of New York, Albany.

44. *GE Schenectady News*, February 11, 1955.

45. *GE Schenectady News*, July 15, 1955.

46. "Highlights of the General Electric Economic Education Program." GE Corporate Archive Files, Kheel Center for Labor-Management Co-operation, Catherwood Library, Cornell University (AOF), accession 5583, box 52.0

47. "Supervisor's Guide to GE Job Information," 5. AOF, Accession 5583-53, box 57.

48. Lemuel Boulware, *The Truth About Boulwarism: Trying to Do Right Voluntarily* (Washington, D.C.: Bureau of National Affairs, 1969), 31.

49. "Supervisor's Guide to GE Job Information," 106. It is not altogether clear how long the guide was distributed to supervisors.

50. Boulware, *The Truth About Boulwarism*, 59.

51. "Highlights of the General Electric Economic Education Program," AOF, accession 5583, box 52.

52. He donated his copies of their books to the Van Pelt Library of the University of Pennsylvania along with his papers.

53. For Burke, see Directors' Notes, December 17, 1954. LBP, box 8, folder 170. For Friedman, see "The Free Market vs. Government Direction of our Economy," 1960, folder 210.

54. Lisa Ann Kannenberg, "The Product of GE's Progress: Labor, Management and Community Relations in Schenectady, 1930–1960" (Ph.D. dissertation, Rutgers University, 1999), 215.

55. Boulware, *The Truth About Boulwarism*, 30–38.

56. Boulware, *The Truth About Boulwarism*, 58.

57. "Proposed Program of Plant and Community Relations," August 1, 1945. LBP, box 8, folder 154.

58. Peter Brimelow, "A Look Back at Boulwarism," *Forbes*, May 29, 1989, 77.

59. "Program for Clergy," General Electric, undated. AOF, accession 5583, box 53.

60. "The Overhaul of General Electric," *Fortune*, December 1955.

61. Kannenberg, "The Product of GE's Progress," 199.

62. Zahavi interview with Stevens, 29–30.

63. Kannenberg, "The Product of GE's Progress," 201.

64. Kannenberg, "The Product of GE's Progress," 199–203. The loyalties of the upper strata of the workforce—foremen and white collar workers—were an important

battleground for management during the 1950s. See, for example, Lichtenstein, *State of the Union*, 118–22.

65. John McCarty to Lemuel Boulware, March 29, 1957. Peter Steele Papers, box 2, correspondence D-G, Knight Library, University of Oregon.

66. Peter Steele to Thurston Steele, April 1, 1957. Peter Steele Papers, box 2, correspondence D-G.

67. Schatz, *The Electrical Workers*, 233–38.

68. LBP, box 35, folder 904.

69. LPB, box 42, folder 1180.

70. "Politics: The Businessman's Biggest Job in 1958," speech given May 21, 1958 to Phoenix Chamber of Commerce. AOF, accession 5583, box 61.

71. Kannenberg, "The Product of GE's Progress," 225–26.

72. John Callahan testimony (Callahan was chairman of the IUE-GE Conference Board) before Special Senate Committee on Unemployment, January 8, 1960, 2–3. IUE/UE Local 301 Collection, reel 2.

73. The union newspaper described one such work stoppage in 1957, which was over issues involving the upgrading of long-time employees. The contract grievance was settled after the work stoppage in the Turbine Department. However, even though the turbine workers had won, the department managers were reluctant to apply the settlement elsewhere in the plant. *Local 301 News*, April 19, 1957. IUE/ UE Local 301 Collection, reel 3.

74. Memo dated September 12, 1956. While it is an unsigned memo, it is written in Boulware's style. LBP, box 9, folder 180.

75. Memo dated July 1, 1960. LBP, box 10, folder 196.

76. GE *Schenectady News*, September 16, 1960.

77. Zahavi interview with Stevens, 45. Also see Ellen Schrecker, *Many Are the Crimes: McCarthyism in America* (Princeton, N.J.: Princeton University Press, 1997), 188, for the Atomic Energy Commission's ban of UE in certain GE plants working on atomic energy; Schatz, *The Electrical Workers*, 238–40, for the impact of the "Cordiner doctrine" of firing workers who took the Fifth Amendment; and David Caute, *The Great Fear: The Anti-Communist Purge Under Truman and Eisenhower* (New York: Simon and Schuster, 1978), 387–89.

78. Address before the National Canners' Association, Chicago, February 21, 1959. LBP, box 80, folder 1613.

79. "Carey vs. Boulware," *Fortune*, October 1952.

80. "Carey vs. Boulware."

81. Boulware, "Salvation is *Not* Free." OAF, accession 5583, box 60. Boulware gave versions of this speech to many different audiences, including the Economic Club of Chicago, the Economic Club of Detroit, Sales Executives Club, American Chamber of Commerce Executives Convention, California Personnel Management Association, National Tool and Die Manufacturers Association, Summit County Employers Association and others. AOF, GE Corporate Pamphlets, accession 5583, box 57.

82. Memo, September 24, 1958, on Salt Lake City Conference September 21–22, Sponsored by the National Right-to-Work Committee. James Clise Papers, box 9, folder on Voluntary Unionism, Knight Library, University of Oregon.

83. Memo, November 26, 1958. LMB, box 10, folder 196.

84. LMB, box 9, folder 193. Also see Regnery papers at the Hoover Institute; Boulware often read and commented on manuscripts for Henry Regnery, the conservative publishing house.

85. Boulware to Clark, June 17, 1958.

86. Editorial, *Fortune*, October 1958; "Business and Elections," *Wall Street Journal*, October 14, 1958.

87. Collins to Boulware, September 16, 1958. LBP, box 34, folder 864. Collins also praised Sears and Ford.

88. Boulware was a frequent contributor to conservative causes as an individual. By 1966, he had given $11,200 to the Intercollegiate Society of Individualists, $4,750 to Americans for Constitutional Action, $1,000 to American Conservative Union, and more money to the Foundation for Economic Education, the American Economics Foundation, the Freedom School and the Intercollegiate Society of Individualists. LBP, box 39, folder 1066.

89. Perlstein, *Before the Storm,* 441. Also see LBP, box 35, folder 880.

90. Goldwater to Boulware, April 27, 1978. LBP, box 38, folder 1040. This nostalgic correspondence continued into the 1980s. In 1983, Goldwater wrote, "The fact that I failed really was not too important. The important thing is that through men like you we did start a realization, which is growing more and more, of the fundamental facts of life, the fundamental facts of philosophy that have made America great. In my book, Lem Boulware is going to go down as one of the men we should have had more of as we progressed through the year, rather torturous ones that have produced nothings." (Goldwater to Boulware, June 13, 1983). Boulware responded in similar fashion: "It is to you we all owe the bringing of sensible conservatism out into the open. . . . You may have lost the one battle along the way. But you are now winning the war" (Boulware to Goldwater, June 20, 1983). Later, Goldwater wrote to Boulware, "Don't be thanking me for anything I've done in politics. Thank yourself and a few others, just a handful, who had the courage to stand behind me when I was beginning to say things that the rest of the people didn't like or understand" (Goldwater to Boulware, September 10, 1984). LBP, box 37, folder 1040.

91. Earl Dunckel, "Ronald Reagan and the General Electric Theater, 1954–55," oral history conducted 1982 by Gabrielle Morris (1982), 15. Bancroft Library, University of California at Berkeley.

92. Reagan to Boulware, January 13, 1966. LBP, box 48, folder 1435.

93. Reagan to Boulware, January 2, 1975. LBP, box 48, folder 1435.

94. Reagan to Boulware, undated sometime in 1981. LBP, box 48, folder 1435.

95. Lemuel Boulware, "Why Should General Electric Take on the Job of Marketing Public Opinion?" LBP, box 8, folder 165.

96. Boulware, "Salvation is *Not* Free."

97. Matles and Higgins, *Them and Us,* 252; Schatz, *The Electrical Workers,* 232. Also see Caute, *The Great Fear,* for more on anticommunism in the electrical industry.

98. A. H. Raskin, "GE's Labor Formula: Its Technique in Strike May Foster Stiffening in Management's Approach," *New York Times,* October 25, 1960.

99. For descriptions of the management offensive of the late 1950s and early 1960s, see Jacoby, *Modern Manors;* Stebenne, *Arthur J. Goldberg;* Metzgar, *Striking Steel;* Fones-Wolf, *Selling Free Enterprise;* Michael Goldfield, *The Decline of Organized Labor in the United States* (Chicago: University of Chicago Press, 1987); and Mike Davis, *Prisoners of the American Dream: Politics and Economy in the History of the U.S. Working Class* (London: Verso, 1986).

100. Bella, "Boulwarism and Collective Bargaining," 300–400.

101. Bella, "Boulwarism and Collective Bargaining," 410.

102. "The Story of General Electric's 1960 Negotiations with the IUE," iii. LBP, box 10, folder 206.

103. Victor Riesel, "Inside Labor," *South Bend Tribune* (Indiana), April 18, 1960. Riesel was reporting on a meeting of GE management employees. Cited in Bella, "Boulwarism and Collective Bargaining," 425–26.

104. "Electrical Workers' Strike of GE to Get First Test of Support Today," unsigned news roundup, *Wall Street Journal,* October 3, 1960.

105. "GE Says Strike Halts Only 1 Plant in 1st Work Day," unsigned news roundup, *Wall Street Journal*, October 4, 1960.

106. "IUE Calls Westinghouse Strike Chances 'Excellent'; GE Talks Remain Deadlocked," unsigned news roundup, *Wall Street Journal*, October 12, 1960.

107. "Picketing Subsides at GE's Schenectady Plant: Salaried Employees Allowed to Enter," unsigned news roundup, *Wall Street Journal*, October 11, 1960.

108. October 10, 1960. LBP, box 10, folder 204.

109. October 3, 1960. LBP, box 10, folder 204.

110. September 27, 1960. LBP, box 10, folder 203.

111. LBP, box 10, folder 205.

112. "Beyond General Electric," October 14, 1960. LBP, box 10, folder 205.

113. Kannenberg, "The Product of GE's Progress," 270.

114. "Over 50,000 GE Strikers Return to Work," *Wall Street Journal*, October 24, 1960.

115. Maurice Franks to Lemuel Boulware, November 2, 1960. LBP, box 37, folder 1010.

116. Raymond Dykema to Lemual Boulware, November 1, 1960. Dykema was a partner at Dykema, Wheat, Spencer, Goodnow & Trigg, a law office in Detroit. LBP, box 35, folder 942.

117. Maxwell Goodwin to Lemuel Boulware, Ocober 25, 1960. LBP, box 37, folder 1044.

118. Donald Ordway to Lemuel Boulware, October 28, 1960. LBP, box 47, folder 1370.

119. Arthur Rosenbaum to Lemuel Boulware, October 25, 1960. LBP, box 49, folder 1472.

120. Executive office meeting memo, November 14, 1960. LBP, box 10, folder 206.

121. Jacoby, *Modern Manors*, 244.

122. Matles and Higgins, *Them and Us*, 262–88.

123. Brimelow, "A Look Back at Boulwarism," 78.

Chapter 13. Godless Capitalism: Ayn Rand and the Conservative Movement

An earlier version of this chapter appears in *Modern Intellectual History* 1, 3 (November 2004): 1–27; reprinted by permission. For their invaluable assistance, I would like to thank Charles Capper, George Cotkin, David A. Hollinger, Nelson Lichtenstein, Joyce Mao, Kristen Richardson, and three anonymous readers.

1. Buckley to Isabel Paterson, January 7, 1958, "Paterson, Isabel (1958)," William F. Buckley Papers, box 6, Yale University Library. Buckley repeated the anecdote (with slightly different spelling) in "On the Right: Ayn Rand, RIP," *National Review*, April 2, 1982, 380.

2. Terminological clarity is elusive when discussing the historic right in America. "New Conservatism" was used generally in the 1950s, in reference to a reassertion of conservative beliefs in the wake of World War II. It is distinct from later conservatism which embraced laissez-faire, as described in this chapter. Then there is the "New Right," a term scholars generally employ either when discussing the Goldwater movement of the 1960s or politically active Christians in the 1970s. I reserve the term "Old Right" for phenomena of the prewar period.

3. Recent scholarship has begun to emphasize the importance of libertarianism, a belief system which Rand both embodied and influenced. This new literature has also delineated the role of corporations and businesspeople in the development

of conservative ideology. See Elizabeth Fones-Wolf, *Selling Free Enterprise: The Business Assault on Labor and Liberalism, 1945–1960* (Urbana: University of Illinois Press, 1994), Rick Perlstein, *Before the Storm: Barry Goldwater and the Unmaking of the American Consensus* (New York: Hill and Wang, 2001). Although most treatments of the 1960s acknowledge her influence, academic work on Rand herself remains scarce. For this reason, I will briefly sketch key features of her thought in this piece.

4. The most useful definition of conservatism, and the one I will employ here, is that given by George H. Nash. He defines conservatism as the postwar political and social movement that opposed liberal reform efforts and encompassed three main impulses: libertarian antistatism, anticommunism, and reverence for tradition (usually rendered as explicitly Christian). I also employ the term "right-wing" to refer to persons and thought that might share some but not all features of this trinitarian conservatism. So, in other words, all conservatives are right-wing, but not all those on the right are conservative (e.g., Rand). George H. Nash, *The Conservative Intellectual Movement Since 1945* (New York: Basic Books, 1976). Nash discusses Rand as an episode in the conservative process of "fusion." Nash concurs with Buckley's opinion that Rand was successfully "read out" of the movement, but does not explore the ambiguity surrounding her work or the deeper issues she raised (142–45). For a critique of Nash, see Jennifer Burns, "In Retrospect: George Nash's *The Conservative Intellectual Movement in America Since 1945*," *Reviews in American History* 32 (September 2004): 447–62.

5. For Meyer's role in the formation of conservative ideology, see Kevin J. Smant, *Principles and Heresies: Frank S. Meyer and the Shaping of the American Conservative Movement* (Wilmington, Del.: ISI Books, 2002).

6. John Leo, "Buckley Explains Views to a Class," *New York Times*, November 22, 1967.

7. These figures are from Nora Ephron, "A Strange Kind of Simplicity," *New York Times Book Review*, May 5, 1968, 8, 42–43, and Barbara Branden, *The Passion of Ayn Rand* (New York: Doubleday, 1987), 180, 299.

8. At the time of Chambers's review, *National Review* had 18,000 subscribers; in 1961 it had 54,000; and in 1964 it reached a high point of 90,000. John B. Judis, *William F. Buckley, Jr.: Patron Saint of the Conservatives* (New York: Simon and Schuster, 1988), 140, 221.

9. The controversy is covered in Nash, *The Conservative Intellectual Movement*, 120–24.

10. Judis, *William F. Buckley, Jr.*, 140.

11. See, for example, her printed debate against Oswald Garrison Villard, former editor of the *New York Evening Post* and the *Nation*, on the theme, "Collectivism or Individualism: Which Promises Postwar Progress?" Syndicated in the series *Wake Up America*, October 11, 1943. Distributed by Fred G. Clark, American Economic Foundation.

12. Rand was born into a middle-class Jewish family. Upon arriving in the United States, she changed her name from the unmistakably Jewish "Alissa Rosenbaum" to the androgynous, Nordic sounding "Ayn Rand." While there is no evidence to suggest that Rand deliberately wished to cover up her Jewish roots, the name change did embody her belief that history and tradition should have little impact on the course of an individual's life. Despite this, it is a notable feature of Rand's career that with the exception of her husband, nearly all her close associates were secular Jews.

13. Rand to Jean Wick, October 27, 1934, in *Letters of Ayn Rand*, ed. Michael S. Berliner (New York: Dutton, 1995), 18.

14. Ayn Rand, *We the Living* (1936; New York: Random House, 1959), 80.

15. Robert Green McCloskey, *American Conservatism in the Age of Enterprise: A Study of William Graham Sumner, Stephen J. Field, and Andrew Carnegie* (Cambridge, Mass.:

Harvard University Press, 1951). Although some of Rand's ideas seem akin to Sumner's, in 1944 she had never heard of him. Rand to Leonard Read, November 12, 1944, "Freedom Quotations Book, Correspondence 1944," Rose Wilder Lane Papers, box 33, Herbert Hoover Presidential Archives, National Archives and Records Administration, West Branch, Iowa. For a discussion of anti-Roosevelt sentiment in Congress, see James T. Patterson, *Congressional Conservatism and the New Deal: The Growth of the Conservative Coalition in Congress, 1933–1939* (Lexington: University Press of Kentucky, 1967). Also helpful on this period is George R. Wolfskill, *Revolt of the Conservatives: A History of the Liberty League, 1934–1940* (Boston: Houghton Mifflin, 1962).

16. Hayek's *The Road to Serfdom* might well be taken as a theoretical exposition of the themes Rand's novel embodied. Both agreed that seemingly benevolent impulses to social planning in fact masked a dictatorial power grab, drew on their experiences in totalitarian Europe to reflect on American politics, and employed an absolutist, "slippery slope" logic to predict that socialism would lead inevitably to communism and then totalitarianism. Nock is well known to students of conservative thought, but Lane and Paterson are not. Lane's life and work are described in William Holtz, *The Ghost in the Little House: A Life of Rose Wilder Lane* (Columbia: University of Missouri Press, 1993); Paterson's career is covered in Stephen Cox, *The Woman and the Dynamo: Isabel Paterson and the Idea of America* (New Brunswick, N.J.: Transaction Publishers, 2004). Libertarians fete all three women as foremothers of their movement. See Jim Powell, "Rose Wilder Lane, Isabel Paterson, and Ayn Rand: Three Women Who Inspired the Modern Libertarian Movement," *Freeman,* May 1996.

17. Nock coined this word to identify a worldview that "interpreted the whole of human life in terms of the production, acquisition, and distribution of wealth." Albert J. Nock, *Memoirs of a Superfluous Man* (New York: Harper Brothers, 1943), 111.

18. Details on Rand's political awakening are taken from *Biographical Interview with Ayn Rand Conducted by Barbara Branden,* Interview 14, tape 8, side 1, "Activities in Politics: 1926 to 1952, The Conservatives," 351–55. Ayn Rand Papers, Ayn Rand Archives, Irvine, California.

19. Carl Snyder, *Capitalism the Creator: The Economic Foundations of Modern Industrial Society* (New York: Macmillan, 1940), 4. Interestingly, Snyder's work was also read by Hayek. See F. A. Hayek, Review of *Capitalism the Creator* by Carl Snyder, *Economica* 7, 28 (November 1940): 437–39.

20. Rand to DeWitt Emery, May 17, 1943, *Letters,* 73.

21. Ayn Rand, *Journals of Ayn Rand,* ed. David Harriman (New York: Dutton, 1997), 113.

22. Ayn Rand, *The Fountainhead,* Fiftieth Anniversary Edition (New York: Penguin, 1993), 684.

23. Rand's Hollywood career is fascinating, but beyond the scope of this paper. In the 1920s and 1930s, she was a screenwriter for several major studios. In 1949 she testified as a friendly witness before HUAC. *The Fountainhead* movie, which starred Gary Cooper, opened in 1949 and was also drawn into the fight against communism. The Committee for Constitutional Government distributed postcards touting the film and encouraging families to see it together as an educational experience. Ayn Rand Papers, box 143–33-C4. For a discussion of the film and its contribution to Cold War discourse, see Robert Spadoni, "Guilty by Omission: Girding The 'Fountainhead' for the Cold War (Ayn Rand)," *Literature-Film Quarterly* 27, 3 (1999): 223–32.

24. The two were Canadians, born Nathaniel Blumenthal and Barbara Weidman. After becoming deeply involved with Rand, they married and changed their surnames to Branden.

25. Rand to John Chamberlain, November 27, 1948, *Letters,* 413.

26. Ayn Rand, *Atlas Shrugged*, Thirty-Fifth Anniversary Edition (New York: Penguin, 1992), 858.

27. For an analysis of nostalgia in Rand's thought, see Andrew Hoberek, "Ayn Rand and the Politics of Property," in *The Twilight of the Middle Class: Post-World War II American Fiction and White-Collar Work* (Princeton, N.J.: Princeton University Press, 2005).

28. *Atlas Shrugged*, 387. Christopher Hitchens suggests that Rand's forward looking vision of capitalism accounts for her popularity in Silicon Valley. See Hitchens, "Why So Many High-Tech Executives Have Declared Allegiance to Randian Objectivism," *Business 2.0*, August 2001.

29. *Atlas Shrugged*, 389.

30. *Atlas Shrugged*, 680.

31. *Atlas Shrugged*, 387–91. It should be noted that this speech was among the most popular parts of the book; Rand granted countless requests for reprints. Rand was a favorite content provider for business owners who sought to spread the gospel of free enterprise. For a description of organized business campaigns against unions, see Fones-Wolf, *Selling Free Enterprise*. Politically engaged small business owners like those who contacted Rand were also committed backers of Barry Goldwater, whose candidacy she supported. See Perlstein, *Before the Storm*, 4–6. Also see note 49.

32. *Atlas Shrugged*, 439, 441.

33. *Atlas Shrugged*, 566–68.

34. Granville Hicks, "A Parable of Buried Talents," *New York Times Book Review*, October 26, 1957, 4–5. The positive *Times* review of *The Fountainhead* is Lorine Pruette, "The Battle Against Evil," *New York Times Book Review*, May 16, 1943, 7, 18.

35. Helen Beal Woodward, "Atlas Shrugged," *Saturday Review*, October 12, 1957, 25.

36. "The Solid Gold Dollar Sign," *Time*, October 14, 1957, 128. A prime example of a reviewer having fun at Rand's expense is Donald Malcolm, "The New Rand Atlas," *New Yorker*, October 26, 1957, 194.

37. Whittaker Chambers, "Big Sister Is Watching You," *National Review*, December 28, 1957, 594–96.

38. See Nock, *Memoirs*.

39. Whittaker Chambers, *Odyssey of a Friend: Whittaker Chambers' Letters to William F. Buckley, Jr.* (New York: Putnam's, 1969), 227–28.

40. Chambers, *Odyssey of a Friend*, 229.

41. According to Buckley's biographer, he never fully comprehended the grounds of difference between himself and Chambers. See Judis, *William F. Buckley, Jr.*, 167, 177.

42. Buckley referred to the article whenever asked about Rand in subsequent years. *National Review* also reprinted the article in its Thirty-Fifth Anniversary Issue, dated November 5, 1990.

43. John Chamberlain, "Reviewer's Notebook: Atlas Shrugged," *Freeman*, December 1957, 53–56. Another defender was Isabel Paterson, who felt the review to be unconscionably mean spirited and possibly libelous. See Paterson to Buckley, January 2, 1958, "Paterson, Isabel (1958)," Buckley Papers, box 6. Robert LeFevre of the Freedom School was also upset by the review. E. Merrill Root to Buckley, January 1, 1960, "Root, E. Merrill (1960)," box 11.

44. John Chamberlain, "To The Editor: An Open Letter to Ayn Rand," *National Review*, February 1, 1958, 118.

45. E. Merrill Root, "What About Ayn Rand?" *National Review*, January 30, 1960, 76.

46. *Atlas Shrugged*, 936–93. See also E. Merrill Root, *Collectivism on the Campus: The Battle for the Mind in American Colleges* (New York: Devin Adair, 1956) and *Brainwashing in the High Schools: An Examination of Eleven American History Textbooks* (New York: Devin Adair, 1958).

47. Wills to Buckley, February 10, 1960, "Wills, Garry (1960)," Buckley Papers, box 12.

48. Buckley to Wills, February 15, 1960, Buckley Papers, box 12.

49. See note 31. There was significant overlap between the followers of Rand and Goldwater. Rand corresponded frequently with the campaign and one of Goldwater's main speechwriters, Karl Hess, was heavily involved in the Objectivist movement. See Paul Richard, "Writer Rests His Pen, Turns to Blowtorch," *Washington Post*, November 21, 1967, B3.

50. Garry Wills, "But Is Ayn Rand Conservative?" *National Review*, February 27, 1960, 139.

51. For the Catholic influence at *National Review*, and in the conservative movement more generally, see Patrick Allitt, *Catholic Intellectuals and Conservative Politics in America, 1950–1985* (Ithaca, N.Y.: Cornell University Press, 1993) and Nash, *The Conservative Intellectual Movement Since 1945*.

52. Rand later published an essay based on the lecture, from which these quotations are taken. Ayn Rand, *Capitalism: The Unknown Ideal* (New York: Penguin, 1967), 194.

53. *Capitalism*, 198.

54. *Capitalism*, 195.

55. The most famous representative of this group is Alan Greenspan, who continues to speak of Rand as an important mentor. Also see Rebecca E. Klatch, *A Generation Divided: The New Left, the New Right, and the 1960s* (Berkeley: University of California Press, 1999), and *Women of the New Right* (Philadelphia: Temple University Press, 1987), and John A. Andrew, III, *The Other Side of the Sixties: Young Americans for Freedom and the Rise of Conservative Politics* (New Brunswick, N.J.: Rutgers University Press, 1997), 238. It is by no means insignificant that Rand was particularly attractive to youth. Although few retained equal levels of devotion in maturity, as Karl Mannheim argues, a person's "natural view of the world" is often formed in the years seventeen to twenty-five and thus an early encounter with Rand could have had a long-standing impact. Karl Mannheim, "The Problem of Generations," in *Essays on the Sociology of Knowledge*, ed. Paul Kecskemeti (London: Routledge and Kegan Paul, 1952), 291.

56. *The Objectivist* replaced *The Objectivist Newsletter* (1962–1965) and was later superseded by *The Ayn Rand Letter* (1971–1976).

57. Rand opposed civil rights to the extent that civil rights leaders advocated government intervention to achieve their goals. On many college campuses, Objectivist students held counterdemonstrations to student protestors. The Rand-inspired Committee for the Defense of Property Rights at Columbia University even distributed "Abolish SDS" buttons and literature. Ayn Rand Archives, box 5–01–18A.

58. For more on Evans's career, and Rand's influence on YAF, see Andrew, *The Other Side of the Sixties*, 65, 61–62.

59. Buckley to Evans, February 28, 1967, "Evans, M. Stanton," Buckley Papers, box 43.

60. M. Stanton Evans, "The Gospel According to Ayn Rand," *National Review*, October 3, 1957, 1067.

61. Jerome Himmelstein erroneously claims that it was the Christian conservatives who were able to reshape capitalism as a moral system. As the debates surrounding fusionism in the 1950s make clear, it was the Christians who had the most trouble with capitalism, and it was the libertarians who argued against them that capitalism should be regarded as a moral system. Rand was the most vigorous, but not the sole, expositor of this argument. Himmelstein, *To the Right: The Transformation of American Conservatism* (Berkeley: University of California Press, 1990), 45.

62. The trouble began when Nathaniel Branden terminated his longstanding affair with Rand. Details of these events and the relationship are given in Nathaniel Branden, *My Years with Ayn Rand* (San Francisco: Jossey-Bass, 1999) and Barbara Branden, *The Passion of Ayn Rand.*

63. For an observation on this, see TRB, "The Ayn Rand Factor," *New Republic,* July 19, 1975.

64. William F. Buckley, Jr., *Getting It Right* (Washington, D.C.: Regnery, 2003).

65. Two influential recent books that assume the desirability of capitalism are Francis Fukuyama, *The End of History and the Last Man* (New York: Free Press, 1992), and Thomas L. Friedman, *The Lexus and the Olive Tree: Understanding Globalization* (New York: Farrar, Straus, Giroux, 1999).

66. Wills was also dissatisfied with the conservative reaction to civil rights. For an able discussion of his career, see Allitt, *Catholic Intellectuals,* chap. 7.

67. In reality, it was more often the case that conservative youth moved from religion to Objectivism than vice versa. See Jerome Tuccile, *It Usually Begins with Ayn Rand* (New York: Stein and Day, 1971).

Contributors

HOWARD BRICK, Professor of History at Washington University in St. Louis, is the author of *Daniel Bell and the Decline of Intellectual Radicalism, Age of Contradiction: American Thought and Culture in the 1960s* and *Beyond the Bourgeoisie: The Postcapitalist Vision and American Social Liberalism in the Twentieth Century.* His latest research follows the history of modern ideas concerning world social development, prior to the advent of "globalization."

JENNIFER BURNS received her Ph.D. in American history from the University of California, Berkeley in 2005, where her dissertation focused on Ayn Rand. She has published articles on the history of American conservatism in *Modern Intellectual History* and *Reviews in American History.*

DAVID C. ENGERMAN is Associate Professor of History at Brandeis University, where he teaches American international and intellectual history. He is the author of *Modernization from the Other Shore: American Intellectuals and the Romance of Russian Development,* coeditor of *Staging Growth: Modernization, Development and the Global Cold War,* and editor of a new edition of *The God That Failed.* He is writing a history of American Sovietology and the making of the Cold War.

DANIEL GEARY is Lecturer in Intellectual and Cultural History at the School of American and Canadian Studies, University of Nottingham. His first book, *The Power and the Intellect: C. Wright Mills, the Left, and American Social Science,* is forthcoming.

NILS GILMAN is an independent scholar who lives in San Francisco. He is author of *Mandarins of the Future,* an intellectual history of modernization theory, and coeditor of *Staging Growth: Modernization, Development, and the Global Cold War.* He is writing a history of managerial thought in the twentieth century.

DANIEL HOROWITZ, Mary Huggins Gamble Professor of American Studies at Smith College, is a historian who writes about U.S. consumer culture and social criticism. He is the author, most recently, of *The Anxieties of Affluence: Critiques of American Consumer Culture, 1939–1979* and *Betty Friedan and the Making of* The Feminine Mystique: *The American Left, the Cold War, and Modern Feminism.*

NELSON LICHTENSTEIN is Professor of History at the University of California, Santa Barbara, where he directs the Center for Work, Labor, and Democracy. He is the author of *Walter Reuther: The Most Dangerous Man in Detroit* and *State of the Union: A Century of American Labor* and editor of *Wal-Mart: The Face of 21ˢᵗ Century Capitalism.* He writes for *New Labor Forum, Dissent, Nation,* and the *Los Angeles Times.*

KEVIN MATTSON is Connor Study Professor of Contemporary History at Ohio University, where he teaches American intellectual history. He is author of *When America Was Great: The Fighting Faith of Postwar Liberalism* and *Intellectuals in Action: The Origins of the New Left and Radical Liberalism, 1945–1970.* He is writing a biography of Upton Sinclair. His essays have appeared in the *New York Times Book Review, Nation, American Prospect,* and other publications.

CHRISTOPHER A. MCAULEY, Associate Professor of Black Studies at the University of California, Santa Barbara, is the author of *The Mind of Oliver C. Cox.*

ALICE O'CONNOR is Associate Professor of History at the University of California, Santa Barbara. She is the author of *Poverty Knowledge: Social Science, Social Policy, and the Poor in Twentieth-Century U.S. History,* coeditor (with Chris Tilly and Lawrence Bobo) of *Urban Inequality: Evidence from Four Cities,* and coeditor (with Gwendolyn Mink) of *Poverty and Social Welfare in the United States: An Encyclopedia of History, Policy, and Politics.* Her current research focuses on the politics and cultural meaning of wealth in the post-World War II United States.

CHRISTOPHER PHELPS, Associate Professor of History at the Ohio State University at Mansfield, is the author of *Young Sidney Hook: Marxist and Pragmatist.* He edited Max Shachtman's *Race and Revolution* and a new edition of Upton Sinclair's *The Jungle.*

KIMBERLY PHILLIPS-FEIN teaches History and Political Economy at the Gallatin School for Individualized Study at New York University. She is working on a book about the role of business in the development of the conservative movement in the postwar period, which will be published by W.W. Norton. Her writing has appeared in *Dissent, Nation, Baffler,* and *Reviews in American History.*

PADDY RILEY is a Ph.D candidate in U.S. history at the University of California, Berkeley. He is writing a dissertation on the Democratic-Republican Party and the politics of slavery in the early national period.

JULIET WILLIAMS teaches at the University of California, Santa Barbara, where she holds a joint appointment in the Law & Society Program and the Women's Studies Program. She is the author of *Liberalism and the Limits of Power* and coeditor (with Paul Apostolidis) of *Public Affairs: Politics in the Age of Sex Scandals.*

Index

Acknowledgments

In the conceptualization of the 2003 UCSB conference, Capitalism and Its Culture: Rethinking Twentieth Century American Social Thought, and the collection of articles that has emerged from it, George Cotkin has proven himself indispensable, a shrewd and sympathetic guide to the people, ideas, and texts that together constitute this book. Along the way, Casey Blake, Howard Brick, Mary Furner, Daniel Geary, David Hollinger, Michael Kazin, and Alice O'Connor have provided much guidance. At the conference and in the postconference discussions and editing, much cross fertilization of ideas and interests took place, so I want to list here all those whose comments, interventions, collaborations, and writings helped make this collection a reality. Aside from the contributors themselves, they include Casey Blake, Eileen Boris, Robert Brenner, Shannan Clark, George Cotkin, Richard Flacks, Mary Furner, Robert Genter, Grace Hale, David Hollinger, Meg Jacobs, Russell Jacoby, Andrew Jewett, Walter Licht, George Lipsitz, Christopher Newfield, Linda Nicholson, Paula Rabinowitz, Adolph Reed, Ronald Schztz, Jeffrey Sklansky, Judith Smith, John Summers, Michael Szalay, Alan Wald, and Jon Wiener. At the University of Pennsylvania Press editor Robert Lockhart has been a wonderfully supportive editor, likewise managing editor Alison Anderson.

This project is grateful for the financial and moral support it has won from the University of California Humanities Research Institute, the University of California Office of the President, and the Interdisciplinary Humanities Center, the Department of History, the College of Letters and Science, and the Academic Senate, all at the University of California, Santa Barbara.